# METAPHYSICS AS A GUIDE TO MORALS

# METAPHYSICS AS A GUIDE TO MORALS

## IRIS MURDOCH

ALLEN LANE
THE PENGUIN PRESS

ALLEN LANE
THE PENGUIN PRESS
Published by the Penguin Group
Viking Penguin, a division of Penguin Books USA Inc.,
375 Hudson Street, New York, New York 10014, U.S.A.
Penguin Books Ltd, 27 Wrights Lane, London W8 5TZ, England
Penguin Books Australia Ltd, Ringwood, Victoria, Australia
Penguin Books Canada Ltd, 10 Alcorn Avenue, Suite 300,
Toronto, Ontario, Canada M4V 3B2
Penguin Books (N.Z.) Ltd, 182–190 Wairau Road,
Auckland 10, New Zealand

Penguin Books Ltd, Registered Offices:
Harmondsworth, Middlesex, England

First American Edition
Published in 1993 by Viking Penguin,
a division of Penguin Books USA Inc.

1   3   5   7   9   10   8   6   4   2

This book is based on the 1982 Gifford Lectures
given at the University of Edinburgh.

Library of Congress Cataloging-in-Publication Data
Murdoch, Iris.
Metaphysics as a guide to morals / Iris Murdoch.
p.   cm.
ISBN 0-7139-9100-3
Includes bibliographical references and index.
1. Philosophy.   2. Ethics.   3. Religion.   I. Title.
B72.M87   1992
100—dc20   92–53533

Printed in the United States of America
Set in Sabon

# Contents

To
Elizabeth Anscombe

Une difficulté est une lumière.
Une difficulté insurmontable est un soleil.

PAUL VALÉRY

# > I <
# Conceptions of Unity. Art

The idea of a self-contained unity or limited whole is a fundamental instinctive concept. We see parts of things, we intuit whole things. We seem to know a great deal on the basis of very little. Oblivious of philosophical problems and paucity of evidence we grasp ourselves as unities, continuous bodies and continuous minds. We assume the continuity of space and time. This intuitive extension of our claim to knowledge has inspired the reflections of many philosophers. Hume, who was sceptical about this universal tendency, was prepared to say that some of our most cherished unities, the self, the material object, were illusions fostered by imagination, by association of ideas, by 'habit and custom'. He admitted that the notion was repugnant to common-sense, not easily entertained outside the philosopher's study even by the philosopher. On the other hand, the strength of our resistance was an aspect, even a proof, of the thing itself; continuous experience provides an orderly world and there is no need for us laymen to worry about 'deep foundations'. Hume combined a radical scepticism with a benignly tolerant worldly wisdom. If a fiction is necessary enough, it is not a lie. Kant was upset by Hume's account. He thought that it undermined scientific thinking and the theoretical and moral claims of human reason. Psychological associations and habits could not constitute the bases of our existence, something deeper and more radically *necessary* was required. We could not infer reality from experience when the possibility of experience itself needed to be explained. The urge to prove that where we intuit unity there really is unity is a deep emotional motive to philosophy, to art, to thinking itself. Intellect is naturally one-making. To evaluate, understand, classify, place in order of merit, implies a wider unified system, the questing mind abhors vacuums. We fear plurality, diffusion, senseless accident, chaos, we want to transform what we cannot dominate or understand into something reassuring and familiar, into ordinary being, into history, art, religion, science. This subject or problem interests us now because the 'pluralisation' or 'demythologisation' of history, art, religion, science, which is characteristic of our age, largely takes the form of an analysis of old and prized unities and deep instinctive beliefs thought to be essential to human nature. Wittgenstein says that philosophy 'leaves everything as it is ... Philosophy simply puts everything before us, and neither explains nor deduces anything.' (*Philosophical Investigations* 124, 126.) This degree of moderation is unusual. A physicist may succeed in reassuring us that his discoveries do not in any way discredit ordinary beliefs. But philosophers do usually intend to persuade us of something, and this is true at times of Wittgenstein too. Philosophy and science and theology have always been to some degree iconoclastic, and the 'everyday outlook' or 'natural standpoint' undergoes historical change. How much it changes many voices now tell us, how little it changes can be learnt from reading Homer. Where philosophy is concerned this change has taken place in a perspective (against a horizon) which goes back as far as the Greeks. We are now being told (for instance by Nietzsche, Heidegger, Derrida) that this horizon has been, to use Nietzsche's phrase, 'sponged away', and that the era, not only of Descartes, but also of Plato, has ended and some entirely new *mode of thinking* is coming to be. I wish in what follows to study this situation, first of all in relation to the concept of the work of art.

The concept of 'art object' or 'work of art' has a force which goes far beyond what we usually think of as 'art'. All sorts of things have 'aesthetic aspects', but what I have in mind is the traditional concept (now under attack) of the unified work of art. A work of art is of course not a material object, though some works of art are bodied forth by material objects so as to seem to inhere in them. In the case of a statue the relation between the material object and the art object seems close, in the case of a picture less so. Poems and symphonies are clearly not material objects. Works of art require material objects to keep them continuously available (our memories fade) and some require performance by secondary artists. All art objects are 'performed' or imagined first by the artist and then by his clients, and these imaginative and intellectual activities or experiences may be said to be the point or essence of art. In ordinary life, unshadowed by philosophy, all sorts of things are said to exist 'in the mind' or 'only in the mind', and there may be various bases and explanations of such phrases. Art, however, essentially (traditionally) involves the idea of a sustained *experienced* mental synthesis. If with great expectation, I stand before the picture and, perhaps because I cannot banish my troubles, 'nothing happens', then something has gone wrong, something which was the point is absent, our sensibility has not been unified. Hearing sounds is not hearing a symphony unless we hear it as a symphony. We perceive a work of art, and also understand the command 'see it as a work of art'. The enjoyed, or achieved, art object is likely too to differ, in the experience of even the most sophisticated clients, to an extent which even the minutest critical language can scarcely uncover. The claim of the artist himself to have performed it 'best' or 'rightly' may be disputed and is hard to state. The accessible existence of art, its ability to hang luminously in human minds at certain times, depends traditionally upon an external being, a fairly precise and fixed sensory notation or 'body', an authority to which the client intermittently submits himself. If this notation is or becomes unavailable the work of art is lost: the picture is burnt, no reproduction does it justice, the papyrus is never given up by the sands of Egypt. Art experience then is something that we can self-evidently and identifiably have or enjoy, in various ways with various material. This ability to sustain and *experience* imagined syntheses has importance in other areas where we make use of analogous or related conceptions of authoritative limited wholes.

The idea of attention or contemplation, of looking carefully at something and *holding* it before the mind, may be conveyed early on in childhood. 'Look, listen, isn't that pretty, isn't that nice?' Also, 'Don't touch!' This is moral training as well as preparation for a pleasurable life. It need not depend on words, but can also be learnt from patterns of behaviour which should in any case back up the words. The far-reaching idea of *respect* is included in such teaching. The, as it might seem, sophisticated concept of a work of art may be acquired easily. Children, if they are lucky, are invited to attend to pictures or objects, or listen quietly to music or stories or verses, and readily understand in what spirit they are to treat these apparently dissimilar things. They may also be encouraged to contemplate works of nature, which are unlike works of art, yet also like them in being 'beautiful'. There are many harmoniously unified forms in nature, but our pleasure here is not always a search for 'objects', but may be a delight in limitless continuation or accumulation or chaos: mountains, waterfalls, forests, the sea, the sky. Kant even saw this experience of 'the sublime' as having a superior spiritual function as contrasted with enjoyment of the 'beauty' of limited forms. The defeat of a presupposed expectation of unity may be itself a pleasure, and is indeed an old and instinctive aesthetic device. Music which pleases by doing what we expect ('coming home') may also please us by failing to do so. Artists have been regarded as seers and prophets. Art does indeed register or picture, sometimes prophetically, the movement of the *Zeitgeist*. The way we grasp the world changes, and the artist knows first, like the animals whose behaviour foretells an earthquake.

The art object has attracted, intermittently, the attention of philosophers. Hegelian idealism took the mentally sustained organic unity of the work of art not only as a paradigm but as a touchstone: the more highly organised, the more real. Analytical empiricists have more recently been interested, not in the old question of what is good art, but in the question of what art is, a question of which art itself has become increasingly conscious. (Poets write about the nature of poetry, novelists about people writing novels.) This shift of interest, of which structuralist criticism (deconstruction) is one aspect, is a symptom of a more critical, more technological and generally less idolatrous attitude. There are many deep reasons for this coolness. It is felt that traditional western art is too grand and too out of touch with the awful, and also the banal, details of life, which (incidentally) television can display with such exquisite technical perfection. The mood of existentialism favoured sincere expressions of feeling or attitude rather than meticulous statements masquerading as objects; and the mood of the new ecological and social utilitarianism can find the artificiality of art frivolous in a suffering world. We should reflect here upon the durability and value of utilitarian moral philosophy as an independent stream of thought. The images of nuclear warfare, or ecological disaster, productive of fear, pessimism, cynicism, also doubtless affect our thoughts about art and make Hegelian and romantic theorising seem remote. In practice Marxist states used enslaved art as propaganda. In theory some Marxist aestheticians, in the spirit of Lukács, defended some continuation of traditional art as 'true realism'; while others, in the Utopian spirit of early Marx, pictured art as scattered spontaneous expressions of social solidarity, rather than as the production of formal

[ 4 ]

individual works. Lukács and Marcuse here give way to William
Morris. Many of these critical attitudes are gathered up by structuralism, which shares with Marxism a reaction against Victorian confidence and grandeur (large pictures, long novels) and in general against
'bourgeois values'. Structuralism more particularly expresses a new
consciousness of language, a metaphysic which offers a new model of
language as the structure of reality. By 'structuralism' I mean here the
movement promoted by Jacques Derrida, also called 'deconstruction',
'modernism', 'post-modernism', etc. I use the old original term as it is
informative and less ephemeral. (After all, what comes after post-
modernism?) Strictly perhaps it should be called 'Derrida's structuralism', to distinguish it from other post-Saussure theories in semiotics
and semiology which use the idea of structure. This doctrine is presented as a sort of morally neutral science, in a manner analogous
to the way in which Husserl presented his theory, but with a new
understanding of science, the languages of science, and of the place
of language generally. Here linguistics and anthropology appear as
mediators between philosophy and a comprehensive 'human science'.
Structuralism may also be seen in its more popular manifestations as
a new sensibility in art, an attack on traditional art forms, where it
operates both as an exercise in, and an image of, demythologisation,
the removal of the transcendent: a removal which analyses (decon-
structs) the familiar concepts of individual object, individual person,
individual meaning, those old and cherished 'limited wholes'. Here we
may readily see our painters as our prophets. A simple image is that
of impressionism, first perceived as a chaotic mass of lines and colours,
repugnant to its clients, but now so thoroughly absorbed that it is hard
to imagine that impressionist pictures were ever difficult to 'read'. The
impressionist is of course not a demythologising 'monist'; he authori-
tatively asserts the presence of the *transcendent object*. As things, landscapes, persons, entities. Cubism is a positive search for the object.
Self-declared abstract painting (Mondrian illustrates stages on this
way) has long remained happily, more or less secretively, obsessed with
the transcendent, which however has increasingly posed itself as a
problem. This awareness has been, one might say, the secret which
inspires the artist. Can it diminish to vanishing point? Many essays in
anti-art art seem anxious to prove that it can. Art's old natural tendency
to 'point beyond' is variously and ingeniously challenged by artists
more conscious of their prophetic role. The object is not 'pictured', it

[ 5 ]

is, just as itself, presented: the kettle, the chair, the Coca-Cola can, the pile of bricks, the revoltingly contingent. The client must then do the work.

Structuralism (as deconstruction) is a radical form of present-day demythologisation, in which the nature of the process itself is to be clarified. It seems like traditional metaphysics, a search for hidden *a priori* determining forms, constituting an ultimate reality. Here again the prophetic artist provides symptoms which are analysed and reinforced by the 'philosopher' as critic. Art, and indeed the whole of human activity, is said to consist of a matrix of linguistic (meaning-bearing) codes which are not the production of individuals, and which *constitute* the reality to which in the past they seemed to *point*. There is an old difficulty here, that of the metaphysician who describes reality but cannot include himself. Structuralist aesthetics allows a kind of special freedom to its creators and to those who understand the doctrines. The 'language' which constitutes reality has here an open creative fringe where poets and critics take some part in inventing new concepts. The critic as philosopher and metaphysician approaches, indeed tends to become, the artist who is making the language. The subject matter of art is then the nature of the process itself. The old conception of mimesis as reference to a transcendent reality, trans-formed and presented by an individual artist, is superseded. A case of the 'old consciousness' would be our illusion of looking through the pages of a book into another world. Reality, it is argued, lies in the linguistic medium itself, in the various (including scientific) languages of the planet, and in the meanings, inspirations, promptings, illumina-tions, which they can self-reflectively convey now. (Physics: the cosmos is the sum of observations of it.) We are to be sceptical of anything, *including the past*, which can be intuited as transcendent and somehow existing separately in its own right.

The new mood has found popular and instinctive expression in art in cults of the ephemeral or deliberately incomplete, expressive of communal feelings, not to be seen as 'statements'. We have become familiar with minimalism, 'happenings', abstract paintings designed to invite 'completion' by provoked clients, natural objects or artefacts offered as works of art, ambiguous entities posing the question 'Is this art?' Theatre audiences are alienated so as to produce their own drama by participation. Writers may be led, or instinctively prefer, to produce short manifestly literary 'texts' instead of the old lengthy carefully constructed objects, and to offer challenging paradoxes or puzzles instead of clarifications. Even plain discursive prose may be suspect as being insufficiently stirring, too naively and soothingly referential. We may be reminded here of Wittgenstein's *Tractatus*, and also of another exponent of 'indirect communication', Kierkegaard, who was not the only theologian to feel that discontinuity, shock and paradox represented the best way to prompt understanding of what is really deep. The paradox before which the intellect surrenders is an idea common to (some) Christian and Buddhist thinking. 'Structuralism', which summarises a mood of scepticism and demythologisation, is of course also a vast ragbag of interesting ideas and tendencies, some very illuminating, some far from new, if we were to regard Kierkegaard (for instance) as a proto-structuralist. His aim however was to promote faith in terms of an individual's appreciation of a religious truth manifested in a story about a person and pointing to a transcendent reality. Here we may glimpse the extreme complexity of the whole idea of demythologisation and its challenge to conceptions of transcendence. Some modern demythologising theology is now structuralist in tone, where it used to be existentialist. Many structuralist writers are explicitly hostile to religion. Metaphysical problems now reach the popular consciousness in the form of a sense of loss, of being returned to a confused pluralistic world from which something 'deep' has been removed.

Art attacks art and thrives by doing so. The artist derives energy from loving, but also from hating, the art of the past. Iconoclasm can be a spiritual activity, Platonism is creative iconoclasm. Is there anything unusual or portentously extreme in current hostility to traditional ideas? Is there some clear analogy, or connection, between iconoclasm in art and the more challenging or reductionist trends in modern theology? The violence of shock and paradox has of course always been at home in Christianity ever since Paul made his point of preaching not just Christ but Christ crucified. However, the calming whole-making tendencies of human thought have also been at work, creating reassuring structures which occasional prophets feel moved to tear down in order to rejoin the original shock. The Judaeo-Christian God owes a considerable debt to art, may even be seen as a work of art. The doctrine of the Trinity is a celestial aesthetic celebration of internal relations. Eastern art has not been so 'thingy' or concerned with complex completeness; and eastern philosophy and religion are more evidently mystical. The relation of eastern art to religion has been on the whole more intuitive and carefree, whereas western art has *served* religion and its dogmas. Our ordinary western attitudes to art in our new age of iconoclasm, and in spite of television and computers, have not yet perhaps so deeply or visibly changed. We still, in our unregenerate way, ignoring the *Zeitgeist, take refuge* in art. People still read novels and listen to Mozart. We still worship the artists whom we understand and enjoy, and there are few matters about which we are more uncritical and opinionated than our own aesthetic prejudices, which can combine great subjective certainty with an absence of conclusive argument. A hymn of praise in gratitude for the joys and consolations and general usefulness of art might run as follows. Art is informative and entertaining, it condenses and clarifies the world, directing attention upon particular things. This intense showing, this bearing witness, of which it is capable is detested by tyrants who always persecute or demoralise their artists. Art illuminates accident and contingency and the general muddle of life, the limitations of time and the discursive intellect, so as to enable us to survey complex or horrible things which would otherwise appal us. It creates an authoritative public human world, a treasury of past experience, it preserves the past. Art makes places and opens spaces for reflection, it is a defence against materialism and against pseudo-scientific attitudes to life. It calms and invigorates, it gives us energy by unifying, possibly by purifying, our feelings. In enjoying great art we experience a clarification and concentration and perfection of our own consciousness. Emotion and intellect are unified into a limited whole. In this sense art also *creates* its client; it inspires intuitions of ideal formal and symbolic unity which enable us to co-operate with the artist and to be, as we enjoy the work, artists ourselves. The art object conveys, in the most accessible and for many the only available form, the idea of a transcendent perfection. Great art inspires because it is separate, it is for nothing, it is for itself. It is an image of virtue. Its condensed, clarified, presentation enables us to look without sin upon a sinful world. It renders innocent and transforms into truthful vision our baser energies connected with power, curiosity, envy and sex.

Such a paean might now seem to many people remote, expressing an old-fashioned or romantic over-valuation of art or misunderstanding of its role. Is art really as pretentious as that, it may be argued, is it really as *good* as that? This enthusiasm depends upon a certain amount of discreet switching between 'art' and 'great art'. In fact there is very little great art and not all that much good art. Is not an ideal morality, an unexamined idea of perfection, being improperly introduced into the background? There is an important difference between learning about virtue and practising it, and the former can indeed be a delusive substitute which effectively prevents the latter. Even great art can be a potent source of illusion, a fact which may suggest to some that we are better employed in examining the social effects of art than in uncritically celebrating its 'spiritual' splendour. Why did Plato not take the art object as the image of the good, as (in effect) Hegel did? And, in his earlier reflections, Wittgenstein. (*Notebooks* 1914–1916, 7.10.16. *Tractatus* 6. 45.) The art object, transcendent, clarified, self-contained, alone, secure and time-resistant, shedding light upon the miserable human scene, prompting compassion and just judgment, seems like a picture of goodness itself, a sort of semi-sensory image of a spiritual ideal.

Kant did not regard art as a great moral liberator. He did however cautiously take it (the beautiful) as a *symbol* of morality. The work of art, not subject to an empirical concept, is produced by the free spontaneous activity of the imagination acting in accord with the notion of 'an object in general'. It is 'purposeful without purpose', a 'finality without end'. This is *like* the free activity of the moral will (practical reason) which 'invents' the moral act which, like the work of art, exists for itself, for its own sake. Aesthetic harmony is however *felt* not reasoned, and Kant's system separates art from practical rationality and from the (in effect rational) 'moral emotions'. (*Respect* for morality, *sublime* feelings about the cosmos.) Our 'sublime' sensations are evoked by a sense of our finitude, fear of what we cannot make sense of (in the face of nature, for instance) combined with sturdy confidence in our rational power. This in turn is *like* 'respect for moral law' (*Achtung*), where the pain of frustrated desire combines with pride in our free moral nature. Such experiences, characteristic of rational beings, are on a higher level than aesthetic pleasure. The confusion of the aesthetic with the moral represents a natural temptation, and Kant, like Plato, wants to keep morality 'safe' from art. The strictness, purity and simplicity of the concept of duty should be our refuge and prime safeguard. Kant thought that the good life was within the reach of all, but that our dual nature (the determinism of our selfishness versus the freedom of our response to reason) makes it difficult. We are to be *obedient* to moral law, *subject* to the demands of reason. Goodness is not spontaneous. We cannot attain perfect freedom or even profitably imagine it. We must be humble enough to 'do the next thing', eschewing attractive and grandiose speculations, taking as our immediate starting point the authoritative experience of duty, which is also our experience of freedom. In considering these different views of art and of morals we may see how deep instinctive moral intuitions find expression in large movements of abstract thought. It has been picturesquely suggested that if Newton had not been inhibited by his religious beliefs he would have discovered relativity.

As there is much to say about Plato in the pages which follow, a preliminary note is needed. Plato uses myths to explain his conception of human life. His most famous picture is that of the Cave (*Republic* 514) wherein people facing the wall at the back see at first shadows, then, turning round, the objects, themselves imitations of real things, which, in the light of a fire, have cast the shadows. They (we) may perhaps go no further, taking the fire to be the only source of light. Some of us may venture on, glimpsing another light beyond, and emerge into the sunlight, where we are dazzled and can only look down at shadows and reflections, then, raising our heads, see the real things themselves and then (if finally enlightened) the sun. This parable portrays a spiritual pilgrimage from appearance to reality. We turn round, we climb up, we raise our heads. At each stage we see at first the *shadows* of what is more real and true. Plato's 'Theory of Forms' deals with logical and moral questions. The (mythical, postulated) Forms (or Ideas) are models, archetypes: universals, general concepts as distinct from particular entities, and, in their ethical role, moral ideals active in our lives, radiant icons, images of virtue. The moral Forms are interrelated. (Justice relates to Truth.) The supreme power, which unifies the Forms, is the Form of the Good, pictured in the Cave myth as the sun. Other Platonic imagery (for instance concerning the soul) should also be understood (as Plato reminds us from time to time) as hermeneutic 'as if'. These are instructive *pictures*. The Theory of Forms has been a subject of endless scholarly dispute, often involving (to quote Myles Burnyeat, *The Theaetetus of Plato*, p. 39) 'temperamental as well as intellectual factors'. Also, to be noted at the start, 'A great work of philosophy demands a response which is more than merely intellectual.' (Burnyeat, p. 37.)

At *Republic* 484CD Plato uses the image of the painter to set forth the notion of the good man gazing at the model (or form or image or idea) of spiritual truth (reality) in his soul and keeping his gaze steadily thereon as he sets about the business of practical life. Kant speaks in a similar way about the idea of rational law in general, the potentiality of moral freedom which is lodged in every human bosom, and which supersedes even the vision of Christ. 'Even the Holy One of the Gospels must first be compared with our ideal of moral perfection before we can recognise Him as such.' (*Fundamental Principles of the Metaphysic of Morals* p. 30, Abbott's translation, hereinafter referred to as the *Grundlegung*.) Both Plato and Kant use an image of referring to an ideal or original pattern, not as imitation either of the model itself or of some chosen instantiation (example) of it, but as an inspired interpretation into the realm of practical life of a deep and certain moral insight. The notion of copying the model itself would be a 'category mistake', since the model is not a particular thing, like a particular command or picture; *imitatio Christi* does not work simply by suggesting that everyone should give away his money, or wondering how Christ would vote. The Demiurge (mythical creator) in Plato's *Timaeus*, 'copying' the Forms (spiritual Ideas) in order to create the world, interprets them into an entirely different medium. A difference between Kant and Plato is that Plato insists that approach to the central Idea (pure goodness, the Form of the Good) comes through a difficult disciplined purification of intellect and passion, wherein passion (Eros) becomes a spiritual force. Whereas Kant regards 'feelings' as dangerous to morality, sharply divides (noumenal) reason from (phenomenal) emotion, and stresses that dutiful action is something of which every man is immediately capable.

Plato's use of the painting metaphor is not in fact intended as a kind word to painters, who are taken in book X of the *Republic* as a prime case, and indeed image, of the bad effect of art. Painting is often thus used as an image of the other arts. The painter looking at his subject, say, a bed, to use Plato's example, is not like the virtuous man who looks toward an idea of goodness. As Plato explains (*Republic* 597), the painter is 'three removes from reality'. 'God' creates the single ideal noumenal idea of the bed, the carpenter makes instances of 'real' (phenomenal) beds, the painter copies a mere appearance of one of these, without understanding, without, for instance, knowing how beds are made. Plato's use of 'God', *theos*, here is picturesque. So the carpenter is nearer to heaven than the painter since he has at least obtained at a simple level some mathematical ideas, some exercise of reason which enables him in a disciplined way to *distinguish* true and false, apparent and real. Skills such as measuring, weighing and using numbers are described (602D) as 'benign assistants' to the truth-seeking mind. Later in Book X (605A) the case of the painter is used to introduce that of the poet, who, even if he be as great as Homer or the tragedians, is still a charming illusionist, a kind of sophist. Imitation is a sort of play. The character of the sophist, as portrayed in the dialogue of that name, is very like that of the artist in *Republic* X. The poet can only present virtue in an imitative way, and does not really understand it (600E), just as the painter does not really understand the bed. Moreover the practice of such imitation inhibits the artist and his client from the effort of penetrating beyond appearances. Plato speaks of an 'old quarrel between poetry and philosophy' (607B). (A quarrel, as I suggest later, which is continuing today.) Literature is even more dangerous than painting since it delights in presenting bad men as interesting and attractive. Such men are easier to portray than good men since the former are always agitated and changeable, whereas the latter are monotonous and steady (604E). Goodness, being lucid and quiet and calm, cannot be expressed or represented in art. Writers, not exceptional for virtue, understand and sympathise with mediocrity and egoism, and cannot perceive goodness. The good are mocked. Art deals with what is peevish and mutable and unstable in human nature since this is easily imitated and grasped, and is more amusing. (Plato is now speaking of literature. He takes it for granted that a painting is less real than what it represents.) Art is the base addressing the base. It is motivated by and caters for the lowest part of the soul, the bad unconscious, which is to be contrasted with *anamnesis*, the good unconscious. The client is thus encouraged to 'take over' the work as his own fantasy. Art fascinates us by exploring the meaner, more peculiar aspects of our being, in comparison with which goodness seems dull. (Artists are indeed unlikely to be good, goodness would silence them.) Good art can corrupt us (Plato is speaking of Homer and the tragic poets), and the good man is as much at risk as the bad man. In sympathising with a fictional character we abandon ourselves to emotional excesses which weaken our better nature. By unreflective imitation literature stirs up our feelings so that the higher part of our soul 'relaxes its guard' (606A) over self-indulgent emotion, and we become lazy sentimental spectators of fictional dramas, abandoning the stoical restraints and standards which we exercise in ordinary life. We may find satisfaction in viewing the misfortunes of others. (Every day on television!) Such experiences, for instance in the theatre, are not, as Aristotle later suggested, a purgation of our emotions by pity and fear, but rather a fostering of base impulses of sex and anger and selfish desire which ought to be induced to dry up and perish (606D). Poets then encourage what is irrational and undiscriminating in the human soul (605C). Here comedy which, regardless of merit, derides what is unsuccessful or ill-favoured, is as bad as tragedy. Plato objects to Homer's description of the gods laughing in the first book of the *Iliad* (I 599); and at *Laws* 656B he describes how a decent man can come to tolerate and be amused by, and only casually to criticise, the base habits of those among whom he lives. Jokes are an art form, and witticisms in private conversation can corrupt. We tolerate clowning and buffoonery and cruel wit, when it comes to us in the guise of art, which we would not accept as any real part of our own conduct. In many areas of ordinary life, art makes a fascination with what is mean and trivial seem innocuous. Art is most pernicious when it poses as a spiritual achievement and inhibits serious reflection and self-criticism. Enjoyment of art is soothing, and may persuade us that we 'understand' (life, people, morality) and need make no further efforts. The great artists especially make us feel that we have arrived; we are home. We feel that we are already wise and good. Plato qualifies his spirited tirade by a mitigating gesture. 'However if sweet poetry and mimesis can show reason why they should exist in a well-governed state we will gladly let them in; for we ourselves are very conscious of their charm.' (607C.) His general conclusion remains that art is both politically and spiritually dangerous; the only good mimetic artist is the *Timaeus* Demiurge.

Plato is a great artist attacking what he sees as bad and dangerous in art. His warnings are apt today. Popular literature and film argue the dullness of the good, the charm of the bad. The violent man is the hero of our time. The technical excellence of television (the Cave) leads us to accept vivid scrappy images and disconnected oddments of information as insight into truth. W. H. Auden observed that 'no poet can prevent his work being used as magic'; even good art can be taken over by its client as fantasy and pornography, a process facilitated by the ready-made 'magic' of vulgar entertainment which makes what is good increasingly difficult to hold in the mind. (And so on and so on.) However, if it is to enlighten us, Plato's attack on art must be seen in the context of his whole moral philosophy. Life is a spiritual pilgrimage inspired by the disturbing magnetism of *truth*, involving *ipso facto* a purification of energy and desire in the light of a vision of what is *good*. The good and just life is thus a process of clarification, a movement toward selfless lucidity, guided by ideas of perfection which are objects of *love*. Platonic morality is not coldly intellectual, it involves the whole man and attaches value to the most 'concrete' of everyday preoccupations and acts. It concerns the continuous detail of human activity, wherein we discriminate between appearance and reality, good and bad, true and false, and check or strengthen our desires.

At the beginning of the *Phaedrus* (250E) we are told that the most vividly seen of the Ideas, or Forms, is *beauty*. We see and love beauty more readily than we love good, it is the spiritual thing to which we are most immediately and instinctively attracted. Plato presents this idea as part of a myth of recollection. He pictures the human soul, in some previous state of being, as having been able to see the spiritual Forms (Ideas) with perfect clarity, a vision of which the incarnate soul retains a shadowy memory.

'Few can recall these things at all well, only when they see any reminder of them they are astounded and are beside themselves, but cannot understand this affliction because their sight is dim. The earthly copies of justice and temperance and the other virtues which are prized by the soul give off no light, and only few of us with our weak faculties can with difficulty see in the imitations the likeness of their originals. But at that former time we saw beauty shining out so brightly . . . when we beheld that vision and were initiated into what is properly called the most blessed of mysteries, which we celebrated in entire perfection, unmarked by the evils of a later time, able as initiates to perceive in a pure light, being ourselves pure, those perfect, simple, calm, and happy showings.'

(250A–C.)

*

[ 14 ]

This ecstatic passage about *anamnesis*, spiritual recollection, exhibits Plato's sense of *certainty* about the *reality* of goodness, which we are properly destined to *love*. We *know* about good and evil. In this, *mutatis* various *mutandis*, he resembles Kant who held, who *saw*, an equally strong certainty which was central to his philosophy. We should also notice in the *Phaedrus* passage the four adjectives, perfect, simple, calm and happy. Beauty, Plato goes on to tell us (250D), is the most readily recovered of those heavenly visions, 'shining out most clearly, apprehended by the clearest of our senses. Sight is the clearest of our physical senses, though it is unable to perceive wisdom. Wisdom would arouse the most frenzied and passionate love if any clear perception of it could come to us through sight ... Only beauty has the special role of being physically perceived.' Plato here draws attention to the dominance of sight over the other senses. We also, in a natural metaphor, 'see' (perceive) non-visual forms of beauty. Plato, in his myth, does not discuss exactly what seeing beauty is like. He assumes his hearer will understand. He is suggesting to us the naturalness of using visual images to express spiritual truths. Plato has been criticised for his use of visual imagery by thinkers who want to connect this with allegedly abstract or intellectual aspects of his ethics. In fact many of these images, in which the visual so eloquently mirrors the moral, are to suggest the absolute closeness, at some points at any rate, of the spiritual world, how close and how numerous are its cues. The sun may be far away, but its reflection in beauty is near, and so is the light which breaks in the carpenter's mind as he learns the rudiments of science (*Republic* 567B). When Plato speaks of the immediacy and visibility of beauty and its uplifting role in our lives he is not however thinking of the beauty of art, or in any romantic sense of the beauty of nature. Plato rarely mentions the charm of nature or suggests that it is a spiritual starting point. The lyric poets enjoy birds and flowers, but Kantian (or Wordsworthian) sublimity in nature is generally absent from the Greek mind.

The *Phaedrus* contains one of the few rural scenes in Plato. Here we find Socrates out in the country, the conversation taking place (230B) near a little shrine beside a spring, shaded by a plane tree and an agnus castus. The naming of the trees is remarkable. The song of the cicadas is also mentioned, though what Socrates likes best is a gentle grassy slope suitable for lying on. He displays some acquaintance with nearby shrines of various gods and speaks reverently as one who feels their presence. The dialogue ends with a prayer which we may take to be inspired by the beauty and holiness of the scene. 'O beloved Pan and all other gods of this place, grant that I may be made beautiful within, and that all outer things may be in amity with that inner life. May I consider the wise man rich; and have only such wealth as a sensible temperate person can carry and direct.' Socrates observes, however, that in his quest for knowledge he is taught by people in the city and not by fields and trees. The beauty which prompts the spirit is more directly spoken of in this dialogue, as in the *Symposium*, in terms of sexual love, and of ascent from physical passion to a vision of divine absolute beauty. Love which is only physical treasures mere 'mortal trash' (*Symposium* 211E), but even bad egoistic love may lead on to teach us virtuous selfless love, and perception of beauty as unselfish attachment can bring about spiritual change. The lover, Plato says, reveres the beloved as if he were a god. When Christopher Isherwood asked his guru if it was all right to love boys, the guru replied that Christopher should regard his loved one as the young god Krishna. How does this go in Christian terms? At Matthew 25. 35–40 the disciples are told that in so far as they ever fed the hungry or clothed the naked or visited those in prison they did this unto the Son of man. To see Christ in those you pity or even in those you hate may seem a more intelligible charge than to see him in those you are madly in love with; where the sacred image might appear as an unwelcome or irrelevant obstacle or else as blasphemously degraded! In such a context Christian western puritanism instinctively envisages as sinful aspects of carnal love which eastern religion has more freely spiritualised. However the command tends to suggest, even to clarify, the difference between good and bad love. It puts the idea of love under judgment. We are said to love each other 'in Christ', and that should mean that we look *as* Christ and that we look *at* Christ in loving another person. Compare Kant's colder injunction that we see and respect and appeal to the rational being in every man. We may see here how love of beauty in art and in nature can be (as Kant thought) a symbol of goodness since such love is naturally, or readily, pure and unpossessive. We may also see how sex can be the image of spirituality as well as its substance. Love as the fruit and overflow of spirit. Plato's visions may seem far away from the mess of ordinary loving, but they shed light, we can understand. Falling in love is for many people their most intense experience, bringing with it a quasi-religious certainty, and most disturbing because it shifts the centre of the world from ourself to another place. A love relationship can occasion extreme selfishness and possessive violence, the attempt to dominate that other place so that it be no longer separate; or it can prompt a process of unselfing wherein the lover learns to see, and cherish and respect, what is not himself. There are many aspects to this teaching: for instance, letting the beloved go with a good grace, knowing when and how to give up, when to express love by silence or by clearing off. This negative heroism may be very enlightening, aided by the palpable satisfaction of having behaved well when one desired to behave otherwise! Human relationship is no doubt the most important, as well as the first, training and testing-ground of morality; and common-sense as well as Freud emphasises the influence of family life, of which Plato does not speak. Certainly he, who returns so often and so ardently to the importance and the ambiguity of love, cannot be called a cold or abstract or purely intellectual moralist. It is rather the other way round. He does not 'intellectualise' love, but sees intellect as passion. A desire for perfection, for clarity and understanding and truth, in craft or intellectual studies, is for Plato the other main road to virtue: a starting point, an inspiration, a discipline of the emotions, a spiritual cue. The way of beauty which passes through human love has a more obvious, evident and immediate, starting point, but also involves great psychological dangers and temptations. The way of intellectual activity in the broad sense of Plato's word *techné*, which would include craft but not fine art, lacks the initial charm of the beautiful, but is on the whole less perilous, although knowledge is power, and power poses moral problems. Power as magic, pride, secret superior knowledge infects science and technology, as it has always infected religion. The computer age also breeds its gnostics. The moral nature of all learning has however nothing mysterious about it. For the Greeks who were inspired, even intoxicated, by their progress in mathematics, this form of thought appeared as a sovereign *techné*, and to Plato as a basic form of spiritual discipline as well as a source of metaphysical imagery.

I return now to the main line of the argument, which concerns an attitude to art thought of as a form or style of 'demythologisation'. It may seem odd to us that Plato did not think that fields and trees had anything to teach him, and that, when speaking so passionately about beauty as a spiritual guide, he did not see works of art in that light. Of course in real life, as it were, as opposed to philosophy, Plato clearly loved art, especially music and poetry. He often, and with evident knowledge, speaks of music, and was himself (modestly) a poet. There may even be an element of envy in his hostility to the tragedians. He several times refers to the 'divine madness' of the poet, which is irresponsible and dangerous, yet also God-given. For one so prolific in visual imagery he shows comparatively little sensibility to the visual arts. Plato stands late in the brief amazing history of Greek visual art. Classical sculptors were concerned with the problem of how to render the human form realistically, and by the time they had solved it their art was already in decline. So little did the later practitioners and connoisseurs value the earlier efforts that the divinely beautiful *kouroi* and other votive statues, some of which survive in the Acropolis Museum, were thrown into a pit to make room for less wonderful but more up-to-date works. I suppose an intellectually disciplined concern about the past, or a meticulous curiosity about it (as opposed to legend and folk memory), is a fairly modern phenomenon, as indeed is the writing of history. Herodotus and Thucydides invented history, but they do not seem to have endowed their own civilisation with anything like a modern sense of the past. One may note in passing that history, in the usual modern academic understanding of it, and respect for and interest in the past, part of which is an appreciation of tradition, are not only recent flowers but frail ones, menaced by technology, totalitarian states, and also by certain iconoclastic aspects of modern thought. But to return to Plato, it is not perhaps difficult to understand why he thought, or at any rate spoke, of visual artists as mere copyists. He was himself a great artist, as he must have been well aware, but had deep reasons, moral, psychological, political and metaphysical, for mounting an attack on art. One of these is an uneasiness about the nature of language itself. This metaphysical anxiety is also character- istic of our age. Reflections prompted by technological (scientific, com- puter) languages may remind us of what Plato has to say in the *Phaedrus* (274–5) and the *Seventh Letter* (341) about the dangers of the written word. Here his anxiety about art appears as an aspect of a deeper concern about the independent creative thinking remembering *person*. Writing was still something of a novelty in Plato's day, invented, then forgotten, then invented again. Of course Plato knows that writing (as we know that books and now computer technology) is valuable and inevitable; but he also sees a crisis which demands pause and thought. He questions the ability of writing to convey fundamental ideas. He presents his contention playfully in the *Phaedrus* in the form of a myth about a junior god who invents writing and proudly shows it to the chief god who finds it most objectionable. The objections as set forth in *Phaedrus* and *Seventh Letter* may be summarised as follows. Written works can only be inert reminders of real communications which take place orally in particular contexts between one person and another. Only thus in such contexts can important truths be discovered and stated. In philosophy for instance (*Seventh Letter* 341C–D) it is only after a persistent study of the matter in hand – *the thing itself* – and an abiding with it, that understanding suddenly comes 'like a light that is kindled by a leaping spark, and thereafter nourishes itself'. The speaking person is ultimate. A written statement cannot reply but can only say one thing. It is moreover portable and can be handed around among those who do not understand or respect it. It is ambiguous, and defenceless in the hands of knaves or fools. So it may become a vehicle of falsehood even though it was set down as a memorandum of truth. Art then (so we may gloss the *Phaedrus*), or as a present-day thinker might more generally put it, any use of written signs, is falsifying in so far as it professes to be a permanent record of an understanding which can only occur in ephemeral contexts of real person-to-person communication when one honest mind speaks to another. Art corrupts because by an attractive eloquent commentary upon human affairs it apes a sort of insight, a unified vision, which in its true form is a spiritual achievement. (*Corruptio optimi pessima.*) Bad art damages us in obvious ways by prompting false egoistic fantasy. But even serious art is dangerous, or is especially dangerous, because it resembles the good, it is a spurious short-cut to 'instant wisdom'. The written text seems to 'do it for us', and need not be diligently assimilated or transformed into our own personal understanding and practice. It represents something which we deeply (unconsciously) want to be the case. We intuit in art a unity, a perfection, which is not really there. Even when wise men talk to each other it is beyond the words that the flame of understanding leaps. And with such considerations we move from ordinary common-sensical criticisms of art to a kind of metaphysical criticism.

Those thoughts of Plato do not seem to us remote. Television with its flickering series of trivial momentary unreflective uncomprehended images, pictures the state of the prisoners in the Cave who can only see the flickering shadows of things which are themselves copies of real things. Plato's view gives reasoned expression to the puritanical watchdog who thinks that art is corrupting, and to the (e.g. Tolstoyan) anti-art artist who feels that it is insincere. Much contemporary art is inspired by this judgment on the past. Writers used to use sticks or quills, then they used pens or typewriters, now they use word-processors. Much of what was once expressed in words is now 'written' and 'remembered' in arcane computer languages. Such reflections may lead people to see art as in process of reification, externalisation, losing spontaneity and directness, leaving what used to be its 'content' as private stirrings in the individual mind. This sort of pervasive anxiety has, indeed prophetically, been leading to the development of informal semi-coherent, even anti-intellectual sub-arts of 'participation' or 'minimalism', intended to stir up private emotion and make the client 'do all the work'. But has not the client always been doing most of the work? This is a main point made against art by Freud, a self-styled modern disciple of Plato. Freud, with the imposing edifice of European civilisation, looking its most sacred and majestic, behind him, cannot be grossly disrespectful. 'Before the problem of the creative artist analysis must, alas, lay down its arms.' (*The Standard Edition of the Complete Psychological Works of Sigmund Freud*, vol. XXI, 177. 'Dostoevsky and Parricide'.) He finds, nevertheless, many damaging things to say about art. His thesis, variously expressed, is that art is the fantasy life of the artist stimulating the fantasy life of the client, with the factitious 'work of art' lying 'overlooked' between them as a sort of disguised bribe. Art is a magic which excites the magical propensities of those who enjoy it: a case of what Freud calls in *Totem and Taboo* (XIII 3) 'the omnipotence of thought', an illusion characteristic of all neurotics. (We may all be supposed to be partly neurotic, or neurotic sometimes.) As he explains elsewhere ('Creative Writers and Day-Dreaming', *Standard Edition*, vol. IX, 153), we would normally be repelled by the private fantasies of another person, but the artist persuades us to accept his by disguising them cleverly, and by offering us formal and aesthetic pleasures which then incite us to release, upon our side, a play of personal fantasy which is normally inhibited. (The lower part of the soul speaking to the lower part of the soul.) 'Our actual enjoyment of an imaginative work proceeds from a liberation of tensions in our minds. It may even be that not a little of this effect is due to the writer's enabling us henceforth to enjoy our daydreams without reproach or shame.' The purely aesthetic pleasure of the art work is called by Freud 'fore-pleasure' and is according to him analogous to the superficial or initiatory sexual stimulation which leads on to the 'end-pleasure' of full gratification. (*Three Essays on the Theory of Sexuality*, vol. VII, chapter iii(1), 211, 'The Transformations of Puberty'. He develops a similar theory in relation to our pleasure in the mysteriously condensed aesthetic medium of jokes. (*Jokes and their Relation to the Unconscious*, vol. VIII, chapter iv, 137.) It begins to look as if, where the art object is a mechanical stimulus to personal fantasy, pornography is the end point. All art aspires to the condition of pornography? It may be true at least that more does than meets the eye.

What becomes now of the dignity and innocence of the work of art? The ideal unity, the image of virtue, which we imagine that we experience is seen to be an illusory unity. Or rather the unity which we intuit (our completion of the circle) is not what we think it is. Art (on such a view of it) is not the imaginative creation of unified public objects or limited wholes for edifying contemplation, with mystical analogies; it is the egotistically motivated production of maimed pseudo-objects which are licences for the private concluding processes of personal fantasy. Sex here provides the image and the substance of the concluding (unifying) process and its satisfactory finality as it moves from fore-pleasure to end-pleasure. Kant's definition of art in terms of 'purposiveness without purpose' is here provided with a secret purpose. The sense of power and energy which the contemplation of the pseudo-unified pseudo-object inspires in us is then easily explained. We can understand too our peculiar delight in the ambiguous condensed symbolism of poetry and painting, concerning which recent criticism has often taken pleasure in vindicating Freud's theory of the hidden bribe. Freud more than once labels himself as a Platonist. 'Anyone who looks down with contempt upon psycho-analysis from a superior vantage-point should remember how closely the enlarged sexuality of psycho-analysis coincides with the Eros of the divine Plato.' (*Three Essays on the Theory of Sexuality*, vol. VII, preface to the fourth edition, 134.) Freud takes the idea of the sexual drive as a unitary principle of explanation; and, with simplifications, the 'modern consciousness' has followed him. At any rate 'explanation by sex' tends to have for us a kind of intuitive obviousness, as if we perfectly knew what sex was. Certain forms of sexual activity come to be thought of as essential (without which life would be impoverished), natural, human and fundamental, functioning thereby as fates and excuses. Freud is of course supposed to be talking about health rather than goodness. Psychoanalysis is to break down false self-pictures only in so far as these impair the efficiency of the ego. This allows a place for necessary structures of illusions, harmless or beneficial illusions, and of course innumerable totally undiscovered and undiscoverable illusions. The psyche 'is and ought to be' a strong closely textured web of subjective dreams, which, if it functions well, don't touch. Do we not all need what John Cowper Powys calls 'life illusions'? This could be a moral point of view or certainly part of one.

The familiar conception of 'analysis' conveys a misleading idea of a minute scientific scrutiny of the human mind: an area in which it is difficult, except at a superficial level, to distinguish illusion from truth, and certainly difficult to do so without the introduction of moral concepts. One cannot explain 'mind' in terms of a single system or meaningfully use the idea of a series which leads toward a perfect analysis. Whether Freud should be seen primarily as a 'humanist' or as a 'man of science' has been continually debated. The English translations, it is argued, consistently mislead by their preference of 'clean' scientific terminology (sometimes invented for the purpose) to Freud's use of ordinary language with its numerous associations. (See Bruno Bettelheim, *Freud and Man's Soul*.) In particular the translation of *Seele* and *Psyche* as 'mind' rather than 'soul' seems to lose a humane, even a religious, dimension. Freud's doctrines, which have been turned (especially in America) toward pure science, have also more recently been explored (especially in France) for more metaphysical directives. Popular Freudianism has certainly attached value to a general idea of 'mental health', sometimes even with the implication that the unanalysed life is a sort of lie. Is not the healthy successful human being realistic and thus truthful? How can the concept of self-knowledge not now be touched by science? Freud's scepticism about art exemplifies his influence as a modern metaphysician. Suspect the false unity and analyse it. The therapist takes as a goal the new redeemed unity of the integrated personality. But the metaphysician has released conceptual forces which, at different levels, are more persistently iconoclastic. A sort of 'demythologisation' has been with us as a reductionist form of 'explanation by sex'. The deeper influence of (among others) Freud, as seen in structuralism, concerns the nature of causal explanation, indeed of explanation in general. A problem (which I consider later), for Freud and those whom he inspires, is whether such analyses can be devoid of radical value judgments.

Freud's obliteration of religion has a theological intensity and confidence: for him, its only discussable future is that of an *illusion*. Freud, who says that his 'libido' coincides *exactly* with Plato's Eros, does not, so far as I know, discuss Plato's *anamnesis*, the ancestor, as one would imagine, of the Freudian concept of the unconscious, as well as of Jung's archetypal folk memory. The concept of *anamnesis* appears in Plato's *Meno* in the context of asking whether virtue is natural or whether it is something that can be taught, and answering that it is neither, but comes by 'divine dispensation' or 'grace'. (99E.) This does not of course mean that virtue is a matter of luck, but that it comes as the reward of a sort of morally disciplined attention. This is a darkness which is unlike Jung's mythological historicism or Freud's glimpses of infantile sexuality. It is also in inimical contrast to the massing 'dead memories' of the computer world. *Anamnesis*, spiritual memory, belongs to the individual who 'remembers' pure Forms of goodness and beauty with which he was familiar 'face to face' (not 'in a glass darkly') in another existence. These journeys of the soul, as described in the *Phaedrus* and in the tale of reincarnation at the end of the *Republic*, are of course *mythical* ideas, similar to the concept of Nirvana in Buddhism. The *Seventh Letter* offers the same instruction in ordinary language; the problem about writing is a problem about 'live remembrance': not the dead written text prompting second-hand reactions, but the deep called-up truth of the individual mind. Plato and Kant are close at this point. The solitary private moral agent must be his own authority, continually doing it all, over and over, for himself. This is moral philosophy, not science, and its message is hostile to the generalising tendencies of science and the conceptions and temptations of power with which science is associated. I think Freud was aware of these paradoxes. He had, we are told, some hesitation about adopting as an epigraph the magnificent Virgilian outcry, the words of Juno at *Aeneid* VII 312, *Flectere si nequeo superos, Acheronta movebo* ('If I cannot bend the higher powers, I shall move the infernal regions'): words which have a peculiarly apt ambiguity in a psychoanalytical context. Who are the 'higher powers', and what kind of attempt at moving them is to be given up in favour of enlisting demons? And are the latter Nemesis or Eumenides? Freud as the speaker (and how could he have resisted purloining such a speech) may have heard with mixed feelings the accents of the all-powerful scientist.

Plato portrays Eros (*Symposium* 202f.) as an ambiguous spirit, a daemon not a god, child of Poverty and Ingenuity, magician, alchemist, shabby, homeless, without shoes, dwelling between ignorance and wisdom, in love with beauty, aspiring to good, but potentially destructive. Eros is sexual energy as spiritual energy. Freud's libido is also a concept of the *energy* of the *Seele* or *Psyche* which can make or mar the life of the individual. Our life-problem is one of the transformation of energy. Here too there is a contrast between the Platonic religious concept and its quasi-scientific modern version. Energy is indeed a versatile and popular concept, as we see it in physics and in some philosophical thought. Ambiguous 'energy' can be the virtuous impulse of the individual, the enlightened influx, the reward of spiritual attention, or it may be seen as the fundamental cosmic energy (ultimate particles, or 'history' or *archi-écriture*) which dissolves both things and persons into some more basic reality. Herein we see re-enacted the quarrel between Plato and the presocratics. In the *Republic* the persistent questioning of Socrates by the young men is primarily concerned with the salvation of the individual. What is justice? How are we to become virtuous? Plato uses this concept of energy to explain the nature of moral change. (As in Freud, 'cure' lies in redeployment of energy.) He essentially accompanies the image of energy (magnetic attraction) by that of light and vision. The sun gives warmth and vital force, and also the light by which to see. We must transform base egoistic energy and vision (low Eros) into high spiritual energy and vision (high Eros). Metaphors of movement to express the nature of the moral will are sometimes in philosophy contrasted polemically with metaphors of vision, the latter being stigmatised as static rather than dynamic. Marxism and existentialism, and theology in descent from Kierkegaard, use the image of a leap. Some modern views of freedom, aware perhaps of an anti-personal deterministic use of the idea of fundamental energy, emphasise discontinuity. Kant is an ancestor of the idea that the mind switches or springs into morality and liberty: the sudden call of duty. Plato's more realistic concept of moral spiritual *desire* avoids both positions. We look at Christ (or Buddha or the Form of the Good) and are magnetically attracted: a tendency of which Kant expresses disapproval in the *Grundlegung*. The moral life in the Platonic understanding of it is a slow shift of attachments wherein *looking* (concentrating, attending, attentive discipline) is a source of divine (purified) energy. This is a progressive redemption of desire: and sexual attachment in the ordinary sense can be one possible starting point for the overcoming of egoism. The movement is not, by an occasional leap, into an external (empty) space of freedom, but patiently and continuously a change of one's whole being in all its contingent detail, through a world of appearance toward a world of reality. The importance Plato attaches to studying, whether in intellectual work or craft, is an instance and image of virtuous truth-seeking activity; and here, in Plato's system, though not by Plato, art too can be saved. (If he who makes the bed or the shield can thereby make himself a just man, why cannot he who decorates them?) There are innumerable points at which we have to detach ourselves, to change our orientation, to redirect our desire and refresh and purify our energy, to keep on looking in the right direction: to attend upon the grace that comes through faith.

> 2 <

# Fact and Value

A misleading though attractive distinction is made by many thinkers between fact and (moral) value. Roughly, the purpose of the distinction (as it is used by Kant and Wittgenstein for instance) is to *segregate* value in order to keep it pure and untainted, not derived from or mixed with empirical facts. This move however, in time and as interpreted, may in effect result in a diminished, even perfunctory, account of morality, leading (with the increasing prestige of science) to a marginalisation of 'the ethical'. (Big world of facts, little peripheral area of value.) This originally well-intentioned segregation then ignores an obvious and important aspect of human existence, the way in which almost all our concepts and activities involve evaluation. A post-Kantian theory of morals: survey all the facts, then use your reason. But, in the majority of cases, a survey of the facts will itself involve moral discrimination. Innumerable forms of evaluation haunt our simplest decisions. The defence of value is not an attack on 'ordinary facts'. The concept of 'fact' is complex. The moral point is that 'facts' are set up as such by human (that is moral) agents. Much of our life is taken up by truth-seeking, imagining, questioning. We relate to facts through truth and truthfulness, and come to recognise and discover that there are different modes and levels of insight and understanding. In many familiar ways *various* values pervade and *colour* what we take to be the reality of our world; wherein we constantly evaluate our own values and those of others, and judge and determine forms of consciousness and modes of being. To say all this is not in any way to deny either science, empiricism or common-sense. The proposition that 'the cat is on the mat' is true, indicates a fact, if the cat is on the mat. A proper separation of fact and value, as a defence of morality, lies in the contention that moral value cannot be *derived* from fact. That is, our activity of moral discrimination cannot be explained as merely one natural instinct among others, or our 'good' *identified* with pleasure, or a will to live, or what the government says (etc.). The possession of a moral sense is uniquely human; morality is, in the human world, something unique, special, *sui generis*, 'as if it came to us from elsewhere'. It is an intimation of 'something higher'. The demand that we be virtuous. It is 'inescapable and fundamental'. The interpretation of such phrases, including less fancy versions of the same intuition, has been, and should be, a main activity of moral philosophers.


'The work of art is the object seen *sub specie aeternitatis*; and the good life is the world seen *sub specie aeternitatis*. This is the connection between art and ethics. The usual way of looking at things sees objects as it were from the midst of them, the view *sub specie aeternitatis* from outside. In such a way that they have the whole world as background . . . If I have been contemplating the stove, and then am told: but now all you know is the stove, my result does indeed seem trivial. For this represents the matter as if I had studied the stove as one among the many things in the world. But if I was contemplating the stove *it* was my world, and everything else colourless by contrast with it . . . For it is equally possible to take the bare present image as the worthless momentary picture in the whole temporal world, and as the true world among shadows.'

(Wittgenstein, *Notebooks 1914–1916*, 7, 8, 9 October 1916.)

Wittgenstein was twenty-seven when he wrote these words which are preliminary notes for the last part of the *Tractatus*. There are significant differences between the two texts. This passage, three consecutive entries over three days, is a complete miniature metaphysical picture, making use of the potent idea of the work of art, or object of contemplative vision, as a limited whole. A 'world' is a limited whole. Morality, according to the later part of the *Tractatus* and this part of the *Notebooks*, is fundamentally an attitude of acceptance of the world of facts which is viewed as a whole, as something independent of my will. I quote again from the *Notebooks*, 8.7.16.

'The world is *given* me, i.e. my will enters into the world completely from outside as into something that is already there . . . That is why we have the feeling of being dependent on an alien will. *However this may be*, at any rate we *are* in a certain sense dependent, and what we are dependent on we can call God. In this sense God would simply be fate, or, what is the same thing: the world, which is independent of our will. I can make myself independent of fate. There are two godheads: the world and my independent I. I am either happy or unhappy, that is all. It can be said: good or evil do not exist.'

This view, which appears in a more epigrammatic form in the *Tractatus*, is to be connected with Wittgenstein's reading of Schopenhauer, by whom he was impressed when he was young. The shadow of Kant may indeed have fallen upon him through Schopenhauer. *Tractatus* Wittgenstein, like Kant, has two 'subjects', one which is locked on to the world of fact, and one which is totally independent of that world. Wittgenstein speaks of two godheads. 'I am my world' in two senses. I am the world of fact in the sense that I, the extensionless subject of experience, coincide exactly with my world of factual and significant apprehension. Wittgenstein's world of fact owns nothing beyond, the subject who experiences it fits it exactly; the notion of his 'seeing beyond' can make no sense. This impossibility is established (by Wittgenstein) in the nature of logic and language; in the *Tractatus* facts, states of affairs, are projected in propositions intelligibly organised by logic. They just *are* so projected, we cannot in the nature of the case see *how*, for this

[ 27 ]

would be to see beyond the transcendental barrier. (What is transcendent is beyond human experience, what is transcendental is not derived from human experience, but is a condition of it.) There is no other access to facts. Thus, in the *Tractatus*, Wittgenstein dismisses any general *problem* of a transcendent 'factual' world, or of the ability of language to refer to the world. Language just does refer to the world. This disposes by fiat of many of the questions raised by structuralism, and also of course of Cartesian anxieties about how the mind reaches the world. He similarly recognises no problem of the freedom of the will. 'The freedom of the will consists in the fact that future actions cannot be known now.' (*Tractatus* 5. 1362. *Tractatus* quotes are from the C. K. Ogden translation, unless otherwise stated.)

The other sense in which (in the *Tractatus*) I am my world, or live or experience my world, is the moral sense. Here I become an artist, or a mystic, ethics and aesthetics being one, looking at and accepting the world *as a whole, all* the facts. Value lies *ineffably* outside this limited whole. 'So too it is impossible for there to be propositions of ethics. Propositions can express nothing that is higher. It is clear that ethics cannot be put into words. Ethics is transcendental. (Ethics and aesthetics are one and the same.)' (*Tractatus* 6. 421, trans. Pears and McGuinness.) Wittgenstein does not, philosophically, discuss art though he makes a number of remarks about it, and like Plato he uses it as an image. Value does not alter, or in that sense enter, the world of facts, in the way in which Kant's duty or Categorical Imperative does mysteriously enter from the outside, illuminating particular situations and enabling us to act freely. 'Value' in the *Tractatus*, or the *moral* subject, of whom we cannot speak (6. 423), resides rather in an *attitude or style* in one's acceptance of all the facts. This morality is stoical rather than Kantian. The distinction between fact and value, the *protective* segregation of value from the world, is seen by Wittgenstein as a form of *silent* stoical understanding and way of life. 'I am either happy or unhappy, good and evil do not exist.' The end of the *Tractatus*, where these views about the moral subject are expressed, has often been treated as an arcane idiosyncratic tailpiece, lacking the philosophical interest of the longer earlier section. But the importance which Wittgenstein attached to it is shown by a letter written in 1919 to Ludwig Ficker (see Paul Engelmann, *Letters from Ludwig Wittgenstein with a Memoir*):

'The book's point is an ethical one. I once meant to include in the preface a sentence which is not in fact there now but which I will write out for you here, because it will perhaps be a key to the work for you. What I meant to write then was this: My work consists of two parts: the one presented here plus all that I have not written. And it is precisely this second part that is the important one. My book draws limits to the sphere of the ethical from the inside as it were, and I am convinced that this is the only rigorous way of drawing those limits. In short, I believe that where many others today are just gassing I have managed in my book to put everything firmly in place by being silent about it. And for that reason, unless I am very much mistaken, the book will say a great deal that you yourself want to say. Only perhaps you won't see that it is said in the book. For now, I would recommend you to read the preface and the conclusion, because they contain the most direct expression of the point of the book.'

I also quote here (from *Wittgenstein and the Vienna Circle*, conversations recorded by Friedrich Waismann, p. 68).

'To be sure, I can imagine what Heidegger means by being and anxiety. Man feels the urge to run up against the limits of language. Think for example of the astonishment that anything at all exists. This astonishment cannot be expressed in the form of a question, and there is also no answer whatsoever. Anything we might say is *a priori* bound to be mere nonsense. Nevertheless we do run up against the limits of language. Kierkegaard too saw that there is this running up against something and he referred to it in a fairly similar way (as running up against paradox). This running up against the limits of language is *ethics*. I think it is definitely important to put an end to all the claptrap about ethics – whether intuitive knowledge exists, whether values exist, whether the good is definable. In ethics we are always making the attempt to say something that cannot be said, something that does not and never will touch the essence of the matter. It is *a priori* certain that whatever definition of the good may be given – it will always be merely a misunderstanding to say that the essential thing, that what is really meant, corresponds to what is expressed (Moore). But the inclination, the running up against something, *indicates something*. St Augustine knew that already when he said: 'What, you swine you want not to talk nonsense! Go ahead and talk nonsense, it does not matter!'

\*

The reference to Heidegger concerns *Sein und Zeit* (*Being and Time*) published 1927, the reference to Moore is to his book *Principia Ethica*, the St Augustine reference is said to paraphrase *Confessions* I iv. *Et vae tacentibus de te, quoniam loquaces muti sunt.* (God is addressed.) 'And woe to those who are silent about You [do not praise You], since the ones who chatter say nothing!'

Wittgenstein has nothing to say in the *Tractatus* about a transcendent reality. Ethics cannot be expressed in words. 'Ethics is transcendental.' (6. 421.) It is at the border of experience. Here the 'fit', as one might put it, is perfect. There is no suggestive gleam from beyond, or crack through which one might peer, or any sense in talking about one. We *enact* morality, it looks after itself. Moreover:

'The solution of the problem of life is seen in the vanishing of the problem . . . There are, indeed, things which cannot be put into words. They *make themselves manifest*. They are what is mystical. The correct method in philosophy would really be the following: to say nothing except what can be said, i.e. propositions of natural science – i.e. something that has nothing to do with philosophy – and then, whenever someone else wanted to say something metaphysical, to demonstrate to him that he had failed to give a meaning to certain signs in his propositions.'

(6. 521, 6. 522, 6. 53; trans. Pears and McGuinness)

The 'propositions of natural science' means ordinary demonstrable factual statements. Wittgenstein says in the *Notebooks* (1.6.15) that his philosophy is entirely connected with whether there is an *a priori* order in the world. Also, 'my work has extended from the foundations of logic to the nature of the world' (2.8.16). The letter to Ficker suggests that the 'setting in order', or segregation (or magical setting apart) of the factual world has as its objective a clarification or purification of the function of morality. This too reminds us of Kant. The two 'godheads' are the world of fact which must be realistically, bravely, accepted, and the moral subject who is to accept it. Our 'will' can change the limits of the world but not the facts. (It can only change the *total aspect*, not the parts within the totality.) The world must wax or wane *as a whole*, according to our *general* attitude of acceptance or non-acceptance. (*Tractatus* 6. 43.) The morality recommended in the last part of the *Tractatus* is for all its coldness not without an intensity which might be called religious, or aesthetic. This would be a place from which to look at the relation between these two concepts. The much quoted 'Not *how* the world is, is the mystical, but *that* it is' (6. 44) is followed by 'The contemplation of the world *sub specie aeterni* is its contemplation as a limited whole.' We experience or express value more purely (indeed in the only possible way according to the *Tractatus*) if we are able to look at the world in a detached manner from the outside, as if it were a work of art. Facts are what can be expressed in plain non-evaluative language. There is no place for any idea of 'moral facts', or for the development of a 'moral vocabulary'. Such a view is certainly not just a period piece; it may be seen as prophetic, a morality for an age when space travel and physics make us conscious of the world, even of the universe, as a single entity, and when intimations of determinism and fears of cosmic disaster make ordinary moral distinctions (ordinary 'good and evil' or detailed talks about morality) seem unimportant. A cool attitude ('the propositions of natural science' (*Tractatus* 6. 53) might seem appropriate here, a preserved ability at least to ascertain the facts, the silent correlate of which would be an (unnamed) stoicism which eschewed despair. From this position the only possible additional morality might be one not envisaged by Wittgenstein: a scientifically informed global utilitarianism. The *Tractatus* may in general be regarded as an extreme and pure case, or by some as a *reductio ad absurdum*, of the idea that fact and value must not be allowed to *contaminate* each other. The imagery involved is very strong and, in a Kantian view of it, might appear traditional. Wittgenstein's later book, the *Philosophical Investigations*, deliberately denies us any dominating pictures. Wittgenstein said of this book that it was 'only an album', portraying a landscape continually sketched from different points of view. The *Tractatus* is more like a definitive metaphysical handbook, with its numerous visual metaphors: logical space, the limited whole, inside and outside, looking in a certain light (*sub specie aeterni*). We might here conjure up something like a picture by Blake, with the factual world spinning as a sort of glittering steel ball and the spirit of value silently circling around it. Or we may see, in a reversal of the Platonic image, the limited factual whole together with encircling value appearing like an eclipse of the sun, with the dark object in the middle and the light round the edges. There is no light in the world: what obscures it is the whole of the world.

*

Wittgenstein's relationship with Schopenhauer 'shows' in his distress or uncertainty about the concept of *will* in the 1914–1916 *Notebooks*, where he appears at moments as a reluctant prisoner of that philosopher's thoughts. I shall discuss Schopenhauer at more length shortly, but will give a very brief account of his views here. Schopenhauer pictures the fundamental reality and basis of our world as a ruthless powerful cosmic force, the Will to Live, and the world as we know and experience it as a causally determined construct of phenomena brought about by (us) subjects through our perceptions, that is objectified ideas of the Will. The Will to Live, to *exist*, takes care of continuation of species and general ordering of entities. At the human level it is manifest as the natural egoism of the individual, each for himself, resulting in a scene of perpetual misery and strife. The world of ideas (objectifications of the Will) is in itself neither good nor bad. The horrors of the human scene result from the selfish wills of individuals as manifestations of the Will to Live. Other individuals, animals, plants, and the whole of our perceived phenomena are also suffering under the sovereignty of the Will. (Schopenhauer quotes St Paul, Romans 8. 22, 'the whole creation groaneth and travaileth in pain together'.) In our world there may be some slight alleviation, or degrees of egoism, through experience of art, or in the form of instinctive compassion. Exceptional individuals may achieve complete escape from pain and evil by a total *denial of the Will*. This 'dying to the world' is, according to Schopenhauer, a mystical spiritual condition which cannot be described. Schopenhauer's interest in Hindu and Buddhist mysticism may well have touched the young Wittgenstein, prompting for instance his attachment to Rabindranath Tagore, as well as his concept of 'the mystical' in *Tractatus* and *Notebooks*.

Wittgenstein was (evidently) attracted, as many other less philosophical persons were, by the outrageous simplicity of Schopenhauer's picture. The structure of objectified ideas is simply *there*, not in itself good or bad, an objectification of the Will which as a cosmic force is both ruthless and blameless (like a waterfall or earthquake). Human wills, willed by the Will to Live, are however, in their existing context, necessarily selfish, an inevitable cause of suffering and unhappiness. The facts, ideas, world is entirely separate from selfish human will and unchanged by it. Humans cannot enforce their will upon the world. Schopenhauer postulates a superhuman cosmic will, Wittgenstein simply speaks of an alien will. While following Schopenhauer, he 'demythologises' the picture. Since he (Wittgenstein) cannot change this alien will (how the world is) his relation to it must be that of an attitude. Can I not make myself entirely independent of it, and so be master of it, by renouncing any influence upon happenings, that is by denying the will altogether? 'How can a man be happy at all, since he cannot ward off the misery of this world? Through a life of knowledge . . . The only life that is happy is the life that can renounce the amenities of the world.' Total denial of the Will is best; a realistic stoicism may be next best. Denial of the Will, with the disappearance of the problem of life, is the mystical. This is a state which we cannot conceptualise, of which we cannot speak. Wittgenstein's 'denial' is apparently offered as an accessible stoicism. Schopenhauer is more pessimistic, offering little hope of human happiness. The mystical stage is only reached by extreme asceticism. However he allows some escape by contemplation of art. Wittgenstein mentions happiness (*Notebooks*): 'the happy life is good', and 'the end of art is the beautiful, and the beautiful *is* what makes happy'. There is also 'living in the present' and stoical 'agreement with the world' which is 'What "being happy" means'. (See *Notebooks* 11.6.16 onward.) Wittgenstein entirely agrees with, and adopts, Schopenhauer's rejection of Kant's Categorical Imperative (*Tractatus* 6. 422); but although both regard morality as an attitude (since the world cannot be altered) Schopenhauer has quite a lot to say about morality (especially about compassion and justice) whereas Wittgenstein suggests his views by his silence. There is in Schopenhauer a shadowy picture of a spiritual pilgrimage. Both postulate a world of facts (or entities) independent of human will, but neither explains 'will' sufficiently to make clear why this world must be assumed. The segregation of the factual world allows in both cases a stoical morality which verges toward mysticism. What Wittgenstein indicates by a silent nod, is stated by Schopenhauer as a distinction of phenomenal and noumenal deriving from Kant. Schopenhauer accounts for our helplessness by a theory of determinism. Wittgenstein simply decrees it and wisely does not tangle with determinism. He equally decreed the machinery of the larger logical part of the *Tractatus*; his segregation of morality also serves the purpose of keeping the world clean for the propositional calculus. Schopenhauer does not explain how the Will relates to ideas, or ideas to particulars. His metaphysical substructure is kept clear of value while at the same time establishing value's place. Schopenhauer's influence on Wittgenstein is in the field of morality, appearing in the last section of *Notebooks* and of *Tractatus*. Later Wittgenstein did not *philosophise* about morals.

Wittgenstein's (in the *Tractatus*) limited whole which is the integrated world of fact, language and experience, separates the area of valueless contingency, where everything is as it is and happens as it does happen, from the *thereby* purified ineffable activity of value. The world can then become, from a moral point of view, with an acceptance of all the facts, an object of contemplation: an idea which would have appalled Kant. This stoical contemplation is true happiness, beyond tainted and illusory ideas of good and evil, fearless of death. We may profitably compare and contrast this strong imagery with that conjured up by Kant's moral philosophy, which also involves a strict separation of fact and value. Here (Kant) the self-contained world of necessity (causally determined contingency) might be thought of as blocking, at any rate rendering unclear, the light which comes from a distant, thereby invisible, God, or spiritual principle better called Freedom and Reason, yet also showing up this spiritual light by contrast. But of course in Kant's picture, value (as practical Reason) does all the time enter the alien world as a kind of laser beam and can be enacted as duty and spoken of in rational discourse about moral maxims in a way which is very familiar to us, and which indeed provides us with a dominant image of spiritual reality. A laser beam: very clear, narrow, strong, coming from an unseen source, illuminating a point in a world which is otherwise valueless. This can be a religious or non-religious picture according to whether the will is seen as a vehicle of a higher power or itself the source. The contingent particularity of the world is hallowed, one might say, by becoming incarnate in moral maxims, in moral *laws*, in principles of action. Insights interact with rules. We then see a (problematic) part of our world clearly from a moral point of view. The laser beam image needs some qualification however. Kant's maxims (rules), as dictates of Reason, are *universal*, applying to all rational beings in similar situations. In the *Grundlegung* Kant seems to imply that such rules are also of great *generality*. (Be benevolent, do not lie.) This may be said to reflect a certain kind of (perfectionist, unified, simplified) moral society. One could agree that 'do not lie' casts its light upon the whole world and must always be kept in mind. But many duties arise in particular complex situations, for instance where rational maxims conflict, and where we have to use our reason to create more particular (fitting *this* situation) moral rulings for our-

[ 34 ]

selves. This is the form of a ubiquitous human problem. Lying is wrong. Yet: when is it right to lie? Benevolence is good, but when is it a *moral* mistake? (Etc. etc. etc.) Schopenhauer discusses this matter, disagreeing with Kant. (I come to this later.) In any case, this dilemma (put in Kantian language, how particular can a universal rule be?) does not affect the validity of Kant's excellent dictum that 'we are not gentleman volunteers, but conscripts, in the army of the moral law'. Our fundamental recognition, in all our various adventures in the contingent world, of the difference between good and evil is Kant's starting point: a self-evident one he would say. How Reason (moral value) alters the course of the (causally determined) realm of fact is not clarified and perhaps cannot be. We recognise this picture of our dual nature, and we *experience* the influence of Respect for the Moral Law, especially when it contradicts our desires. Wittgenstein does not speak of moral rules or discuss freedom or cause. His 'limited whole' world is everywhere equally and relentlessly contingent and value-free. Good or bad willing cannot alter the facts, but only the 'limits' (or one might venture the image 'colour') of the *whole* world, which waxes and wanes as a whole. A moral attitude is to be taken as a totality. 'The world of the happy is unlike the world of the unhappy.' We are subject to fate; God (one of Wittgenstein's two 'godheads') is to be seen as fate, as *amor fati*. We must accept 'all the facts', the world is not altered by morality, but the whole of it is (as one might say) bathed in a certain light. In the *Vermischte Bemerkungen, Culture and Value* (p. 78), Wittgenstein says, ' "*Le style c'est l'homme, le style c'est l'homme même*". The first expression has cheap epigrammatic brevity. The second, correct version opens up quite a different perspective. It says that a man's style is a *picture* of himself.' (Of the whole man, and his whole world.) To speak of the 'waxing and waning' in terms of general moral 'style' is to emphasise a contrast with Kant. It may be said that surely in (moral, spiritual) 'conversion' a man's whole life (world) alters. Another remark in *Culture and Value* (p. 53): 'I believe that one of the things Christianity says is that sound doctrines are all useless. That you have to change your *life*. (Or the *direction* of your life.)' This is an inspiring dictum, but how does this come about? A general 'conversion' does not, any more than a general 'style', solve detailed unpredictable problems of duty, to which we must have the humility to realise that we are subject. We *need* a 'moral vocabulary', a detailed value terminology, morally loaded words. (Not a requirement of Wittgenstein.) Important moral partings of the ways are implied in the complex relations between these concepts. Wittgenstein gives no status to the idea of duty, he follows Schopenhauer who regarded 'duty' as an archaic magico-theological idea derived from the Ten Commandments and connected with rewards and punishments. Schopenhauer: 'In the conception of *ought* there lies always and essentially the reference to threatened punishment or promised reward.' ('Criticism of the Kantian Philosophy', *The World as Will and Idea*, henceforth styled *WWI*, Haldane and Kemp translation. See also *The Basis of Morality* II 4.) This is echoed by Wittgenstein at *Tractatus* 6. 422. Wittgenstein does not use the vocabulary of noumenal and phenomenal, but what it names is present, and the relation of value to the 'ordinary world' is also mysterious. Value is essentially ineffable since significant discourse is tied to fact. It cannot alter facts but its operation is thereby extremely pure. Moral philosophy and theology too are bound to be ineffable, an attempt to say what cannot be said but can only be, in the whole living of life, *shown*. 'Ethics is transcendental' (*Tractatus* 6. 421). Indeed the whole of the *Tractatus* is really nonsense (6. 54), since if we attempt to limit the conditions of experience from inside we cannot properly talk about what is outside. Can we not see a little beyond those transcendental barriers, do we not have intimations, gleams of light, glimpses of another scene? The *Tractatus* is a sustained attempt to put a final end to such talk, and to do so (as he explained in the letter to Ficker), in the interests of morality. We must, at least, talk as little as possible and then, as Wittgenstein tells us at the end of the book, 'throw away the ladder'. Kierkegaard would have appreciated that image.

This excursion into pictures follows on from what I was saying about the fascinating image of the work of art (the illusory unity, the limited whole), and illustrates too the pictorial nature of philosophy, which one does not always notice because 'picturing' is so natural. In thinking about abstract matters one instinctively produces images, such as duty being like a laser beam coming from above; an image which may itself elicit figurative rejoinders. Are not many duties more like an unchanging fall of shadows from a permanent light-source at ground level? Does not duty live here below in networks of rules? If the 'demythologisation' of theological and moral thinking means the removal of pictures, can this be more than a substitution of one picture for another, so that (for instance) instead of God we have the mobile jumping will, and instead of metaphors of light, metaphors of movement (and so on)? Philosophers are artists, and metaphysical ideas are aesthetic; they are intended to clarify and connect, and they certainly satisfy deep emotional needs. The image of the unified limited whole is a product of philosophical art, and is like a work of art. Popular physics now portrays to us the cosmos (everything that is) as a 'whole'; and the idea works deeply in religious and metaphysical thinking. This may seem both natural and inevitable since our world is full of things and persons and stories. We constantly weave our experience into limited wholes (art works), as when we 'tell our day' in a series of vignettes. Many problems in philosophy concern the status and authority of these familiar entities. What are these 'limited wholes'? Are 'persons' really real? Hume said they were 'bundles of perceptions'. (*Treatise of Human Nature*, Book I, iv 6.) Stories, which involve the difficult concept of cause, are surely 'artificial', perhaps 'superficial'. Painters, that unphilosophical tribe who make pictures of the world, dissolve the solid object into planes and colours and space. Can all such 'things' be regarded as 'basic norms' or 'fundamental aspects of human nature', of which other things appear as analogies? Or are they illusions which, inside the philosopher's study at any rate, can be analysed away? Even in philosophy it is hard to think in other terms. At least we can remember, to use a warning from the *Philosophical Investigations* (II vii, p. 184) that the picture is in the foreground while the *work* which the picture does is often in the background. The concept of evolution: we form a picture, the higher animals emerging and so on. 'What this language primarily describes is a picture. What is to be done with the picture, how it is to be used, is still obscure. Clearly however it must be explored if we want to understand the sense of what we are saying. But the picture seems to spare us this work: it already points to a particular use.'

It is difficult for the philosopher, and *a fortiori* for the theologian, to surrender the quest for satisfying sovereign imagery which is to indicate a very, or absolutely, important reality. Philosophers divide between those who do, and those who do not, think that morality is such a reality. Philosophers who separate value from fact may belong to either group. (Hume, for instance, portrays morality in a way which shows it as important, but not supremely so.) Plato's *image* (metaphor) for the Form of the Good is another separate spherical object, the sun:

[ 37 ]

an ideal unity, a transcendent source of light. Good is above being, non-personal, non-contingent, not a particular thing among other things. Plato illumines it with stories which are deliberately cast as explanatory myths and must not be mistaken for anything else. Plato's 'sun' is separate and perfect, yet also immanent in the world as the life-giving magnetic genesis of all our struggles for truth and virtue. Plato never identified his Form of the Good with God (the use of *theos* at *Republic* 597B is a *façon de parler*), and this separation is for him an essential one. Religion is above the level of the 'gods'. There are no gods and no God either. Neo-Platonic thinkers made the *identification* (of God with Good) possible; and the Judaeo-Christian tradition has made it easy and natural for us to gather together the aesthetic and consoling impression of Good as a person. At least, we find it easy to imagine; but must remember that (some) great philosophers in the past were able to believe in a personal God in a way which is increasingly inaccessible to the thinkers of today. They (Descartes for instance) could *think* God, and thereby unify the idea of Good, in a way which we begin to find difficult. The question can even arise whether we are able to think systematically at all about morals (Wittgenstein thought we could not) and what kind, if any, of expression we can give to a belief, if we hold it, in the sovereign status of morality. Hegelians may appear to be the most comfortable theists. Hegel's immanent 'god' is, like Plato's mythical Demiurge, an artist, but, unlike the Demiurge, is not handling irreducibly recalcitrant material; so Hegel's Whole, which seen philosophically from the outside is a limited one, can be (ultimately) perfectly coherent and good: another large round object.

The *Tractatus* may be seen as, in the Platonic sense, a myth. Its ethical purpose is to exclude talk about ethics. Such talk would be a running against the limits. (Such running against nevertheless indicates something.) Derrida's structuralism, much later, sharing some of Wittgenstein's (for instance anti-Cartesian) ideas but not his method, may be seen as more like a science, excluding morality in the way in which science excludes it. In general the picturesque traditional (for instance existentialist) philosophies are being 'seen off', their solutions exposed as merely watered-down or dehydrated versions of great old solutions (those of Descartes, Kant, Hegel). Derrida announced the end of philosophy and named Heidegger as the last metaphysician. The Cartesian era is coming to an end. Wittgenstein said that he was ending it. In moral philosophy it may appear that the Kantian era is coming to an end. Theology not only reflects these problems but is forced to struggle with them in ways which bring it closer to philosophy now than it has been for some time. This is so in spite of, and partly in reaction to, the fact that in a materialistic technological society, theology might be expected to be increasingly isolated from general trends of thought. The question, what can be said about value and how can we picture it and grasp it, raised by the *Tractatus* and implicitly by structuralism, would not have occurred to Plato or to a quasi-Platonic thinker such as Hegel, for whom the world *is* a system of truths and values; whereas the question suggests that *value* is something personal and dramatic (perhaps a silent movement of the will), or mysterious and arcane (residing in creative uses of language), or a bourgeois illusion, or an illusion *tout court*: at any rate that it is something separate, lodged in a part of the world, and not a light in which the whole world is revealed. This setting at a distance of what is closest (material objects, knowledge of the world, emotional aspects of evaluation, etc.) is a persistent, and of course not necessarily unfruitful, technique for dealing with, or inventing, philosophical problems. How is it done? By magic. 'Metaphysics as a kind of magic.' (Wittgenstein; see introduction to his *Remarks on Frazer's 'Golden Bough'*.) Plato assumes the internal relation of value, truth, cognition. Virtue (as compassion, humility, courage) involves a desire for and achievement of truth instead of falsehood, reality instead of appearance. Goodness involves truth-seeking knowledge and *ipso facto* a discipline of desire. 'Getting things right', as in meticulous grammar or mathematics, is truth-seeking as virtue. Learning anything properly demands (virtuous) attention. Here the idea of *truth* plays a crucial role (as it does also in Kant) and reality emerges as the object of truthful vision, and virtuous action as the product of such vision. This is a picture of the omnipresence of morality and evaluation in human life. On this view it would seem mad to begin philosophy by asserting a complete separation of fact from value, and then attempting to give a satisfactory account of morals.

The dualism in question may of course be traced in some form very far back in western thought, even to a distinction between mortals and gods. As a pre-Kantian philosophical viewpoint it may be seen in the Aristotelian tradition in familiar distinctions of faith from reason, and intellect from will. In pre-Kantian British empiricism, we might see it in Hume's contention that we cannot derive 'ought' from 'is', or value from fact, although he wants no drama made of this since habit and custom and semi-reflective feeling are not only the best but the only available guides to conduct. This in effect allows an instinctive, if not intellectual, connection of fact with value. This sensible anti-rationalist attitude makes Hume an ancestor of both conservative and liberal political thinking. Of course both Platonic and Kantian morality reject any crude derivation of value from fact or 'nature', as in a *definition* of good as happiness, or what the dictator says, or what the priest says. This is about the connection of virtue with freedom. The moral agent should be able to distinguish (not always easy) a benign influence from a surrender of conscience. The extreme modern form of the fact–value distinction derives from Kant, who unlike Hume had some clear idea of science. Kant was impressed by Hume (who, Kant says, woke him from his 'dogmatic slumber'), but repudiated Hume's vague (sloppy) psychological account of space, time, causality, morals and conceptual knowledge. A protection of science then went with a segregation of value, and vice versa. The austerity of this severance also had a part to play in the drama of the Romantic Movement, as involving the liberation of the individual into an open space wherein to *construct* his morality, stirred and edified by reflection upon freedom versus necessity, passion versus reason, value versus fact. Kant of course connects the two relentlessly severed realms by the experience of duty and the postulation of practical reason. We are to believe that they connect, though the exact mechanism of the connection remains somewhat clouded. Post-Kantian developments in moral philosophy outside the Hegelian tradition have been largely attempts at different versions of this fact–value distinction, which also appears in its more histrionic form in Sartre's existentialism (*en-soi* and *pour soi*) and Heidegger's contrast of 'everydayness' with heroic authenticity. A distinction of intellect from will still imparts its flavour to some, Catholic and Protestant, theology. *Tractatus* Wittgenstein is as usual elegantly unlike his colleagues in that, with more sober logic, he tells us that if we absolutely separate fact and value we can say nothing about the latter. And this is just as well since, as he hints elsewhere, things which people do try to say in general about value are usually pretty messy and false (just gassing). Wittgenstein is not simply enjoining philosophical silence in the *Tractatus*. He enjoins ordinary-language silence. He also, in peripheral observations, indicates that the (to use Kierkegaard's phrase) indirect communication of art may perhaps be able somehow to say something about value, morality, and 'the human heart'; but he would not think it the philosopher's task to say how this could be done or to evaluate attempts to do it.

Wittgenstein has had many followers in the analytical tradition, most of whom he would regard as having misunderstood him. The preface to A. J. Ayer's *Language, Truth and Logic* (published 1936) tells us that

'The views which are put forward in this treatise derive from the doctrines of Bertrand Russell and Wittgenstein, which are themselves the logical outcome of the empiricism of Berkeley and David Hume. Like Hume, I divide all genuine propositions into two classes: those which, in his terminology, concern "relations of ideas", and those which concern "matters of fact". The former class comprises the *a priori* propositions of logic and pure mathematics, and these I allow to be necessary and certain only because they are analytic. That is, I maintain that the reason why these propositions cannot be confuted in experience is that they do not make any assertion about the empirical world, but simply record our determination to use symbols in a certain fashion. Propositions concerning empirical matters of fact, on the other hand, I hold to be hypotheses, which can be probable but never certain. And in giving an account of their validation I claim also to have explained the nature of truth ... I require of an empirical hypothesis, not indeed that it should be conclusively verifiable, but that some possible sense-experience should be relevant to the determination of its truth or falsehood. If a putative proposition fails to satisfy this principle, and is not a tautology, then I hold that it is metaphysical, and that, being metaphysical, it is neither true nor false, but literally senseless.'

Having discussed and disposed of various objections to the idea that all synthetic (non-tautological) propositions are empirical hypotheses, Ayer confronts a final one to the effect that, surely, 'statements of value' are genuine synthetic propositions, but cannot be represented as hypotheses, which are used to predict the course of our sensations, and therefore the existence of ethics and aesthetics presents a difficulty for Ayer's 'radical empiricist thesis'. He proceeds to argue, and attempts to demonstrate, that 'in so far as statements of value are significant they are ordinary "scientific" statements, and that in so far as they are

[ 41 ]

not scientific, they are not in the literal sense significant, but are simply expressions of emotion which can be neither true nor false.' Non-normative descriptions of ethical terms may be held to be factual, descriptions of moral experience are consigned to the science of psychology. Normative expressions of ethical terms and exhortations to virtue 'are not propositions at all, but ejaculations or commands'. The truth of ethical judgments cannot be tested because they depend upon pseudo-concepts.

'The presence of an ethical symbol in a proposition adds nothing to its factual content. If I say to someone "You acted wrongly in stealing that money", I am not stating anything more than if I had simply said "You stole that money". In adding that this action is wrong I am not making any further statement about it. I am simply evincing my moral disapproval of it. It is as if I had said "You stole that money" in a peculiar tone of horror, or written it with the addition of some special exclamation marks. The tone, or the exclamation marks, add nothing to the literal meaning of the sentence. It merely serves to show that the expression of it is attended by certain feelings in the speaker.'

I first read Ayer's book in 1940 when I began to study philosophy and was, together with many others, amazed and impressed by its wonderful clarity and simplicity. We were unprovided with any weapons with which to confront it, and in any case it was a welcome change from the scraps of Bradley and Cook Wilson with which we had been fiddling, and considerably easier to understand than Kant and Aristotle. The first chapter is entitled 'The Elimination of Metaphysics', a 'rejection of the metaphysical thesis that philosophy affords us knowledge of a transcendent reality'. This was long before Derrida. Schlick and the Vienna Circle are mentioned. Kant is claimed as an ally in having rejected metaphysics in the sense of knowledge of the transcendent. Plato, Aristotle and Kant were not metaphysicians but analysts, not concerned with the existence or properties of things, but 'only with the way in which we talk about them'. 'The propositions of philosophy are not factual, but linguistic in character . . . they express definitions, or the formal consequences of definitions. We may say that philosophy is a department of logic.' Such thoughts belong to the earlier days of analytical philosophy and are, before their time, often suggestive of structuralist aims and modes of reflection. This brilliant young man's book certainly poses deep problems, even if these problems are given, to say the least, a rather hasty treatment.

'A work of art is not necessarily the worse for the fact that all the propositions comprising it are literally false. But to say that many literary works are largely composed of falsehoods is not to say that they are composed of pseudo-propositions. It is, in fact, very rare for a literary artist to produce sentences which have no literal meaning. And where this does occur, the sentences are carefully chosen for their rhythm and balance. If the author writes nonsense, it is because he considers it most suitable for bringing about the effects for which his writing is designed.'

Ayer seems to have taken to heart the message of the last part of the *Tractatus* which describes as nonsense and consigns to silence all our utterances except 'the propositions of natural science'. However, Ayer seems to have misunderstood Wittgenstein in the same way in which numerous thinkers misunderstand Plato. The 'picturesque' structure indicates something beyond it; it is not to be taken literally. That is in the nature (or magic) of metaphysics. Ayer's book, which may now seem to us brilliant and ingenious, but also unsophisticated and dotty, diminishes the human scene to the scale of a logical puzzle. (Ayer himself, in later prefaces, suggests some, not radical, modifications.) Wittgenstein's silence indicates the area of value. Ayer's use of the distinction between fact and value deliberately removes value. His 'explanation' of truth, his 'elimination' of the transcendent, not least his claim that philosophical thought can only concern uses of language, are more suggestive of the reductionist ruthlessness of the followers of Derrida than of the milder reflections of the empiricist tradition. Moreover, if we reflect now upon computer technology, the restriction of truth-capacity to facts and *tautologies* may have a reinforced plausibility. Some subsequent linguistic philosophers, styling themselves analysts and not preachers, but unhappy with the idea that moral judgments were just expressions of emotion unconnected with rationality, attempted a rescue by describing them, in post-Kantian and less brutal ways, as persuasions or commands. Gilbert Ryle's book *The Concept of Mind* (1949), after discussing Descartes and 'the ghost in the machine', discusses, with numerous examples, concepts such as emotion, will, imagination. Even if one disagrees with his behaviourist thesis, his lively descriptions may be read as 'phenomenology'.

*

[ 43 ]

When we think about morality we want to be comforted by our thoughts and are reluctant to admit that we can say nothing about it. Ayer hailed G. E. Moore as another holder of the view that 'philosophising is an activity of analysis', but adding that Moore 'took a rather different view' of analysis. This is true; indeed Moore is a shameless *preacher*, not hesitating to tell us, not only what the *concept* of (moral) good is, but also what things actually *are good*. He identified something which he called the 'naturalistic fallacy' which was the mistake of *defining* good, and trying to do so by joining fact and value through a definition such as 'good is happiness', 'good is pleasure', 'good is obedience to the Church'. Moore charged Bentham and Mill with having made this mistake. However, Moore was reluctant to abandon the idea that good was *something* (and so a *kind* of fact). He reintroduced a transcendent good in the form of a *simple property* of goodness, to be compared in respect of simplicity with yellow, only 'non-natural', whose presence in certain places we are able to intuit: an idea which might be held to work more plausibly for beauty, of which perhaps Moore was thinking.

*Principia Ethica* (1903) chapter I, sections 6–10:

'If I am asked, "What is good?" my answer is that good is good, and that is the end of the matter. Or if I am asked, "How is good to be defined?" my answer is that it cannot be defined, and that is all I have to say about it. But disappointing as these answers may appear, they are of the very last importance. To readers who are familiar with philosophic terminology, I can express their importance by saying that they amount to this: That propositions about the good are all of them synthetic and never analytic; and that is plainly no trivial matter. And the same thing may be expressed more popularly, by saying that, if I am right, then nobody can foist upon us such an axiom as that "Pleasure is the only good" or that "The good is the desired" on the pretence that this is "the very meaning of the word". Let us, then, consider this position. My point is that "good" is a simple notion, just as "yellow" is a simple notion; that just as you cannot, by any manner of means, explain to anyone who does not already know it, what yellow is, so you cannot explain what good is . . . "good" has no definition because it is simple and has no parts . . . It may be true that all things which are good are *also* something else, just as it is true that all things which are yellow produce a certain kind of vibration in the light. And it is a fact that Ethics aims at discovering what are those other properties belonging to all things which are good. But far too many philosophers have thought that when they named those other properties they were actually defining good; that these properties, in fact, were simply not "other" but absolutely and entirely the same with goodness. This view I propose to call the "naturalistic fallacy" and of it I shall now endeavour to dispose.'

J. M. Keynes, reflecting in 'My Early Beliefs' (*Two Memoirs*) upon the influence Moore had upon his disciples in Cambridge, says: 'We classified as aesthetic experience what is really human experience and somehow sterilised it by this mis-classification.' By 'sterilised' I assume he means separated it from the messiness of ordinary morals and practical life. Keynes also says: 'It is remarkable how wholly oblivious Moore managed to be of the qualities of the life of action and also of the pattern of life as a whole. He was existing in a timeless ecstasy. His way of translating his own particular emotions of the moment into the language of generalised abstraction is a charming and beautiful comedy.' The last two sentences may be less than just, but it can indeed be said that Moore was his own (not unendearing) kind of contemplative. So, good is like yellow in being a simple property not definable in terms of its parts, and also (being non-natural) resembles other entities (such as numbers) which do not in the ordinary (natural) sense exist. The comparisons are striking, but on reflection not illuminating. Indeed they bring out rather how very unlike 'good' is to other concepts. 'Yellow' can be learnt instantly by ostensive showing, whereas 'learning the meaning of good' is a more complex matter. Moore confuses the situation further by his firm choice of the highest goodest goods. 'By far the most valuable things which we know or can imagine are certain states of consciousness which may be roughly described as the pleasures of human intercourse and the enjoyment of beautiful objects.' (VI 113.) His selection is touching, and if modestly offered as just 'valuable' or even 'very valuable' might well find acceptance. But his choice does indeed seem to omit (to use Keynes's words) 'the pattern of life as a whole'; and is so exclusive as almost to amount to a definition of good in terms of aesthetics and friendship: a form of hedonistic utilitarianism. ('Valuable' as pleasing to sophisticated persons.) His idea (attractive to Keynes) that 'states of mind' are what matter deserves reflection. Later I shall discuss 'consciousness' and its 'quality' as coming into

[ 45 ]

consideration in moral philosophy. Moore's confident taking-for-granted of this concept is one of the more interesting aspects of his thought.

Moore was of course right to deal firmly with Bentham and Mill in so far as they *equated* good with happiness – an equation uneasily disturbed by Mill's distinction between higher and lower pleasures. Moore was mainly read as a critic of the utilitarians although his discussions of other thinkers are worth attention. But the distinction between fact and value, which he took to be implied by his objection to definitions of good (quite apart from his temperament), isolated and diminished his concept of good; as this distinction, in its many guises in moral philosophy, tends to do. I discuss this matter in more general terms later on. Wittgenstein, who offered the distinction in a different style in the *Tractatus*, of course disagreed with Moore's views and his philosophical tone, but he respected Moore very much, and elicited from his work items worthy to be discussed: a privilege he did not extend to many people. Moore was regarded later by some as a 'bad influence' upon the undergraduates of his time. Keynes sees it otherwise. 'It was this escape from Bentham, joined with the *unsurpassable individualism* [my italics] of our philosophy, which has served to protect us from the final *reductio ad absurdum* of Benthamism known as Marxism'. And 'indeed it is only states of mind that matter, provided we agree to take account of the pattern of life through time, and give up regarding it as a series of independent instantaneous flashes; but the ways in which states of mind can be valuable, and the objects of them, are more various and also much richer than we allowed for'. Not Marx, not Freud: for Keynes and his friends, 'the atmosphere of Plato's dialogues'.

More recent philosophers have attempted to retain some shadow of the old guaranteeing unity by treating morality in a neo-Kantian sense as non-universal reason or sincere authentic free activity. Thus the individual will takes over the transcendent unifying function, operating as a sun-like source of value, conferring sense upon the world and assembling it systematically around the individual as centre. Impersonal intellect looks after facts, personal will creates values. Structuralism, in so far as it offers itself as 'scientific', must profess to be morally neutral; but the large and various volume of structuralist writings contains innumerable value judgments. Benthamite utilitarianism, and that perhaps alone, in its original and in its modern (unacknowledged as such) form, is genuinely pluralist, and makes a more thorough rejection of a unified good, since although morality is defined in terms of a single idea, happiness, the natural muddle of the world re-enters the theory through the ambiguity and diversity of the concept. The fundamentalist pluralism of Hobbes has the same axiomatic individualistic basis; whereas modern technology and orthodox Marxism imply, whether as 'social reality' or as *dolce vita*, a more homogeneous idea of happiness. Bentham and Hobbes stand behind political liberalism, repetitively reminding us of the good old unregenerate idea of diverse human satisfactions; and Benthamite values have also of course worked quietly within the Marxist orthodoxy, ignoring the general myth and pointing to individual and various needs. There is here a constant and recurring return to the obvious. Some form of utilitarianism is probably now the most widely and instinctively accepted philosophy of the western world. (Compare Schopenhauer's 'compassion'.) What this view lacks, and needs, as some of its critics point out, is a positive conception of virtue. This should not be thought of as a 'refutation' of utilitarian insights, which must always travel with us, but rather as a moral light in which to understand and 'place' them. These insights retain an axiomatic status which I shall discuss later. J. S. Mill, aware of Coleridge and pointing on to Moore, posed the question when he used an intuited idea of 'moral quality' (higher and lower pleasures) to organise and justify the 'natural' conception of happiness: thus making, like Moore, a little metaphysical gesture to indicate a problem he could not solve. For a larger enlightenment we turn to a more detailed and imaginative metaphysic. An uncriticised idea of happiness cannot be the sole basis of an ethical theory. Plato's idea of truth-seeking knowledge and his ambivalent Eros, and Kant's particularising idea of duty, play in a more effective manner the necessary role of introducing pluralism into unity and thereby revealing the world.

Historical change is (in part and fundamentally) change of imagery. This is often prompted by scientific discovery. Think how our idea of our home planet has altered, both as we look back over hundreds of years, and over scores of years; Earth, now, as a travelling spaceship, seen from the outside, vulnerable, lonely, precious. Technological progress can deeply affect our sense of ourselves, as Marxists tried to explain. The agency can be mysterious, darkness moving upon darkness. We are at present involved in deep thought-changes, of which the unattractive word 'demythologisation' names some. I have been talking about the aesthetic one-making instincts of metaphysicians, and also about that popular explanatory device, the dichotomy between fact and value (or intellect and will) which haunts theologians as well as philosophers. A related distinction, familiar and influential, is that between public and private. This distinction has an obvious beneficent use in liberal political theory and practice. Moral philosophy must however consider the shadows cast by such distinctions upon modes of individual reflection. The *Tractatus*, here once again functioning as an elegant and prophetic myth, quietly joins the two dichotomies together. Science and 'ordinary life' are public and use public, that is significant, language (or in other words, language), whereas morality and religion are private and ineffable. Language, meaning, is and can only be a structure which rests upon actual or possible ('ordinary' or scientific) facts. The *Tractatus* takes reference to the world, projection of fact into language, as fundamental and unsayable, inaccessible to discussion. 'A picture cannot depict its pictorial form; it displays it.' (Or: 'its method of representation'. *Seine Form der Abbildung* 2. 172.) These ideas can also, having suffered various sea-changes, be seen in structuralism. The second sentence of the *Tractatus*, 'The world is the totality of facts, not of things', resembles a structuralist insight. Structuralism however makes a further metaphysical move from which Wittgenstein wisely abstained. If we cannot see, or say, how language is able to refer to the world (by looking at both and noting correspondences) then it seems a simple philosophical feat and apt use of Occam's razor to remove the world. Structuralist thought is then also driven to distinguish discreetly between 'low', fairly simple though shifting, 'ordinary' and technological, self-referring linguistic codes (naively taken to refer to a pre-existent world, and constituting the main being of ordinary proceedings and ordinary folk) and 'high', sophisticated, creative, self-aware, uses of language by scientific geniuses, or by philosophers and poets and poetic writers who, in indirect communications, invent concepts and hint at values. One result of this distinction is that literature is required to be linguistically self-conscious, no longer taken in by the 'referential fallacy' (looking through the page into another world), and to treat language as an experimental adventure playground where what is important can only be said by poetic

[ 48 ]

or quasi-poetic means. Early structuralism does not seem to have been aware of Wittgenstein. Lacan produced as novel, in 1956, ideas (for instance about 'inner processes', and words not being names) which were current in Cambridge before the 1939 war. In general, for those trained in the analytical philosophical tradition, structuralist writings seem singularly lacking in detailed philosophical reflection.

In the *Philosophical Investigations* Wittgenstein abandons the metaphysical, pictorial, method of the *Tractatus* and deals in a more direct and piecemeal way with questions about meaning and 'mental contents', taking the problems away from the simple dichotomy made in his earlier book. One of the emotions likely to be aroused by reading the *Investigations* is a sense of loss, such as is often expressed by Wittgenstein's imaginary critic, in spite of the philosopher's assurances that his arguments leave 'everything as it is'. Philosophical dichotomies and formulations often communicate this 'reductive' feeling, the sense that something essential is now missing. The fact–value distinction in ethics seems thus to reduce our familiar world. A metaphysical nightmare is that 'value' may turn out in the end to be illusory, or else something small. What we 'lose' in the *Investigations* is some sort of inner thing. As we pursue Wittgenstein's arguments, and do his 'exercises', about 'following a rule' and how meaning is not a 'mental process', we may (rightly) become convinced (for instance) that we do not need mental samples to recognise chairs, or memory images to have memories. But we may also end up feeling that we cannot now justify the reality or identity of our most important thoughts and most precious awarenesses. We are losing the *detail*. (Schopenhauer complained that Kant's philosophy loses us our 'rich field of perceptions'.) Wittgenstein's conclusive polemic against certain philosophical mistakes (such as those made by Hume and Russell) about thinking and meaning may seem also to damage some necessary sense of the 'inner life'. ('Removed' so firmly by Gilbert Ryle in *The Concept of Mind*.) The later part of the *Investigations* indicates points at which Wittgenstein himself felt uncertain. (I shall discuss Wittgenstein's view of 'mental contents' at a later stage.) A justifiable criticism, in epistemology or philosophy of mind, of the role of certain kinds of mental events, may have a less proper influence in ethics, tending for instance towards behaviourism or existentialism. It may be considered that if there is nothing 'in' the mind except otiose imagery, daydreams, viscous stuff, (etc.), then morality must *consist* of *de facto* conduct or acts of will. In ethics it is always of interest to enquire about a philosopher's motives, I mean in a general, not detailed personal or 'psychoanalytical' sense (though speculation of the latter sort can at least be amusing). Kant's motives may thus be said to be to justify and delineate science and empirical knowledge, and to segregate and purify morality by connecting it with freedom and reason. The two operations are, as in the *Tractatus*, interdependent. Kant also wanted, *ipso facto*, to make an intelligible and safe place for (some form of) religious faith, and something like this might also be said, *mutatis mutandis*, of *Tractatus* Wittgenstein. There is an instinctive movement of relief involved in the putting-into-safety of something pure. (Metaphysics as magic.) Compare Wittgenstein's idea that his philosophy involved a 'throwing-into-the-lumber room of the whole world'. (*Culture and Value*, p. 9.) Border-lines must be formed which keep out what is irrelevant and messily confusing. We desire to simplify and clarify our thinking and one way to do this is to gather all the value together in one place. If this is done the question of how to redistribute it must arise (as the question of the relation of the mind to the world arises when the philosopher has separated them). Belief in God is one solution, where we picture God both as pure transcendent Goodness, and also as a personal good-making intelligence active here below. Plato gathers value together in its purest form in the Idea (Form) of the Good, and also sees it as distributed into human variety through the working of truthfulness, knowledge and purified spiritual desire (love, Eros). Kant brings value back to the world through conceptions of truth and justice incarnate in particular situations through the operation of practical reason (the recognition of duties). Plato and Kant are religious philosophers, imbued with a characteristically religious certainty about the fundamental and ubiquitous reality of goodness: their real world is the moral world. Kant could still put science 'in its place'. In our post-Kantian world, where religious faith wanes and truth gains so much of its prestige from scientific method, this is harder to do. Here it may seem a felicitous move to separate fact and value so as to guarantee the *purity* of value and the *accuracy* of fact. This compelling picture, taken as a moral guide or background, is in danger of making *truth* and *value* part company. 'Value' becomes difficult to discuss. The area of fact becomes more extensive and more present to us (television) and seems more real. Scientific views and methods spread from their proper place in science into peripheral areas. All sorts of theorists (including some philosophers) begin to feel that they must eschew value preferences and discussions of value, and offer themselves as neutral scientific workers. Surely, it may be felt, a clear-cut division of fact and value excludes personal prejudice and amputates whole areas of messy sentimental or muddled pseudo-factual thinking.

Toulmin and Janik, in their book *Wittgenstein's Vienna*, describe the intellectual reaction in that city at the turn of the century against a soft corrupt Austro-Hungarian political atmosphere in favour of harsh precise epigrammatic truth-telling in the style of Karl Kraus. Wittgenstein detested muddled emotional talk. Let there be plain truth and forthright action, and no high-minded generalising or fuzzy chatter. Philosophy too should be austere and laconic. In answer to someone who praised his work: 'No. If this were philosophy you could learn it by heart.' Also, 'I think I summed up my attitude to philosophy when I said philosophy ought really to be written only as a poetic composition.' A philosopher may enlighten himself and others by reflection upon his temperament. What seems like a logical or technical argument can go far in recommending a way of life. By 'poetic composition' Wittgenstein means of course not (in the ordinary sense) poetry, but something beautifully concise, purely clarified and condensed, thus memorable and indubitable. Something quite different (judging from his later work) is intended by Heidegger who tells us that now the language of philosophy, if it is to tell the truth, must be poeticised and become a new sort of prose-poetry. This terrible wish is also expressed by structuralists. When young, Wittgenstein liked the poetry of Rabindranath Tagore and even (Toulmin and Janik inform us) read some of it to a meeting of the Vienna Circle. I was also told (by a friend) that Wittgenstein was very fond of a play by Tagore called *The King of the Dark Chamber*, a mystical Hindu morality play. Who is the real King, he who is handsome and powerful and decked with jewels, or he who is ragged and poor and plain? Conclusion: 'I am waiting with my all in the hope of losing everything.' Tagore now seems a poet 'of his period', but evidently conveyed to Wittgenstein something of 'the mystical'. Schopenhauer's excursions into Hinduism and Buddhism impressed him. His evidently deep feelings about mysticism may derive also from the German tradition, for instance through Jacob Boehme in whom he was interested.


One desired effect of the distinction between fact and value is the segregation or liberation of the will. The will as the carrier of value is detached from the ordinary factual world. Kant set the (real, noumenal) will free from the (apparent, phenomenal) world of causally determined events. Wittgenstein, without talking of 'cause' or 'reality', set it free (removed it) from the world of fact; a separation which is essential to the 'moral purpose' which he attributes to the *Tractatus*. Will, as silent attitude or style, changes the *whole* of the world but not the facts. (6. 43.) Jean-Paul Sartre, one might say, with his distinction of inert mind from active mind, sets the will free from the conventional (bourgeois) world. The distinction, the setting free or setting apart, appears as the instrument of a kind of revolution, or purification, or renewal. Such a distinction and such imagery is to be found in structuralism and (some) Protestant theology. (Salvation by faith is a formidable release.) If we feel uneasy here it is no simple matter to clarify the problems which the uneasiness indicates. (Wittgenstein said in the preface that the *Tractatus* showed 'how little is achieved when these problems are solved'.) If we feel loss, what kind of mistake do we think has been made? Is there then no 'moral knowledge' or 'moralised fact', such as common-sense seems to demand? Does not value *colour* almost all our apprehensions of the world, and is this colour something which must be withdrawn in order to purify the will? We struggle here with imagery. Are our ordinary personal (and precious) 'value perceptions' to be made either impossible or ineffable?

Simone Weil says that will does not lead us to moral improvement, but should be connected only with the idea of strict obligations. Moral change comes from an *attention* to the world whose natural result is a decrease in egoism through an increased sense of the reality of, primarily of course other people, but also other things. Such a view accords with oriental wisdom (and with Schopenhauer) to the effect that ultimately we ought to have no will. This would be the 'life of knowledge', to use the Schopenhauerian phrase, which was in Wittgenstein's head when he wrote the 1914–1916 *Notebooks*. This picture is helped out in Schopenhauer's case (though not in Wittgenstein's) by a theory of human nature which emphasises our capacity for com-

passion, for identifying with other people and thus reducing our egoistic impulses. If we picture morality in this way the will is no longer
the prime agent and may be seen as morally (or as Wittgenstein says,
philosophically) a kind of fiction. Schopenhauer and Wittgenstein reject
the Kantian concept of duty. But a realistic view of morality cannot
dispense with the idea; duty is for most people the most obvious form
of moral experience: Kant's starting point. One might say that morality
divides between moral obligation and spiritual change. The good life
becomes increasingly selfless through an increased awareness of, sensibility to, the world beyond the self. But meanwhile requirements and
claims, which we still recognise abstractly and as it were externally,
demand to be met. (So, though of course not all duties have a utilitarian
basis, a part of every moral philosophy must be utilitarian.) And we
must at least listen to the person who says, If you recognise enough
duties, why bother about spiritual change? Or, Why spend years in
meditation to achieve a spiritual condition with which you will have
little or no time left to benefit mankind? Simone Weil firmly 'sets will
on one side', 'finds a place' for it. (Concepts must find their places with
help from philosophers.) 'Will' seems to belong with duty rather than
with spiritual change. The regular performance of certain duties may
favour such change, but not necessarily. The concept of duty does not
require the concept of will, innumerable duties are performed without
any place for it: Hume's 'habit and custom' for instance, and perhaps
Wittgenstein's 'Forms of Life'. In a good man duties are more like
habits. (A holy will is not a will; but then there are no holy wills.)
However, as many duties are abstract in relation to our nature (we do
not want to do them, we do not identify with them), there may be a
place for the concept of will as a name used for the *strain* which is then
felt. Someone might say that something like Kant's *Achtung* (respect for
the moral law) or Sartre's *angoisse* is not a sign or accompaniment of
will, but will itself.

'Of the will as the subject of the ethical we cannot speak. And the
will as a phenomenon is only of interest to psychology.' (*Tractatus*
6. 423.) In Schopenhauer's terms, the will as phenomenon is merely
egoistic impulse; whereas the 'moral will' is the *indescribable* energy
which changes the whole personality, enabling a denial of the will
to live. Against this background we may understand Wittgenstein's
non-phenomenal (noumenal, though he would not use this word) will:
not a particular thrust or emotive drive among others, but a total

change of being in relation to everything. 'Is the will an attitude of mind?' Yes, if this is something which makes the world become 'altogether different' and wax and wane as a *whole*, an image which takes over the weaker 'attitude of mind' and focuses our attention upon the strictness of the separation (between a phenomenal will and 'something higher'). Looked at in this way, it may begin to seem that here the word 'will' is out of place, must be explained in other terms, is even misleading and unnecessary. Change of being, *metanoia*, is not brought about by straining and 'will-power', but by a long deep process of unselfing. 'Will' may be used *ad hoc* in contexts which are to be casually passed by or which demand deeper consideration: someone needs will-power to carry on, has a great will, lives by the will, wills people to obey him, etc. Posed as something deep or serious, 'will' may turn out to be superficial, even a pseudo-concept. If not trivial, the idea appears as dramatically metaphysical, as in its use by Schopenhauer, passed on to Nietzsche and young Wittgenstein: a liberating force capable of removing the illusions and miseries of mundane egoism. As naming a recipe for moral improvement it is better (as Simone Weil says) 'set aside'. Wittgenstein's 'profession of faith' at the end of the *Tractatus* is eloquent, epigrammatic and brief, fitting in with the earlier sections of the work with which it is essentially related by separation. Wittgenstein is not concerned, as Simone Weil is, with the details of a road to virtue. He offers us a strong impression of his own moral style. The 'Life of Knowledge' of the 1914–1916 *Notebooks* (13.8.16). Happiness 'in spite of the misery of the world'. A brave young man might well believe that it could be achieved.

So, some philosophers assume, while others do not, that morality is deep, fundamental to human nature, the most important thing. Moral relativism, or 'naturalism', whether or not based on determinism, the view that morality is epiphenomenal, superficial, just a matter of historically induced conventions or irrational emotions (etc.), is probably not really held by any one. Moral cynics or reductionists, from Thrasymachus (*Republic* I) onward have usually employed such arguments to promote moral attitudes of their own. Even the simplest hedonism can contain moralistic views about freedom, and much existentialist and structuralist 'anti-establishment' social criticism uses relativist arguments in aid of strong moral positions. Relativism, scientific naturalism, belief in determinism, may also be professed by social theorists who are traditional moral agents in private life, but just not interested in morals as a form of human activity. We do not have to have a theoretical interest in morality. There is indeed a kind of (instinctive) orientation or certainty which is rejected if we emphasise free will and individual decision. Are there however some ways in which, if we reflect about moral value, we cannot properly avoid picturing the world? Metaphysicians try to persuade us that this is so. To put it slightly differently, are there fundamental concepts and problems which moral philosophers *have* to (or *ought* to) deal with? If one feels uneasy with the various forms of the fact–value distinction can this suggest what problems lie at a deeper level? I want to refer here to something said earlier about Plato, and also about Wittgenstein, contrasting them with Descartes. Philosophers attempt to make models of the *deep* aspects of human life. The metaphor of depth, generally understood, is difficult to explain in other terms. 'What's it all about, padre?' There is something about the human spirit which seems to some thinkers to *demand* a search for 'deep foundations'. Herein, it is often felt, there is something *essential*; and this essential thing must be built into the explanation at the start, or else it tends to fly away and become problematic and remote and extremely difficult to integrate. On the other hand, if it is built in at the start, the thinker may be accused of an unwarrantable act of faith or intuition, since there remains something fundamental of which he appears to be saying: well, it is so. Descartes isolated the thinking mind and made for himself the problem of how the mind could know the world, to solve which he required God, and an intuition about the nature of truth. Berkeley and Hume, similarly, made out that all we actually experience are mental data (impressions, ideas), and created the problem shared with modern phenomenalism, of how we then fabricate the notion of a material object. Here laymen, and other philosophers, may say, 'But surely the idea of the material object is primary.' Structuralist thinkers, and writers under their influence, are excited by their fundamental assumption that language does not refer to 'the world', it refers to itself. Dr Johnson, that excellent philosopher, who would not have liked structuralism, refuted Berkeley by kicking a stone, and determinism by saying to Boswell, 'Sir, we know the will is free, and there's an end on't.' It is one of the felicitous aspects of the *Tractatus* that the referential nature of language is not questioned. There just *is* a method of projection whereby language can picture the world. The *Investigations*, which in many ways 'corrects' the *Tractatus*, does not, in its attention to particular problems, contradict the general assumption about reference of language to the world. Kant equally finds it perfectly clear and primary that we all recognise the absolute call of duty, know the difference between good and bad, and are capable of distinguishing between a hypothetical and a categorical imperative. This is *ipso facto* the possession of freedom. When Kant tries (in the *Grundlegung*) to establish these ideas upon a more profound basis he admits the circularity of the argument. Plato makes the assumption that value is everywhere, that the whole of life is movement on a moral scale, all knowledge is a moral quest, and the mind seeks reality and desires the good, which is a transcendent source of spiritual power, to which we are related through the idea of truth. 'Good is what every soul pursues and for which it ventures everything, intuiting what it is, yet baffled and unable fully to apprehend its nature.' (*Republic* 505E.) The 'proof' of these strong fundamental pictures is provided through numerous examples. Plato's Eros as *pharmakeus* (alchemist, magician), an energy potentially good or bad, pictures the infinite variety of human experience. The philosopher's own primary certainty is present as an influence, towards understanding though of course not necessarily towards agreement. Some great philosophical pictures are also great religious pictures, and illustrate how close philosophy and theology can come to each other, while still wisely staying apart. Heraclitus tells us that 'The One who alone is wise does not want and does want to be called by the name of Zeus.' (Fr. 32.) This is indeed the problem. We yearn for the transcendent, for God, for something divine and good and pure, but in picturing the transcendent we transform it into idols which we then realise to be contingent particulars, just things among others here below. If we destroy these idols in order to reach something untainted and pure, what we really need, the thing itself, we render the Divine ineffable, and as such in peril of being judged non-existent. Then the sense of the Divine vanishes in the attempt to preserve it. No wonder 'that which alone is wise' is in two minds about how to proceed. (The order of the wishes may be significant; fundamentally it does not want, but is forced by the frailties of human nature into wanting.) The instinct to protect the intuitively known essential by a circumstantial or picturesque theory is very strong and corresponds to a persistent human need. Goodness and holiness have traditionally been protected by establishing them, their source or exemplars, somewhere else, separate and sole, under the guard of dragon-like concepts. The idea of the absolute reality of a pure good is found on both sides of the divide which separates Kant from Plato, either as moral rationality distinct from intellectual rationality, or as a transcendent source incarnate at various levels in our cognitive and emotional experience. This divide is of interest to theology. The most familiar (western) concept which gathers all value together into itself and then redistributes it is the concept of God; and of this too it may be said that unless you have it in the picture from the start you cannot get it in later by extraneous means. Here there is a well-recognised metaphysical circularity (as in Kant's concept of freedom). The Ontological Proof, unlike other alleged proofs of God's existence, shows, indeed uses, an awareness of this.

# > 3 <

# Schopenhauer

Schopenhauer inspired Nietzsche (who called him 'the only serious moralist of our century') and overwhelmed Wagner as well as touching Wittgenstein. He held that the dialogue between Plato and Kant underlies the whole of western philosophy. (I am inclined to agree with this.) He takes from Kant the contrast between (hidden) Thing-in-itself and phenomenal appearance. He takes from Plato the concept of Ideas as conveying Thing-in-itself (ultimate reality) to the world, and as being models or archetypes of innumerable particular ideas. He does not accept Kant's intimation of a noumenal (God-like) reality manifesting itself as duty, nor does he picture the work of Ideas as illumined by anything like Plato's supreme unique Form (Idea) of the Good. Schopenhauer's Thing-in-itself, the fundamental power which moves and underlies all things, the Will to Live (ancestor of Nietzsche's Will to Power), is not known to us, it is not an object for a subject. Schopenhauer chides Kant for having failed positively to *deny* the objective existence of his (Kant's) Thing-in-itself. The world of phenomena, our world, appears as ideas, objectifications of the Will, rendering it as object for subjects. The title of Schopenhauer's main work, *Die Welt als Wille und Vorstellung*, already poses a problem of translation. The older English translation by Haldane and Kemp (which I shall use in quoting from Schopenhauer) renders *Vorstellung* as 'Idea'. The more recent one by E. F. J. Payne renders it as 'Representation'. Idea should be understood as any object of consciousness. 'Platonic Ideas' are, as in Plato, postulated universal concepts or models of which particular ideas are instantiations. There are many grades and degrees of objectification, as in stones, plants, animals, humans, also thoughts, states of consciousness, etc.; nevertheless the Will is 'present and undivided in every object of nature and any living being'. Schopenhauer gives no finally coherent account of his metaphysical structure. How does a timeless eternal Will as unknowable Thing-in-itself relate to a plurality of beings? How does intellect relate to will, and human wills to the Will? What are Platonic Ideas, how do they relate to the particular ideas which 'copy' them? At *Parmenides* 130 Plato portrays the youthful Socrates struggling with some similar problems. Schopenhauer 'decrees' this metaphysical structure as a starting point, but freely departs from it when it suits him. Much of his moral philosophy refers itself to salient features of his metaphysic (the Will objectified as egoism for instance), but can be discussed without clarification (if such were possible) of the questions raised above. Schopenhauer is in many of his instincts an empiricist, and readily switches to plainer styles of argument and observation, leaving more abstract matters to look after themselves. (Note. *The World as Will and Idea*, hereinafter referred to as *WWI*, consists of: *four books*, each of several chapters, with a numbered sequence of sections continuous throughout the four; and *Supplements* to these books consisting of a single sequence of numbered chapters.)

The Will to Live is something fundamental. Our world, all that we are aware of, the ideas or representations of Will made known as object, is a composition of phenomena, appearances, Maya. Schopenhauer's use of this word (Maya) refers us to eastern philosophy, but we must also think of Plato. His Cave image (*Republic* 514f.) suggests levels of consciousness rising from illusion to truthful reality. This indeed offers us a recognisable picture of the human scene. Schopenhauer's (ordinary, our) world seems in this light to consist only of the lower levels, the darkest part of Plato's imagined Cave. In our world, according to Schopenhauer, the Will manifests itself as miserable perpetual struggle. All entities suffer, and fight fiercely for existence. The human scene is a place of restless desire and ruthless egoistic striving, devoid of freedom, ruled by the overwhelming determinism of the Will. However there are a few possible mitigations of this state. One is the existence of an instinct of compassion, another lies in a total denial of the Will. A third is through a contemplation of Platonic Ideas, whereby we look through the veil of Maya, lose our egoistic personal identity and overcome the divide between subject and object. This is made possible through good art. Here Schopenhauer follows Plotinus and parts company with Plato; the (good) artist does not copy particular things, he sees and copies the Platonic Ideas (the universals or conceptual exemplars) themselves. The general notion of a spiritual liberation through art is accessible to common-sense as an account of our relationship to works of art when the walls of the ego fall, the noisy ego is silenced, we are freed from possessive selfish desires and anxieties and are one with what we contemplate, enjoying a unique unity with something which is itself unique. The conception of the artist seeing beyond the particular to the universal is a striking one which suits some kinds of visual art. (Van Gogh's chair, Van Gogh's peasant shoes which so impressed Heidegger.) It is less easy to apply in literature, though one might instance some poetry and mention T. S. Eliot's 'objective correlative'. We see through, pass through, the busy multiplicity of particulars and contemplate, touch, become one with, 'the thing itself'. Many forms of art however pursue the busy contingent rather than the still icon. About music, with a felicitous daring which is characteristic of him, Schopenhauer has something different to say. 'Music is by no means like the other arts, a copy of [Platonic] Ideas, but a *copy of the Will itself*, whose objectivity the Ideas are.' (Schopenhauer's italics. *WWI*, Book III, section 52.) Music is the most powerful of the arts, not expressing Ideas, but acting directly upon the Will, that is the emotions of the hearer. 'The connection of the metaphysical significance of music with its physical and arithmetical base depends upon the fact that what resists our *apprehension*, the irrational relation or dissonance, becomes the natural type of what resists our *will*; and conversely the consonance of the rational relation which easily adopts itself to our apprehension, becomes the type of the satisfaction of the will.' (Schopenhauer's italics.) Music portrays the movements of the human heart, that is the Will, in 'whose essential nature is always satisfaction and dissatisfaction'. When the elements of the melody are disunited we feel uneasy, when they are reconciled we are at peace. So 'we gladly hear in its language the secret history of our will and all its emotions and stirrings'. (Supplement to Book IV, ch. xxxix, 'On the Metaphysics of Music'.) This account is of course delightful, and where traditional western music is concerned (Schopenhauer instances Beethoven) 'has something in it'. Later twentieth-century music, it may be said, draws attention to our desire for satisfaction by refusing to give it.

It would appear from this picture that, although music is the strongest of the arts, affecting us more deeply and directly, it is less 'spiritual' than the other arts which involve the effort of overcoming the ego – whereas music moving with the will (though in a pattern of resistance and reconcilement) does not banish but soothes the ego. However this may be, the release or remission granted by the arts would seem to be temporary, and not part of any steady progression toward a higher life. And why does Schopenhauer connect this refuge from the ego especially with aesthetic experience? In these two respects also he differs from Plato, who envisages a definite path out of the Cave, seen in terms of intellectual and moral betterment. Schopenhauer keeps moral values *out* of the ordinary world which is ruled by the Will. A strict dualism must be fundamental. We are *captives*, subject to determinism. Kant's dualism pictures a realm of necessity, where the phenomenal self is subject to determinism, and a realm of freedom and reason which is *available* to every rational being. Schopenhauer pictures a scene of egoism and suffering from which it is almost impossible to escape. He may be said to be in love with the Will. What he here invokes is indeed a vast and ubiquitous concept with a huge ancestry and innumerable descendants: cosmic energy of being, fundamental creative power, Taoism, the presocratics, Heraclitus's eternal fire, his *Logos*, the Christian *Logos*, Plato's Eros, Freud's Libido, Jung's Unconscious, Heidegger's (later) concept of Being as a cosmic gamester. Present-day Hindu religious philosophy, a suggestion of a possible account: 'A Mind, a Will seems to have imagined and organised the universe but it has veiled itself behind its creation; its first erection has been this screen of an inconscient Energy and a material form of substance, at once a disguise of its presence and a plastic creative basis on which it could work as an artisan uses for his production of forms and patterns a dumb and obedient material.' (Aurobindo, *The Life Divine*, 'Indeterminates and Cosmic Determinations', p. 302.) This, offered as an example of a possible theory, might remind us of the *Timaeus*. These great 'wills' or cosmic forces differ in respect of their omnipotence, their roles as accessible or inaccessible, ruthless or kindly, and their status as mythical, mystical, philosophical, or scientific objects. Schopenhauer's Will is, with Nietzsche's and that of the later Heidegger, one of the nastiest. Plato's daemon Eros is capable of baseness but also of the highest spirituality. Plato does not invoke any omnipotent divine figure. The mythical Demiurge has limited powers, the Forms are not gods. Human beings yearn for these great things and metaphysics has to deal with them.

The only complete escape from Schopenhauer's ravenous energy of egoism is an absolute denial of the Will, achieved by an asceticism which lies *beyond* the virtues. 'It no longer suffices to love others as himself and to do as much for them as for himself; but there arises within him a horror of the nature of his own phenomenal existence, the Will to Live, the kernel and inner nature of that world which is recognised as full of misery.' (*WWI*, Book IV, section 68.) Schopenhauer's totally will-less state is not to be thought of as an automatic release into an unselfish condition of virtuous activity (return to the Cave), it is above or beyond compassion and any 'ordinary morals'. At times he seems to preach simply stoicism and *amor fati*. 'Death does not concern us . . . When we are death is not, and when death is we are not. Epicurus.' (*WWI*, Supplement to Book IV, ch. xli. See also *Tractatus* 6. 4311.) But the Schopenhauerian 'denial' is something much more radical. The whole world of individual egos and universal suffering is phenomenal and unreal and its removal, which must be wished for, leaves behind the true reality of our being, from which submission to the Will has been an aberration. This non-phenomenal and non-personal something represents what is eternal and real and free from the Will. 'Death is the great opportunity no longer to be I.' This salvation by dying to the world is not suicide (rejected by Schopenhauer, and by Wittgenstein) or 'ordinary' death or anything to do with survival. As non-personal it is not in any accessible sense experienced and cannot be described. Here we may be tempted to posit something magically arcane as what Schopenhauer has to offer; or else take refuge in assuming some 'benefit', for others, for the world, which is somehow *bound* to result from such a great ascesis. Schopenhauer ends the chapter: 'To die willingly, to die gladly, is the prerogative of the resigned, of him who surrenders and denies the Will to Live. For only he wills to die *really* and not merely *apparently* and consequently he needs and desires no continuance of his person. The existence we know he willingly gives up: what he gets instead is in our eyes *nothing* because our existence is, with reference to that, *nothing*. The Buddhist faith calls it Nirvana, that is extinction.' We may gloss this by picturing the completely selfless person as indescribable and unimaginable in the language and concepts of the world. What he is seems to us as a stripped-down nothing, to be like him would indeed be for us nothing. Can we really imagine the life of the extreme ascetic who exists without *all* those infinitely many worldly things and experiences which compose the life of the ego? Do we not shudder and turn away? What, existing without . . . and without . . . and without . . . ? Yet must we live with so austere a picture, as if we are to be utterly damned or utterly saved? This is certainly one among many religious pictures. But did not Christ and Buddha speak of a way? What Schopenhauer tells us about the mystical *metanoia* may seem too puritanically absolute. He does not claim that he himself is living an ascetic life. It is not just that he hates the world. Let us rather say that he feels that only what is extreme will crack the hard ego. As his numerous writings reveal, he is *fascinated* by the world and its bright diversity. He is a self-proclaimed pessimist – but he is also merry, like Hume whom he genially admires. His religious passion is sincere and the negativity of his picture, the absence of light, is a just image of, as we can see it, the surrender of worldly pleasures. He stirs us to thought and has the great merit of having made a serious attempt to introduce eastern philosophy to western philosophy. Western philosophy cannot be said to have profited much by the introduction. Indeed neither side pays as yet much attention to the other. Nevertheless numerous western individuals have been helped by even a little knowledge of eastern spirituality.

Plato spoke of appearance and reality, but Schopenhauer's Maya is certainly not Platonic. Plato's pilgrim is able, at various stages in his journey, his escape from the Cave, to construe the difference between the apparent and the real in accessible terms which do not detach him from the continuum of the world as a whole, or imply a 'horror' resulting in complete severance. Talk of liberation by Ideas may seem close to the Cave imagery. But Plato postulates no blind merciless Will as fundamental energy. The power, for good or ill, of his mythical Eros is to be seen within the world. What is ultimate and above being is the Form of the Good, whose magnetic influence reaches to all. Plato, like Kant, makes morality central and fundamental in human life. Schopenhauer speaks of an asceticism which is above virtue. However, in many parts of his work he adopts quite a different tone. There is no divinity and no supreme good in his system, but there is a scattering of sensitive understanding; as in *The Basis of Morality* which contains much humane wisdom on the subject of morals. Schopenhauer here indulges in cheerful spirited argument and attention to detail. He, who takes so much from Kant, discards the Categorical Imperative and also Kant's strong emphasis on absolute truthfulness. Truth-telling, says Schopenhauer, may be important but is not fundamental. All sorts of reasonable lying is in order. We may properly lie to 'robbers and ruffians'. An extorted promise is not binding. A right to lie also extends to cases of unauthorised prying into our private affairs. Even Jesus told a lie. (John 7. 8–10.) Malice, not lying, is the worst vice. The fundamental command of morality is '*Neminem laede, immo omnes, quantum potes, iuva*' – 'Hurt no one, rather help everyone as much as you can.' This saying indicates the two cardinal virtues upon which all the others depend, justice and compassion. Both these virtues 'have their roots in natural compassion. But this itself is an undeniable fact of human consciousness, is essential to it, and does not depend on presuppositions, concepts, religions, dogmas, myths, training and education. On the contrary it is original and immediate, it resides in human nature itself and, for this very reason, it endures in all circumstances and appears in all countries at all times.' (*The Basis of Morality*, section 17.) Compassion impedes the sufferings which I intend to cause another person. 'It calls out to me "stop!", it stands before the other man like a bulwark, protecting him from the injury that my egoism or malice would otherwise urge me to do.' There are in general, Schopenhauer says, only three fundamental motives of human activity: egoism, malice, and compassion. He deplores Kant's classification of sympathetic feelings and motives as 'pathological', non-rational, purely phenomenal, and non-moral. Instinctive sympathy and compassion is closest and most evident in human nature: compassion is an 'everyday

... immediate participation' in the suffering of others. This is what Schopenhauer contrasts with 'duty' and 'conscience', which depend upon 'the dogmas and commandments of religion and the self-scrutiny undertaken in reference to them'. A man's conscience 'probably consists of one-fifth fear of men, one-fifth fear of the gods, one-fifth prejudice, one-fifth vanity and one-fifth habit. So he is essentially no better than the Englishman who said quite frankly, "I cannot afford to keep a conscience".' These sceptical comments, Schopenhauer adds, do not in any way deny the existence of genuine morality; though they do 'moderate our expectations of the moral tendency in man and consequently of the natural foundation of ethics'. The natural omnipresence of compassion 'is certainly astonishing, indeed mysterious. In fact it is the great mystery of ethics; it is the primary and original phenomenon of ethics, the boundary mark beyond which only metaphysical speculation can venture to step.' The ultimate foundation of morality in human nature itself 'cannot again [after Schopenhauer's explanation] be a problem of *ethics*, but rather, like everything that exists *as such*, of *metaphysics*'. We are here up against the barrier, the limits of our knowledge, the mystery, a primary phenomenon. It is an ultimate (and the most important) aspect of human nature, that we sympathise. This cannot be a problem of ethics (as in 'ought we to sympathise?) but is, in so far as it can be spoken of at all, something for metaphysics to state, and if not justify, at least clarify.

Schopenhauer is here 'running free', discarding the complex Kantian machinery, and not worrying about Nirvana or how Will relates to Ideas. 'Don't hurt anyone, help everyone' is certainly a good shot at a, or the, fundamental maxim. However, he stays close to Kant, and indeed Plato, in his attempt to think the spiritual without the supernatural. He agrees with Kant that the moral claim upon us is unique, unconnected with happiness or (in any scientific sense) nature; but objects to its appearance in the form of the Categorical Imperative as an *a priori* law comparable to that which ordains the *necessary* form of all objects. Kant's separation of *a priori* forms from *a posteriori* experiences (as set out in the *Critique of Pure Reason*) is, Schopenhauer says, 'the most brilliant and potent discovery of which metaphysics can boast'. But this formulation, illuminating in relation to the factual world, cannot (according to Schopenhauer) be applied to the world of value; where (according to Kant) 'ethics too is to consist of a pure, i.e. *a priori* knowable part and an empirical one'. Kant rigidly separates freedom from determinism, observance of rational rules from subjection to pathological emotions. *Ought*, the Categorical Imperative, arbitrarily set up 'without further authentification', essentially implies reward or punishment, and is thereby impossible as a moral concept. There is no unconditional ought. All these decrees and severances, Schopenhauer holds, divide morality from the details of ordinary life and the real experience of human individuals. Nevertheless, Kant's great service to ethics consists in this, 'that he has freed ethics from all principles of the world of experience, that is from all direct or indirect doctrines of happiness, and has shown in a quite special manner that the kingdom of virtue is not of this world. This service is all the greater because all ancient philosophies, with the single exception of Plato . . . sought . . . either to make virtue and happiness depend on each other . . . or to identify them . . . This charge applies with equal force to all modern philosophers down to Kant.'

An attractive aspect of Schopenhauer's ethic is, together with his concept of compassion, this affirmation, shared with Kant, of the fundamental nature of the moral. Kant however is haunted by, or has intimations of, a veiled unknown God. Schopenhauer, who chides Kant for this, allows no God, and no Form of the Good either. The highest things we know (experience) are Platonic Ideas, purer objectifications of the Will, but lacking any sovereign image of a unique Idea (or Form) of Good. (The mystical state is not describable or in the ordinary sense experienced.) Here there is certainly some hint of a Platonic pilgrimage, away from the domination of the Will as egoism and strife, toward some higher condition. The contemplation of art, which temporarily silences the ego, shows that this can be done. Compassion (*not* love, which Schopenhauer sees as tainted by egoism), instinctive sympathetic identification with others, suggests that we are able (after all) to move a little against the Will. Schopenhauer often returns to examples of selfless care and kindness, not only among humans but between humans and animals. This endearing, and among philosophers rare, emphasis must connect with, but need not depend upon, his Hindu and Buddhist perception of the whole cosmos as bound together and worthy of respect in all its parts. His humane philosophy is marred however, even *contradicted*, not only by the omission of the concept of duty, but by certain other equally firmly held views. Schopenhauer's chief stumbling block is his concept of Will as fundamental, all-determining and (*qua* neutrally relentless) evil. Even in the benign pages

[ 65 ]

of *The Basis of Morality* he tells us that 'the difference of characters is innate and ineradicable'. We cannot change the nature we are born with. We are ruled by the determinism of the Will under which some people are innately good and others innately bad. After explaining this he allows that he has 'long been listening to the reader putting the question: Where are guilt and merit to be found?'. He refers us to 'Kant's greatest and most brilliant' ethical doctrine of the coexistence of freedom and necessity. The empirical character of man as phenomenon (active in the phenomenal world of time and space) is determined by the underlying Thing-in-itself, which is outside space and time, and constitutes the intelligible character which is present in all the actions of the individual 'and is stamped upon every one of them like the signet of a thousand seals'. The phenomenon must 'show the constancy of a natural law in all its manifestations'. Acts of will are necessarily determined by motives (which originate in character). This necessity, Schopenhauer tells us, has been clearly demonstrated by Hobbes, Spinoza, Hume, Holbach, and Priestley. 'In consequence of the irrefutable arguments of these predecessors Kant also regarded the complete necessity of acts of will as a settled affair.' Thus the 'inflexible rigidity of everyone's empirical character, which had been observed at all times by thinkers (whenever the rest imagined a man's character to be capable of being reformed through rational remonstrances and moral exhortations) was reduced to a rational basis and consequently also established for philosophy'. Guilt and merit lie in what we are, not in what we do. What we do is necessitated. Nevertheless we recognise our deeds as our own. '*Freedom*, which proclaims itself alone through *responsibility*', can only be found in *what we are*. Reproaches of conscience only ostensibly concern what we have done, but really and ultimately concern what we are. 'Conscience is acquaintance with ourselves', and our remorseful thought that we might have been another, better, man.

This ingenious account deserves reflection as an analysis of what we may at times be tempted to think and believe. (Well, that's what I'm like! At least I know myself! etc.) As a 'rational reduction' of the extreme complexity of the moral life it is confused and unrealistic. Schopenhauer, professing to adopt and expound Kant's doctrine of the coexistence of freedom and necessity, misconstrues it. This is partly a result, an aspect, of Schopenhauer's rejection of the concept of duty by which Kant joins the phenomenal to the noumenal world. The freedom of Kant's individual rests in his being continually 'touched' by a higher power which enables him to overcome, or shows him the possibility of overcoming, the (apparent) necessity (determinism) of his phenomenal being. Schopenhauer on the contrary shows himself to be, as we too may sometimes be, rather in love with determinism, with *amor fati*, with the stoical, or relaxing, idea that 'it must be so'. Here necessity (supported in Schopenhauer's picture by natural science) rules, and freedom is simply the recognition of necessity (a 'profound' idea to be found elsewhere, for instance in Marxism). Here also we may see compassion, appearing sometimes as virtue, as really a mere human instinct among others. Schopenhauer, in this mood or mode which is not always dominant, parts company with common-sense and demeans or diminishes the human individual, who is so emboldened and illumined in Kant's account. One might compare Schopenhauer's relentless damaging all-powerful Will with Derrida's concept of *archi-écriture*: another mystifying postulation, effecting the removal of the individual. Schopenhauer, often in his manifold pages the empiricist, the aspiring mystic, the advocate of common-sense, the friend of animals, the generous lively polymath, interested in everything, can also be, and at his most metaphysical, the cynic or stoic. He rejects Kant's rational 'duty' and also any idea of unselfish love, or the freedom to achieve moral progress. Only our instinctive reaction (if we have it) to our awareness of the suffering of others influences us to 'good deeds'. 'All true and pure love is sympathy, and all love that is not sympathy is selfishness. *Eros* is selfishness, *agape* is sympathy.'

Sexual attraction is to be seen as the Will to Live ensuring the continuation of the species. 'Love is rooted in the sex impulse alone.' (*WWI*, Supplement to Book IV, ch. xliv, 'The Metaphysics of the Love of the Sexes'.) The Will manifests itself as sexual desire in general, and when this desire is directed to an individual, 'although in itself a subjective need, it knows how to assume very skilfully the mask of an objective admiration, and thus to deceive our consciousness, for nature requires this stratagem to attain its ends'. As egoistic Will is the main driving force of human activity, nature 'implants an illusion in the individual' so that what is good for the species appears as good for the self. So, 'every lover, after the consummation of the great work, finds himself cheated, for the illusion has vanished by means of which the individual was here the dupe of the species'. Schopenhauer bids us look at the world of non-human animals, to see how the ingenuity and 'altruism' of individuals is framed to benefit the species. Those who object to the 'gross realism' of this account should, the philosopher suggests, reflect that 'the determination of the individualities of the next generation is a much higher and more worthy end than all their exuberant feelings and supersensible soap bubbles'. Well, science often and in various ways urges us rational animals to consider how we are also subject to laws which govern non-rational animals. Schopenhauer, celebrating the ruthlessness of the Will, tells us that 'the species, as that in which the root of our being lies, has a closer and earlier right to us than the individual', and thus Cupid was traditionally pictured as 'a malevolent cruel and ill-reputed god, in spite of his childish appearance, a capricious despotic demon, yet lord of gods and men'. Schopenhauer congratulates himself for being the first philosopher to make a serious study of sexual love, which now 'lies before us as raw material'. He surprisingly goes on: 'The one who has most concerned himself with it is Plato, especially in the *Symposium* and the *Phaedrus*. Yet what he says on the subject is confined to the sphere of myths, fables and jokes, and for the most part concerns only the Greek love of youths.' Freud, who also congratulated Schopenhauer on his interest in sex, referred to Plato, less impolitely, but still with dubious grace.

'It is some time since Arthur Schopenhauer showed mankind the extent to which their activities are determined by sexual impulses, in the ordinary sense of the word. It should surely have been impossible for a whole world of readers to banish such a startling piece of information so completely from their minds. And as for the "stretching" of the concept of sexuality which has been necessitated by the analysis of children and what are called perverts, anyone who looks down with contempt upon psycho-analysis from a superior vantage point should remember how closely the enlarged sexuality of psycho-analysis coincides with the Eros of the divine Plato.'
(Preface to the fourth edition of *Three Essays on Sexuality*.)

Schopenhauer returns at the end of *The World as Will and Idea* to the Buddhist concept of Nirvana. He admits that we lack concepts with which to express or describe this state. It is a point 'which remains forever unattainable to human knowledge'. In the almost final chapter ('Denial of the Will to Live') he makes a final attempt to clarify his version of how freedom coexists with determinism. Christianity (really) agrees with Buddhism and Hinduism that our guilt or sin is our existence itself. Christianity, it is true, places original sin *after* some postulated free existence, but this is merely a myth. We are guilty not of what we do but of what we are. There is no salvation by works. Schopenhauer regards any emphasis on works as a Protestant aberration. What we require is a (by implication almost impossible) *complete transformation* of our mind and nature. He refers to Luke 24. 4, 'repentance and forgiveness of sins', *metanoia*, a (total) change of mind. The moral virtues (as previously defined by him) are not the end, but a step upon the way, a light upon the path between subjection to the Will (unredeemed egoism) and the denial of the Will, 'or mythically from original sin to salvation through faith in the mediation of the incarnate God (Avatar)'. The word 'mythical' distances any literal or traditional understanding, and the word 'Avatar' embraces the non-Christian religions. Any 'release' must be thought of in terms of mysticism. 'Theism, calculated with reference to the capacity of the multitude, places the source of existence within us as an object'; whereas mysticism 'draws it gradually back within us as the subject, and the adept recognises at last with wonder and delight that he is it himself'. Schopenhauer then quotes from 'Meister Eckhart, the father of German mysticism' the 'precept for the perfect ascetic, "that he seek not God outside himself"'. As suitable reading for those who wish to become acquainted with quietism he recommends Eckhart and, among various others, John Bunyan. The great fundamental truth (about denial of the Will) is admittedly 'entirely opposed to the natural tendency of the human race', and only to be understood, if at all, by the majority, when contained in a 'mythical vehicle'. The Sermon on the Mount (Matthew 5. 40, 6. 25, etc.) expresses the great truth in terms echoed by Buddha: 'throw everything away and become beggars'. (The command uttered by Tagore, which Wittgenstein put into practice.) Just before this great conclusion Schopenhauer, with his incurable empirical eye for detail, devotes several pages to 'the highly remarkable sect of the Shakers in North America', which, 'even in the very lap of Protestantism', expresses the essentially ascetic spirit of Christianity. His spirited account of the rites and general mode of life of these people ('avoid all unnecessary noise, such as shouting and slamming doors') illustrates Schopenhauer's particular generous *joie de vivre* which survives in spite of his evident inability to achieve, for himself, the wished-for denial. Mystics differ in style and doctrinal context, yet seem to have much in common. Here one is inclined to say (I am inclined to say) that the fundamental nature of religion is mystical. This is a, or the, feature of it which has ensured, and (I hope) will ensure its continuity. Eckhart's 'do not seek for God outside your own soul' (the sort of pronouncement which got him into serious trouble) may be read by beginners as an important warning against idolatry. On the other hand, the withdrawal into self, which (much) mysticism evidently involves, may be an ultimate deification of egoism. So must all 'genuine' mystics return to the world, serve others, exhibit virtues? Not necessarily. Yet forgetting the world may be more spiritually dangerous than returning to it. The three religions with which Schopenhauer is with sincere and touching piety concerned seem to envisage both paths. Schopenhauer, when solving *en passant* 'the profoundest mystery of Christianity' (the Trinity), suggests that the Holy Spirit is the denial of the Will to Live, and that Christ is the incarnate assertion of the Will, which together with the Father produces the phenomenal world: assertion and denial are opposite acts of the same Will whose capability for both is the only true freedom. So is this myth an admission by Schopenhauer that the mystic (or some enlightened person) might also enjoy this dual capacity (a view which would contradict Schopenhauer's general 'teaching')? Lest we should be encouraged by this possibility he hastens to add: 'However, this is to be regarded as a mere *lusus ingenii*.'

Schopenhauer's irrepressible empiricist gaiety is in tension with his nihilistic hatred of the ordinary world (the fallen scene, everywhere visible) and his cosmic sense of nature as destructive (we are nothing). But he is also tenderly aware of the animals (and the plants) and loves and venerates nature. Through this veneration of all-things we may be, perhaps, in a sense, saved. Not the long path of the selfless mystic; but a kind of on-the-way mysticism. In the Supplement to Book IV, ch. xli, 'On Death', Schopenhauer says:

'Certainly we know no higher game of chance than that for death and life. Every decision about this we watch with the utmost excitement, interest and fear, for in our eyes all in all is at stake. On the other hand, nature, which never lies, but is always straightforward and open, speaks quite differently upon this theme, speaks like Krishna in the *Bhagavad-gita*. What it says is: The death or life of the individual is of no significance. It expresses this by the fact that it exposes the life of every beast, and even of man, to the most insignificant accidents without coming to the rescue. Consider the insect on your path: a slight unconscious turning of your step is decisive as to its life or death. Look at the wood-snail, without any means of flight, of defence, of deception, of concealment, already prey for all. Look at the fish carelessly playing in the still open net; the frog restrained by its laziness from the flight which might save it; the bird that does not know of the falcon which soars above it; the sheep which the wolf eyes and examines from the thicket. All these, provided with little foresight, go about guilelessly among the dangers which threaten their existence every moment. Since now nature exposes its organisms, constructed with such inimitable skill, not only to the predatory instincts of the stronger, but also to the blindest chance . . . it declares that the annihilation of these individuals is indifferent to it . . . It says this very distinctly and does not lie . . . If now the all-mother sends forth her children without protection to a thousand threatening dangers this can only be because she knows that, if they fall, they fall back into her womb where they are safe; therefore their fall is a mere jest.'

So, it is all a game and a jest? We live with the sense of hopeless, ruthless contingency, we are victims of chance. The examples of the little animals, the insect which we thoughtlessly tread upon, strike a different note from that of Simone Weil. Schopenhauer follows Kant in showing us a fallen phenomenal realm in which we are imprisoned. Kant however does not picture us as sharing this fate with the animals (whom he regards as senseless sub-beings) or with the vegetable world, let alone with the whole cosmos down to its last atom. Schopenhauer, taught by the east, constantly has this cosmic connection in mind. Kant's fallen state is dark and banal, but visited by the light of Reason, and his picture can appeal to our common-sense. Schopenhauer's account is more dramatic, even tragic. He speaks of a game, and a jest, in a way which would never occur to Kant, or to Simone Weil. One may be reminded here of Heraclitus's imagery of war (Fr. 53) or fire (Fr. 30) and his (Fr. 52), 'Aeon is a child playing draughts, the kingship is the child's.' (Aeon probably means time.) Heidegger, who was fascinated by this fragment, came to picture Being (as fate or time) as also playing a game. Further on along this road we find Derrida's *jeu des signifiants*. (I am also reminded here of the inscription, in Greek, over the door of T. E. Lawrence's little house in the woods: *ou phrontis*, roughly to be translated as 'What the hell!', or more literally 'It doesn't matter!' Herodotus VI 129.) However, in these and other cases the image of the dangerous game is energising rather than edifying. Contingency may be harmlessly thought of as a game, provided this is seen as merely a striking image. In truth, nothing and no one plays this game. On the other hand: Schopenhauer's mysticism is to be approached and imagined through reflection upon his love, not of humans, but of the rest of created beings. In this we see his true Buddhism. He speaks of our being, when we fall back into the womb of Nature, *safe*. Can we not at least accept our mortality? There is nothing cynical here in the term 'jest'. His *identification* with the snail, the frog, the fish, is a significant part of the picture. The idea of the 'game' is sinister in the work of Heidegger, frivolous in that of Derrida. Schopenhauer (we may say to 'save' him) has two pictures in mind. One is that we may, through our reverent sympathy with the rest of creation, at least, whatever we may do with the insight, realise that we are just contingent short-lived mortals. The other is that of our doing something with the insight by disposing of our ego. The end of Book IV again portrays the ineffable state:

'We must banish the dark impression of that nothingness which we discern behind all virtue and holiness as their final goal, and which we fear as children fear the dark; we must not even evade it like the Indians through myths and meaningless words, such as reabsorption in Brahma or the Nirvana of the Buddhists. Rather do we freely acknowledge that what remains after the entire abolition of the will is for those who are still full of will certainly nothing; but conversely to those in whom the will has turned and denied itself, this our world, which is so real, with all its suns and milky-ways – is nothing.'

It may not seem easy to read Schopenhauer's book as 'religious teaching', though the author, in many of his moods, must have wished us to. It is a philosophical book. Yet it is also a religious book. Why should we not be repeatedly told that we are ruthless egoists and that the world which we take as all-important and *real* is a valueless and *unreal* world? Does not Plato teach this, does not Christianity teach it? Schopenhauer might well say to us (as his disciple Wittgenstein said about the *Tractatus*) that the book's point is an ethical one. Is not this indeed obvious? What distracts us is of course partly Schopenhauer's attachment to determinism, his promotion of the all-powerful Will which condemns us to endless fruitless strife. We are cheered to learn that we are all endowed with instincts of compassion, but dashed to be told that we cannot change our imprinted character. Liberation through art (Ideas) is mentioned but not explored. Rejection of Kant's 'duty' removes the hope of continuous access to the higher. Complete denial of the Will is something indescribable and in any case so difficult as to be almost impossible for us humans. On the other hand, Schopenhauer's omnivorous *interest* in the world, his innocent *love* of the world, is an endless source of the 'value' which is so formally excluded. Love and hope do manage to break in. He speaks often of mysticism as something remote and arcane. The Oxford Dictionary describes the mystical as 'having a certain spiritual character or import by virtue of a connection or union with God transcending human comprehension'. All right. I would say (persuasive definition) that a mystic is a good person whose knowledge of the divine and practice of the selfless life has transcended the level of idols and images. (Plato's *noesis*. Eckhart.) This may or may not accompany belief in a personal deity. Julian of Norwich's showings are for all humanity. The condition of course remains exceedingly remote from that of ordinary sinners. (Needless to say, the word 'mystical' is often, in a degraded sense, applied to Gnostic beliefs and power-seeking magic.) It is true that we may at times, in various situations, experience loss of self, or intuitions of a beyond. Such experiences may 'do us good'. We are also continuously aware of standards of good conduct which we continuously ignore. But, someone may say, what can we do now that there is no God? This does not affect what is mystical. The loss of prayer, through the loss of belief in God, is a great loss. However, a *general* answer is a practice of meditation: a withdrawal, through some disciplined quietness, into the great chamber of the soul. Just sitting quiet will help. Teach it to children.

Mystical writings usually take ordinary virtue for granted; that is, the approach to God or Avatar (or Form of the Good) is achieved not through any annihilation of the world, but by a purification of virtue. 'Throwing everything away', which is indeed a general enough precept, should involve (as we would expect 'pure compassion' to involve) care for others. Love of God, love of Good, love of your neighbour. This would seem, as in the Platonic pilgrimage, to involve the world in all its variety. Schopenhauer's 'religious doctrine', although stated so sincerely and based upon learning even if not practice, is marred by his idea of the world as given over to an evil Will from which escape is achieved by the (almost impossible) move which annihilates self and world. The world has to be not only dismissed but hated. Of course Schopenhauer did not hate the world. But he may, in the desperate extremity of his 'dismissal' of it, have been influenced, as other adjacent thinkers have been, by the example of the Greeks. We may be reminded here of Sophocles, *Oedipus at Colonus* 1224: 'not to have been born is best'. Heidegger in similar mood (*An Introduction to Metaphysics*, 'The Limitation of Being') draws our attention to *Antigone* 332. 'There are many very strange things but none more strange than man.' The word *deinos* is translated by Liddell and Scott as (first meaning) 'fearful, terrible, dread, dire', and (second) 'marvellously strong, powerful for good or ill', and thirdly 'wonderful'. Heidegger pictures something violently powerful, and with this *unheimlich*, strange, weird, uncanny, in the fundamental sense of unhomely, estranged, unable to be at home.

'*Deinon* means the powerful in the sense of one who uses power, who not only disposes of power [*Gewalt*] but is violent [*gewalt-tätig*] in so far as the use of power is the basic trait not only of his action but also of his being-there [*Dasein*]. Here we use the word violence in an essential sense extending beyond the common usage of the word as mere arbitrary brutality. In this common usage violence is seen from the standpoint of a realm which draws its standards from conventional compromise and mutual aid, and which accordingly disparages all violence as a disturbance of the peace . . . To say that man is *to deinotaton*, the strangest of all, is not to impute a particular attribute to man, as though he were also something else; no, the verse says that to be the strangest of all is the basic trait of the human essence within which all other traits must find their place. In calling man 'the strangest of all' it gives the authentic Greek definition of man. We shall fully appreciate this phenomenon of strangeness only if we experience the power of appearance and the struggle with it as an essential part of being-there [*Dasein*] . . . We shall fail to understand the mysteriousness of the essence of being-human, thus experienced and carried back into its grounds if we snatch at value judgments of any kind.'

Elsewhere (p. 177) Heidegger connects the 'violence' involved in being-human with the conception of a 'daring refusal of being' (as envisaged in *Oedipus at Colonus*). These observations, occurring in a discussion of Heraclitus and Parmenides, certainly 'carry us back' into a non-Platonic, non-Christian 'ground'. For us to exist at all is to commit some sort of breakage, in continuing to exist we use force. This is nothing to do with morals, it is 'deeper' than morality, we must not 'snatch at value judgments'. Violence is more profound, more noble, more beautiful, than the weak 'values' of compromise and mutual aid. (*An Introduction to Metaphysics*, published 1953, was based on a 1935 lecture.) Nietzsche, who is often in Heidegger's mind, tells us in *Philosophy in the Tragic Age of the Greeks* (translation by Marianna Cowan, pp. 60–61, 64–5) that Heraclitus (may have) believed that 'the entire world process' was 'an act of punishment for hubris. The many the result of evil-doing? . . . Is guilt not now transplanted into the very nucleus of materiality and the world of becoming and of individuals sentenced to carry the consequences of evil forever and anew?' 'The many': the multiplicity of phenomena, breaking the unity of the One. Heraclitus (perhaps) finally concludes that we can make no sense (certainly not a moral or teleological sense) of what exists. Nietzsche also points us to Fragment 52: 'Time (*aeon*) is a child playing draughts'. So it is all (he says) 'the beautiful innocent game of the *aeon*'. As Heraclitus (Nietzsche tells us) exclaims: 'It's a game! Don't take it pathetically and, above all, don't make morality of it!' See the scene as it is, with contemplative pleasure; and do not let aesthetic perception of cosmic play be vulgarised as consideration for the world's useful ends. Heidegger looks back to Nietzsche and Nietzsche looks back to Schopenhauer. Schopenhauer does not share the ferocity of Nietzsche or the (ultimate) pessimism of Heidegger. The idea that 'it's *all* a game' is handled by Nietzsche, Heidegger, and Derrida. Nietzsche and Heidegger regard as somehow fundamental what they take to be 'the Greek view of life', as they extract it from the tragic poets and the presocratic philosophers. This 'view' implies the exclusion of *anything moral* from the 'ground' of things: the *ground*, which has been, and is, so ardently fought for in a different way by religious thinkers and philosophers. Heidegger's *Introduction to Metaphysics*, in a section (pp. 196–9) called 'Being and the Ought', discusses the ordinary sense of value as a *superficial form of thinking* which has separated itself from Being, seeks a ground in itself and claims a 'being' of its own. Briefly: Being (Heidegger tells us) as understood by the presocratics, was originally *phusis*, the supreme creative power which emerges and discloses. Plato however set up the Idea (of the Good) above mere existent beings who were related to it as to a model, as to what *ought* to be. *Logos* (as statement) led on toward the supremacy of self-sufficient reason. The process was completed by Kant, for whom 'Being' was *nature* as determined by (scientific) reason, and, opposed to nature, the *ought* (Categorical Imperative), determined by and as (moral) reason. Nineteenth-century science, now including the human sciences, took over Kant's scientifically determined *nature*. 'Ought', diminished and undermined, had to seek a ground in itself, claiming an intrinsic (baseless) value, itself as value, as opposed to fact. Even Nietzsche, with his 'revaluation of all values', failed to understand the questionable origin of this concept. Here Heidegger adds that 'works that are being peddled about nowadays as the philosophy of National Socialism . . . have nothing whatever to do with the inner truth and greatness of this movement (namely the encounter between global technology and modern man)'. Of this brief history Heidegger says that, 'This interpretation never rests exclusively or even primarily on philosophical exegesis.' *Phusis*, as the power that reveals, and conceals, and disposes, travels in Heidegger's thought as an aspect of Being.

Heidegger here is not just rejecting a crude formulation of 'facts versus values', he is telling us that our ordinary, evaluative modes of thought are superficial and that what is really real is a *nature of man* of which the Greeks alone were fully aware and which since then has been covered over, though sometimes glimpsed by artists and thinkers. This basic nature or being is not touched by morality, it is as if it were a terrible secret, the ultimate state of man's homelessness. One may comment here that this radical vision, which may indeed be glimpsed in Greek poets and presocratic thinkers, appears, perhaps necessarily, in later thinkers as something not really recovered or shared but as a kind of romantic heroism. Nietzsche, whom Heidegger chides for using the concept of value, also takes the 'tragic' preplatonic Greeks as those who saw what was really real, and that it was *deinos*. Nietzsche, here opposing his admired Schopenhauer, claimed to be ending the era of Plato. Returning to the pages of Schopenhauer, we are, for all his attempted 'frightfulness', in a milder, more secure, more commonsensical, less terrified world. He cannot resist rambling, he constantly makes jokes, when (agreeing with Nietzsche and Heidegger) he rejects teleology as a disguised form of theology he uses as evidence, for both the plausibility and the unacceptability of theology, a mass of facts which he has culled from books about animals, insects, fishes. 'If we give ourselves up to the contemplation of the indescribably and infinitely ingenious construction of any animal, even if it were only the commonest insect, lose ourselves in admiration of it, and it now occurs to us that nature recklessly exposes even this exceedingly ingenious and highly complicated organism daily and by thousands to destruction by accident, animal rapacity and human wantonness, this wild prodigality fills us with amazement; but our amazement is based upon an ambiguity of the conceptions, for we have in our minds the human work of art which is accomplished by the help of the intellect and by overcoming a foreign and resisting material and therefore certainly costs much trouble. Nature's works on the contrary, however ingenious they may be, cost her absolutely no trouble.' (Supplement to Book II, ch. xxvi, 'On Teleology'.) The contingent carelessness of ingenious nature, and our realisation that we too, our sturdy egoistic selves, are 'worthless' or 'nothing', opens a *space* for *another road*. In Kant and Plato this road is made clearly visible. Schopenhauer can only dimly point at this. Meanwhile he finds the ordinary world full of interesting wonders. In spite of his metaphysics and his mysticism, Schopenhauer may in general appear as a genial empiricist. His views on Hegel (in *WWI*): 'clumsy and stupid ... a repulsive mindless charlatan, an unparalleled scribbler of nonsense ... such as has previously been heard only in madhouses ... shallow, crudeness, folly ... barefaced mystification', etc. etc. His views on Hume: 'In every page of David Hume there is more to be learnt than from Hegel's, Herbart's and Schleiermacher's complete philosophical works put together.' (*Studies in Pessimism*, 'The Misery of Life'.)

# A Note on the Riddle

One might put part of *Tractatus* Wittgenstein's view, which excludes inner life, moral states, and (my word) 'elsewhere', as being that one should live very close to 'the facts' or, to use an image from the *Investigations*, the 'stream of life'. (Not to be confused with the stream of consciousness.) The facts cannot be changed. One should go with the stream of life and agree with the world. This would be a stoical 'style' of living, which would leave no space between oneself and the world in which illusions could lodge. Self and world agree, they match. The limitation placed by *Tractatus* Wittgenstein on language, the sense in which logic is transcendental (shown not said) connects with, indeed guarantees, the limitation of the moral life, the sense in which ethics is also transcendental (shown not said). For the 'happy' (enlightened) man who 'lives in the present' these limitations coincide. Where Schopenhauer (or common-sense) would say experience, Wittgenstein says significance. The world we have to live close to is the world as rendered into facts by significant language. Moralising speculation or image-making or *a priori* metaphysical inferences are precluded by these limits. 'Not *how* the world is, is the mystical, but *that* it is. The contemplation of the world *sub specie aeterni* is its contemplation as a limited whole. The feeling of the world as a limited whole is the mystical feeling. For an answer which cannot be expressed the question too cannot be expressed. *The riddle* does not exist.' (*Tractatus* 6. 44–6. 5.) This riddle is Schopenhauer's riddle. Schopenhauer (*WWI*, Supplement to Book I, 'Criticism of the Kantian Philosophy'): 'The world and our existence presents itself to us necessarily as a riddle'. He refers to Kant's dictum to the effect that 'the source of metaphysics must throughout be non-empirical; its fundamental principles and conceptions must never be taken from either inner or outer experience'. Kant:

'First, as regards the *sources* of metaphysical knowledge, it lies in the very concept of metaphysics that they cannot be empirical. Its principles (which comprise not only its fundamental propositions but also its fundamental concepts) must never be taken from experience; for it is not to be physical but metaphysical knowledge, i.e. lying beyond experience. Thus neither outer experience, which provides the source of physics proper, nor inner experience, which provides the basis for empirical psychology, will be the ground of metaphysics. Metaphysics is thus knowledge *a priori*, or out of pure understanding and pure reason.'

(*Prolegomena to Any Future Metaphysic*,
Preamble, section 1; P. Gray Lucas translation.)

That is (says Schopenhauer) 'everything must be excluded of which we can in any way have *immediate* knowledge', but rather be 'sought only in that at which we can arrive merely indirectly, that is by means of inferences from universal principles *a priori*'. Schopenhauer *objects* that there is no proof of this contention.

'We have no grounds for shutting ourselves off, in the case of the most important and most difficult of all questions, from the richest of all sources of knowledge, inner and outer experience, in order to work only with empty forms. I therefore say that the solution of the riddle of the world must proceed from the understanding of the world itself; that thus the task of metaphysics is not to pass beyond the experience in which the world exists, but to understand it thoroughly because inner and outer experience is at any rate the principal source of all knowledge; that therefore the solution of the riddle of the world is only possible through the proper connection of outer with inner experience effected at the right point, and the combination thereby produced of these two very different sources of knowledge. Yet this solution is only possible within certain limits which are inseparable from our finite nature, so that we attain to a right understanding of the world itself without reaching a final explanation of its existence.'

Schopenhauer here expresses a new (modern) definition of metaphysics or metaphysical craving (one which would also be acceptable to Plato) when he speaks of our finite nature together with our passionate desire to understand 'the world' which we attempt to intuit 'as a whole'. Metaphysics may thus be connected with a mystical state. Wittgenstein's 'proper connection of outer with inner experience' which solves (or removes) the riddle is effected when the 'two Godheads' (the world and I) are in harmony. Wittgenstein uses the idea of the work of art, the ability to see the world *sub specie aeterni* as a limited whole, to explain what this harmony is like. (Ethics and aesthetics are one. *Tractatus* 6. 421.) The ability thus to see (or feel) depends on keeping close to the reality of the world, accepting the facts and following the stream of life. This is described as 'mystical'. Within the 'limits' of our 'finite nature' we are able to feel or intuit the world as a whole, though not as a totally comprehended whole. We are at peace with the world, as we are with a work of art. Wittgenstein uses Schopenhauer's metaphysical imagery in a succinct form. It is as if he wanted to shrink it to the dimension of an aphorism. In terms of philosophical style Schopenhauer represents what Wittgenstein shudders from: an insatiable omnivorous muddled cheerful often casual volubility. Schopenhauer's relation to his reader is relaxed, amicable, confiding, that of a kindly teacher or fellow seeker. He tells stories and makes jokes.

Wittgenstein does not relate to a reader, he passes by leaving a task behind. Even the imagined interlocutor in the *Investigations*, the 'someone' who 'might say', is isolated from us inside the text.

# > 4 <

# Art and Religion

Kant claimed to be checking scientific empirical reason (defining its role) in order to liberate moral spiritual reason, to preserve it and keep it autonomous and pure. What was so preserved was *ipso facto* morality, with its unique and special *Categorical Imperative* which came to us from a higher source, allowing perhaps some tacit sense of the presence of God, supported by the very idea of faith. (Philosophical metaphors: reality perceived as being above us, or below us.) Plato kept his unique source separate and pure, uncontaminated by the 'supernatural'. The Christian God has been mainly absent from post-Kantian philosophy, the problems he poses relegated to theology. Hegelian thought, which so horrified Kierkegaard, provides an elaborate analysis to prove the idea superfluous, 'overcome' in the Absolute. Heidegger, looking to Hölderlin, sometimes speaks as if he believed in gods; in an interview with *Der Spiegel* in 1966 he said that '*Nur ein Gott kann uns retten*', only a god can save us. Philosophically God is not present, though said by some thinkers to be in eclipse, gone to the catacombs to use Martin Buber's image, or like Heidegger's personified Being, to have 'withdrawn'. On the other hand, away from abstract thought, and although it is true that many young people now grow up entirely outside religion, the idea of God remains familiar, intuitively comprehensible, and religious institutions continue to function and have influence. Religion may still be an answer to guilt and fear, may be expected to save us from technology; the hope of the salvation of the individual and the redemption of all fallen things remains in many forms. Belief in a personal God seemed a prime guarantee of general morality. The charm, attraction, and in many ways deep effectiveness, of faith in a personal God must constantly strike the critical or envious outsider. It is just this practical and consoling God whom the bolder demythologising theologians want us to take leave of. In doing so they may well point to the Second Commandment. 'Thou shalt not make unto thee any graven image, or any likeness of any thing that is in heaven above or in the earth beneath or in the water under the earth.' (Exodus 20. 4.) This indeed sounds like a veto not only upon idolatrous symbolic visual art, but upon any art and even upon the development of a pictorial theology. The spirit of the Commandment has been observed by Judaism and Islam; but not by Christianity, where all the talents of art, not least those of the painters, have been dedicated to presenting God as a kind of super-art-object. The work of art unifies our sensibility. Its authoritative unity and thereness guarantees and stabilises our existence, while removing our petty egoistic anxiety. The art object is an analogy of the person-object, we intuit our best selves in its mirror, and not only when we are under its spell. Art with which we are familiar stays with us as an intimation that love has power and the world makes sense. God combines the characteristics of a work of art and of a philosophical idea with those of an ideal spectator. We see in God in a magnified form the analogy between work of art and person; and Christ as God provides both personality and story. Art sets us in order, the ideal unity of the object makes us also one. In a relation with God this unification takes place by being observed as well as through observing. The magnetic beyond looks back. In the west, God creates the individual and guarantees him as a real unity, responsible and morally judged, even perhaps able to survive death. The structuralist attack on traditional art, the 'removal' of morality from art and art criticism, is an attack on God and understood as such. Christianity has of course recruited not only great artists but plenty of mediocre ones too. In religion as in art, base emotions are often closely related to their redeemed counterparts. Christianity is a religion of suffering, its central image is of a man in torment. There are all kinds of consolation here: such as an invigorating sense of guilt combined with a countermanding experience of innocence and of salvation through some imagined punishment. The endeavour to remove the 'interesting' is also of religious origin. ('Do not be fascinated or excited by your spiritual condition.') Our teachers, from the Psalmist and

St Paul, have pointed to a sense of sin as a starting point: an idea which would not have occurred to a classical Greek thinker. (The distinction between sin and shame has force here.) We enact our guilt in the presence of God so as to feel freed from it, a procedure which may induce amendment of life, or renewed security in carefree sinning. Causality and the contingent aspects of time are ideally overcome, in our own case and by extension in that of others, so that, as in tragedy, we can survey the misery of the world more calmly. St Paul has been a major purveyor of these great spiritual images which have touched and comforted so many.

I speak here of St Paul because his Christ seems more like a personal creation and a work of art than does the calmer figure of the Gospels. Christianity was indeed fortunate (if one may put it so) to find available, at the crucial moment, five geniuses including two great thinkers. Five artists of genius one might also say; Christianity, providing us with a mythology, a story, images, pictures, a dominant and attractive central character, is itself like a vast work of art. The great painters, with their impressive, memorable, authoritative works, helped to create the unified pictorial conglomerate with which we are so familiar. Religious imagery colours and fixes and bodies forth moral ideas. This is obvious and characteristically essential in Christianity, although of course other religions have mythical figures and stories and didactic parables. Western art, so solid and so clear, has helped us to *believe*, not only in Christ and the Trinity, but in the Good Samaritan, the Prodigal Son, innumerable saints and a whole cast of famous and well-loved scenes and persons. Christ as *Logos* is unifying principle and guarantor of thought, Christ as Redeemer the suffering saviour of man from sin and horror. In the traditional picture redemption is not only new being as amendment of life, but also the triumph of suffering over death, the substitution of punishment (penance) for death. Religious motivation is inevitably mixed. A central Christian idea is the transformation of sin into purifying pain. The light of God's presence makes consciousness of sin into pure suffering, combined in the traditional story with the removal of death; Christ is the image of suffering without death. (This is an idea which leads into a discussion of tragedy.) Of course many modern Christians do not believe in survival. But the idea of suffering as triumph over death, as ransom from death, is deep and deeply consoling. Even the idea of a just judgment, *cum vix iustus sit securus*, can be a satisfaction and a comfort. (Obviously as it concerns others, but also as it concerns oneself.) Pornographic art presents a degraded erotic object. It is a function of God to be a non-degradable erotic object. This is an important religious idea. The Greeks were fairly detached about their gods. Jews and Christians (in different styles) take God as a supreme love-object, with a profound confidence that impure feelings can be purified by being directed upon a pure (untainted, unstained) object. Plato's Good is such an object, and can shine through lesser, even false, goods; there is a place in Platonism for a doctrine of grace. However, God sees us and seeks us, Good does not. It would be a matter of faith in Christianity that if we sincerely imagine we are praying to God we really are.

I have been suggesting ways in which religious imagery partakes of the nature of art, and how understanding what art is, its charms, its powers, its limits, helps us to understand religion. This is not of course to suggest that religious experience is merely aesthetic or any nonsense of that sort. It would be more just to say that great art is religious, as Tolstoy believed. This too would need explanation and qualification. I have already quoted Keynes's thought that Moore led him and his friends to classify general human experience as 'aesthetic'. One merit of this classification is that it emphasises a sense of 'experience' as 'consciousness', which is often philosophically neglected or made invisible. We make classifications and set up analogies in order to illuminate an aspect, and this illumination may cast a shadow which makes another aspect less visible. To assimilate the one-making aspect of religion to the one-making aspect of art, and then to assimilate the 'demythologisation' process in both areas is of course only a part of an argument. One could not, for instance, properly *define* religion in such terms, although a modern thinker, Jung, virtually does so when he explains it as a unifying story emerging from the unconscious. The drama of God versus Job moves to a satisfactory conclusion when God is forced by his conscience to become Job, the innocent victim, in Christ. (*The Answer to Job.*) Another significant one-making picture is said (by Jung) to be forming itself in our age with the incorporation of Satan into the Trinity, or into the Quaternity if we count the Virgin Mary as having been already incorporated. This inclusion of the 'dark opposite' as an essential part of the religious ideal, of course no novelty, is a Gnostic, Taoist, presocratic conception. Jung admits to being a Gnostic. This is indeed religion as art, history as myth, the unfolding

[ 83 ]

of a coherent story, or play with successive acts, the production of a series of satisfying syntheses, answering the needs and pressures of different times. More general and acceptable is 'the Motherhood of God', under the protection of Julian of Norwich. The image-play of theology, as in the development of the doctrine of the Trinity, has always been an important part of religion but cannot be all of it. It may be said that if you must have a metaphysical picture it can never be a complete one. A new unity, involving perhaps a new dichotomy, is likely to lose, make ineffable or conceptually inaccessible, visions and values which were elsewhere evident, and indeed the eclipse of these may have been one of the aims of the metaphysician. The rulers in Orwell's *1984* alter the language so as to make certain things unsayable. Consider what values Marxism squeezed out of view, or how a strict pietistic Kantianism excludes the generality of a Benthamite outlook, while on the other hand utilitarianism lacks a detailed picture of virtue. Ideas about beauty and virtue expressed in terms of quality of consciousness or quality of happiness find no appropriate vocabulary in many recent styles of moral philosophy. Theologians tend to frown upon the concept of 'religious experience'; and the concept of 'moral knowledge' has been even more frowned upon by philosophers. For purposes of ethics, and indeed in general, we lack a suitable philosophical view of 'consciousness' and 'the self'. John Stuart Mill, an ancestor of J. M. Keynes's mentor G. E. Moore, is an interesting case of a philosopher who adopted, or was indoctrinated into by his father and Bentham, a 'progressive rational' philosophical system, and then passionately and inconsistently tried to lodge therein traditional values which the system seemed to have excluded: a case of faith. Mill's essays on Bentham and Coleridge elegantly illustrate this dilemma. Mill could not surrender the idea of qualitative levels of happiness and experience, a conception whose glow, somewhat modified, also illumines what Moore had to say about 'states of mind'. We might indeed look to these, not altogether consistent, utilitarians for something like a philosophy of consciousness. These are examples of how a metaphysic or *Weltanschauung* may be felt to omit something which then peripherally and disturbingly haunts it, or else disappears to be rediscovered later. One could also instance the way in which intuited axioms lead a continued life outside theoretical systems which they may or may not positively challenge. Notions of natural rights would be examples of such axioms. Sometimes of course the inconsistent fellow travellers are best acknowledged as both valid and unassimilable. We might also think of St Paul's list, at Romans 8. 38, of the things that will not separate him from the love of God in Christ. There is an exercise of freedom, or act of faith, or expression of certainty (of which of course we may or may not approve) when someone is moved to proclaim, 'In spite of any system which makes X invisible or ineffable or professes to disprove X, I hold to X.' There are moments in history when concepts are suddenly found or when they are suddenly lost. When some strong unifying idea is sceptically challenged there is a loss of conceptual tissue. The contemporary challenge to *unity* affects (in various areas of thought) ideas as diverse as God, the self, virtue, the material object, the story. The conceptual loss involved poses moral and theoretical problems for the sceptics, for philosophers and artists and de-mythologising theologians. Can, and should, what is lost be recovered in some other way? In such contexts we see how deep metaphysical imagery goes down into the human soul. Farther than we can see?

I have spoken about unity and illusions of unity in relation to the idea of a work of art. The art object may be looked at as analogous in function to certain moral and religious concepts (or pictures) and also as an analogy of the self. I am an artist in the imaginative, or fantastic, creation of myself. I shall shortly discuss a very potent aesthetic conception, that of tragedy, which plays an ambiguous role in religious and moral thinking. I want now briefly and in summary to go on talking about art itself. Is the work of art a kind of hoax, something which seems complete but is really incomplete, completed secretly by the private unacknowledged fantasies of the artist and his conniving client? A consideration of this question can also throw light on the nature of virtue, so that art can turn out to be an image of good, though in a sense different from that which might at first occur to one. Our illusions about art and morals are in some ways similar. Do we expect too much from art? The Greeks did not. At certain times in history (for instance in the Romantic Movement) we tend to deify it. Yet artists are human individuals, no work is perfect, though our hearts may claim perfection for some. The material of art is contingent limited historically stained stuff. Nevertheless art is a great source of revelation. Bad art displays the base aspects of human nature more clearly than anything else, though of course not so harmfully. One might even say that the *exemplification* of human frailty in bad art is a clearer warning to us than its *representation* in good art. Great art (often) cannot help casting light, sparkles of charm, upon its villains, perhaps through the felicitous working of their role, or through admiration for their courage or compassion for their sins. (Something of this can be expressed by inspired detail. Rubens' picture, in the Brera, of the Last Supper represents Judas's dog sitting underneath his chair.) In bad art the self-magnifying illusion-making lying ego is shamelessly on display. Bad art (that is ordinary bad art, not vile pornography) is also in general a sound producer of that unpretentious low-grade happiness (consolation, escape), harmless or not very harmful, which Benthamite utilitarians reasonably regard as a human right. There are worse ends than the pursuit of an unexacting happiness; it is better to be cheered up by a silly magazine than by plans of revenge. (It is of course also true that we ought often to be out helping our neighbour rather than reading Proust or Tolstoy.) The art object as false unity is an image of the self. The bad story is the sentimental untruthful tale of how the brave attractive ego (of course he has his faults) triumphs over accident and causality and is never really mocked or brought to nought. It is difficult for any artist not to falsify, the discipline of art must include the persistent recognition and rejection of easy natural falsification: the temptation to the ego is enormous since it really does seem here to dispose of the godlike powers it secretly dreams of. Truth is always a proper touchstone in art, and a training in art is a training in how to use the touchstone. This is perhaps the most difficult thing of all, requiring that *courage* which the good artist must possess. Artists indicate or *invent*, in the invention of their work, their own relevant *tests of truth*. A study of good literature, or of any good art, enlarges and refines our understanding of truth, our methods of verification. Truth is not a simple or easy concept. Critical terminology imputes falsehood to an artist by using terms such as fantastic, sentimental, self-indulgent, banal, grotesque, tendentious, unclarified, wilfully obscure and so on. The positive aspect of the avoidance of these faults is a kind of transcendence: the ability to see other non-self things clearly and to criticise and celebrate them freely and justly. This is a place for a definition of freedom, and for a distinction between trapped egoistic *fantasy*, and *imagination* as a faculty of transcendence. The *analogy* with virtue is here very plain; and of course the artist's discipline includes the *exercise* of virtue: patience, courage, truthfulness, justice. As a father or a citizen the good artist may of course be less than admirable. As moral agents we tend to specialise.

Art is artificial, it is indirect communication which delights in its own artifice. The work of art is, to use W. H. Auden's words (he is speaking of a poem), 'a contraption'. But it is, as he goes on to say, 'a contraption with a guy inside it'. The art object is a kind of illusion, a false unity, the product of a mortal man who cannot entirely dominate his subject matter and remove or transform contingent rubble and unclarified personal emotions and attitudes. He cannot, by rendering his work unambiguous, render it timeless. Nor can the artist, to use Auden's words again, 'prevent his work being used as magic, for that is what all of us, highbrow and lowbrow alike, secretly want art to be'. (*Poets at Work*, 'Squares and Oblongs'.) Or from being used as pornography, for instance. This is like the anxiety expressed by Plato in the *Seventh Letter*. The written word can fall into the hands of any knave or fool. Only in certain kinds of personal converse can we thoroughly clarify each other's understanding. The thinker's defence against this may be, like that of Socrates or Christ, not to write. Or it may be, like that of (for instance) Kierkegaard, Wittgenstein, Derrida, to employ a careful obscurity. I think some literary writers, consciously or unconsciously, avoid 'telling a good story' because if the story is 'good' enough the idle lazy reader will fail to appreciate its deeper meaning. Better to have fewer and more worthy readers. However that may be we, as clients of art, take pleasure in the enclosed form of the object to whose 'completeness' we imaginatively contribute. We are also aware of incompleteness, and peevishly criticise novels or pictures or music for careless or unsatisfying design. Much modern music (post-Schoenberg) defeats our old-fashioned wish for the melody to 'come home'. A lack of 'finish' may result from artistic failure or from a deliberate internalised disunity which only the perceptive client will understand. *King Lear* is a very high instance of a broken pattern which indeed makes the play intolerable to many. 'Loose ends' may be a, frequently used, way of indicating patterns or realities which attend the work 'from the outside'. The landscape goes on, ordinary life continues, the musical questions find no solution within the piece. The intelligent critic can talk about such matters. (To take one fairly recent instance, about the influence of photography upon painting.) This too is art, an intimation of our mortality and our limitation, a reminder of contingency, presented to us as a source of energy and understanding and joy. Art expands our present consciousness and teaches us to live inside it. We seek in art of all kinds for the comforting sense of a unified self, with organised emotions and fearless world-dominating intelligence, a complete experience in a limited whole. Yet good art mirrors not only the (illusory) unity of the self but its real disunity. The pseudo-object need not mislead: though in a sense complete it proclaims its incompleteness and points away. Good art accepts and celebrates and meditates upon the defeat of the discursive intellect by the world. Bad art misrepresents the world so as to pretend there is no defeat.

The work of art may seem to be a limited whole enclosed in a circle, but because of contingency and the muddled nature of the world and the imperfections of language the circle is always broken. This picture of the broken circle suggests the imagery of Kant. We cannot make the phenomenal world perfectly intelligible nor our conduct in it perfectly rational, though the magnetic power of Reason continually inspires us to try. Kant's concept of the sublime, though he did not himself apply it to art, suggests something essential to the nature of serious art: how the world overflows the art object, how it transcends it, how emotions attend the experience of this. There are various metaphors which suggest themselves here. The art object points beyond itself, the world is seen beyond it, somewhat as the artist saw it when he attempted his statement, although of course he is not just copying the world. The art object is porous or cracked, another reality flows through it, it is in tension between a clarified statement and a confused pointing, and is in danger if it goes too far either way. Much modern art instinctively tends to abandon complete clear statement and complete separate object in favour of a merging of art into the continuity of the world or its withdrawal into self-referential autonomous sign-play. Traditional critics may regard this instinctive tendency as a passing fashion, but other (e.g. structuralist) thinkers claim it as a deep uneasy awareness of a metaphysical truth. A chapter in Jacques Derrida's early but still fundamental book *De la Grammatologie* is entitled 'la fin du livre et le commencement de l'écriture'. *L'écriture* here indicates *archi-écriture*, 'primal writing' or sign-activity which is not derivative from spoken speech, as a fundamental 'field'. This basic 'writing' is not (used by us as) indicative of reality, but *is* reality in a sense now being made clear by the languages of science which here provide a metaphysical model. Some of the insights of Wittgenstein appear also in structuralism; but Wittgenstein said that his arguments left ordinary language undisturbed. (*Investigations* 98.) He did not pose as a prophet or a critic, he disliked explanations of art, and once told F. R. Leavis that he ought to give up literary criticism! In philosophy, what was needed was not a new jargon or a system, but a certain kind of clarity, *ein übersichtliche Darstellung*.

In its most consistently metaphysical form structuralism (deconstruction) demands a revolution in our ways of thinking about truth and reality. It is not easy to 'explain' this large and heterogeneous mass of theory. It enters the argument for a moment at this point as an atmosphere or influence which challenges traditional conceptions of art. The main tenet of structuralism is the denial of transcendence, and with it the removal of a deep motive to art. An idea of truth is at stake here. Such a considerable change of viewpoint must have moral implications, however much structuralism professes to be scientific. What art instinctively does proves nothing in metaphysics. Writers have long been aware of, and played deliberately with, the ambiguity of 'the relation of language to the world'. An obsessive awareness of structuralist-style metaphysic, on the other hand, whether refined or vulgarly popularised, can result in an anti-intellectualist denial of the cognitive role of art, art as a form of knowledge. (At different times there are often motives, for instance political ones, for this denial.) Structuralism explicitly questions 'old-fashioned' generally accepted views of truth in literature, and in literary and historical studies. Many non-philosophers, such as literary critics, are excited by this atmosphere. In so far as structuralism professes to be 'scientific', in a post-Husserlian sense, it professes to be morally neutral. Moral philosophers in the analytical empiricist tradition have also at times professed this. In both cases, while a certain morality is rejected or set aside, another is usually tacitly assumed or promoted. There is a territory held in common between structuralist and Wittgensteinian philosophers. A part of the structuralist polemic is directed against ideas already discredited by Wittgenstein. Art, especially literature, has in the past instinctively operated as a form, the most profound generally accessible form, of moral reflection, being in this respect close to ordinary life which is saturated with moral reflection. Structuralism here contradicts common-sense, which philosophy often does, and carries with it a certain contempt for ordinary naive attitudes. This is something which Derrida has in common with Heidegger and with Sartre. It requires ingenuity to produce a work of literature devoid of moral judgments.

Dullness may be the nemesis of such an attempt. One way to succeed without being dull is to produce a work which is puzzling and obscure. The structuralist text may resemble a koan in having no solution, but being a play of meanings which stirs the client into meaning-making activity for himself; whereas the traditional novel carries the ideal reader along, fascinated by the single authoritative 'reality' of its imagined world. A contrast between such proceedings has of course long existed unselfconsciously inside the huge realm of art.

# > 5 <
# Comic and Tragic

To speak of the simplicity of art is not to embrace any Tolstoyan theory about the supremacy of folk tales. It is the height of art to be able to show what is nearest, what is deeply and obviously true but usually invisible. (Philosophy attempts this too.) Art makes place for simple statements, then seen as profound. Art is feared by tyrants because it gives weight and interest to what is various, obvious and ordinary. Tyrants fear funniness. (Western diplomats in certain countries are advised not to indulge in unrestrained laughter in public.) All tyrants try to mystify and may invent languages for that purpose. Bad artists are useful to tyrants, whose policies they can simplify and romanticise, as in Stalinist-style art. The quarrel between Lukács and the Hungarian Communist Party brought out some frank speaking on this subject. 'The positive hero of the new Hungarian socialist realist literature should be the man at work carrying out the Five-Year Plan.' (Joszef Revai's polemical pamphlet against Lukács, *Lukács and Socialist Realism*.) One can, nearer home, imagine an Orwellian state where the élite read esoteric 'literary' texts, leaving the laity to a soothing diet of state-approved romantic novels and television. The absurdity of art, its funniness, its simplicity, its lucidity connects it with ordinary life and is inimical to authoritarian mystification. 'Absurd' here should be understood in a wide sense, and not in a local or esoterically technical way (as in 'theatre of the absurd'). The absurd is the comic, as well as what defeats or teases the intellect. When Tolstoy said that art expressed the highest religious sensibility of the age he was also implying a concept of religion. Even good art may make us feel too much at ease with something less than the best, it offers a sort of spiritual exercise and what looks like a spiritual home, a kind of armchair sanctity which may be a substitute for genuine moral effort. The last volume of Yukio Mishima's *Sea of Fertility* ends with a graceful homage of art to religion. The elderly hero meets the Buddhist abbess whom he knew as a wild girl, and mentions a man who was once her lover. She remembers no such person. He mentions other people. No. At last he appreciates the religious point. So if these people never existed he too . . . The selfish and fantastical ego is unreal, the true religious life has no stories. It is above mythology. In the end we give up everything, including God, as we are told by Christian mystics such as Eckhart and St John of the Cross. Of course for the unenlightened this paradox too is a kind of art, a shadow cast by a higher truth. It certainly has a thrilling aesthetic charm.

What is absurd is very often funny, though it can be appalling too. There is a tragic absurd (*King Lear*). The absurdity of Kafka is terrifying and yet can manage to be funny at the same time. The funny may be distinguished from the witty and the ironic or satirical. Philosophy and religion may be witty and ironic, not funny. Jesus is witty not funny. In literature the funny can go deeper and is a great redeeming place of ordinary frailty. Consider the funniness of Shakespeare and Dostoevsky. (The terrible tale told at the beginning of *Crime and Punishment* by the ridiculous Marmeladov.) As comedy and as tragedy literature abounds in, one might almost say consists of, value judgments. Comic art can be revolutionary and dangerous as well as carrying the tender and the sentimental as far as they can be carried in good literature (Dickens). Comedy has an obvious built-in factor of disunity, a return to the contingent, an appeal to individual experience and common-sense. In laughing, we turn to our friends. The Greek playwrights did not mix comedy and tragedy, although Homer does this. It was evidently doubted that the same man could write both, and Socrates is found arguing this point at the end of the *Symposium*.

Plato regarded both forms, and theatre in general, with suspicion. The content of tragedy, with the charm (of poetry, music, acting, etc.) removed, 'is like the faces of adolescents, young but not really beautiful, when the bloom of youth is gone'. (*Republic* 601B.) Comedy is chaotic and concerned with accidental details and unreflective absurdities. We may imagine that the carpenter goes to the theatre and then cannot be bothered to measure his table accurately. (Not a bad parable.) Comedy, one might say, keeps the low man from rising. Tragedy on the other hand would be, according to Plato, even more objectionable because it would stop the high man from rising higher, by providing intelligent but false consolation, and a sense of achievement and self-satisfaction which impedes the highest vision. Plato banished the tragic poets. This 'banishing' is of course ironical and fictitious, but also serious. Plato's view of comedy might appear more plausible than his view of tragedy. Tragedy seems to be something serious and profound, concerned with suffering, courage and virtue, and able to carry a religious message. Zen Buddhists are, as they point out, unusual in explicitly including a kind of jokiness in the region of spirituality, in contrast with the Indian conception that a saint may smile but not roar with laughter. Of course any religious or moral view will be rightly critical of the kind of humour which is fundamentally malicious. But on the whole we in the west attach value, prudentially and morally, to the possession of a sense of humour. It is an important fact, often neglected at a theoretical level by philosophers and theologians, that the funny is everywhere to be found. A morally high sense of the comic is ubiquitous in literature.

The comic is often paired as an opposite with the tragic, but the two concepts are asymmetrical and different in kind. It is not that the comic is unserious and the tragic serious. The comic is capable of the highest seriousness, in life and in art; whereas the attempted tragic or bad tragic may be pretentious lying nonsense not capable of seriousness at all. Indeed, fortunately for the human race, the comic is everywhere, it is in the air which, as being every one of us an artist, we breathe. The tragic is not the same as sorrow – sorrow, grief, of course is also in the air we breathe. Tragedy belongs only to art, where it occupies a very small area. One might even be puzzled by the high prestige which the form enjoys, as if we needed for psychological reasons to inflate the idea. There are extremely few good tragedies and, one may say, bad tragedies are not tragedies. Compare: a bad ballet dancer is not a ballet dancer, a bad poet is not a poet. On the other hand we allow that a bad novelist is a novelist. This is to do with the generally accepted conception of 'a story'. (Novels are like stories we tell each other.) Much of the greatest literary art is a tragi-comic, or perhaps one should say sad-comic, condensation, a kind of pathos which is aware of terrible things, and which eschews definition and declared formal purpose. Such pathos is everywhere in Shakespeare. We also see it in the great novels. The novel is the literary form best suited to this sort of free reflection, sad-comic and discursive truth-telling. (Art is cognitive.) What it loses in hard-edged formal impact, it gains in its grasp of detail, its freedom of tempo, its ability to be irrelevant, to reflect without haste upon persons and situations and in general to pursue what is contingent and incomplete.

The concept of the tragic is obscure, one is tempted to say confused or incoherent. Real life is not tragic. Religion is not tragic. These are interesting and important border-lines. Plato's famous banishment of the tragedians may be taken as a religious parable. 'The tragic' some-times makes its appearance as a (serious, stoical) attitude to life: 'We can live at a trivial level or at a tragic level.' Newspapers talk about 'tragic situations' or 'tragedies at sea'. When in real-life unhappiness we 'live the tragic' or 'see something as a tragedy' something false may be involved, possibly a forgivable reaching for consolation. Strictly speaking, tragedy belongs to literature. Tragedies are plays written by great poets. One might say of the *Iliad* that, in a supreme sense, it rises to a tragic level, which no prose work can reach. But it is too long and multiform to be a tragedy. There are no prose tragedies. Real life is not tragic. In saying this one means that the extreme horrors of real life cannot be expressed in art. (This relates to why religion lies beyond art.) Art offers some consolation, some sense, some form whereas the most dreadful ills of human life allow of none. Auschwitz is not a tragedy. Religious belief may console, but can it do so in the extreme case without some element of deception? As part of our awareness of death, we are uneasily conscious of absolutes of suffering. We become accustomed, in the technically perfect 'art work' of television, to structured glimpses, real and fictional, of human misery. There is in a sense 'no reason why' we should attempt to live 'out there' in a full consciousness of the horrors of life. If we can we forget them. Perhaps a saint can sustain such a consciousness without defiling it. Great sufferings are transformed by tragic poets, as the miseries of war are in the *Iliad*, or by analogy in the paintings of Goya. (Strictly, paintings are not tragic – why?) Christ upon the cross, that ultimate picture of human suffering, is probably the greatest single consolation in western history; it is also the most generally familiar of all aesthetic images. But we need only to reflect seriously upon really terrible human fates to see that they exceed art, are utterly different from art: bereavements such as we all suffer, oppression, starvation, torture, terrorism, the father murdered in front of his child, the innumerable people who at this moment die of hunger in deserts and suffer without hope in prisons. And the fate of the Jews under Hitler which has become a symbol of the capacity and strength of human wickedness. Catastrophes are of course constantly made the subject matter of bad art, such as we continually see on television or in the cinema. Sometimes, however, art which lies can also instruct. The Holocaust on television seems a blasphemous impossibility; and when a TV film was made about a Jewish family in Hitler's Germany many people protested at the prettified inadequacy of the presentation. Yet the blunted art did convey some conception of *the facts* to a large audience, and according to some critics did so more effectively because the film resembled other sorts of TV films with which the viewers were familiar. This may be worth reflecting on.

Tragedy belongs to art, and only to great art. But perhaps even here one is suffering from an illusion? Are there works of art which are real tragedies, real instances of the form? Or is tragedy just an ideal conception, something which we think we need, something which we would like to exist? We feel: *somewhere* it must be justly recorded. Human life is full of such shadows, religion is full of them. Perhaps the concept works out as: quasi-tragic, having tragic aspects or moments, or a tragic atmosphere. The works we revere are more confused than we imagine, more indirect in making whatever point they make. Shakespeare's tragic plays contain comic and irrelevant matter. To try to define and isolate tragedy we might look at some examples of things in life about which we might want to exclaim, 'How tragic' or 'It's a tragedy.' And here we must keep in mind that anything which we describe is likely to be touched by art. Art work and value judgments are everywhere in human self-expression. Our evening story about the events of our day is a little evaluative work of art. How far do we want to press this idea? Is everything we reflect on or remember, everything we *experience*, aesthetically worked? What we feel inclined to say here will go with conceptions of art, thought, experience, and such speculation soon becomes, but not trivially, conceptual or metaphysical. Let us take a real-life example. I read in some account of the matter that on one of the last days in Hitler's bunker at the end of the war, when Dr and Mrs Goebbels were hustling their children up to bed, about to poison them with cyanide, one of the children, jesting with one of the guards, whom she was fond of, said to him, '*Misch, Misch, du bist ein Fisch.*' This episode has a piercing touchingness composed partly of tragic irony. It touches us too as evidence of the innocent vitality of the human spirit under terrible conditions. (Stories from the concentration camps.) And we picture children in that place. There is also the fact that someone remembered it. But this is not tragedy, it is a fragment of something far more awful, not just because it is 'real', but because it is different; it has no formal context, is not modified and solaced by any limited surround. The story could be told in different ways, but this touch of art does not make it tragic.

Thus in real life there occur what one might call 'pieces of tragic utterance'. But then who hears them, who repeats them, and when, for what purpose? A joke is a joke however often repeated, it is portable and has its conventional belongingness in life. But the 'tragic fragment' embarrasses and disturbs us or begins to sound suspiciously and inappropriately like art. There are stories which we hesitate to repeat lest we seem to be gloating over horrors or trying to gratify unworthy emotions in ourselves or our hearers. One might tell someone's dying words to his mother, but not repeat them at a dinner party. Of course pieces of historical data constantly detach themselves as repeatable stories, and the same is true of memorable words, like Vanzetti's last speech in the law court. 'If it had not been for these thing I might have live out my life talking at street corners to scorning men. I might have die unmarked, unknown, a failure. This is our career and our triumph. Never in our full life can we hope to do such work for tolerance, for justice, for man's understanding of man, as we now do by an accident.' Taken out of a fuller context (and there would be many ways of supplying that) it certainly moves us; but we soon also think, what a splendid rhythm, how good this would sound in a play. And who recorded it, has it not been touched up? I do not think one would want to repeat these words idly, though one might quote them in a history lesson, or in a book on prose style, which is where I came across them.

(Herbert Read, *English Prose Style*.) An example of another kind is the account by Thucydides of the sufferings of the Athenians on the Sicilian expedition, where the terrible facts are made more moving by the cool tone of the historian. If we think of it as 'tragic' it is because these graphic descriptions emerge as great literature, because of a backward glance at the mistakes and the *hubris* (a word belonging to discussion of tragedy) which brought it all about, and because we identify ourselves with the Athenians as with tragic heroes. It is difficult to talk about terrible things and we tend to turn 'the facts' into quasi-tragic art in our minds. History and folk history, including our personal and family 'chronicles', are full of such portable anecdotes and tales. These examples suggest a continuum from conversational reportage through more formal stories and history towards (Shakespearean and Greek) tragedy, along which we might move in either direction. We instinctively use art for consolation at an immediate personal level as well as at that of Titian, Mozart and Homer. Terrible events may be fiddled with by art, but as they appear in the stream of life, in conversation, newspapers, television, informal or formal books (and so on) these aesthetic 'limited wholes' tend to be unstable, so that we may see through the tale into the horror beyond. We are moved by the well-formed anecdote, but we mistrust it, do not pause upon it, take it as a mere pointer. Such considerations may also lead us to delight in (Shakespearean and Greek) tragedy, which reminds us of our own defensive reactions to what appals us in real life, and at the same time to question the ability of art, in this area, to tell truth.

The novel form more frankly admits, indeed embraces, the instability of art and the invincible variety, contingency and scarcely communicable frightfulness of life. The novel is a discursive art. Novels are, however sad or catastrophic, essentially comic. When one rereads a great novel one is often surprised to find how funny it is. The novel, in the great nineteenth-century sense, attempts to envisage if not the whole of life, at any rate a piece of it large and varied enough to seem to illuminate the whole, and has most obviously an open texture, the porous or cracked quality which I mentioned earlier. The object is as it were full of holes through which it communicates with life, and life flows in and out of it. This openness is compatible with elaborate form. The thing is open in the sense that it looks toward life and life looks back. We ask ourselves, would it be like that? There is an evident stimulus to our sense of verisimilitude and our everyday feeling for truth. This high art also takes it for granted that the world transcends art. In the traditional novel the people, the story, the innumerable kinds of value judgments both illuminate and celebrate life, and are judged and placed by life, in a reciprocal process. We read great novels with all our knowledge of life engaged, the experience is cognitive and moral in the highest degree. These huge objects mock the attempts of dogmatic critics who wish to reduce them to non-evaluative codes. Our pleasure herein is an open-textured pleasure, and this sometimes in spite of the novelist's movement toward closing the object and making it into a limited whole. Characters in novels partake of the funniness and absurdity and contingent incompleteness and lack of dignity of people in ordinary life. We read here both the positive being of individuals and also their lack of formal wholeness. We are, as real people, unfinished and full of blankness and jumble; only in our own illusioning fantasy are we complete. Good novels concern the fight between good and evil and the pilgrimage from appearance to reality. They expose vanity and inculcate humility. They are amazingly moral. They are funny, as funniness is everywhere. People make jokes in prison camps. Most traditional novels are to some degree ironical, and irony is inimical to tragedy. Tragic irony, so called, exists for the spectators not the characters. An ironical character (Iago) can endanger a tragedy just as much as a pathetic character (Malvolio) can endanger a comedy. (These are risks which clever directors love to run.) The great novels contain, often embedded in sadness, some of the funniest things in literature. And the awful things are contained in open surroundings, aware of contingency and absurdity, absolute ultimate loss of dignity, and the impossibility of an aesthetically complete presentation. The highest art here trails away into life. The context modifies the 'tragic moment' even when its point is a senseless death like that of Petya Rostov in *War and Peace*. We tend to recall the terrifying scenes in *Wuthering Heights* and forget the funniness and the sophisticated ironical modes of narration. The tension and the cruelty are also softened by an exciting sense of the magical and the demonic, which 'spoils' the tragic as it spoils religion. The tragic irony that Cathy and Heathcliff are in fact brother and sister leads to the climatic *dénouement*, and is kept concealed in a way which makes its discovery almost funny. (Where did that little gypsy child appear from? Are we to believe Mr Earnshaw's improbable tale that he 'found him' in Liverpool? Clearly he is Mr Earnshaw's illegitimate son. Once explained this is obvious.)

The ghost-story genre is not far away. It would not occur to us to regard *The Turn of the Screw* as tragic. The frightfulness of *The Heart of Darkness* has a narrative container which refers us back to the atmosphere and tempo of ordinary life, with its banalities and crude judgments. The high demonic is not the tragic, and neither is the high pathetic, such as the death of Jo the Sweeper in *Bleak House*, which is mediated by the surrounding air of unhurried sentiment (less well done it would be sentimental), and by the direct reference to religious faith. Gods may be characters in tragedies but God cannot be; even if He is seen to refuse human categories and defeat human ends His authoritarian presence cannot but be reassuring. The Book of Job is not a tragedy.

To say of this and that that it is not tragic, or not a tragedy, implies a positive concept. Yet it may be easier to see why certain sad or frightful things in art are not tragic, than to say what sort of art is tragic. Someone has got to die, it has to be a play, it has to be poetry, it has to be very good. Is it simply that we (in the west) have been enormously impressed by a certain literary genre? If it must be a play, is it not necessarily too short and simple? The paradox about tragedy may be compared with the paradox about religion. It must be about the deepest things, it must be *true*, and also comprehensible, or ambiguous, enough to be appropriated by all sorts of individuals. The statement must be impressive but not too complete, the object must be pierced, the circle broken. This, which happens spontaneously and easily in the comic, is harder to achieve and more formally essential in the tragic, where high fantasy completions, secret conniving modes of 'happy ending', must be excluded. The intelligent truthful creator must keep his material open enough, must keep, as it were, pulling it apart. We constantly formulate and express the sense of ordinary life in comic forms. But for very awful things we have, as ordinary citizens, no appropriate mode of expression. It is as if we had to borrow our language from elsewhere. Black humour may console and cheer, but is markedly indirect communication, obliquely related to the horror, not an attempt to understand, portray or comment. It begins to sound as if a tragedy is a rare bird. Perhaps there are none, or only one? If we use the word in a non-normative sense of course there are many bad tragedies. Bathos is the revenge of the fragmentary world upon a pretentious pseudo-unity. So, if we fail so many, we must have an idea of what is good? The concept is not unimportant, indeed we seem to attach some considerable significance to it. We must not be too much consoled. All art tends to console, as the presence of God consoles Job. We turn to the work of a few geniuses, where an account of what is achieved is not easy to frame.

Aristotle (*Poetics* VI 2) tells us that 'a tragedy is a representation of an action that is serious, complete, and of a certain magnitude, each form of verbal adornment [sung and unsung verse] being placed separately, consisting of action not narrative, and by pity and fear bringing about a purification of these emotions.' That is, pity and fear, or 'such emotions', meaning presumably strong emotions. The definition stresses action and completeness. The idea of a purification of emotion promotes thought and seems in place. Such purification must surely be part of our general moral enterprise and should engage the interest of the moral philosopher. We tend to feel that tragedy is connected with high morality and is good for us. Aristotle's account (*Poetics* VI–XIV) is superbly apt and lucid. Tragedy, he tells us, is primarily an action or happening (*praxis*), requiring a story or plot (*mythos*), portrayal of character (*ethos*) and intelligent spoken presentation (*dianoia*). There must be a beginning, a middle, and an end. There must of course be dramatic moments, reversals (*peripeteia*), recognition scenes, representations of suffering (*pathos*), and also wounds and deaths. (Plays where no one is killed should be classified as comedies.) The pity and fear thus induced must be clarified and purified. For this we should *not* simply see the virtuous man overthrown or the bad man successful or the total villain destroyed, *but rather* the not especially good man brought down, not by evil or wickedness, but by some fault, frailty, or weakness of character (*akrasia*). The Greek word *hamartia* is usually translated as (in an ambiguous sense) failure, fault; only (as Liddell and Scott put it) 'in the language of philosophy and religion' as sin or guilt. The corresponding verb *hamartano* means primarily 'miss the mark' (as with one's spear) and also, fail, miss one's purpose, make a mistake, or (lastly) do wrong or sin. This may seem to invite a comment upon the general character of the Greeks; but it certainly suggests something important about the nature of tragedy. (I return to this later.)

Plato, as we know, is less inclined to praise the art form which he thinks charms us into identifying with bad and extreme people and indulging in unbridled emotions which we would condemn elsewhere. Kant tells us that tragedy joins the sublime and the beautiful together. The sublime is the proud energetic fear with which the rational being faces the contingent dreadfulness of the world. The beautiful (says Kant) is the experience of a pleasing formal completeness in a purposeless conceptless object. The sublime is a special exercise of reason, a kind of moral adventure. The beautiful is a free play of the imagination in a frolic with the understanding, working sensuously upon an empty notion of 'an object' offered by the latter. The concepts are dissimilar; the sublime is moral, the beautiful is aesthetic. We cannot separate 'tragic experience' from our general sense of humanity. Kant elevates the noble sublime above the playful beautiful. Tragedy then would be a (unique) moralising or redeeming of the beautiful. Only within a high morality can the spectacle of terrible human suffering become a thing of beauty. If only saints can watch awful pain without some subtle degradation or evasion, then tragedy might be a temporary, perhaps edifying, simulation of sanctity. These are attractive lines of thought. Fear of the contingent, fear of chance, of the dreadful machinery of human fate, certainly seems to be in place here; but Kant's sublime is an adventure of the rational self, a rather peculiar experience which strengthens confidence in reason and is thus saved from contingency. Hegel suggests that tragedy portrays the collision of two systems of thought (or being), each with its own respectable justification, as in the *Antigone*. This idea may help us to look at certain works; but it does not seem morally eloquent or deep enough, is too abstract and narrowly rational, to deal with the terrible unintelligible fates of individual men, the suffering of the innocent, the nature of evil, which we feel that tragedy must concern.

Schopenhauer, with his refined unhurried common-sense, comes nearer to the centre of the matter and nearer to Aristotle. So far from being a Victorian antique, Schopenhauer stands as a modern and prophetic thinker. The voice is calm and discursive, the argument detailed and rich in examples.

'The demand for so-called poetic justice rests on an entire misconception of tragedy and indeed of the structure of the world itself. It boldly appears in all its dullness in the criticisms which Samuel Johnson made of particular plays of Shakespeare, for he very naively laments its absence. And its absence is certainly obvious, for in what have Ophelia, Desdemona and Cordelia offended? Only the dull optimistic Protestant rationalistic view of life ... will make the demand for poetic justice and find satisfaction in it. The true sense of tragedy is in the deeper insight that it is not his own individual sins that the hero atones for but original sin, i.e. the crime of existence itself.'

Schopenhauer goes on to say that it is equally inadequate to define tragedy in terms of the work of wicked men (Iago) or blind fate or perverse causality (Oedipus). The highest tragedy shows how

'characters of ordinary morality, under circumstances such as often occur, are so situated with regard to each other that their position compels them knowingly and with their eyes open to do each other the greatest injury without any one of them being entirely in the wrong ... It shows us the greatest misfortune, not as an exception, not as something occasioned by rare circumstances or monstrous characters, but as arising easily and of itself out of the actions and characters of men, indeed almost as essential to them, and thus brings it terribly near to us.'

(*WWI*, Book III, 'The Platonic Idea: The Object of Art'.)

Schopenhauer points to the metaphysical nature of tragedy, its connection with 'the structure of the world'. Tragedy is a communication about the deepest matters, purporting perhaps to reach as far down as metaphysics itself. Schopenhauer says that tragic catastrophe is occasioned by 'original sin', and he suggests what that is like when he speaks of ordinary, not necessarily very wicked, people coming to a point where they knowingly and inevitably damage each other and cause the innocent to suffer, a point where evil seems inevitable, necessary, even a kind of duty.

It is not easy to picture either great evil or great good in literature without sentimentality or caricature. Simone Weil, who was often a perceptive literary critic, criticises François Mauriac's novel *Thérèse Desqueyroux* for its failure to portray evil justly.

'The picture he draws of evil is defective ... where the culminating point of contact between self-deception and good is reached, he has made a muddle of things, has not rendered sensible the difference at the same time as the resemblance. Very nearly a great book (but in fact a trivial one). Something monstrous about the conception of life of those years (1918–1940). What is lacking is the colour of evil, the monotony and facility of it, the feeling of emptiness and nothingness. Money. He conceals the rôle played by this factor in this crime. He is its accomplice. But worthy of note: the way in which the crime begins and develops, and "it was like a duty". (Thus evil immediately takes on the monotony of duty.) [*That* is what ought to have been depicted] . . . In thinking that crime conceals a form of grace, they take away whatever grace lies therein, for if it does, in fact, conceal a form of grace, this can only be in the form of a dark night.'

(*Cahiers*, p. 128; *Notebooks*, trans. Arthur Wills, p. 80.)

The novel describes how Thérèse, after making a dazed family-induced marriage connected with money and land, becomes bored and frustrated and unsuccessfully attempts to murder her bourgeois and slightly boorish husband by poisoning him slowly with arsenic. (He is not bad or cruel, just tedious!) Thérèse is tried and acquitted and subsequently forced by the husband's family (for a period) to 'keep up appearances'. What may strike the reader as obvious is that a peculiarly revolting and inexcusable crime has been committed by a very nasty woman. (Poor Bernard Desqueyroux surely deserves considerable sympathy, as does his literary relation Charles Bovary.) Mauriac's skill, however, so envelops Thérèse in a cloud of sin-conscious religious understanding that it might be just possible to regard her as an interesting and touching heroine. A second novel (*La Fin de la Nuit*) portrays her later on as not exactly repentant (she seems never fully to realise what she has done) but made (somehow) wiser and nicer by suffering. Simone Weil's comments clearly indicate what makes one thoroughly uneasy about this, in some ways remarkable, book. The attempted murder is dwelt upon in detail by the author not so much to exhibit and explain its wanton wickedness (she did not have to marry him, she could have tolerated him or left him) but to reinforce our concern with the state of Thérèse's soul, and her consequent sufferings. Mauriac is of course more than a little in love with Thérèse, as he admits in a frank preface:

'Thérèse, people will say that you do not exist. But I know that you do, I who for years have watched you, often halted you upon your way and unmasked you. When young I remember having seen you in a suffocating courtroom, the prey of lawyers less ferocious than the befeathered ladies, your little face lipless and white. Later, in a country drawing room I saw you as a haggard young woman irritated by the attentions of elderly relations and a naive husband: "What's the matter with you, surely we have given you everything." Since then how often have I not been moved to see you clasp your wide and lovely brow with a hand just a little bit too large! How often through the living bars of family life, seen you pad to and fro with wolfish step; and you have stared upon me with your sad and wicked eye.'

(This startling admission represents a paradox of all art: if you are not deeply personally engaged the work will be trivial, if you are it may be half blind.) As Simone Weil points out, Mauriac has failed to emphasise the unsavoury background of the marriage in terms of money and power (he is an 'accomplice'), and to show how remote even understandable self-deception is from goodness, and thus to analyse the thoroughly evil nature of the event. He fails because he has at once leapt forward to considering Thérèse as an interesting, because so extreme, recipient of divine grace. (Our sympathy with the Prodigal Son should always be tempered by a respectful awareness of the virtues of his brother.) The notion, familiar and popular in various forms, of an internal relation between sin and grace, so that the bad act automatically *contains* the grace, is always in danger of becoming sloppy and sentimental, and removing the *fact* of evil-doing from the eye of the sinner, and even of society. The concept of grace stands in need of translation into terms of visible movement, and in extreme cases must be regarded as a (in some sense religious) mystery. Mauriac's book does however, in its best part, portray how easy it is to continue doing evil, when it becomes habitual, a way of life, something which one just 'has to go on with'. (Compare Hannah Arendt's much quoted remark about the banality of evil.) We may look from here to Shakespeare's wicked characters, such as Iago and Macbeth, to see what Simone Weil called 'the colour of evil', evil as 'duty', or 'inevitable fate', the natural irresistible exercise of a depraved vision, taken for granted as an aspect of sexual cynicism or ambition, the circumstantial working of 'original sin' as indicated by Schopenhauer. Evil is terrible and also very close.

The concept of original sin, the crime of existence itself, may be seen as a reasonable generalisation about the natural sinfulness of humans. No one is without sin. It may of course also be used as a fantasising protection of the ego, a deterministic myth, concealing chance and obliterating freedom, and making everything we do seem innocent because inevitable. Contingency should be apprehended not as fate or genes, but as a reminder of our frailty, of death and of the vain suffering of the frustrated ego and the emptiness of so many of its worldly desires. There are indeed situations, in real life and in fiction, when evil, once deeply entered into, seems 'forced' to continue. However, evil people are not usually (morally) excused on the plea that 'once started they couldn't stop'. In *Macbeth* much of the awfulness lies not only in Macbeth's wickedness but in his remorse. ('I could have done otherwise' recognised as true.) Schopenhauer's picture of a rigidly determined phenomenal world must here be detached from his genuine insight. (A 'tragic' situation for today: the young terrorist, once inside the organisation, repents, and has to choose between continuing, or dying at the hands of his comrades. Perhaps there are many of these.) Tragedy concerns the difference between suffering and death. Simone Weil says that exposure to God condemns what is evil in us *'pas à la souffrance mais à la mort'*. Not to suffering but to death. Plays in which people suffer but do not die are not (strictly speaking) tragedies. Our concept of tragedy must contain some dreadful vision of the reality and significance of death. Here sin, evil, is the evasion of the idea of death; refuge is taken in exercise of power, heroic fantasies of will or fate, cults of suffering or the passing-on of pain as damage to others. The tragic art form is rare because it is difficult to keep attention focused on the truth without the author slipping into an easier senti-mental, abstract, melodramatic (and so on) mode. In the truthful vision evil is justly judged and misery candidly surveyed. The language which can achieve this is a high poetic language. Tragedy is a paradoxical art because to succeed it must really upset us while exhibiting, but not as mere consolation, some orderly and comprehensive vista of evil and catastrophe. Death threatens the ego's dream of eternal life and happi-ness and power. Tragedy, like religion, must break the ego, destroying the illusory whole of the unified self. Ordinary works of art may be seen as illusory unities, the reassuring image of the satisfied ego, pleas-ing through a felt unification of the sensibility, an intuited harmony: a frolic between the imagination and the understanding producing a quasi-thing (Kant), or a collusion between the unconscious desires of the artist and those of his client (Freud). Tragedy, resisting these com-forts, must be in a positive, even thoroughly uncomfortable, sense a broken whole; the concluding process of the idle egoistic mind must be checked. Many people find *King Lear* almost unendurable. Tragedy must break the charmed completion which is the essence of lesser art, revealing the true nature of sin, the futility of fantasy and the reality of death. Since it is art it must have borders, it must be some kind of magic, but must also inhibit magic in its more familiar and consoling uses.

Before going on to say more about Shakespeare, and especially about *King Lear*, I would like to stay a little longer with the philosophers. The danger to drama is melodrama, sentimentality, anything which makes the story into a lie. A prime difficulty in human life: we must have stories (art forms), but stories (art forms) are almost always a bit or very false. As a Dostoevsky character remarks, we have to mix a little falsehood into truth to make it plausible. The true story may not even look like a story because it will inhibit the automatic movement of egoism, with its imposition of a pleasing innocuous form. We want to control the tale ourselves and give it *our* ending (which need not of course be in the ordinary sense a happy one). We want to make a move to a conclusion, *our* conclusion. Part of this process, to return to Freud, may involve those secret personal fantasies whose details might seem repulsive or childish. 'The essential *ars poetica* lies in the technique of overcoming the feeling of repulsion in us which is undoubtedly connected with the barriers that arise between our single ego and the others. We can guess two of the methods used by this technique. The writer softens the character of his egoistic daydreams by altering and disguising it, and he bribes us by the purely formal – that is aesthetic – yield of pleasure which he offers us in the presentation of his phantasies.' This aesthetic love-play is the 'fore-pleasure', like that which leads on to the 'end-pleasure' of orgasm, the desired and manoeuvred-for conclusion. (See 'Creative Writers and Day-Dreaming', vol. IX, 153 and Three Essays on the Theory of Sexuality, vol. VII, ch. iii, 211.) We may compare with this what Simone Weil has to say when she puts the tragedians in their places. What checks the movement of fantasy is felt as immobile. She uses the image of what is 'motionless' when speaking of Greek statues. 'Only drama without movement is truly beautiful. Shakespeare's tragedies are second class with the exception of *Lear*. Those of Racine are third class except for *Phèdre*. Those of Corneille *n*th class.' (*Notebooks*, p. 620.) Another quotation explains more of what she means. 'If we look upon ourselves as an end in the world, the world is chaos and without finality. If we eliminate ourselves, then the finality of the world is manifest; but there is no end.' This sounds like Kant's view of art as purposiveness without purpose, finality without end; also like the later part of Wittgenstein's *Tractatus*. The moral will or vision removes itself outside the pattern of the (contingent) world where everything is as it is and happens as it does happen. We must look at the world from the outside, *sub specie aeternitatis*. That is the good life. However the positions are different. Kant's beautiful object pleases us because it has the completeness of an ordinary thing but no conceptual label, it is 'just itself', formally pleasing but without moral message, a happy creation of the imagination and the understanding, but not of the reason. Wittgenstein's view seems more like an aesthetic stoicism, a vision of a dignity and courage independent of vulgar egoistic desires and pains. Here the moral will, separated from the total contingent world (all the facts), moves silently as a kind of invisible moral *style*. (This can be a secretly self-satisfying condition.) Simone Weil continues, making her own use of Kant's aesthetic:

'God is the sole and unique end. But he is not really an end at all, since he is not dependent on any means. Everything which has God for an end is finality without end [purposiveness without purpose]. Everything which has an end of its own is deprived of finality. That is why we have to transform finality into *necessity*. And it is what we manage to do through the notion of *obedience*. The suffering which goes hand in hand with necessity leads us to finality without end. That is why the spectacle of human misery is beautiful. Beauty is the only source of joy open to us.'

(*Notebooks*, vol. 2, p. 613; my italics and parenthesis.)

When, how, can human misery be beautiful? Seeing it as beautiful is what we do when we enjoy great tragedy. Perhaps one could say that the art form of tragedy is the *image* of a (rarely achieved) moral condition. (Compare the image of Nirvana.) Plato (*Phaedrus*) said that enjoyment of beauty was the only spiritual pleasure that was natural to us. Hence we must think not of mere aesthetic gratification but of something high. What does it all look like to a saint? Can we imagine? (What does it look like to a great artist?) This is metaphysical persuasive description. The 'true saint' believes in 'God' but not as a superperson who satisfies all our ordinary desires 'in the end'. (There is no end, there is no reward.) This is also to do with time, how we live it. It is a religious position where the concept of God is in place, indeed, in a fundamental sense, defined. A proper understanding of contingency apprehends chance and its horrors, not as fate, but as an aspect of death, of the frailty and unreality of the ego and the emptiness of worldly desires. So, our evil part is condemned 'not to suffering but to death'. (I expressed this once in an aphorism: the false god punishes, the true god slays.)

Love as well as God is being defined here. The viewpoint might be compared with that of the mythical Demiurge in Plato's *Timaeus*, where the divine artist, looking with love toward a perfect model, *paradeigma* (the spiritual Forms, *qua* the Good), creates out of contingent given material an imperfect copy. The Demiurge (*Demiourgos*, craftsman, artificer) a mythical god, an entirely good but not omnipotent being, is doing the best he can with the alien matter at his disposal, which already has inherent properties. Plato distinguishes here between two kinds of causality, the necessary, which belongs to the given matter, and the divine, which is the work of the Demiurge. The world as cosmos comes about through reason *persuading* necessity. (48A.) Plato, turning to us, says that we must distinguish these, and 'in all things seek after the divine for the sake of gaining a life of blessedness so far as our nature admits thereof, and to seek the necessary for the sake of the divine, reckoning that without the former it is impossible to discern by themselves alone the divine objects after which we strive'. (68E–69A.) We are (potentially) spiritual beings but also finite, seeking the divine in a contingent spatio-temporal material scene. (The visible things which conceal and intimate the invisible.) The Creator is looking at the world 'as a limited whole'. But he is also looking *away* from it at the perfect original and seeing the world in its *light*. The Forms are untainted, separate and eternal. The copy is imperfect but illumined by Good. Creation, which is both activity and contemplation, evokes joy. One might perhaps pursue the thought about the *Timaeus* by saying that the Demiurge looking at his creation is like the perfect spectator looking at the perfect tragedy. The Demiurge, who is among other things a chemist and a physicist, has created our cosmos as a region possessing 'laws of nature', persuasively fashioned out of the inherent causality of the original material. (This gave Plato an opportunity to exhibit some of the science he had picked up from the western Greeks.) The cosmos is also (34B) endowed with a soul, the *Anima Mundi* (World Soul), which is essentially good but not entirely rational. The *Anima Mundi*, incarnate, stretched out through the whole of the world and wrapped round its exterior, may be thought of as suffering therein from its experience of the distracted nature of things, brought about by the uneasy combination of divine magnetism and natural laws with the recalcitrant necessity of the original alien and non-rational material. *Timaeus* 35–7 describes the complex creation of the *Anima Mundi* which when completed 'initiates a divine beginning of unending intelligent life forever' (36E); and 'when the Father who had made it saw it moving and alive, astonishing the immortal gods, he rejoiced.' (37C.) After this success, the Demiurge, realising that he cannot confer upon the cosmos, because of its mixed nature, the eternal being of the Good, invents, 'a moving image of eternity', our time. (The *Timaeus* is a late dialogue, the main account is given by Timaeus, an astronomer.)

We may seek to 'be with' the divine cause, as exhorted by Plato, but we cannot avoid necessity, and indeed need it (as he tells us) to force upon us the reality of our situation as mortals. Let us return here to Simone Weil's beauty as a source of joy and her concept of 'obedience'. This is of course for her something ultimate and not just ancillary to a quasi-aesthetic experience. One might attempt here a comparison with Kant, seeing 'obedience' as more like Kantian sublimity than like Kantian duty. This would involve an interpretation of Kant which stresses the surreptitious way in which the *experience* of sublimity, and of *Achtung*, joyful painful respect for the moral law, supports or inspires the *non-experiential* operation of duty (obedience to reason). The connection (in sublime and *Achtung*) with a partly pleasurable emotion may indeed reduce their force or starkness by contrast with the relentlessness of duty. Simone Weil's obedience and necessity are better understood as a confrontation with what is not just unintelligible but pointless. Sublime experience is of course just this (the Alps, the stars). But Kant allows, indeed insists upon, the spiritual value of the self-aware satisfaction of the free rational spectator, as sturdy pride in his reason mingles with his awe and fear. Simone Weil's picture is grimmer, more as if she saw necessity and *malheur*, affliction, as subjection to a koan. No 'fruits of action', no quasi-aesthetic experience, just attention, truthful obedience, where even to regard suffering as a punishment would be a consolation. Not stoicism or presocratic harmony of opposites. We are to confront, not only the pointless necessity of the world, but also (*Timaeus*) *its* obedience to alien law. Here our purification takes place as exposure to a pure source. Void. The difference between *dianoia* and *noesis* in Plato, between (good) discursive thinking and (mystical) imageless attention to what is unconditional.

These reflections have led us to high matters and to a lofty conception of Aristotle's purging of the emotions. Let us review the argument using more sober terms. Morality, as virtue, involves a particular acceptance of the human condition and the suffering therein, combined with a concomitant checking of selfish desires. Our desires, our life-energy or Eros, can be purified through our attention to God, or to some magnetic Good unescapably active in our lives. An appreciation or image of necessity as law of nature can exhibit the futility of selfish purposes. This insight could lead to haughty stoicism or detached passivity. Schopenhauer, who explicitly (or officially) rejects stoicism, saw that his thought could be misunderstood in this sense. Stoicism may be said to include the sensible, or 'reasonable', egoistic aim of ceasing to suffer, and might be seen as part of any ordinary decent moral life. Wittgenstein (seeing that the world cares not for his will) may appear as a genuine stoic. Simone Weil connects necessity with a spiritual obedience prompting purification and love. She stays with the reality (the truthful experience) of suffering, affliction, *malheur*, seeing this as a kind of absolute condition capable of a spiritual use. Obedience is the freedom wherein the good man spontaneously helps and serves others. Suffering remains but accompanied by a kind of passion, a high Eros, or purified joy, which is the vision of good itself which comes about when, or brings it about that, selfish desires, and the distress involved in their frustration, are removed. We can then see the world, nature and its laws, in the light of the good, and experience a purified suffering which is a *unique* form of rapture. In obedience we can see the whole cosmos in this light and take an inspired joy in *its* obedience, rather as we can then experience (the one thing might image the other) a purified (not self-satisfied) 'sublime' emotion when watching a stormy sea. Here the idea of a purgation of emotion is necessarily in place. The spectacle of power or of pain evokes those deep ambiguous emotions designated 'sado-masochistic', especially expressive of the double nature of Eros. When these are purged of egoistic matter and of *base* (of course not necessarily all) erotic (sexual) matter we can experience a pure joy, or one might say an innocent spiritual thrill. No doubt this very rarely, perhaps never altogether, happens; and indignation at the cosmos may often seem more proper than a selfless sympathy with natural law! Who are *we* to feel such sympathy? We are not gods. (It is a new blessing in our modern age that we are learning to love the planet and care for its natural ways. This too teaches something.)

Simone Weil is envisaging an ideal definition in terms of an ideal moral achievement. Moral philosophy may work from a conception of an intensely imagined ideal man. We may judge a man's virtue by his actions, but also demand or hope to know the 'substance' which lies behind them, as in our own case we apprehend a value-bearing base of being from which actions spring. Here a part of our understanding of 'the good man' may be thought of in terms of a spectator of a tragedy. How are we to think of, to dare to think of, to make sense of, the awful sufferings and awful wickednesses of the human race? We should not always, and cannot always, refrain from judging. In making use here of the concept of tragedy we may further reflect upon the deep working of imagery as analogy in our understanding of morals.

I want in parenthesis to glance at a few fragmentary things said by Wittgenstein, who only mentioned such matters *en passant*. Art is not the only deceptive resource to which we turn in order to be able to think more comfortably about death, and about suffering so awful that it is (spiritually, psychologically) a form or equivalent of death. Pseudo-scientific beliefs often help out our political attitudes and affect the way people view their own lives. Ideas which may belong genuinely to science often live also at a popular or cult level. No doubt this has always been so and Marx is right to emphasise the deep historical working of technological change. Only now we have more powerful technology and more 'information'. Advertisements appeal, with a perfected charm, to popular science. Science, which we 'make our own', may acquire in doing so an aesthetic aspect. Wittgenstein's conversational remarks about Freud offer a criticism of popular science, and of pseudo-science which Wittgenstein took Freud's theories to be.

'Freud refers to various ancient myths in these connections [dreams], and claims that his researches have now explained how it came about that anybody should think or propound a myth of that sort. Whereas in fact Freud has done something different. He has not given a scientific explanation of an ancient myth. What he has done is to propound a new myth. The attractiveness of the suggestion, for instance, that all anxiety is a repetition of the anxiety of the birth trauma is just the attractiveness of mythology. "It is all the outcome of something which happened long ago." Almost like referring to a totem. Much the same

could be said of the notion of an *Urszene*. This often has the attractiveness of giving a sort of tragic pattern to one's life. It is all the repetition
of the same pattern which was settled long ago. Like a tragic figure
carrying out the decrees under which the fates had placed him at birth.
Many people have, at some period, serious trouble in their lives – so
serious as to lead to thoughts of suicide. This is likely to appear to one
as something nasty, as a situation too foul to be a subject for tragedy.
And it may then be an immense relief if it can be shown that one's life
has the pattern rather of a tragedy – the tragic working out and repetition of a pattern which was determined by the primal scene.'

('Conversations on Freud' in *Lectures and Conversations on
Aesthetics, Psychology and Religious Belief*, p. 51.)

Wittgenstein here expresses a particular view of tragedy (or use of the
concept) as concerned with a determined primal doom. Whether or
not one wishes to 'dismiss' the work of Freud, or to question the
empirical evidence upon which weird concepts such as 'penis envy' are
based, one can appreciate the sense of this criticism of a way in which
his ideas might be used. The sort of consolation indicated in this
example is indeed very widespread and familiar. The (any) explanatory
aesthetic 'tragic pattern' gives dignity to aspects of human conduct
which might otherwise simply appear base, mean, contemptible, vile,
criminally stupid. The 'mythical explanation' rescues us from this sort
of self-condemnation and self-abasement. It also removes the pain of
contingency, which is a shadow of death. The awful suffering, the
irrevocable loss may be accidental, but it is not (we persuade ourselves)
trivially so (if only he had not caught the train that crashed, etc.); it is
somehow accidental on a cosmic scale, a result of some sort of natural
law or profound uncontrollable life-pattern, and so in a way not really
accidental at all. This might be seen as a *debased* (fatalistic) form of
'obedience'. (Simone Weil's obedience is realism exposed to good.) So
we may escape both responsibility *and* subjection to spiteful chance.
'It was God's will' can also serve this purpose. And when we consider
how horrible human life can be we may be inclined to forgive the
frequent use of such devices.

I suggested in discussing Wittgenstein's ethical views that he seemed,
in the *Tractatus*, to want to gather all contingency together into the
limited whole of the factual world which the mystical subject could
then contemplate from the outside, from the factless realm of value.

[ 111 ]

Wittgenstein, using the same imagery, expressed his stoicism in a more positive form in the (earlier) 1914–1916 *Notebooks*. (20.10.16.) If we accept *all* the facts we can be both happy and good. And the acceptance of all the facts must (of course) exclude the 'softening' influences of art or popular science. (There are no art-facts or pseudo-science-facts.) Virtue (freedom and happiness) consists in our (ineffable) mode of approach to the facts. This defiant stoical, one might add quasi-existentialist, position separates fact and value, intellect and will, in a simple radical way which is essentially un-Kantian. Existentialism is close to stoicism. Sartre uses not dissimilar imagery. There is a satisfying neatness about such separations, all 'fact' classified together, all 'value' totally pure. Schopenhauer was right to complain that Kant robbed us of our 'rich field of perceptions'. (What else are we all the time concerned with?) Philosophy has different ways or styles of being abstract, and its mistakes too arise from its abstractness; but it is formally abstract and must beware of art (the poetic), as Plato saw.

It also seems appropriate to quote here some of Wittgenstein's remarks about Shakespeare in *Culture and Value*.

'I do not believe that Shakespeare can be set alongside any other poet. Was he perhaps a *creator of language* rather than a poet? I could only stare in wonder at Shakespeare; never do anything with him. I am *deeply* suspicious of most of Shakespeare's admirers. The misfortune is, I believe, that he stands by himself, at least in the culture of the west, so that one can only place him by placing him wrongly. It is *not* as though Shakespeare portrayed human types well and were in that respect *true to life*. He is *not* true to life. But he has such a supple hand and his *brush strokes* are so individual, that each of his characters looks *significant*, is worth looking at. "Beethoven's great heart" – nobody could speak of "Shakespeare's great heart".'

(p. 84.)

'The reason why I cannot understand Shakespeare is that I want to find symmetry in all this asymmetry. His pieces give me an impression as of enormous *sketches* rather than of paintings; as though they had been *dashed off* by someone who can permit himself *anything*, so to speak. And I understand how someone can admire that and call it *supreme* art, but I don't like it. So if someone stands in front of these pieces speechless, I can understand him; but anyone who admires them as one admires, say, Beethoven seems to me to misunderstand Shakespeare.'

(p. 86.)

'I do not think that Shakespeare would have been able to reflect on the "lot of the poet" [*das Dichterlos*]. Nor could he regard himself as a prophet or as a teacher of mankind. People stare at him in wonderment, almost as at a spectacular natural phenomenon. They do not have the feeling that this brings them into contact with a great *human being*. Rather with a phenomenon. I believe that if one is to enjoy a writer one has to *like* the culture he belongs to as well. If one finds it indifferent or distasteful, one's admiration cools off.'

(p. 85.)

George Steiner, in his interesting and perceptive W. P. Ker Lecture, *A Reading against Shakespeare*, quotes Wittgenstein's views. The indictment may be expressed, in Steiner's words, as: 'the manipulative sovereignty and singularity of Shakespeare's spectacular skills generates a merely *phenomenal* significance. And mere phenomenality is *untrue to life*.' Wittgenstein's *ich mag es nicht* (tamely translated as 'I don't like it') conveys, Steiner says, 'a colloquial intensity of distaste'. Steiner draws attention to Wittgenstein's sentence: 'Was he perhaps a *creator of language* rather than a poet?' '*War er vielleicht eher ein Sprachschöpfer als ein Dichter?*' Steiner goes on:

'*Sprachschöpfer* [which Wittgenstein has underlined] can be translated: the archaic but also (if I am not mistaken) Joycean term "wordsmith" renders the appropriate stem and connotations. But "poet" does *not* translate *Dichter*. And it is this gap, indeed it is very nearly an abyss, which is the crux of Wittgenstein's entire case.'

'The authentic *Dichter* is of the rarest . . . For the *Dichter* is "one who knows ethically, who object-knows" (an inadmissible fusion in English, but imperative to the implicit notion of meaning). The *Dichter*'s knowing is antithetical to "knowingness", to encyclopaedic myriad-mindedness (as so many have found it in Shakespeare). In the *Dichter* knowledge, cognition and re-cognition are, in a sense not unlike that of Plato's epistemology of the loving intellect, *moral acts*.'

'In Martin Heidegger, Wittgenstein's secret sharer at so many decisive points in the philosophy of hermeneutics and the investigation of language, the term *Dichter* is cardinal. The *Dichter* – Sophocles, Hölderlin

[ 113 ]

above all, Rilke and Paul Celan among the moderns – "speaks being" ... More than any other man the *Dichter* is, for Heidegger, the "shepherd of being".'

Steiner quotes Wittgenstein's remark, 'I do not think Shakespeare would have been able to reflect on the *Dichterlos*', and continues:

'a term again resistant to translation into English and into the entire register of Anglo-Saxon sensibility, but signifying something like the "calling", the "destined ordinance" of the poet.'

'The contrast with Dante, with Goethe, with Tolstoy, *die Dichter par excellence*, is glaring. Where is there a Shakespearean philosophy or intelligible ethic? Both Cordelia and Iago, Richard III and Hermione are instinct with the same uncanny trick of life. The shaping imagination which animates their "spectacular" presence is beyond good and evil. It has the dispassionate neutrality of sunlight or of wind. Can a man or woman conduct their lives by the example or precepts of Shakespeare as they can, say, by those of Tolstoy?'

Steiner mentions T. S. Eliot's 'more guarded but no less divisive preference of Dante over Shakespeare'.

I turn now to Eliot, *Selected Essays*, 'Dante', and 'Seneca in Elizabethan Translation'. 'Dante and Shakespeare divide the modern world between them; there is no third.' (p. 265.)

'In a comparison of Shakespeare with Dante, for instance, it is assumed that Dante leant upon a system of philosophy which he accepted whole, whereas Shakespeare created his own: or that Shakespeare had acquired some extra- or ultra-intellectual knowledge superior to a philosophy. This occult kind of information is sometimes called "spiritual knowledge" or "insight". Shakespeare and Dante were both merely poets (and Shakespeare a dramatist as well); our estimate of the intellectual material they absorbed does not affect our estimate of their poetry, either absolutely or relative to each other. But it must affect our vision of them and the use we make of them, the fact that Dante, for instance, had behind him an Aquinas, and Shakespeare behind him a Seneca. Perhaps it was Shakespeare's special role in history to have effected this peculiar union – perhaps it is part of his special eminence to have expressed an inferior philosophy in the greatest poetry. It is certainly one cause of the terror and awe with which he inspires us.'

(p. 96.)

Well, Dante was moved by his own religious faith and his love of Aristotle. But great poets are not philosophers, and thinkers do not stand 'behind' them in the sense implied by Eliot. The idea is certainly out of place in the case of Shakespeare, who made some uses of Seneca and certainly read Florio's translation of Montaigne. But then the whole world was his, he imbibed everything, he transformed everything. His 'dispassionate neutrality' is his calm sense of justice, his compassion, his profound understanding of human nature. 'Spiritual knowledge' or 'insight', not to be dismissed as 'occult information', is indeed what Shakespeare possesses. He is in his own unique way a religious poet, he knows about good and evil. He did not didactically 'express a philosophy'. He did not (fortunately) 'regard himself as a prophet or as a teacher of mankind'. Both Dante and Shakespeare in their different ways *show* us what religion is.

After so much quoting I might be expected, or expect myself, to reply, on behalf of 'the Anglo-Saxon sensibility', to George Steiner's elegant and spirited attack upon Shakespeare. In fact I think the essence of my defence is contained in the brief criticism of Eliot. Another thing one may say of Eliot concerns his famous argument in 'The Metaphysical Poets' essay, about a 'dissociation of sensibility', 'from which we have never recovered', and the difference between the intellectual poet and the reflective poet. 'Tennyson and Browning are poets and they think; but they do not feel their thought as immediately as the odour of a rose. A thought to Donne was an experience; it modified his sensibility.' Shakespeare is not at all like Donne; but it might be said (when speaking of their dissimilarity) that the ability to feel thought like the odour of a rose (whatever exactly that may mean) was possessed by Shakespeare in a more profound and purer form. We know very little about Shakespeare, he is hidden behind his work, and perhaps in this respect is an ideal artist. Invisible and modest, he 'disappears' his wisdom into his art. He is not didactic, he is, as artist, selfless, it would never have occurred to him to comment on his writings or discuss what it is to be a poet. His 'philosophy' and his 'ethic' is 'consumed in anonymous work'. Shakespeare does not speak formally about religion, this aspect of his life is obscure. But the plays are 'showings'. They are indeed 'criticisms' of vast areas of human life, offered to us by a just and compassionate intellect: not 'beyond good and evil', but goodness *made perfectly* into art. They are not philosophy or philosophical, but may be compared, *mutatis mutandis*, with Plato's dialogues in being full of light and truth, and, to steal Steiner's fine phrase, the epistemology of the loving intellect. The range and profundity of this intellect is so seemingly effortless that it may look to us transparent, as it were invisible. Shakespeare's people, enduring *individuals* known all over the world, are like icons, secure inhabitants of an art which comprehends human nature from its deepest evil to its highest good, together with its funniness, its happiness and its beauty. All this, needless to say, implies no disrespect for the great *Dichter* mentioned by Steiner. Great poets come in felicitously various kinds.

With Shakespeare we return to the concept of tragedy and how it prompts the idea that art must not console us too much. Here, in the interests of truth, the artist must inhibit his magic. Well, must he? Who says so? Not every concept that seems deep is deep, even though it may inspire lofty thoughts. Is there not something wilful in the attempt to define tragedy, making it out to be something interesting and ideal? Why not treat the tragic plays as individual works, full of aspects and ideas and multifarious stuff? The general notion may be incoherent, but we are inclined to feel that the concept, the fact that it has been coined and treated with such respect, indicates some kind of end-point, a remarkable break in the continuum of art. It tells us something too about the nature of speech, of poetic speech. All tragedies are written in poetry. Prose candidates can readily be seen to belong to other genres. Tragedy is sometimes called the highest form of art because (we feel) only great poetry can raise language to the pitch of clarified moral intensity which enables it to display the horrors of human life in dramatic form. This idea also prompts suspicion. After all, tragedies are theatre. A tragedy, unlike a novel, cannot be very various or very long. Shakespeare gets away with irrelevancies and comic patches which would have shocked the Greeks. Iago *can* be partly played as a comic character. (So incidentally could the watchman at the beginning of Aeschylus's *Agamemnon*.) It is very difficult to reach and maintain the required pitch, and with tragedy, unless you are doing it very well you are not doing it at all. Tragedy (we feel) is the point where art nearly breaks down but triumphantly does not. Tragedy must mock itself internally through being essentially, in its own way, a broken whole. The tragic poet breaks the egoistic illusory unity which is natural to art and is able to look at human evil with a just and steady eye. He positively prevents his client from using the work as private magic. Tragedy must cause us distress: its subject matter is contingency and death, the profound difference between suffering and death, the connection of truth and justice with the apprehension of death, the elevation of morality to the religious level. That someone must die in a tragedy is not a mere convention like that which decrees deaths in detective stories. In tragedy the compulsory nature of death is an image of its place in life. Such are the solemn thoughts which a contemplation of this great concept may inspire in us.

But is all this really happening, or is it just something that we want to happen? Surely no artist can really defend himself against his client, nothing can prevent any object from degenerating in the eye of the beholder. And what about the charm of the work? Hölderlin's epigram on Sophocles:

> Viele versuchten umsonst das freudigste freudig zu sagen,
> Hier spricht endlich es mir, hier in der Trauer sich aus.
> Many vainly attempted to speak the most joyful in joy,
> Here at last in grief it speaks itself to me.

Great poetry can reach heights of clarified intensity and dread, but can also give supreme pleasure. *Antigone*, a marvellous evening in the theatre. Can art actually convey the horrors of life better than the television news? Perhaps all actual tragedies are failed tragedies, fake romantic 'tragedies', even if not bathetic absurdities? And if so, what can the high concept tell us, is it still valuable as a mirage? (An Idea of Reason?) I think interested parties would agree that there are very few candidates. Apart from the Greeks, a few plays by Shakespeare, one or two by Marlowe, Webster, Racine, a few more and one begins to hesitate and fish around. And even Shakespeare. *Antony and Cleopatra*, a romantic love story with a brilliant portrait of a nasty woman. *Othello*, about sex, the degraded sex of Iago, the idealised sex of Othello, the innocent sex of Desdemona, the *Liebestod*, the magical consoling marriage between sex and death, murder scene as love scene: the redemption of death by its identification with sex, the exact opposite of a tragic theme. *Hamlet*, also about sex, the Freudian classic, the romantic ironical hero, the most delightful character in drama, every actor's favourite role. Of course these plays are full of thrills and marvels and deep psychological insights. But pity and terror? The horrors of human life? Real evil? Real death? Perhaps after all only Aristotle's Greeks could do it. *Macbeth* comes closest to Schopenhauer's definition, people committing awful crimes with their eyes open because they have somehow taken a path which makes these crimes into an inevitable duty.

> 'I am in blood
> Stepped in so far that, should I wade no more,
> Returning were as tedious as go o'er.'

We can to some extent *understand* how it is that *Macbeth* approaches the tragic 'ideal'. But what about *King Lear*?

*Lear* really does distress us in a sense in which *Othello*, say, does not. It may be felt to be almost too painful, inspiring a quite uncomfortable fear, possibly even aversion, or an uneasy awe as at a mysterious ambiguous mystical object. Part of the weirdness of the play belongs to the curiously hard unresponsive semi-symbolic nature of the character of Cordelia. Though doomed, she is not an easily comprehensible 'tragic character'. She has not made herself at home in the work, she is not at home anywhere, from the point of view of the natural illusory whole she might even be said to be a flaw, leading some down-to-earth critics to say that the tiresome self-important girl has caused a great deal of trouble for which she has shown no sign of being sorry. A companion piece, as it were in a diptych, is the portrayal of Lear's *illusions* at the end when a less great conception might have placed him beyond illusion. There is illusion behind illusion.

> 'Come, let's away to prison.
> We two alone will sing like birds i' the cage,
> When thou dost ask me blessing, I'll kneel down
> And ask of thee forgiveness: so we'll live,
> And pray, and sing, and tell old tales, and laugh
> At gilded butterflies, and hear poor rogues
> Talk of court news; and we'll talk with them too,
> Who loses and who wins, who's in, who's out;
> And take upon's the mystery of things,
> As if we were God's spies; and we'll wear out,
> In a walled prison, packs and sects of great ones
> That ebb and flow by the moon.'

This is, if one wants to use the phrase, the highest conceivable tragic irony. For one who knows the play this visionary speech is perhaps its most frightful moment, the essence of its frightfulness, which is also so piercingly beautiful: perhaps near the point where 'the misery of the world is beautiful'. Lear envisages a continuation of life, its renewal over many years, in prison and in suffering, a purgatory of pure sancti-fying love. But it is not so easy to take upon oneself the mystery of things. Perhaps there is no mystery and no God, only pain and utter loss and helpless senseless death. 'Come, let's away to prison' must often have been the cry of defeated people who suddenly saw a holy vision of peace inside pain, of forgiving and being forgiven, of *redemp-tive suffering*. One can imagine how this might come about and how someone who had sinned and suffered, or struggled angrily and in vain for some cause, could become a sort of calm wise anchorite in the end, triumphing over suffering and bitterness, transmuting it all into a kind of religious vision. (A wise and also witty anchorite, for 'we'll talk with them too'.) It seems indeed a profound religious idea, like the triumph of Christ upon the cross, whose redemptive suffering actually over-comes death; and behind the dying Christ we see God and the angels and the risen Christ in majesty. Death is transformed into visionary pain and then into the living peace of a renewed being. It is the absolute cancellation of this idea which constitutes the tragic climax of *Lear*, the final turn of the screw, and of which the peculiarly chill and odd, one might say charmless, quality of Cordelia is the image and essence. This role of Cordelia in the play must surely overcome the sensible reaction of those who see her simply as a proud opinionated prig. Cordelia both as symbol and as sufferer is an essential part of the tragic matrix. Perhaps indeed suitably understood and transmuted, the harsh judgment upon her can stand too. Those who refuse to compromise reasonably with what they see as evil may well destroy themselves and their innocent friends and achieve nothing – except perhaps to leave an example behind. (Antigone, too, brought about the death of the innocent.) The play has a double ending, a soft tragic end in 'calm of mind, all passion spent', followed by another end in screams and howl-ing. It could be called, from a traditional point of view, an unChristian play, raising to the highest level of intensity Shakespeare's reticent attitude to Christianity. Of course this reticence might have obvious motives in his religious (Catholic) attachments; but I think one may also see in it Shakespeare's (true) tragic understanding that religion, especially and essentially, must not be consolation (magic). He, an inventor of myths, did not want to touch the soft magical aspects of the Christian story, any more than he would touch the Arthurian legends. Prospero's magisterial sacrifice (his surrender of magic power) must be continually renewed.

That loss of promised redemption and wise gentle stoical peace is something which speaks especially to our, Hitler and after, age when warfare and tyranny have achieved an intensity of cruelty which previous generations might have consigned to the barbaric past. In some ages or some contexts the ingenious and persistent wickedness of Goneril and Regan might seem absurdly unnatural; not so now. It has in this century been the fate of so many to be confronted with totally ruthless unshakeable evil and to have to choose between degrees of compromise and an absolute opposition which will tear mind and body to tatters, ruin the lives of friends and family, and perhaps never even be heard of or known of to *be* an example to others. Such situations break hearts, breed weary cynicism, weaken the sense of absolute; and also of course reveal a small number of the hero-saints of our time. Many, no doubt, have gone unrevealed.

To return to Schopenhauer's idea, which fits *Macbeth*, of 'characters of ordinary morality under circumstances which often occur' knowingly doing each other the greatest injury; does this idea fit or enlighten *Lear*? Again we can see something prophetic in the play if we think of quite ordinary people who worked as guards in concentration camps: evil as a job to be carried on, we may as well continue and finish it, evil as duty. Lear could have satisfied the tragic canon by dying peacefully, full of wise words, at the end of the play; without that prophetic glimpse of the huge power and *triumph* of evil, and the destruction of his vision of redemptive peace. As it is, one might go further and ask would it not be an even better tragedy if Lear were left alive at the end, if we were left with the sense of his consciousness, bearing this terrible knowledge, continuing to be. (We are not to be consoled by the idea that he is mad, he is not mad, he knows and sees it all.) Death is peace. The play almost breaks the art form, and a surviving Lear would break it altogether. (As his crying continues on and on.) The metaphor of the broken circle, the cracked object, occurs to us especially I think here, where the satisfying calming completeness of art is internally contradicted by absolute contingency and humiliating death. To die sword in hand is quite another thing. Lear could be imagined living on as an image of death which would be more awful than the merciful end conventionally required. A clever cinema director could perhaps end a version of the play by continued shots of Lear, still alive, remembering, always growing older and older and always *thinking* those terrible torturing thoughts. *Lear*, as it is, continues to point beyond the conventions, it is a religious object bearing the arcane message that redemptive suffering does not overcome death. *Pas à la souffrance* ... Socrates said that philosophers must practise dying. It is the living who can do that, the dead are at peace. Lear obeys the tragic convention and dies in the end and stops suffering and stops knowing what he briefly knew, and which was too much for him. He is not a typical tragic hero achieving a violent death in some gesture of wild courage and thus in some aesthetic manner atoning for his sins. Lear dies a helpless victim, as so many people do on this planet, prisoners who are quietly shot in the back of the head on some unrecorded morning. After witnessing the superb deaths of Othello, Macbeth and Hamlet, we leave the theatre excited, exalted, invigorated, perhaps even persuading ourselves that our pity and fear have been purged. After *Lear* we go away uneasy, chilled by a cold wind from another region. Something of this unconsoling coldness is found in Greek literature. Our 'pessimism' can be accompanied by a gloomy relish. The Greeks are devoid of our ubiquitous (romantic) sado-masochism. Shakespeare's sado-masochism, so elegantly on display in the sonnets, so rarely visible elsewhere, is blown about and largely blown away by the fresh gales of his genius. I wonder if he was conscious of it as a secret.

What does accompany us from a performance of *Lear* as the nearest thing to a consolation is the figure of Cordelia as a pale statuesque monument, as an image of truth as death. The ending is agonising and senseless, yet leaving the unconsoling and indeed helpless truth somehow intact as a sort of dead and stony emblem. Cordelia's innocence is unlike that of Desdemona and Ophelia, with whom Schopenhauer links her. Cordelia is a touchstone, an absolute, and although a victim, not quite human. Her essential nature (function) is to be completely pure, but not as Ophelia and Desdemona are pure. Ophelia is a helpless innocent, Desdemona is a great sexual princess; whereas the idea of sex cannot come near Cordelia, any more than it can come near real death. The Othello-style death which is identical with sexual love is a fake death. Cordelia's purity is unromantic, unresponsive, un-thou, she is not an ordinary vital force, she is symbolic, demytholo-gised, charmless (yet portrayed by a charming actress!): a paradoxical, theatrically scarcely intelligible, character. She is like a Platonic Form, she is 'immobile' to use Simone Weil's word, which seems in place here. Plato's separate eternal unresponsive Forms are magnetic objects of love, but they are also symbols of death which are only truly grasped as such by a purified Eros. (We have no reward.) A positive ('practis-ing', to use Socrates's word) acceptance or integration of death into life can be a vital moral force only at a high level, which Lear himself is far from reaching.

It appears then that the concept of tragedy, if considered strictly, is paradoxical. One seems to have in mind some sort of ideal tragic below which actual tragedies usually, or always, fall. Perhaps the concept of tragedy founders (to use a Kierkegaardian image) upon the nature of art itself. Art cannot help changing what it professes to display into something different. It magically charms reality, nature, into a formal semblance. Hell itself it turns to favour and to prettiness. This impera-tive of transformation is, as I said earlier, challenged (now) by artists who want to dissolve the barrier between art and life. Let the 'illusion' of art be exposed, theatre is merely happenings, a tale merely a text and not a vision into another world. The 'work' of art should be exhibited as part of the continuum of life, to be taken over by the client. Natural objects or commercial artefacts are placed in art galleries to startle us out of traditional assumptions and thereby to sharpen our vision. However, in this contest, as the Surrealists found out, art may win, and anti-art mediate new and hitherto unimagined forms of art. Incoherent gestures and deliberate confusions of 'art' with 'life' are often popular because they are easier to produce than finished aesthetic statements, and are sometimes useful as political tools. They can be symbols of 'protest'. However the instincts of the artist can (we hope) return again to reflectiveness and to the work of the individual imagina-tion in its search for truth. The endlessly various formal separateness of art makes *spaces* for reflection. To resume: art cannot help, whatever its subject, beautifying and consoling. Goya's 'horrors of war' are ter-rifying but beautiful. Great art is beautiful, this is a place where the (unfashionable) concept of beauty is at home, and is preeminently tested and clarified. Whereas the evils and miseries of human life are not beautiful or attractive or formally complete. How can such a terrible planet dare to have art at all? ('Who can write poetry after

Auschwitz?' Adorno.) (An answer, Paul Celan.) Politics yes, art no. Great tragedy then has to be some sort of contradiction, destroying itself as art while maintaining itself as art. Metaphysics too, and theology, are, to say the least of it, touched by art.


Plato's reaction against art was that of a religious man. When he speaks in the *Republic* of the 'old quarrel between philosophy and poetry' (607B), he places the tragic poet, with other mimetic artists, at three removes from reality, as a copyist of appearance (597). How does the concept of the tragic relate to that of the religious? Fear of the aesthetic haunts many religious people. Questions and concepts have their places, where, under pressure, they become clearer (as the concept of beauty does in the context of the tragic) and this is a place (among others) where one might attempt a definition of religion. Gloom and despair and recognition of human misery and wickedness in art and (usually) in philosophy and (one might venture to say) in theology are not genuine whole-hearted gloom and despair and recognition of human misery and wickedness. Leaving aside the artists, who obviously enjoy themselves, consider the zest and relish with which Schopenhauer and Bertrand Russell and Jean-Paul Sartre declare their realistic clear-eyed pessimism. People call Schopenhauer pessimistic. Not at all. He is as cheerful as Hume whom he admires and in some ways resembles. Is one then to be, for fear of lying, silent about such deep matters, as Wittgenstein sometimes recommended? Such silence is contrary to respectable human instincts, we must talk, it keeps things going, and out of traditions of ordinary talk great geniuses arise who make the impossible possible. With the achievement of *Lear* we might compare the calm lucid sunny light which shines in the dialogues of Plato and is quite unlike the gloomy relish of lesser thinkers. We might recall too that Plato lived, and lived dangerously, as an active participant through one of the beastliest and most violent periods of recorded human history. His philosophical imagination, though much concerned with politics, does not focus on these historical details, the rare references to which (for instance at *Symposium* 220–21 and *Theaetetus* 142) are in effect aesthetic.

Art is connected with happiness and religion is traditionally connected with bliss, whether as something to be attained hereafter or, by the elect, enjoyed in this life. Religious bliss is, however, agreed to be something of a mystery, difficult and obscure, quite unlike ordinary happiness which depends on the satisfaction of selfish desires which would *ex hypothesi* not attend a beatified state. Plato says that higher realities appear at lower levels as images or shadows. Perhaps we see a shadow or image of religious joy in some mystical writings and in some (few) philosophical writings, and then one is tempted to say in some art. But the shadow is not the reality and the reality is unimaginably different, its nature cannot be guessed from its shadow. The 'mode of projection' cannot be understood from below. About the reality most of us know no more than the prisoners in the Cave knew of the things that cast the shadows. Of course religion can console at any level, but also contains a self-transcending imperative, a continuous iconoclastic urge to move beyond false consolation, suggesting a magnetic end-point where there is no more illusion, only truth, where consolation and explanation vanish.

We may remind ourselves here of Kierkegaard's distinction in *Fear and Trembling* between the Tragic Hero and the Knight of Faith. This contrast, like many of Kierkegaard's distinctions, is Hegelian in style, involving the triad which he often makes use of: the aesthetic individual, the moral universal, the religious individual. The first and the third are private and obscure, belonging in the secrecy of the individual soul, the second, being clearly and rationally explicable, can represent a public model. This picture exhibits the possibility, so present to Plato, of the aesthetic being confused with the spiritual. Opponents of religion may argue that it is always a disguised aesthetic, affording escape from the moral burden of explanation and accountability. Within religion too, 'personal spirituality' is sometimes contrasted (favourably or not) with a more 'politicised' socially responsible and public exercise of religion. (After all, 'love thy neighbour' is fundamental.) In *Fear and Trembling* Kierkegaard first presents his Knight through the figure of Abraham, obeying God's command to sacrifice his son: a command which cannot be publicly justified in universal moral terms and which condemns Abraham to isolation and silence. At the beginning of the book he tells the story of Abraham four times over. I insert here the notes upon these four versions which I made in 1943 in my copy of the book: (1) Abraham sacrifices Isaac's respect to drive Isaac to God. (2) Abraham cannot forgive God. (3) Abraham guiltily suspects his own heart. (4) Isaac's faith is destroyed. Underneath this I had written: SK, like LW, wants to see what happens if the story is taken as true.

All later existentialism is within SK. [SK is Kierkegaard, LW is Wittgenstein.] I now resume. For the Tragic Hero 'it is a glorious thing to be understood by every noble mind'. He 'renounces himself in order to express the universal; the Knight of Faith renounces the universal to express the Individual'. 'As soon as I speak I express the universal, and when I remain silent no one can understand me.' 'The tragic hero is great through his moral virtue, Abraham is great through his purely personal virtue.' A paradox of which Kierkegaard is of course not unaware is that by celebrating Abraham in beautiful heart-felt prose he is trying to make Abraham comprehensible, and is thus in danger of turning him into a universal tragic character. Christ too may be seen as a universal tragic character. Othello is a universal tragic character. Shakespeare's highest art attempts to ensure that we cannot see Lear or Cordelia in this light. (They are unattractive.) We are here close to the metaphysical enigma of tragic art, and indeed, by extension, of all art and all discourse. As soon as you talk about it you lose the object. Better to stay quietly with what is manifested without words.

Kierkegaard attempts by further talking to remove any misapprehension and cure any tendency in his reader to idealise (universalise) the Knight of Faith. What is this person really like?

'I have never discovered a Knight of Faith, but I can easily imagine one. Here he is. I make his acquaintance, I am introduced to him. And the moment I lay eyes on him I push him away and leap back suddenly, clap my hands together and say half aloud: "Good God! Is this really he? Why he looks like an Inspector of Taxes!" ... I watch every movement he makes to see whether he shows any sign of the least telegraphic communication with the infinite, a glance, a look, a gesture, an air of melancholy, a smile to portray the contrast of infinity with the finite. But no! I examine him from head to foot, hoping to discover a chink through which the infinite can peer. But no! He is completely solid. How does he walk? Firmly. He belongs wholly to the finite; and there is no townsman dressed in his Sunday best who spends his Sunday afternoon in Frederiksburg who treads the earth more firmly than he; he belongs altogether to the earth, no bourgeois more so.'

Kierkegaard wants to commend a private silent inner personal spirituality and to do so without romanticising religion. He goes on for some while describing his good man who looks like an Inspector of Taxes.

'He is not a poet . . . When he comes home in the evening he walks as sturdily as a postman. On his way he thinks about the special hot dish which his wife has been preparing for him, a grilled lamb's head garnished with herbs perhaps.'

And so on. Is he overdoing it, we might think, surely there must be some outward and visible difference between a very spiritual man and an ordinary bourgeois? But of course this is a parable making a rhetorical point. By this time we are more likely to be thinking: what an endearing character! What a simple yet noble chap, a genuinely saintly being! Why, this fellow is just as charming as the other one! Avoiding one kind of romantic exposition Kierkegaard falls (so beautifully) into another; to avoid the traditional hero he conjures up a now not unfamiliar kind of anti-hero.

It is difficult to talk eloquently at any length upon a religious subject without employing the consolations and charms of art. This is perhaps very obvious and one may say so what, or *que faire*? A saint described is a saint romanticised. Nor of course must a saint romanticise himself. So saints must be invisible both to others and to themselves. Is not this as unrealistic as that Tax Inspector? Yet in a way the difficulty, or paradox, is a familiar one, and indicates real distinctions and differences. Simple edifying religious homilies (as in sermons, Thoughts for the Day, etc.), using homely examples and excluding anything lofty or high-flown, are themselves a clearly recognisable art form. No wonder some thinkers say: don't talk. Some religious orders limit the amount of 'ordinary speech' which is to take place, and many liturgical styles rely upon the constant repetition of traditional forms of words rather than upon verbal improvising. However, churches are public institutions, concerned with the progressive clarification and propagation of their ideas, and with their place and duties in society. In order to teach, to persuade, to explain, they must talk. It is indeed difficult to attend to any religious matter or object without drawing it down to some easily imagined easily handled level. Theology has always been concerned with how far, in this process, to go. Religion is for everybody, but how to reach everybody? T. S. Eliot said that Christianity has always been changing itself into something which can be generally believed. There may be a limit to this process, where a demythologised religion becomes intolerable. Recent Anglican theology exhibits these problems. A denuded 'existentialist' faith may lose its identity in the mind of the believer and become more like an unadorned high moral asceticism.

'We want religion to be a severe inner discipline without any consolations whatsoever. The colder and clearer the better ... Religious activity has now to be undertaken just for its own sake as an autonomous and practical response to the coolly perceived truth of the human condition. This is true religion: all else is superstition.'

(Don Cupitt, *The Listener*, 13 September 1984.)

Stern words deserving respect. On the other hand, a theologian, such as Maurice Wiles, who wishes to continue to draw upon the traditional images, feels in danger of living upon borrowed capital and invokes 'a bold and creative use of the speculative imagination' (*The Remaking of Christian Doctrine*, p. 120). A genius is needed. Christian theology may well begin to feel that whereas other (for instance scientific) modes of thought in this age are producing new and profoundly revolutionary ideas, its activity is limited to the manipulation of a given number of ageing concepts. A (drastic) way forward may have been suggested by a Catholic theologian, Brian Nolan, who told a conference (at Maynooth in September 1984) that after a more prolonged exposure to oriental religions, African Christianity, Liberation theology, and the Women's Movement, traditional European theology would find itself (felicitously) put through the shredder.

Both artist and client tend to use art as magic and read into it private fantasies and unrealised unities. Religion has always been a patron of the arts and has been served with enthusiasm and genius. Think what European painting has done for the Crucifixion, the Resurrection, and the doctrine of the Trinity. Religious puritanism is to a large extent a rejection of the role of art in religion. Puritans (and Plato is one) see that art is a danger to religion. Puritans, including Plato, are also of course aware of the strong sexual charge (for instance the sadomasochism) in religious doctrine and practice. Plato saw Eros, when purified, as the highest form of spiritual energy, but lower unredeemed Eros as a plausible tempter. The concept of tragedy is paradoxical because it attempts to display horror through charm. A great genius can integrate these; usually one or the other has to win at the expense of great art. At least it seems to make sense to ask, is the Christian story tragic? One may reply, no, it is just a piece of history. Or if not: God cannot be a character in a tragedy. And is there not a happy ending? Are the Gospels and St Paul's epistles art? It is extraordinary (or miraculous) that they exist at all. What happened immediately after Christ's death, how it all went on, how the Gospel writers and Paul became persuaded He had risen: this is one of the great mysteries of history. It is difficult to imagine any explanation in purely historical terms, though the unbeliever must assume there is one. Perhaps there are many such events, only this is the most important and picturesquely documented. How did Christianity survive through those first centuries? E. R. Dodds (*Pagan and Christian in an Age of Anxiety*) suggests that 'the strongest single cause of the spread of Christianity' was that, in a time of rootlessness and loneliness and fear, members of Christian communities cared for each other. The unbeliever may also of course feel that the story of the Crucifixion has a *tragic* ending since Christ, who may or may not have thought he was divine, in fact was not: tragic irony. 'Why hast Thou forsaken me?' The Gospel narratives show defeat turning into victory, the triumph of suffering over death, suffering set up as the adversary of death. The frightful story of Christ's death becomes a supreme cosmic event. The terrified confused abandoned disciples turn into heroes and geniuses. The story of Christ is the story which we want to hear: that suffering can be redemptive, and that death is not the end. Suffering and death are now joined in such a way that the former swallows up the latter. Suffering need not be pointless, it need not be wasted, it has meaning, it can be the way. The dying Christ redeems suffering itself, even beautifies it, as well as overcoming death. This is the traditional and persisting picture upon which the light of modern theology attempts to fall with a difference.

Wittgenstein remarks (*Culture and Value*, p. 30,) that 'the spring which flows gently and limpidly in the Gospels seems to have *froth* on it in Paul's epistles'. The Gospels are in a sense easy to read, can seem so (even I would think for a complete stranger to them), because they are the kind of great art where we feel: It is so. Paul's writings, also great art, express a kind of demonic power, a sense of something being created before one's eyes by a force of inspired will, which convinces by rhetoric. In fact these writings about Christ are not really easy to read, especially for Christians and ex-Christians who cannot readily assess them as art and to whom they are so familiar as to seem transparent (magisterially authoritative). The ethical teaching, the religious promise, the beloved figure, the frightful suffering, the glorious and moving end. (The meeting in the garden, the disciples at Emmaus, it is all so perfect.) Can we accept a being who is both true God and true man without supernatural magic, can the extreme of positive evil and innocent suffering be represented, let alone explained or justified, as part of a larger whole? Religion is about reconciliation and forgiveness and renewal of life and salvation from sin and despair. It lives between cosy sentiment and magic at one end of the scale and at the other a kind of austerity which can scarcely be expected from human beings. As an institution, religion may covertly recognise that the highest teaching is for the few only. A subtle form of sentimentality is sado-masochism, whereby popular religion is infected by bad tragedy; a degeneration to which Christianity is particularly subject. The idea of redemptive suffering is difficult and ambiguous: a cult of redemptive suffering may become a cult of suffering.

A question concerning the survival of demythologised Christianity may be put as: Can religion survive without art? Puritanical reactions against art are a familiar aspect of religious theory and practice, Plato is not the only religious thinker to disapprove of 'theatre'. Puritanism comes in moods and phases as well as being permanently dominant in some traditions. The florid grandeur and illusory completeness and airy authority of art is suddenly seen as offensive, requiring a return to simplicity, modesty, humility, penitential nakedness, minimalism. Many present-day artists may be seen to be in puritanical revolt against the grand large-scale confident art of the nineteenth century and indeed of the whole post-Renaissance tradition. There are strong streaks of puritanism in structuralist thought. Deconstruction: dissecting, reducing, dismantling, breaking down. Chinese and Japanese Buddhism reacts against the polymorphous highly decorated religious styles of India. Zen Buddhism uses art as religious teaching, but therein also dispels its air of magisterial authority and grandeur. Plato would have appreciated this. Zen art is highly expert but deliberately simple and ungrand and (seemingly) unfinished. Of course puritanism has its own strong magic, its own form of degeneration into a sexually charged romanticism. More severe Protestant sects preach the fierce magical instant Christ of St Paul. (Roughly, St Paul is romantic, the Gospels are not.) Popular (diluted, popularised) Zen too appears to offer magical change brought about by interesting techniques. Needless to say, real change is usually a long job, but the *attractiveness* of religious styles is important too, it speaks to the emotions, it speaks to the individual temperament. Where art is rejected or suspected, some kind of theological magic may take its place. If we are to *like* religion we cannot be instantly confronted with nothing but the frightful austerity of what it is really asking! One aspect of demythologisation is a critique of traditional uses of art. But this does not necessarily result in a more rational kind of religion. (Darkness underlies it all.) Jung, who demythologises in order to remythologise, says that 'we cannot tell whether God and the Unconscious are two different entities'. (*The Answer to Job*, p. 177.) Heraclitus more reliably informed us that the One who alone is wise does not wish, and does wish, to be called Zeus. Religion must move toward aesthetic formulation and systematic theology. This is an essential source of its energy, yet the need to clear these from the scene when they become idolatrous is equally essential.

There is a problem about the difference between suffering and death, and there is an analogy between truth in art and truth in religion. Truth is unbearable and degenerates into illusions which may have some truth-contents. There is little great art or true religion, little holiness, few saints, much superstition and sentimentality. There is a counterpart in religion to the drive which moves art in the direction of pornography. Organised religion mitigates its failure by a doctrine of grace whereby the feeble efforts of sinners may benefit from the energy of a higher power, and something like this can really happen. Suffering is interesting, our *views* of it are often magically, sexually, charged. Real *deathly* suffering, such as we see in *King Lear*, is very difficult to portray, and in life terrible suffering is very difficult to contemplate. Of course if it is remote from us, something seen on television, even if we think it is 'very important', we arrange to be hardened enough to forget it fairly promptly. If, because the sufferer is oneself or a close other, we cannot do this, we use our life-energy to transform the experience as soon as possible, as we do in bereavement. Suffering, mercifully, offers a route back into the ego. Sado-masochism is also an escape route well known to its devotees. It is difficult to suffer well, without resentment, false consolation, untruthful flight. One consolation which is usually false is that suffering purifies the soul, as tragedy was supposed to purify the emotions it aroused. The idea of redemptive suffering, one's own or another's, is ambiguous and deep. The notion of purgatory is attractive because it combines the absolute of sin and just punishment with the then justified and clarified disappearance of the idea of death. The souls in Dante's *Purgatorio* plunge gladly back into the flames. Well they may, they are living inside a work of art. Much religious belief is like living in a work of art. Art is not a small domain, it is everywhere. The image of the crucified Saviour is more familiar in the west than the most ubiquitous advertising cliché. In an ideal penal system every criminal would will his own punishment, like the souls in Dante, so that it becomes purification. In real life we have to do with the deep devious ingenuity of egoism, those 'devices and desires of our own hearts' which the Prayer Book tells us we have followed too much. Modern psychology has much plausibly to say about the ambivalent role of pain and suffering in the shadow play of the soul. There is a contrast between absolute (deathly) pain and the kind which can be managed, made part of a story, turned into art.

Where the sufferer is someone else and not oneself the drama is played with a difference. The redemptive suffering of Christ, if not accepted in a simple spirit, is hard to think about, because so much traditional 'working' gets in the way. Some Christians, who accept the divinity and the teaching, find this bit difficult. Why should another be punished for my sins? And is this real punishment? The risen Christ can be seen beyond the appalling anguished sufferer. Together with the crucified one we see the terrifying authoritative figure of Piero della Francesca's picture (of Christ stepping out of the tomb), or the strange magical being, portrayed by so many painters, who told Mary Magdalen not to touch him. It might be argued that Christ as a redemptive sufferer is more *purely* efficacious if not divine. If God exists he can cleanse the impurities from the confused egoistic souls of those who throughout the ages have identified with Christ's passion. If God does not exist we are left with an experience which those who regard religion as a pernicious distraction from human betterment might call morbid. The idea of another's suffering as redemptive is certainly intelligible. Christians may tend to connect it with Christ and see lesser human efforts as an *imitatio Christi*, but redemption can exist without God. The concept has strong emotive appeal, but also structure. The redeemed one is *bought* at the *expense* of another and thereby *set free*. The transaction is effective through the *virtue*, or relevant *pure intent* (or pure love), of the one who makes the sacrifice. The beneficiary must internalise the spectacle of suffering as a lesson whereby he is changed. A classic example might be the delinquent boy moved by the love and distress of his mother. Here the suffering may be more or less clearly 'directed at' the sinner. Sinners can feel persecuted by sufferers, and silent suffering may be more efficacious. This is a problem in Christianity too, where the lesson has to be understood by the individual, taken in in his own way. A crippled person in a family may behave in a way which has redemptive power. The patient good sufferer produces in the spectator shame, then love, then the creative energy required for amendment of life. Variants on this theme often appear in novels (in Dickens and Dostoevsky for instance) where the author may well intend to edify the reader. If Christ can redeem then a figure in a story can have redemptive power. There are many points at which the virtuous suffering of another may be related to our own consciousness of sin. People remote from us, such as dissident protesters against oppressive regimes, may stir us in this way, with or without the mediation of *imitatio Christi*. The subject is difficult, redemption is difficult, because the contemplation of suffering is difficult both in theory and practice. The operation occurs at a point where all sorts of illusions crowd in to tempt us. We have to attend in a certain way, if the experience is not to degenerate. We seek escape into passive admiration, ingenious sado-masochistic identification, pleasure that someone else is in trouble and not us. We must also, of course, find the right redeemer, and there is an obvious shortage of these. To keep the concept clear and uncorrupted we require an unmuddied example. A Christ who is a terrorist cannot be a redemptive figure. The redeemer must be, in respect of his suffering, innocent. In stories, and in real life where things are less clear, the suffering may be perfected by death. That is the perfect, the most impressive lesson, when another person dies for you. This is an image of the way in which the redeemer's suffering must enter into the being and body of the redeemed, who then *suffers* creatively in bringing about the *death* of evil in himself. The idea of redemption, so familiar to Christians, yet so difficult, provides an example of how a moral-religious concept does work, how it demands and stirs practical thought at a deep level. It is a special case of the problem, which arises in a consideration of tragedy, of how to contemplate, depict and understand suffering. Contemplation of the suffering of the innocent can be redemptive when the spectator is moved by both guilt and love. Something like this can happen in art too when we identify with the sinner. The suffering of Cordelia is redemptive, that of Ophelia and Desdemona is not.

Protestant theology and popular Romantic theology have made

something of a cult of suffering. From this angle we may see Luther as the first romantic, and first modern man. A later nomination could be Rousseau, an earlier St Augustine. This cult is, as I suggested, absent from classical Greek literature and almost entirely absent from Shakespeare. Kant, a Protestant and a puritan, made thrilling self-castigating emotion an aspect of his austere doctrine. In our relation with the authority of the moral law and with the contingency of the world our suffering is combined with a kind of (quasi-sexual?) excitement. (Freud was not, I think, particularly perspicacious about sado-masochism, he was too much of an all-male grandee to appreciate this phenomenon.) In Kant's picture when we feel (an emotion, not a rational concept) *respect* for the moral law our desires suffer like souls in purgatory in the presence of Reason. In sublime experiences we suffer and exult in the contest of Reason with the terrible contingent sinful world. These are great Romantic ideas which we may trace in many of Kant's successors in the existentialist line, for instance in Schopenhauer, Nietzsche, Sartre and Simone Weil.

The eclipse of death by creative suffering and the transformation of suffering and death into art are ways in which human beings make the intolerable tolerable, and Christian theology made use of those remedies long before the Romantic Movement. Psychoanalysis has come to share the tasks of religion both as therapy and as theology. Wittgenstein, as I quoted earlier, speaking of Freud, said that we are comforted to be told that our life, instead of being a senseless mess which we have made ourselves, is an intelligible drama deriving from some original scenario. Jung celebrates the unillusioned entry, or re-entry, of religion into myth: I quote from *Answer to Job*, page 72 and following.

'Christ's biography and psychology cannot be separated from eschatology. Eschatology means in effect that Christ is God and man at the same time and that he therefore suffers a divine as well as a human fate. The two natures interpenetrate so thoroughly that any attempt to separate them mutilates both . . . The oldest scriptures, those of St Paul, do not seem to have the slightest interest in Christ's existence as a concrete human being . . . There is no evidence that Christ ever wondered about himself or that he ever confronted himself. To this rule there is only one significant exception in the despairing cry from the

Cross: "My God, my God, why hast Thou forsaken me?" Here his human nature attains divinity: at that moment God experiences what it means to be a mortal man and drinks to the dregs what he made his faithful servant Job suffer. Here is given the answer to Job, and clearly this supreme moment is as divine as it is human, as "eschatological" as it is "psychological". And at this moment too where one can feel the human being so absolutely, the divine myth is present in full force. And both mean one and the same thing. How then can one possibly "demythologise" the figure of Christ? . . . What is the use of a religion without a mythos, since religion means if anything at all precisely that function which links us back to the eternal myth? . . . Myth is not fiction; it consists of facts that are continually repeated and observed over and over again. It is something that happens to man, and men have mythical fates just as much as Greek heroes do. The fact that the life of Christ is largely myth does absolutely nothing to disprove its factual truth – quite the contrary. I would even go so far as to say that the mythical character of a life is just what expresses its universal human validity. It is perfectly possible, psychologically, for the unconscious or an archetype to take complete possession of a man and to determine his fate down to the smallest detail . . . the life of Christ is just what it had to be if it is the life of a god and a man at the same time. It is a *symbolum*, a bringing together of heterogeneous natures, rather as if Job and Yahweh were combined in a single personality. Yahweh's intention to become man, which resulted from his collision with Job, is fulfilled in Christ's life and suffering.'

This authoritative dictum from Jung raises questions and doubts which are even more apt now than when he wrote. He suggests that we can preserve and develop religious mythology, no longer by reference to any traditional 'good' or 'absolute', but by fostering in our own souls a natural harmony of opposites, good and evil, masculine and feminine, dark and light. In the battle between Plato and the presocratics, Jung is definitely on the side of the latter, cosmic soul is God, there is no absolute beyond the explanations of religious experience which he pictures in terms of myth. Here presocratic cosmic Taoism can, it seems, energise and renew the Christian myth as well. The spiritual energy which Plato and Christian thinkers saw as disturbing a fallen world by its magnetic attraction to a transcendent absolute, Jung pictures as immanently circulating to produce an experiential harmony in which there is no positive vision of good as opposed to evil, but good and evil are seen as aspects or shades of a self-adjusting whole. This powerful challenge attractively suggests that we can retain the 'genuine' mythological stuff of religion while rejecting a faith which is now impossible to a modern man. Jungian therapy certainly uses myth in ways which can command the co-operation of patients and help their condition. But Jung is not just offering a therapeutic tool, he is offering what he feels to be a relevant and necessary metaphysic. This Gnostic monism cannot be taken as a plausible account of morality. A relativistic view of good supports a relativistic view of truth, and vice versa. Self-contained soul-experience obscures, and is no substitute for, the struggle with an *alien reality* which engenders and imposes and develops absolute distinctions between good and evil and truth and falsehood. The idea of transcendence cannot be dissolved by enclosing it inside a soul distended by mythological archetypes. Let us here consider Jung's hypothesis about the survival of Christianity, since it raises fundamental questions about a demythologised religion.

Can western religion survive, retain continuity, without the old dogmatic literalistic myths, what would this state of affairs be like? We are not talking about a dream world where one can regard real history as the adventure of an individual (cosmic) soul. Buddhism has no (literal, historical) central dogma similar to the Christian one, but has a large mythology, readily understood by simpler believers, used in a more reflective manner by the sophisticated. However, eastern religion has always made close links between religion, morality and philosophy, areas which western thought has tended to separate. The simpler believer in many parts of the west now tends to become an unbeliever, and the sophisticated (educated) believer has a new problem about how to use mythology. Every man his own theologian. The relation of religion, morality and philosophy is perhaps the great intellectual problem of the age, as Heidegger indicated. The *reflective believer* in the east is supported by a long tradition of thought on these matters which does not exist in the west. Even if we accept Jung's assumption that mythological processes have a *zeitgeistlich* momentum of their own, can this momentum continue in a self-conscious age of the world after people like Jung have been telling us how it happens? Can the Christian mythology thus transform itself in front of our eyes? Must not myth be more spontaneous, and more unforcedly traditional, if it is to be a live spiritual guide? This point may be exaggerated. Those seeking guidance can to some extent use, even select, a mythology. Yet is not this a dangerous relationship? Jung tells us we have mythical fates; he also celebrates our ability to use myth creatively in our lives. Clearly individuals, and groups, are often taken over or held in place by deep unreflective myths, old tribal myths or new social myths. The concept overlaps with that of 'ideology'. But in the new 'liberated' awareness which Jung postulates and which many thinkers draw attention to, we can surely, and ought to, decide upon our attitudes to myths and may well choose not to have a mythical fate. It sounds indeed a rather egoistic and self-indulgent thing to have; and to insist that everybody has one, whether consciously or voluntarily or not, is to deprive the concept of sense. We have to keep returning to the centre of the dilemma as we see it and feel it. Can the figure of Christ remain religiously significant without the old god-man mythology somehow understood? Can Christ, soon enough, become like Buddha, both real and mystical, but no longer the divine all-in-one man of traditional Christianity? Jung says that a myth is not a fiction, and that 'the mythical character of a life expresses its universal human validity'. A 'lived' myth, one that guides deep attitudes and important actions, may be said *ipso facto* to be no mere fiction, and it may also be expressive of some unity of the individual with 'humanity' or some group thereof. But all this can happen irrespective of the quality of the myth. The hero of *Crime and Punishment* was animated by a myth, so were Hitler's followers. History and literature are full of stories of men destroyed by myths. The long knife of morality prises the concept apart. Our relation to myth is subject to moral judgment. (Plato's myths are metaphors.) To take another sort of example, is the myth of the Mother Goddess as completing the Trinity now expressive of some 'compulsory' human value? The relation of such a figure to the liberation of women is extremely dubious. Life and politics is picking about in the real. So do we now have to choose, if we reject Jung's method of rescuing traditional religion, between a self-conscious manipulation of a personal mythology and a denuded choice of 'religious values' without any icons? Many interested people, I think, feel faced with some such choice; but the situation is both more complicated and more hopeful. Jung inflates the concept of myth in a way which obscures the complexity of the religion–morality–philosophy relationship. His appeal or surrender to myth is a frank example of the transformation of death into suffering and suffering into art. On the scale on which Jung envisages it, it may be seen as a kind of Hegelian view, where history becomes myth-history or mythical historicism, history 'seen from the outside', from a standpoint in metaphysics. God answers Job's complaint by an assertion of supreme power, but still feels uneasy and has to silence Job by becoming Job in Christ. Present-day demythologisation may be seen as part of the long mythical story of Christian theology, growing and changing with the 'growing-up' of the human race. A sceptical spectator might view it as some non-Marxists viewed Marxism, not accepting its large claims, but treating it as a suggestive, perhaps instructive, theoretical pattern to be laid down, as it were, on the world, so as to emphasise facts and values which might not otherwise be evident. In both cases the concept of 'the will of history' must be criticised by the outsider both as an empirical hypothesis (does it deeply and comprehensively explain what is going on?) and as a moral guide (if we accept this world-view are we more likely to lead a good or satisfactory life?). Moral judgment may look to metaphysics, but can always undermine it. We are reluctant to think we are the creatures of unconscious or irresistible forces, but must at times consider the possibility. These are not remote considerations, but aspects of ordinary judgment and decision.

It may be said that, in accordance with Eliot's view of theology continually (instinctively) rendering itself believable, we have the God and the theology that we (deeply) desire; and our desires are affected by a great variety of forces. A main tenet of the Kantian metaphysic has merged into popular, or semi-popular, moral argument. We must internalise the demand of duty, understand it, judge it, make it our own, be autonomous not heteronomous. Duty is not a rigid external code, it is a rule I impose on myself, felt as external by my mixed and imperfect nature. We must now also internalise our God. An omnipotent supernatural father figure imposes a heteronomous religion. We must stop thinking of 'God' as the name of a super-person, and indeed as a name at all. Can we then be saved by a mystical Christ who is the Buddha of the west? A Buddhist-style survival of Christianity could preserve tradition, renewing religious inspiration and observance in a vision of Christ as a live spiritual symbol. The historical Buddha became the mystical Buddha-nature; but this process developed during a pre-scientific pre-rationalistic age. Can Christian thought and feeling consciously effect such a change now? Must we otherwise envisage a denuded existentialist 'God' as a symbol of commitment to 'religious values', or the vanishing of religion into political activity or technological utilitarianism? A Christian theology student in New York once said to me: 'We don't emphasise Jesus now, we prefer to talk about God because that unites us with the Jews.' Here we see religious mythology in the making with people consciously choosing between two myths and having a reason for their choice. For others, a demonic magical Pauline Christ may be the god that the age requires rather than a calm though demanding figure symbolising our spiritual nature. The figure of Christ does not cease to be paradoxical.

We are now self-conscious and critical about religion in a way which is new, and the Christian west is better informed about the religions of the east. Schopenhauer's interest in Hinduism and Buddhism was regarded as a slightly feverish personal eccentricity of no importance to western philosophy or theology. We now begin to know better; and have at the same time witnessed the 'abolition' of religion in totalitarian states. Western people may now find themselves both inside and outside religion. On the one hand we increasingly see it as a historically determined phenomenon, and ourselves as emerging from an era where myths were regarded in an unreflective way as 'real', into a scientific era where, making a distinction which people in the past did not make, we treat them as symbols or purveyors of truth, though not factually true. On the other hand, if we do not want to dismiss all religion as childish fiction, we have to decide, as people in the past did not, what exactly religion is and where in the mass of religiosity and religious stuff it 'really resides'. One judgment which may be made is that mythical historicism of the kind offered by Jung is inadequate precisely in that it is a transformation into art, a magical overcoming of the contingent, a resort to providence (God or the unconscious), in effect a continuation of the old vague consolations of religion which the modern consciousness is rejecting. One of the difficulties of a modern view of religion is that one may seem forced to suggest, and for many kinds of reasons (modesty, historical sensibility) is reluctant to, that the religion of the past was for most people a consoling, though perhaps ethically efficacious, fiction. Pasteur is reported to have wished he had the faith of a Breton peasant, or rather (when it was suggested that this was inappropriate for a man of science) of the Breton peasant's wife. Of course simple faith cannot be dismissed as superstitious illusion, it may be more 'in the truth' than modern scepticism. Our huge jumbled history is a *religious* history from which we must learn. We may judge past beliefs, knowing that the past is another country, and we too will be said to have been deceived. We may say that of course in the past there were many who accepted easy religious consolation (and who is to blame them) while a hardy few took loftier and more truthful paths. The same may be said of the present, except that now (in the west) consolation-seekers abandon religion, and the others feel more confused and isolated, not supported by a mythical consciousness shared by their whole society. Must all 'religious' people now be mystics? Eastern religion has seen mysticism as something close to the ordinary religious consciousness.

However that may be, one must still hold on to the present problem of distinguishing 'true religion' from the comforts of mythology, old or new. Much art and religious myth has the effect, and the intended effect, of concealing the fact of death and the absolute contingency of existence which is an aspect of that fact. Of course human life is also happy, funny, pleasant, full of the rewards of love and knowledge. These art and popular religion can handle. It is the other thing that is difficult. The idea of metempsychosis, transmigration of souls, in eastern religion, which may be thought of in supernatural terms of personal immortality, is in a more sophisticated sense a symbol of the unreality of the self. It appears in this sense at the end of the *Republic*. What is mechanically determined is unreal, as in the metaphysic of Kant. 'Neurosis' is characterised, almost in a popular sense defined, by a mechanical repetitive imprisoning of the mind. The idea of the unreality of the self mediates the idea of death, which has a greater hold upon the religion of the east. It is not difficult to distinguish between absolute or deathly pain, and what one might call relative or art pain. The latter can of course be severe, but is different because it can be manipulated and does not altogether destroy one's ordinary world and sense of one's being. It does not radically alter one's consciousness, but can be looked at with some degree of detachment. The sufferer can become an artist in relation to his own consciousness, he can for instance dramatise the situation. 'I wonder who's kissing her now?' can express a very painful state of mind, but one about which one can usually do something. This is (usually) not deathly pain, such as people experience in bereavement, in vain remorse for some terrible act, or as the helpless and hopeless victims of extreme poverty, oppression or violence, pain which relates to the ground of our being. The contrast between relative and absolute is conveyed in Tolstoy's story *Ivan Ilyitch*: yet not altogether well conveyed, since we feel too much the presence of the story-teller. We feel, it's a good story. Religion, and tragedy if it exists, must concern the absolute in a specifically moral way. Documentary films about massacres or prisons or concentration camps are not in themselves tragic or religious. The contemplation or experience must be connected to, enlightened by, seen in the light of, something good (pure, just). This is the sense in which stoicism is not a religion. The *tragic* image of death in art is a counterpart or reflection of selfless decreated being, it is contingent mortal existence held in a clear gaze. The philosopher, as religious man, practises dying; he may gradually internalise the conception of death or may be confronted with it face to face in extreme affliction. Absolute pain is absolute in that it realises the idea of death. There is no place here for personal histrionics, wry glances, black humour or sado-masochistic play. There is no space for such relief, no space into which to retreat. The illusions of the ego are destroyed and most of its ordinary goals seen as worthless, the whole of reality, suddenly bereft of the warm glow of selfish desire and purpose, stands, as it were, coldly by, frighteningly visible. In the extreme situation we are not conscious of morality with its claims and pluckings, it is present with a kind of necessity, we *have* to see the truth which is held up before us. Outsiders often help bereaved people by reminding them that they have urgent duties and must not remain in stilled contemplation of what is uniquely terrible. There are immediate tasks, arrangements to be made, others to be comforted, ordinary life at last to be carried on. Can less extreme lessons enable us to take in our mortality and see the world in its light? Can it be done through art, through meditation, through psychoanalysis, through reading books or listening to preaching? No doubt a usual response to absolute pain is, after the first shock, instant flight, despair, blank self-enclosed misery. When we recover from bereavement we know we have been in another country upon which we resolutely turn our backs. We do not *look*. In these (usual) cases the pure morality or religious vision (justice, wisdom, unselfing, acceptance of death and chance) can only reside in the silent eye of some rarely gifted beholder, or in the working or speaking eye of a great artist. In the latter case we have tragedy, the moral vision residing in the work, not in the man.

In art there are many familiar patterns by which art pain or relative pain is conveyed, and the idea of death played with and then removed; for instance, in images of purgatorial suffering or ordeals. Most stories indeed concern the tribulations of an ultimately successful hero, that is what we want to be told about. As I said earlier, we cannot regard Christ's passion as tragic unless we regard his death as real death, which theology and art discourage us from doing; one could scarcely call it an ordeal. No one would call *The Magic Flute* or *Sir Gawain and the Green Knight* tragic. The Arthurian legends, dominated by the attractive ambiguous symbol of the Grail, are not tragic. They have an intense but untragic atmosphere, they have a powerfully pleasantly sexual atmosphere, the Grail is a sexual symbol; whereas absolute pain, experienced or (if that is possible) justly perceived or portrayed, removes all sexual interest. (There is none in *Lear*.) It is in the more ordinary, more relaxed and pleasure-seeking vision of romantic artists, aesthetical spectators, psychological myth-makers, that sex and death, as these are usually understood, are connected. Their so interesting 'connection' is magical and an atmosphere of magic is alien to tragedy as it is to true religion. The death, and the love, that religion teaches are unlike our ordinary experience of these things; though it must also be admitted that *Othello* is a great tragedy, and that 'the highest', though very far away, is continuous with everyday life! It is interesting that Shakespeare did not use the Arthurian legends, or refer to them except for a sneer by Hotspur (*I Henry IV*, III, i, 48) and a joke by the Fool (*Lear*, III, ii, 95) directed against Merlin. *Cymbeline* is not Arthurian. He knew that that stuff was not for him, its sexy magical romantic world incompatible with the high art to which his instincts belonged. Of course Malory's writings are beautiful, but Shakespeare's own romanticism as seen in the comedies is clean and clear by contrast (it is 'tougher'). This also has to do with his portrayal of women. His women are free individuals, brilliant images of a liberation which then lay (in many contexts still lies) in the future. Malory's women are semi-magical charmers, worthy of being celebrated by pre-Raphaelite painters. Shakespeare created his own symbols. The powerful image of the Grail would have been a nuisance in one of his plays, and I suspect that he found it alien. Shakespeare's plays have their own special moral and religious atmosphere. Morality and religion do not appear in abstract or doctrinal guises in the plays. Shakespeare's great intelligence and high moral and religious understanding are otherwise on display, transformed by the poet into densely particular work. The plays are pre-eminently about the difference between illusion and reality, and the battle between good and evil, they *shine* with a positive sense of goodness, which is, by all those words, shown rather than explicitly or laboriously said. As I suggested earlier, we may in that respect, and in spite of the 'old quarrel', compare Shakespeare with Plato. Stanley Rosen, in his excellent book *The Quarrel between Philosophy and Poetry*, speaking of Heidegger's failure to understand Plato, suggests that the elusive Being which Heidegger attempts to discover for us is in fact the *light* which illuminates the atmosphere of the Platonic dialogues. I think this same light is to be found in Shakespeare. Tragedy, which deals with what is most difficult, is dense non-generalised non-abstract work, herein resembling states of absolute pain in real cases where generalities are irrelevant; the tragic vision of such pain is condensed and non-discursive as is the condition itself. We are placed, as it were, right up against it; close to a real awareness of death, of the senseless rubble aspect of human life which is concealed under grand illusory names such as fate, destiny, history, providence. Something of this is expressed in Kant's image of the broken whole, the inevitable defeat of reason and its inevitable aspiration. Here is exhibited the problem of truth in art, how *can* art tell truth, how can it not lie a little so as to console, even to convince? We wish to be persuaded that great art is analogous to moral knowledge, an absolute convergence of fact and value. It would then be immobile as Simone Weil said, an enlightened (just, 'obedient') vision of necessity, being for us, without evasion, 'the thing itself'. 'There is no way, there is only the end, what we call the way is messing about': Kafka. The sense in which this is good advice to artists may suggest to us the sense in which it is also good moral advice.

Great tragedies are written in poetry where language reaches an extreme level of density and suggestive power. How short the plays of Shakespeare seem when we re-read them, compared with the vast radiant object about which we have in the interim been thinking. I have been talking about tragedy in a context of talking about religion, and have borrowed religious categories, hoping thereby to illumine both concepts. I have not attempted here to discuss the Greeks, who after all invented the form, and may be said to have had, in something like the sense in which I am discussing it, a 'tragic view of life'. Their clear-eyed grimness concerning the awful facts of human suffering may attract, impress, or appal: for instance their sense of slavery as a human fate, a fate taken for granted, which might be one's own. I said earlier that the *Iliad*, full of relentless images of war and pointless slaughter, might be called tragic. Yet there is something in the poem about the romance and heroism of war which softens the picture. The deaths of Patroclus and Hector prompt tears, but do not utterly appal. These deaths are beautiful, and unlike the deaths of Agamemnon and Antigone. The *Iliad* is full of a most intense pathos (the horses of Achilles weeping over Patroclus) which is also at home in Shakespeare. Euripides seems a 'less pure' tragedian for reasons which also make him more accessible and interesting to many modern readers. He presents us with more anthropomorphic and sympathetic gods who may be thought of as personifications of human passions; whereas the gods of Aeschylus are more remote, cold, appearing as fate and justice. Looked at in this perspective *Lear* is clearly the 'most Greek' of Shakespeare's plays. Sex is absent from *Lear*, as is the notion of an ordeal, sado-masochistic suffering, transcended redemptive suffering or magical release; and the sense in which love is present is a stark and unworldly one. Cordelia is a religious figure (whom we might compare and contrast with Antigone), an image of the highest morality, the truth which wears the face of death and does not console or respond, yet (and so) can enlighten, bring about 'new being'. The comforting relation of 'I and thou' is absent. Lear feels its absence in that painful first scene. He seeks a 'thou' and fails to find one, and is offended by the unattractive negativity of truth instead. He meets the pure, difficult, at an ordinary level unacceptable, face of love. In *this* context it can also make sense to ask whether Cordelia ought not to have compromised by responding in a way which her father would understand! Of course it is her fictional task to make a revelation which would be lost if she behaved otherwise. In real life such a question is not an easy one. The Judaeo-Christian God has been treated as a supreme Thou. Hindu mysticism freely uses sexual imagery to speak of the soul's union with the Godhead. Many mystical writings, neo-Platonic, oriental, Christian, invoke the idea of a sexual union with the Absolute (spiritual love as passion); and talking directly to God has been and is the most familiar religious experience of most believers. Part of the dismay occasioned and felt by modern demythologising theologians is connected with the loss of such imagery, the recognition of it as less than final. God may now appear as a symbol of an absolute demand, as an internalised categorical imperative, a traditional image of commitment to religious values, rather than as an external supernatural loving Father to whom we speak in our prayers, and who wants to be loved by us in return. The Absolute is not a person and is indifferent to us. This carries too the now more emphatic reminder that the daily bread of human affections and human relations is, from the fearful inmost point of view of religion, imperfect. Heavenly love is unlike earthly love. Christ broke up families.

There is a passage in Plato's *Sophist* where the Eleatic Stranger, who in this dialogue plays the Socratic part, says to Theaetetus, 'But for heaven's sake, shall we easily let ourselves be persuaded that motion and rest and life and soul and mind are really not present in absolute being, that it neither lives nor thinks, but stays there motionless, solemn and holy and devoid of mind?' (249A.) Theaetetus answers that this would indeed be a terrible admission. This exchange about the nature of 'ultimate reality', which may be thought of as changeless or else in flux, having or not having a mind and soul, appears as part of a very much longer discussion. Plato was concerned with the difference between science and morals. He believed that religion cannot rest upon personal deity, and that the natural order (in the scientific sense) cannot be regarded as a fundamental spiritual reality. The concept of responsive and responsible God or gods, by drawing down providential power into the accidental and largely incomprehensible natural scene which we inhabit, was indeed in effect a way of covering up a rift between nature and spirit. Some forms of eastern religion and modern versions (for instance in Jung) join with presocratic ideas of a fundamental natural rhythm (as in strife of opposites) which unites the aspirations of the human soul to a harmonious background in the flux of nature, here understood not as contingent and various but as single and orderly. Plato, rejecting this imagined harmony, raises (as Kant does) the problem of how we are to relate these spiritual aspirations to our evident existence as accidental beings in an accidental world; how we are furthermore to spiritualise that relation so as to understand it as in some sense essential. Kant connected the possibility of free religious faith with the impossibility of a complete understanding of the natural world or harmonious unity with it. Our situation is essentially contingent; it is a persistent illusion to imagine otherwise. The image of unity and harmony is 'ideal'. Herein Plato's crucial rejection of the 'cosmic' religion of his predecessors initiates the 'troubles' of western ethics and theology. As the problem is posed in the *Sophist*, if we take 'ultimate being' in the moral-religious sense, the answer to the Stranger's question must be 'yes'. Plato makes clear elsewhere that the final demand or absolute is not itself a form of life, though as an object of (pure) love it can inspire (true) life. (Simone Weil's 'obedience'.) The moral Form, or Idea, is spoken of by Plato as being (he speaks here at *Symposium* 211B about the Form of Beauty) 'Itself by itself with itself, single and eternally existent.' Religion, concern with 'the ultimate', is in Plato's view of it, as in the theology of Buddhism and Hinduism, above the picturesque or figurative level of 'gods'. Such images are shadows which indicate something beyond. The lonely supremacy of moral goodness is also portrayed in the Trinitarian creation myth of the *Timaeus*, which I mentioned earlier when speaking of the divine Demiurge (perfectly good but not omnipotent) as an ideal picture of the artist. Plato's Trinity (Forms, Demiurge, World Soul) may be seen reflected (surely not by accident) in the Christian Trinity as God the Father (Form of the Good), Holy Spirit (Demiurge) and Christ (*Anima Mundi*). Crucial differences between Plato's mythical Trinity and the Christian one are that the supreme figure in the *Timaeus* (Good as sovereign Form) is impersonal and separate, the divine creator makes a fundamentally imperfect world, and the World Soul, fallible incarnate creature, is not wholly rational. Christ as *Anima Mundi* may be thought of as the exemplar of the highest form of incarnate being. Plato elaborates his imagery by distinguishing between the original world created by the Demiurge and that world as lived by us humans. The causality and laws and order of the original world are the work of pure reason confronted by contingent material. As we are far from completely rational, our concept of causality is local and 'errant' and much of our experience is that of 'pure chance'. (In brief, we have mucked up a world which was inevitably imperfect to begin with.) This is an obscure part of the dialogue (46D onward). Pursuing the artist analogy, the original (not perfect) work of art is that created by the artist, the secondary work is that enjoyed and used by his clients. The beautiful *Timaeus* myth may seem to us both realistic and pessimistic. At least it induces humility, it puts 'God' (as Demiurge) in his place (secondary, not omnipotent) and also opens a space for the mystical incarnate Christ. The World Soul as *Logos* can also represent ordinary human activity, sunk in contingency and confusion, yet also vitally connected with the power of spirit. We must keep in mind that the whole thing originated in love. Religion is the *attachment* to an ultimate and fundamental demand, the demand or urge that we become truthful and compassionate and wise, it *is* the *love* of that demand. Kant's impersonal call of duty inspires respect, awe, fear, but not love. Plato's Forms are separate and unresponsive, but they are *essentially* objects of love. (*Symposium, Phaedrus.*) Eros, the high translated form of sexual energy, a daemon not a god, is our guide into the realm of spirit. The *Timaeus* Demiurge, a high but not highest being, is also Eros.

I have been talking about the ambiguous conspiracy between art and religion, and about the idea or illusion of the limited whole, discussing these matters in relation to great and familiar images such as those offered to us by Plato and by Shakespeare. The problem about philosophy, and about life, is how to relate large impressive illuminating general conceptions to the mundane ('messing about') details of ordinary personal private existence. But can we still *use* these great images, can they go on helping us? How do the generalisations of philosophers connect with what I am doing in my day-to-day and moment-to-moment pilgrimage, how can metaphysics be a guide to morals? ('Is it really as grim as all that?' No, because ordinary simple compassion exists all over the place, and whether or not we are aware of 'the highest' we may be well employed in loving our neighbour.) Levels and modes of understanding are (somehow) levels and modes of existence. My general being coexists with my particular being. We are faced with these difficulties in our apprehensions of art and religion. Fiction writers have, instinctively or reflectively, to solve the problem of this coexistence when they portray characters in books, and we the readers appreciate and judge their solution, and exercise many different kinds of insight in doing so. The creation and appreciation of a novel is a complex highly diversified operation. This process of relating and fusing takes place largely instinctively when we attend to a work of art. This attention will of course include the ready use, or else the critical questioning, of familiar conventions. In ordinary life we are continually and instinctively relating dissimilar elements and only sometimes becoming acutely conscious of these numerous operations when (for instance) an intuitive understanding of a particular case conflicts with a general principle or a religious picture. The achievement of coherence is itself ambiguous. Coherence is not necessarily good, and one must question its cost. Better sometimes to remain confused. Most people pay attention to some art. Some, still many, people receive a religious upbringing and know religion from earliest childhood. The ease with which children acquire and retain religious concepts may be taken as proof that we are all naturally religious or that we are all naturally superstitious. The roots of religious ideas and images so acquired go deep. However, the process of relating them to ordinary life may be seen as analogous to the processes by which we understand art objects or (should they come our way) philosophical conceptions. These three areas overlap in confusing, often unnerving, ways. How do we thus put ourselves together? Well, perfectly easily, we are doing it all the time. But how is it done, *how*? When this question really checks us we may be inspired to become artists or philosophers.

> 6 <

# Consciousness and Thought – I

In order to talk about consciousness or self-being, the 'medium' in which all these amazing things are taking place, it is necessary first to consider the philosophical concept, or concepts, of the self. 'Self' can impede a consideration of 'consciousness' by which it ought to be enriched. How do the concepts 'self', 'experience', 'consciousness' relate? Should philosophy recognise these concepts at all? 'The self' sounds like the name of something, soul, ego, psyche, essential person. Self, thing, person, story and work of art are wholes which can function as analogies of each other. 'Self' is a concept which does not trouble us as ordinary people. We get along with being a self without difficulty, though if we reflect it may seem a remarkable achievement. Ordinary usage recognises a (morally) higher and lower self evidenced by higher and lower thoughts and actions. Philosophically, should 'self' be taken as an initial problem, or simply assumed or postulated as a carrier of experience or consciousness, or should we take something else, society or language or genes, as fundamental? Is the self part of the world, or should it be seen as constructing the world? Descartes pictures a solitary mind having certain knowledge only of its immediate apprehensions, from which (helped by belief in God) it is able to find itself in a world grasped as 'external' and real. Hume's self, also, like that of Descartes, taken as primary, is strictly a bundle of perceptions, but endowed with innate awareness of association and order. Habits of imagination enable the construction, out of atomic data, of our ordinary experienced world, including causality, space, time and morals. Kant, turning the problem round (the 'Copernican Revolution') started from evident truths of empirical experience and science and *deduced* a complex knower or metaphysical subject who *must* exist as their counterpart. The object both requires and guarantees the subject. Plato and Platonists, closer in many respects to common-sense and to modern formulations of these problems, do not start from a solitary subject, but from a general conception of persons active in a diverse world. Plato's imagery pictures levels and qualities of intellectual and moral consciousness, consciousness as a value-bearing continuum. His metaphysic has no historical dimension, and (in a sense) no system. There is a way (a possible pilgrim's progress), but individuals have to *learn* how to use it. Hegel also presents the conception of ascending levels of consciousness (*Bewußtsein*). This is not however an ascent accessible to free idiosyncratic persons, but represents a single rationally ordered totality within which all activity of mind takes place, *Geist* (mind, spirit) moving inevitably toward greater coherence (excellence) and thus toward total coherence and pure intelligibility. Kierkegaard saw this great system as a deterministic machine obliterating the concept of the solitary responsible moral person. Plato's mythical 'as if' lacks the quasi-scientific magisterial quality of the metaphysics of Kant and Hegel. After Hegel 'consciousness' was used (magisterially) by Marx as a socio-political concept. But the word has retained its vague ordinary-language meaning as an awareness of self as continuous being.

An important question to ask about any philosopher is whether he is *deeply* interested in morality. The Platonic soul, picturing the whole experience of a whole person, is a mixture of knowledge and illusion, immersed in a reality which transcends it, failing or succeeding to learn, in innumerable ways, the difference between true and false, good and evil. Descartes, and also Berkeley, held deep Christian beliefs, and both picture faith in God as an essential part of the escape from solipsism. Descartes's version of the Ontological Proof, in the Third Meditation, appears in the context of his theory of knowledge. Berkeley's God, as guarantor of knowledge of 'external' reality, seems perfunctory compared with that of Descartes, but the idea is comprehensibly similar. God too is inside the lonely soul, and this indubitable presence must involve the idea of truth and of an ability to judge what 'seems to be the case'. In general however Cartesian thought (after Descartes) has not been (in the sense in which Platonic thought has been) fundamentally moral and religious in its inspiration. Cartesians seem on the whole to have taken the attractive clarity of the certain starting point as founding an empiricism more friendly to science than to ethics or religion. Hume, relaxed and benevolent, may here figure as a predecessor and kinsman of Schopenhauer, John Stuart Mill and G. E. Moore. Though certainly interested, in a critical spirit, in religion, he presents morality (including political wisdom) as civilised, reasonably altruistic, virtue, comprising happiness and social harmony, resting on a deep foundation of tradition, imagination and habit. The self as 'bundle of perceptions' turns out to be quite complex enough to represent a decent man. Hume separates reason from passion (intuition, feelings etc.). Reason, which cannot distinguish good and evil, 'is and ought to be the slave of the passions'. (This 'slave' however is to be seen as more like a friendly adviser, an old family solicitor as someone has suggested.) (*Treatise of Human Nature* II iii 5 and III i 1.) Kant was disturbed by Hume's scepticism, his demotion of reason, his relaxed moral theory, and his messy insecure reliance on feelings, associations and habits. Surely world, science and morals must depend upon some deeper and more *necessary* structure. Kant's portrayal of a radically divided self contrasts with Hume's tolerant compromise and his worldly calm. For Hume similar habits and movements of imagination set in order both the factual and the moral. For Kant the clarified justified account of scientific and factual knowledge has the intended effect of displaying as *totally different* the free activity of mind in moral choice and discernment. (As in the *Tractatus*.) Kant's man as knower of the phenomenal world (exercising theoretical reason) is to be distinguished from his man as moral agent (exercising practical reason). Schopenhauer, after exhibiting ultimate reality (Thing-in-itself) as ruthless all-powerful Will, allows in his ramblings the ordinary unenlightened self to be someone rather like Hume's man, subject to deterministic pressures, yet sometimes blessed (by temperament) with a little altruism (compassion) and even a sense of justice. Looked at in a more morally ambitious light, the soul is capable of being disturbed by Platonic Ideas, and even able to deny the egoistic Will altogether.

Later forms of empiricism have, until lately, exhibited less interest in morality and *a fortiori* in religion. Early (from the nineteenth century) psychological studies, endorsing Hume's idea of the importance of habit, proposed to philosophy various quasi-empirical 'selves' based on principles of association. Phenomenalists (at times for instance Bertrand Russell and Ayer) were empiricists in the tradition of Berkeley and Hume, their problems concerned with the creation of the world out of experiential atoms or 'sense data'. Heidegger's *Sein und Zeit* and Wittgenstein's *Investigations* finally disposed of these doctrines. The local phenomenalism was taken over by linguistic philosophy, which excluded psychological speculations and usually dealt with morality as a separate matter, discussed in terms of emotive language, imperatives, persuasions, and other tentative formulae. This style of philosophy, innocent of Hegel or Bradley, was neo-Kantian in style, assuming a distinction between fact and value, the purpose of which is not so much to elevate or purify moral philosophising, as to isolate it as respectable though peripheral. It could then be considered as a 'special subject' wherein the philosopher worked as a neutral technician. Surely an age which at last clearly separates myth from science should be at pains to distinguish between conceptual analysis and preaching! Bertrand Russell exhibited in parable form his own version of the alienation of fact and value. The contrast between his logic and his admonitory essays illustrates how far ethics had then strayed out of philosophy. The 'factual world', also the posited world of language, could receive strict philosophical treatment, whereas morality was a personal affair. Anti-Cartesian dismissal of the solitary knower, with his purified access to clear and distinct private data, was sometimes taken to imply that all private inner reflection was in some sense incoherent, inaccessible, and vague. With this, 'self' theories, whether psychological or metaphysical, were to be 'eliminated'. Those who found this situation unsatisfactory have sought in utilitarianism and pragmatism a field for further fruitful development of empiricist thinking. More recently forms of Aristotelian moral philosophy, both

Thomist and phenomenological, have given much-needed attention to the concept of the inner life (Philippa Foot, *Virtues and Vices*, Charles Taylor, *Sources of the Self*). Also read, *sui generis*, Stanley Rosen who has I think the clearest grasp of the modern scene.

Popular deconstructionist literature challenges the traditional conception of fictional characters. The notion of the person as having a particular private flow of consciousness begins to be a trifle shadowy. 'Just being a person doesn't work anymore', a poem of John Ashbery suggests. Perhaps the whole human race is changing? Marxists regarded the bourgeois concept of the individual as moribund. Derrida's structuralism took over from Marxism. Language and feeling and value (and thoughts and emotions, etc.) are henceforth not 'owned' by 'private persons' in the old familiar sense. The 'metaphysics of presence' is to be rejected: the notion that 'the present' is what it seems to be as a reality in the consciousness and experience of the individual. As I said earlier, these dicta are made plausible by reference to truisms and half-truths. We may be quite prepared to be told that there is no God, that we are limited contingent beings affected by forces beyond our control, and that 'language' (now studied by scientific experts) is a huge area of which we know little. All this may seem obvious, easily put up with, part of living in this age. We then find that further steps have been taken which purport to deny our ordinary sense of a transcendent (extra-linguistic) real world 'out there'; indeed there is no 'out there' since language, not world, transcends us, we are 'made' by language, and are not the free independent ordinary individuals we imagined we were. This alarming mystification gains some of its plausibility from moves, critical of traditional concepts of 'self' and 'mind', effected by (for instance) Wittgenstein, Heidegger, Sartre, Ryle and others. How far do these moves take us in the direction of finding that the 'individual' with his boasted 'inner life' is really some kind of illusion? Are not these moves just 'technical', inside philosophy, not to do with us? Perhaps philosophers were influential in the past, but now we think more scientifically. Is it just that 'the elimination of the self' is in the air, have we not been prepared for it by Marx and Freud? Does it matter? Wittgenstein says that (his) philosophy leaves everything as it is; whereas Sartre and Heidegger are by contrast prophets who want to change our picture of the world. Derrida (who is not strictly a philosopher) seems to have been, after all, by imparting his doctrine to literary writers and critics, the most generally influential.

How limited here is the philosophical point, what is its purpose and what its, intended or otherwise, effect? The operation has roughly two moves, based on two questions. Are there introspectible mental contents? What, if they exist, is the role or function of such contents? In judging this approach, we must recall that much recent philosophy, analytical and structuralist, has been concerned with removing mistaken views (such as those of Descartes, Locke, Berkeley, Hume and more recently Husserl) concerning 'contents of the mind'. We learn now *rightly* that Cartesians and empiricists were wrong to begin their epistemology by positing private experiential mental data of indubitable clarity and separable integral existence. Thinking is not a mental composition repeated aloud verbatim, spoken words do not have to have mental equivalents, recognition and remembrance do not depend on comparison with inner pictures, words are not names of things, there is no God-named reality lying under the net of some single correct meaning-bearing language. In fact Schopenhauer pointed out such errors before linguistic philosophy was invented. Wittgenstein established a 'new insight' (the end of the Cartesian era) in the *Philosophical Investigations*. Wittgenstein's activity was, he claimed, negative, he was simply pointing out philosophical mistakes. (I consider Wittgenstein's position later.) *However* (some) Wittgensteinians as well as structuralists carried this (reasonable and proper) sort of discussion on, the former toward behaviourism, the latter, with greater panache, toward a more thorough denial of the 'inner life'. The argument might be pressed on as follows. There are fewer 'private mental contents' than we are inclined (casually or under the spell of a theory) to imagine as present. To identify or describe them is a dubious, as well as an inessential and unimportant, proceeding. They do not play any necessary or primary role. Such as may be discerned are shadowy, messy, indeterminate and vague, entities such as mental images, pressures, pictorial or kinaesthetic, verbal fragments uttered 'in the mind' and so on. Thought and language must depend entirely on the use of public concepts, the interlocking of public concepts and public activity. A 'decision' is not a mental act – the concept depends on (is verified by) public outward action. (If he has not done it, he has not 'decided' to do it.) There is in this sense no private coherent mental activity, no mental reality. It has moreover been properly pointed out by both Saussure and Wittgenstein that language develops and depends upon internally related groups of concepts, wherein sense is *modified* by relation to the group. Sometimes such groups are readily visible; but we must now (the structuralist argument *goes on*) realise that *all* of language consists of internal relations, *is* in fact an internally related network which no individual can survey. We are not masters of language, we are ourselves, as utterers, simply parts of language, we do not and cannot really know what we are saying, or possess any intelligible 'present' which is 'our own'.

Language is now a prime philosophical concept, whether thought of in a Wittgenstein (unsystematic, empiricist) or a Derrida (systematic, metaphysical) style. These forms of argument in removing old Cartesian errors, may indeed seem to render problematic the common-sense conception of the individual self as a moral centre or substance. The concept of 'consciousness' in Hegelian and Marxist theory (as belonging to a supra-personal whole) has the same effect of displacing the vitality and significance of the individual; this displacement has assisted in the acceptance of structuralism and remains in alliance with it. In such contexts we feel that we have lost something: our dense familiar inner stuff, private and personal, with a quality and a value of its own, something which we can scrutinise and control. Moral reflections especially may move us in this direction. Example of moral activity: inhibiting malicious thoughts. Let us leave aside here the ordinary sense in which we may be accused, or accuse ourselves, of being automatons, 'manipulated' (a frequent word) by advertisements, governments, our unconscious minds and so on. We do not normally take such accusations too seriously or really envisage ourselves as conscious machines. We are not, in ordinary life as opposed to philosophy, determinists; and in philosophy a doctrine of total determinism has never been intelligibly stated. What we have to deal with in philosophy is a ghost of determinism, which finds support in various non-philosophical desires to believe that 'it cannot be otherwise'. Popular Marxism and popular Freudianism gained strength from such desires, which function also in religious contexts and in the everyday wish to feel that fate and not one's own folly has brought things about. (Thy will be done.) But surely the 'person' we wish to defend here, endorsed by common-sense, is not so easily magicked away. Our present moment, our experiences, our flow of consciousness, our indelible moral sense, are not all these essentially linked together and do they not *imply* the individual? How are we to frame our question? Let us look at how various thinkers have considered the concepts of consciousness and self.


Jean-Paul Sartre was attracted by the romantic figure of the lonely gratuitous chooser; but he wanted also to present this 'authentic' figure as a spokesman for the best aspirations of the human race. (*L'Existentialisme est un humanisme.*) Marx saw the Proletariat as playing this role of being the bearers of freedom and truth and thus the saviours of humanity. Sartre carried his libertarian views on into a form of Marxism. (*Critique de la Raison dialectique.*) At first his philosophical point was Kantian, to keep the realm of value (as choice and freedom) pure, to defend it from contamination by dead fact in the form of convention or blind bourgeois 'value'. Later he removed value from the free unillusioned individual will and lodged it in the 'new structure' of the ideal Marxist society. Both these movements are characteristic of our age and can be executed as *de facto* or deliberate rejection of the concept of self as whole person. Both Sartrian existentialists and Marxists often took the stand of high-minded puritans. Wittgenstein (also high-minded and puritanical) established his epistemological metaphysical subject in Kantian style in the *Tractatus* by identifying him with his 'world', but also allowing a (silent ineffable) moral will to exist outside the closed circle of factual propositions. Wittgenstein elegantly shuns explanation. Sartre is all explanation. In *L'Etre et le Néant*, and in *La Nausée*, he makes a head-on attempt to *describe* the 'flow and texture' of consciousness, and does succeed in describing something which we can recognise. See for example the characterisation of *le visqueux*, viscosity or viscousness, in *L'Etre et le Néant* IV 2. 3, p. 695ff. The section is called 'De la qualité comme révélatrice de l'Etre'. Quality as revealing Being. Sartre's description of a quality of consciousness as gluey, liquid, jumbled, cloudy is intended to illustrate the senseless messiness of the 'inner' by contrast with the clear clean effective visible nature of outer commitments and choices. However, Sartre's own temperament and talent (which also make him a good novelist) lead him to linger fondly with this 'inner', developing a rich vocabulary in his account of its states. Another phenomenologist, Merleau-Ponty in his first phase, was interested in quasi-empirical quasi-scientific descriptions of consciousness for their own sake. Sartre's purpose is metaphysical; and we may note here that it is indeed difficult to describe *this*, which is nearest to us, our conscious being, without having, or developing, particular motives and value judgments: such is indeed the essence of the problem. Almost any description involves an evaluation; and this in turn may need to be *appropriately* justified. Sartre tells us what the stuff of the inner is mainly like, and that it is devoid of knowledge and spirit, a contingent fellow traveller of the free soul. Following Kant who regards the phenomenal self as spiritless and causally determined, he sees the inner 'consciousness' as something comparatively inert which resists the pure free lively movement of moral choice. Here we see one of those leaps, familiar in philosophy, when we move in a flash from one picture to another which is superficially connected but deeply unlike and with different implications. Hume comments on the magical movement from a factual argument to an evaluative one.

'In every system of morality which I have hitherto met with I have always remarked that the author proceeds for some time in the ordinary way of reasoning and establishes the being of a God or makes observations concerning human affairs; when of a sudden I am surprised to find that instead of the usual copulations of propositions *is* and *is not*, I meet with no proposition that is not connected with an *ought* or an *ought not*. This change is imperceptible, but is however of the last consequence.'

(*Treatise of Human Nature* III i 1.)

In spite of these words Hume himself in effect elides morality with the 'soft' concepts of habit and custom. Philosophy is constantly making persuasive connections and eclipsing radical differences. A deep divide may impoverish both sides. One concept may quietly swallow another and obliterate a whole region of thought. (As structuralist argument obliterates the conception of extra-linguistic reality.)

The dull gluey jumbled unfree (and so determined, only Sartre does not stress this) nature of the inner life, as described in *L'Etre et le Néant* and most graphically in *La Nausée*, is taken as an image of, and then as a case of, *mauvaise foi*, bad faith, failure to reflect, spiritless acceptance of habits, conventions and bourgeois values. Our mind is required to run with instant unnoticed speed along this persuasive line of juxtaposed ideas. Deep instinctive metaphors are at work. If we introspect we fail to find clarity, we discover only dark inert sticky senseless material, something which *contrasts* with the clean clear light agile movement of externally manifested decisive thought and action. What is pure and strong and free (*être-pour-soi*) emerges as it were *automatically* beyond and above what is dull, jumbled and senseless (*être-en-soi*). Thought moves bodiless and unimpeded above this morass, it makes choices and carries values. People who cannot think, who fail to think, who choose not to think, are pictured as being sunk in a dark muddled consciousness, composed of feelings and associations and fragmentary awareness. Such people live by unreflective conventions, they are afraid of action and change and free creative thinking. Genuine authentic truthful thought rises, shaking itself free, above this swampy consciousness into a new heightened clarified consciousness, able to look about, look ahead, act and prove itself in action. The Marxist concept of '*praxis*', carried on by Sartre into his later *Critique*, is in place here. Adorno was condemned by fellow Marxists as a useless dreamer, not positively at work (*praxis*) upon the battlefront of the Revolution. Structuralist thinking contains an aestheticised version of this concept, only the ordinary people (the new 'proletariat') are now inert (like the old dull bourgeoisie) and the 'battlefront' is the linguistic front line, the playground of creative poeticised writers and thinkers. We can see at this point how existentialism as well as Marxism has favoured (opened a way for) the emergence of structuralism, whose popular and more deeply worked version now replaces that of existentialism. The emotionally stirring and (to many) attractive contrast made by Sartre is Kantian in style, but Kant's contrast between the causally determined self and the free self is frankly metaphysical, in a sense to which Sartre is not committed. His position is apparently more 'realistic' (phenomenological, psychological). One might say he is bringing out the difficulties in Kant's view. Both Wittgenstein and Sartre seem at times to dismiss our confused inner reflections, or flow of consciousness, as irrelevant to the outward procedures of human life. Sartre might agree with Wittgenstein's 'An inner process stands in need of outer criteria.' (*Investigations* 580.) But by this Sartre would mean something moralistic, at least 'authentic', while Wittgenstein is saying something 'logical'. That is, Sartre is contrasting dreamy conventional (bourgeois) musing with courageous free unillusioned activity (*praxis*); whereas Wittgenstein is rejecting the 'inner' in so far as we may, in attributing roles to it, make philosophical mistakes. In fact, a closer look at Wittgenstein's dictum may lead us to attribute to it after all a sort of moral role. 'Do not try to analyse your own inner experience' (*Investigations* II xi, p. 204) may be seen also as a suggestion that one should not attach too much significance to (probably egoistic and senseless) inner chat! Silence becomes the inner as well as the outer person. As often in philosophy a growth of mutually supporting metaphors may seem to add up to a position which has been argued for. Thus something important may, by a bold distinction, be persuasively obscured. It is one thing to present sound anti-Cartesian critical arguments about sense data, momentary inner certainties, or the role of memory images in remembering; it is quite another to sweep aside as irrelevant a whole area of our private reflections, which we may regard as the very substance of our soul and being, as somehow unreal, otiose, without relevant *quality* or *value*. Wittgenstein occasionally protests that this is not what he is doing. He refers to introspectibilia, but rather as items, awkward misleading inner events, not as a part of some intelligible continuous flow. He is (like Derrida) thoroughly uneasy with the concept of 'experience'. He goes straight to language (language-games and communal forms of life). Immediate followers of Wittgenstein, including Gilbert Ryle, translated his admittedly obscure reflections into a form of behaviourism: only the 'outer' is real. (I discuss these Wittgensteinian matters at more length later on.) The, in effect, elimination of many of our ordinary conceptions of ourselves, and of the quality and texture of our awareness, by structuralist thinkers, is similar to that of Wittgenstein in going 'straight to language', but proceeds in a more polemical manner which certainly does not 'leave things as they are'. Structuralism has replaced existentialism as a popular 'philosophy of our time', but its doctrine, when assimilated, cuts deeper. The eclipse of (popular) existentialism is itself an interesting phenomenon. The idea of that brave individualistic, rather irresponsible, freedom attracted many non-philosophers after the war with Hitler, it seemed to be something which everyone could understand. Perhaps the prospect, or burden, of so much undefined freedom became, as many post-war hopes dwindled, less attractive and less realistic. People began to feel that, after all, they were in the grip of uncontrollable and mysterious forces, political, economic, scientific, cosmic, and that they had better become more relaxed and resigned. Structuralism with its particular anti-individualistic determinism (language speaks the man) and its aesthetic élitism (the artist as metaphysician, as specialised language-master, concept-master, and prophet) may be more calming to the nerves of those who regard it as a kind of science, and more flattering to those who feel themselves to be capable of such an exclusive creative freedom. The structuralist distinction between fact and value allows fewer people access to the latter. Structuralism (deconstruction) also, as a political, literary and metaphysical force, seems more disturbingly revolutionary, it flies the flag of a new era. Sartre seems tamely (or safely) traditional by contrast; and Derrida names Heidegger as ending the philosophical period which the Greeks began. So, certain philosophical dichotomies make the 'self', or 'consciousness', problem invisible. Both Sartre and Derrida were of course influenced by Heidegger, adopting from him his 'heroic' distinction between the authentic and the inauthentic life, and (in the case of Derrida) his desire to poeticise the language of philosophy.

Phenomenology in the style of Husserl uses the concept of consciousness. Husserl was prepared to look into the mind, and to set up a considerable amount of machinery to explain what he saw. He took as fundamental the 'intentional' nature of consciousness, consciousness as being always consciousness *of* something. He believed that it was possible by a special kind of introspection to isolate contents of consciousness and to study their transcendental (logical, category-bearing) structure. Husserlian phenomenology, divided up into various streams, has been made use of by moral philosophers, including Pope John Paul II. Husserl's transcendental philosophy is Kantian, but his method, and his confidence, is also Cartesian, and in that respect alien to later philosophy in the Wittgensteinian and structuralist lines. The changing character of phenomenology and its mediation into structuralism may be traced in the career of Merleau-Ponty. Husserl was a Kantian, not a Hegelian, his transcendental machinery was static and 'pure', not subject to historical development or prophetic concern with 'new consciousness'. He may be regarded as a 'bridge' figure; his theory has enlivened thinkers who have rejected it. As transcendental logic his conceptual forms or categories are too abstract and rigid to deal with anything like an introspectible mind; and as psychological intuition his method lacks the precision of either science or philosophy. Phenomenological analysis risks an inconclusive division, falling apart into either abstract logical structuring or uninhibited descriptions which may seem to belong to empirical psychology or even to the art of the novelist. One of Wittgenstein's aims was to remove philosophy from the vicinity of science, particularly of psychological science. Successors of Husserl have not been so particular. Sartre attempted to integrate psychoanalysis with existentialist philosophy, and structuralists have, with much greater ambition and refinement, 'taken over' sociology, anthropology and psychoanalysis (Lacan) into a philosophy of language. The sheer learning and energy exhibited in this take-over by its more brilliant exponents can make such theorising at its best and even for an alien critic very interesting. One can appreciate the temptation (not after all resisted by philosophers in the past, and deified by Hegel) to take over *all* new knowledge and organise it into a pattern of what is deepest. The metaphysic of Freud, for instance, now so familiar, might be put forward (by some), refined and altered perhaps, as a structure fundamental to the mind, beyond and beneath which one cannot go.

Popular structuralism at large in the field of literature exhibits the attack in a cruder form, dismantling ('deconstructing') the substantial individual being of works of art, of fictional characters and of their authors, in technical quasi-scientific terminology into theoretical patterns which are actually to *take the place* of what has been thus removed. We see here, as in a parable or mirror, how 'scientific' theory and technology may take the place of human beings. We, who still in spite of everything live in a Greek light, have yet to see how far science and its satellite theories can actually alter our human world. Intelligent tyrants reflect on this; and Marxism, for all its utilitarian virtues, carried this hypothesis, unclarified and semi-conscious, within itself. Could it before long begin to seem *naive* to believe in the value and being of individual consciousness, even in that one which is oneself? The denial of any *philosophical* role to 'experience' or 'mental contents' has left no place for a consideration of consciousness. 'Value' is placed outside philosophy or else is accommodated on the edge by some smaller technical structure, such as a form of behaviourism based on will and rules. A wholesale entry of 'human science' into philosophy swallows up and digests value. The heroic aestheticism of Heidegger and Derrida quietly effaces any close view of moral lives as lived by ordinary individuals. Motivation is indeed important in philosophy and at certain times philosophers lack motive, lack Eros, to pursue certain problems, perhaps because a dominating picture, even though sensed as incomplete, suits the general drive of their theory. It may seem that we have the philosophies which the age requires: a scientific linguistically minded age, wherein religion too is thrust aside. Does not such an age need and want a clarified determinism, combined perhaps with some sensible behaviouristic doctrine of non-universal reason, or a neo-Marxist philosophy of action, plus various utilitarian idealisms (ecology, human rights) – *rather than* theories of virtue and spirituality and quality of consciousness? As one might say, if so many other explanatory metaphysical pictures are available why strive for this, admittedly difficult, one? Heidegger, it is true, (in *Sein und Zeit*) takes his stand 'in the middle of experience', a place avoided by other philosophers. Existentialists professed to do something of the sort but without much success. Perhaps in his attempt to explain what it is to be a here and now experiencing person, (early) Heidegger is the only true existentialist. His *Dasein*, being-there, self-being, makes its first appearance as an individual. The views of later Heidegger are another matter.

'I can know what someone else is thinking, not what I am thinking. It is correct to say "I know what you are thinking", and wrong to say "I know what I am thinking". (A whole cloud of philosophy condensed into a drop of grammar.)' *Philosophical Investigations* II xi, p. 222. This asymmetry, pursued by Wittgenstein in *On Certainty*, expresses one aspect of present philosophical difficulties about the concept of the 'self'. I can *test*, and so be sure of, what others are thinking. I can, it may be argued, only thus test myself by regarding myself as another person (watching what I do etc.). Have I really decided? Wait and see! The seat of certainty, perhaps more generally of *truth*, has, it seems, been removed from its privileged central position. The whole thing, our grasp of our existence, has been revealed as working in a more complex, an indirect, a different, way. One does not have to be a philosopher to be assailed by such problems. On the one hand we, including the philosopher outside his study, believe with complete undoubting confidence in the real existence of the things (the 'external world') round about us; and (it may seem) with a similar confidence in our own existence, the authority of our own minds, the indubitable immediacy and continuity of our conscious self. Do we know what 'self' means? Well, yes, of course we do – don't we? 'Thing' and 'self' guarantee each other philosophically and also psychologically. All right, the philosophical 'metaphysical subject' may not be just like us, but objects must surely have subjects. We continue to enjoy art objects which unify our sensibility. Our surroundings continue and we continue with them. On the other hand, we know we make all sorts of *mistakes*, we fear death, we fear dissolution; anything which fragments consciousness, such as an inability to remember or to fit appearances together, produces fear, the prompt suspicion that the ego is not the one all-powerful unity and unifier which it feels itself to be. The *cogito* argument of Descartes is not just one simple attractive intuition (the test we can all give to ourselves): it takes a secret route through moral and religious 'certainties' from which we now feel more detached. A specialised fear of recent origin appears as a loss of confidence in language, a recognition of a fragmentation of language and a failure of linguistic ability. Does grammar matter? Does spelling matter? Why should we teach children all those old rules? Why should we believe in some general 'correct' language? Any dialect or patois is just as efficacious and often more expressive. Clips from radio or TV speech from even a few years ago can seem odd, affected, 'funny'. Philosophers used to appeal confidently to 'ordinary language'; but is there really such a thing? (At a dinner in Oxford in the nineteen fifties Professor Quine proposed a toast 'to ordinary language'. A philosopher present wondered at the time whether, in twenty or thirty years, we should find this toast equally significant and aptly amusing!) Is not the language which seemed so solid and continuous now falling apart into all sorts of specialised or local usages? Perhaps one can discern a general division into scientific languages, physics, computer language, Artificial Intelligence, Freudianism, structuralism, as contrasted with broken-down fragmented weakened modes of discourse, emotive, unreflective, inexact, bearers of inarticulate emotion and *idées reçues*. Versions of this alarming distinction are repeated by, sometimes gleeful, prophets, by whom, perhaps, we ought to be more alarmed. Those who accept this 'new realism', with distaste but with resignation, may lack energy to defend or re-examine the old idea of the self, the truth-seeking individual person, as a moral and spiritual centre. Structuralists and Marxist-structuralists and some empiricist philosophers see here the end of the old (Greek, Cartesian, bourgeois, etc.) metaphysical era as also the end of the God era. The Christian God supports, by his attention, the reality of the solitary individual, of whom Christ is the guarantor, ideal image or *alter ego*. Modern totalitarian tyrants, rightly from their point of view, have wanted to destroy religion *entirely*. Religious observance is a hiding place. Think what it did for Poland in the second half of the twentieth century. Art too has traditionally been, for artist and client, a space opened for individuals; and when we are frightened by prophecies we may be reassured by the substantial being of works of art. Critics who dismiss the nineteenth-century novel and even sneer at Shakespeare do not yet abandon Mozart. Schopenhauer was right to treat music as a special case. The art object, which is a kind of 'thing', is also a kind of 'soul'. The imagery of art and of religion, the persisting idea, whether personified or not, of an absolute good or moral ground, provide fortifying reflections, pictures, analogies of an active unified self. We are still surrounded by sources of energy which may maintain our 'self-confidence'. Our intuition helps out what is fragmentary to produce an idea of unity and in this mirror we see ourselves. It is in the critique of elements of illusion in this process that something essential may be lost.

Modern philosophy rejects old metaphysical unities, neo-Kantian moralists allow that rational beings may disagree, multiplicity must often be preferred to unity. Yet where the central problem of human consciousness is concerned the alleged 'disappearance' of the old substantial self has not led to any new philosophical enlightenment, or clear indication concerning how we are to discuss in a more realistic way a demythologised and (apparently) disunited self. Metaphysical ideas persist of more deprived but still unitary selflets, leading a minimal yet dignified sort of existence as principles of will or sincerity or non-universal rationality. It is possible that such philosophical notions are closer than they used to be to ordinary lay self-understanding, I mean that people are really less inclined to think of themselves as souls and persons. A glorified 'falsely completed' image of conscious being has been set aside, together with abandoned theories of art and morals, and with the Cartesian idea that immediate consciousness is the foundation of conceptual knowledge. The old concept of the self as a unified active consciousness, living between appearance and reality (the traditional field of the novel), is being dislodged by psychoanalytical psychologists and 'literary' deconstruction. We now see in modern neo-Hegelian thinking fact actually becoming value, as quasi-scientific technical modes of discourse (psychoanalysis, anthropology, semiology, grammatology, etc.) are treated as ultimate truths, and *contrasted* with a conceptually vague 'ordinary language' composed of conventional assumptions and illusions, and which if solemnly uttered by some non-technical thinker is inevitably in bad faith.

I quote from Perry Anderson's prophetic 1968 essay *Components of the National Culture*:

'The novel has declined as a genre, not – as is often alleged – because it was the product of the rising bourgeoisie of the nineteenth century and could not survive it. The true reason is that it has disappeared into the abyss between everyday language and the technical discourses inaugurated by Marx and Freud. The sum of objective knowledge within the specialised codes of the human sciences has decisively contradicted and surpassed the normal assumptions behind exoteric speech. The result is that a novelist after Marx and Freud has either to simulate an arcadian innocence or transfer elements of their discourse immediately into his work. Hence the entrenched bifurcation between pseudo-traditional and experimental novels. The ingenuousness of the former is always in bad faith. The opposite solution, the inclusion of frontier concepts from Freud and Marx within the novel, has no viable outcome either. The novelist can only forge his art from the material of ordinary language. If there is a radical discordance between this and objective knowledge of man and society, the novel ceases. It has no ground between the naive and the arcane.'

(Quoted in Bernard Sharratt's book *Reading Relations*,
and in David Lodge's review of Sharratt's book in
*The Times Literary Supplement*, 23 April 1982.)

This interesting piece, written in an interesting year, utters prophecies which are still worth reflecting upon. For instance, the distinction between the naive and the arcane, the traditional and the experimental: is not this now everywhere in view in literature, in painting, in music? And the specialised codes of the human sciences are indeed surpassing the normal assumptions behind exoteric speech. Anderson's strong words may still be taken as a warning. What has clearly changed (since 1968) is the status of Marx, and to some extent that of Freud. The tendency to join these two together has lasted a long time. Freud would probably now be seen (by ordinary sophisticated observers) not strictly as a scientist, but as a great thinker who has considerably altered our view of human nature; whereas Marx, though larger and more influential, seems more like a historical phenomenon. Many people have profited more from a rejection of Marx than from his insights. Both these thinkers have now been gathered up into structuralism, merging into a new form of 'human science'. I would take a less extreme view than Anderson of the effect of the racing *Zeitgeist* upon art. Thinkers may try to jolt art, the surrealists did it, the structuralists are doing it. But the artist makes everything his own. (André Breton and Roland Barthes did not 'control' or 'inspire' Picasso and Robbe-Grillet.) Here the novelist is (I conjecture) even more at liberty since he does not have to exhibit his work in galleries or in concert halls, he is a private secluded individual offering his art to another private secluded individual. Of course, if he is lucky, his books are displayed in shops – but they are consumed in solitude. I do not think that literature has fallen into the predicted abyss. It has certainly changed, but is saved by the superb versatility of authors. Novels are stories such as humans have always used. The traditional novel can look after itself, tradition develops, experiments are infinitely various. The novel has flourished abundantly in the second half of the century. I have quoted out of context (and out of time) the stirring words of Perry Anderson because they seemed clearly and aptly to epitomise dangers which still lie ahead. We must indeed preserve and cherish a strong truth-bearing everyday language, not marred or corrupted by technical discourse or scientific codes; and thereby promote the clarified objective knowledge of man and society of which we are in need as citizens, and as moral agents.

Hume (as philosopher) held that the self was a sort of 'illusion', just as the material object was an 'illusion'; that is, it was, both as empirical knower and as moral agent, a lot of fragmentary experiences held together by strong habits of imagination. Here the idea of the material object may even be regarded as the dominant illusion, in that we usually regard the inhabitant of the same body as the same person, however great the time span involved, and however incoherent the intervening consciousness. Illusions are of many different kinds, perceptual mistakes, fantasies, ghosts, wishful thinkings, literary fictions, and so on. Hume's 'self' and 'object' illusions may be thought of as natural necessities, necessary though perhaps scarcely justifiable ideas. 'I must distinguish in the imagination betwixt the principles which are permanent, irresistible and universal, such as the customary transition from causes to effects and from effects to causes; and the principles which are changeable weak and irregular. The former are the foundation of all our thoughts and actions, so that upon their removal human nature must immediately perish and go to ruin.' (*Treatise of Human Nature* I iv 4.) We *must* believe in causality, in persons and objects and in the substantial continuity of our own being. What would it be not to? We might compare and contrast this belief with metaphysical ideas such as the Marxist theory of history or Kant's Universal Reason. There are also axioms or axiomatic fictions with moral and political uses such as Locke's natural rights or Hobbes's concept of the individual or Hume's doctrine that, politically, every man should be deemed a knave. I shall discuss the status of such 'axioms' later. The problematic 'self' does not really fit these categories, though it could, to stir reflection, be considered in all three, as a necessary illusion, not further discussable, as a historically determined persuasive idea, which the *Zeitgeist* could remove, or is removing, or as an ideal mode of thinking, of obvious value in morals and politics. The notion that the continuous self is a fiction may occur to us in ordinary situations, in puzzling about memory or responsibility for the past. Is the Nazi war criminal unearthed many years later the same person who did those terrible things in a concentration camp? We may sometimes feel, in exasperation or despair, about ourselves or others, that an entity so prone to error, so stuffed with illusion, is itself an illusion. Platonic philosophy and some religious positions take ordinary egoistic consciousness to be a veil which separates us from the order and true multiplicity of the real world: reflectively understood this is obviously true. Moral progress (freedom, justice, love, truth) leads us to a new state of being. This higher state does not involve the ending but rather the transformation of the 'ordinary' person and world. There is a false unity and multiplicity and a true unity and multiplicity. There is the selfish ego surrounded by dark menacing chaos, and the more enlightened soul perceiving the diversity of creation in the light of truth. Buddhist and Hindu religious art is often expressive of the play between appearance and reality and multiplicity and unity, and how what is infinitely multiple can appear either as terrifying or as soul-shakingly beautiful. This imagery may remind us of Kant's sublime, and of what Kant did with Hume's compulsory illusory belief. Habit and unexplained belief could not, for a scientifically minded and religious man such as Kant, be the founding basis or ground of human existence. One might say of Hume that he had performed the Copernican Revolution without noticing. Kant's categories and his phenomenal self explain and establish the compulsoriness of the empirical world. Hume's unitary self held, as part and support of his continuous being, very strong habitual beliefs and feelings about society and morality, similar to his beliefs about objects. Kant's separated noumenal rational self transcends the mechanical multiplicity of the phenomenal world toward a unified intelligible moral order. The individual experienced being of the Kantian man resides in the tension between the two orders. These are traditional metaphysical pictures of self and self-being which consider as a matter of course the moral and epistemological nature of the person, and indicate better and worse activities and states of consciousness. Even Hume who, in his study, holds the self to be an illusion, persuasively pictures an ideal temperate tolerant man with civilised feelings who eschews the excesses of abstract rationalism. To describe the self may seem to involve describing the self as moral being, to discuss consciousness to involve discerning qualities of consciousness. The self or soul, in these traditional images, is seen to live and travel between truth and falsehood, good and evil, appearance and reality.

The theological idea of the soul has been a support to the concept of the self in philosophy. Now as theology and religion lose their authority the picture of the soul fades and the idea of the self loses its power. Questions about the unity or identity of the self have been discussed in contemporary philosophy in technical post-Cartesian anti-Humian terms as matters fairly easily dealt with and set aside, or else as pseudo-problems. With this goes a (taken-for-granted) setting-aside of consciousness, inwardness, as a bearer of moral substance. There are of course, outside philosophy, in sociology, psychology, political theory, speculations about the self as historical individual, language-user, victim of identity crises, etc., which it might do philosophers no harm to peruse. But such accounts will normally treat 'morals', if mentioned, as a social or historical, etc. phenomenon, rather than worrying about the self as moral being. In the field of philosophy Charles Taylor's wise and learned work *Sources of the Self* explores in reflectively presented detail those surrounding fields, while pursuing a *philosophical argument* which involves establishing *ab initio* that 'orientation in relation to the good is essential to being a functional human agent' (p. 42).

Schopenhauer protests against Kant. (*The Basis of Morality* II 6.) 'Kant does not represent the so-called moral law *as a fact of consciousness* ... Human consciousness, as well as the whole of the external world, together with all the experience and facts in them, are swept from under our feet ... What are we to hold onto? Onto a few concepts which are entirely abstract.' 'By discarding every empirical basis of morals he rejects all inner, and even more definitely all outer, *experi-*

*ence.*' (My italics.) Elsewhere Schopenhauer praises Kant for removing morality from definition or determination in empirical terms (for instance explaining it as a natural phenomenon among others). Here he is objecting to the sharply segregated nature of Kant's Categorical Imperative as a unique command from elsewhere, and as our only direct contact with what is spiritual. This charge may not seem entirely just since in the exercise of reason the moral agent is forced to attend to the multiplicity of the world. But Kant does say that the impetus of the sense of duty is not an (ordinary) experience and not part of our multifarious (causally determined) phenomenal awareness. What Schopenhauer is here demanding instead is that our morality should be fed by our whole experience and conscious awareness of our world, which is *already* filled with intimations of good and evil. Our personality and temperament, and the daily momently quality of our consciousness, our ability to *look at particulars*, must be thought of as an organic part of our morals, and soaked in value. His claim made for 'consciousness' as the very stuff of quality of being is in fact close to Plato and to his imagery of different levels of awareness wherein each subject *has the object he deserves.*

In philosophy we exhibit deep motives in our selection of tasks; and in the omnipresence of scientific explanation philosophers may not be motivated to speak in the context of ethics about these problems which trouble Schopenhauer. It seems to me that one cannot 'philosophise' adequately upon the subject unless one takes it as fundamental that consciousness is a form of moral activity: what we attend to, how we attend, whether we attend. This need not imply that all states of consciousness are evaluating or can be evaluated. ('Every second has moral quality' would have to be a synthetic *a priori* proposition!) Of course as soon as we look at it in this way we encounter grave problems about how to describe and explain what we are looking at; but these problems arise in any attempt at describing mind and mental process, and are best met (in my view) as posed at this level (the level of our general conception of consciousness), and discussed in ordinary language and not in specialised jargon. Of course, any attempt, by a philosopher or psychoanalyst, to exhibit 'the mind' in terms of a clear conceptual framework with firmly distinguishable parts is likely to be at least thought-provoking and in this sense hermeneutic. The difficulty of relating the *explicans* to the *explicandum* may be reminiscent of that of relating languages of art criticism or literary criticism to the objects

[ 167 ]

they are designed to illumine. These languages can assist us, even ones we find alien can often throw light; but if we are to learn from such discourse, our eyes must be fixed upon *the thing itself* which is much closer to us than the suggestive schemata which are being wheeled up against it, and whose language gains sense only from our primary animation of what it is. Technical meta-language terminology must be *ancillary* to basic looking, and not something which (as in deconstruction) takes its place. We look at the picture, we read the poem. We follow the instruction to consider this rhythm or that ambiguity. What the critic says is secondary, a suggested way of looking. Of course philosophy is unlike aesthetic critical pointing in that what is indicated is so *very much* more difficult to elucidate. What is similar is the required attempt to find a way of being faithful (true) to the thing itself.

Morality, unless put into the picture at the start, cannot be adequately represented by anything inserted later. Anti-Cartesian thinkers who remove metaphysical subjects seem in doing so simply to update the old divisions which have the effect of paralysing attempts to think in fresh and independent and realistic ways about what morality or being a person is like. Such reflection is often explicitly handed over to 'sociology', a 'scientific' subject which increasingly invades the philosophical field and attracts young people away from the (far more difficult) study of philosophy. Here, as I suggested earlier, utilitarianism, dismissed when I was young as an old discredited doctrine, survives to provide for many an entry into philosophical thought and a free open space for philosophical reflection. In a (since television even more manifestly) suffering world utilitarian ideas and projects make evident sense and can always win respect. How refreshing it is to turn from the nightmarish schemata of deconstructionist thought to the open meditative pages of John Stuart Mill, who really seems to be *thinking* about recognisable human beings. G. E. Moore's ideas, moreover, in *Principia Ethica*, about 'good states of mind', however eccentric, can promote reflection. J. M. Keynes's delightfully intelligent discussion of Moore in *My Early Beliefs*, from which I quoted earlier, indicates some of the major difficulties and also exhibits how much he and his contemporaries were inspired to think by their chosen sage. 'Indeed it is only states of mind that matter, provided that we agree to take account of the pattern of life through time, and give up regarding it as a series of independent instantaneous flashes, but the ways in which states of mind can be valuable, and the objects of them, are more various and also much richer than we allowed for.' This is a model example of radical and good-tempered reaction against one's teacher. Keynes recalls with particular affection the 'sweet and lovely passage, so sincere and passionate and careful' in which Moore 'discusses whether, granting it is mental qualities which one should chiefly love, it is important that the beloved person should also be good-looking'! (*Principia Ethica*, ch. VI, section 122.) The case of Keynes and his friends also illustrates the way in which clever young people can be absolutely taken over by a philosophical view, later seen to be intolerably abstract and implausible. 'I have called this faith a religion, and some sort of relation of neo-platonism it surely was. But we should have been very angry at the time with such a suggestion. We regarded all this as entirely rational and scientific in character.' Keynes speaks of Moore's world as being pre-Marx and pre-Freud (that pair again) and possessing the atmosphere of Plato's early dialogues.

It may be helpful here, before going further, to look at what novelists do. It may be that the best model for all thought is the creative imagination. We cannot exactly say that novelists are unaware or unconscious of these problems, since they have constantly to invent methods of conveying states of mind or to choose between different styles of doing so. Novels moreover exhibit the ubiquity of moral quality inherent in consciousness. We may rightly criticise novels in which characters' thoughts (as well as actions) exhibit a lack of moral sensibility which seems called for by the story. This is an important kind of literary criticism. Indeed the judgment passed upon the moral sensibility of the artist is a primary kind of aesthetic judgment. Of course, some artists can talk about how they work and others cannot, or will not, and it is the art object which is great or otherwise, and not the 'how it is done'. Artists are famous for not knowing how it is done, or for perhaps rightly feeling that at their best they do not know what they are up to. (This darkness of aesthetic inspiration worried Plato.) At any rate, the novelist's problem (the traditional novelist's problem), solved intuitively or otherwise, is precisely a unification of fact and value, the exhibiting of personal morality in a non-abstract manner as the stuff of consciousness. Here the use of figurative highly toned evaluative language seems natural, in showing the movement between immediacy and abstraction and the instant sorting and evaluating of the world in our awareness of it. I spoke of the philosopher as (sometimes) lacking motives. The novelist (unless corrupted by recent critics who think that not only criticism but literature is a scientific pursuit from which value must be excluded) does not lack motivation. Novels, both old and new, from Murasaki (*The Tale of Genji*) onward, seem to have had no radical difficulties with the concept of consciousness. The variety of solutions is one of the charms of the art form. Let us take an example.

In Henry James's novel *The Golden Bowl* Maggie Verver realises that her husband is enjoying a long-standing love relationship with her best friend.

'It was not till many days had passed that the Princess began to accept the idea of having done, a little, something she was not always doing, or indeed of having listened to any inward voice that spoke in a new tone. Yet these instinctive postponements of reflection were the fruit, positively, of recognitions and perceptions already active; of the sense, above all, that she had made, at a particular hour, made by the mere touch of her hand, a difference in the situation so long present to her as practically unattackable. This situation had been occupying, for months and months, the very centre of the garden of her life, but it had reared itself there like some strange tall tower of ivory, or perhaps rather some wonderful, beautiful, but outlandish pagoda, a structure plated with hard bright porcelain, coloured and figured and adorned, at the overhanging eaves, with silver bells that tinkled, ever so charmingly, when stirred by chance airs. She had walked round and round it – that was what she felt; she had carried on her existence in the space left her for circulation, a space that sometimes seemed ample and sometimes narrow; looking up, all the while, at the fair structure that spread itself so amply and rose so high, but never quite making out, as yet, where she might have entered had she wished. She had not wished till now – such was the odd case; and what was doubtless equally odd, besides, was that, though her raised eyes seemed to distinguish places that must serve, from within, and especially far aloft, as apertures and outlooks, no door appeared to give access from her convenient garden level. The great decorated surface had remained consistently impenetrable and inscrutable. At present, however, to her considering mind, it was as if she had ceased merely to circle and to scan the elevation, ceased so vaguely, so quite helplessly to stare and wonder: she had caught herself distinctly in the act of pausing, then in that of lingering, and finally in that of stepping unprecedentedly near. The thing might have been, by the distance at which it kept her, a Mohammedan mosque, with which no base heretic could take a liberty; there so hung about it the vision of one's putting off one's shoes to enter and even, verily, of one's paying with one's life if found there as an interloper. She had not, certainly, arrived at the conception of paying with her life for anything she might do; but it was nevertheless quite as if she had sounded with a tap or two one of the rare porcelain plates. She had knocked, in short – though she could scarce have said whether for admission or for what; she had applied her hand to a cool, smooth spot, and had waited to see what would happen. Something *had* happened; it was as if a sound, at her touch, after a little, had come back to her from within; a sound sufficiently suggesting that her approach had been noted.'

How is it done? Well, like that and in innumerable other ways. Do we understand? Yes, of course, we follow, in context, these descriptions of states of consciousness with no difficulty. We are able to think of the imagery both as something which the character is continually, like the author, coining as she goes along, and as something 'deeper' or 'beyond', which the imagery evokes or points to. This may be seen as two levels of a region wherein we can discern many levels. Figurative language, metaphor, is everywhere in our thinking, apprehended by the thinker as ultimate or as pointing beyond. How we proceed here can be a matter of our deepest thoughts. We recognise this dialectic, these levels, these differences of style and image, in our own thinking as we understand a writer and as we are at other times led to reflect upon what the stuff and quality of our consciousness is. We do this; but can we also talk intelligibly, philosophically, about what it is that we do? Is there *a* philosophical problem of consciousness; rather than, say, a lot of peripheral problems so arranged as to remove any allegedly central problem which could be so called? Problems are set up in philosophy with ulterior motives. I want there to be a discussable problem of consciousness because I want to talk about consciousness or self-being as the fundamental mode or form of moral being. As contrasted with what, or distinguished from what? Well, as distinguished from conceptions depending solely upon choice, will and action, from voluntarism and ethical behaviourism, and indeed from Kant for whom phenomenal awareness (the mess of actual consciousness) is without value, also from theories in the style of Husserl or of Freud which depend upon technical terminology. Philosophers are supposed to clarify, and should attempt to write in ordinary language and not in jargon. The present problem particularly illustrates the importance of this aim. We may also note at this point respects in which the formulation of present disagreements is not new. A similar conflict concerning the deep sources and background of virtuous action arose between Pelagius and St Augustine. Augustine emphasises the importance and ambiguity of motivation, the dense and fallen nature of the soul, so subject to selfish habit, so precariously and imperfectly free. He pictures our consciousness as existing continuously in the presence of God, continually aware of sin and of the necessity of prayer. The *Confessions* is a long passionate loving speech addressed to God. 'Perfect me, O Lord ... Behold thy voice is my joy, yea, thy voice exceedeth the abundance of all pleasures. Give me what I love, for verily I do love it, and this love is of thy giving.' (Book XI, ch. 2.) This relationship to the Good may be contrasted with Kant's picture (no doubt more like the usual human scene) of the moral agent sunk in egoism but *able* at times to notice the outcry of Duty. Schopenhauer, when sufficiently muddled and relaxed, offers in his concept of compassion something more like Augustine's blurred image of our imperfect freedom. It is enough to emphasise the strength of temperament and habit and the difficulty of altering the natural set of one's desires. The neo-Kantian concept of will is here too abstract and superficial, it cannot be carried to a deep enough level. Philosophies of will in descent from Kant which discard Kant's metaphysical background and religious moral intent, and work with some concept of non-universal reason, are in danger of falling into behaviourism.

Is what we want to put into the picture essentially the *moral* aspect of the mind? If there were no value judgments would a behaviourist account suffice? (Simply taking what we do to be real, and what we think to be unreal.) Post-Cartesian philosophers have usually been concerned with 'immediate awarenesses', perceptions for instance, as bearers of knowledge rather than of value, and have in this interest reduced the ordinary concept of 'inner' activity. Certainly a strong belief in the moral (evaluative) nature of (almost all) private inner reflection is a motive here. (Almost all? Why not say all?) But something more radical is involved. The volatile variegated *force*, the ever-flowing *energy*, the temporal *pressure*, the unfailing *presence* of what we call 'the stream of consciousness' – surely this is something fundamental, surely if we are searching for 'being' this is it? Yet after this declaration which way do we go? Not only many questions, but many different kinds of questions, present themselves. How does the alleged 'stream' relate to time? How do 'general' and 'particular' relate therein? Should we, and can we, distinguish mental contents which have some degree (what degree?) of clarity, form and body, for instance by consisting of sentences which could be uttered aloud? What is the value, use, status of contents which fail this sort of test? What do we do with items which have personal 'colour' but no public classification, are there such items? (Is there private language?) How immediate is immediate awareness? Are there mental entities (images, icons, lights, dark clouds, verbal admonitions, etc., etc.) which are *always* in our minds? What about 'unconscious mind', is there such a thing? If we flounder and 'cannot say' what kind of difficulty is involved, is this a mystery, or some sort of transcendental check or ordinary failure of description? The scene is so vast and the problems lead away in so many directions, we may feel there is no unitary subject or concept here at all. What are we worrying about or fighting for? A neat purposeful analysis proves too reductionist, it tells us too little, while an attempt at scrupulous description may have to use so many and various devices that it answers no questions at all, but merely presents the problem in another form. I think these were difficulties which confronted Husserl. An acute realisation or impression that after all there is not only nothing else but consciousness, but nothing else but present consciousness, is the road to Cartesianism, solipsism, idealism, mysticism, and insanity. Yet the layman lives at peace with 'consciousness', with all its obscure implications of 'ownership' and 'presence'. It is what is most his own, he is responsible for it, even though it may seem to include so much that is not momentary or personal or private or clearly visible.

The presocratic Greeks worried about the origin and substance of all things (water? water and earth? fire?) and how the (eternal) One related to the (arriving and departing) many. Parmenides held that thinking and being were one. Or was it all a *game* played by the gods (a view favoured by Heidegger and Derrida following Heraclitus, Fragment 52)? In general the Greek philosophers took the world and our being in it for granted. Plato would have regarded the Cartesian idea of immediate *cogitatio* as a philosophical *starting point* as absurd, and indeed this is contradicted by his whole philosophy. He was not concerned with 'contents of consciousness' in a Cartesian or Humian sense. The idea that we could have knowledge of something momentary would be alien to his thought. The discussion about 'What is knowledge?' in the *Theaetetus* exhibits (151Eff.) the thoroughly jumbled and baffling nature of the concept of 'perception'. (No general conclusion is reached, but as Myles Burnyeat remarks in the introduction to his excellent commentary, 'there is much to be learnt from raising questions and then discovering *in detail* why a tempting wrong answer is wrong.') Plato was suspicious of writing which seems to remove knowledge and truth from the present moment of the individual and lodge it elsewhere, in books, which are inert and cannot defend themselves against fools. The speaking person is fundamental. Insight into truth is the flash which in live conversation upon serious matters carries one beyond the words. G. E. Moore and his friends would understand that. Plato assumes that speech, as the immediate present thought of the individual, is more direct than writing. As epistemologist, he does not define or describe any general 'ordinary consciousness', but as moral thinker posits a scale of (increasingly) refined personal awareness. His picture *demands* the concept of change of consciousness. Such states of being, or 'states of mind', are of course implied in the spiritual pilgrimage of the *Republic*. This is more realistically suggested, pictured as real 'thinkings' and 'discernings' of individuals, in the attacks on writing, and in the high rhetoric of the *Phaedrus* and the *Symposium*, which are concerned with personal salvation as personal vision and change of being. This double movement, away from the private and personal and then back again, may remind us of views, more simply put, of Kierkegaard and Schopenhauer, thinkers who do not make philosophical theory out of immediate awareness in a Cartesian (or phenomenological) sense, but attach an ultimate importance to the continuous lived existence of individual beings. The vague word 'existential', which I shall in general avoid, might seem in place here. Modern theologians struggle to relate spiritual ideas of some complexity to everyday inner lives. I shall shortly be quoting from a Zen thinker, Katsuki Sekida, whose criticism of Husserl is also in the spirit of this 'double movement'. Plato would agree with Sekida in regarding the ordinary apprehension of the ordinary man, even if not taken in anything like an atomic Cartesian sense, as a form of largely illusory awareness. Egoistic anxiety veils the world. This may be taken in a logical sense. Knowledge cannot be something immediate, the possession of solitary individual perceptions or thought-data. Knowledge implies ideas, concepts, linguistic networks, connections. The rejection of Descartes by Wittgenstein, later by structuralists, rests on the connection of knowledge with concepts. (We may note here that Descartes's solitary thinker is released by a *moral* intuition!) The Platonic 'true knowledge' must also be understood in a moral-religious sense which pictures salvation or enlightenment as wisdom or true vision, brought about by a refinement of desire in daily living, and involving a clearer perception, including literal perception, of the world. Education is moral education. Taken in either sense the Platonic view implies that ordinary consciousness is full of illusion. The (ordinary) egoist lives in a small world. Our objects of knowledge are at the level of our deserts. Both the savant and saint know more and see more than the ordinary man. The Theory of Forms is suspended, sometimes awkwardly, between the logical and the mystical. Whitehead said that western philosophy was all footnotes to Plato. The truth of this epigram becomes especially evident in the second half of the twentieth century as we realise how many of our current problems Plato was aware of. This is the end of the Cartesian era, and may be the end of the Aristotelian era, but in the strange cosmic astronomy of the wandering *Zeitgeist* we are closer to Plato now than in many previous centuries.

Kierkegaard's version of the Hegelian dialectic (aesthetic–moral–religious) is closer in its purpose and mode of exposition to Plato, and can be read as a picture of change of consciousness in the Platonic manner. Kierkegaard however, inspired by hatred of Hegel, was hostile to philosophical system, *ergo* to philosophy, and makes his own teaching by myths into a self-confessed and sustained form of fiction as 'indirect communication'. It may be apt here, as a warning, to quote some of Kierkegaard's remarks on Schopenhauer (*Journals*, trans. A. Dru, 1354). 'Schopenhauer is so far from being a real pessimist that at the most he represents "the interesting": in a certain sense he makes asceticism interesting – the most dangerous thing possible for a pleasure-seeking age which will be harmed more than ever by distilling pleasure even out of – asceticism; that is to say by studying asceticism in a completely impersonal way, by assigning it a place in the system.' This comment is aimed at one of Schopenhauer's vulnerable points. The term 'interesting' is indeed in place. Schopenhauer, who seems far from ascetic, may indeed be said to romanticise asceticism, gratifying himself by speaking grandly of it, as if he could glimpse the state of selfless being and award it top marks. He even, deliberately and impertinently, separates it from the *virtue*, which must surely be required for its achievement. His 'impersonal study' might be compared with the experience of someone who imagines his spiritual understanding is increased by reading books about eastern philosophy. The *practice*, the exercise itself, is absent. Schopenhauer could reply urbanely that he is a metaphysical thinker who has studied the religions of the orient and regards 'impersonal' as a term of praise; and if he has succeeded in making asceticism interesting then surely this is, from any point of view, something to be desired! In fact Kierkegaard, disliking Schopenhauer's style, misses his passionate seriousness. Kierkegaard does not seem to have been attracted by Plato, and is here attacking Schopenhauer's Platonism as well as his orientalism. Philosophising about goodness may produce a gratified lethargy in the individual at whom Kierkegaard's disturbing teaching is aimed. Philosophical celebration of virtue may be like the empty admiration we have for our 'heroes'.

'It is everlastingly untrue that anyone was ever helped to do the good by the fact that someone else really did it; for if he ever comes to the point of really doing it himself, it will be by apprehending the reality of the other as a possibility. When Themistocles was rendered sleepless by thinking about the exploits of Miltiades, it was his apprehension of their reality as a possibility that made him sleepless. Had he plunged into enquiries as to whether Miltiades had really accomplished the great things attributed to him, had he contented himself with knowing that Miltiades had actually done them, he would scarcely have been rendered sleepless. In that case he would have become a sleepy or at the most a noisy admirer, but scarcely a second Miltiades. Ethically speaking there is nothing so conducive to sound sleep as admiration of another person's ethical reality. And again ethically speaking, if there is anything that can stir and rouse a man it is a possibility ideally requiring itself of a human being.'

(*Concluding Unscientific Postscript*, Part Two, end of chapter III.)

Kierkegaard shuns Plato's system but emulates his charm, that charm which Plato himself saw as dangerous when he attacked the artists. Every age is pleasure-loving and attracted by 'the interesting'; and in spite of the dangerous nature of art and philosophy, thinkers must think and writers must write, under the inspiration of their individual Eros. How the warning uttered by Plato to art and by Kierkegaard to philosophy is to be internalised is a matter for reflection. With this in mind we resume. Plato's moral education is to be seen in terms of a change of self-being, of mental and spiritual activity and 'stuff', and the modern moral philosopher in search of a concept might profitably reflect upon the myth of the Cave as implying a progressively changing quality of consciousness. Subjects begin to see different objects; they have a deeper and wider and wiser understanding of the world. The pilgrim will not only produce a better series of acts, he will have (down to last details) a better series of mental states. He can literally see better, see people's faces and leaves on trees, he will more rapidly and easily expel an unworthy thought or improper image. Herein the concepts of knowledge, truth, justice and moral passion are internally bound together. Knowledge informs the moral quality of the world, the selfish self-interestedly casual or callous man *sees* a different world from that which the careful scrupulous benevolent just man sees; and the largely explicable ambiguity of the word 'see' here conveys the essence of the concept of the moral. The connection between ethics and epistemology is something which we are intuitively grasping all the time in our non-philosophical lives.

The element of metaphor is unavoidable in philosophy, especially in moral philosophy; it is simply more or less evident. Some theories of will, for instance, may avoid speaking of leaps, but constantly use metaphors of movement. All right, but in order to move one must see, one must survey the scene, and the ability to see justly is also connected with changes in what is desired. Failure to understand how thought constantly *works* in moral living supports a popular misrepresentation of Plato as an '*intellectualist*' philosopher who (in the ordinary sense) put the highest value on intellectual skill, and (in the metaphysical sense) thought that nothing was real except objectified abstract ideas lodged somewhere in heaven. Metaphysics is full of metaphors whose force is often half concealed. The Platonic myths are an explicit resort to metaphor as a mode of explanation. Plato continually pictures education as moral progress and indicates the kind of relation which exists between moral goodness and a desire for just and true understanding.

Mathematics is good for the soul, getting things right enlivens a sense of truth, efforts to understand automatically purify desires. What happened to the slave in the *Meno*, did he undergo some permanent spiritual change as a result of being prompted to solve the geometrical problem? That rather blood-chilling yet also so poetical scene poses a problem or hitch which must also accompany a Platonic ethical view. This is one of the points where we want to switch our attention to Kant as a helpful corrective, as we instinctively want to defend Kant's 'duty' against the sneers of Schopenhauer and Wittgenstein. Kant thought that every man possessed through Practical Reason the entire potential for moral goodness, though he also thought (to adopt the words of Julian of Norwich) that sin was behovely, that failure was likely, given the strength of base egoistic desires. In effect, Kant's moral view is optimistic and democratic. Plato's is pessimistic and aristocratic, in the sense that he offers a vision of what is highest, but also of the distance which separates us from it. Kant's view is horizontal, Plato's is vertical. Kant's man plods along a level road, alternately failing and succeeding, continually nagged by conscience. We easily identify with this individual. Plato has no similar figure. When goodness is so difficult there seems less point in saying that every man is potentially good, though the Cave myth may imply it. Both these views (Kantian and Platonic) can be seen as realistic and philosophically instructive. Yet one may also want to regard (I discuss this later) the idea of duty as indestructible, and want to examine more closely the intractable density of individual fates. The connection made by Plato of knowledge (truthfulness) and learning with goodness provides a deep intelligible conception of moral change, but detailed questions need to be asked about how exactly this comes about. Plato tells us in the *Meno* that virtue cannot be taught, neither is it natural, it comes by divine gift (*Meno* 100B). This does not of course mean accidentally or without effort. Help from God or the unconscious mind must normally be thought of as arriving in a context of attending and trying. Leaving aside the problem-solving slave, upon whom perhaps in that in many ways so terrible civilisation no light could fall, let us return to the case of the craftsmen at the end of the *Republic* who benefit from the 'most gracious assistance' (602D) of measuring, numbering and weighing. The carpenter, for instance (at 597B), who makes the non-ideal bed, imitating the ideal bed 'made by God', in industriously pursuing his craft may gain access to mathematical ideas. We can

[ 178 ]

imagine here, conjuring up the virtuous apprentice, how such industry could 'do him good'. The Greeks were amazed and impressed by their progress in geometry, and Plato takes mathematics as a case of a high, though not highest, knowledge. It may also be seen as an image of, or standing for, any strict intellectual discipline, such as learning a foreign language. Learning is moral progress because it is an asceticism, it diminishes our egoism and enlarges our conception of truth, it provides deeper, subtler and wiser visions of the world. What should be taught in schools: to attend and get things right. Creative power requires these abilities. Intellectual and craft studies initiate new qualities of consciousness, minutiae of perception, ability to observe, they alter our desires, our instinctive movements of desire and aversion. To attend is to care, to learn to desire to learn. One may of course *learn* bad habits as well as good, and that too is a matter of quality of consciousness. I am speaking now of evident aspects of education and teaching, where the 'intellectual' connects with the 'moral'; and where apparently 'neutral' words naturally take on a glow of value. The concepts 'truth' and 'reality' are at issue. Structuralism, which professes no morality, puts both these concepts, in the sense attached to them in these considerations, in question. The ambiguity and difficulty of both appears in the case of the carpenter whom Plato summons up expressly to contrast with the painter (597B–C) whose relationship to the bed remains at a level of unreflective immediacy. Plato subsequently (607B) refers to the old quarrel between philosophy and poetry. Without entering here into Plato's precise objections (political, psychological, moral) to art (painting, music, theatre), we may readily understand his conception of art generally as relaxing the moral and intellectual faculties, and weakening the grasp upon what is true and real. We (today) see all about us vast commercial and pseudo-intellectual proliferations of inane and corrupting rubbish which usurp the name of art. Yet in just this context we are led to claim our knowledge and experience of good art as something moral. It is not just delight, it is refinement and revelation. Kant recognised this when he spoke of genius, and Schopenhauer allowed a contemplation of art as inducing, at least a temporary, state of selflessness. Any artist, or thinker, or craftsman knows of crucial moments when an aggregate of reflection and skill must *now* be pressed a little harder so as to achieve some significantly better result. If that *now* is missed, passed over in vagueness and lassitude, the collected power is dissipated and the result is less good, as the thinker moves in a relaxed or lazy manner from 'it's too soon to try' to 'it's too late to try – this stuff is finished anyway'. This is a place for the notion of an effort of will. There is a good description (a discussion between two scientists) of situations of this sort in Solzhenitsyn's novel *The First Circle*. Ideas *work* in the mind of the slave and the carpenter. This working is something which we can experience, of which we can be conscious in present moments. Ideas break the narrow self-obsessed limits of the mind. The enjoyment and study of good art is enlarging and enlightening in this way. We may add to this that as mathematics 'stands for' any high intellectual discipline, we may, without breaking faith with Plato, suggest that the carpenter 'stands for' any careful attentive self-forgetting work or craft, including housework, and all kinds of nameless 'unskilled' fixings or cleanings or arrangings which may be done well or badly; so deeply may we read the doctrine of Ideas into our situation. (See George Herbert's poem: 'Teach me my God and King, In all things Thee to see . . .')

Meno 86 B C:

'And if the truth of all things that are is always in our soul, then the soul must be immortal, so you should take courage and whatever you do not happen to know, that is to remember, at present, you must endeavour to discover and recollect . . . I cannot swear to everything I have said in this argument – but one thing I am ready to fight for in word and deed, that we shall be better, braver and more active men if we believe it right to look for what we do not know, than if we think we cannot discover it and have no duty to seek it.'

Plato here indicates that part of what he says is to be taken as an instructive metaphor. See the similar indication at *Republic* 592B. I want to quote again from Stanley Rosen's book *The Quarrel between Philosophy and Poetry*, the chapter on 'Heidegger's interpretation of Plato'.

'The most general way to state the error of Heidegger's interpretation of Plato is by observing that Plato recognises the difference between Being and beings, between the light and what is uncovered or illuminated. For this reason, Plato sought to avoid a speech which would temporalise, objectify, or rationalise Being itself. [Rosen here refers us to *Phaedrus* 229cff.] The openness of Being, as prior to distinctions of beings, particular speeches, kinds of measuring, and the subject–object relationship is the unstated luminosity within which the dialogues are themselves visible. The dialogues become intelligible only when we perceive this unstated luminosity which is directly present as the *silence* of Plato. The spoken voice of the dialogues occurs always within the Cave (if not always in the language of the Cave). We may emerge from this Cave at any instant that we hear the silent accompanying voice of Plato. In my opinion Heidegger goes wrong because he is not sufficiently attentive to the silence of Plato. Still more specifically, he never confronts the significance of Socratic irony or the dramatic form of the dialogues.'

The errors attributed here to Heidegger are shared by many other critics of Plato.

Plato poses almost all the traditional problems of western philosophy and combines them with insights of eastern philosophy. Eastern philosophy was and is intimately connected with religion. In this respect, as well as others, it is, as I suggested earlier, the Platonic view of the cosmos which speaks to our age. Help, 'mediation', can come from understanding a religion without a personal God. Plato of course did not believe in a personal God or gods, and Kant, in ways which are hard to 'track', certainly distances and veils, even negates, the Christian God. Yet both these thinkers are religious, bind religion-morality into the deepest structure of their consciousness, and have influenced Christian theology. The present opposition to religion is at its most dangerous when it argues that the age of Platonic-Kantian western philosophy is now over. The rejection by Nietzsche of both Plato and the Christian tradition represents (symbolises) the effacing of a concept of the divine with which we have travelled a long way through many transformation scenes. Nietzsche was well aware of the enormity of this removal. In *The Gay Science* (*Die Fröhliche Wissenschaft*, *La Gaia Scienza*) III 125 a madman cries out in the market place, 'Where has God gone? ... We have killed him ... How were we able to drink up the sea? Who gave us the sponge to wipe away the whole horizon? What did we do when we unchained this earth from its sun?' Later he says, 'I have come too early.' Many of Nietzsche's beautiful and exuberant writings express an extraordinary joy, and a sense of what is holy. Zarathustra, with his loved and loving animals, is a saintly as well as a frightening prophet. Nietzsche revered Schopenhauer. (See essay 'Schopenhauer as Educator', *Unzeitgemäße Betrachtungen (Untimely Meditations)*.) Schopenhauer's man, Nietzsche tells us, 'voluntarily takes upon himself the pain of telling the truth'. He quotes as Schopenhauer's the view that a happy life is impossible, and man's highest aspiration is to a heroic life. He sees Schopenhauer as a last metaphysician (a place assigned to Heidegger by Derrida). Schopenhauer is however, among the confusions and inconsistencies of his system, an old-fashioned religious writer teaching Christian and Buddhist values of gentleness and compassion, and a selfless humility leading to a mystical goal. He does not idolise heroism. Nietzsche rejects traditional metaphysics ('Christianity is Platonism for the people') with its built-in distinction between phenomenal and noumenal (which can harbour God etc.), and in this respect he may even be called an empiricist. 'Eternal recurrence' implies a rejection of the noumenal as an 'elsewhere' – *everything* is the *finite* contingent jumble of items wherein certain patterns must inevitably recur. (This could also suggest the mysterious significant fullness of every moment.) Absent from Nietzsche's picture is the conception of ordinary virtue. His idea of traditional metaphysics is God by other means, and reality located as elsewhere. He and many others have thus misunderstood Platonism. In fact Plato (more than any other philosopher) 'saves' metaphysics by showing how the noumenal and the phenomenal exist *inside* each human life. There is nowhere else, it is all here. Nietzsche's own 'metaphysic' is a kind of heroic historicism, envisaging a development of the race toward a higher general form of human being, and so of human society, since this change of being can clearly be the property only of a few. This evolution is to be a 'transvaluation of all values', involving a destruction of 'herding-animal morality', democracy ('the autonomous herd'), the religion of 'mutual sympathy' with its 'compassion for all that feels and suffers', and of soft effeminate sentiments 'under the spell of which Europe seems threatened by a new Buddhism'. Man must learn to see the future of humanity as 'his *will*'. (*Beyond Good and Evil* 202–3.) The hubris and sheer *hatred* expressed in these pages is remarkable. Something of the same tone is to be found in Heidegger's 'heroic' contempt for *Alltäglichkeit* (everydayness). A degraded version of the transvaluation was enacted in Hitler's Germany. (Nietzsche's sister was an enthusiastic supporter of Hitler.)

Religion is traditionally about, or is, the change of being attendant upon our deepest and highest concern with morality. How, and whether, we are to distinguish between religion and morality I shall discuss later. Of course, while they are still visible, religious icons are available to all, whatever their beliefs, and innumerable things can serve as icons. The Cave is a religious myth suggesting, what is also accessible to any careful not necessarily philosophical reflection, that there are discernible levels and qualities of *awareness* or *experience* (we need this terminology), which cannot be reduced to acquaintance with neutral factual propositions or analysed in terms of dispositions to act. Of course there are neutral scientific or scholarly or legal disciplines and procedures and states of mind, and these, often to be thought of as ideal limits, are essential and without them we would indeed 'perish and go to ruin'. But they represent one aspect only of the idea of truth, and occupy a smaller area than is sometimes suggested by those who conjure up a vast world of facts in contrast to a small specialised activity of evaluating. Beside the idea of truth as some sort of mechanical accuracy (science is not really like this anyhow) or obvious, and of course necessary, daily reportage (the cat is on the mat), we need a larger idea which can contain, turning toward the individual, ideas of 'truthfulness' and 'wisdom'. This is very obvious, but philosophy is partly a matter of finding appropriate places in which to say the obvious. Plato makes a place for 'metaphorical moral thinking' when he says in the Cave myth that a higher moral level appears to us first, at our own lower level, as an image, reflection or shadow. Our understanding of a higher morality than that which comes easily to us tends to be intuitive and pictorial, we live all the time in semi-pictorial modes of awareness. In fact there are many kinds of reasons why we have private inexplicable unclarified states of consciousness, including picturesque awarenesses of modes of moral (including intellectual and aesthetic) procedures. Sometimes (rightly or wrongly) we judge it better to trust our feeling or intuition, not to examine or analyse too carefully. Theology (east and west) often suggests to us that we can know God only by analogy, in myths, in pictures, through metaphors, in a glass darkly. To speak of Nirvana as nothingness, as the bringing-to-nothingness of our fallen nature, is to use an image. But we need not refer ourselves only to such grand topics in order to become aware that we think about value in a mixture of rational discourse and metaphor. The imagery moreover may be difficult to expose. The novelist may offer hard-edged clarified versions, as in Maggie's image of her dilemma in *The Golden Bowl*. But the images which we use in moral thinking and in other kinds of cognitive reflection may be elusive, allusive, and highly personal.

Tailpiece on Schopenhauer:

'Every work has its origin in a happy thought, and the latter gives the joy of conception; the birth however, the carrying out, is in my own case at least, not without pain; for then I stand before my own soul, like an inexorable judge before a prisoner lying on the rack, and make it answer until there is nothing else to ask. Almost all the errors and unutterable follies of which doctrines and philosophies are so full seem to me to spring from a lack of this probity. The truth was not found, not because it was unsought, but because the intention always was to find again instead some preconceived opinion or other, or at least not to wound some favourite idea, and with this aim in view subterfuges had to be employed against both other people and the thinker himself. It is the courage of making a clean breast of it in face of every question that makes the philosopher. He must be like Sophocles' Oedipus who, seeking enlightenment concerning his terrible fate, pursues his indefatigable enquiry, even when he divines that appalling horror awaits him in the answer. But most of us carry in our hearts the Jocasta who begs Oedipus for God's sake not to enquire further; and we give way to her, and that is the reason why philosophy stands where it does.'

(His letter to Goethe, 11 November 1815.)

Quoted by Ferenczi (*First Contributions to Psycho-analysis*, p. 253), who says: 'The deep and compressed wisdom of these remarks deserves to be discussed and to be compared with the results of psychoanalysis.' Also (quoted by Hollingdale in his book, *Nietzsche*, pp. 44 & 51): Nietzsche read *The World as Will and Idea* in Leipzig in 1865: 'I threw myself onto the sofa with the newly-won treasure and began to let that energetic and gloomy genius operate upon me . . . Here I saw a mirror in which I beheld the world, life and my own nature in a terrifying grandeur . . . here I saw sickness and health, exile and refuge, Hell and Heaven.'

# > 7 <
# Derrida and Structuralism

The origins of structuralism (post-structuralism, deconstruction, modernism, post-modernism) are to be found in anthropology (Lévi-Strauss) and in linguistics (Saussure), but (as it has affected the second half of the twentieth century) the doctrine is mainly the property or creation of Jacques Derrida, and its influence and effects are to be understood through his ideas. It has been widely dispersed (often in simplified and cruder versions) among literary critics, and to a lesser extent among historians and sociologists. It does not seem in general to be using philosophical arguments. Derrida, who calls Heidegger the last metaphysician, is declaring the end of philosophy as we know it and the beginning of a *new thinking*. Heidegger also believed that *he* was doing just this. Structuralist discourse can sound like science. (I heard an adherent, when asked to explain it, compare it to physics as something which could not be expounded to the laity.) It also seems like metaphysics, in its use of metaphorical structures and equations set up, as it were, by decree: that is, a new-style 'metaphysics', not in the argumentative tradition of Plato and Aristotle. Again, as in the case of Heidegger and Nietzsche, there is hostility to Plato, friendship with the presocratics. As a doctrine it might be called Linguistic Idealism, Linguistic Monism, or Linguistic Determinism, since it presents a picture of the individual as submerged in language, rather than as an autonomous user of language. Much structuralist argument (or decree) appeals to plausibly reinforced or dramatised half-truths or truisms: such as our realisation that *of course* we are influenced by innumerable forces which are beyond our control and of which we are unconscious *and so* should come to see as illusions many aspects of our being in which we have had naive belief. This particular contention is indeed not new, but is used by Derrida more persuasively in an atmosphere engendered by recent science. The period between the formation of Wittgenstein's later ideas in the thirties and forties and the emergence of structuralism in the fifties and sixties was one in which the techniques of science (computers, data bases, artificial intelligence) began with remarkable speed to enter the lives and awareness of ordinary people. One measure of this might be that earlier in the century we could not have conceived of the total disappearance of books. (And Wittgenstein was certain that we could not fly to the moon.) Kierkegaard said that philosophy is like sewing, you must knot the thread. A fundamental starting point is required. This view, not shared by all philosophers, may or may not be a good one. An idea which sheds much light may also effectively obliterate other ideas. Movement of philosophical thought is slow, it takes a long time to work out a deep insight. *Cogito ergo sum* (certainly a fundamental and revolutionary starting point) has only lately been attacked and discarded. This 'move' represents indeed one of the most important elements in recent philosophy. However, the thinkers who have rejected Descartes have done so in ways which significantly differ. It may be said of Sartre that he was one of the last Cartesians (though he 'officially' denied being one). 'The *cogito*' was finally rejected because it set up as ultimate the problem of how 'the mind' related to the real world, how inner could ever reach outer. This is now seen (variously) as a pseudo-problem. Religious existentialism (Kierkegaard, Gabriel Marcel), explaining or studying the individual in a moral light, dissolved the problem in man's fundamental original relationship to God (a new individual in a new relationship). In fact, Descartes also dissolved his own problem in that way (as I discuss later) but without removing or undermining the much more obvious and famous primal declaration. Sartre never (in *L'Etre et le Néant*) really parts company with this declaration, his 'hero', *être-pour-soi*, living constantly with the problem of how to relate to the alien *être-en-soi*.

Wittgenstein, Heidegger and Derrida are all anti-Cartesian (Wittgenstein said his work brought the Cartesian era to an end) but with different methods and conclusions. They agree in rejecting the philosophical concept of the autonomous 'I' which discovers one primal immediate truth in its momentary present experience. ('This *at least* is indubitably true.') Argument against this position will go along lines of saying that there can be no such thing as momentary knowledge, knowledge requires concepts which develop in an extended 'world' and cannot be the property of an instant flash of awareness. How do I reach the world? You are in the world, it is your world. (For this relief much thanks.) But what does this mean and what exactly follows? Derrida, in placing Heidegger as 'last metaphysician', attacks particularly what he calls the 'metaphysics of presence', the use of concepts of present being, consciousness, experience. He, Derrida, following 'logical' implications of the rejection of *cogito*, concludes that if there can be no solitary knower (since knowledge and meaning depend on conceptual networks, that is language) then there can, really, be no knower, only a network of meanings (the infinitely great net of language itself) under which there is nothing. (See a philosophical discussion of these matters in my first novel, *Under the Net*.) Because of the vast extent of language and the way in which meanings of words and concepts are determined by innumerable relationships with other words and concepts, no individual speaker can really 'know' what he means, we are *unconscious* of the immense linguistic beyond which we think that we 'use' when really it is using us. That is, in rejecting Descartes' *argument*, Derrida rejects *also* the *concept* of the autonomous individual; and with it the (ordinary) concept of truth. Derrida shares with Wittgenstein the 'discovery' (made earlier by the latter) that words are not names of things, predeterminedly affixed to particular objects (the fallacy which Derrida calls 'logocentrism'), but have meaning through relations with other words. But Wittgenstein would add that meaning comes through use and forms of life, presumed to be, in a common-sense sense, the local property of individuals. Wittgenstein offers no further theory here. The individual is 'saved' by (early) Heidegger in the concept of *Dasein* taken as primary, human being, or human reality, thrown into a world and existing immediately in it *as* its relations to it. *Dasein* (being-there) is *In-der-Welt-sein* (being-in-the-world). Thus the old Cartesian problem is thrown away. The Heidegger of *Sein und Zeit* has been called an existentialist, and is certainly a defender of (takes as his 'main character') the existing individual. He calls this individual the Shepherd of Being, the creator of spaces and clearings where Being (as in some sense transcendent truth and reality) can manifest itself. (This imagery can be readily understood in religious or aesthetic terms.) Later Heidegger seems to reverse the roles, picturing man more as the victim of Being than its shepherd. (Being plays its own secret game.) In the *Tractatus* Wittgenstein 'saves' the individual by metaphysical decree: 'I am my world.' I discuss later what happens in the *Investigations*.

Saussure separated language conceived of as a general system from its particular local use by individuals. He retained however the idea (which belongs with 'presence', consciousness, experience) that speech, not writing, was the basis of language and meaning. Plato expresses this intuition in the *Phaedrus* and the *Seventh Letter*. Spoken words are understood in their proper meaning in the *presence* of the recipient. In the *Seventh Letter* Plato seems to speak particularly of philosophical conversation, but the parable in the *Phaedrus* (274ff.) can apply to all speech; as opposed to speech, writing cannot answer back, may be misunderstood, is at a remove from original meaning. It is a secondary technique. Saussure agreed; real speech and clear meaning belong to speaking persons. Derrida reverses this. What is primary is writing, thought of in a (metaphysical) sense as a vast system or sign structure whereby meaning is determined by a mutual relationship of signs which transcends the localised talk of individual speakers. This postulated transcendent, or basic, language Derrida calls *archi-écriture* or 'primal writing'. We make use of local codes which derive from an area of similarities and differences which transcends our awareness. In this sense language speaks us. Derrida has fortified his theory by inventing the word *différance*, a variant of ordinary French *différence* which means 'difference'. The verb *différer* means to differ, and also to defer, and Derrida's coinage includes both meanings. That which determines meaning, since it is a function of the vast linguistic region of *archi-écriture*, is something infinitely deferred; any meaning is marked by 'traces' left by other, perhaps extremely remote, similarities and differences. So in an important sense we are not in control of our meaning, we are *unconscious* of how language itself, at a deeper level, makes meaning. We do not know what we are uttering. This image of the whole of language determining every part of it is awesome and impressive. It may undermine our confidence in what we took to be our 'mastery of language' and our ability to say anything clearly, or to say what is *true*. Here truism, half-truth, and shameless metaphysics join to deceive us. Yes, of course language is a huge transcendent structure, stretching infinitely far away out of our sight, and yes, when we reflect, we realise that often we cannot say quite what we mean or do not quite know what we mean. Common-sense does not usually take the trouble to reflect as far as this, or if it has done so realises that nothing is really being changed and meaning and truth are what they have always seemed. (A study of philosophy may be likened to a catharsis, like that of the Zen Buddhist who begins with rivers and mountains, doubts rivers and mountains, then returns to rivers and mountains.) Suppose we worry about the discovery that our tables and chairs are made of atoms. We are being frightened by a picture, in the case of tables and chairs a scientific picture, in the case of *archi-écriture* a metaphysical picture. Anyway (if we want to proceed) we may ask, if all that is so, how does Derrida know what he means? The answer rests in the technique of 'deconstruction', which it must be assumed the theorist can apply not only to others but to himself. This is a technique, most generally on view in literary criticism, whereby texts are minutely studied in a manner which reveals deep meanings of which the writer is unaware. This may seem fair enough. Literary critics, especially since Freud, may do this as part of their general task, and writers, as ordinary human beings, might agree that their 'text' can be shown to indicate (for instance) prejudices of which they were less than fully aware. This would be compatible with what is expected of a literary critic who would, we hope, be a well-read scholarly person, with wide tastes and a knowledge of languages and history, who appreciates and *enjoys* all kinds of literature and is able to write about it with insight and balanced judgment. But 'deconstruction' is something more radical and no friend of the old-fashioned or traditional critic just described. Our whole concept of what literature *is* is here in question. This *quest* for the hidden deep (primal-language) meaning of the *text* (to use the jargon) is now said to be the main and essential part of the critic's task. The 'old', and in my view good, proper, literary critic, approaches a literary work in an open-minded manner and is interested in it in *all sorts of ways*: which certainly does not exclude treating a tale as a 'window into another world', reacting to characters as if they were real people, making value judgments about them, about how their creator treats them, and so on. Here the enjoyment, or otherwise, of the critic is *like* that of the layman, only generally (one hopes) well informed and guided by a respect and love for literature and a liberal-minded *sense of justice*. He will beware suitably of his own prejudices, but will not be chary of speaking his mind. Literary critics are speaking as *individuals* and not as scientists speak. Literature is a vast scene of confusion, that is of freedom. Of course, critics who

[ 189 ]

say that they are 'deconstructionists' often felicitously lapse into the 'old habits'. But the ideal deconstructionist is more like a scientist who shows that things are *absolutely not* what they seem (they really are made of atoms). He will tell us that the literary object, as we have hitherto understood it, is pure phenomenon, below which lies something quite different from what its naive creator believed and intended, or what the naive reader imagines he perceives. In fact the *real* work of literature is what the *critic* produces. The deconstructed work is the real work.

The notion that every sentence we use bears, indeed consists of, the invisible *traces* of other meanings created by a vast non-human *system*, carries serious implications. We seem to be losing our concept of the individual. Literature, as we ordinarily see it, is full of values, and we the clients receive it as such and consider it in the light of our values. The consumption of literature involves continual (usually instinctive) evaluation, of characters in stories, content and quality of poems, skill and intentions of authors, etc. etc. etc. Value, morality, is removed by the structuralist picture if taken seriously. This removal of value is, in a quiet way, characteristic of this age. Heidegger's book *What is Metaphysics?* is partly concerned with showing how the general idea of value (morals) is a superficial phenomenon. Behind this new 'revaluation of all values' by Heidegger and by Derrida lies the (metaphysical) concept of a vast superhuman area of control: Heidegger's later concept of Being, and Derrida's theory of Language. These systems represent new forms of determinism. Determinism is always reappearing in new forms since it satisfies a deep human wish: to *give up*, to get rid of freedom, responsibility, remorse, all sorts of personal individual unease, and surrender to fate and the relief of 'it could not be otherwise'.

Derrida, trying to explain his idea of *archi-écriture*, admits that:

'*Quant au concept d'expérience, il est ici fort embarrassant. Comme toutes les notions dont nous nous servons ici, il appartient à l'histoire de la métaphysique et nous ne pouvons l'utiliser que sous rature. "Expérience" a toujours désigné le rapport à une présence, que ce rapport ait ou non la forme de la conscience. Nous devons toutefois, selon cette sort de contorsion et de contention à laquelle le discours est ici obligé, épuiser les ressources du concept d'expérience avant et afin de l'atteindre, par déconstruction, en son dernier fond. C'est la seule condition pour échapper à la fois à "l'empirisme" et aux critiques "naïves" de l'expérience. Ainsi, par exemple, l'expérience dont "la théorie", dit Hjelmslev, "doit être indépendente" n'est pas tout de l'expérience. Elle correspond toujours à un certain type d'expérience factuelle ou régionale (historique, psychologique, physiologique, sociologique etc.), donnant lieu à une science elle-même régionale, et, en tant que telle, rigoureusement extérieure à la linguistique. Il n'en est rien dans le cas de l'expérience comme archi-écriture. La mise entre parenthèses des régions de l'expérience ou de la totalité de l'expérience naturelle doit découvrir un champ d'expérience transcendantale.'*

(*De la Grammatologie*, published 1967, p. 89.)

'As for the concept of experience, it is certainly an embarrassment here. Like all the ideas we are dealing with, it belongs to the history of metaphysics and we can only make use of it under erasure. [*Sous rature.*] "*Experience*" has always indicated a relationship to something present, whether or not this relation takes the form of consciousness. We must always, in accordance with the contortions and contentions which our discourse is here obliged to adopt, exhaust the resources of the concept of experience, before, and with the intention of, reaching, by deconstruction, its deep foundation. This is the only way in which we can keep clear both of "empiricism" and of "naive" accounts of experience. For example, when Hjelmslev speaks of an experience "the theory of which must be independent", the experience in question is not the whole of experience. It always corresponds to some particular type of factual or regional experience (historical, psychological, physio-logical, sociological, etc.), occasioning a science which is itself regional, and as such strictly outside the domain of linguistics. This is not the case with experience conceived as *archi-écriture*. The putting into brackets of regions of experience, or of the totality of natural experi-ence, must uncover a transcendental field of experience.'

(Hjelmslev, a follower and critic of Saussure,
*Prolegomena to a Theory of Language*, 1943, trans. 1953.)

This passage (taken out of context but I think fundamentally informative) refers to Derrida's programme for a transcendental deduc-tion. His theory follows Kant and Husserl in seeking to uncover an all-inclusive 'transcendental field', actualising Husserl's dream of a philosophical discovery more radical than any science. This field or network is sought in language, not in local individual uses, but in the postulated primal language system. This system is not in any ordinary sense experienced, nor can it be indicated by traditional metaphysical concepts of experience; its discovery involves a *deconstruction* of 'experience' so radical that the concept can only be used *sous rature*, under erasure. This 'embarrassing' device, of using a crossed-out word, is intended to alert us to an unusual, stripped, deconstructed sense of a concept which no better words can at present be found to exhibit. It is a term of art designed to be stronger and more specialised than what is often achieved by putting a word in inverted commas. This 'contortion' should enable us, alerted, to avoid thinking of *archi-écriture* either naively, as something we can be at some moment 'aware of', or in terms of traditional empiricism, say of the Kantian or Humian or 'ordinary language' variety. To understand what *archi-écriture* means we are not to think about ordinary, personal and local, everyday experience, nor about any historical, psychological, sociological or (previous) philosophical explanations or analyses of such experience. The totality of these regional and natural experiences, whether naive or worked by science, must be set aside or put in 'parenthesis' (a concept borrowed from Husserl) if the deep basic transcendental field is to be found. Well, philosophy is to some extent a foreign tongue. The deconstructed field of *archi-écriture* is uncovered by the post Saussurian analysis of 'language' as basic (non-individual, non-experienced) human activity. Saussure, as an aid to thinking about language, made a distinction between *parole*, actual historical and various speech uses, and *langue*, the abstract notion of language as, at any given moment, a single system. Language as system, the subject matter of a possible semiology or science of signs, was said by Saussure to rest upon two intimately related ideas or principles. Linguistic signs are arbitrary, words are not names vertically posed upon pre-existing, already fixed (as if by God), things or qualities, this is not how language has meaning. Language has meaning through lateral horizontal networks or group-ings of signs related by systematic differences. Both these ideas, that words are not names and that concepts gain sense through use in relational groups, have been expressed by Wittgenstein and belong to a rejection of Cartesian or Humian starting points which is common to modern philosophies. Saussure, who still thought that a sign or signifier should signify or point to something signified, detached verbal signs from a one–one naming connection with entities in the world, and attached them instead to mental concepts in the mind. Wittgenstein (I discuss his view later) attacked ideas of meaning as mental process, or use of private 'inner contents', suggesting that there were many ways in which language related to the world, that concepts (meaning) depended on public rules and forms of life. He pointed out mistakes but did not create a general counter-theory. At a certain point he left things alone. Saussure's structuralist successors also pointed out that the same error (that of assuming entities of definite predetermined quality) was committed by postulating inner things instead of outer things. They then made a further step, not made by Wittgenstein, in deciding that therefore the *signified*, whether thought of as external entity or mental datum, was otiose, and that *meaning* was entirely enclosed in the self-referential system of language. This is the crucial move which, in the structuralist theory, separates meaning from truth, outlaws the idea that truth rests on some kind of relation with a non-linguistic reality, and in effect removes the concept of truth altogether. The removal from language of any reference except to other parts of language sweeps away not only the correspondence theory, but any theory, of truth. Meaning, then, is an internally self-related movement or *play* of language. *Le jeu des signifiants*. The word 'play' (or 'game'), often used by structuralists (and by late Heidegger and by the presocratic philosophers), is here seen in a fundamental context. Here 'language' must of course not be thought of in terms of effective individual usages, but as a postulated totality of system which transcends these. What is 'transcendent' is not the world, but the great sea of language itself which cannot be dominated by the individuals who move or play in it, and who do not speak or use language, but are spoken or used by it. This is the 'transcendental field' which is revealed when 'experience', as something regional or natural, is put in brackets. On this view, almost all language-use is an unconscious subjection to system. Only at some points (in the activity of some minds) can language be seen to emerge as *conscious play*. Such playing of self-aware system could be either science or art. The central structuralist ideas, closely integrated with each other, could be said to be aspects of the same idea. It is interesting to see how a number of half-truths, which might be expressed as intelligent suggestive hermeneutic observations about language, are made into what appears to be a closely knit metaphysical argument. Of course, in an obvious sense, language transcends its user, meanings are ambiguous, words are clarified through discrimination, and so on. But the amassing of such general considerations is remote from a conclusion to the effect that 'really' no final statement which can be said to be true or false is ever made. Here, as in other metaphysical 'totalities', system obliterates a necessary recognition of the contingent. What is left out of the picture, magically blotted out by a persuasive knitting-together of ideas and terminology, is that statements are made, propositions are uttered, by individual incarnate persons in particular extra-linguistic situations, and it is in the whole of this larger context that our familiar and essential concepts of *truth* and *truthfulness* live and work. 'Truth' is inseparable from individual contextual human *responsibilities*. The ingenious continuous weave of structuralist gener-alisation checks reflection at the point where it should be most industri-ous, and makes important problems invisible and so undiscussable by removing familiar distinctions and landmarks. Structuralism can be attractive because it seems to exhibit or point out much that is new in our now so fast-moving world; and so it can look like the perennial philosophical study of conceptual change. But structuralist theory dis-ables this study (and in this respect indeed can claim to have parted from traditional philosophy) by its removal of the 'old' idea of truth and truth-seeking as moral value. If all meaning is deferred our ordi-nary distinctions, for instance between what is clearly true and what is dubious and what is false, are removed and we begin to lose confi-dence (as structuralists urge us to do) in what is made to seem the simple, old-fashioned, ordinary concept of truth and its *related moral-ity*. If, in some 'deep sense', it cannot be finally established whether or not the cat is on the mat, then how can we have the energy to trouble ourselves about the truth or falsity of more obscure and difficult mat-ters? In this frame of mind we may feel that we can understand and welcome this new doctrine as 'the philosophy' of our age, and embrace the idea of language as stirring 'play' whereby we are incited to discover 'meanings' which are independent of truth. We can see at this point how naturally structuralism preys upon literature and indeed inspires a new kind of literature which seems to prove its point. Literary forms, *fictions*, *texts*, recognised as such, exhibit the ways in which language, no longer thought of as a 'picture of reality', can liberate the mind into a creative enjoyment of unfettered meanings. (Of course this game may produce good writing, but need not obliterate all other literary forms!) Not the least damage done by the doctrine is that students spend their time studying the very obscure books which propound it, rather than reading the great works of literature.

The structuralist view cannot be called a 'coherence theory of truth' in any traditional philosophical sense, although it makes ingenious use of the idea of coherence. Hegelian and Bradleian coherence theories point, as does Kant's 'Kingdom of Ends', toward some sort of moral ideal situation where adjustment and development of partial truths emerge into an ideal harmony which alone is entirely true. Scholarship, science, art, everyday life, involve searching for coherence ('making sense of things') and dealing suitably with the innumerable contingent elements which impede, divert, or inspire the search. This is an abstract description of what we are doing all the time. The metaphysical deification of truth in coherence theories derives its plausibility from the recognisable *moral effort* demanded by the continued search for coherence. Because of the endlessly contingent nature of our existence this quest can never reach a 'totalised' conclusion. The conscientious historian (to take an example which can serve as an image for other cases) goes on trying to make sense of heterogeneous data, to understand and illuminate the separate pieces by classifying them, placing them, at a proper moment and not prematurely, into groups and systems. He continually notes, draws attention to and returns to, the recalcitrant incoherent pieces which refuse to fit in. These may be the pieces which will alter his method of assembly, refute one of his theories, inspire him to invent a more truthful way of looking. This is like what we all do when reflecting on a moral problem, and indeed intuitively in all our thinking. These important incoherent contingent stumbling blocks are of course loved by artists, both as sources of inspiration in the process of creation and as deliberately alien items in finished works. The piece which is 'nothing to do with' the story or pattern may perform various functions, such as being a reminder that there is another world outside the work of art. This device should be used judiciously. Art which is nothing but such reminders ceases to be art. Art is a cunning mixture of coherence and incoherence, necessary and contingent, systematic and absurd. Ordinary-life truth-seeking, a certain level of which is essential for survival, is a swift instinctive testing of innumerable kinds of coherence against innumerable kinds of *extralinguistic* data. The (essential) idea of 'correspondence' is in place, not as a rival theory of truth, but as representing the fundamental fact and feel of the constant comparison and contrast of language with a non-linguistic world, with a reality not yet organised for present needs and purposes. Of course we are constantly conceptualising what confronts us, 'making' it into meaning, into language. But what we encounter remains free, ambiguous, endlessly contingent, and *there*. In our meeting with it we 'create' truth and falsehood. This local and regional and individual 'organisation' is the stuff of our continuous local and regional and individual conscious being. Use of ordinary verbal language, even in a fragmentary manner, composes of course only a part of our thinking and consciousness. We can use non-verbal, such as musical, mathematical, scientific, technological, systematic languages. We can also be said to think or use concepts in all sorts of perceptual and 'feeling' states where no systematic language is present; indeed (probably) most conscious states are of this kind. This will include the 'field of perceptions' which Schopenhauer accused Kant of ignoring. The boundaries of what may be called 'conscious awareness' or 'consciousness' are hazy, and some of these outer areas are more easily suggested by novelists and poets than analytically described by philosophers; but should nevertheless be recognised, and talked about somehow, by the latter. Empirical observations and tautologies will here, as in other difficult regions, lie close together. If we want to call any conceptualising awareness, that is any conscious awareness, a kind of language, we may also want to say that language depends on some kind of coherence. So a coherence theory of truth need not be only about systematic languages, and any piece of coherence may be thought of as a little system which postulates a larger one. What makes metaphysical ('totalising') coherence theories unacceptable is the way in which they in effect 'disappear' what is individual and contingent by equating reality with integration in system, and degrees of reality with degrees of integration, and by implying that 'ultimately' or 'really' there is only one system. Hegel's philosophy as expressed in the *Phenomenology of Mind* implies this; though it also contradicts itself by so evidently not being that system, by exercising and suggesting so many various modes of thought and truth-seeking, and by sending the fascinated reader's reflections flying away in all sorts of directions. Of course a metaphysical system is not supposed to be a literal report of how things are, it must be judged as a big complicated heuristic image. But however much we may learn from, or be inspired to think by, such a system we must also be prepared to take it as a whole seriously enough to judge it in relation to our own experience of living in the world which it professes to explain. McTaggart says time is unreal, Moore says he has had his breakfast. Perhaps Moore had not 'really tried' to understand McTaggart, and clearly Dr Johnson, when he refuted Berkeley by kicking a stone, had not 'really tried' to understand Berkeley, but these 'accusations' are pertinent and must be dealt with. Kant's system, unlike that of Hegel, recognises our unavoidable encounter with what is contingent and alien, and the persistently incomplete nature of our moral and theoretical aspirations. Metaphysical systems have consequences. Those who think that the individual has reality only through the system do not only sit in studies, they sit in places of political power. Political systems break against individuals, but may also break individuals, which it is easier to do now than in the days of Hobbes.

Structuralism, seen in this larger context as siding with the system against the individual, may be called 'linguistic idealism' or 'linguistic monism'. Derrida says that Heidegger is the last metaphysician, but structuralism does look like another not uninteresting, not uninfluential metaphysic. It claims a break with traditional philosophy, and is certainly unlike philosophy in that it is short of philosophical arguments and of the kind of extended careful lucid explanatory talk and use of relevant examples which good philosophy, however systematic, includes and consists of. But it has a rhetorical power which depends on an impressive image or set of images, 'language' as fundamental system, written not spoken, a totality to be enjoyed without external verification, etc.; and may, like other metaphysics, be treated as a kind of pragmatism or aesthetic guide. It looks more like traditional metaphysics than like science. Here the old idea of a total coherence is used to inspire a way of life which excludes the value of individually establishable truths or truth-seeking, the 'regional' and 'local' activities of our present consciousnesses, and in effect excludes value in favour of 'play'. As such it may be welcomed by clever people who are, perhaps understandably as they survey the present world, fed up with 'all the old solutions'. Here too there is a convergence, paradoxical at first sight, with Marxism. That distinctly Utopian theory relied upon a weave of internally related specialised terminology only rather roughly and in very general terms seeming to *describe* the world, but used with skilled and urgent intent to *change* it. In practice Marxist theory has been constantly modified by ordinary moral motives including utilitarian ones and by being forced to attend to locally establishable truths of various ordinary kinds relying on reference to a non-theorised world. It was inspired by, and certainly professed, moral ideals. Structuralism poses as a neutral quasi-scientific theory. Marxism was a theory of history which used historical evidence established by traditional methods to support its world-view. An aspect of structuralism is to regard history as *fabulation*, and 'the past' as a meaning-construct belonging to the present. It is, and admittedly, rhetoric versus reason. Of course we cannot *see* the past, so we must be thought of as inventing it. This fake choice blots out the conception of seeking carefully for some truthful conception of the past. Marxism and (Derrida's) structuralism can join forces however in their rejection of God and religion and their hostility to 'bourgeois' views and values, seen as solidifying a view of the world which new revolutionary forces must now destroy. Happily, since I wrote the above, the *Zeitgeist*, assisted by very many courageous individuals, has discredited and is demolishing Marxism. One of the first things which liberated people want to know is the truth about their past.

Structuralists, like their predecessors the surrealists, aim at shocking and frightening us. They draw attention to changes, technological changes for instance, by which indeed we *ought* to be shocked and frightened. A decent society will, by innumerable pressures from its free and various components, be forced to struggle with such matters as part of its natural moral development. Art changes, class changes, religion changes, technology changes. A live, free, decent society changes. What perhaps we *should*, however, in our great technological era and on our smaller and more vulnerable planet, be *afraid of* might be described as a sort of plausible amoralistic determinism, something which lies at a deeper level than that of our soluble social problems. I shall return to structuralism as determinism shortly, what I want to indicate at this point is something less (one should say even less) tangible, a kind of instinctual debased Taoism, arising in a period of exceptional scientific and technological progress and popular scientific knowledge, a relaxed acceptance as ultimate of a deep impersonal world-rhythm which overcomes the awkward dichotomies between good and evil and one individual and another. A sort of neo-Taoism is also part of a popular metaphysic of our time. In his book *The Tao of Physics*, Fritjof Capra suggests similarities between presocratic and Taoist views of the cosmos, and those of modern physics.

'The final apprehension of the unity of all things . . . is reached – so the mystics tell us – in a state of consciousness where one's individuality dissolves into an undifferentiated oneness, where the world of the senses is transcended and the notion of "things" is left behind . . . Modern physics . . . cannot go that far in the experience of the unity of all things. But it has made a great step toward the world view of the Eastern mystics in atomic theory. Quantum physics has abolished the notion of fundamentally separated objects, has introduced the concept of the participator to replace that of the observer, and may even find it necessary to include the human consciousness in its description of the world.'

(Chapter 10.)

Structuralism is deeply motivated by an appreciation of languages of science and technology, which seem to undermine our ordinary language and its 'naive' truth values. Such scientific languages can also be seen as more genuinely universal (for instance international). They are written not spoken. Speech is regional, local, full of accidents. *Archi-écriture* is also to be thought of (postulated) as 'written' not spoken, and as, in the scientific sense of deep, deep. This is the '*écriture*' celebrated by Derrida in his chapter-heading, *la fin du livre, et le commencement de l'écriture* (the end of books, and the beginning of writing). 'Taoism' is of course a very general name for a vast region of religious and metaphysical theory and social practice. I am speaking of it now as a view referred to in recent western books about oriental religion, and as an idea, connected with moderation and harmony and the coexistence of opposites, which seems to have some kinship with the moods and theories of this age. One can readily see how multiform and ambiguous such an idea is. Opposites, or alleged opposites, good and evil, or Yin and Yang, can be thought of as enemies, or as demanding an achievable harmony. There is a half-truth here also. Why not peace instead of war? Compromise is rational. Love your darkness. Integrate your personality. Why become neurotic by attempting to reach impossible moral goals? There may be a place for saying such things; but it does not follow (the leap from particularised common-sense to metaphysics) that good and evil are false abstractions from a better and more real harmony. All sorts of separate neutral, or

[ 199 ]

ordinary, or innocent, or proper things can be seized upon as evidences or motives for a general theory suited to our time, and claimed as fundamental: popular physics, space travel, sexual liberation, the decline of dogmatic religion. The Taoist concepts as used by Jung are also effectively normative; old abstract God-supported good and evil are to be 'overcome' in the interest of a deeper understanding of reality, a spiritual harmony which makes a better (more integrated, less confused, therefore happier) person. Structuralism is supposed to be morally neutral, its transcendental deduction to resemble, *mutatis mutandis*, that of Husserl, its primal writing to suggest physics rather than the hand of God. One may however presume that a certain proud 'authenticity' is to be achieved by those who are no longer duped by outmoded ideas. In effect structuralism is anti-religious, the idea of 'God' being connected with old 'logocentric' ideas of divinely established pre-linguistic meanings. It is also non-moral, since it erases the idea of truthfulness and the common-sense idea of freedom which goes with it, while offering no morally higher sense in which we abandon one truth in order to find another, or abandon God in favour of a differently conceived moral and spiritual mode of understanding.

The structuralist argument requires an assumption that, given that language is not anchored to the world by old logocentric one–one correspondences, it cannot be anchored at all. Any sophisticated reflection on language can suggest to us that it consists of various internally related systems of discrimination, that words cohere together in groups, that the group modifies the meaning of its members. Development of language and vocabulary is systematic discrimination of conceptual groupings, and observation of this process reveals the incompletely determined and shifting nature of verbal concepts. Using language is indeed not like discovering the once-for-all name of a predetermined eternally existing entity whose name this is. Translation between natural languages, or between variant areas in one's own language, is difficult because one language-system may generate words, concepts, which the other lacks. We may introduce a concept (*chic* for instance) by borrowing a word, or by modifying the meaning of existing words. 'Smart' gains something from having *chic* as a neighbour. A language which has no word for (concept of) mauve or purple, has a different concept of blue from a language which has. (And so on and so on.) Language-using is a continuous generation and modification of conceptual groupings and sub-systems. Structuralism presses its advantage here by suggesting that since meaning can be seen to depend on systematic relationships of pieces, we cannot say that any word has a determinate meaning, since its meaning is to be understood by a relation to the (postulated) whole of language. Common-sense here says, Wait a moment, we can see lots of little systems, but we can't see any big general one, and anyway, words surely have definite meanings when we apply them in *particular contexts*. If this were not so we couldn't distinguish true from false. To make a picture of the structuralist hypothesis we may observe how Saussure's distinction between *langue*, language postulated as a system complete at any given moment, and *parole*, the ordinary and various uses of actual human speech, has been taken over into a form of neo-Hegelian idealism. Saussure's abstract heuristic distinction is intended to assist our thinking about language by allowing us to consider it *as if* it were a whole motionless non-historical non-local sign-system, and to separate such thinking from other kinds of scientific, sociological, psychological, etc. study of language. How helpful this hypothetical image is to our reflections about language, and whether there could be or is a viable science of Saussurian semiology, is open to discussion. The *langue–parole* distinction, properly a tool of linguistic specialists, has been popularised in structuralist argument as in some way establishing a general removal of language from 'the world', and thereby also the removal, as otiose, of 'the world'. What language 'does' is then explained partly in terms of its evident aesthetic fictional self-referential 'play', and partly in terms of its even more evident existence as preformed 'codes', the useful blunted shorthand of everyday life, a linguistic (and thereby fundamental) form of Hume's 'habits and customs'. Here the idea of the Freudian unconscious is also put into service. All human activity, except that of exceptional and original persons, is based on networks of uncriticised assumptions and deep unconscious drives and patterns.

Here we return to *archi-écriture* as the metaphysical basis of our entire 'human reality', thought of as writing, not as speech, since speech is uttered in present moments by individual local historical incarnate speakers. We have been (we are told) profoundly mistaken in assuming that speech is in some profound sense prior to writing and represents a more direct and unambiguous communication. We must allow ourselves to be influenced by reflection upon languages of science, 'natural language' is not the only language of the planet, the language of physics, for instance, may be, if we really think about it, felt to be more fundamental. Our ordinary 'consciousness' of a separately existent external world of extra-linguistic entities is shown, in this light, to be an illusion. There are no 'in-themselves' signifieds sitting about awaiting our attention, there are only mutually related signifiers. Indeed nothing 'really' (*deeply*) exists except a sea or play of language of whose profound or sole reality 'we' may be more or less aware as we follow unconscious codes or join in the lively playful creative movements of the linguistic totality which transcends us. Of course there is much novelty, scholarship, brilliance, to be seen in the structuralist compound. What is objectionable is the damage done to other modes of thinking and to literature by the presentation of this fanciful metaphysic as a fundamental system. Philosophy, anthropology, history, literature, have different procedures and methods of verification. It is only when the idea of truth as relation to separate reality is removed that they can seem in this odd hallucinatory light to be similar. With the idea of truth the idea of value also vanishes. Here the deep affinity, the holding hands under the table, between structuralism and Marxism becomes intelligible. Not to explain the world but to change it, not to seek painstakingly to establish a disconnected variety of alleged facts about the past, not to attempt an impossible bits-and-pieces illusory truthfulness, but to stir the imagination to a unified grasp of what is 'really significant', what is 'relevant'. Marxists also attacked bourgeois morality, religion, and the concept of the individual.

Well, *what* about truth? What about morality and responsibility and individuals? And what about ordinary consciousness and experience and presence and uses of language in contingent situations? One feels here, live and kicking in the tired modern soul, burdened by all sorts of abstract and scientific theorising, the indignation of Kierkegaard against Hegel. Something is lost, the existing incarnate individual with his real particular life of thoughts and perceptions and moral living. This naive reaction needs to be philosophically justified, and it is a merit of structuralism to indicate to us, with so much energy and so much learning, that the concept of the individual which we have inherited from centuries of thinkers cannot any longer be taken for granted but must be defended. The plausibility of structuralist theory relies, as I have suggested, upon an interwoven assemblage of generalised half-truths, often inspired by proper reactions and arguments against old false philosophical assumptions. Of course language is relational and systematic, it depends on public rules not only on individual utterance, works of art are not simply what their authors 'mean by them', religious myths cannot be taken literally, we may have 'unconscious motives', history is not a photograph of the past, we can only explain things in terms which are accessible and significant now, languages of science reveal a form of reality quite unlike 'ordinary experience', and so on. These doctrinal attitudes are part of our new consciousness as inhabitants of this planet in this time, part of a new recognition of our limitations and difficulties, deep and various discernments which separate us from past thinkers now seen as naive or mistaken. Moreover, and however, these large insights so curtly listed above are not definite discoveries established once and for all, they are the initiations of numbers of different arguments and modes of reflection. They belong to different disciplines and universes of discourse and are not easily related to one another. It is improbable that they can all be linked up into a philosophical theory; particularly one which uses the linkage to deny so many common-sense and traditional conceptions concerning persons, morality and truth. It is no doubt characteristic of metaphysical systems, and can as I have said be one of their uses, to fly in the face of common-sense. What is 'commonsensical', the 'natural standpoint', changes and should change in response to just such challenges. Meanwhile, and also rightly, other non-philosophical thinkers, scientists, scholars, artists, continue their separate activities without worrying about whether or not time is unreal or language refers to the world. I have been describing structuralism as a (sort of) 'metaphysic' because it is the best way of indicating what we are confronted with. However it is not really philosophy. It is certainly not science in any ordinary sense. The basic tenets fail to be intelligible in a way similar to that in which the tenets of old-fashioned, or new-fashioned, determinism fail to be intelligible; and structuralism is in effect a new-fashioned determinism. As a philosophical theory, as contrasted with a theological view or an assumption of popular science or an emotional intuition about fate, determinism fails because it is unstateable. However far we impinge (for instance for legal or moral purposes) upon the area of free will we cannot philosophically exhibit a situation in which, instead of shifting, it vanishes. The phenomena of rationality and morality are involved in the very attempt to banish them. The 'problem of free will' is not something to strain at, as if it could be suddenly solved by a proof that there is such a thing; it should rather fade or dissolve when it is seen that 'determinism' is not an intelligible theory. What is important is the methods by which, and extent to which, the conception of free will is (sometimes rightly, as in law courts) modified or limited in particular areas; and also the deep motives and purposes of those who profess or invoke determinist theories. Theories which endeavour to show that all evaluation (ascription of value) is subjective, relative, historically determined, psychologically determined, often do so in aid of other differently described or covert value systems, whether political or aesthetic. Structuralist theory certainly implies values such as scholarship, intelligent talent, originality, gifted insight. These may (officially) be thought of and understood as similar to Sartre's 'sincerity' and Heidegger's 'authenticity' and 'heroism', or else in terms of an omnipresent aestheticism. The theory of *archi-écriture*, in effect a linguistic determinism, may also be looked at in another way. Modern 'determinism' is not mechanical or mechanistic in style, and the science it refers to has advanced since the time of Engels; it is inspired more by presocratic philosophy and modern physics, evoking a view of reality as a system of energy or complex integrated sea of micro-events of which human beings are phenomenal parts or aspects whose sense of individuality and freedom is necessarily illusory. To say that discoveries about protons or DNA 'prove' that free will is an illusion is a philosophical rather than a scientific claim. As a claim of any kind it can only exist as a kind of intuition, which may be scientific or religious, or as a metaphysical fiat. It would then be close to the embryonic religious-scientific-philosophical theories held by the presocratics, or to a modern popular 'Taoism' to which these can be related. Scientists sometimes show affection for determinist theories, but this is a professional hermeneutic instinct which significantly lives in certain areas of work, and cannot be extended from there to undermine or radically reinterpret the diversity of human existence as lived by individual scientists and philosophers just as by the rest of us.

So literary critics are to set themselves the difficult task of discussing traditional literature in terms of non-evaluative structures or codes discovered inside as 'keys'. This approach excludes the most important and interesting critical movement when the moral sense of the critic seeks out and considers the moral sense of the writer. Of course moral judgments are not the whole of criticism, but they are a vital part of it, as they are of the reader's interest and enjoyment. The writer's own *morality*, displayed in the novel, is a major item. People argue about whether D. H. Lawrence was *unjust* to Clifford Chatterley in *Lady Chatterley's Lover*, and how far this affects our judgment of the work; or about whether the hero of Henry James's *Ambassadors* was a righteous man or a self-deceiving fool. Such arguments are certainly interesting and may even be deep! An author's sentimental over-valuing of the hero with whom he identifies is a familiar fault. Structuralist (deconstructionist) criticism does not see literature as a window opened upon an imagined world which is both like and unlike the 'real' world, but which relates to it intimately. Literature is rather to be seen as a network of meanings esteemed for its liveliness, originality, ability to disturb (as 'saints' are now supposed to disturb, rather than to edify), and judged in terms of a psychological-sociological analysis which also seeks out factors not consciously intended by the writer. Such analysis may of course be a part of any criticism, but not necessarily or largely. A close study of the 'texture' of a literary work is or may be a part of criticism, but the critic has to decide its importance in relation to *numerous* other points of interest and evaluation. The writer, then, is required by deconstructionists to 'deploy' language, using it to construct a meaningful text, out of which the reader or critic constructs his own meanings. This may be regarded as a truism (I understand and imagine what I am able to understand and imagine); or it may be thought of as a scientific or metaphysical programme. As 'scientist', the literary critic is then treated as a specialist, a thinker far more relevantly equipped and experienced, of course than the reader, but also than the often naive or prejudiced writer. So, ultimately, the work of criticism *is* the real work of art. The 'soul' of the work lies not in portrayals of life or lively description or profound understanding of moral dilemmas (etc. etc.) but in some vitality or present relevance of meaning-structure as discerned and presented to us by the expert critic. The past is, on this view, and not just in a truistic or tautological sense, what we can *make* of it in the present, which is to say that in a way there is no past. The true text is what it means, what it can do, now. Ordinary historical interest in the past appears here as merely antiquarian. The past must earn its right to exist by being made to work for the present, that is, to be 'significant' in or for it. Here again, one is moving from a truism (it is often very difficult to establish or imagine what happened in the past) to a quasi-philosophical or metaphysical ruling. Literature written to please structuralist critics tends to be involuted and obscure because the objective is to *use*, play with, the language in a stirring, suggestive, puzzling, exciting manner. Traditional tale-telling or moral reflection or simple-minded referential uses of language are to be avoided. Literature must therefore be full of novelties, and obstacles and obscurities, aspiring to the condition of (a certain kind of) *rhetoric* or arcane poetry. This is a tendency which leads us away, not only from the 'old' novel, but also from the ordinary lucid expository prose which is so essential to philosophy and to other humane disciplines. Structuralist critics and novelists are to *attempt* ingeniously to exclude everyday moral judgment from their 'texts'. The word 'text', as a technical term, conveniently allows the critic to bracket himself with the imaginative writer. The novel and the criticism of it are both 'texts', the latter being potentially the true one. Ultimately the work of criticism *is* the real work of art. Of course the exclusion of morality and ordinary considerations about what is true and real is in practice difficult. A clever writer like Alain Robbe-Grillet seems to attempt it, while producing, for instance in *Les Gommes*, a fine novel which is only a little damaged by its determination to be a puzzle picture.

To be noted. George Steiner writes in his enlightening book *Real Presences*: 'We have seen that the commentary, the translation, the formal transformation, or even the polemic parody of the source-text can surpass the original. Their brilliance can come to replace or to bury it. We have seen that modern relativism is right when it insists on the fluidity of the lines which separate the vitality of the primary from that of the secondary. Yet neither truth alters the profound difference between the status of being of the independent and the dependent forms. The primary text – the poem, picture, piece of music – is a phenomenon of *freedom*. It can be or it cannot be. The hermeneutic-critical response, the executive enactment via performance, via vision and reading, are the clauses dependent on that freedom. Even at the highest point of recreative or subversive virtuosity, their genesis is that of dependence. Their licence may indeed be boundless (the post-structuralist and deconstructive game-theories and play have shown this); but their freedom is strictly a *secondary* one.'

(p. 151.)

[ 206 ]

Of course art changes, and changes mysteriously, in its intimate unspoken relation with the *Zeitgeist*. Many artists find they cannot do traditional things and must do new things, and this is proper to the continued life of art. But this change, this interweaving of old and new, is subtle and various, and each artist must find his own way. When does a tradition cease, and when does it alter? New things are often seen to be traditional. The critic should not think of himself as a kind of scientist in a superior position able to offer some final overall analysis. Of course, sometimes led on by critics, sometimes by instinct, artists may thus bully each other, as in an art school where it is simply 'not done' to represent the human figure. An attractive esoteric theory, incomprehensible to laymen, may be felt to be more lively and amusing than the vaguer, less easily stated objectives of traditional critics, such as to enjoy literature and understand literature and history, help others to share this enjoyment and understanding, to read a great many different kinds of books, and in general to be a polymath with a sophisticated liberal-minded judgment and a refined sense of value. Esoteric new theories also, of course, tend to appeal to students, since they simplify the scenery and can obviate scholarship and the effort of independent discovery and thinking. It is not always realised that the study of literature is something *difficult*. As an academic subject the study of literature in one's own language has often been said to be a 'soft option'. This is a very misleading view. A good teacher of literature (and a good literary critic) not only understands poetry (which not many people do) and other literary forms, but is a historian, a linguist, a connoisseur of other arts, and a sophisticated student of human nature. He is in the best sense a jack of all trades. He should of course have 'read everything'. The notion that a study of English literature was 'too easy' led the authorities at Oxford University, when they at last reluctantly allowed it to be a university subject, to build in a compulsory study of Anglo-Saxon to stiffen it up a bit. The belief that literature is an easy subject may lead academics to defend themselves by becoming specialists who know everything about one period, or indeed one writer, and nothing about anything else. It may also, the case in point, lead them to embrace an obscure and difficult theory which looks like a science, which other people do not understand, and which provides the consoling feeling of having a special private expertise, and so being just as good as a physicist or a biologist. Paradoxically, the motives, or ideals, of structuralism have as their nemesis or accompaniment the wish to establish oneself as a member of an elite. This is a form of a familiar and enduring style of thought, Gnosticism, knowledge as power. Here the search for truth becomes a search for magic formulae and the seeker desires to become a privileged initiate of a secret cult, a sorcerer or *pharmakeus*. This development may be understandable. Fear of mass production, of materialism, of commercialism, of vulgarity, of technology, of television, produces a wish for a new purified esoteric art. Everything, it seems, is demeaned by being public, becoming part of what Theodor Adorno called 'the culture industry'. Such a vista may lead some writers to seek refuge in deliberate mystification.

A despairing prophetic tone may be heard in some structuralist utterances, as from a desire to run forward to anticipate a terrible future, to make it present and prove that it can be lived with. The same note can be heard in writings of the Frankfurt School (Adorno, Benjamin). This is a hint of realism which certainly challenges thought; we are being forced to consider how radical a time of change we are now living through. Marxists, after all, told us that technological change brings ideological change. There are disturbing ideas here which indeed concern the nature of language, the future of books, the meaning of the word 'writing'. Traditional ideas of truth, freedom and personality are at stake, and we must remind ourselves that the frightening future is not yet with us and can be resisted. New and patently self-referential, invented not natural, languages of physics and biology are destined to enter our lives through our own use of technology and our general sense of a cosmos described by science. This new cosmos evoked for us by physicists is not discovered in the same sense as America or the South Pole was discovered. It is not, in the ordinary sense, imaginable, and not, in the ordinary sense, 'really there'. Science fiction, an important literary form, soothes our disturbed frustrated imagination by picturing our more distant surroundings as being just like our domestic ones only, in our local terms, more weird; and though it may strain every nerve it cannot do otherwise. Science fiction has been praised as the most imaginative writing possible, but in fact, though there are many talented writers of it, it presents us rather with the poverty and limits of our imagination when projected in that direction. Imagination concerns the depth and working of the human soul and its truthful visions. We may think here of Coleridge's distinction between fancy and imagination, fancy as juxtaposition of given pieces, imagination as deep fusion, deep creative understanding. Human life mingles horror and absurdity, and great art has the ability to mingle these and do justice to them in the process. Science fiction can please and edify us by exhibiting the latest scientific discoveries; it must also visit weird 'unhuman' worlds and endow them with human interest. This is certainly a difficult task, we are to be awed and frightened, at home and yet not at home. SF stories picture us as meeting with beings from elsewhere who are, and indeed must be, with picturesque differences, rather like ourselves. But modern physics bears a different and more frightful message. As Wittgenstein remarked, 'If a lion could talk, we would not understand him.' What science fiction is concealing from us and at the same time making us uneasily aware of, is that we are surrounded by an external reality which can only be indicated in a language which almost none of us can understand and which is not in our ordinary local sense descriptive. Yet, we may feel, what could be more fundamental, basic, and so surely *true*, than what our greatest minds are now, in these fields, discovering? This is the scientific era when at last we discover reality, and that things are not as they seem. Indeed, for science, there are no things, only relations. The microcosm and the macrocosm are in these respects equally mysterious. Beneath human personality, free will, morality, lies a different 'more real' world of genes, molecules, DNA. Are we becoming used to the idea that, whether we are concerned with distant galaxies or with the deep structure of our own things and our own bodies and our own thoughts, the deepest language, the language we might say of the planet itself, is totally unlike our natural referential language with its familiar methods of verification? Notions of 'probability', 'facts' about atoms, protons, things that can be both waves and particles, become vaguely familiar to us, and are used in arguments about free will. We are told that, because of genes, no one can be blamed for anything. The spectre of determinism, appearing in new and convincing forms, may be in effect more attractive than horrific. So, in the end, it is all a matter of cosmic rhythms to which we must learn to surrender ourselves: a very old story, older even than the presocratics who were rejected by Plato. Under this spell we may begin to gain the impression that our ordinary language is being, as it were, prised off the world, and is thus withering away. We are being taught, in a new style, what the Hegelians also tried to tell us, that the individual is a special kind of illusion. What if this development continues, as it seems likely to, and as we must wish it to, not only because of the obvious benefits of technology, but because the collapse of technological civilisation could mean a return to barbarism? We cannot turn back this clock, we are (in ways both fortunate and unfortunate) destined to become surrounded by, used to, dependent on, clever machines which *separate* us from the old simpler furniture of the world and even from the activity of our own minds. Typewriters replace pens, word processors replace typewriters. Calculators replace mental arithmetic, data banks replace books. The era of alphabetic writing, which was originally thought of as secondary to verbal speech, an ingenious means of representing it, is also said to be coming to an end. The picture of speaking and traditional writing as prime methods of representation and communication is now, it seems, seen to be outmoded and essentially fallacious. We have to think in terms of an un-writing, writing proper, the writing of reality itself, of the planet, of the cosmos. Of course, in the time to come, which we are not told but might gloomily prophesy, the majority of people will make contact only with the childishly simple machinery, as the great machines which explore the depths of what will then be thought of as human reality will only be understood by brilliant and highly trained experts. Most people, unable to read, will be watching television. Television, the dictator's best friend, already erodes our ability to read. What is, and not implausibly, envisaged here is an apocalyptic change in human consciousness, involving vast social changes and the disappearance of old local ideas of individuals and virtues. A loss of sovereignty.

I do not believe that the structuralist nightmare, *la fin du livre* etc., can be set up as a really convincing prophecy, but it carries a serious warning. The doctrine is too emotive to be philosophy, let alone science. The future perhaps, one sometimes feels inclined to say no doubt, contains terrible things, but one thing we may be sure about is that it cannot be reliably predicted. (Who predicted the sudden collapse of Marxism in eastern Europe?) It has certainly never been so predicted in the past, and there are extra reasons now for an inability to predict. Is what is pictured here something very remote, or something very close indeed? Here too, looking ahead, the courage of philosophy may fail. Many voices proclaim the end of philosophy. Philosophy departments are closing. I think it is very important that western philosophy, with its particular tradition and *method* of imaginative truth-seeking and lucid clarification, should not fail us here. Philosophy is perpetually in tension between empiricism and metaphysics, between, one might say, Moore and McTaggart. This argument can take place within the same philosopher. Religion moves similarly between simplicity and elaboration, puritanism and its opposite (to which various names may be given). There are times for piecemeal analysis, modesty and common-sense, and other times for ambitious synthesis and the aspiring and edifying charm of lofty and intricate structures. Certainly philosophy's recurrent task is to point out that a metalanguage has truth-bearing sense only if it can be suitably translated into a more accessible clarifiable terminology. It has sense through its relation to the original reality which has brought it into existence. The dialogue form in Plato helps to relate his myths to real cases. This task of philosophy is not less but more essential now, in helping to preserve and refresh a stream of meticulous, subtle, eloquent ordinary language, free from jargon and able to deal clearly and in detail with matters of a certain degree of generality and abstraction. We cannot see the future, but must fear it intelligently.

We are all workers and, of necessity, in order to live at all, truth-seekers on that familiar everyday (transcendental) edge where language continually struggles with an encountered world. In this activity we are like, or are, artists. While our motives and abilities to grasp and express truth differ, the conception of true and false is essential to human life, which without it would perish and go to ruin. A *radical* separation of meaning from truth not only 'removes' morally responsible truth-seeking speech in particular situations, it also leaves our ordinary conduct inexplicable. Art cannot be taken as proof that the separation is possible. Even bad art relies on some truth value, and serious art is a continuous working of meaning in the light of the discovery of some truth. The often difficult explanation of the *truth* of great art is a proper task of criticism. The concept of language-using must imply that of an individual person as a presence, that is, it must imply responsibility and the possibility of truth, upon which the possibility of falsehood depends. This concept of presence does not of course mean that any significant statement must be attributable; it is a way of expressing the necessary anchorage of language in a surrounding world. From here, and returning to here, every sort of 'fiction' can take off, including good and bad art and complex and simple lying.

As Derrida says, 'experience' relates to a present, whether or not in the form of consciousness. Some or much of the time when we are 'aware' we do not have any vivid sense of presentness. Simone Weil expressed her wish for a lively present by saying that she wanted to be able to perceive without reverie. An inability to be fully present is something which we often feel. We move about in time in all sorts of strange ways which are also entirely familiar. We 'live in memory', we anticipate and plan, we discover unconscious wishes, we 'sum up' in spoken thoughts processes of mental stuff which we could not describe or temporally analyse in detail, our mental life is time-textured, and a certain mastery of time is required for living and in various sophisticated forms for living well. But our time-adventures return to and are based in presence and encounter. These concepts, experience, consciousness, presence, cannot be arbitrarily excluded from philosophical discussion. Certainly, reflection may soon feel confronted by a mystery. Heidegger seizes on that word of Sophocles to describe being human: *deinos*, *unheimlich*, terrible, weird, strange, wonderful. How do we do it? It is at this point that one must move steadily on, attempting to say, in ordinary language and without jargon, things which may seem obvious. Here philosophy has a negative technical task of removing (philosophical) errors, which must be combined with a positive task of finding a simple open mode of discourse concerning ordinary evident (for instance moral) aspects of human life. Of course philosophy is 'abstract': a term not easy to define or explain. It is a delicately managed conversation that moves between degrees of generality in order to promote understanding of very general features of our lives. Metaphysical systems, as positions, are abstract and difficult to understand, but their critics do in effect, as time passes, interpret, clarify, justify, modify, or refute them by relationship to what we know in ordinary ways about human life; and there are moments when such a reference is, philosophically, essential, and when the language of philosophy should be simplified. Philosophers are wise to attend to critics of the Dr Johnson variety, and if one is not a genius (and perhaps even if one is one) it is usually helpful to attempt a laborious expression in ordinary language of 'what one is thinking' or 'how one sees it'. The negative error-correcting work of philosophy inevitably suggests a variety of general positions which require calm viewing, and this general look cannot be cast without reference to morality. That is, philosophy must be moral philosophy, as indeed, in the sense in which, it has usually been.

An implication of the primacy of presence to and encounter with a non-linguistic world is that speech must be thought of as more fundamental than writing, as it has been by both philosophers and laymen. 'Speech' here must be extended to cover, not only audible utterance but all our awareness and reflections. These may well be unclarified, but (the point is) they are primary. *We speak to ourselves.* 'Writing' codifies and makes available what originates in and returns to individual minds and voices. The original bases of our life are in spoken encounter. Writings constitute a removal of thought from conditions in which it can be clarified and in which what lies beyond the words can be intuitively grasped. A book may be misused and misunderstood and cannot defend itself. This expresses a fundamental idea about the centrality of individual minds, a moral and religious idea which also belongs to common-sense. If this sounds like hubris, it is a hubris which is easily dispelled. Of course we are fantasising sinners, victims of accident, history, habit and unconscious motive, and *of course* books are *essential*, we need and rightly want books, and computers which menace books, and languages of science which can satisfy our curiosity and cure our ills. But we must retain our everyday and continually renewed awareness that no theory can remove or explain away our moral and rational mastery of our individual being. Books too are individual works of art, with the independence yet rootedness characteristic of such objects, made by individual persons for other individual persons. Of course 'the meaning' of a work of art is not *just* what its creator might say or have said it meant; but it is not disconnected from this either. What any man says is open to interpretation as well as to misinterpretation. Language has public rules as well as particular or private contexts. As critics and as ordinary persons we solve problems of this sort every day. The 'writing' which Derrida appeals to as being, in the direction away from the individual speaker, beyond books is a new ownerless language which evades context and verification.

It may be argued that whether we like it or not such a language is possible as that of, at least, some people. Masses of human beings may be virtually persuaded that they are automatons and so used by others. (As in Aldous Huxley's *Brave New World*.) Of course we speak of people being 'dehumanised' by depraved conditioning, by hunger, poverty, fear. But usually these are fates of individuals which can be looked at in detail. The human automaton as a total continuous being still seems to belong to science fiction. But it is worth conjuring up the picture as something cognate with an emotional or popular acceptance of deterministic theories. If we allow ourselves to be intimidated by new technological determinisms, based on scientific or metaphysical ideas, we may also weaken our faith in morality, rationality, and ability to discern truth, and this weakness can have political consequences too. Utopian political theories linked to historical determinism flourish when we lose the ordinary fundamental sense of contingency and accident which belongs with the concept of the individual. The structuralist Utopia is perhaps more cheerful than some others, picturing the average man as a quiet codified fellow, perhaps even happy in his simple way, and the artists and thinkers as an élite sporting in a *jouissance* of linguistic play, occasionally stirring up the average man a little by theatre, television or cinema. Perhaps a shadowy sketch of this state of affairs can already be seen in some of our free societies.

The structuralist phenomenon can also be seen as a recent sophisticated version of the recurrent anti-rational anti-intellectual reaction of intellectuals against what seems to them an old tired tradition, heavy with unavailing thoughts which have been worked over innumerable times: an exasperated weariness with the old metaphysical world with its continually defended systematic rationality and its ancient superannuated God and its grand self-conscious conceited art. The new anti-metaphysical metaphysic promises to unburden the intellectuals and set them free to play. Man has now 'come of age' and is strong enough to get rid of his past. Such a revolution suits the mood at a time of fast and amazing technological change. This same mood of admiration for science and disgust with the inefficiency and frivolity of humanistic ratiocination can affect both intellectuals and non-intellectuals alike. The suspicion of the latter that the former are merely playing about instead of serving society can stabilise a tyranny as well as prompting a revolution. Here the severance of meaning from truth, and language from the world can be seen, not only as philosophically baseless and morally intolerable, but as politically suicidal.

The fundamental value which is lost, obscured, made not to be, by structuralist theory, is truth, language as truthful, where 'truthful' means faithful to, engaging intelligently and responsibly with, a reality which is beyond us. This is the transcendental network, the border, wherein the interests and passions which unite us to the world are progressively woven into illusion or reality, a continuous working of consciousness. This is to speak of what is closest to us. 'Truth' is found by 'truthful' endeavour, both words are needed in a just description of language. Truth is learnt, found, in specialised areas of art where the writer (for instance) struggles to make his deep intuitions of the world into artful truthful judgment. This is the truth, terrible, delightful, funny, whose strong lively presence we recognise in great writers and whose absence we feel in the weak, empty, self-regarding fantasy of bad writers. The world is not given to us 'on a plate', it is given to us as a creative task. It is impossible to banish morality from this picture. We *work*, using or failing to use our honesty, our courage, our truthful imagination, at the interpretation of what is present to us, as we of necessity shape it and 'make something of it'. We help it to be. We work at the meeting point where we deal with a world which is other than ourselves. This transcendental barrier is more like a band than a line. Our ordinary consciousness is a deep continuous working of values, a *continuous present and presence* of perceptions, intuitions, images, feelings, desires, aversions, attachments. It is a matter of what we 'see things as', what we let, or make, ourselves think about, how by innumerable movements, we train our instincts and develop our habits and test our methods of verification. Imagery, metaphor, has its deep roots and origins in this self-being, and an important part of human learning is an ability both to generate and to judge and understand the imagery which helps us to interpret the world.

The implications of structuralism with its threat to accepted conceptions of truth, value, individual, impels us (felicitously) to argue in new ways for what we take to be fundamental and have perhaps too much, both as philosophers and laymen, taken for granted. But are we perhaps being too strict, too solemn, failing to understand Derrida's rhetoric, his uses of 'play' and 'game'? Surely playing with language can suggest new meanings, open new views, and thus in its own way suggest new truths? The philosophical form, here, of a suitable argument is not easy to determine. Much contemporary analytical philosophy does not bother to engage with what is regarded as the 'absurdities' of structuralism. Empiricist accounts of mental activity, which (rightly) avoid descent into psychological hypothesis and also (wrongly in my view) shun moral philosophy, can seem very abstract when checked by a glance at the curious messy phenomena of our actual experience. The problems of how to describe this, how to settle down and *look* at it, are philosophical problems which seem here to be left over. Of course something systematic must be said, and empiricists may reply that they leave the great variety of detailed and 'realistic' picturings of streams of consciousness and so on to novelists, or to scientists. This stuff however should be approached by philosophers if we are not to leave the field to deterministic theories (such as historical materialism or linguistic monism) or to be content with a neo-psychologism which avoids any deep discussion and involvement of ethics. Philosophy is moral philosophy as Kant and Plato thought. We must check philosophical theories against what we know of human nature (and hold on to that phrase too) and feed philosophy with our ordinary (non-theorised, non-jargonised) views of it. Language is meaningful, *ergo* useful, it performs its *essential* task, through its ability to be truthful; and its truthfulness is a function of the struggle of individuals creatively to adjust language to contingent conditions outside it. All right, Captain Cook's ship (we are told) did not frighten the natives because they could not conceptualise it, that is see it. Possibly we are surrounded by extra-galactic visitors (or angels) to whom we are similarly blind. But the limits of my language which are the limits of my world fade away on every side into areas of fighting for concepts, for understanding, for expression, for control, of which the search for the *mot juste* may serve as an image. Everyone, every moral being, that is every human being, is involved in this fight, it is not reserved for philosophers, artists and scientists. Language must not be separated from individual consciousness and treated as (for the many) a handy impersonal network and (for the few) an adventure playground. Language, consciousness and world are bound together, the (essential) aspiration of language to truth is an aspect of consciousness as a work of evaluation.

# > 8 <

# Consciousness and Thought – II

'The service of philosophy, of speculative culture, towards the human spirit is to rouse, to startle it into sharp and eager observation. Every moment some form grows perfect in hand or face; some tone on the hills or the sea is choicer than the rest; some mood of passion or insight or intellectual excitement is irresistibly real and attractive for us, – for that moment only. Not the fruit of experience, but experience itself, is the end. A counted number of pulses only is given to us of a variegated, dramatic life. How may we see in them all that is to be seen by the finest senses? How shall we pass most swiftly from point to point, and be present always at the focus where the greatest number of vital forces unite in their purest energy? To burn always with this hard, gem-like flame, to maintain this ecstasy, is success in life. In a sense it might even be said that our failure is to form habits: for, after all, habit is relative to a stereotyped world, and meantime it is only the roughness of the eye that makes any two persons, things, situations, seem alike. While all melts under our feet, we may well catch at any exquisite passion, or any contribution to knowledge that seems by a lifted horizon to set the spirit free for a moment, or any stirring of the senses, strange dyes, strange colours, and curious odours, or work of the artist's hands, or the face of one's friend. Not to discriminate every moment some passionate attitude in those about us, and in the very brilliancy of their gifts some tragic dividing of forces on their ways, is, on this short day of frost and sun, to sleep before evening ... The theory or idea or system which requires of us the sacrifice of any part of this experience, in consideration of some interest into which we cannot enter, or some abstract theory we have not identified with

ourselves, or what is only conventional, has no real claim upon us
... Great passions may give us this quickened sense of life, ecstasy
and sorrow of love, the various forms of enthusiastic activity,
disinterested or otherwise, which come naturally to many of us.
Only be sure it is passion – that it does yield you this fruit of a
quickened multiplied consciousness. Of this wisdom, the poetic passion, the desire of beauty, the love of art for art's sake, has most;
for art comes to you proposing frankly to give nothing but the
highest quality to your moments as they pass, and simply for those
moments' sake.'

(Walter Pater, *The Renaissance*, Conclusion.)

Pater's well-known celebration of 'experience' should interest, at
least amuse, anyone who wishes to rescue this concept, though rescuers
are likely to amend it in various ways. It asserts the fundamental reality
of the individual in a style not unlike that of G. E. Moore, but without
the philosophical surround. We should live in the present, have visual
and olfactory (and no doubt auditory) pleasures, look at landscapes
and at the faces of our friends and enjoy works of art. The mood is
aesthetic, hedonistic and self-centred, likely to be unpleasing to brisker
and more altruistic critics who would cherish the fruits of experience
and look warily upon passion. On the other hand we can switch to a
different way of thinking by recalling Simone Weil's wish that she
could 'perceive without reverie'. And 'Attention: not to think about.'
Should we not in any case endeavour to *see* (visual metaphor) and
attend to what surrounds and concerns us, because it is there and
is interesting, beautiful, strange, worth experiencing, and because it
demands (and *needs*) our attention, rather than living in a vague haze
of private anxiety and fantasy? This requirement could be stated in
quasi-aesthetic terms close to those of Pater, or in terms of healthy
human function or 'mental hygiene' (practical yoga or car-factory Zen),
or of course in moral terms: one must see what is happening, what is
there, in order to be able to see what ought to be done, one should see
the faces of strangers as well as of friends. Alert vivid experience, living
in the present, can be celebrated as the higher hedonism, or as moral
or spiritual 'attention'. Religion speaks of a continual sense of God's
presence. The reflective critic who wishes to 'moralise' Pater's hard
gem-like flame is likely also to object to his dismissal of habit. Habit
is essential, both practically and morally. Habits can dull us and blind

us, but we need useful habits and ought to develop virtuous habits. Habits save time which might be enjoyed or made good use of. In this context Pater's perpetual 'ecstasy' (to use Keynes's term concerning Moore) seems not only egoistic but absurd. We cannot distinguish so easily between the fruit of experience and experience itself. The Kantian language of 'principle' and 'duty' with its requirement of impersonal classification leads us away from Pater. We do not however (as I argue later) have to choose between 'attention' and 'duty', we live with both. Pater's memorable flame is worth mentioning as an evocation of the *present*, the moment-to-moment consciousness which philosophers tend to be embarrassed by, to neglect, or to analyse away.

As I have been suggesting, the concept of experience or consciousness has been passed over because philosophical styles have not offered a suitable mode of description and because philosophers have lacked motives to attempt description, for instance in cases where a Kantian positive conception of moral will, separate from and interrupting the stream of experience, deprives ordinary awareness and 'mere feelings' of value, interest, and function. Such dismissal of the 'inner life' may appear in ordinary admonitions: Never mind your emotions, just do what's right. The concept was also denied to moral philosophy, and to philosophy of mind in general, when a rejection of the Cartesian view of consciousness seemed to make any other treatment of personal experience seem impossible. How impossible we may see from Gilbert Ryle's *Concept of Mind*, and from some understandings of Wittgenstein. Hegelian and Marxist 'consciousness' moreover is not the property of existing individuals living in present moments; it belongs to history or society or *Geist*, and can only be ascribed generally to groups or classes dwelling in phases. The states of mind so finely analysed in the *Phenomenology of Mind* are of very general application, suitable for metamorphosis into Kierkegaard's edifying pictures of various recognisable human moods.

Some philosophers have made use of the idea of immediate 'contents of consciousness' with a confidence which suggests that they feel they can detect and identify such things, at any rate when they are thinking philosophically. Hume spoke of the philosopher's vision as fading when he left the study; at any rate in their studies he and Berkeley felt able to assume that there were atomic mental contents, impressions, ideas, which could be thought of as basic constituents of reality. More recent phenomenalists (such as Russell and Ayer) have postulated 'sense data' which may or may not be said to be strictly introspectible. This line of empiricist thought makes use of an intuitive sense of one's ability to isolate and 'look at' fragmentary mental contents (shades of blue, red patches) which are thus immediately knowable in a sense in which public material objects are not. Can anyone do it, that is isolate and inspect immediate contents of consciousness? If only philosophers can why should we regard these as primal parts of everyone's awareness? How can the private experience carry over its certainty into the public world? Hume was not concerned with either the effortful establishing of, or the escape from, the '*cogito* situation'. He is close to Kant in a sense in which Descartes is not. He uses an implicit transcendental argument; we just evidently *are* able to fuse our impressions together into generally shared experience. These private data must be assumed if we are to have a philosophical explanation, and if we look hard enough we can satisfy ourselves that they exist. Hume's 'habits' act as transcendental forms. Post-Hegelian Husserlian phenomenology may be seen by contrast as a more Cartesian form of transcendental empiricism, resting its argument upon the effortful intensity of the Cartesian vision. Post-Wittgensteinian discussion of these problems has, in the course of attacking the errors involved in their formulations, tended to remove ideas of 'consciousness' and of 'presence' from the philosophical scene.

Can I have clear intuitive knowledge of something 'owned' by me, something which is indubitably present to me? Can I 'see' such a thing, can I be said to know it, can this certainty be extended to a public world? Berkeley answered the last question by picturing God as an external guarantor of 'objective' knowledge, a universal perceiver who, through the framework of his own perception, organises and defines the steady and reliable patterns of our experience. This can be seen as a mechanical or childish version of Descartes' solution which is also his Ontological Proof (and which as such I shall discuss later). We cease to doubt the reliability of our experience (Descartes argues) because in grasping our own existence as perceiver and thinker we are able *ipso facto* to grasp the existence of God, both as something in itself clear and distinct, and as guaranteeing the criterion of clearness and distinctness as a test of truth; thereafter we can assume that, on the whole, the world is as it seems, we cannot be entirely misled by a *malin génie*, and even a confused impression can be clearly thought of as such. In a secular equivalent of this proof we may say that what we intuitively grasp is the idea of truth itself. We might think here of the way a child learns the concept, and of ways in which it can be positively taught. Plato's stages of enlightenment are developments in the understanding of truth, which are also developments in our confidence in our own inner life of thought and judgment and in our real existence as individual persons capable of truth.

The idea of a Cartesian, or Humian, datum as an epistemological starting point has been unsettled or attacked, from Kant onward. Nothing momentary can be an item of knowledge, we must look elsewhere for the structures of veridical awareness. Neither the Cartesian argument, nor the philosophies which have taken its place, afford or affect to need any laboriously realistic account of consciousness, which appears in the first case as clear pinpoints of attention devoid of transcendent claims and in the second case as shadowy shifting irrelevant stuff, peripheral to the public conceptual structures upon which knowing-activity depends. Possibly Hume's ramshackle and unsatisfactory idea of consciousness as a continuum of units, fused by association and habit and containing certain morally tinged items such as feelings of approval, most resembles a childish picture of what we feel like! The Cartesian era may have ended, but as often happens when a general philosophical viewpoint loses its charm, something is lost. Descartes did not have to introduce value as an external element into a world (mind) primarily or fundamentally devoid of it, or to scramble a few value-conscious items into a 'factual' account of our knowledge of material objects. Awareness of God is seen (by Descartes) as fundamental to any spark of mind, or to put it in secular terms, all awareness includes value *as* the (versatile) agility to distinguish true from false. (Compare the role of truth-seeking in Plato's system.) The alert truth-seeking *cogito* uncovers the moral potentiality of consciousness.

Kant was upset by Hume's arguments, he was not prepared to rest scientific knowledge upon a psychology of association of ideas, or to derive our conceptions of space and time from experiences of succession which presupposed these conceptions. Kant's picture of the ideality of space and time (in tune with modern physics as well as with Schopenhauer's oriental religiosity), together with his conception of fundamental categories of understanding under the inspiration of Reason, allowed no sense to the idea of discrete units of experience. Our experience was already composed, it was 'screened'. The understood, experienced world was a product of conjoined forms of organisation (*a priori* and empirical concepts), and morality too was not something felt but the actualisation of rational systems in the sphere of human action. Kant calls our material factual world 'phenomenal', an appearance, the work done by our faculties upon a hidden datum. But it is not an illusion which relates to a reality which we can or ought to be able to discover. Plato (and Platonists and eastern religious thinkers) would hold ordinary awareness to be a state of illusion, but would allow and advocate a gradual change of consciousness whereby the veil of appearance was penetrated by moral-intellectual cognition. Kant's phenomenal world is devoid of value, self-contained and absolute (like the factual world of the *Tractatus*); the command of duty enters from beyond. Moral agency consists in the switch to the activity of the moral (rational and real) will, somehow effective in the causally regulated phenomenal world. Kant distinguishes between the love that is (merely) felt and the love that is practised. Strictly, for him, there is no such thing as 'moral experience', or moral consciousness as a 'morally coloured' awareness. But can we really imagine morality without an intimate relation with consciousness as perceptions, feelings, streams of reflection? These problems about morality, knowledge, and the 'inner life' are of course very old. St Augustine, who joined Plato to the mystic Christ of St Paul and the God of the Psalms, had much to say on the subject. Augustine derived from Plato and Plotinus, and made Christian, the idea of the soul as a huge dark reservoir of potential power in which truth and light must be ceaselessly, momently, sought. We are changed by love and pursuit of what we only partly see and understand. This activity is our awareness of our world. My point here is that a metaphysical (e.g. Kantian) picture can make impossible, apparently otiose, a philosophical attempt at a realistic (in the sense in which Augustine's is realistic) representation of human consciousness. Consideration, in a philosophical context, of the kind of experience described by Augustine in the *Confessions* may help to clarify the sense of 'inner' in 'inner life'. But in Kant's rejection of moral sensibility we may detect signs of a softening grace. Through the peripheral concepts of the sublime and Respect for the Law, which lead back into the phenomenal self, Kant allows a sort of immediate phenomenal consciousness of morality, a 'self-feeling' or praiseworthy symptom which may of course be morally dangerous if it degenerates into a pleasurable end-in-itself; as when, for instance, Respect for the Law (when we feel both pious awe and selfish fear when confronting a moral demand) relaxes into self-indulgent feelings of guilt, which may become a substitute for action. This is a not unfamiliar situation. Kant also endows imagination with a certain independent creativity, as in its conceptless play in the creation of art, and acknowledges the existence of genius as a creative principle. The partly illusory authority of the work of art gives a form to experience. These are intrusions of value into phenomenal awareness.

Kant's 'consciousness' is not Cartesian or Hegelian, nor is it the ordinary (regional or local, to use Derrida's words) concept which I want to try to characterise. Kant's phenomenal consciousness (if we exclude the small 'dangerous' concessions just mentioned) is strictly the correlate of formulated true or false factual judgments about states of affairs, like 'what is the case' in the *Tractatus*, what could be set out in empirical propositions. Kant did not 'highlight' consciousness; in taking it thus for granted he penetrated it with other concepts. He did not think in terms of a densely coloured personally (or historically) owned stream of consciousness. Hegel made the concept primary, he put it on the map in the sense in which it is in sociology and Marxism: social consciousness, class consciousness, the structure of consciousness, consciousness as a product of society and history. He also set it up as a very general psychological concept (as in for instance 'the unhappy consciousness'), in which sense it was also used by Kierkegaard and influenced Freud. Hegel turned Kant's static categories, and his magnetic Reason, into a lively dynamic network of modes of being. In doing this he also turned towards Plato, to Plato's dialectic as stages of an argument and to the Platonic conception of a moral cognition magnetically attracted toward a higher stage of understanding. The Hegelian dialectic is soaked in value. This is in itself an attractive feature when we contrast it with philosophies which are hygienically ignorant of value or put it in as a footnote; on the other hand it constitutes in effect an ambiguous and dangerous charm which it shares with its offspring Marxism. Hegel joins fact to value, but thereby ultimately kills value and loses the individual. Value is, in the totality, overcome. Plato's Forms, as objects of moral desire, and principles of understanding, are to be thought of as active creative sources of energy in the world, but are mythically pictured as separate and transcendent; they cannot be relativised by being absorbed into (historical or psychological) transformations of existence. At a superficial level history fashions morals, at a deep level morals resist history. Plato's constant and explicit use of myth also separates him from Hegel, whose would-be homogeneous metaphysic can be seen as a sort of science, historical, or social, or psychological. The double nature of the Forms, being both immanent and transcendent, makes difficulties (as discussed in the *Parmenides*) for them in their logical role (as everyday universals), but in their moral role presents a comprehensible image, and indeed, as a concept of 'the divine', a familiar one. What is ideal is *active* in the imperfect life, and yet is also, and necessarily, separate from it. This separateness is connected with the possibility of freedom and spiritual movement and change in the life of the individual. This continuous activity is *experienced* and lives and thrives, for good or ill, in the richly textured matrix of our moment-to-moment consciousness.

I quote from Hegel's *Phenomenology of Mind*:

'Observational psychology, which in the first instance states what observation finds regarding the general forms brought to its notice in the active consciousness, discovers all sorts of faculties, inclinations and passions; and since, while narrating what this collection contains, the remembrance of the unity of self-consciousness is not to be suppressed, observational psychology is bound to get the length at least of wonderment that such a lot and such a miscellany of things can happen to be somehow alongside of one another in the mind as in a kind of bag, more especially when they are seen to be not lifeless inert things, but restless active processes. In telling over these various faculties observation keeps to the universal aspect: the unity of these multifarious capacities is the opposite aspect to this universality, is the actual concrete individuality. To take up again thus the different concrete individualities, and to describe how one man has more inclination for this, the other for that, how one has more intelligence than the other – all this is, however, something much more uninteresting than even to reckon up the species of insects, mosses and so on. For these latter give observation the right to take them thus individually and disconnectedly (*begrifflos*), because they belong essentially to the sphere of fortuitous detailed particulars. To take conscious individuality on the other hand, as a particular phenomenal entity, and treat it in so wooden a fashion, is self-contradictory, because the essential element of individuality lies in the universal element of mind. Since however the process of apprehending it causes it at the same time to pass into the form of universality, to apprehend it is to find its law, and seems in this way to have a rational purpose in view and a necessary function to fulfil. The moments constituting the content of the law are on the one hand individuality itself, on the other its universal inorganic nature, viz. the given circumstances, situations, habits, customs, religion, and so forth; from these the determinate individuality is to be understood and comprehended. They contain something specific, determinate as well as universal, and are at the same time something lying at hand, which furnishes material for observation and on the other side expresses itself in the form of individuality.'

('Observation of Self-consciousness', c. V, A, 3b;
trans. J. B. Baillie, rev. edn. 1931, p. 332.)

Hegel aims to produce an entirely comprehensive and scientific system; he emphasises the scientific nature of the enterprise and the sense in which science must involve the progressive disappearance of individuals. (See the preface to the *Phenomenology*.) His thought is at the same time 'psychological' in a modern sense. He is both a product of the Enlightenment and its most subtle enemy. His dialectic, the questioning of every position and the transcendence of position and question by a more unified view which in turn is questioned, is the form taken by the logical, rational, progressive development of Spirit in the course of which at each stage what is separate and individual is later seen to be part of a larger more intelligible whole. Among the wholes thus generated existing states and societies hold high, Hegel sometimes thought uniquely privileged, places. However, in spite of empirically inspired references and diversions, which are not among the least charms of the book, this is *ontology*, it is about the nature of rational thought, and thereby about *being* in its profound philosophical sense, a complete account of *everything*. In the section quoted, early in the *Phenomenology*, Hegel describes how mental contents, classified here in (technical) terms of faculties, inclinations, passions, can be listed by 'observational psychology' as a 'miscellany of things' happening to be 'sometimes alongside one another in the mind as in a kind of bag'. These entities have a unity which derives from their being roughly similar in kind; on the other hand they can now be seen as a disconnected (*begrifflos*, conceptless) collection of 'restless active processes' demanding a further intelligibility. This is one way of proceeding in a

[ 225 ]

description of the mind, and commits the thinker to a route which excludes other routes. Doubts and alternatives must be overcome. This bold confident establishing of *direction* is an aspect of the necessity to which Hegel submits, or which he blithely chooses, on his way to a total explanation or edifice. (Thinking is being, as Parmenides once said.) To select a method (in this case a particular psychological terminology) is already to invoke a certain kind of universality or understanding. Contemplation of what now seems a merely random list of psychological items induces a (logical, ontological, spiritual) demand for a more highly integrated concept of unity. The picture of the 'bag' is transcended by the idea of the human individual, a new kind of universality whose law or rational formation is made up in a different conceptual terminology of habits, customs and moral and religious outlook. The, by contrast random, contents are to be understood in the light of the essential unity of the individual mind which involves both the individual's ability to think and the nature of what he thinks about. The mind cannot be understood at the ragbag level without a further consideration of its surroundings; 'to apprehend it is to find its law' or rationale. 'The moments constituting the content of the law are on the one hand individuality itself, on the other universal inorganic nature, viz. the given circumstances, situations, habits, customs, religion and so forth: from these the determinate individuality is to be understood and comprehended.' This movement of progressive 'destruction' of individuals, moving from individual to universal and, at a higher rational level, back to individual, is (it is argued) the inevitable necessary pattern of all thought and (*ipso facto*) being. Hegel explains later how the more fully self-conscious individual, whose consciousness has 'cast away all opposition' and starts anew from itself, who has integrated his ragbag personality and 'knows himself' in both general (universal) and personal (particular) terms, *an und für sich*, is found, or finds himself, to be incomplete and unreal until realised and individualised in the larger whole of the society, which is itself a larger individual. (c. V.) (This discussion is entirely concerned with the *Phenomenology*, Hegel's best-known and most influential work.)

For both Plato and Hegel the need and desire to understand (to understand *everything*) presents a conception of what is real at a series of progressively higher levels. Hegel's *Geist* (better translated as 'spirit' rather than as 'mind') is like Plato's Forms (Ideas) which generate both logical-epistemological understanding (as universals) and (as desired by Eros) spiritual understanding and moral motive. The *Phenomenology* is a tale of developing aspiring mind moving from the apparent to the real, and may be read as logic, or science, or an allegory of the nature of thought, or human history, or the intellectual or spiritual pilgrimage of an individual person. It can be *used* in many ways (as it was by Marx). Hegel must count himself a Platonic thinker, and his image of progress must remind us of Plato's Cave. However Hegel's omnivorous dialectic is unlike Plato's dialectic. Hegel's Reason proceeds by a continuous discarding of possibilities; doubts, ambiguities, alternatives, ramblings of any kind are officially not permitted and cannot be left 'lying about'. Seen in this way, the process seems not an increasingly widening, increasingly well-lighted all-embracing prospect, but rather an entry into some dark narrowing almost mechanical confinement. (Allegory of a Marxist state.) What is contingent, *sui generis*, incompatible, mysterious, has been ground up by the machine; but great things, love, religion, happiness, even *art* (of which Hegel has many interesting things to say) demand, not logic, but freedom. Plato is not systematic in the Hegelian sense. (After all he was inventing the whole of western philosophy.) His dialectic is the open-ended to-and-fro, sometimes inconclusive, movement of serious argument, wherein his art gives life to opposing positions. He tells us when he is using a myth (metaphor). He changes his mind, he expresses doubts. His Forms are separate and distant. In Hegel's account things may be distant but nothing is separate, and in spite of the contrasts or changes of consciousness, often so stirring and interesting, offered by the theses and antitheses, the inevitable process itself is what is real, the end is contained in the way, there is a continuum to the Absolute.

Such a continuum is deliberately broken by Plato and Kant. Hegel objected to Kant's limitation of our capacity for knowledge and goodness. That our position is limited and agnostic is for Kant an essential idea, to be connected with the nature of moral freedom and religious faith. A plausible metaphysical account of our situation and nature must be radically dualistic. Hegel's authoritative monism, which presents the absolutely rational and complete as the only real being of which all lesser individuals are intelligible parts or moments, joins fact to value in a way which not only 'loses' the individual person but ultimately devalues value. It is now (generally) taken for granted, in a variety of forms, that the individual is, in a sense and partly, a function or creation of his society and historical situation. In Hegelian argument, the society is 'more real' than the individual; and Hegel was at one time inclined to believe (as perhaps Heidegger, *mutatis mutandis*, at one time was) that the ideal and complete society could be incarnate in an actual empirically existing state. Plato never thought of society as perfectible, the ideal state exists only 'in heaven' (*Republic* 592). The myth of Eros, and the Trinity myth in the *Timaeus*, represent the spiritually inspired but irrevocably limited situation of human individuals. The dialogues are full of confused truth-seekers. Nor did Plato see the individual person as loved and guided by omnipotent divine power, or as an absorbable piece or moment in some super-human process. He regarded (as Kant did) a kind of ignorance, weakness and agnosticism, as natural to our mode of being. This admission has a political as well as an ethical importance. Plato's realistic discussions of politics in the dialogues show how far he is from being a Utopian thinker. Of course awareness of human weakness and fallibility provides no general excuse, and puts no specific limit upon our attempts to become perfect! The myth of the Cave envisages possible emergence into the sunlight. But this emergence is something to be achieved, if at all, by individuals. (*Noesis*, beyond images, holiness, the mystical.) It is not, as in Hegel, a final totality in which all entities are ultimately (logically) fused. We, inside the cave, are intuitively aware of many things whose presence and proximity we may 'feel', but which we cannot, or cannot yet, fully explain or inspect. Our sense of the presence of a vast extra-linguistic reality may be said (in the spirit of the myth) to be one such thing, as is our sense of history and of unrealised moral possibilities. This is also a place for Kant's painful *Achtung* and experience of the Sublime. Our incomplete and 'fallen' state, and our bitter awareness of it, the theme of the Old and New Testaments, is independently portrayed in Plato and the biblical tradition. There is no evidence of mutual influence in classical times. 'Nothing so far has disproved the contention that the classical Greeks did not even know the name of the Jews. In short, as far as we know, the Greeks lived happily in their classical age without recognising the existence of the Jews.' (A. D. Momigliano, *Alien Wisdom*, p. 78.) Both traditions are primarily concerned with the density and reality of the historically existing individual and his 'states of mind'. Hegel provides his successors and our world of thought with a powerful image of spiritual intellectual energy as a perpetual potential movement of liberation. (The orderly yet *swarming* impression of the *Phenomenology* may even remind one of the interrelated proliferation of gods on a Hindu temple.) However his metaphysical hubris also made his vast edifice into a prison. Hegel's ultimate monistic Absolute also engendered Utopian Marxism and doctrines which call in the structures of science to suggest that the individual person 'does not really exist' but is essentially a function of processes which transcend him.

Philosophy and theology, for all their persistent mutual hostilities, have always maintained relations and, contrary to some appearances, still do. Pope John Paul II, in his book *The Acting Person*, takes note of A. J. Ayer, whom he accuses of holding 'the metaphysical belief that values have no real existence (evaluative nihilism)' and 'the epistemological belief that values are not an object of cognition (acognitivism)'. Metaphysics is a theological thought-source, a place where theological ideas can, often surreptitiously, undergo changes which suit them to the temper of new times. The process whereby Christianity goes on keeping itself believable still persists upon the border of philosophical thought. Heidegger may be called a theological metaphysician. Hegel endowed Marxism with both its Platonic and its biblical aspects. We transcend ourselves, we strive to move out of ourselves, by dialectical revolutionary change, into a lost unity. The Hegelian dialectic can be treated as an ultimate picture of being, a fundamental form of explanation, a description of thinking consciousness, and has charm as psychological imagery, even at a popular level. Kierkegaard uses the Hegelian thesis—antithesis—synthesis in his most general account of moral progress from the aesthetic, through the moral, to the religious. Sartre takes the dialectic of Master and Slave from the *Phenomenology* as a fundamental psychological and moral truth, an image of our damned and captive state. Kierkegaard 'saves' his individual from his analysis by asserting the subjective inwardness of each person, held in private relationship with God. God, who preserves the individual, is absent from Hegel, and also from Sartre who pictures salvation from depersonalising bondage as a condition of free but empty solitude. Sartre is damned with Hegel but saved with Kant, only without God. (At any rate he thought at one moment that existentialism was humanism.) Early Marxism combined the idea of salvation by self-transcendence with the individualistic realism of Benthamite utilitarianism. Popular Marxism tended to reduce to a level of mechanical generality the idea that we apprehend 'being' through the discovery of law as dialectical materialism. We may compare here the structuralist critic's understanding of a work of literature through the discovery of its 'code', and the further claim that the text as explained by the critic *is* the work itself. The humane Marxism of the Frankfurt School (Adorno, Benjamin, Horkheimer, Marcuse) represents a (after 1989, the) breaking-up of the Marxist tradition. Marxism itself was 'saved' by a return toward realism, common-sense, and the claims of the individual; but thereby also continued the process of its own disintegration. Kant's strict distinction of fact from value, for all its misleading rigidity and unfortunate consequences, kept moral law out of the way of scientific law and endowed it with the free enlivening power of the spirit. Hegel's manner of joining fact and value threatens the latter with a scientific relativism whereby we become spectators of, and units in, a whole which we cannot understand or influence. Our best (clearest) *consciousness* is then an awareness of ourselves as ancillary, relative, and not wholly real. This is the metaphysical nemesis which neo-Marxist thought, moving beyond 'the role of the individual in history', struggled perhaps vainly to avoid; and which may be said to be a nemesis of technological civilisation as a whole. Structuralist thought, in this respect Hegelian in style, engages prophetically with the problem, and as expressed with picturesque brilliance by Derrida, and more crudely by his literary disciples, is able to view this valueless bookless future with a kind of apocalyptic glee. Of course, like some Marxist thinkers, because individualism is endemic and spirit cannot be quenched, structuralist prophets do not believe that the prophecies really apply to them. The neo-Hegelian gloom has to be contradicted from within. This generates the semi-secret élitist doctrine that although the average person is composed of 'codes', there are some free clever ones who can *invent* language. This may be seen as a secularised up-to-date version of Kant's view of the exceptional role of genius. Of course great poets remake the language and great artists break rules. Heidegger regarded poets as privileged mouthpieces of spirit. But if poets ever stop being 'unacknowledged legislators' and become (accompanied by ideological friends) acknowledged ones, poetry itself will be the first victim. In any case this has really little to do with the worship of art. It is the old idea of the priestly caste as an initiated few in its unattractive and dangerous modern dress.

*

I have been following a sort of history of the concept of consciousness, as it is indicated or implied in metaphysical systems, and I want here to say something briefly about the aims and influence of Husserl. One purpose of this will be to indicate a contrast between a Husserlian view and another very different view. 'Phenomenology' might sound like the name of a 'philosophy of consciousness', but its history exhibits the ambiguity of the term. The career of Merleau-Ponty, for instance, may be said to begin in phenomenology and end in structuralism. Wittgenstein wrote in the 1914–16 *Notebooks* (1.6.15.): 'The great problem round which everything that I write turns is: Is there an order in the world *a priori*, and if so what does it consist in?' This is the main problem of traditional metaphysics and is the programme of Husserlian phenomenology and of Derrida's structuralism (the discovery of 'a transcendental field of experience'). Husserl's ambitious project is an attempt to found an 'eidetic science', a fundamental theory of essences, to be the basis of all other forms of scientific or philosophical enquiry. Husserl's theory is about 'What is happening now', and in this respect looks like a philosophy of consciousness. The method is Kantian and transcendental, concerned with the conditions of experience, the fundamental formative net or structure of consciousness. Kant however pictured the net or screen at a level of deep generality in terms of basic general categories such as cause and substance and formal intuitions of space and time, and distinguished those from ordinary (boots and shoes, mud and hair) concepts whose operation, philosophically uninteresting, was within experience and not *a priori*. Kant's view, which would classify language as empirical (or 'local'), is a mode of thought which is strictly 'logical', or using the word in this sense 'metaphysical', in style, framed to be untainted by any degeneration into mere empirical psychology. We may here compare Wittgenstein's 'general form of the proposition', and the logical cleanness of the *Tractatus* picture. It was Wittgenstein's aim throughout, also of course in the *Investigations*, to separate philosophy clearly from psychology. The Kantian 'synthesis' which produces the representation or idea, which is the stuff or unit of experience, unifies the (manifold) world in a single grasp or grab which puts together *a priori* concepts, space and time, and empirical concepts. Kant is concerned with consciousness or experience only in its most general aspects. Husserl's transcendental philosophy is Kantian but also Cartesian and through this tendency more empirical, allowing a closer approach to psychology. Indeed phenomenology, of which Husserl is said to be the father, may be called a would-be logical kind of psychology. Husserl's fundamental philosophical unit of experience is something very much less general, something more individual and detailed, than that of Kant, thus facilitating a move to a philosophy of language. Roughly, structuralism (against a background of Herder, Rousseau, Hegel) reaches a philosophy of language (language as being, as transcendent network) through linguistics and phenomenology (including Heidegger). Wittgenstein, disturbed by Russell and influenced by Schopenhauer, went to it straight without metaphysical ontological presuppositions. (See Schopenhauer, *WWI*, Book I, section 9.)

According to Husserl, the basic unit of consciousness is the 'intentional object'. This term expresses the notion that all consciousness points beyond itself, is an indication, a holding or framing, of something beyond: a desire is *for* something, a fear *of* something, a puzzlement *about* something (etc.). Consciousness is a series of psychic acts which have intentional objects. Husserl here follows and transforms Kant's method of connecting consciousness with logic through thinking of the mind as making judgments which have logical form; Husserl enlarges the kind of judgments or intentional acts whose performance he thinks he can discern. The discerning takes place by a Cartesian move to a philosophical standpoint. The intentional objects, or *ideas*, can be isolated and identified for purposes of study by a special process of reflection, an *epoché*, a check or pause, a suspension of judgment, a 'putting into parenthesis' or into 'brackets', the so-called phenomenological reduction whereby the essence (fundamental structure) of mental activity can be immediately and intuitively grasped as pure phenomenon. (Derrida inherited this use of parenthesis.) This mode of reflection involves the suspension of the movement of thought toward ordinary empirical awareness; it is like the Cartesian move from an unphilosophical awareness of an objective world (the natural standpoint) to a philosophical awareness of the 'objective awareness', now grasped as a mental content only, and one about which one has clear immediate self-evident knowledge, pure knowledge, as contrasted with one's more dubious knowledge of a transcendent reality. 'Intentional' (inner, in the mind) objects are thus clearly distinguished from transcendent (outer, in the world) objects, and one of the former may or may not adequately represent one of the latter; the illusory judgment is just as real, when held in suspension for purposes of study, as the veridical judgment. This 'eidetic science' is supposed by Husserl to be *prior* to all other sciences since it analyses mental activity at its most fundamental level in the consciousness itself. Consciousness constitutes all objects and so all knowledge. Looked at in this way there is indeed nothing else but consciousness, it is the only thing that exists in and of itself: a thought to be found also in oriental philosophy but with different theoretical surroundings and implications. It may also be seen by ordinary modes of reflection as something (in a sense) obvious! The meaning and truth of the world is composed, as it were, of the intentional objects which can be found in the pure, clearly seen, consciousness, which the reduction *reveals*. The existence of these indubitable *intermediaries* makes language and knowledge possible. Husserl insists that this system is not subjective idealism, nor is it mere psychologism, the two abysses into which it might fall. It is a logical-metaphysical truly transcendental science. Husserlian phenomenology is not idealism even in the Kantian sense, in that the exclusively mental area of ideas which the reflective reduction examines is to be thought of as quite separate from the world of real empirical objects or states of affairs which may or may not be there to correspond to the mental acts. On the other hand, the mental realm is really primary in that it is the source of every sort of concept, without which the external world would not be an object of knowledge, and might just as well not exist at all, like Locke's 'substance' and Kant's *Ding-an-sich*. This is what Husserl means when he claims that his eidetic science is prior to all other knowledge, restoring philosophy to its sovereign position as 'queen of the sciences'. Heidegger, who totally rejected Husserl's Cartesian approach, nevertheless admits his influence. Whether or not Heidegger is a phenomenologist is an interesting (even important) question. (Gilbert Ryle, in his review of *Sein und Zeit* in *Mind* 38, 1929, treats the work as phenomenology.)

The comparison and contrast with the *Tractatus*, and also with the *Investigations*, again comes to mind. 'Logic is transcendental.' Wittgenstein rejects the Cartesian method and the idea of an explanatory mental intermediary. In what sense could one examine such an object, what role could it perform? Once one has postulated such a philosophical entity one is confronted with false philosophical problems about its relation to the world. How does language refer to the world? Wittgenstein's early answer, in accord with what Dr Johnson would say, is that it just does. The accord with the world is affected by fiat in the *Tractatus*. The 'propositions of natural science' at 6. 53 are an instance and *image* of what (factual) language can say; as contrasted with the (moral) things which can only be shown, not said. Language pictures the world (somehow) and we cannot include in the picture the method of projection by which it does so (by which the picture is made). Language is transcendental, a final network which we cannot creep under. Here Wittgenstein rejects the possibility of any general systematic philosophical account of meaning and thought in terms of a deep *psychological* structure. In the *Investigations* a variety of ways in which language deals with the world are examined with minute, not always conclusive, care. 'How do sentences do it? Don't you know? For nothing is hidden.' (435.) There are all sorts of methods by which sentences do it, and one can *look* at these without the use of any large unified theory, or any doubt about the ability of language to refer. Husserl's 'eidetic science' has proved too ambitious a project, even for those whom he influenced. It is, I think, impossible to clarify the idea of an 'intentional object', that is, it is not possible to perform the change of standpoint required by the reduction in such a way as to discern and exhibit a coherently connected range of 'essences'. The flow of consciousness is indeed observable, but cannot be arrested so as to display *isolated* items as pure phenomena. Descartes's *cogito* is a different matter; it is a momentary, though always available, movement which exhibits the alleged contrast between inner certainty and outer doubt. Descartes never suggests that one could, by prolonged and intense introspection, classify the *cogitationes* in a scientific or logical manner. Both views are vulnerable to Wittgensteinian objections. We cannot be said to have *knowledge* of what is momentary or *purely* introspectible; the 'identification' of the inner involves a *variety* of concepts whose meaning is established, and whose use in such a context justified, in the external world remote from the 'deep' position taken by the *cogito* and the phenomenological reduction. *Cogito* is an illusion; the *feeling* of certainty provides the plausibility. These objections point the transcendental seeker toward a study of language. After Husserl, phenomenology, as a search for deep or transcendental structure, has taken a variety of paths toward the two errors feared by Husserl, some toward psychologism and at least one (if structuralism may be called linguistic idealism) towards idealism. Merleau-Ponty's early book *The Phenomenology of Perception* is filled with, frankly declared, material from experimental psychology: a form of investigation later felt to be unsatisfactory by purists (including Merleau-Ponty himself) who wanted to find more philosophical and conclusive answers to their questions. Derrida's structuralism, taking fundamental patterns from Saussure, attempts to 'swallow' a certain amount of Freudian psychology. 'Deconstruction' of literary texts often adopts a style of doctrinaire psychologism, for instance by assuming that a writer's unconscious motives provide deepest clues to meaning. Derrida's philosophy, formally stated as a search for transcendental structure, is in general more like a deterministic idealism of language, wherein psychological categories are to receive a more basic analysis. The authoritarian aspiration to a unique systematic truth distorts what could be valuable in a more humble hermeneutic; and promotes (at its worst) the haze of pseudo-scientific jargon in which gross divergences from common-sense are announced without any philosophical justification. Wittgenstein, discussing meaning without the postulation of quasi-psychological intermediaries, assumes that language refers to the world, and (in the *Investigations*) that unsystematic philosophical things can be said about how this happens.

These problems about 'deep structure' may prompt an outsider (including the outsider who dwells inside every philosopher) to ask whether there is any deep structure. Of course we recognise that our very small number of philosophical geniuses have suggested structures which have dominated and guided centuries of thought not only inside philosophy but in science, in theology, in morality, and in the most general sorts of world-view held by unreflective people. Philosophy, it may be said, collects and formalises new ideas which, at various times, for various often mysterious reasons, are hanging about in the air, sensed by thinkers of all kinds. This 'universal' role of philosophy has led to it being thought of as a sovereign discipline. Since Hegel this mystery too, the *Zeitgeist*, has been a subject for metaphysical theorising. But after it all, and in spite of the undoubted influence of philosophical pictures, does anybody really believe, in any close or even quasi-literal sense, in Kant's system or Hegel's system? Is Kant's 'machinery' supposed, even by Kantians, to be *really there* 'in the mind', what would it be like to believe this? Do we think that all these operations are taking place now? This may be considered a very naive question which, if pressed, might seem like an attempt to dismiss philosophy altogether; as philosophy is in fact, for just such considerations, dismissed by many people who know only a little about it. Of course the 'outsider' receives various sophisticated answers, of which one may be derived from Plato who, in the midst of hard detailed discussion and the use of innumerable examples, presents fundamental ideas metaphysically in the form of myth. You have to work hard to understand, and then throw away the ladder. (*Tractatus* 6. 54.) The *work* must be understood in relation to a conclusion which is not to be thought of as 'containing' it. Learning philosophy is learning a particular kind of intuitive understanding. Doubtless learning anything difficult may be said to involve what may be called intuition; and the idea will be less than enlightening unless one can suggest where it is and what it does. Plato's myths 'cover' and (often) clarify intuitive leaps which in other philosophers are also required but not (for better or worse) similarly adorned. The term 'intuition', often opposed to 'reason', is perhaps a dangerous one to use. It may be said that an 'intuitive leap' must be either a wild guess or a piece of unusually fast reasoning! What I mean to indicate here is that what is 'deep' in philosophy is not something literal or quasi-factual or quasi-scientific. A careful explicit use of metaphor, often instinctive, is in place. This may seem to leave the final utterance open to a degree of (carefully situated) ambiguity: which may in itself be a philosophical position. Formal philosophy can come only so far, and after that can only point; Plato's *Seventh Letter* suggests something like this. This is not mysticism but a recognition of a difficulty. Philosophers who feel able to dispel all ambiguity also have to explain that a philosophical schema is not like a literal account of the functioning of an engine, but is a special *method of explanation*, not easy to understand, but having its own traditional standards of clarification and truthfulness. Discussions and arguments proceeding from here are also philosophy, and philosophers, in the British and American empiricist school for example, have been much concerned with them. The continual demand for what has been called the 'cash value' of abstract philosophical statements represents this very proper unease. This can also go too far in the direction of literalism, as when difficult concepts which cannot easily be explained in simple terms are classified as 'emotive' or dismissed as meaningless. In general, empiricism is one essential aspect of good philosophy, just as utilitarianism is one essential aspect of good moral philosophy. It represents what must not be ignored. It remembers the contingent. There is also, in the down-to-earth or anti-metaphysical style, the attitude, sometimes expressed by Wittgenstein, that the philosopher has no positive role, but is to sit at home until particular problems are brought to his attention. (See 'the right method of philosophy', *Tractatus* 6. 53.) If Wittgenstein was preaching this, he certainly did not practise it, and it would be a difficult programme for a gifted philosophical thinker to carry out. Well, *is* there, discoverable by *philosophy*, deep structure, and if we assume (as of course we may not) that (somehow) there is or *must be*, what mode of philosophical speech can deal with it? Is it, initially, something psychological, or physical, or moral, which philosophy may comment upon, and set out in a formal manner in philosophy of mind, or philosophy of science, or moral philosophy, or philosophy of religion?

I hope in what follows to 'talk around' some of these questions. Such 'talking' may constitute or indicate answers. If we see why a certain kind of explanation must fail this will help us to see what to do next. Husserlian phenomenology and some of its descendants or (in similar style) rivals seem to me to constitute a philosophical dead end, because the chosen method of description or analysis of consciousness is too abstract, too rigid, inappropriately specialised, is at the wrong level, misses the nature of what it is attempting to explain. The detailed mobility of consciousness, its polymorphous complexity and the inherence in it of constant evaluation, is lost. Such theorising fails because it aims at a kind of scientific status, mixes philosophy with over-simplified psychology, or attempts to offer a 'neutral' analysis which ignores morality (value) or treats it as a small special subject; whereas the inherence of evaluation, of moral atmosphere, pressure, concepts, presuppositions, in consciousness, constitutes the main problem and its importance. The charm of Hegel is that he accepted this aspect of consciousness as fundamental. At the other end of the spectrum those who share Husserl's approach will be saying: but if morality is to be put into an account of mind we shall have nothing but confusion. States of mind are too mixed and complex, subject to various modes of continuity, and coloured by presupposition and evaluation for classification in terms of desires, beliefs, etc., to be useful. Hegel observes this in the quotation given earlier from the *Phenomenology*, where he speaks of mental contents so sorted as constituting a ragbag. Of course the mind is like a ragbag, full of amazing incoherent oddments. This must be set as part of the philosophical problem of finding ways of talking about fundamental matters. Hegel so sets it, but in the context of a solution which obliterates the picture of individual people in an accidental world.

There may seem to be some awkwardness in continuing to pose the question of consciousness in the context of such heterogeneous theories, but it is an awkwardness which must be maintained. Looking at a variety of other views and metaphors may help, through under-standing of what seems unsatisfactory, toward a grasp of something essential. At intervals one must stand back and ask: Well, what *am* I worried about, what do I want, what am I after, what is supposed to be missing? Here one tries, roughly and metaphorically, to delineate an impression. There are 'moral judgments', which may in some ways resemble judgments in law courts, or which take place at stated times and initiate clearly visible new courses of action or the embryos of new dispositions. But there are also ways and states in which value inheres in consciousness, morality colours an outlook, light penetrates a dark-ness. We have senses of direction and absolute checks. There are quali-ties of consciousness. Perhaps a purified consciousness might be able to do the sort of thing which Husserl wanted? After all, do I not wish to connect morality with knowledge? With truth, *ergo* with know-ledge? The Cartesian movement, in Husserl's use and understanding of it, is not regarded as a moral movement or achievement. Is it then so simple and so easy? Descartes and Husserl *appeal* to consciousness and do so with certain ends in view; the consciousness of consciousness is to reveal the foundations of knowledge. (Do we all somehow believe in the possibility of such a revelation?) Descartes also says that in the pure separated (inner non-transcendent) consciousness we also dis-cover God. We intuitively, and with certainty, know of God when with this particular movement or intensity of reflection we shift from the natural standpoint into the mind. This does not just mean that when we think about God, instead of thinking about the stove, we intuit God's existence. Descartes means that any pure certainty *includes* (is internally related to) an intuition of God. God is the light of truth. *Dominus illuminatio mea*. We might here translate 'God' into absolute value, the unconditioned, the reality of good.

Are there 'deep structures' in the mind, or in the soul? How is one to deny the claim, in the sense in which Thrasymachus for instance meant it, that there is nothing deep? Should philosophical approaches to the problem recognise the omnipresence of a moral sense in thinking and knowing? There is a point at which reflection, however beset, must stand firm and be prepared to go on circling round an essential point which remains obscure. As in the working of a ratchet, one must hold anything which seems like an advance, while seeking a method of producing the next movement. The contrast between the *cogitatio* of Husserl and that of Descartes offers a point from which to prospect. Descartes does not suggest that it is extremely difficult, though of course it implies some ability to reflect, to enact *cogito ergo sum*. He thinks (with the thought of his time and which unites him to Anselm) that the idea of God and the sense of God's presence is close, or potentially close, or integrally close, to any man. A modern formulation might suggest that the idea of good, of value, of truth, is thus close. This insight combines with, is one with, the ability to examine or arrest a momentary non-transcendent experience or instant of consciousness, as part of an argument which justifies our confidence in our forms of knowledge and our conception of the world. Husserl does not maintain that the movement to, or from, his *cogitatio* or 'essence' has anything to do with value or moral insight, or with any specialised expertise except that of sustained introspection; whereas Descartes believes that by discovering God, and the light of truth, in an exercise of reflection we discover our ability to know the realities of our world. What is discovered is a sense of reality, an orientation.

I want to consider here some criticisms of Husserl uttered by a Zen thinker, Katsuki Sekida, in his book *Zen Training*. Sekida quotes (p. 188) a passage in which Husserl describes the phenomenological reduction:

'Only through a reduction, the same one we have already called *phenomenological reduction*, do I attain an absolute datum which no longer presents anything transcendent. Even if I should put in question the ego and the world and the ego's mental life as such, still my simply "seeing" reflection on what is given in the apperception of the relevant mental process and on my ego, yields the *phenomenon* of this apperception; the phenomenon, so to say, of "perception construed as my perception". Of course, I can also make use of the natural mode of reflection here, and relate this phenomenon to my ego, postulating this ego as an empirical reality through saying again: I have this phenomenon, it is mine. Then in order to get back to the pure phenomenon, I would have to put the ego, as well as time and the world once more into question, and thereby display a pure phenomenon, the pure *cogitatio*.' But while I am perceiving I can also look, by way of purely 'seeing', at the perception, at itself as it is there, and ignore its relation to the ego, or at least abstract from it. Then the perception which is thereby grasped and delimited in 'seeing' is an absolutely given pure phenomenon in the phenomenological sense, renouncing anything transcendent?'

This 'reduction', providing a cognitive phenomenon which makes no statement about a transcendent world, is the crucial item in Husserl's 'eidetic science'. Hereby we are supposed to be able to inspect pure primal essences which are the basis of all knowledge. Wittgenstein would attack such a programme by pointing out the impossibility of contextless knowledge. Adorno regarded Husserl's reduction as a last move of bourgeois idealism in search of a safe world accessible to universal knowledge. Sekida attacks Husserl from another angle:

'Pure consciousness. Such a state of looking simultaneously both into one's own nature and into universal nature can be attained only when consciousness is deprived of its habitual way of thinking. Working on a koan is one way of doing this. The necessary condition of consciousness that we must achieve is called pure consciousness. Pure consciousness and pure existence are fundamental concepts for the discussion of Zen from a modern point of view. The phenomenologist Husserl says that when every involvement of the ego as a person is suspended through the method of phenomenological reduction, the pure phenomenon is attained. He carries out this reduction in his head, by changing the attitude of his mind, and seems to suggest that it can be done without much difficulty. The idea of suspending every involvement of the personal ego agrees closely with our view of the need to eliminate the habitual way of consciousness. However, the methods advocated for doing this are utterly different. In zazen [the Zen discipline of sitting in meditation] we effect it not by a simple change of mental attitude, but by hard discipline of body and mind, going through absolute samadhi [state of deep meditation], in which time, space and delusive thoughts fall away. We root out the emotionally and intellectually habituated mode of consciousness, and then find that a pure state of consciousness appears. There must, therefore, be a rather considerable difference between what we call pure consciousness and the pure phenomenon of the phenomenologists. Nevertheless, there must also be some resemblance between the two.'

(pp. 100–101.)

Sekida 'takes Husserl seriously' in a way in which, for instance, Adorno does not and Wittgenstein would not. The idea of 'pure consciousness' or 'pure cognition' makes sense for Sekida, but not as something to be attained or used by Husserl's, as it would seem to him naive, method. Sekida questions Husserl's assumption that there is a pure *cogitatio* which can be reached by 'setting the ego aside' in an act of philosophical reflection available to anybody who can do philosophy. The egoistic (personal) formulation and distortion of reality reaches right down to the base of unenlightened cognition, and one cannot by a reflective move cancel it and obtain some 'purified' introspectible mental datum. There is no such thing, discoverable by philosophers who may be clever but not necessarily (in a moral or spiritual sense) selfless or wise, which could be set up as an *eidos* or essence to become part of a general profound 'science' of the human world. There can be no such science. Husserl's move should here (I argue) be contrasted with that of Descartes, whose *cogitatio* is an *ad hominem* philosophical argument and not a would-be item in a science. Zen proclaims itself as 'not a philosophy' and Sekida is speaking critically as a spiritual thinker and not as a counter-theorist. Nevertheless such comments, by morally religiously minded outsiders who feel they must object to philosophical descriptions or reductions, can be of value to philosophers. Much of present-day moral philosophy misses obvious and essential considerations which cannot be simply 'left outside'. Sekida's argument holds not only against Husserl, but against other accounts of mind and 'placing' of morals, by empiricists and structuralists. It is impossible to describe mind philosophically without including its moral mobility, the sense in which any situation is individualised by being pierced by moral considerations, by being given a particular moral colour or orientation. One resorts here, to obtain understanding, to metaphors. (The sharp call of an unwelcome duty seems to come from elsewhere; but it descends upon a countryside which already has its vegetation and its contours.) Consciousness *au fond* and *ab initio* must contain an element of truth-seeking through which it is also evaluated.

In this sense, some cognitions are purer than others; but we cannot descend by any unitary 'scientific' or systematic method below the levels at which, in various ways, we test truth and reflect upon moral understanding. The parts of such process must be seen as everywhere, as something in which we are all engaged; but there is no science, or overall philosophical 'explanation', of 'the whole'.

One cannot postulate a non-transcendent pure cognition. Wittgenstein (who would never use such language) may be said to agree. Sekida however is not merely making a negative criticism of Husserl. He rejects Husserl's concept of an eidetic science involving (philosophically motivated) cases of pure (*qua* non-transcendent, purely 'in the mind' like the *cogito*) cognitive experiences. The 'resemblance' he mentions would seem to rest simply upon the idea of a pure awareness or purified consciousness. Husserl's 'purity' is that of a skilled intellectual. Sekida's is that of an enlightened individual who has had an 'arduous training' aimed at overcoming his egoistic illusions. Science is (supposedly) morally neutral. Zen is a form of spiritual discipline. Here one cannot separate cognition from an idea of truth as something reached by a spiritual or moral path. This would be, in general terms, a Platonic view. The details of such a training, which could take many forms, are another matter. Many different disciplines can serve spiritual ends. Buddhism and Plato would agree about this, and also about the difficulty, at a certain point, of talking about it without falsification. Plato uses myths. Sekida, trying to explain something to outsiders, uses a terminology of overcoming the dualism between subject and object. (To be thought of as a disposable ladder, since Zen denies it is philosophy.) He quotes (p. 175) a Japanese poem, by Nansen, which is, he says, 'a splendid description of pure cognition'. Pure cognition is also called 'direct pointing'.

> Hearing, seeing, touching and knowing are not one and one;
> Mountains and rivers should not be viewed in the mirror.
> The frosty sky, the setting moon – at midnight;
> With whom will the serene waters of the lake reflect the shadows
>     in the cold?

Sekida comments:

'"Mountains and rivers should not be viewed in the mirror" means that you should not say, as the idealist does, that the external world is nothing but the projection of the subjective mirror of your mind, and that sensation cannot transcend itself to hit upon the external object. The truth is the opposite of this. In profound silence, deep in the middle of the night, the lake serenely reflects the frosty sky, the setting moon, rivers, trees and grass. The cognition occurs solemnly and exclusively between you and the objects. Cognition is accomplished through two processes: first, pure cognition; second, the recognition of pure cognition. In pure cognition there is no subjectivity and no objectivity. Think of the moment your hand touches the cup: there is only the touch. The next moment you recognise that you felt the touch. A touch is first effected just through the interaction between hand and object, and at that moment, pure cognition takes place. The next moment, the pure cognition is recognised by the reflecting action of consciousness, and recognised cognition is completed. Then there arise subjectivity and objectivity . . .'

Sekida's account (which I have touched upon only briefly) emerges from a religious background; he wishes to connect pure cognition, the disappearance of subject-object, with the disappearance of the egoistic illusions, of thick ingrained egoism, which prevents true attention to things and people. No self, no subject, observes the serene waters of the lake. Coming from a religious thinker, there is an 'extremism' in what Sekida is suggesting, he advocates a lengthy ascesis at the end of which some purer and better state of consciousness and being is achieved. Adorno, coming out of Marxism and out of a deep involvement with an art (music), is also concerned with quality of consciousness, and with a purification of the dialectic of subject and object by an achieved respect for the object. The place occupied in Sekida's view by a state of spiritual enlightenment is occupied in orthodox Marxism by the Utopian notion of a really existing perfect society, and in 'maverick Marxism' (e.g. Adorno) by the *idea* of a good (perhaps unattainable) society working perpetually in the minds of properly intentioned people: a regulative idea which reaches back to Plato's ideal city (*Republic* 592) and to Augustine's, not unrelated, *City of God*.

To stay with Buddhism. I have suggested that the concept of consciousness should contain the (moral) idea of truth-seeking. If this is left out at first it cannot be put in later. Some cognitions are purer, truer, than others, one cannot separate cognition from some idea of truthfulness. The purification of consciousness and cognition can take

[ 243 ]

place upon many different 'paths', life is full of 'learnings' and 'attendings'; other things being equal (for instance, if there is no evil involvement or intention), any skill teaches some virtue. Zen teachers say that Zen cannot be formulated as a philosophy. Enlightenment is achieved through a way of life which must include prolonged meditation. This process may involve the use of that characteristically Zen instrument, the koan, a paradox or contradiction which defeats imagination and conceptual thought, but which must be held in sustained attention. The, or one, purpose of this, I take it, is to break the networks not only of casual thinking and feeling, but also of accustomed intellectual thinking, to break 'the natural standpoint', and the natural ego: producing thereby a selfless (pure, good) consciousness. This aim is not unlike that of the monastic disciplines of any austere religious order, but its methods seem more extreme, and its end-points less visible. Of course 'higher' spiritual states tend to be invisible, to appear empty or pointless from lower positions. (Schopenhauer's Nirvana.) But in Judaeo-Christian society, for instance, we think we can recognise 'the enlightened man', if he is out in the world, by his unusually unselfish and courageously compassionate conduct. The Zen sage, who is usually supposed to return to the world, may seem to us harder to understand, perhaps because Zen dispenses with the mass of supportive, partly aesthetic, imagery with which the idea of a selfless being is surrounded in the west. Plato's man who returns to the Cave, already familiar to us through our ability to picture the degrees of his ascent, has more easily imaginable tasks to perform.

Emphasis is laid by Zen, partly in its instruction through art, upon the small contingent details of ordinary life and the natural world. Buddhism teaches respect and love for *all things*. This concerned attention implies or effects a removal from the usual egoistic fuzz of self-protective anxiety. One may not be sure that those who observe stones and snails lovingly will also thus observe human beings, but such observation is a *way*, an act of respect for individuals, which is itself a virtue, and an image of virtue. The enlightened man returns to, that is *discovers*, the world. He begins by thinking that rivers are merely rivers and mountains are merely mountains, proceeds to the view that rivers are not rivers and mountains are not mountains, and later achieves the deep understanding that rivers are really rivers and mountains are really mountains. The Japanese *haiku* is a very short poem with a strict formal structure, which *points*, sometimes in a paradoxical way, at some aspect of the visible world. It indicates that outer and inner, subject and object, are one, in a way which does not lose or subjectivise the world. Zen painting also combines a skill, born of long and strict teaching, with a throw-away simplicity. In a few strokes, the pointless presence, the thereness, of the plant, the animal, the man. Zen uses art in teaching, but rejects the discursive intellectual and literary pomp and content of western art, so full of tropes and references, illusions and attachments. The 'hardness' of Zen art is to leave no holes or surfaces where such things could lodge and grow. The notion of achieving a pure cognitive state where the object is not disturbed by the subjective ego, but where subject and object simply exist as one is here made comprehensible through a certain experience of art and nature. (Dualism is overcome: not such an arcane idea after all.) A discipline of meditation wherein the mind is alert but emptied of self enables this form of awareness, and the disciplined practice of various skills may promote a similar unselfing, or '*décréation*' to use Simone Weil's vocabulary. Attend 'without thinking about'. This is 'good for us' because it involves respect, because it is an exercise in cleansing the mind of selfish preoccupation, because it is an experience of what truth is *like*.

All this may sound like an achievement of 'the aesthetic'. The ambiguity of the aesthetic sensibility is a puzzle for moral philosophers, and indeed for moral agents. Not all art is readily seen to be spiritual or truth-bearing, or concerned with details of the world in either Zen or Italian Renaissance senses. Art cannot and should not be so defined or confined. But in *this* context, and talking of 'consciousness', one may use an argument or example from art. A contemplative observation of contingent 'trivial' detail (insects, leaves, shapes of screwed-up paper, looks and shadows of anything, expressions of faces) is a prevalent and usually, at least in a minimal sense, 'unselfing' activity of consciousness. This might also be called an argument from perception. It 'proves', as against generalising and reductionist philosophical or psychological theories, that individual consciousness or awareness can be spoken of in theoretical discussions of morality. It is a place where the moral and the aesthetic join. It marks a path *through* the aesthetic. This is a path which neo-Marxists too have taken in the direction of a philosophy of the individual. Theodor Adorno's assertion, against vulgar Marxism and against Husserl and against Hegel, of the concept of individual experience is framed in terms not unlike those of Sekida, and implies an idea of truth which arises from, but passes beyond, aesthetic experience. He attacked Kierkegaard for disparaging 'the aesthetic', and regarded its rescue as *politically* necessary. I shall return to Adorno in later discussions of politics.

I want now to quote some passages from *Selected Letters of Rainer Maria Rilke 1902–1926*. Here Rilke describes looking at some pictures by Cézanne with a friend (Mathilde Vollmoeller):

'Trained and using her eye wholly as a painter [she] said: "Like a dog he sat in front of it and simply looked, without any nervousness or irrelevant speculation." And she said something else very good in connection with his technique (which you can see from an unfinished picture). "Here", she said, pointing to the spot, "he knew what he wanted and said it (part of an apple); but there it is still open, because he didn't yet know. He only did what he knew, nothing else." '

And about a self-portrait of Cézanne, Rilke speaks of

'an animal attentiveness which maintains a continuing, objective vigilance in the unwinking eyes. And how great and incorruptible this objectivity of his gaze was, is confirmed in an almost touching manner by the circumstance that, without analysing or in the remotest degree regarding his expression from a superior standpoint, he made a replica of himself with so much humble objectiveness, with the credulity and extrinsic interest and attention of a dog which sees itself in a mirror and thinks: there is another dog.'

Rilke speaks of how much, in doing his own work, he has learnt from Cézanne:

'I am on the road to becoming a worker ... I was with his pictures again today; it is extraordinary what an environment they create about themselves. Without studying any single one, and standing between the two great halls, you can feel their presence gathering into a colossal reality. It is as if these colours took away all your indecisions for ever and ever. The good conscience of these reds, these blues – their simple truthfulness teaches you; and if you place yourself among them as receptively as you can they seem to be doing something for you. Also you notice, better and better each time, how necessary it was to get beyond even love; it comes naturally to you to love each one of these things if you have made them yourself; but if you show it, you make

[ 246 ]

them less well; you judge them instead of *saying* them. You cease being impartial; and love, the best thing of all, remains outside your work, does not enter into it, is left over unresolved beside it: this is how the sentimentalist school of painting came into being (which is no better than the realist school). They painted "I love this" instead of painting "Here it is". In the latter case everybody must look carefully to see whether I loved it or not. It is not shown at all, and many people would even assert that there was no mention of love in it. So utterly has it been consumed without residue in the act of making. This consuming of love in anonymous work, which gives rise to such pure things, probably no one has succeeded in doing so completely as old Cézanne.'

(pp. 150, 163, 151–2.)

These remarks (all to Clara Rilke) exhibit, in a way which we may understand if we are acquainted with any art or craft, what kind of achievement 'pure cognition' or 'perception without reverie' might be: to do with 'animal attentiveness', 'good conscience', 'only doing what you know', 'simple truthfulness', the 'consuming of love in anonymous work'. Love becomes invisible (Cordelia), its activity and its being are inward. 'A colossal reality' which 'removes indecisions'. Though here we must also quote another remark of Rilke in the same context: 'Ah, we ought to work – that's all we can do, in everything else we are tenth-rate.' The words of an artist. I do not think that Simone Weil would feel that we had to, or ought to, resign ourselves to being *tenth-rate*! (As if the artist were excused from morals.)

Simone Weil (*Notebooks*, pp. 395, 406) on Zen: 'The primitive Zen method seems to consist of a gratuitous search of such intensity that it takes the place of all attachments. But, because it is gratuitous, it cannot become an object of attachment except in so far as it is actively pursued, and the activity involved in this fruitless search becomes exhausted. When exhaustion point has been almost reached, some shock or other brings about detachment.' 'The idea behind Zen Buddhism: to perceive *purely*, without any admixture of reverie (my idea when I was seventeen).' The imageless austerity of Zen is impressive and attractive. It represents to us 'the real thing', what it is like to be stripped of the ego, and how difficult this is. (Plato's *distance* from the sun.) Simone Weil felt a natural affinity with this 'extremism' which indeed she practised in her own life. She had studied Hindu and Buddhist philosophy. She at the same time loved Plato and the mystical Christ.

[ 247 ]

Relentless asceticism may be suspect simply because we 'do not know what is going on'. This indeed may never be known, even by the ascetic himself. (God only knows.) In religious houses, doubts constantly return: is it a spiritual dark night or is it just egoistic despair? Many dedicated self-denying recluses return to the world, or are in constant intermittent touch with the world, tending some few or many who come to them for spiritual help. (Such people have their own temptations, it must be wonderful to be treated as godlike.) In fact what we sinners usually want is *love*, to be in touch with pure just loving judgment. (Like God.) The secluded disciplined religious may provide this, or may provide some substitute, or may be wrapped in private egoism, or else simply mad. And even if mad, who can tell, spirit itself may seem, or *be*, mad. (Father Ferapont in *The Brothers Karamazov*.) Zen has become known and practised in the west for many reasons, for its spiritual aids of course, for its severity, for its bizarre methods, for its religious godlessness and imagelessness and apparent lack of ecstasy and for not being a philosophy. Not everyone approves of Zen. Arthur Koestler (in his book *Bricks for Babel*) connected it with Japanese militarism (Bushido). Traditional Zen stories involve senseless jokes, which may be given as koans, and even physical brutality. A koan: an arbitrary thing offered to concentration. (The most famous koan: What is the sound of one hand clapping?) 'The search for the meaning of the koan results in a "dark night" which is followed by illumination.' (Simone Weil, *Notebooks*, p. 396.) The Zen 'attack on reason' occurs within a religious discipline. In fact there is an air almost of cool rationality in the mounting of the Zen method. The question recurs, can such religious practice make people *better*? Certainly it may make them more calm, more 'collected', less given to egoistic passions, in many ways more 'unselfish'. But when you are back again with rivers and mountains are you more able to understand and care for other people? What about *love* as it is understood by Plato and in Christianity? Well, again, how can one say? What Christians call love may on closer inspection appear to be shot with egoisms and delusions. The figure of Christ *means* love, but this meaning is regularly degraded by its users. Perhaps Schopenhauer followed a Buddhist path in making compassion, not love, the prime virtue. Here it may seem, in no idle way, a matter of concepts. But equally, ascetic disciplines cannot easily be judged from the outside. Zen may seem cold; yet Zen art lovingly portrays the tiny things of the world, the details, blithely existing without intelligibility; this too is moral training. Southern Buddhism makes a more liberal use of spiritual images and most evidently the ideal of respect, love, for all created beings. A 'patriarch from the east' comes to us in the form of the Dalai Lama, eastern religion may be becoming more visible and comprehensible. Christianity has of course its own styles of iconoclasm, and its own ecstasies. Many people leave their churches because reason forbids belief, not only in God, but in saints, visions, revelations, mystical states and so on. Buddhism and Hinduism have avoided the awkward unique figure of the Judaeo-Christian God as Individual Person. Roughly, if there are many gods or icons or godlike beings (the 'polytheism' shuddered at by the west) it may be easier to perceive, or come to perceive, these as sources of spiritual energy, and not as literal-historical supernatural people. Perhaps the deep nature of religion is (after all, and as it may seem now) better understood in the east where it is (if not destroyed by dictators) less vulnerable. There, I suspect, the difference between the sophisticated and the unsophisticated believer is less sharp, not because the sophisticated believer is idolatrous, but because the unsophisticated believer has a more multiform, though not less sincere and passionate, relation to the spiritual. Such speculations look no doubt toward the future; and of course nothing here belittles our essential light-giving truth-seeking western reason (or Reason), or ignores the horrors of religious intolerance and mutual hate exhibited not only (for instance) in India, but in many parts of our own civilised scenery. What will the future of religion be like on this planet, will we go on attempting to overcome the ego, will we even care about it? Can there still, now, be avatars, great teachers pure of heart in whose truth we can believe? I think there are such people, we are unlikely to meet them, but such presences can distribute light, they can prove something: even, in our more closely knitted planet, have influence. Profound change is the reward or privilege of few of us. We must be content with our local intuitions of what is good; Kant would say we require nothing more! On the other hand the concept of the holy must not be lost.

What is important is that we now take in conceptions of religion without God, and of meditation as religious exercise. There is, just as there used (with the old God) to be, a place of wisdom and calm to which we can remove ourselves. We can make our own rites and images, we can preserve the concept of holiness. The veil of Maya is not a single mysterious screen which can suddenly be whisked away by magic. We need the Platonic picture here. We are moving through a continuum within which we are aware of truth and falsehood, illusion and reality, good and evil. We are continuously striving and learning, discovering and discarding images. Here we are not forced to choose between a 'religious life' and a 'secular life', or between being a 'goodie' and being a cheerful egoist! The whole matter is far more complex and more detailed. Our business is with the continual activity of our own minds and souls and with our own possibilities of being truthful and good. Incidentally, and philosophically, we may see here the necessity of the concept of consciousness.

Plato uses an image of a philosophical problem as being like a hunted animal, carefully cornered in a thicket which on approach turns out to be empty. The idea of quality of consciousness seems an unavoidable one, but how is it to be handled? The ubiquity of value demands a link between consciousness and cognition. A good quality of consciousness involves a continual discrimination between truth and falsehood. This is something we may become better or worse at; it is, involving the formation of habit, the background of virtuous action. 'Pure cognition', picked up here from Sekida's terminology as used by him in an attack on Husserl, must not of course be understood as indicating some improved Husserlian method whereby 'essences' could after all, with less difficulty, be surveyed. There are no such essences. It is rather to be thought of (and this is its point) as a penetration toward the true, real, aspects of the ordinary world. I shall not retain the phrase 'pure cognition' in discussions which follow as it is too 'artful' and open to misunderstanding. It is better to use simpler terms. Rilke's words give us, in the context of art, an idea of what 'pure cognition', as something both pleasing and edifying, might mean, which we can use analogously in other moral situations. Perception unclouded by base and irrelevant thoughts. I want to say that the emergence of awareness, perception, judgment, knowledge, in consciousness is a process in which value (moral colour) is inherent. Both the necessity and the difficulty of discussing quality of consciousness was grasped, and in his awkward (valuable) frankness exhibited, by Schopenhauer.

'The higher the consciousness has risen the more distinct and connected are the thoughts, the clearer the perceptions, the more intense the emotions. Through it everything gains more depth: emotion, sadness, joy and sorrow. Commonplace blockheads are not even capable of real joy: they live on in dull insensibility. While to one man his consciousness only presents his own existence, together with the motives which must be apprehended for the purpose of sustaining and enlivening it in a bare comprehension of the external world, it is to another a *camera obscura* in which the macrocosm itself is exhibited.'

(*WWI*, Supplement to Book II, ch. xxii.)

Schopenhauer is speaking in general terms about a gradation of intellectual and aesthetic awareness, to which he gives a Platonic spiritual sense. His language is a trifle blunt; we are all blockheads in some respects, and it is not easy to judge the sensibility of others. I do not care, either, for the *camera obscura* image, which suggests the 'mirror' rightly rejected by Sekida, and pictures the mind as a space separated from the world and with a different light. But Schopenhauer's imagery is casual here and should not be taken in a systematic metaphysical sense. He is often better understood as a (sometimes blundering) empiricist with a large metaphysical erudition and a religious vision who dashes at problems again and again trying doggedly to illuminate them in ordinary terminology. One of his merits is that he is prepared to exhibit his puzzlement and to ramble. Wittgenstein accuses Schopenhauer of evading what is 'deep'. Schopenhauer may thus 'give up', but he recognises his obstacle, rushes off at a tangent, tries to wander round it, talks, even chats, about it, and can instruct us in this way too. (An insuperable difficulty may or may not be a sun, but it gives some light.)

If it is evident that our stream of awareness is a bearer of moral judgment, and if we do not think that morality is an illusion, then this outlaws certain kinds of theories. There are many ways of 'picturing' consciousness, of which Rilke's and Sekida's are examples. Many philosophers, including Berkeley and Hume and many twentieth-century empiricists and existentialists, have been impressed by the elusive, fragmentary or messy nature of the so-called stream. Schopenhauer admits elsewhere, 'In consequence of the inevitably distracted and fragmentary nature of all our thinking . . . and the mingling of ideas of different kinds thereby introduced, to which even the noblest human minds are subject, we really have only *half* a *consciousness* with which to grope about in the labyrinth of our life.' (*WWI*, Supplement to Book I, ch. xv; Schopenhauer's italics.) Schopenhauer makes the point more precisely, and in a way which sounds for us a more modern note, anticipating Wittgenstein and Derrida, as follows:

'Speech, as an object of outer experience, is obviously nothing more than a very complete telegraph which communicates *arbitrary signs* with the greatest rapidity and the *finest distinctions of difference*. [My italics.] But what do these signs mean? How are they interpreted? When someone speaks do we at once translate words into pictures of the fancy, which instantaneously flash upon us, arrange and link themselves together, and assume form and colour according to the words that are poured forth and their grammatical inflections? What a tumult there would be in our brains while we listened to a speech, or to the reading of a book. But what actually happens is not this at all. The meaning of a speech is, as a rule, immediately grasped, accurately and distinctly taken in, without the imagination being brought into play. It is reason which speaks to reason, keeping within its own province.'

(*WWI*, Book I, ch. i, section 9. See on this topic also *On the Fourfold Root of the Principle of Sufficient Reason*, section 28.)

In speaking of imagination and reason Schopenhauer is using Kantian terminology. We see here however how forward-looking this great empiricist is, how amid his metaphysics he keeps the empirical temper and pauses to look carefully at details; his omnivorous industry reveals a more various world than that usually on display in a book of philosophy. He shows his width of vision and his grasp of the future not least in his *philosophical* discovery of Buddhism and Hinduism. Western 'demythologising' theology, seeking a less literal reading of scripture and a more mystical conception of spirituality, might even be ready to profit from a marriage of eastern insights with the Platonism which St Augustine introduced into Christianity. Schopenhauer's Will to Live, in his official account of it, is a ruthless thoughtless force; but he also unofficially manifests a sense of our caring participation in a unity of nature, which is more true to his understanding of oriental wisdom. The *Timaeus* suggests that man saves or cherishes creation by lending a consciousness to nature, and these or similar ideas (noted by Schopenhauer) are in St Augustine. (Augustine, *De Civitate Dei* xi, 28, Schopenhauer, *WWI*, Book II, section 24.) Freud's paper on 'Resistances to

Psychoanalysis' (*Collected Papers* V) salutes Schopenhauer for proclaiming 'the incomparable significance of sexual life'. Freud goes on to say, 'What psychoanalysis called sexuality was by no means identical with the impulsion towards a union of the two sexes or towards producing a pleasurable sensation in the genitals; it had far more resemblance to the all-inclusive and all-preserving Eros of Plato's *Symposium*.' Well, Schopenhauer failed to appreciate Plato's Eros, and his Will to Live was concerned with sex as ensuring the continuation of the species, and in that sense 'all-inclusive and all-preserving'. ('The Metaphysics of the Love of the Sexes', Supplement to Book IV, ch. xliv.) Certainly the Will has nothing to do with superficial romance and may in this sense count as Freudian. Schopenhauer, as mentioned earlier, allowed a certain escape from the bondage of the Will through contemplation of art. We may also find, in his 'unofficial' doctrine, a 'grace' or liberation afforded by response to the natural world including kindness to animals. Here, in a concern for animals, absent from Plato's outlook and (as Schopenhauer observes) from Kant's, we can see a release or redemption in a new kind of recognition of our unity with nature.

On animals (*The Basis of Morality* II 8) Schopenhauer reports Kant as saying that 'beings devoid of reason (hence animals) are *things* and therefore should be treated merely as *means* that are not at the same time an *end*'. He also quotes Kant's view that 'man can have no duty to any beings except human', and 'cruelty to animals is contrary to man's duty *to himself* because it deadens in him the feeling of sympathy to their sufferings, and thus a natural tendency that is very useful to morality in relation to other human beings is weakened'. (The argument about effect on character is in itself sound, and is a strong argument against fox-hunting, appealing at least to the *reason* of those who are, in this context, unhappily lacking in compassion.) Schopenhauer goes on:

'Thus only for practice are we to have sympathy for animals, and they are, so to speak, the pathological phantom for the purpose of practising sympathy for human beings! In common with the whole of Asia . . . I regard such propositions as revolting and abominable. At the same time, we see here once more how entirely this philosophical morality, which as previously shown is only a theological one in disguise, depends in reality on the biblical one. Thus because Christian morality leaves animals out of account . . . they are at once outlawed in philosophical morals; they are mere "things", mere *means* to any ends whatsoever. They can therefore be used for vivisection, hunting, coursing, bullfights, and horse racing, and can be whipped to death as they struggle along with heavy carts of stone. Shame on such a morality that . . . fails to recognise the eternal essence that exists in every living thing, and shines forth with inscrutable significance from all eyes that see the sun!'

And (*WWI*, Book IV, ch. iv, section 68):

'Sacrifice means resignation generally, and the rest of nature must look for its salvation to man who is at once the priest and the sacrifice. Indeed it deserves to be noticed as very remarkable, that this thought has also been expressed by the admirable and unfathomably profound Angelus Silesius in the little poem entitled "Man brings all to God": it runs, "Man – all loves thee, around thee great is the throng. All things flee to thee that they may attain to God." But a yet greater mystic, Meister Eckhart . . . says the same thing . . . "I bear witness to the saying of Christ. I, if I be lifted up from the earth will draw all things unto me (John 12. 32). So shall the good man draw all things up to God, to the source from which they came. The Masters certify to us that all creatures are made for the sake of man. This is proved in all created things by the fact that the one makes use of the other; the ox makes use of the grass, the fish of the water, the bird of the air, the wild beast of the forests. Thus all created things become of use to the good man. A good man brings to God the one thing in the other." '

(I am not sure that the animals would appreciate the idea that God saves them by feeding them to humans. However Schopenhauer glides over that.) He adds, 'He means to say that man makes use of the beasts in this life because, in and with him, he saves them also. It seems to me that that difficult passage in the Bible, Romans 8, 21–4 must be interpreted in this sense.' The lines in question speak of how 'the whole creation groaneth and travaileth in pain together until now'. Karl Barth on this passage: 'We must recover that clarity of sight by which there is discovered in the cosmos the invisibility of God.' Barth refers us here to Romans 1. 20. The omnipresence of the spiritual, and the union of all things in their hope of salvation, is, after all, an idea that Christianity shares with Buddhism and Hinduism. Schopenhauer, after mentioning

Romans, engagingly quotes Buddha's words to his horse: 'Bear me but this once more, Kantatakana, away from here, and when I have attained to the Law I will not forget thee.'


To resume after this interlude with the animals. In the passage quoted earlier (*WWI*, Book I, section 9) Schopenhauer suggests that we are not to picture conscious thought in terms of mechanical process or of the Humian notion of a laborious play of mental intermediaries. Thought and language fly direct without the aid of mediating psychological devices which repeat speech or connect mental images. Wittgenstein: 'How do sentences do it? Don't you know? For nothing is hidden. But given this answer "But you know how sentences do it for nothing is concealed" one would like to retort "Yes, but it all goes by so quick, and I should like to see it as it were laid open to view".' (*Philosophical Investigations* 435.) The passage of Schopenhauer is quoted by Morris Engel in his article 'Schopenhauer's Impact on Wittgenstein' (in *Schopenhauer: His Philosophical Achievement*, ed. M. Fox) where he compares it with a passage in the *Blue Book*. Prefigurings of Wittgenstein may of course also be pursued further back, into Hegel and Herder. (See pointers in Charles Taylor's *Hegel*, p. 568.) Engel's article illustrates other cases where Wittgenstein's thoughts and terminology concerning words and concepts resemble those of Schopenhauer. I spoke earlier of different (ethical) aspects of Wittgenstein's debt. The riddle (*Rätsel*) mentioned and dismissed at *Tractatus* 6. 5 is a Schopenhauerian riddle. Wittgenstein's judgment: 'Schopenhauer is, one might say, quite a *crude* mind. That is, he has refinement, but at a certain depth this gives out, and he is as crude as the crudest. Where real depth starts, his comes to an end. One can say of Schopenhauer: he never searches his conscience, he never looks into himself, into his soul.' (*Culture and Value*, p. 36.) This seems somewhat harsh, though it may be true that Schopenhauer's vastly inventive, and omnivorous mind did not possess the ruthlessness required to 'finish the job'. Altogether Wittgenstein fails to admit his considerable debt to Schopenhauer. Schopenhauer does not seem to have radically pursued the insight expressed in the quoted passage, and elsewhere (as Engel points out) seemed unsure whether or not to identify concepts with words, although in at least one place he says firmly that this would be wrong. He does not make any dramatic confrontation between these ways of looking at consciousness, nor describe in philosophical detail what it is for the Ideas to *work* in the mind, as when we *attend* to art in situations like that described by Rilke. Wittgenstein does not of course draw any moral conclusions from his critique of 'mental processes' in the *Investigations*. Nor does he, in places where one might like more detail, offer it. 'Perhaps the word "describe" tricks us here. I say "I describe my state of mind" and "I describe my room". You need to call to mind the difference between the language games.' (*Philosophical Investigations* 290.)

Other recent thinkers have however (as I said earlier) used the elusive and fragmentary nature of our introspectible awareness as an argument for a neo-Kantian moral philosophy of will and imperatives which would have horrified Schopenhauer. If there is no substantial intimately connected inner mechanism, if the inner material is merely shadowy or messy (gluey, viscous) then it cannot have value or play a moral, or rational or cognitive, role and the question of its doing so cannot arise. This then disposes of any philosophical problem about 'experience' or 'consciousness' as a seat of value or indeed of reason. Schopenhauer rejects Kant's philosophy of moral will (duty) and his abandonment of the phenomenal world to a spiritless and causally determined status. In this perspective on his thought the determinism which Schopenhauer paradoxically inherited from Kant amounts to a conception of the *extreme difficulty* of moral change. (The *distance* from the back of the Cave to the outside world.) The substance of blind will is given form by intellect (idea) and intermittently spiritualised by vision of (Platonic) Ideas. Schopenhauer was aware of the 'telegraphic' nature of the mind, and the absence of the 'machinery' which was the object of Wittgenstein's attack.

In philosophy one sometimes thinks that something *must* be so; and such moments of conviction are not necessarily sound guides. On the other hand it may be a case of having a philosophical 'nose'. At any rate a strong sense of direction may be worth trying out. These metaphors come naturally when thinking about thought. The concept of consciousness and the concept of value 'must' be internally linked. To be conscious is to be a value-bearer or value-donor. This sounds like a metaphysical or perhaps religious remark. I have used metaphors of being 'soaked in', or 'coloured by', value. Of course there are many periods when we are reflecting morally or aesthetically, entertaining and carrying out good or bad plans and so on. But are there not other periods which are neutral or blank? Often we are performing 'automatic' tasks and operations. It is true that such activity may be rated as good or bad, diligent or lazy, etc. etc. Here it may be argued that the required concept is that of a *disposition*. Much conscious activity is habitual. Here a close scrutiny of moment-to-moment awareness would yield no relevant information, one would have to step back a little and look at larger areas. This in turn suggests that an idea of 'parts' of consciousness gives a wrong image; and moreover it would be better not to think in terms of a continuous consciousness at all. This path might lead back to a dispositional account of mind or states of mind. Yet this may still leave one with the familiar feeling of having lost something. One returns to the most obvious and most mysterious notion of all, that this present moment is the whole of one's reality, and this at least is unavoidable. (The weirdness of being human.) Then one may start again reflecting upon the moment-to-moment reality of consciousness and how this is, after all, where we live. The concept of 'experience' is more wide-ranging and more free. Derrida spoke of experience as thought of in the form of consciousness or not. 'Experience' may simply mean dispositional expertise; or may suggest 'adventures' of very various kinds wherein we collect a part of our awareness together, making it into some sort of whole which could then be recalled or reassessed. What 'it was like' moment-to-moment we normally forget, it is as if we have to forget. This natural 'lostness' of the 'stream' may suggest its general nearly-non-existence and so its irrelevance. It might be thought of as only dispositionally extant, or at best an occasional indulgence of reflective people. On the other hand, surely it contains the whole chronicle of our existence, perhaps recorded by God. We might attempt to describe some of it in detail (say as an account of our 'fantasy life') to an analyst or a priest. Certainly our 'presents' are very various in quality.

Is there not something we ought to aim at here? Is every moment morally significant? We may be inclined to say no, are there not innocuously valueless gaps, can we not rest sometimes! The question seems censorious and inappropriate. On the other hand if we say yes, are we making some kind of moral or religious or metaphysical move? Does the whole consist simply of its parts? (Moore was concerned in a not dissimilar context with this problem.) The attractive image of the 'stream' may suggest something in some sense homogeneous. In literature the detailed portrayal of it (as a general literary form) seems to be surprisingly recent, liberally in use since Dorothy Richardson, Virginia Woolf and James Joyce. The term 'stream of consciousness' was, I gather, coined by William James (*Principles of Psychology*). The 'purest' example, or classic case, is Molly Bloom's soliloquy at the end of *Ulysses*. This art form, briefly regarded as odd, is now taken for granted. Of course any of these possible descriptions compared with the 'real thing' are likely to be loaded, coloured, evaluated. Streams of consciousness in fiction are usually moral indicators. The deepest thoughts and feelings of the fictional character are revealed, from *this* evidence he cannot escape! And is it not the same with us? Of course the fictional stream serves a fictional end, its formlessness has form and context, it is, compared with the 'real thing', purposeful and thin. But can we record (write down, dictate) our own stream, as if we could see it all or overhear it as an inner monologue? Could we 'keep up' with it? It moves so fast and is so full of miscellaneous 'stuff', we cannot capture it. We recognise Hegel's image of a ragbag. Only the eye of God could be alert enough to see it all. Does this matter? Perhaps on other planets for other beings the stream moves more slowly. Reflection here may suggest how much of our self-existence continues unknown in the dark, we do not need Freud to tell us. Perhaps our merciful Demiurge decided that it would overburden, indeed destroy, our frail souls if we could recall and hold all the moving substance of the mind. This concerns what it is to be human, the enigma at the centre. If we are a whole is not this its core? If *this* escapes us what are we? Do such thoughts represent a new form of anxiety brought on by an increased self-awareness? If we cannot deal in continuously identifiable items, must we be content to be, as our own observers, our own fiction-writers? Indeed what is truth, and why bother?

This line of investigation could occasion the 'eerie feeling' experienced in another (related) context by Saul Kripke. It could lead to relativism, cynicism, doubts about morals, doubts about *order*: the chaos which Hume and Kant were so afraid of. Of course these are, in their extreme form, philosophers' conceptions and worries, not likely to trouble the great innocent majority of mankind. Hume's remedy lies here nearest to common-sense: habit and custom conceal the lack of any genuine foundation. As for consciousness and its weirdness, there does seem to be a *décalage*, a slipped connection, between the moment-to-moment flow and the procedure, however continuous, of the inner monologue or inner life. Here, so far from raising doubts about morality, it seems to me that morality is 'proved' by its indelible inherence in the secret mind. As for the loss of 'items' this is an aspect of our radically contingent nature, the bit which the Demiurge blotted out. We have to confront mysteries. We are not gods. Meanwhile of course philosophers hanker after deep foundations and describable (even if postulated) entities. In the *Theaetetus* Socrates discussing the nature and possibility of true judgment (knowledge) suggests (the dream of Socrates, 201E–202B) that we should think of reality as composed of primal elements, not accessible to reason and knowledge, which can only be named. As these elements are woven together, so their names are woven together. This complex becomes a *logos*, an account or rational explanation; a *logos* is essentially a complex of names. However: how can the primal elements be unknowable and the complexes knowable? The dialogue continues and reaches no satisfactory conclusion. Wittgenstein, acknowledging his debt to Plato (*Investigations* 46ff., also *Philosophical Grammar*, p. 208), offers a similar picture in the *Tractatus*. 'Objects can only be *named*. Signs are their representatives . . . The requirement that simple signs be possible is the requirement that sense be determinate.' (*Tractatus* 3. 221, 3. 23.) I do not propose to discuss these metaphysical statements, I offer them only as examples of how philosophy can try, with an appearance of clear system, to reach the basis of things and show us what, though we may not be able to see it, *must* be there. These systems are, like Kant's, *deduced*, transcendental, offering huge general *pictures* of what 'must be the case' for human being to be as it is. Of course one seeks out concepts with motives, celebrating one, ignoring or obliterating another. I want to assert and indicate the importance and omnipresence of a reflective experiential background to moral decision and action, and with this the omnipresence of value (an opposition between good and bad) in human activity. This might be a point at which some technical vocabulary might be set up, some fundamental distinction made, for instance between self-reflective and unreflective awareness, between *Erfahrung* and *Erlebnis*, and so on. But it may be wise to avoid too much hasty technical precision. Distinctions mooted in philosophy can too rapidly become taken-for-granted shorthands, 'obvious' starting points and tools of reflection (such as intellect and will, fact and value, emotive and descriptive). As we cannot keep track of items, to say that every moment counts may seem absurd; or else like a profession of faith. God sees it all. The Psalmist clearly thought that every moment counted. Is that simply poetic or picturesque? The idea of detailed scrutiny and potential judgment of all states of mind is not the exclusive property of traditional religion. If we call it a religious way of looking we may be said to extend the concept of religion. However that may be, more often than might seem at first sight our passing moments have a positive controllable content. We may encourage or discourage certain thoughts or emotions. That place, where we are at home, which we *seem* to leave and then return to, which is the fundamental seat of our freedom, has moral colour, moral sensibility. We have a continuous *sense of orientation*. The concept of consciousness, the stream of consciousness, is *animated* by indicating a moral dimension. Our speech is moral speech, a constant use of the innumerable subtle *normative* words whereby (for better or worse) we texture the detail of our moral surround and steer our life of action. We cannot over-estimate the importance of the concept-forming words we utter to ourselves and others. This background of our thinking and feeling is always vulnerable. Looked at in this way we may entertain a metaphor of a continuous tone, or murmur, or conversation, or perhaps a symphonic binding together of different vibrations. We know very well what it is like to be obsessed by bad thoughts and feelings. Nothing is more evident in human life than fear and muddle, and the tumultuous agitation of the battle against natural egoism. The ego is indeed 'unbridled'. Continuous control is required.

Seen in this context, Sartre's treatment of consciousness, of which I spoke earlier, seems very abstract, perfunctory, *a priori* and non-empirical, although he is good at describing certain carefully selected states. The conditions which he chooses (in *La Nausée* and *L'Etre et le Néant*) are offered as cases of inert *mauvaise foi*, habit-ridden reverie, or at best an appalled fascinated sense of contingency which is a kind of experience of, or preliminary to, freedom, a broken-down descendant of Kant's *Achtung* or of Kierkegaard's *Angst*. The 'truly valuable' in this picture is as it were invisible (as it is in the *Tractatus*), being for neo-Kantian Sartre the empty substanceless movement of freedom (choice, decision) itself. In this philosophical psychology what is bad is visible and substantial, whereas what is good only 'shows itself' in certain willed behavioural movements; and consciousness itself is seemingly set down as morally negative. Kant of course also 'abandons' phenomena, including psychological ones; but Sartre's theory of morality as freedom has no place for Kant's concept of duty. Response to duty demands an enlightened assessment of the relevant world; and to this 'seen' world the colours of morality and value are restored by the discerning look, in a way which enables us to modify Kant's dualism. The concept itself, of duty, rejected by Schopenhauer, Sartre, and Wittgenstein, thus provides for its own salvation. We understand what a bad texture of consciousness is like, equally we understand what a good one is like, and what sort of changes lead from one to the other. Consider what novelists can do, and how variously and successfully they can do it. I quoted earlier Henry James's elaborate simile which describes Maggie Verver's apprehension that all is not well. Of course this is not stream of consciousness. We are not necessarily to think of Maggie as picturing her pagoda in detail. Perhaps she does picture it, perhaps nothing exactly or even roughly like it occurs in her mind at all. We are subject here to the magic of the author. But we know where we are. The reader easily, without even noticing, transcribes the simile into an awareness of an immediately recognisable state of mind. With machinery less elaborate but just as subtle Tolstoy conveys and evaluates conditions of conscious being, the way in which states of mind, for better or worse, colour surroundings. 'The world of the happy is not the world of the unhappy'; and equally the world, and moment-to-moment experience, of the kindly, loving person is unlike that of the malicious, vengeful person. (Of course we may all of us be such persons at different times.) To continue the colour metaphor, within any life there is general or prevailing colour, and also local colour, and both may be spoken of in terms of states of consciousness which are not reducible to dispositions. The move from (to use general or rough terms) benevolence to envy, or amiability to malice, may be a deep slow growth, or something prompted by a sudden event or thought. Such changes are well-known phenomena. Anna Karenina's consciousness of Kitty's family before she falls in love with Vronsky is quite different from what it is afterwards, the children too notice this difference. Pierre sees a different world after he realises that his marriage to Helen was a *moral* mistake. Levin's character, his goodness, also his naivety, is portrayed in Tolstoy's art even in the consciousness of Levin's dog.

At the moment towards the end of *A la recherche*, when Proust's narrator steps on an uneven paving stone, he experiences an intense joy and sense of certainty which removes all anxiety, all intellectual doubts, all fear of the future, all fear of death. Proust describes this moment as set free from the order of time, an experience of time in a pure state, an enjoyment of the essences of things. This intense perception-memory which the narrator realises he has often experienced before without understanding or profit, prompts the reflections upon illusion and reality, general and particular, the unreality of the self, the nature of art, which enable the narrator to begin writing the book. The revelation in Proust's story plays its part in the tale, explaining its inception and joining together certain significant experiences of which the reader knows already, and which reach back into the narrator's childhood. In this context the revelation appears, or may appear, as an aesthetic one, whereby the dead serial moments of ordinary life, with its obsessions and illusions, are contrasted with a vision which sees them as of value as the material of art. Here, even those people one most dearly loved must in the end be seen as having posed for the writer, as for a portrait-painter. Nothing endures save by becoming general, the 'lesson of idealism' is that what is material can only find its truth by passing into thought. Redemption or salvation is the discovery of oneself as an artist. Then, when one writes, one seeks scrupulously, and with closest attention, for the truth; whereas, out in life, one destroys oneself for illusions, *on se tue pour des mensonges.* The narrator here recalls how he never really believed in Albertine's love, but was ready to destroy his health, his work, his whole life for what he really knew to be a lie. And Swann: '*j'ai gâché ma vie pour une femme qui n'était pas mon genre.*'

Proust's narrator (and we must remember that he is a fictional being talking inside a work of art) speaks of his renewal as something remarkable experienced by an artist. But his revelation may be seen as implicitly carrying a larger meaning, a meaning already offered to the reader in the book (which, in the book, is about to be written) wherein is portrayed (for instance) the *contrast* between the narrator's love for his grandmother and his love for Albertine. From here we may allow ourselves to be reminded of Katsuki Sekida's 'pure consciousness', and even compare and contrast his 'hand touching the cup' with the narrator's experience (soon after the paving-stone incident) of hearing a spoon touch a plate. This sound, recalling (as the paving stone does) a previous experience and its associations, prompts another visitation of perception-memory, bringing the confidence, the certainty, the joy, wherein the narrator intuitively grasps his ability to recapture time in art. Proust's examples concern and illustrate a particular way in which reality is suddenly apprehended in the midst of illusion, an experienced contrast of dead impure time with live pure time, serial time with lived time, which may lead toward a recovery or 'redemption' of life through art. His state, or moment, of perception-memory may be seen as like Sekida's pure consciousness, or Simone Weil's perception without reverie, but it is also unlike. Proust's essential illuminations are involuntary, gifts from the gods, not experiences or states which could be attained or prolonged by a (morally, spiritually) disciplined way of living. Proust is here celebrating, as capable of a truthful 'recovery' or vision of his own life, the artist in the ordinary sense (an exceptional person), not in the 'we are all artists' sense. 'In the end', in Proust's story, the narrator discovers pure time and pure experience, he feels joy and certainty because he has learnt about, indeed experienced, truthfulness, and can now set about recovering his life in the light of truth. But of course, in an important sense, the narrator's life cannot be recovered, and those, including himself, whom he harmed by an imperfect way of living, remain irrevocably harmed; how much harmed the story ruthlessly reveals, the story which also exhibits true goodness and true love, as well as the *mensonges* for which the narrator was ready to destroy himself. In writing the book Proust has of course revealed himself (as the narrator will reveal himself), as every great novelist does, as a great moralist as well as a great artist. But the narrator's final revelation is not, as presented, a general guide or pointer to a good or spiritual way of life, it is about the artist, not about the saint. Nor, of course, is this (artist's) recovery of time the same as that of a penitent who feels 'at the end' that God has forgiven him. We have here to be our own moralists if we want to use Proust's states of pure consciousness as part of a moral, or moral philosophical, argument. Put it this way, why do we have to wait for accidental inspirational experiences which may, if we are lucky, make us artists? Should we not attempt to turn most of our time from dead (inattentive, obsessed, etc.) time into live time? This is an attempt which can be made, in various manners, as a disciplined way of living. 'Inspiration' is always available, truthful experience is a touchstone, something, in Proust's words, *pareil à une certitude*. Such states are of course not guaranteed just by their own intensity or feeling of insight, their status as truth-bearing can also be tested by longer-term examinations and considerations. But we can in general see and appreciate the difference between anxious calculating distracted passing of time when the present is never really inhabited or filled, and present moments which are lived attentively as truth and reality. In selfish obsessional calculation or resentment we are 'always elsewhere'; and the anxiety and fear and grief which come to us all may be lived, from moment to moment, in a variety of ways as illusion or as reality. Proust contrasts his visionary meaningful experiences with inattentive truthless memory which is like the idle turning of pages in a picture book, when, with the egoistic vanity of a collector, we tell ourselves what a lot of fine things we have seen. *J'ai tout de même vu de belles choses dans ma vie.* So much of our lives is thus passed and wasted 'elsewhere', as with the tourist who does not *look* at the famous monument, but fiddles with his camera to get a good 'view' which he can display later to his neighbours. The disappointment at the longed-for place which we find ourselves unable to take in is then compensated for by the reflection that, well, I can always say I've seen it. (For above, see Proust, *A la recherche du temps perdu*, Pléiade edition, vol. III, 1954, pp. 866–73, 905–10.)

We have no difficulty in understanding novelists, and it is natural here to speak of awarenesses, perceivings, experiences, consciousness, and of someone's 'world'. One is speaking here of what is categorical, not hypothetical. Maggie Verver, sitting alone in her room, breathing quietly and biting her lip, is to be imagined as, at intervals, having the experiences indicated by the pagoda image, and at some point reflectively remembering the process. Philosophically, one has to do battle against an excessive use of the idea of a 'disposition' (a general tendency to think and act in a certain way). Of course any account of virtue or of human frailty must include reference to good and bad dispositions and habits; but these are not concepts to which everything can be or ought to be reduced. A purely hypothetical or dispositional account of the mind of a moral agent omits something essential in a way analogous to the omission of the essential in a phenomenalist analysis of perception. What is omitted is what the novelist talks so much about, and what we all know about when we are not being misled by theories. The temptation to simplify by saying that 'he has a bad quality, or state, of consciousness' *means* 'he is likely to commit a bad action', must be resisted. This is important not only on empirical grounds, but because we need the concept of consciousness to understand how morality is cognitive; how there is no ubiquitous gulf fixed between fact and value, intellect and will. Reflection on this concept enables us to display how deeply, subtly and in detail, values, the various qualities and grades between good and bad, 'seep' through our moment-to-moment experiences. This argument concerns our ability to see that value, valuing, is not a specialised activity of the will, but an apprehension of the world, an aspect of cognition, which is everywhere. Of course the novelist knows more than we do in ordinary life, he knows the insides of people's minds to a degree that we usually do not. In an ordinary sense and as *part* of a philosophical picture we know that we can, or must, 'read' (as it were) backwards as well as forwards and out to in as well as in to out. I mean, we often do regard actions as primary, and states of mind as less important, or unimportant, merely inferred entities or hypotheses. We may properly say to someone, 'Stop brooding, act!' We see, and suffer or benefit from, people's actions; their states of mind are often secret and felt to be inaccessible. Yet what is inaccessible? We can *seek* for truth, we can imagine the past and *test* our imaginings, and we can do the same about other minds, and about our own. We have *various* methods of *verification*. We can examine our own states of mind and test them, we see 'into' them, we need not accept them at their face value (do I really intend this act, do I really love this person?), nor are we bound to dismiss them as mere dreamy fancies or drifting rubble. Our 'innerness' may be elusive or hard to describe but it is not unimportant or (necessarily) shadowy. Of course these inward happenings are not (in the sense attacked by Wittgenstein) significance-bestowing processes of meaning, or intermediaries, prior to or essential to thinking or speaking. Remembering is not having images; it may or may not be accompanied by them. We can test memory without speculation about mental events. Such (valid) arguments present the strongest form of a philosophical view which may also discourage talk about consciousness or experiential contents.

In pursuing these reflections one may at times find oneself poised between uttering nonsense and laboriously saying the obvious. Philosophically, the path lies perilously between naive realism and some form of idealism. The mode of description proper to 'consciousness' presents evident difficulties. Maggie's pagoda is clearly a literary device, whereas Tolstoy's account of Anna's or Pierre's or Levin's consciousness sounds more like a literal description; and yet not quite, for would not 'literal description' come out more like James Joyce or Virginia Woolf? But are not these too literary devices? Must one not, to *describe* here, be a master of metaphor? In an Aristotelian Society symposium to which I also contributed a paper (*Thinking and Languages*, Aristotelian Society supplementary volume 25, 1951), Professor Gilbert Ryle made a distinction between 'chronicles' and 'histories'. If we consider a period of time during which we have been 'brooding' or 'thinking' we may attempt a description in the form of a moment-to-moment chronicle of introspectible events, such as images, or words uttered to oneself. Even when one is trying to think carefully and consecutively the 'inward stream' may contain, or be interrupted by, chance items, such as perceptions suddenly illuminated by irrelevant significance. Consider the case of the tree root, or the braces of the café *patron*, in *La Nausée*. Such intrusions, if at all intense, may, as in Sartre's novel, cause a kind of disgust, a feeling of senselessness, inability to concentrate, describable as a fear of contingency; but may also (as in Proust) occasion joy, or if for instance they check a revengeful fantasy, provide a valuable relief from egoism. Gabriel Marcel attacked Sartre for finding contingency an occasion for horror rather than for grace. Such cases are not odd or exceptional. The outer world often enters the inward eye with an intensity of significance which punctuates a reflective reverie which does not initially concern it: as when Wittgenstein's stove becomes 'the true world among shadows'. These are not unusual experiences or ones especially connected with aesthetic or philosophical reflection; nor need we, to put 'inwardness' on the map, run to extreme examples of 'extension of consciousness' by drugs. These marvels are happening all the time. What Ryle called by contrast a 'historical account' would bring out a direction or a conclusion without reference to experiential details. 'What are you thinking?' Answer, 'Where to go on holiday', not 'I am having memory images of Venice.' Ryle was prepared to admit this distinction, but not to attach any, or more than minimal, importance to the items of the *chronicle*. The sense was to be drawn away into the *history*, in accord with a linguistic philosophy which emphasised public rules and activity. After all, we locate a good man by his actions, and when someone says he has 'decided', we wait to see what he does. My argument wants to focus attention upon the experiential stream as a cognitive background to activity, without suggesting that it is in any idealist (Hegelian, Husserlian) sense primary, or that it is the only place to which we need to look to assess moral quality.

Of course we can remind ourselves at intervals that we are, in a sense which perhaps has to be learnt, dealing with *pictures*. These pictures often do not in any way affect our ordinary activities. Wittgenstein claimed that his did not; he just pointed out philosophical mistakes and offered perspicuous accounts and descriptions. In general, we are not in any immediate way disturbed by metaphysical imagery. A phenomenal table remains just a table. We may be aware that great metaphysical systems 'change the world', but the process is slow and, for ordinary purposes, not perceptible. Yet the influence of the 'pictures' may at times be more directly perceived. Hegel influenced Marx who influenced innumerable people. Derrida has influenced a generation of literary critics. A behaviourist moral philosophy may also contribute to creating an atmosphere. The image of the transcendental barrier lends itself to various further pictorial adventures. Can we touch it (like Maggie touching the pagoda)? Perhaps this is dangerous – it may certainly be exhilarating. I see this image at work in structuralism where the codified many may be thought of as sunk in a deep ocean while the (aesthetically, intellectually) enlightened few disport themselves upon the surface, rising up into the sunshine while still belonging to the sea. (Like dolphins perhaps.) The touching of the barrier is also admitted by Kant in his celebration of genius and great art. Consider too the place given to poets, especially a poet (Hölderlin), by Heidegger; who actually demands, as the sole form of profound thinking suited to this age, a *poeticised philosophy*. Heidegger's prophetic proclamations, and Derrida's arcane prose, actually damage philosophy by renouncing the requirement of a careful sober lucidity and a quiet truthful clarified reflection which has characterised great philosophical writing since Plato. Pictures, yes (such as Plato used, declaring them to *be* pictures), but explained, used, related to human life, surrounded by clear plain language. Structuralist (monist, idealist) thinking, by inflating coherence at the expense of correspondence, loses our ordinary everyday conception of truth. 'Correspondence' contains the awareness that we are *continually* confronting something other than ourselves. Some exceptional people may gaze upon uncategorised manifolds and create new meanings, discover fresh categories, reinvent language, *donner un sens plus pur aux mots de la tribu* and so on. But we all, not only can but *have to*, experience and deal with a transcendent reality, the resistant otherness of other persons, other things, history, the natural world, the cosmos, and this involves perpetual effort. We are amazing creatures, no wonder Sophocles calls us *deinos*. Most of this effort is moral effort. This is the sense in which morality (value) is transcendental, concerned with the conditions of experience. We do not have to go as far as genius, but only as far as the category of the existing individual which Kierkegaard asserted against Hegel. Philosophy, if it is to give much-needed help to the human race, indeed if it is to *survive*, must stay with its austere traditional modes of truth-telling. Heidegger ('The Anaximander Fragment', *Early Greek Thinking*, p. 58): 'What if Being in its essence *needs to use* the essence of man? Then thinking must poeticise on the riddle of Being. It brings the dawn of thought into the neighbourhood of what is for thinking.' This is not the path of philosophy. The words sound stirring and may seem to suggest something religious. But as religion and as philosophy I reject late Heidegger's personified, historicised, and ultimately fateful and wanton, Being. *Sein und Zeit* brought about a philosophical revolution. Heidegger's dismissal of Descartes is less 'logical' than that of Wittgenstein, but it is (while being philosophy and not phenomenology) more humanely interesting. Here Heidegger is (though loveless and heroic) a moral philosopher. Later pronouncements suggest more the religiosity of a false prophet.

To return to Kant, in his thought the barrier, the perfect conceptual 'fit', essential to the validity of science, and to the segregation of a purely phenomenal world of empirical experience, is at a certain level of generality. (Causes, the general idea of an object, etc.) He did not worry about ordinary empirical concepts (boots and shoes) which were at a 'lower level' and looked after themselves. Analogously in the realm of moral conduct he was not concerned with detailed secondary moral concepts, the *middle-range mediating moral vocabulary* which carries so much of our ever-changing being. States of mind and qualities of consciousness would be regarded as pathological phenomena, not any part of practical reason. Kant thus 'loses' (as Schopenhauer would agree) a whole fundamental area of human existence. In the *Grund-*

*legung* he 'translates' the sovereign demand of Reason into moral concepts of great generality, such as truthfulness, benevolence, justice and teleological concern for humanity. The light of Reason shows us these great generalities and the empirical facts to which they are relevant. No assistance is (on Kant's view) required from intermediate variously named value-qualities (such as vanity, envy, sentimentality, gentleness, loyalty and so on) which might be thought of as hanging around as moral quasi-facts at the empirical level. (Our instinctive and so necessary moral modes of speech.) One might say in general that puritans make stronger, more confident, less detailed moral judgments. ('Don't lie' means *don't lie*.) To resort to detail is to obscure the issue and make excuses. 'Character' is unreal. For Kant the transcendental barrier occurs at a higher (or deeper, either image would do) level. Hegel, who was interested in boots and shoes, rolled his transcendences (as it were) over and over until the all-consuming organism of universal mind had ultimately sieved and united everything, and nothing was left behind or outside. The great Hegelian image may be treated as a kind of 'mystery'. There are many and various problems which lie between logic and the nature of the world.

# > 9 <

# Wittgenstein and the Inner Life

Modern philosophy, in parting company with Descartes, has also rightly disposed of various metaphysical entities postulated by previous philosophers. The removal of these images is to be welcomed on grounds of Occam's razor and because their shadowy existence could occasion a mystifying agnosticism. ('Perhaps there's something in it?') Locke's Substance, Kant's Thing-in-itself, Schopenhauer's Will. New styles of philosophical argument send them away, and the *Zeitgeist* does so too. What they represented can be dealt with less picturesquely. The philosopher tends to think there are deep foundations, there *must* be a source, a cause, a radical reality. But if he cannot credibly explain or describe this he might as well do without it. We no longer think that things are named by God. We have to understand language itself as a subject for philosophical reflection. Yet, for instance, when reading Wittgenstein, we may worry about the 'inner life'. Can there not be too fierce a removal of entities deemed to be unnecessary and unknowable? In the context of arguing *à la* Schopenhauer and Wittgenstein that language is telegraphic, we may also agree that memory does not depend on mental images (etc.). 'Do not try to analyse your inner experience.' (*Investigations* II xi, p. 204.) This sounds more like moral or religious advice: do not spend time scrutinising your conscience. But Wittgenstein's remark must be addressed to philosophers. Others may well say, 'Why not? It's up to me!' Surely Wittgenstein's attack on the inner-thought-outer-thing dualism concerns a philosophical mistake and is not intended by him to suggest there is no such thing as private reflection, or to support a behaviourist ethics? The revolution occasioned by Wittgenstein and Heidegger most famously removes the Cartesian starting point. We are not 'most certain' of our momentary concentration upon our private self-experience. We cannot 'know' in a solitary instant. Knowledge involves concepts, context, surroundings. 'A great deal of stage-setting in the language' must be presumed. (*Investigations* 257.) What is primary is an awareness *already* in the world. Heidegger pictures us as 'thrown' into the world, our 'I' is a being-there (*Dasein*), our state is *being-in-the-world* (*in-der-Welt-sein*). Heidegger emphasises our contingency. Wittgenstein (*Tractatus*) pictures a language-user as 'an extensionless point' in the centre of its world. The I is its world. Wittgenstein even (in *Philosophical Remarks* VI) suggests the removal of the concept of Ego or first person. So, 'it thinks', 'it sees', 'there is thinking', 'there is seeing'. Like, 'it rains', 'there is rain'. It has been suggested that here he has been influenced by the Buddhism of Schopenhauer. The Buddhist removal of the ego is a spiritual achievement, however, spoken of in this sense by Schopenhauer. In *Zen and the Art of Archery* the master tells the pupil to try to achieve 'it shoots'. The 'influence' is more probably Lichtenberg. An aphorism of Lichtenberg: 'We should say *it thinks*, just as we say *it lightens*. To say *cogito* is already to say too much as soon as we translate it as *I think*. To assume, to postulate the I is a practical requirement.' (*Note-*

*book* K.) (I return to this later.) Heidegger's *Dasein*, though he too sounds like a depersonalised entity, is in effect more like an adventurer in a real human scene.

'An "inner process" stands in need of outer criteria.' (*Investigations* 580.) ' "But surely you cannot deny that, for example, in remembering, an inner process takes place . . ." The impression that we wanted to deny something arises from our setting our faces *against the picture of the "inner process"*. [My italics.] Why should I deny that there is a mental process? But "There has just taken place in me the mental process of remembering" means nothing more than "I have just remembered" . . . "Are you not really a behaviourist in disguise? Aren't you at bottom saying that everything except human behaviour is fiction?" If I do speak of a fiction, then it is of a *grammatical* fiction.' (305–7.) By a grammatical fiction Wittgenstein presumably means something entertained by a philosopher. At 295 he speaks of pictures we see 'When we look into ourselves as we do philosophy', and at 299 of 'being unable, when we surrender ourselves to philosophical thought, to help saying such-and-such'. All right, we do not require an inner thought process which coincides with and produces outer speech. I think Schopenhauer explained this more clearly than Wittgenstein. Such beliefs, if held by philosophers, are rightly pointed out by other philosophers as philosophical mistakes or 'fictions'. Ordinary people, if left alone, get on perfectly well holding, or not holding, similar vague pictures of their inner mental existence. Thus far, concerning the matters mentioned above, philosophers should be grateful to Wittgenstein, and to the structuralists, for a removal of errors. However there is another, not separable but deeper, even fundamental, aspect of Wittgenstein's thinking. Very early in the *Investigations* he introduces us to 'language games' and 'forms of life' (*Lebensformen*). 'To imagine a language is to imagine a form of life' (19). 'One thinks that learning language consists in giving names to objects' (25). Then we can refer to things, we can point to them. However 'an ostensive definition can be variously interpreted in *every* case' (28). To explain 'red' it is not enough to point to something red. The thing pointed at is ambiguous, it is not *just* red. To remove such ambiguity should not all words be proper names of unique individuals, 'simples', primary elements, of which no further account can be given? Wittgenstein refers here to the *Theaetetus*, the dream of Socrates (201E), and adds 'Both Russell's "individuals" and my "objects" [*Tractatus Logico-Philosophicus*] were such primary elements'. Wittgenstein goes on to picture language games which are to assemble primary elements into orderly complexes subject to rules. 'Seeing *what is common*' (72). But what is following a rule (82) or continuing a series (143)? How do we ever know that anything is the same again, or that a system has been understood? 'The certainty that I shall be able to go on after I have had this experience – seen the formula for instance – is simply based on induction.' What does this mean? 'The certainty that the fire will burn me is based on induction.' . . . Is our confidence justified? 'What people accept as a justification – is shown by how they think and live.' Also later (292) 'Don't always think that you can read off what you say from the facts, that you portray these in words according to rules. For even so you would have to apply the rule in this particular case without guidance.' The concept of *induction*, and anxiety about cause and ground, takes us back to Hume's scepticism. Hume overcame his scepticism by cheerfulness and common sense. Wittgenstein is more profoundly troubled. He refers us back to the imagery of primary elements in Plato and in the *Tractatus*. He offers an unnerving account of the bases of language and thought. He sets his face against the inner process. An inner process requires outer criteria. He appeals to forms of life. Of course this is a *kind* of metaphysics, though more empirical and confused than the *Tractatus*, and in this respect harder to understand. But how does all this leave us, the individuals, where does it leave our thought-stream, our private reflections, where does it leave *truth*, if our foundations are so shaky and our judgments so shadowy? What sort of criteria are required to sanction the genuineness, even the real existence, of our 'inner' world, or indeed of 'the world'? Wittgenstein's fable (258) about 'Sensation S' concerns a person who says he has a particular sensation whose recurrence he notes in his diary as 'S'. He cannot define S or offer any description or explanation of it. How does he know it is the same each time? He just knows when it comes again. But *how*? Well, he concentrates his attention on it, he impresses on himself the connection between the sign S and the sensation. He gives himself, as it were, a private ostensive definition, a pointing inward at a feeling. 'But what is this ceremony for? . . . "I impress it on myself" can only mean I remember the connection *right* in future. But in the present case I have no criterion of correctness. One would like to say: whatever is going to seem right to me is right. And that only means that here we can't talk about "right".' This is an extreme case (a *reductio ad absurdum* some might say), a tailor-made situation designed to show the empti-ness of the inner when not evidently connected with the outer. Out in real life the owner of S would be an individual living in time. Wittgen-stein's example suggests but a perfunctory interrogation. The truth or falsehood of the claim is not allowed into the picture, which should include an immense number of details about character and situation. (Is he mad, a trickster, a liar, a foreigner, a genius, a poet, almost anyone trying to 'make something out'?) Wittgenstein's S man is a prisoner of Wittgenstein's relentless thinking, part of a general attack upon the (his) concepts of 'private language' and 'inner process'. There is a distinct smell of tautology. We must distinguish here between the case of the otiose dualism, for instance, the 'inner process' which is supposed to articulate and present the *finished outer speech*; and the very general idea of 'processes' as stream of consciousness, inner reflec-tion, imagery, in fact our *experience* as inner (unspoken, undemon-strated) being. It is this huge confused area which is being threatened, even removed. What are we to do for criteria? The picture of 'produc-ing them' seems out of place. Wittgenstein himself says that he some-times has a dream image which he cannot describe. (*Culture and Value*, p. 79.)

At the end of the *Investigations* (which I discuss shortly) Wittgenstein seems anxious to remove the concept of 'experience', also obliterated by Derrida. Are we to be left with the rather rigid, and indeed not clearly explained, ideas of language games and *Lebensformen*? Can this be a full philosophical account of human life and language? In the *Investigations* Wittgenstein seems to be shaking off views expressed in the *Tractatus* and the *Notebooks*; we were to be liberated from an earlier cage. But is the 'second book', for all its liberating anti-Cartesian aspects, not in some respects another cage? There is a feeling of con-straint. Perhaps what lingers is a shadow of *logic*? In the *Notebooks* (2.8.16) 'Yes, my work has extended from the foundations of logic to the nature of the world.' At times Wittgenstein seems to be reluctantly questioning logic. 'Thought is surrounded by a halo. Its essence, logic, presents an order, in fact the *a priori* order of the world; that is the order of *possibilities*, which must be common to both world and thought. But this order, it seems, must be *utterly simple*. It is *prior* to all experience, must run through all experience: no empirical cloudiness or uncertainty can be allowed to affect it. It must rather be of the purest crystal. But this crystal does not appear as an abstraction; but

[ 273 ]

as something concrete, as it were the *hardest* thing there is.' (*Tractatus Logico-Philosophicus* 5. 5563.) 'We are under the illusion that what is peculiar, profound, essential, in our investigation, resides in its trying to grasp the incomparable essence of language.' (*Investigations* 97.) The pages which follow continue this tone of reflective even frenzied doubt. 'We see that what we call "sentence" and "language" have not the formal unity that I imagined, but are families of structures more or less related to each other? But what becomes of logic now? Its rigour seems to be giving way here. But in that case doesn't logic altogether disappear? For how can it lose its rigour? Of course not by our bargaining any of its rigour out of it. The *preconceived idea* of crystalline purity can only be removed by turning our whole examination round. (One might say: the axis of reference of our examination must be rotated, but about the fixed point of our real need.)' (108.) This last sentence beautifully expresses a reaction to a philosophical dilemma.

There is a sort of strained anguish in the *Investigations*, thought being constantly stretched to its limit. The problem about the 'inner life' has to be connected with 'continuing the series', for instance by the idea of 'criteria'. One is tempted to say: the author of the *Tractatus* solved by metaphysical fiat the problem of the relation of language to the world. (Of course language refers to the world, 'and there's an end on't' as Dr Johnson would say.) Cannot the author of the *Investigations* simply emulate Hume and solve the problem of *induction* in a similar manner? Are not the intelligent things which Schopenhauer said to him (about the telegraphic nature of language which we somehow manage) enough? Apparently not. 'It is difficult to keep our heads up . . . We feel as if we had to repair a torn spider's web with our fingers . . . The conflict becomes intolerable . . .' (106, 107.) Quite apart from anything else Wittgenstein, obsessed with language, is being unfair to it. It has been suggested by some that Wittgenstein and Derrida are saying similar things. But here let us glance at the picture of language presented by Saussure, *as if* it were a vast ocean of linkages and possibilities over which we cannot see very far. This is indeed the *sort of thing* language is, this is the way to *picture* it in order to understand it. Derrida took the further step of 'freezing' the picture into some sort of postulated reality. Wittgenstein's strong but unclear concepts of language games plus *Lebensformen* freeze his different, quasi-logical picture of language. He says (108) that 'we are talking about the spatial and temporal phenomenon of language, not about some non-spatial, non-temporal phantasm'. Added here in square brackets: '[Note in margin: Only it is possible to be interested in a phenomenon in a variety of ways.]' Out in the real world language is a colossal infinitely various creative ferment. (No wonder some are tempted, metaphysically, to say that it is all there is.) Here we (I) must prefer, as far more *suggestive* of the nature of language, Derrida's free play, to Wittgenstein's more (logical?) restricted language games and life forms. In Derrida's realm the sensation S man would not be persecuted. Wittgenstein's image of 'outer criteria' seems, in his use of it, unbearably narrow; and, one feels, *motivated* by a desire to restrict and curtail the whole jumbled field of our inner musing. (Experience, consciousness.) This area, so immense, so personal, is admitted to be the home of 'fine shades of behaviour' (*Investigations* II xi, p. 203). Here we are told that 'what we have rather to do is to *accept* the everyday language game.' But what is this? Of course, in a general sense, language must have rules. But it is also the property of *individuals* whose inner private consciousness, seething with arcane imagery and shadowy intuitions, occupies the greater part of their being.

Later on, at II xi, Wittgenstein pursues the inner-outer matter, with evident signs of doubt and anxiety, in relation to sensations, perceptions, *experiences*. What is seeing something *as* something? Recognition demands mastery of a technique, possession of (public) concepts, ability to interpret. But what is seeing 'according to an interpretation'? ' "Seeing as" is not part of perception . . . it is like seeing and again not like.' (p. 197.) 'The concept of "seeing" makes a tangled impression . . . After all, how completely ragged what we see can appear! And now look at all that can be meant by "description of what is seen" . . . Here we are in enormous danger of wanting to make fine distinctions. It is the same when one tries to define the concept of a material object in terms of "what is really seen". What we have rather to do is to *accept* the everyday language-game, and to note *false* accounts of the matter *as* false.' (p. 200.) 'It is certainly possible to be convinced by evidence that someone is in such-and-such a state of mind, that, for instance, he is not pretending. But "evidence" here includes "imponderable" evidence. The question is: what does imponderable evidence *accomplish*? . . . Imponderable evidence includes subtleties of glance, of gesture, of tone.' (p. 228.) 'The criteria for the truth of the *confession* that I thought such-and-such are not the criteria for a true *description* of a process. And the importance of the true confession does not reside in its being a correct and certain report of a process. It resides rather in the special consequences which can be drawn from a confession whose truth is guaranteed by the special criteria of *truthfulness*.' (p. 222.) 'It is no doubt true that you could not calculate with certain sorts of paper and ink, if, that is, they were subject to certain queer changes – but still the fact that they changed could in turn only be got from memory and comparison with other means of calculation. And how are these to be tested in their turn? What has to be accepted, the given, is – so one could say – *forms of life*.' (p. 226.)

These last pages certainly make a tangled impression. Wittgenstein now allows 'imponderable evidence', 'fine shades of behaviour', glances, gestures, tones, also differing concepts of 'experience'. A moral consideration enters, the concept of truthfulness. There is a laborious piling up of examples. It is as if he were at last feeling bound to envisage the muddled nature of the human condition and hastily to put it inside the confines of philosophy (logic). That indeed is the problem. How much of human doing can be analysed, formalised, philosophically? The great metaphysicians of the past seemed to assume that they could somehow capture it all. Wittgenstein speaks again, so near the end, of language games and forms of life, but still without clarifying either conception. How large or small, local or general, is a language game? How are we to *trust ourselves* to such a concept, what is it to 'accept the *everyday* language game' and to note false accounts? These would presumably be philosophical (theoretical) accounts noted by philosophers. Forms of life also remain unclarified, though they are finally referred to as *to be accepted, the given, das Hinzunehmende, Gegebene*, great words of power which suggest something (or some things) transcendentally deduced and utterly unavoidable. Well, we may be inclined to say that *language itself* is 'given'. But Wittgenstein's *Lebensformen* are introduced as fundamental (logical?) judges of the possibility of meaning. Meanwhile the vast concept of 'experience' subsists as something inward (perhaps images or toothache) but dependent upon, situated by, a public outer, which has consequences. Imponderable evidence exists but is suspect. Truth is not exhibited by an account of an inner process (all right) but by criteria of truthfulness. How is truthfulness tested? How is memory tested? By consequences! But surely human society depends largely on trust in the virtue of others, often ascertained on imponderable evidence? There is indeed a clearly discernible area of mistakes made by philosophers (which I have mentioned before). In the later part of the book we should recall the warning in the Preface that we shall have to travel over a wide field criss-cross in every direction.

The *Philosophical Investigations* has been studied and combed over and argued about and discussed and explained by very many people who know more about the work of Wittgenstein than I do, and I am aware of rushing in where angels fear to tread. I want to say a few things about the end of the book and the light it throws back on the beginning; and also to relate what Wittgenstein says about 'inner and outer' to some other (moral philosophical) considerations. Wittgenstein's analysis of 'perception', etc. pursued with so many and various examples, seems to raise new questions of terminology and method, and even raise doubts about matters apparently established earlier. Wittgenstein has claimed that his philosophy offers 'description', affords 'perspicuous presentation'. But at times one wonders, is this phenomenology? Wittgenstein seems sometimes perilously near the edge of empirical science. (See Richard Gregory, *The Mind in Science*, pp. 196, 388, 428 for a scientist's reference to these reflections.) Wittgenstein himself notes the peril. 'Here it is *difficult* to see that what is at issue is the fixing of concepts.' He adds, 'A *concept* forces itself on one'. (In *Culture and Value* he wonders whether the concept of God may be forced on one.) This suggests that the argument is a sort of transcendental one, wherein concepts are *deduced*. Does perception include interpretation? (Pure perception, pure cognition?) 'Was it seeing or was it a thought?' How can this question be answered? A *description* of perceptions, whether by Merleau-Ponty or Richard Gregory, may produce a great variety of facts about visual experiences. (For instance, an approaching train, seen at a distance, at first grows larger while seeming to stay in the same place, then ceases to grow and is seen as moving.) I do not see how Wittgenstein's question here connects with the more clarified arguments set up earlier (about illusory inner processes, recognising by mental samples, thinking as picturing etc.). We do not normally think of approaching trains in terms of outer object plus inner picture. In a laboratory we might try to describe particular perceptions (now the train is getting larger, now the train is moving), and these might lead to various scientific conclusions. But outside the laboratory, or untroubled by philosophy, our perceptions, which so largely constitute our experienced-being, are intensely individual and polymorphous. Seeing, thinking and 'interpreting' are mixed. And, for instance, instinctive value judgments and intuitions are involved. I feel that Wittgenstein's urgency, his anxiety, as he poses these questions is related to his wish to keep the 'individual' and 'value' out of the picture. (This would continue the metaphysic of the *Tractatus*.)

The concepts of experience and intuition 'embarrass' Wittgenstein as they 'embarrass' Derrida. The *experience* of seeing the approaching train (Merleau-Ponty's example) can, when released from phenomenology, be (as truthfully as possible) described in innumerable ways, and involve innumerable considerations. (Is the train late? Will it be crowded? Will it stop? Will she be on it? Is it the blue one? Etc. etc.) 'Experience' has *layers*. Here the intense lively privacy of the individual 'inner life' presents itself as something not to be analysed away; and indeed Wittgenstein at moments declares he is not analysing it away, only pointing out 'grammatical mistakes'. Yet the examples which he pursues and worries in this part of the book seem to postulate a possible further clarification, a subjection of an unconquered field to a particular neater clearer account. He seems to select, as illuminating special cases, examples of perception experience which are in fact hugely and vaguely ubiquitous. I mean, he takes over as a fairly small field (presumed to pose a clearly answerable question) something which is really a very large field, posing many kinds of questions. Must a particular technical mastery be a 'logical' condition of someone's having a particular experience? (What indeed is 'logic' doing here!) There must be different concepts of experience. Here Wittgenstein has in mind the dictum about the inner needing outer criteria. May a doubt be thrown on this? What about the 'experience' of being guided or influenced, for instance in copying a figure. While being guided I notice nothing special. Afterwards if I wonder what happened I feel there must have been something else. 'I have the feeling that what is essential about it is "an experience of being influenced", of a *connection* . . . but I should not be willing to call any experienced phenomenon the "experience of being influenced" . . . I should like to say that I experienced the "because", and yet I do not want to call any phenomenon "the experience of the because".' (176.) This anxiety connects with Wittgenstein's more general problem about ability to continue a series, 'how to go on', how to trust our memory. We (I) reading Wittgenstein here feel the compelling presence of 'logic', and also a sense of void. Wittgenstein cannot find (and really does not want) any 'because'. The 'experience' of being guided is an illusion. But what is to *count* as an experience? Back in ordinary language we may say, all right, often (for instance, counting, adding) we do not have any 'palpable' experience – but also, often, we are in situations where the concept of experience is clearly in place. 'Is it seeing or a thought?' Well, usually it is both, one cannot, necessarily, 'logically' prise experiences apart. *Experience is consciousness.* (Wittgenstein avoids the latter word.) It is deep and complex, it has density, thoughts and perceptions and feelings are combined in the swift movement of our mode of existence. (Swift, as pointed out by Schopenhauer.) Can we experience an influence? Yes, of course, when (for instance) we sit wondering whether we have been wrongly persuaded by another person. Physical feelings as well as mental images attend such anxiety. In 'setting his face against the picture of the inner process' Wittgenstein seems to have banished not only (as in the example at 305–7) a naive error (or grammatical fiction) but the whole multifarious mixed-up business of our inner reflections, thought-being, experience, consciousness. So experience is consciousness? Let us say to Wittgenstein for the sake of argument, consciousness may be pictured as a stream punctuated by objectified memorable events called experiences. But some events scarcely enter the consciousness, slip quickly from the memory, and cannot or cannot strictly be called experiences. Here we are back with 'How do sentences do it?' (*Investigations* 435.) The concept of experience is huge, generalised and uncertain. Why should we be forced to talk in this laborious way about it? Wittgenstein has been *forcing upon us* a certain picture of experience as a kind of illusion, thereby discrediting the density and real existence of inner thinking ('inner life').

'Change of aspect' and 'seeing as' are ubiquitous activities or experiences. We are constantly puzzled by ambiguous 'perceptions' or 'seeings', we 'interpret' our surroundings all the time, enjoying as it were a multiple grasp of their texture and significance. We are doing it continuously and this includes intense imaginative introspection, evaluation, focusing upon an image, turning thoughts into things. Shall I do it? becomes a picture of it done. Such activities do not contradict the anti-Cartesian, anti-double-process, arguments offered earlier by Wittgenstein. It is as if he has, at the end, entered into an area of a quite new kind of *unnecessary* speculation. His terminology here is awkward. He seems at times like a Martian staring at human affairs. It may be said that this is just what a philosopher is. Philosophy is prompted by amazement, by being amazed at what ordinary folk take for granted. The Greeks were amazed by human existence, Kant was stunned by the starry heavens, Heidegger wondered why there was something instead of nothing. But Wittgenstein's struggles with perception and interpretation seem to throw doubt upon what seemed agreed, throwing a dubious light upon earlier formulations. The idea of values and value judgments is excluded, as if we were still in the world of the *Tractatus*. The 'surround' or 'stage-setting' which is the required 'outer', the interpretation which gives meaning to the inner, is 'logically' construed. But the human situation is muddled and complex. It concerns the activities of individuals. Use of language does not require a logical (accurate, formulated) method of identifying 'inner experience'. Our whole busy moral-aesthetic intellectual creativity abounds in private insoluble difficulties, mysterious half-understood mental configurations. A great part of our thinking is the retention, the cherishing, of such entities. 'Inner' can co-exist or fuse with 'outer' and not be *lost*. (What is inner, what is outer?) This is what *thinking* is like. The *Tractatus* has by contrast a certain innocence, it is shameless metaphysics; Schopenhauer would have called it a joke, some of its earliest admirers called it an Ode to Propositional Logic. At the end of that book Wittgenstein limits what can meaningfully be said to 'the propositions of natural science' (that is purely factual language), and philosophy to a demonstration, to anyone using metaphysical language, that his remarks were meaningless. All else must be consigned to silence, shown not said. (Logic demands this silence.) By implication not only moral or aesthetic utterance is banned. This austerity may express Wittgenstein's detestation of (what he felt to be) any careless use of words (as when he banished Norman Malcolm for some time because Malcolm, in 1939, defended the British 'national character' as not given to deceits. Malcolm's *Ludwig Wittgenstein: A Memoir*, p. 32). Heidegger disliked the 'vulgar' talk of 'ordinary people' (*Gerede*), preferring to it not a dignified silence but a language of nobility and poetry, and (ideally) a poeticised philosophy. Wittgenstein certainly did not mean anything like that when he said that he wished he could write philosophy which could be 'learnt by heart'.

What is the language, or language game, of a *Lebensform* supposed to be like? Is the substratum, what is ultimate, a reliance upon 'general agreement' in a community as an arbiter of sense? Wittgenstein speaks of 'truthfulness'. *Individuals* are truthful or otherwise. The owner of sensation S is an individual. How long people go on believing or disbelieving him is an individual matter. How does meaning connect with truth? One language can be more potentially truth-bearing, more precise, more beautiful, richer in concepts than another. Tyrants destroy language, diminish vocabulary. A language is enlarged, *improved* (value judgment), by truthful utterance. People suffer and are damaged if prevented from uttering the truth. Assent, general agreement, has a background which must be scrutinised. Is there a reason why a despotic state could not be a *Lebensform*? Any *Lebensform* may be subject to moral judgment. How about members of the community who do not assent? They may be illiterate or mad, or may be geniuses, artists, free beings who enrich the language. The *Lebensform* concept suggests loss of the individual. At *Investigations* 241, Wittgenstein says, by way of clarification of 'agreement', 'It is what human beings *say* that is true and false; and they agree in the *language* they use. That is not agreement in opinions but in form of life.' However, out in the ordinary world, not in a frozen logical example, such distinctions are very difficult to make. Truth and falsehood are in a perpetual engagement with meaning. Meaning is slippery and free, language is a huge place (structuralists are right here). Surely we cannot take the imagined 'assent' of postulated 'groups' as establishing all correctness and intelligibility? Why is Wittgenstein so anxious to set up this machinery which so pointedly excludes the individual peculiarity of speaking humans? And if it appears that we cannot accept this picture are we rejecting one of his fundamental tenets? Of course language depends very generally upon areas of 'agreement', but is also continuously lived by persons. Fine shades of behaviour, imponderable evidence, looks, glances, gestures, tones, whistling. Such modes of human communication are everywhere fundamental, defeating general 'exactness', but performing precise jobs in *individual contexts*. Thinking, communicating, must admit the individual, the moral, the aesthetic. Wittgenstein's examples and reflections include, but he does not discuss as such, our everyday, every moment use of metaphors which carry so many shades and evidences. Language is full of art forms, full of *values*, we rely daily upon intuitions and distinctions, life passes on, we have to trust our memories, we have to trust the truthfulness of other people. It may be said that if one lets everything in it isn't philosophy. Surely one must have a 'system'? Well, some confusions can be clarified, some questions clearly answered. (For instance the matter of *cogito ergo sum*. Though even here . . .) Elsewhere, philosophy does tend, perhaps felicitously, to fall into phenomenology. Wittgenstein claims to *describe*, but without the psychological or the ethical. The question 'what is really seen' may lead our thoughts back to Husserl or to Sekida's 'pure cognition' and to Simone Weil's 'pure perception'. Also to Plato's Cave where subjects have the objects they deserve. An analysis or description of perception, if not scientific, seems inevitably to include a consideration of values, the question of inner-and-outer demands such consideration. Wittgenstein 'allows' the aesthetic at II xi, p. 202, 'Hear this bar as an introduction'. Our private reflections, or 'inner lives', are soaked in values. Do we not therefore need to inspect and evaluate our own private thought-being, that inner which is *so different* from our lived outer? A *sense of that separation* is one of our deepest experiences. We know very little even about the people who are closest to us. We depend upon intuition and rightly accept many things as mysteries. Is not some denial or obfuscation of this picture a move in the direction of behaviourism? A step further on and we will be being warned against fantasies, private chatter and idle self-scrutiny. The warning will consist in the removal. Perhaps Wittgenstein was pointing toward the necessity, at least the desirability, of an inner silence.

'The results of philosophy are the uncovering of one or another piece of plain nonsense and of the bumps that the understanding has got by running its head against the limits of the language.' (*Investigations* 119.) Elsewhere (Waismann, *Wittgenstein and the Vienna Circle*, p. 68), Wittgenstein is quoted as saying that this running up against 'is ethics', that is, theorising about morals. (By Moore, for instance.) He also speaks in this piece (which I quoted earlier) about Heidegger and Kierkegaard. The image of language, thought of in this philosophical context, is that of a cage. There are stern and clearly defined limits. This goes with ideas of 'logic' and the 'conceptual': of rather abrupt collision with the transcendent (as limit). Wittgenstein's method, in *Tractatus* and later, is professedly negative, a defence against useless metaphysical formulations. 'This method would be' to the aspiring metaphysician 'unsatisfying – he would not have the feeling that we were teaching him philosophy.' (*Tractatus* 6. 53.) The *Investigations* retains the abruptness of this method, but concealing or burying it in a stylistically different whirl of questions and examples. Herein it is instructive to look for, or dig out, the points of inconsistency or doubt. Wittgenstein is 'embarrassed' by the concept of experience. This huge concept directs us toward the messiness of ordinary life and its mysteries. He persecutes sensations S. He denies 'experiential volume' to meaning, intending, being influenced (p. 217). He also denies it (II xi, p. 219) to the expression 'the word is on the tip of my tongue'. In more relaxed and less logical mood, in *Culture and Value*, p. 79, he describes 'cases where someone has the sense of what he wants to say much more clearly in his mind than he can express in words. (This happens to me very often.) It is as though one had a dream image quite clearly before one's mind's eye, but could not describe it to someone else so as to let him see it too. As a matter of fact, for the writer (myself) it is often as though the image stays there behind the words, so that they *seem* to describe it *to me*.' He goes on to say: 'A mediocre writer must beware of too quickly replacing a crude, incorrect expression with a correct one. By doing so he kills his original idea, which was at least still a living seedling. Now it is withered and no longer worth *anything*. He may as well throw it on the rubbish heap. Whereas the wretched little seedling was still worth something.' Here, with a free and apt use of metaphor, with swift intuitive imagination, Wittgenstein describes the *experience* of thinking. Yes, it is like that. We can come close to these things and do them justice. At the border-lines of thought and language we can often 'see' what we cannot say: and have to *wait* and attempt to formulate for ourselves and convey to others our *experience* of what is initially beyond and hidden. We look out into the abyss, into the mystery, intuiting what is not ourselves. A difficulty is a light, an insuperable difficulty is a sun. Great poetry may be for all thinkers an ideal image of 'pure creativity' (compare 'pure cognition'). Of course philosophy is definitely not poetry. (I stay with the 'old quarrel'.) But, even in philosophy, language is not a cage.

Here I refer to Saul Kripke, who has discussed with greater clarity the matters with which I have been engaged. In his book *Wittgenstein on Rules and Private Language*, Kripke argues that the attack on 'private language', supposed to have started round about *Philosophical Investigations* 243, in fact began much earlier in the form of a *more general* sceptical paradox which is (Kripke says) the fundamental problem of the *Investigations*. The question is, as Kripke points out, very like that posed by Hume. How can we be sure that the future will resemble the past? No past state of my mind can entail a future one. Further explanations or clarifications or rules for interpreting rules may all be misunderstood. How can we ever be sure that something is the same as before? Kripke admits that, in contemplating this situation, he has something of an eerie feeling. Surely there is something in his mind which instructs him what he ought to do in all future cases? 'It seems that the entire idea of meaning vanishes into thin air.' This sceptical approach is applied later in *Investigations* to problems about sensations. Here the attack on 'private ostensive definition' or 'private language' takes the form of the removal (irrelevance) of the 'inner thing'. The case of 'sensation S' (258) and 'the beetle in the box' (293). Can I know something (pain for instance) only from my own case? It is difficult here (returning to Wittgenstein) to separate out what is 'all right'. Of course a confession of what we thought is not a 'literal' account of an inner process (etc.). What is 'eerie' is the background picture of solipsism, the 'empty box', which seems to imply a form of behaviourism.

On pp. 100–102 Kripke says that the demand for outward criteria is not to be seen as a verificationist or behaviourist premise. It is rather *deduced* in a Kantian sense (it is forced upon us). 'A sceptical problem is posed and a sceptical solution to that problem is given. The solution turns on the idea that each person who claims to be following a rule can be checked by others.' Methods of checking constitute a 'primitive part of the language game'. 'Outward criteria' for pain sensations are just 'the way this general requirement of our game of attributing concepts to others works out in the special case of sensations'. In footnotes (pp. 101–4) Kripke expresses some doubts. Wittgenstein 'often seems to be taken to suppose that for any type of sensation there is an appropriate "natural expression" of that sensation type ("pain behaviour" for pain)'. *Investigations* 244: 'A child has hurt himself and he cries.' This natural expression would be some sort of typical external behaviour 'other than and prior to the subject's avowal that he has the sensation. If the theory of §244 that the first-person avowals are verbal replacements for a "primitive natural expression" of a sensation has the generality it appears to have, it would follow that Wittgenstein holds that such a "primitive natural expression" must always exist if the first-person avowal is to be meaningful.' Kripke refers here also to

*Investigations* 256–7 (which lead on to 'sensation S'). He tells us that he (Kripke) in his presentation of Wittgenstein's private-language argument has portrayed Wittgenstein as holding that 'for each rule I follow there must be a criterion – other than simply what I say – by which another will judge that I am following the rule correctly. Applied to sensations, this seems to mean that there must be some "natural expression", or at any rate some external circumstances other than my mere inclination to say that this is the same sensation again, in virtue of which someone else can judge whether the sensation is present, and hence whether I have mastered the sensation term correctly.' Kripke says that, in this (his) essay, he has 'largely suppressed my own views'; however he will venture to 'remark here that any view that supposes that, in this sense, an inner process always has "outward criteria", seems to me probably to be *empirically* false'. (Kripke's italics.) This is a welcome admission. Kripke goes on to offer a 'liberal' version of the argument which may be compatible with Wittgenstein's intentions, allowing that in some cases a speaker might use sensation terms with no outward criteria for the presence of the sensations other than his sincere avowal. No one else can check. This, Kripke says, will not have 'the objectionable form of a "private language"' provided the speaker can 'demonstrate, for many sensations that do have public criteria, that he has mastered the appropriate terminology for identifying these sensations'; then the public criteria for the intelligibility of his avowal may be allowed to be the avowal itself. So there can be *some* rules where relevant mastery cannot be checked, but is assumed on the basis of community membership. Kripke's 'liberalisation', together with his welcome intrusion of his own opinion, may be understood to extend beyond the field of sensations to cover similar instances of inner phenomena lacking outer criteria. Kripke's exposition of Wittgenstein's argument began with the *very general* case of following rules, the scepticism occasioned by the thought that there is no way of being sure that something is the same as before. Wittgenstein (here I resume) certainly returns to the idea of *Lebensformen* as something absolutely fundamental. (Of course this is not an appeal to anthropology.) A 'community' here suggests an enclosure, a dominant group of judges, or a thoroughly reliable general will. What constitutes a 'confidence' in another person's language, the belief that what he says means something? Of course we are always dealing with this problem! But it strikes one (me) here that the 'goings-on' of language recede from 'clear cases'

[ 285 ]

into the wildest strangest most individualistic regions of human existence. Would it not be better to bypass the community and appeal to language itself as that which simply *does what is necessary*? (What is necessary for meaningfulness, and so also for truth.) The term 'language game' suggests some sort of *particular control* of language. Is not the best solution indeed that of Hume, or of, one might add, the author of the *Tractatus*? Language *just does* refer to the world, we *just do* possess the *essential* talent of knowing that something is the same again. Without this human nature would perish and go to ruin. Here we can see it as a Kantian-Humian deduction. It just has to be so for us to be as we are. If we recall here Kierkegaard's image of philosophical thinking as having to knot the thread, the admission that it is empirically false to say that an inner process must *always* have outer criteria must seem to constitute a cutting of a thread, by which we are liberated into conceptions of the 'inner life' which are considerably closer to common-sense. Perhaps the rather 'tangled' impression made by the relevant last part of the *Investigations* arises from Wittgenstein's (late) realisation that his previously offered picture was far from clear. I like and pick up another 'personal opinion' of Kripke (p. 43) that the force of Hume's picture (of an irreducible 'impression' corresponding to each psychological state) whose simplistic version Wittgenstein rejected, has been if anything *too little* felt. This suggests a thinking which tends to restore being and body to philosophical conceptions of consciousness.


Relevant quotations. Hume, *A Treatise of Human Nature*, Book I:

'All our reasonings concerning causes and effects are derived from nothing but custom; and that belief is more properly an act of the sensitive, than of the cogitative part of our natures.'

(Part IV section 1.)

'This sceptical doubt, both with respect to reason and the senses, is a malady which can never be radically cured, but must return upon us every moment, however we may chase it away, and sometimes may seem entirely free from it. It is impossible, upon any system, to defend either our understanding or our senses; and we but expose them further when we endeavour to justify them in that manner. As the sceptical doubt arises naturally from a profound and intense reflection on those subjects, it always increases the further we carry our reflections, whether in opposition or conformity to it. Carelessness and inattention alone can afford us any remedy.'

(Part IV section 2.)

'I must distinguish in the imagination betwixt the principles which are permanent, irresistible and universal; such as the customary transition from causes to effects and from effects to causes: and the principles which are changeable weak and irregular . . . The former are the foundation of all our thoughts and actions, so that upon their removal human nature must immediately perish and go to ruin.'

(Part IV section 4.)

'For my part, when I enter most intimately into what I call *myself*, I always stumble on some particular perception or other, of heat or cold, light or shade, love or hatred, pain or pleasure. I never catch myself at any time without a perception, and can never observe anything but the perception . . . If anyone, upon serious and unprejudiced reflection, thinks he has a different notion of *himself*, I must confess I can no longer reason with him. All I can allow him is that he may be in the right as well as I, and that we are essentially different in this particular. He may perhaps perceive something simple and continued which he calls *himself*; though I am certain there is no such principle in me. But setting aside some metaphysicians of this kind, I may venture to affirm of the rest of mankind that they are nothing but a bundle or collection of different perceptions which succeed each other with an inconceivable rapidity, and are in a perpetual flux and movement.'

(Part IV section 6.)

'Thus the sceptic still continues to reason and believe, even though he asserts that he cannot defend his reason by reason; and by the same rule he must assent to the principle concerning the existence of body though he cannot pretend by any arguments of philosophy, to maintain its veracity. Nature has not left it to his choice, and has doubtless esteemed it an affair of too great importance to be trusted to our uncertain reasonings and speculations. We may well ask what causes induce us to believe in the existence of body? But it is in vain to ask whether there be body or no? That is a point we must take for granted in all our reasonings.'

(Part IV section 2.)

Stanley Rosen, *The Ancients and Moderns*, p. 131:

[ 287 ]

'Wittgenstein's later writings are filled with one passage after another in which intuition is first rejected, either explicitly or implicitly, and then a puzzle arises with respect to how we know some simple fact or another of our experience. For example, how do we know that someone is in pain? The answer, I think, is quite simple: sometimes we do not, but when we do, it is through an intuitive unification of a variety of perceptions, some visual, some aural, and so on. If we are not allowed to have an intuitive grasp of the sense of connected phenomena, but are left with a person, his face contorted in a grimace, who shouts "I am in pain!" then the puzzle arises whether the grimace and the shout are enough evidence for the inference that the man is actually in pain. And they are not enough evidence. This leads Wittgenstein to fanciful speculations about whether we require a "picture" of the pain as distinct from the grimace and the shout, or whether we would need to look inside the interior of the shouting person in order to try to see the pain, and so on. These speculations arise because the obvious answer to the problem has been ruled out. There is no analytical or theoretical account of how we know that certain symptoms show a man to be in pain, because we intuit this.'

*Postscript.* Henry Staten's lucid and learned book, *Wittgenstein and Derrida*, throws light upon both writers. Staten tells us that the 'underlying theme of the whole book' is

'the question of what kind of functioning of language is involved in deconstructive discourse, which is neither poetry nor (quite) philosophy. Derrida picks up the view of language developed first by the symbolists and then by the modernists, that language is a quasi-material medium that is worked not by fitting words to the requisite meanings but by attentiveness to the way the words as words (sounds, shapes, associative echoes) will allow themselves to be fitted together. This is called in contemporary jargon "the play of signifiers" and has probably always been the way poets choose their words . . . I will argue that Wittgenstein himself did treat language this way . . .'

(Preface, pp. xiv–xv.)

Later, Staten refers us to Wittgenstein's 'attack on the conception of rules as transcendental and super-hard' at *Investigations* 193–4. Wittgenstein: 'When does one have the thought: the possible movements of a machine are already there in it in some mysterious sense? Well, when one is doing philosophy. And what leads us into thinking that? The kind of way we talk about machines.' (194.) Staten comments,

'The possibility of a particular movement as given in the *diagram* of the machine or ideal machine seems absolute and immutable, whereas an actual machine is subject to accidents; Wittgenstein wants us to stop thinking of the operation of rules on the model of machine-as-diagram and think, rather, in terms of something actual that is subject to contingency, to which *accidents may happen*. To think an essential law of contingency, as Derrida does, is to generalise as a "grammatical rule" the principles of the kind of critique that Wittgenstein here instantiates. Whereas "metaphysical grammar" subordinates accident to essence, the empirical to the logical, and so on, "deconstructive grammar" does not. Rather, it attempts to let accidental being operate upon deconstructive writing, deforming it and preventing it from achieving transcendental form.'

(Introduction, p. 18.)

I don't think the example given is helpful in suggesting a similarity between Derrida and Wittgenstein. What emerges is rather an interesting difference between them. One way of explaining deconstructive discourse would be to contrast it with ordinary language; with which Wittgenstein has no quarrel. What he is talking about is what philosophers, and laymen, wrongly picture or imagine. The discussion round about 194 concerns Wittgenstein's continuing *anxiety* about ability to follow a rule. How can we know that the future will resemble the past? At 199 he says, 'To obey a rule, to make a report, to give an order to play a game of chess, are *customs* (uses, institutions).' Hume's terminology. Whereas Derrida is thinking of felicitous accidents and contingencies brought about by the interlacing nature of language and *made use of* aesthetically (expressively) in discourse. His 'law of contingency' is an encouragement to word play. (He is a *literary man*, Wittgenstein was not.) Wittgenstein's distinctive style should not be mistaken for a deliberately poetic use of language.

One difficulty for interested analytical philosophers is to see Derrida's problems as problems and so to see the need and nature of his solutions. In the British empiricist tradition there has been no Thomism, no Hegelianism, and generally no urge toward complete (metaphysical or logical) system. Perhaps contingency and muddle were always closer, and a willingness to believe that perhaps A did not have to be either A or not A. Notions of sealed integrity of super-hard God-established concepts were not in charge. Behind Derrida stand the Aristotelian tradition, also Hegel, Husserl, Heidegger, also Nietzsche, Freud, Joyce and the poetic aestheticism of the symbolists. A critique of Descartes is now common to both traditions. What must strike one in a comparison and contrast is that Wittgenstein is plainly a philosopher, whereas Derrida is not. Indeed it is difficult to know what to call him, he is *sui generis*. Their aims and motives are different. Toward the end of his book (in an interesting discussion of Austin) Staten remarks that

'perhaps what we have in this debate is a conflict between modern Anglo-American clean-mindedness or sincerity and a more archaic moral rigour that insists on reminding us of the residue of darkness in man's intention. If there is any scepticism in Derrida, it is a moral, not an epistemological scepticism – not a doubt about the possibility of morality but about an idealised picture of sincerity that takes insufficient account of the windings and twistings of fear and desire, weakness and lust, sadism and masochism and the will to power, in the mind of even the most sincere man.'

(3. IV, pp. 126–7.)

He goes on shortly to say that his (a particular) criticism of Austin might even seem unfair 'since Austin was not even trying to do anything like what Derrida wants to do. Derrida has more in common with Montaigne and Shakespeare, Nietzsche and Freud, than he does with Austin, the straightforward investigator on the scientific model.' Yes, analytical philosophy is doing something different, less dramatic, less all-embracing, more precise. I have been talking about moral philosophy. It is not easy for philosophy to deal with evil. On today's scene I think (analytical) neo-Aristotelian, neo-Thomist philosophers such as Philippa Foot and Charles Taylor are finding a way. Nietzsche and Freud, who in their different ways romanticise or sterilise the subject, are perhaps not the best guides. We must beware of coming too close to 'the game'. Simone Weil kept a cooler and clearer head. The dark side, the deep evil in the soul is not to be played with, Shakespeare did not play with it. Derrida's position suggests a more tolerant Jungian approach. 'Archaic moral rigour' may name something profound, and we may certainly have to turn to the Greeks. But what they show us, and what Shakespeare shows us, is a teaching which is conveyed by the highest art. Derrida is an 'authority' who sets up laws of contingency and rules of grammar. He cannot but appear as a sort of moralist, his work carries a strong emotional charge, a whiff of some new-style liberation. He is far more like Nietzsche and Freud than like Wittgenstein. He is a remarkable thinker, a great scholar, a brilliant maverick polymath, a *pharmakeus*. But if thought of as philosophy, the aesthetic requirement of the doctrine itself tends to exclude sober plodding reflection, slow lucid explanation, simple clear thinking. Heidegger desired a poeticised philosophy. A poeticisation of thought.

I read *L'écriture et la différence*, an early book of Derrida, when it was first published in 1967, and was impressed and disturbed by it. I have read, or read large parts of, other books of his since, brilliant *difficult* books full of learning and thinking and the ironic and playful light of a remarkable intelligence. Any book of his attacks many subjects and may adopt many styles. More lately and wildly, for instance, to be 'experienced', *Glas*, a poetic anthology presenting (and burying) Hegel (etc.) in a mass of literary and philosophical reflections and erudite word play and crazy wit. *Psyche*, a headlong commentary on everything and everybody. One should not ignore (as some of his critics do) these unique literary marvels. So what is wrong, what is there to worry about, should we not enjoy and profit from his versatile writings, his scholarship, his gorgeous prose, his large literary achievement? I have been relevantly concerned here only with a certain band or aspect of his work: the jargon, the poeticisation of philosophy, the hubris, the 'transcendental field', the concepts of *archi-écriture* and *différance*. What is disturbing and dangerous is the presentation of his thought as philosophy or as some sort of final metaphysic, and its elevation into a comprehensive literary creed and model of prose style and criticism, constituting an entirely (as it were compulsory) new way of writing and thinking.

# > 10 <

# Notes on Will and Duty

To be indifferent to one's own misery is not like being indifferent to that of others. And what about the *unavoidable scrutiny* of the extensive and various workings of one's own mind? From many positions life not only ought not to be, but cannot possibly be, looked at as a whole, like a work of art. I shall discuss 'certainty' shortly and also argue that the concept of duty, though not constituting the whole of morals, cannot be dispensed with. Schopenhauer chides Kant for his exclusion of experience, the fact that he 'does not represent the so-called moral law as a fact of consciousness'. He also doubts whether the idea of duty is alone strong enough 'to put the bridle on the impulse of strong desires, the storm of passion, and the gigantic stature of egoism'. (*The Basis of Morality*, section 6, 'On the Basis of Kant's Ethics'.) Heroic endurance and indifference to worldly goods is not only not the whole of virtue, it cannot be a plausible programme for virtue. Can we say that the man who has this courage and this indifference, who has in these respects conquered egoism (not a mean achievement), automatically or *ipso facto* cares for other people? (Wittgenstein gave up a fortune, and worked in a hospital during the 1939–45 war.) To see the whole picture one may have to stop being neat, not everything therein can necessarily support or imply everything else. Stoical endurance and lack of worldly values do not seem essentially to 'contain' a purification of desire or practical concern for the needs of others. It is possible to imagine such concepts or characteristics as mutually independent or even antithetical. And (of course) philosophers (such as Schopenhauer, Wittgenstein and Heidegger) who celebrate or indicate mysticism, do not thereby qualify as mystics. (Mystics are *good*. A 'bad mystic' is a magician.) Many moral philosophers or preachers will seek for principles of unity, perhaps through some central 'deeper' idea (such as love or truth or reason). In 'ordinary life' we often tend to be specialists in morals, as if we had a limited amount of moral energy, and could not spread it over the whole field; and 'specialists' may often want to accuse of hypocrisy those who pretend to a larger capacity. The motives to endure one's own misery are not the same as those whereby we 'endure' the misery of others: these latter may be various, we may for instance hold that pretended 'help' is really interference, pretension, exercise of power. Desire for intense self-scrutiny does not necessarily excite desire to forgo worldly advantage. Here the idea of a list of duties, or a list offered by a religious figure (as in the Sermon on the Mount), might seem attractive, with or without some absolutely clear principle of connection. Certainly many people who recognise duties would be hard put to explain their mutual implication. We may attempt to understand Wittgenstein's stoicism by an extension or deepening. (Can aesthetes be stoics, can evil men be stoics, is stoicism a virtue or a defence of the self?) Wittgenstein rejects 'duty' and 'experience' (consciousness), and places the idea of significance (a kind of truthfulness, a closeness to facts, a saying only what can be said) at the point where Kant puts the entry into phenomena of the noumenal beam of duty. Kant allows us an experiential shudder in the apprehension of duty (*Achtung*, respect for the law), and one may find a similar emotion in the author of the *Tractatus*, expressed in his aphoristic literary style. Truthfulness eschews florid sentimentality, irresponsible generalisation, development of vague concepts.

Our world cannot properly be said to wax and wane as a whole. Certainly morality must be seen as 'everywhere' but in a fallen and incomplete sense. I would regard the (daily, hourly, minutely) attempted purification of consciousness as the central and fundamental 'arena' of morality, but the nature of the world must be thought of as essentially 'in' this place too. Truth is central, energising a perpetual unsystematic (that is un-Hegelian) dialectic of subject and object. (Love is truth, truth is love.) My moral energy is a function of how I understand, see, the world. There is continual strife in the deep patterns of desire. There are many ways in which people become better, all kinds of inspirations and illuminations, points of clarity and rays of grace. What is objective here, what is subjective? Concepts, truth, reason, love, may seem to us sometimes as 'our own', sometimes as external judges. I do not think philosophy can establish any closely knit system here. As Kant and Schopenhauer point out, a complete 'solution' is precluded by our finite nature. The word 'dialectic', which may suggest such system, should thus be used with care or avoided. (The concept of 'intentionality' is also likely to cause confusion; I think we are better without it.) One can only attempt to place ideas in various magnetic relationships to each other. I have been discussing the concept of consciousness (also experience) as indispensable. But from here one can also see the necessity of the idea of duty as something alien, the outer not the inner, the command whose authority may be recognised as running against the stream of the inner life. I shall discuss shortly the concept of 'axioms' as essentially isolated statements of values. This idea (axioms) has a particular importance in politics. Utilitarian arguments may also be thought of as possessing this isolated status. (Like brown, not in the spectrum.)

The concept of the individual as it has been developed and exhibited in the west since Homer *requires* the idea of consciousness, inwardness, privacy, separate worlds. Our increased awareness of local historical and psychological 'conditioning' does not separate us from Locke and Hobbes. Our conception of the, properly, 'inviolate' individual is enlivened by our knowledge of how persons can be de-individualised, brutalised out of individuality, by hunger, fear, extreme deprivation or manipulation of concepts. We constantly reflect upon the inner life of others, we are *driven* to do this. The concept is forced upon us. Such coercion may be a source of enlightenment or of despair. To say that I can know what other people are thinking but not (in the same sense) what I am thinking, makes a *philosophical* point. But of course our conception of ourselves is, properly, far richer and more detailed, as well as of course more 'interesting', than our conception of others! It may also, of course, be more subject to illusion; though our illusions about others are often a function of our illusions about ourselves. The concept of the individual is certainly a political flag; its value in politics derives from and depends upon a more general moral sense of the value and status of privacy and the 'inner life'. Here we may remind ourselves of the importance of literature, poetry, the novel, as a continued exploration of, and reflection upon, the inner world of appearance and illusion, and the problem (often so crudely simplified in philosophy) of 'objective' and 'subjective', which is also the problem of truth. Here the border-line of what is expressible, to others and to ourselves, is very blurred. Plato's *Seventh Letter* speaks about this blurred edge. We are often out at this edge, and do not have to be philosophers or 'writers' to be there, it is often a good place to be.

A study of the idea of moral change is a useful mode of reflection here. In this context we may go on to reflect upon the part played in our lives by desires and attachments. Here we make sense of the idea that it is our duty to have good desires and remove or weaken bad ones. A good desire includes the urge to see truly. Truthful vision prompts right action. Kant said 'Never lie.' We may, with Schopenhauer, wish to allow some exceptions. But Kant's absolutism emphasises the *status* of truthfulness, upon which Schopenhauer's worldly realism casts a shadow. We should not want to tread the road of 'it doesn't matter all that much'. A 'list of virtues' must establish not only a hierarchy, but also a sense of interpenetration, otherwise it may mislead us. The quality of our attachments is the quality of our understanding. Being dutiful involves being just, justice must make a pact with mercy. Christ's 'list' spoke of love as fundamental and inhering in all. Plato's moral forms cohere and interweave, making a *koinonia* or communion. One point of certainty supports another. 'If there is no God, how can I be a captain?' cries a character in Dostoevsky. These mutual coherences of the values we feel sure of, and the things we desire, develop (for good or ill) the thickening density of our lives. Here we may understand the feelings of Schopenhauer and Wittgenstein when they rejected 'duty' as a mere arbitrary listing of divinely commanded particular tasks, as opposed to a more general moral sensibility. On the other hand if we go too far toward an intuited unity, an identification of moral concepts with each other in a hazy mass of internal relations, this may lead to a stoical or aesthetic morality of 'style', a reduction of morals to some single concept (as in Schopenhauer's 'compassion'), a loss (as in Hegelian idealism) of our sense of the independent contingency and diversity of the world. Husserl wanted to analyse the 'natural standpoint'. Sekida wished to change it, virtually rejecting the idea of any general standpoint, since we are always in motion toward or away from what is more real. It is not difficult to understand the view that our ordinary consciousness is full of illusions. Our 'grasp' is superficial. Anxiety, malice, envy, greed, all sorts of selfish preoccupations and instinctive attachments may deform or hide what confronts us. Here we see the ubiquitous nature of moral value. The term 'transcendence' is present in a moral sense. At every moment we are 'attending' or failing to attend. ('What, can't we ever rest?!' There are different kinds of resting.) Blameless ignorance, misery, affliction can also darken the scene and at such times we may lose 'our world' altogether. The terminology of appearance and reality, in quite familiar senses, is in place here. Philosophy too should attempt to use ordinary language and avoid pre-emptive jargon. All right, traditional metaphysics has a certain amount of specialised terminology, but it is not for us to presume to add to it. Meta-languages gain their *sense* from the language they are explaining; the 'thing itself' must be constantly in view. Of course our conversation lives in history and is local and changeful. Yet western philosophy since the Greeks, that continuum of which Derrida announces the end, offers an area of general discourse, a hall of reflection, wherein the difficult conceptions of great thinkers have constantly been broken down, examined, used and passed on into our thinking while at the same time retaining their identities. St Augustine mediated Platonism into Christianity, by innumerable channels the thoughts of Freud have filtered into our minds. Meanwhile, fortunately (so far) the original texts remain on the shelves. Anyone who has taught philosophy is likely to know of the surprise with which one re-reads a text one has been teaching for some time. In philosophy, as in other studies, one must continually try to return to 'the beginning', which involves discovering what 'the beginning' is. In this persisting light we can still try to proceed without becoming pseudo-scientists.

Simone Weil uses an image of the human situation as being like that of a mountain walker who is aware of what is very distant, what is less distant, what is near, as well as of the uneven ground beneath her feet. Our confused conscious being is both here and elsewhere, living at different levels and in different modes of cognition. We are 'distracted' creatures, extended, layered, pulled apart. Our most obvious unifying feature is methodical egoism, the barrier which divides the area of our interests and requirements from the rest of the world. Morality thought of as the achievement of virtue, 'becoming good' (anyway becoming better), involves the breaking of that barrier. How can it be done, should it be done? There is no lack of comments including those of Freudians (and to some extent Freud) to the effect that the ego need not and should not allow its structure to be damaged by 'ideals'. To be an effective moral being you must be an effective being. Morality is best thought of as doing what is right if it is also fairly easy. This may indeed be (roughly) a code which most of us follow. But if we consider how multiform and unpredictable and huge is the ambiguous border-line between subject and object, us and world, and how consciousness is at all times unavoidably active in evaluation and in control and development of desire, we are 'forced' to see how a larger picture is required. The felt need for this picture, or field of force, is answered by metaphysics and religion, and by general moral values, our sense of right and wrong. This is not a matter of specialised isolated moments of moral choice, appearing in a continuum of non-moral activity. These movements and responses are occurring all the time. The reality of the moral requirement is proved by the world. Reflection here can suggest how morality is 'naturally religious' as well as religion 'naturally moral'. This would be part of a (in the west) changing concept of religion. We may also see, through reflection on both, how we might and why we should 'break the barriers of egoism'; how it is that spiritual reality is the same as ordinary reality, is the reality of our everyday appearance, is all *here*, not elsewhere: which is also a funda-mental religious view.

Philosophical doctrines which profess neutrality, whether they are professedly analytic (against preaching) or scientific (against value) cannot help, by what they obliterate or what they emphasise, making moral judgments. (Structuralist thinking is full of moral judgments.) Moral philosophers should be frankly and realistically high-minded in the sense of recognising the unique and profound presence and importance of a moral sense. They should be liberal-minded, not cyn-ics, reductivists, relativists, but able to scan a wide vista of human life. Such thinking involves a sensitive empiricism and grasp of detail. For instance (some of Plato's dialogues are exemplars here) it is necessary to consider with the help of examples what egoism is, whether it is wrong, how it relates to truth, love, freedom. What is happiness, what is 'true happiness', why did Mill find he could not do without the concept of higher pleasures? These are not just theoretical exercises in seminars, they indicate the nature of our everyday problems.

I return (briefly) to Schopenhauer as an example of empiricist know-all, confused metaphysician, and simple-hearted moralist. (I have refrained from commenting on his views about women, expressed in *Studies in Pessimism*! It should be kept in mind that he was probably expressing opinions held at that time by a majority of men. And that time is still not far away.) Schopenhauer's ebullient fiddling with his concepts provides us with the elements of a partly recognisable picture of our world. It is as if he had all the pieces but could not modify them suitably in relation to each other. He dodges between metaphysics and common-sense. He is a cheerful pessimist and not a cynic. (Kierkegaard's remarks about him are apt.) In a passage where he compares and contrasts Kant's Thing-in-itself and Plato's Idea, he remarks on 'the remarkable diversity of the individuality of their authors', and says that 'they are the best commentary on each other, for they are like two entirely different roads that conduct us to the same goal'. (*WWI*, Book III, 'The Platonic Idea: the Object of Art'.) I like the notion of 'the best commentary': also 'Western philosophy is a dialogue between Plato and Kant'. I see the deepest aspects of moral philosophy as contained in this dialogue. However to attribute 'the same goal' is to fasten on one aspect only of their thoughts. Schopenhauer puts it as follows, 'that both explain the visible world as a manifestation, which in itself is nothing, and which only has meaning and a borrowed reality through that which expresses itself in it (in one case the Thing-in-itself, in the other the Idea)'. This way of putting it may sound like some understanding of eastern philosophy, and may seem to ignore the sense in which both philosophers are empiricists; but Schopenhauer is aware of how the difference between appearance and reality has to be sought piecemeal in this 'visible world' which is thereby not abolished but revealed. The 'veil of Maya' can (should) also be understood in this way. One may certainly say that both Plato and Kant envisage some deeper reality which lies behind ordinary superficial appearances. This is not just a metaphysical or religious dictum. That our awareness in all its variety, of our daily 'world' is normally hasty and perfunctory, and may be deepened, revealing more truth and reality, is on reflection something obvious. However, Kant in his role as modern scientific man, attributes to our rationality a noumenal, not a phenomenal, role, whereas Plato unites intellect and moral will; and, as moral philosophers, Kant sees the active principle as cool reason, Plato as rational virtuous passion (Eros). Schopenhauer is usually more concerned to find his own visions in great philosophers rather than to expound theirs, and later in the same section interrupts a discussion about whether and how Plato fails to distinguish between Ideas and concepts by declaring, 'We leave this question alone and go on our way, glad when we come upon traces of any great and noble mind, yet not following his footsteps but our own aim.' This is of course something which any philosopher must say at times, and should say explicitly.

Neither Kant nor Plato would care for Schopenhauer's cosmic will which seems to leave no place for the human individual and the absolutes of morality. The energy of Plato's Eros moves between good and evil. However the idea of the unity of all being in a cosmic flux which transcends individuality (as offered also in some accounts of modern physics) may imply and include a 'natural' capacity to have sympathy and empathy with the whole of creation, an idea shared with Buddhism and Hinduism. The transcended individual may of course be seen as the now selfless and enlightened individual. 'God is everywhere' in Christianity too. Plato who does not pay much attention to plants and animals (Socrates notices a tree in the *Phaedrus*, but prefers the city) says however in the *Timaeus* that man should attempt to perfect the created world, working thereby on behalf of all aspirations towards consciousness of all created beings. Our natural (since we are part of it) awareness of and sympathy with the rest of being, our reverence thereby for all life, may be said to provide us, in Schopenhauer's general picture, with another way to escape from determinism. Our attention is continually caught by the details of our surroundings, we can be touched and surprised into an ability to change, to move 'out of ourselves', by all sorts of attentions to other things and people, instinctive overcomings of the barrier between self and world. Our ability and tendency, continually in all sorts of ways, to do this, is an important part of Schopenhauer's contention that compassion, not Kantian rational law, is the basis of morality. He gives numerous examples, of which one, already mentioned, is tenderness to animals. As I said earlier, Schopenhauer is I think unique among notable philosophers in saying, not just coolly, but with feeling, that cruelty to animals is wrong, and any training that includes it is bad training. He chides Kant for ignoring the huge perceptible world, the innumerable individual things, of innumerable kinds, which crave for our attention and (as also indicated in the *Timaeus*) our *protection*. (Modern 'green' politics, ecology, care for wild life, is a welcome extension of utilitarianism in the direction of everything.) Schopenhauer, who cannot see the point and essential importance of the idea of duty, gives of course an unfair rendering of Kant's imperative. He is right however to indicate the multiform workings of compassion. In *The Basis of Morality* (section 19, 'The Foundation of Ethics') he concludes that 'boundless compassion for all living beings is the firmest and surest guarantee of pure moral conduct', and that the genuineness of this moral incentive is 'further confirmed by the fact that *the animals* are also taken under its protection'. (His italics.) Schopenhauer here exhibits how argument in moral philosophy moves to and fro between abstract principles and immediate moral instincts. Evident sympathy with animals can 'confirm' a general rule. He remarks, in praising compassion, that it is 'the basis of loving-kindness even more obviously than justice'. This is not so clear. Duty and justice must not be eclipsed. The cause of the liberation of women has depended largely upon these concepts; sometimes compassion only arrives later.

'Will', 'the Will', can be a confusing concept, especially in its grandiose uses, as by Kant, Schopenhauer, Wittgenstein. It can be a term which, seeming to deal with or explain a large matter, halts reflection at a crucial point. It may be better, as I suggested earlier, to restrict the term will, as 'willing' or 'exercise of will', to cases where there is an immediate straining, for instance occasioned by a perceived duty or principle, against a large part of preformed consciousness. What moves us – our motives, our desires, our reasoning – emerges from a constantly changing complex; moral change is the change of that complex, for better or worse. Herein intellectual experiences, states of reflective viewing of the world, are continually moving in relation to more affective or instinctive levels of thought and feeling. Experience, awareness, consciousness, these words emphasise the existence of the thinking, planning, remembering, acting moral being as a mobile creature living in the present. Such, as it might seem here, obscure and complicated pictures are, we should remind ourselves, frequently and convincingly described by great novelists. St Augustine too, using a great many real-life examples, pictures will as a blend of intellect and feeling. (Plenty of experiential volume.) The problem of the freedom of the will must be thought of as lying inside such a picture. Freedom (in this sense) is freedom from bad habit and bad desire, and is brought about in all sorts of ways by impulses of love, rational reflection, new scenery, conscious and deliberate formation of new attachments and so on.

There are good modes of attention and good objects of attention. 'Whatsoever things are true, whatsoever things are honest, whatsoever things are just, whatsoever things are lovely, whatsoever things are of good report, if there be any virtue, if there be any praise, think on these things.' (St Paul, Philippians 4. 8.) Any look at the contingency of our strange and interesting world, its oddity, its surprisingness, its jumble or its neatness can provide such objects and occasions. These 'things' which are just and good assist our attention when we try to make just and compassionate judgments of others or to judge and correct ourselves. Faced with difficult problems or terrible decisions we may feel the need, not so much of a sudden straining of unpractised will-power, but of a calm vision, a relaxed understanding, something that comes from a deep level. This darkness must be stirred and fed, as the deep mind of the artist is fed intuitively by his experience. There is a 'moral unconscious'. This is how morality leads naturally into mysticism and has a natural bond with religion. (By religion I mean a religious attitude and form of life, not a literalistic adherence to a particular dogma.) There can no doubt be a mysticism of the extreme ascetic. But there is also a natural way of mysticism, as indicated by St Paul, which involves a deepened and purified apprehension of our surroundings. The truth-seeking mind is magnetised by an independent transcendent multiform reality. Unselfish attention breaks the barrier of egoism. Living in the present: I really see the face of my friend, the playing dog, Piero's picture. These visual cases also have a metaphorical force. We instinctively dodge in and out of metaphor all the time, and in this sense too are fed or damaged spiritually by what we attend to. Simone Weil uses the image of becoming empty so as to be filled with the truth. She speaks of the mountain walker who sees many things besides the mountain top. Eckhart speaks of emptying the soul so that it may fill with God. A moral position much higher than our own may only be imagined as deprivation. The idea of negation (void) or surrender of selfish will is to be understood together with the idea of purified desire as purified cognition.

Someone may say that this line of thought could degenerate into a relaxed surrender to an aesthetic attitude, an ethic of 'beautiful thoughts'; and theories which thus 'swallow' or transform the concept of will may run this risk, even though they may also seem more empirical and realistic. After all, it may be said, the idea of plain stark duty, so contemptuously rejected by Schopenhauer, and following him by

Wittgenstein, as a mere theological survival, is also a widely recognised and surely rightly prized part of the everyday moral life. Certainly the idea of duty must not be analysed or 'reduced' away, though it must also be seen in a wider landscape. It would be misleading to suggest that morality could be reduced to a list, perhaps a short list, of duties. The concept of duty is *sui generis*, its separateness is an aspect of its efficacy. It is not the whole of morals, but is an essential rigidly enduring part. Moral rules appear (should appear) early in life when morality itself is being taught. Ideally, these rules may be surrounded by some degree of explanation. These early conversations are very important. Behind the slow natural working of education and example the idea of certain absolute requirements should remain visible. Duty is not to be absorbed into, or dissolved in, the vast complexities of moral feeling and sensibility. Love may carry us on, natural generosity, instinctive compassion, as Schopenhauer thought. But the concept of duty as moral rules of a certain degree of generality should stay in place. Do not lie, do not steal, be helpful, be kind. Fortunate children imbibe such ideas in a scene which promotes honesty and kindness and mutual love. Truth is taught in an atmosphere of truthfulness. Primary duties may seem later to find their places in a general development of moral texture, while remaining on call as discrete individual commands. Particular moral taboos may remain intact in an alien environment, certain inhibitions, even thought of as 'irrational', may remain valuable: such as, in a life of reckless selfishness, the *impossibility* of stealing. The nearness of duties is a persistent form of education. Duty can appear when moral instinct and habit fail, when we lack any clarifying mode of reflection, and seek for a rule felt as external. Most often perhaps we become aware of duty when it collides head-on with inclination. (A place for the concept of will-power.) Anyone may suddenly find himself, in an unforeseen situation, confronted in his stream of consciousness by the notice DON'T DO IT. (Socrates's daemon told him only what not to do.) Duties, because of their use as a bridle placed on egoism (Schopenhauer thought an ineffective one), may seem more often to carry a sign of negation. 'Don't lie' is a *clearer* command than 'be truthful'. Be kind, be generous – these requirements seem a vaguer part of our lives, unclear in their limits. But the idea of duty must often in these vague areas be cherished and especially illumined – as when we are 'forced' to exhibit 'loving kindness' in the captivity of some unavoidable service. Here the quiet pressure of duty may bring about the move from negative to positive. The concept is *indispensable*, though it cannot stand alone; it is a formal way of asserting both the orderly pattern-like nature of morality, and its uniquely absolute demand, quite different from that of inclination. A totally good being would not experience the call of duty, might be said to lack or not need the concept, since all acts and decisions would emerge from virtuous insight and its orderly process. God has no duties. An imperfect being often feels and recognises the moral demand as external, contrary to instinct and habit, contrary to usual modes of thought. The idea of duty serves here. If thought of without the enclosing background of general and changing quality of consciousness, of moral experience, of acquired moral fabric, it may seem stark, inexplicable except as arbitrary orders given by God, or be considered as mere historically determined social rules. It may also be taken to suggest that morality is an occasional part-time activity of switching on the ethical faculty on separate occasions of moral choice. But to return to an earlier metaphor, we can only move properly in a world that we can see, and what must be sought for is vision.

The conception of an absolute requirement, whether or not adorned with metaphysical justifications, is shared with religion where it is connected with an absolute ground, that is some idea of a persisting and necessarily existing reality. How far can a demythologised religion go in that direction and still be called religion? The 'reality' or 'ground', traditionally thought of picturesquely as 'elsewhere', may be seen as available to ordinary cognition, intuitable, veiled and so on. Some Kantian views, and part of the mind of Kant himself, would wish to check for questioning any movement from morality into religion because this would be to accept a heteronomous principle. It is easy to see this dilemma. If we recognise an absolute which is more extensive than our own sense of right we are giving away our judgment to an external authority. If God appeared physically before us on His throne and said 'Do this' we would still be able to wonder if we ought to. Wittgenstein, commenting on the old question of whether something is right because God wills it or willed by God because it is right, preferred the former because it 'cuts off any road to an explanation'. That is, any explanation or justification (pictures, accounts, dogmatic formulations) of religion is a kind of lie, a misleading clutter; a religious person does not explain what 'God' is, he goes *there* directly and not through any external paraphernalia. God, the Divine, is unique, not a

thing among others to be given 'place' in the world. Properly understood this point is like that of, properly understood, the Ontological
Proof. We may feel that Wittgenstein's aphorism silences us too
quickly, and (especially Protestant) theologians like to emphasise that
the only acceptable religion must be one which could accord with a
purified conception of autonomy. These are very old and ever new
problems to which I shall return later when talking about religion and
the Ontological Proof. I look here at the question of duty in the context
of the possible charge that the sort of neo-Platonic moral view on
which I have been reflecting is really a sort of aesthetic view, a kind of
wander through pleasant groves of quasi-religious experience. I spoke
just now of a move from morality on into religion. I could think rather
in terms of a move from religion into morality, that is a rediscovery of
religious modes of thought deep inside morals. That religion and
morals somehow overlap or 'blend' may seem obvious: yet in the secular atmosphere of today may need stating as well as studying. The
exercise of duty is not a cold look at the facts and a jump to a moral
intuition or dictate of reason: the picture implied by a sharp distinction
between fact and value. We are all the time building up our value world
and exercising, or failing to exercise, our sense of truth in the daily
hourly minutely business of apprehending, or failing to apprehend,
what is real and distinguishing it from illusion. 'The absolute' may be
thought of as a distant moral goal, like a temple at the end of a
pilgrimage, a condition of perfection glimpsed but never reached. Or
of course it may be thought of as being, or being the property of, a
personal God. But the idea of absolute, as truth and certainty, is contained in ordinary exercises of cognition, it is already inherent in the
knowledge which suggests our duty, it is *in* our sense of truth; however
feeble or 'specialised' our response to it may be. Our justifications of
our moral failures pay it homage. It should not be seen as a dangerous
possibly heteronomous property of religion (or a kind of transcendent
'thing'), but as something innate in morality which can also bind or
connect morality with a certain understanding of religion.

I have suggested that we may look at these matters by making use
of a concept of consciousness. Of course, as I said above, we may
properly reflect upon our conditioning, our deep prejudices, our
received ideas, etc. I mean 'consciousness' in a common-sense understanding of 'where we live'. Many states of consciousness are touched
by art, and not only in a sentimental or weakening sense. Art is a mode

of cognition, the artist in us is aware of the problem of formulating what is true. The good artist destroys false work. We depend on intuitions which go beyond what is distinctly seen, we are out on frontiers where methods of verification are at stake. We exist in many different ways at many different levels at the same time. There are qualities of consciousness and levels of cognition. We think and speak of ourselves in hypothetical dispositional terms. There are unconscious good habits, an aspect of civilisation. But we also know that we are not just a network of dispositions. This knowledge is part of our sense of our freedom. We need and want to *come home* to what is categorical not hypothetical, to return to the present, where we also and essentially live. There are patterns and there are events, there are moments and 'long presents'. There is busy preoccupied activity, obsessed gazing, concentrated watching, attention, meditation. We look at trees and at television sets. These fundamental uses of our time may be hard to delineate. We 'make them our own'; we can move from fine shades of behaviour to finer shades, we can move toward what is less readily *identifiable* but indubitably present. The question of 'the inner' can be seen as one of identification. We are involved in the mysteries of lived time, our being here and elsewhere. This is, in my view, not a problem which philosophers can successfully analyse into any sort of minute or quasi-scientific detail. 'Temporalisation' or (French) *temporalisation* is an extremely unclear concept. But philosophers might be wise to deal with time-problems as aspects of particular contexts. An example would be: can we properly condemn a man of seventy for crimes he committed when he was twenty? We can attempt to clarify this. A general philosophical theory of time is likely to be unbearably abstract. The argument is not just Moore versus McTaggart. The mountain walker can be aware of very many things 'at the same time'. Our memories and expectations enter into the quality of our categorical present. 'What this is like', what I 'see it as' is not a problem which can be, as it were, handed over to empirical psychology and then received back in a helpfully sorted state; non-scientific concepts, value concepts, philosophical concepts are involved in setting the scene, indicating what we want to characterise and why. Here ordinary language is best, and to describe the indescribable we must resort to it. Serious discussion of states of consciousness, thinking, moral reflection, quality of being tends to use imagery and resort to art.

'Seeing as' is everywhere and is the stuff of metaphors. Metaphors

are not rhetorical speech-aids occasionally resorted to. They are fundamental modes of understanding. We are exceedingly used to imagery
and are continually employing it. I use the words 'metaphor' and
'image' in the wide sense where one form indicates another and where
it may be very easy or very difficult to translate into a non-figurative
mode. 'We are all one happy family down at Headquarters' is easy to
'translate'. Descriptions of complex states of mind may be more difficult. Here a long intricate image (such as Maggie's pagoda in *The
Golden Bowl*) may have a clear non-figurative sense whereas to say (in
despair) that the world is 'black' or 'smells foul' may seem more like
an ultimate statement. Often we do not notice metaphors. ('High' and
'low' for instance.) Plato said, using a metaphor, that higher spiritual
conceptions appear as images or shadows at lower levels. Often we
cannot get beyond the image or intimation. How do we, how can we,
'picture' the good man? Here traditional taken-for-granted icons come
to us, helpfully or not: Christ as the good man. How carefully do we
scrutinise what we 'see'? The picture of Christ may enlighten and
inspire us, or enable us to stop thinking. Sometimes we are not sure
whether something is an image or not. 'Stealing isn't exactly wrong,
it's bad form.' The Second Commandment tells us not to make 'any
graven image, or any likeness of any thing that is in heaven above or
that is in the earth beneath or that is in the water under the earth'.
(Exodus 20. 4.) Kant said this was the most sublime commandment of
Judaic law. It is a caution against idolatry and against anthropomorphism. What is true is 'beyond'. The prisoners in Plato's Cave wrongly
took the images and shadows of things to be the things themselves.
But whether or not it be taken literally the command is a hard saying.
Islamic art, which accepts the prohibition, shows how hard it is and
also how ingenious art is. The Taj Mahal, which is written all over
with the most exquisite (non-human, non-animal) natural forms, is
itself an image. We may have to be content with images. Exceptional
persons, such as mystics or 'Dante' in Dante's story, who 'see God'
cannot express what they saw. Nor can Plato's pilgrim describe the
Sun.

We may think of a person as an image of God or of the soul, or
attempt to find in 'nothingness', a negation of speech and picture, an
'image' of the spiritual life. There are images wherein, rightly or
wrongly, we rest, and others which are promptings to work. Religious
myths are metaphors which come in many kinds. Rituals are images,

often simple (washing, eating) often complex ('doing' the Stations of the Cross). The attention of the devotee is part of the rite. Here the inner needs the outer because, being incarnate, we need places and times, expressive gestures which release psychic energy and bring healing, making spaces and occasions for spiritual activity or events. Plato connects imagery with the work of Eros, the magnetism which draws us out of the Cave. The shadows puzzle the mind, suggest something beyond, give us the motive to move and to change. The Forms fill our minds with images, they are beyond imagery and yet they 'inform' the soul with their magnetic figures. Schopenhauer sees the Forms (Ideas) as thus working in the mind also through the vast extension of the imagery of art. Freud, who invented a modern concept of psychic energy, acknowledges his debt to Eros. He is also (surely) indebted to *anamnesis*. The 'unconscious mind' is a deep abode of ambiguous images. Freud's treatment of these may be narrowed by his lack of consideration of the deeply moral nature of soul activity. This omission may be deemed essential to a scientific account. But if we regret the omission we may be led to doubt the scientific claim. In practice psychoanalytical therapy, as treatment of human individuals with histories, cannot avoid being involved in moral judgment, in moral reflection and insight in the widest sense. This moral aspect of their work is now recognised in the claim of some practitioners that all analysis is lay analysis. It is the soul that is being treated. The notion that the soul can, in its travail, become the analysand of an authoritative science contributes to an atmosphere wherein people resolutely ignore moral and religious aspects of their *experience*. It has become unfashionable, even among theologians and moralists, to refer to such experience. Newspapers and magazines and television, though also full of evident nonsense, create a sense of 'fact', of a complete documentary presentation of our surroundings. We are amused and entertained by popular science. This simplified neon-lighted atmosphere is inimical to an apprehension of the whole world as spiritually alive and significant. Absence of ritual from ordinary life also starves the imagination; institutions, schools, universities, even churches abandon it. But when we say that 'religion is disappearing' part of what is disappearing is both the occurrence of certain experiences, and also of our tendency to *notice* them and, instinctively or reflectively, to lend them moral or religious meaning. A lack of Eros.

# Imagination

Kant (in the *Critique of Pure Reason*) establishes imagination as a mediator between sense perception and concepts, something between sense and thought. Knowledge of the phenomenal world, empirical knowledge, is made possible by the imagination as a power of spontaneous synthesis operating at the transcendental barrier of consciousness. It serves the conceptual understanding by providing 'schemata' which enable the mind to grasp, or 'body forth', empirical objects. Kant here connects imagination essentially with the conception of an object. It spontaneously joins or fuses space and time (forms of intuition, perception) and the categories (conceptual forms of the greatest generality) so as to make an empty pattern or schematic form of 'an empirical object in general'. It also, at a less fundamental level, provides (in ways which may be available to conscious awareness) sensuously bodied schemata of classes of empirical objects. Imagination is a spontaneous intuitive capacity to put together what is presented to us so as to form a coherent spatio-temporal experience which is intellectually ordered and sensuously based. We may give ourselves rough examples of this essential activity by considering what happens when we try to interpret an imperfectly visible or totally unfamiliar object. If we can make no sense of it we may not be able to see it, as in the case of the natives and Captain Cook's ship. Kant then gives to imagination a large part in our original ability to grasp any object. It is designed to solve many problems for him. Exactly how this transcendental function of imagination makes the phenomenal world available has been much discussed and disputed, and Kant himself appears to give different accounts. Is it misleading simply to read the conscious activity back into the unconscious (transcendental) activity? Can we intelligibly speak of a primal conception of an object? Is the schema to be thought of as a sort of image or a sort of method of assembly? Is Kant's account 'psychological', or 'phenomenalist'?

Hume pictures imagination in terms of laws of association, but gives to it the transcendental function of providing those 'habits and customs without which human nature would perish and go to ruin'. Our objects, our causal links, our sense of space and time, all our apprehensions of an objective world, are based upon strong (very strong) imaginative associations, which by operating upon somehow-given discrete data save us from chaos. The idea of the proximity of chaos is profoundly present to both Hume and Kant. Hume's sensible unambitious moral philosophy and his liberal traditionalist political philosophy also depend upon the same idea of the important bonding role of habit, and the imagination as the spontaneous vital force which constructs and preserves it. Kant saw that this would not do. It was impossible, for instance, to see space and time as derived from (spatio-temporal) experience of sequence. Kant's metaphysical 'reply' to Hume opens an enormous and various vista with which we are still living. Hume's world is much the same throughout. Kant saw that space-and-time was a 'special case', to be seen as a 'form of intuition'; so was morality, to be seen as a unique operation of reason.

Imagination is said to be 'spontaneous', thus to be distinguished from other more 'automatic' mental functions. (Imagination is 'lively'.) Its unconscious or transcendental 'spontaneity' is perhaps to be conceived figuratively upon analogy. We can attempt to give sense to the idea, as we extend and modify the conception of a barrier or network (or set of 'schemata'), in terms of empirical concepts, and (now also) of language as a, to some extent consciously manipulable, experiential threshold. Imagination provides essential fusion, also gratuitous creation. At one end of the scale is the unconscious activity necessary to experience a world, at the other the free inventive power of exceptional minds. This may be seen as a scale of degrees of freedom, where, of course, not everything that is spontaneous is free. (Digestion is spontaneous.) The moral law is also described as spontaneous and free. The exercise of reason, ideally automatic, is seen and experienced 'here below' as a creative force of freedom acting against irrational barriers. There is, ideally, no limit to our ability to conform to rational laws. For Kant, morality is fundamentally based on reason, not upon imagination. We would ordinarily say that rational judgment must involve, for instance, an ability to imagine various situations. In a strict Kantian view of the concept this might be seen as a dangerous activity. Imagination must here (with Kant) be, to reverse Hume's picture, the 'slave' of reason. Imagination is a mixed matter, in its basic transcendental use it 'knows' both mind and senses. It is an intelligent sensibility, it can feel about in the dark and move both sides of barriers. One might almost say that 'imagination' is the *name* of the transcendental problem, or is used as a convenient blanket to cover it up. Kant *had* to invent the idea. At least, one might add, it stirs thought to advance in the right direction. In any case it is too double-sided a concept, too much like a kind of feeling, to be allowed (by Kant) near to the essence of morality. Equally, the mixed emotion of *respect* (*Achtung*) for the moral law, the joy at being free to be righteous mixed with the pain of frustrated desire, is not a cause or basis but a *symptom* of moral judgment, a result or accompaniment of it. The related feeling of the Kantian 'sublime', the defeat of imagination and reason, 'the feeling of our powerlessness to reach an Idea that is law for us', is not *in itself* either aesthetic or moral; but combined with a return to the independent strength of the free rational self, is an enlivening signal of our mixed nature. (Our moral powers are invigorated.) We may connect imagination with these 'border-line feelings', which can be recognised as present in our enjoyment of art. Beauty *symbolises* morality because the free imagination in its co-operation with the orderly rule-giving understanding, when in contemplation it creates and sustains beautiful objects, is *like* the free activity of the moral will in obedience to laws of reason, when we 'construct' a moral problem and its solution. Imagination is thus separated from morality, but is given a high function in art, especially where art reaches the level of genius: mind endeavours to extend the limits of thought by thinking both sides of the limit. The idea of such an exceptional and godlike power might be felt to be inappropriate in a strict account of morality. As moral agents we are not called upon to be original geniuses but to be good persons.

In the *Critique of Judgement* Kant, cautiously at first, exhibits the powers of the aesthetic imagination, which at its purest might be said to play a sort of spiritual role; and here one is certainly in 'danger' of giving imagination a prime moral function. The imagination is an exercise of freedom. We *look* at clouds and stoves, we *construct* pictures in our minds. In our experience of beauty in art or nature imagination is free to discern conceptless forms, it plays or frolics with the understanding without being governed by empirical concepts. It is out at the edge of things. The experience of beauty is often ineffable, the creation of art inexplicable. Kant would have little patience with a moral agent who could say nothing rational to justify his choice, but merely referred to a feeling. Morality had better not think it is out on the edge of things, it might become contaminated by aesthetic religiosity. Religion is not *about* a picturesque imagined 'beyond'. Kant aims to separate morality not only from art but from (traditional supernatural heteronomous) religion, and (in effect) reconstruct religion from the moral side. (Many thinkers want to do this now.) Morality concerns what an ordinary man may be expected to be able to do and what in Kant's extended metaphysical picture he *can* do. The imagination, in its free play, is a more independently speculative faculty, and may be so because what it does, in its discernment of the beautiful, in a sense does not matter. The good is compulsory, the beautiful is not. The beautiful is to be understood partly by contrast with the sublime, which is not an aesthetic experience but a quasi-moral one. Beauty suggests (some degree of) form, we speak of works of art and nature (trees, pictures) as beautiful. The sublime is an experience of formlessness and limitlessness, combined with a thought of, or desire for, limit (conceptualisation). Kant expresses the distinction by saying that beauty 'presents an indeterminate concept of the understanding, the sublime an indeterminate concept of reason'. (*Critique of Judgement*, Book II, Analytic of the Sublime, section 23.) We have an intellectual experience of sublimity (the mathematical sublime) when we consider mathematical or scientific concepts of a magnitude which exceeds the grasp of sense. (An emotion inspired by modern physics.) We have a more sensuous experience (the dynamical sublime) when we contemplate formless endless works of nature, waterfalls, mountains, starry heavens. In nature we find both sublimity and beauty. We are thrilled by its vastness and its sheer chaotic confusion (the sublime is partly a fear of contingency), we are also pleased by leaves and flowers. (Kant evidently liked flowers, especially tulips.) This pleasure resembles our pleasure in a work of art.

Sublimity is an experience, not a virtuous act, it is an encouraging sign pointing to the power of reason. It is a (high) spiritual experience, not a (lower) aesthetic experience, it is a (thrilling, frightening) apprehension of reason confronting contingency, devoid of the mediating, shaping, soothing power of the object-making imagination. It is a purer experience. (Compare, in Plato, the edifying effect of mathematical study, the demoralising effect of art.) 'The sublime' shows us human destiny as a dangerous solitary task, it is a proof that each man gives to himself as he summons up the rational force in his own bosom. The imagination works with the understanding to find or make forms. It is a play of the mind whereby forms may be discerned by an intuitive *sensus communis*. Kant expresses the peculiarity of aesthetic experience as a sense of 'purposiveness without a purpose' or 'finality without end'. There is definite form, suggestive of a forming will, but what is seen as beautiful is devoid of purpose and not classifiable under empirical concepts. It is a formal entity which is gratuitous, 'for nothing', and we delight in it as such. This strict and illuminating definition is of course not necessarily easy to apply to the vast area of our experiences of beauty, wherein all kinds of 'extraneous' knowledge seems to play an indissoluble part. To take an example, although botanical studies are distinct from aesthetic pleasures, it may be difficult to dissociate our delight in a tree from our perception of what kind of tree it is! In general 'something beautiful' is an experienced sensuous entity which is like an empirical object, but is not an empirical object, since it is not classified under general empirical concepts. It is in a characteristic way *sui generis*. Strictly, to class it as a beech tree is to leave the realm of the aesthetic. The general idea of an object offered by the understanding inspires the co-operation of the imagination in creating a sensuous something (some sensuous presence is essential) which is held together in the delighted mind.

We can recognise the idea of 'switching' from ordinary awareness to aesthetic contemplation. The synthetic power of imagination works here in a special way to produce the unique (purposeless, unclassifiable) beautiful object. God (nature) however creates trees and flowers, to which we respond in acts of (aesthetic) attention. We see nature as beautiful. Human beings create works of art, and questions of merit complicate the matter. 'Ordinary' imagination produces 'ordinary' art, 'superior' imagination produces 'superior' art, or 'fine art'. To this superior power, at its highest, Kant gives the name of genius. (*Critique of Judgement*, Book II, Analytic of the Sublime, section 46.) Genius, or high inspiration, is a spontaneous imaginative power which enables the artist to create new unique original forms. 'Fine art is the art of genius. Genius is the talent (natural endowment) which gives the rule to art.' Empirical knowledge and moral judgment depend upon *rules* given by the understanding and the reason respectively. The art object too must accord with rules, that is have form, but here, in the creation of good art, the rules are not general rules, but rules invented in and for the making of the individual object itself. The object asserts and establishes its own method of *verification*. We demand *truth* from art, and great works of art refine and extend our conception and grasp of truth. Genius *invents* its own 'rules' or modes, and good art as it moves towards this level may be partly judged in terms of this ability. Bad or mediocre art is clearly seen to be *obeying* 'general rules' or familiar formulae. (How to write a successful thriller, etc.) We may compare here the place given to genius in structuralist theory, where the original creative artist, philosopher, scientist, as inventor of language and meaning, is exempt from the general conventional preformed linguistic rules or codes whereby 'language speaks the man'. Structuralism, sometimes offered as 'scientific', is in its general tendency an aesthetic system of value. Kant's 'genius' is a spontaneous faculty which its owner cannot explain, and whose products offer no general rules for imitators. There is 'complete opposition between genius and the spirit of imitation'. The imagination produces something unique which has the form of 'an object in general', some sort of object. What sort? *This* sort. A work of art is essentially and definitely limited. (A view challenged in our later times.) In art the imagination operates freely according to its own laws to produce beauty, which in this way *symbolises* morality; that is the reason operating freely according to a general notion of law (rational harmony) to produce practical judgments in particular cases. The ability of the imagination to invent, out of the chaos of the ordinary world, the unique order of the art object, must be distinguished from the higher, and requisite, discernment of rational universal principles of action amid the contingent confusion of practical activity. Geniuses are not necessarily good. Beauty is only an *image* of morals, it is not about action in the world, and the imagination which cannot state its laws is a lower faculty, the partner of the understanding not of the reason.

Kant's exaltation of spontaneous creative imagination in fine art felicitously extends or amends his characterisation, earlier in the *Critique of Judgment*, of art generally in narrower formal terms as the production of conceptless objects, and the experience of beauty. The apprehension of beauty involves an individual imaginative synthesis,

[ 313 ]

as when we attend to the shape of a shell or leaf, or apprehend a wallpaper pattern. But the grander nature of fine art involves, for artist and client, a creative imagination of a higher order capable of inventing or appreciating far more complex, more intellectual, laws, categories and modes of vision, incarnate in and not removable from the objects themselves. Our aesthetic unbotanical pleasure in a leaf or modestly simple artwork is a unique occasion, our 'creation' of a unique entity. But the products of genius are more intensively thought, more substantial, their rules and formation more profound. Kant's distinction, as a guide to art criticism, is of course not easy to clarify. Some great art is extremely complicated, some exhibits a pregnant simplicity. Great art can be unsophisticated. It can also be highly traditional. (And so on.) Kant's reflections on genius respond to the need to see art as capable of engaging with an intellectual grasp of the world. The artist reforms pre-existing 'languages', often of great complexity, as when a painter deeply appreciates but radically alters the tradition to which he belongs. Art theory must 'account' for tragedy, for poetry. 'Poetry (which owes its origins almost entirely to genius and is least willing to be led by precepts or example) holds the first rank among the arts.' (Book II, Analytic of the Sublime, section 53.) The poet as prophet: a Romantic view, also one which does justice to the unique high nature of *poetry*, as opposed to verse. Poetry is difficult to write; great poetry is almost impossible to write. Kant tells us that 'the imagination (as a *productive* faculty of cognition) is a powerful agent for creating, as it were, *a second nature* out of the material supplied to it by actual nature . . . By this means we get a sense of our freedom from the law of association (which attaches to the empirical employment of the imagination).' (My italics.) So, imagination can create 'a second nature' (a new being). This idea can go very far, farther perhaps than its author intended. If we let art out of the small corner denoted by 'fine art' and 'genius', then we may want to maintain that the world around us is constantly being modified or 'presented' (made or made up) by a spontaneous creative *free* faculty which is not that of 'reason' thought of as 'beaming in' upon purely empirical situations not otherwise evaluated. Imagination, if the concept is in question at all, can scarcely be thought of as morally neutral. When we settle down to be 'thoroughly rational' about a situation, we have already, reflectively or unreflectively, imagined it in a certain way. Our deepest imaginings which structure the world in which 'moral judgments' occur are already evaluations. Perception itself is a mode of evaluation. Any account of morality must at least set up a problem here. Kant both celebrates the imagination and fears it. He fears the degeneration of moral judgment into aesthetic judgment, and if the matter is put in this way we can also sympathise with him. There is good and bad 'imagining'. In (Kant's) moral judgment the faculty is to have no role at all. Here again, we can picture a proper effort to *examine* an imaginative picture to the point of at least seeming to exclude 'imagination'. The concept itself is at stake. Kantian morality works with one sovereign concept, that of a harmonious *obedience* to universal rational law, a concept which is non-empirical, transcendental, spiritual, belonging to the 'other world' of reality and freedom. Exactly *how* rational insight works upon its phenomenal problematic data (the situations of beings who are phenomenal as well as noumenal) strictly speaking 'cannot be said', as reason must be supposed to be an ultimate faculty not explicable in other terms. Reason can presumably be 'expressed' in reasoning or reasonable talk which cannot be analysed in terms of any other concept. But the moral exercise of reason is practical and the act or choice is, as it were, silent, is morality itself, and its 'content' of reason (as distinct from selfish desire) cannot be assessed here below. The transcendental which 'cannot be said' in the *Tractatus* comes in a different style. Wittgenstein seems to regard 'talk about' moral decisions, whether 'rational', or 'philosophical' or 'ordinary', as in itself suspect and likely to be other than it seems. Beyond the perhaps allowable simplicity of 'Why did you do it?' 'Because I promised' lie all sorts of messy and unclarified prevarications. Moral activity 'shows itself' and is essentially solitary and silent. In both cases (Kant and Wittgenstein) the metaphysical picture is illuminating but likely to be felt as intolerable. We have to 'talk' and our talk will be largely 'imaginative' (we are all artists). *How* we see our situation is itself, already, a moral activity, and one which is, for better as well as worse, 'made' by linguistic process. A denial here of the exclusive role of reason need not of course lead toward moral relativism. The point is, to put it picturesquely, that the 'transcendental barrier' is a huge wide various band (it resembles a transformer such as the lungs in being rather like a sponge) largely penetrable by the creative activity of individuals (though of course we are culturally marked 'children of our time' etc.), and this creativity is the place where the concept of imagination must be placed and defined. Kant himself does not (in the *Grundlegung*) resist the temptation to talk about, explain and clarify, the activity of reason, in terms of the examples of 'obviously valid' general universal maxims which I mentioned above. Do not lie or kill yourself; develop your talents and be kind: and do so in all circumstances. Why? So as to improve society and thus serve the human race? If imposed in terms of a teleological development this advice must seem heteronomous and arbitrary. The concept of reason is flexible and 'deep' enough to be taken seriously in its own right as 'the basis' of morality. A hypothesis about the development of human society, or the function of reason in human life, cannot be so taken. Of course the idea (of teleology) expressed by Kant in the *Grundlegung*, and discussed by him elsewhere in his work, is visible, serviced and metamorphosed, in utilitarianism and in Marxism. Here, however, the deep and flexible, necessary and plausible, concept is in *both* these cases (as I shall argue later) happiness. Most acceptable, that is as such effective; Marxist moral philosophy was utilitarian, helped out at levels remote from power by an ideal of selflessness. ('The Party serves the people.') How flexible can a deep concept be? is a founding question of philosophy. Kant, in his precision, is careful not to demand too much of the concept of imagination. He distinguishes the empirical imagination, which spontaneously yet 'mechanically' prepares a sensuous manifold for subjection to the synthetic *a priori* and empirical concepts of the understanding, but which is not independently creative or aesthetically sensible, from the aesthetic imagination which is spontaneous and free and able to create a 'second nature'. But are 'fine art' and 'genius' as described by Kant really such a small corner of human faculty and experience? The concept of genius itself emerges from an appreciation of the deep and omnipresent operation of imagination in human life.

The modern self-conscious concept of 'imagination' as something generally rather exalted is Romantic. Shakespeare uses the word to mean the production of imagined appearances, mental images or fictions, he also connects the faculty with poets and madmen. (*A Midsummer Night's Dream*, V, i, 8; 2 *Henry IV*, I, iii, 31.) What Hamlet 'abhors in imagination' is picturing the skull he holds in his hand as that of the incarnate Yorick. Imagination is often dark but capable of being sweetened. (*Lear*, IV, vi, 131.) For 'the shaping spirit of imagination' (Coleridge's *Ode to Dejection*) we in England have to wait for what

Coleridge learnt from Kant's German successors. Into this morass or dark forest I do not propose to enter but will follow Virgil's advice to Dante, *non ragioniam di lor, ma guarda e passa*. (Don't let's talk about them, just look and pass by.) The modern sense is not carried by Greek *phantasia*. Plato refers more than once to the unconscious non-rational creativity of poets who do not know how they do it and cannot explain what they have done. That great artist had mixed feelings about such dangerous gifts. He was well aware of the lying fantasising tendency of the human mind and that it would be hard to exaggerate our capacity for egoistic fabrication. The mind is indeed besieged or crowded by selfish dream life. Plato uses the word *eikasia*, best translated here as 'illusion' or 'fantasy', to indicate the most benighted human state, the lowest condition in the Cave. He also uses the word *phantasia* in this sense. He connects egoistic fantasy and lack of moral sense with inability to reflect. Mere uninspired reproductive art (one might say, *mimesis* without *anamnesis*) would then be at the bottom of the scale: the case of the painter in Book X of the *Republic* who is inferior to the carpenter who at least possesses the rudiments of mathematics. One might take the *Republic* (597) passage about the painter as indicating art which was bad because thoughtless. Plato's attitude to art also includes his suspicion of sophisticated literature (the tragic poets), and music which arises from or excites irrational and unworthy passions. Of course Plato did not fail to appreciate the creative power of Homer, and the tragedians and other poets, whose work he admired and (I suspect) envied. He was concerned about the results of (some) art; and is using the artist as an exemplar or metaphor. The poet as seer or madman is a dangerous figure. (Consider here Heidegger's conjuration of the 'prophetic' poet, and his ideal of a 'poeticised' philosophy.)

The *Sophist* is fundamentally concerned with how falsehood is possible, how false propositions have sense. Plato solves this problem by explaining how being and non-being do not exclude each other, but are, through language, made into a single interwoven fabric (*symploke*). The *Tractatus* concept of 'logical space' offers a similar answer. Structuralists too pay homage to that dialogue. The definition of 'the sophist' as a sophisticated liar involves an elaborate discussion of different levels of 'fantasising'. Moral improvement, as we learn from the *Republic*, involves a progressive destruction of false images. Image-making or image-apprehending is always an imperfect activity, some images are higher than others, that is nearer to reality. Images should not be resting places, but pointers toward higher truth. The implication is that the highest activities of the mind, as in mathematics and mysticism, are imageless. The geometer is not talking about circles drawn in the sand nor about mental images. Plato places mathematical objects high in the scale of knowledge, though not at the summit. The Greeks were impressed and inspired by their own rapid progress in mathematics, especially geometry, and likely to see this as an exemplar of understanding. Certainly theological mythology, stories about gods, creation myths and so on, belong to the realm of image-making and are at a lower level than reality and ultimate religious truth, a view continuously held in the east, and also in western mysticism: beyond the last image we fall into the abyss of God. Plato's own use of myth draws specific attention to the purely ancillary role of such pictures. Plato's moral philosophy is *about* demythologisation. Plato in his mature years, and the author of the *Seventh Letter*, might agree that the mythical and metaphorical imagery of the central dialogues could be regarded, by those able to understand them, as ladders to be thrown away after use. In the multiform work itself Plato constantly mixes ethics, religion and theory of knowledge in a way which makes any summarised 'real belief' or 'central doctrine' too abstract. There is, besides, the question of the return to the Cave, the assertion of a reality at all levels which must belong to a political and social concern. Selfless persons return to the darkness, and seek to rescue the deprived or illiterate Cave dwellers. (Ideal of a good society.) In the *Laws*, where the earlier spiritual aspiration seems absent, political counsel is gloomy and repressive and (903D) God is playing draughts, this social concern remains, expressing itself in an amazing interest in the proper ordering of the details of ordinary life. (Tidy hair and shoes.) We cannot know what Plato, who freely uses his own versions of Orphic myths, 'really thought' about spiritually highest states of consciousness. It is very difficult to understand 'what goes on' in the souls of dedicated religious people, even when we know them face to face and they are trying to tell us. It is also difficult to *imagine* ways of life which are much above our own moral level as being morally demanded. They exert no magnetism and cannot be seen except in terms of senseless deprivation. There is much that cannot be expressed but can only be experienced or known after much training, as the *Seventh Letter* says of philosophy. In the spiritual hierarchy of the *Republic*, *dianoia*, discursive understanding as selfless wisdom, is the highest image-using condition. *Noesis* is an indescribable mystical state, thinkable perhaps as contemplation of the Form of the Good, a passionate stilled attention, wherein the self is no more. (This does not imply leaving the world.)

In many of the dialogues (especially *Symposium, Phaedrus*) Plato speaks with intense emotion about a vision of perfection which might be granted to the soul. Christian theology would speak of the beatific vision. About this Dante tells us that the beholder has neither the knowledge nor the power to speak, since the intellect, nearing its desired object, *deepens* so that memory cannot retrace its steps.

> *perché appressando sè al suo disire,*
> *nostro intelletto si profunda tanto,*
> *che dietro la memoria non può ire.*
> (*Paradiso* I 7–9.)

In his *Letter to Can Grande* Dante mentions St Paul, 2 Corinthians 12. 2–4, concerning someone (Paul himself?) who was 'caught up into Paradise, and heard unspeakable words, which it is not lawful for a man to utter'. Dante emphasises that 'Dante' *nescit et nequit*, does not know what he saw and cannot tell it because, even if he could remember it, language fails. Here the religious image also conjures up the highest inspiration of the artist who on the border-line of what can be expressed, with trembling excitement and quickening pace, reaches his goal by a path which he cannot later remember or explain. Dante speaks of Plato's use of metaphor to express what could not be said otherwise. 'For we see many things by the intellect for which there are no vocal signs, of which Plato gives sufficient hint in his books by having recourse to metaphors; for he saw many things by intellectual light which he could not express in direct speech.' The last lines of the *Paradiso* express both the joy and the helplessness of this condition in which ultimately the soul surrenders its desire and its will to the harmonious movement of love. This is the apotheosis of the imagination where words and images fail and the concept, which implies some kind of striving or separation, comes to an end. High imagination is passionately creative. A presocratic thinker (Pherekydes) said that Zeus became Eros in order to create the world. Dante's vision of God as love is of a perfect harmony to which the soul gives itself as to an unmoved mover. In Plato the unmoved Forms inspire the creative love of spirit which is active at a lower level. In the *Sophist* (265C) Plato posits a (mythical) God whose creative intelligence (*phuousé dianoia*) creates the world, preferring this explanatory (teleological) myth to the notion of production by nature. Compare the image of virtue as God-given, rather than taught or natural, in the *Meno*. Here too the realm of nature pictures the realm of morality. Plato's mythical God is a restless imaginative creative artist, Eros, seen in the *Timaeus* as the Demiurge, the spirit who, looking with love toward a higher reality, creates an imperfect world as his best image of a perfection which he sees but cannot express. Virtue is dynamic and creative, a passionate attention directed toward what is good. Perhaps most graphically Plato celebrates imagination as *anamnesis* in the *Meno*, a power working at a barrier of darkness, recovering verities which we somehow know of, but have in our egoistic fantasy life 'forgotten'. So it appears that Plato, like Kant, offers two views of the imagination. For Plato the lower level, which for Kant is necessary automatic synthesis, is seen in human terms as the production of base illusions, or perhaps simply of the ordinary unimaginative egoistic screen of our conceptualising. Plato, teaching by images and myths, also acknowledges high imagination as creative stirring spirit, attempting to express and embody what is perfectly good, but extremely remote, a picture which implicitly allows a redemption of art. The spiritual life is a long disciplined destruction of false images and false goods until (in some sense which we cannot understand) the imagining mind achieves an end of images and shadows (*ex umbris et imaginibus in veritatem*), the final *demythologisation* of the religious passion as expressed by mystics such as Eckhart and St John of the Cross. Kant's more 'democratic' and less ecstatic morality envisages a more modest continually renewed daily achievement under the concepts of reason and duty. Creative imagination may be thought of as an aspect of the Sublime, as well as of the Beautiful (which is after all an image of the Good), and, out at the fringes of human capacity, genius exerts a force which may well be both inspiring and edifying.

These philosophical distinctions can be roughly but readily seen in terms of different states of consciousness, resembling Plato's hierarchy of levels of knowledge with differing objects. We can make sense of a scale or series with egoistic fantasies at one end and creative imagination, culminating in genius at the other. Plato would of course put mystical selflessness (*noesis*) above artistic genius. We distinguish the genius from the saint. Herein imagination too is to be thought of as sanctified. We can recognise 'automatic' uses of imagination, and the points at which (good, serious, strong) imagination fails, as in the layman 'imagining' physics, or in certain moral and religious situations. We can thus 'picture' Plato's distinction between *dianoia* and *noesis* without claiming to 'think both sides of the barrier'. To mark the distances involved we need, for purposes of discussion, two words for two concepts: a distinction between egoistic *fantasy* and liberated truth-seeking creative *imagination*. Can there not be high evil fantasising forms of creative imaginative activity? A search for candidates will, I think, tend to reinforce at least the usefulness of a distinction between 'fantasy' as mechanical, egoistic, untruthful, and 'imagination' as truthful and free. The role of 'personal fantasy' in 'high art' (for instance) is a subject which merits consideration. This 'fantasy' and 'imagination' is not the same as Coleridge's pair 'fancy' and 'imagination'. Coleridge is contrasting fancy as a shifting-about of given pieces, with imagination as creative fusion. 'Fancy has no other counters to play but fixities and definities . . . Fancy must receive all its materials ready made . . .' (*Biographia Literaria*, chapter XIII.) Fancy: as when a story-teller creates a character by roughly tying together, in an unfused collection, separate characteristics from different people he knows. Whereas I want to see the contrast more positively in terms of two active faculties, one somewhat mechanically generating narrowly banal false pictures (the ego as all-powerful), and the other freely and creatively exploring the world, moving toward the expression and elucidation (and in art celebration) of what is true and deep. 'Deep' here invokes the sense in which any serious pursuit and expression of truth moves toward fundamental questions, as when a political problem refers us to a view of human nature. 'Truth' is something we recognise in good art when we are led to a juster, clearer, more detailed, more refined understanding. Good art 'explains' truth itself, by *manifesting* deep conceptual connections. Truth is clarification, justice, compassion. This manifestation of internal relations is an image of metaphysics. Art at play can be a metaphysician too, expressing spontaneous delight at the connectedness of things, or else at their absurd unconnectedness. Jokes have their contexts, even when their point is to have no point. The work of imagination in art may be seen as a symbol of its operation elsewhere; this might also be expressed by saying that there is artistry in the sorting, separating and connecting movement of the mind in other areas, in science and scholarship, and in morals and politics where an ordering activity is fused with an ability to picture what is quite other; especially of course to picture and realise, make real to oneself, the existence and being of other people. Imagination in politics: to imagine the consequences of policies, to picture what it is like for people to be in certain situations (unemployed, persecuted, very poor), to relate axiomatic moral ideas (for instance about rights) to pragmatic and utilitarian considerations.

The concept of imagination is, on reflection, an essential one, not least perhaps because it can strengthen or clarify the sense in which 'we are all artists'. It is on the other hand so ubiquitous that it is in danger of seeming empty. Perhaps, having seen its point or points, we should dismantle it into parts? I think we need the familiar word to designate something (good by definition) to which the contrast with fantasy (bad by definition) gives substance. The human mind is naturally and largely given to fantasy. Vanity (a prime human motive) is composed of fantasy. Neurotic or vengeful fantasies, erotic fantasies, delusions of grandeur, dreams of power, can imprison the mind, impeding new understanding, new interests and affections, possibilities of fruitful and virtuous action. If we consider the narrow dreariness of this fantasy life to which we are so addicted the term 'unimaginative' seems appropriate. (Contrast, as St Augustine observed, the amazing inventiveness of some sleeping dreams.) 'Stop having those fantasies about getting your own back.' And grief has its fantasies too. 'Stop picturing that awful scene again and again.' What may seem to happen as a healing process, mysteriously in extreme situations, may be seen more clearly in ordinary situations where imagination appears as a restoration of freedom, cognition, the effortful ability to see what lies before one more clearly, more justly, to consider new possibilities, and to respond to good attachments and desires which have been in eclipse. This effort may be compared with that of 'composing' and 'holding' a difficult work of art in one's attention, an effort which is similar in the good artist and in the good client. (Teaching art is teaching morals.) 'Be more sympathetic, imagine her situation, see it from her point of view.' Fairly everyday advice. Imagination is here a moral discipline of the mind, which would, for instance, help people not to become embittered or brutalised or stupefied by affliction. Why not call it courage? (One seeks clarification by moving concepts around.) Of course it is courage too. Courage is imaginative, imagination brave. But the concept of imagination is another side of the figure. Courage suggests sturdiness and will, the ability to act. Imagination suggests the searching, joining, light-seeking, semi-figurative nature of the mind's work, which prepares and forms the consciousness for action. In a context of reflection, one elaborates a distinction and defines a concept, so as to see further. In a way this is a speculative ladder to be thrown away, in a way there are also instinctive movements which take place in ordinary language. (A good language provides instruments of reflection for all.) As philosophers and as moral agents we decide what concepts we need, we reach out for these tools. (Wittgenstein used to say to his class, 'You're the boss.' Humpty Dumpty also took a tough line with words.) What do you do with your mind when you are in prison? Or bereaved or suffering irremediable injustice, or crippled by awful guilt? What you are able to do with it then will depend very much on what you were doing with it before. The mysterious imaginative power of the artist, creation *ex nihilo*, the attentive waiting for the response of the unconscious power, is not remote from moral imagination, it is like, or is, prayer. Here we can *experience* the force and movement of imagination in conscious waiting and periods of attention.

We are fantasising imaginative animals. The larger moral concepts are 'porous' in character. Of course language works through networks of combined exclusion and mutual relation; concepts are not solitary individuals, words are not proper names. This is the general point much emphasised since Saussure and Wittgenstein. It is the context of the 'porous' image. If we study one moral concept we soon see it as an aspect of another. It is true on the one hand that as moral agents we tend to specialise. The high-principled statesman may be a negligent father (and so on). It may seem as if we have a limited amount of good motivation available and cannot be expected to be decent 'all round'. There are familiar ways of characterising people in terms of individual characteristics. Yet also a closer look may show this as superficial, and we then wish to say that the impulse toward goodness should stir the whole person. This demand does not isolate goodness in the way in which 'good' is isolated in an existentialist scheme, where it is merely an empty box into which chosen items are put. The existentialist choosing will is separated from other moral terms in a way which renders *them* otiose. If 'free choice' alone confers value, then all that is needed is a pointing finger; no place for cognitive struggle involving specialised informative moral concepts. ('I wouldn't call that bravery, it's just an egoistic gamble.') Value is neither contextless choice nor is it at the other extreme identical with some sort of filled out coming-into-existence. It is neither void nor plenum. The sun is separate from the world, but enlivens all of it. Courage is composed of imagination. Truthful imagining requires courage and humility. Truthfulness is aware of the obligation not to cause distress. In this way of seeing, there are not just external clashes between alien principles (an idea which is at home in politics). It is a matter of deepening the concepts in question through a relation to each other. There is a continuous and spontaneous interplay. 'Becoming better' is a process involving an exercise and refinement of moral vocabulary and sensibility. Yet we must also in discussing virtue, as distinct from practising it, beware of seeming to suggest that the articulate educated man is better than the inarticulate uneducated man because he can think rationally and formulate and verbalise his distinctions. Such a suggestion might lead people to accuse Plato of confounding virtue with intellectual learning, and Kant of identifying it with cold rationality. Morality (as both these philosophers were well aware in their different ways) is right up against the world, to do with all apprehensions of others, all lonely reveries, all uses of time. Virtue shows in actions, goodness can be simple. Here the idea of imaginative grasp of one's surroundings may be preferred to that of a rational survey or an ability to learn, or we may like to insist that good reasoning and learning is imaginative. The virtuous peasant can imagine the results of what he does and knows in his experience what truthfulness is. There is no need here to go to the other extreme of exalting intuition or instinct or speechless goodness (as for instance in Tolstoy's peasant Platon Karataev in *War and Peace*) in preference to a more talkative morality. The human situation is much more mixed-up than theorising about it can suggest; Kant is right to say that every man understands good and evil, and Plato that learning is a spiritual exercise.

The traditional, still influential, dualism of fact and value, intellect and will, can profitably be looked at again in the context of the present discussion. Some of Kant's later followers, in emphasising the 'purity' of the moral will, in separating it from a factual determination (argument from fact to value), have in effect turned the Kantian universal rational will into an individual non-rational will. The end-point, not far from the stark existentialist view of the matter, would be: no need for thought, imagination, words, just point or jump. This would omit the continuous detailed conceptual pictorial activity whereby (for better or worse) we make and remake the 'world' *within which* our desires and reflections move, and out of which our actions arise. A consideration of the place of imagination in morality also makes clear the need for a reflective 'placing' of consciousness. Imagination is an (inner) activity of the senses, a picturing and a grasping, a stirring of desire. At a more explicitly reflective level, in everyday moral discussion as well as in metaphysics, we deploy a complex densely textured network of values round an intuited centre of 'good'. We imagine hierarchies and concentric circles, we are forced by experience to make distinctions, to elaborate moral 'pictures' and a *moral vocabulary*. We work with value *concepts*, value *words*. Moral acts do not usually, and cannot essentially, rest on isolated pure arbitrarily 'willed' decisions. We can change what we are, but not quickly or easily, there is such depth and density in what needs to be changed. A part of such change is an ability to understand (in practice) what virtues consist of and how they relate. A child is told to tell the truth. *Truth* is important. In growing up he elaborates his own conception of what *truthfulness* involves. (This is one of the most important and central parts of any moral evolution.) Here again the spectator (theorist) is inclined to say that the egoist has a narrow moral world, the better man a larger and more complex one; yet must also add that there is a sense in which the good man's world is again simple: simple in the sense that he may see what is right without prolonged doubt and reflection, large because, being less egoistic, he can see more of life. (He returns to seeing, now *really* seeing, rivers and mountains as rivers and mountains. He has fewer temptations.) Truth is very close to good, closer than, for instance, generosity. 'Generosity' may be a form of egoism, which needs to be purified by a patient use of intelligence and a sense of justice. Humility requires realism and humour. Often we must forget our dignity but not always. Integrity is an ambiguous concept, so is sincerity. What is so called can be a form of pride or self-assertion. 'A sense of humour', often treated as an identifiable faculty all on its own, needs to be looked at critically, even with suspicion. There is a perfectly familiar distinction between amiable joking and malicious or corrupt mockery. We must shun spiteful wit, yet not forget the social uses of satire.

*

So we may talk and think, constantly examining and altering our sense of the order and interdependence of our values. The study of this interweaving *is* moral reflection, and at a theoretical level makes intelligible places for defining and understanding central concepts which may have become isolated and attenuated in our argumentative and emotional usage of them: happiness, freedom, love. Freedom is not an isolated ability, like the ability to swim, which we can 'exercise' in a pure form. The idea of 'the freedom of the will' can only be understood in the context of the complexity and ubiquity of value, it is inseparable from modes of cognition. Freedom is a matter of degree and a mode of being. If we isolate the idea of a free will it becomes incomprehensible and conjures up as its companion the ghostly empty *philosophical* concept of determinism. The liberal political (external, negative) sense of freedom as 'doing what one wants' must be distinguished from the positive moral meaning of the term. I will shortly be discussing this important difference, and the Hobbesian sense in which 'morals' may be said to differ from 'politics'. The idea of moral freedom may in part be clarified by this contrast; it may also be defined in terms of the triumph of imagination over fantasy. 'Happiness' also, so often spoken of as an intelligible end, becomes multiform under the pressure of surrounding values. A Benthamite conception of it as uniform stuff may be in order in some situations as a political fiction. Mill's relation to Bentham exhibits some of the difficulties of attempting to treat it for general moral purposes as a fundamental concept. 'Love', often taken for granted to be fundamental, is even more (another Platonic image) 'densely textured'. Sex-love can be entirely egoistic. But purified love is surely not sexless, or should we say not necessarily sexless? Which way shall we press the concept on this border-line? A paradox about religion: religion concerns the acceptance of death, which drives away the idea and force of sex. Yet religion is also the passionate love of good, which is the sublimation of sex (as seen in the *Symposium*). Nietzsche tells us that 'the degree and kind of a man's sexuality extends to the highest pinnacle of his spirit'. The concept of sex alters (or need it be thought to depart?) when subjected to the sort of pressure involved in being interpreted together with other moral concepts at a high level. (Metaphors.) Religious chastity, love of God. Here again we may be enlightened by considering the case of the artist who in creation endeavours to *purify* his passion; and also by remembering the sense in which we are all artists. (The ego is passionate; yet without passion no high work.) Such persuasive shifting about among concepts, such metaphorical picturing of their mutual influence and function, is characteristic of metaphysics, and also of ordinary moral and aesthetic thinking. There are huge ambiguous inspiring or frightening moral concepts without which we could not live; there are also secondary, tertiary terms, narrower, more specialised, easier to define, which may do essential work for us. We develop an evaluative (moral) vocabulary which is in constant use. Disorder (for better or worse, at least it promotes reflection) results when we seize upon a minor concept and promote it to do major work. A demythologising theologian, wishing to avoid the difficulties of a more traditional terminology, suggests the word 'disinterested' to indicate our highest moral condition. Such a move, intended perhaps to 'cool' the argument, may involve too great a loss of 'being'. Words vanish or alter their meanings 'naturally' in the course of language-use and social change, but thinkers too can tinker with the process. Theology needs speculative imagination. A most important case: the word 'God' is less often used. Should its traditional meaning be left alone unquestioned? Should we let it dwindle and go, together with the *person* whom it used to designate? Or should we, while allowing its sense to change (that is, no longer designate a person) try to preserve and renew its ancient power? However that may be, we need to surround our 'great words' (concepts) with narrower more specialised ones with smaller clearer meanings. We must protect the precision of these secondary moral words, exercise them and keep them fit. The artistry of good prose writing, moral reflections in fiction and non-fiction, can serve this purpose. Living is making distinctions and indicating order and pattern.

Hume and Kant saw imagination as a necessary faculty mediating between 'sense' and 'thought'. Both philosophers were concerned not only with what we can know, but also with the actual operation and construction of our 'consciousness'. When we think about 'the world' or about 'our own soul' or 'good and evil', we picture an order with shifting degrees of mediation. (Metaphors.) Coleridge spoke of the importance of thinking in images. Modern philosophers and theologians criticise what they regard as misleading imagery (inner–outer, above–below). We live by developing imagery and also by discarding it. The 'modern crisis' can be seen as a crisis about imagery (myth, metaphysics). Reflections upon the sensuous-intellectual nature of our mental being refer us to our 'consciousness'. What are we to do with this concept, also in crisis? (Wittgenstein evades it, Derrida rejects it.) A conception of imagination demands a conception of consciousness; at any rate if we need to speak of imagination we need also to speak of consciousness. Our inward being *happens* moment-to-moment. Thinking and feeling imagery is not like an internal cinema show. Yet it is not unlike it either. Nor does the fact that we use metaphors in talking or writing imply that these, or any, metaphorical pictures are privately present. To say I think (doubt, imagine, etc.) need not imply a present mental content. Yet it is not true that there is no significant inward pictorial mental activity, or that we must philosophically obliterate 'consciousness'. The concept is unique, essential, and difficult to talk about, yet what is closer and (in a sense) what else is there? Hegelian idealism 'ruins' consciousness as it 'ruins' imagination by making it swallow and be everything. We must attach consciousness to the individual thinker, it is part of his definition and his particular mode of being. Ordinary language admits 'states of consciousness', literature and literary criticism allow 'streams of consciousness'. These are not isolated tropes, but references to something which we can all recognise. It must be mentioned here as a problematic concept and exhibited in use, as when one might say that non-verbal consciousness is the ground of metaphor, or that our deepest not yet explicit thinking is alive with movement already grasped in a pictorial manner. The poet seeking an image, anyone anxiously composing an adequate description, 'gropes in the dark'. Behind the idea of a mediation between sense and thought lies the deep not yet formed thought-sense activity of the mind, which we must attempt to speak of and not simply surrender to empirical science. Discussion of the place of imagination and metaphor in our lives is not just about figurative writing or clarified metaphorical speech or explicit virtually verbal thought, but (also) about what our private unclarified but often very strong and present thinking and experiencing is like. At deep levels metaphor and perception merge. Perception is a mode of evaluation.

Images of light and space and movement are fundamental to our modes of cognition. When St Paul tells us to think about whatsoever things are honest, just, pure, lovely and of good report, he believes rightly that we know how to perform this feat of imagination. How do we know how to do it? Oddly enough we do. (We can distinguish too between doing it in a vague feeble way and attempting to do it better.) Observe the assemblage of related moral Forms. Moral imagination is partly aesthetic, it is a place where the aesthetic is moralised. If we have been touched by religion our minds are likely to be full of readily available religious imagery which there is no need to expel simply because (as it may be) we do not believe in God. Some kinds of puritanism and some kinds of Kantian philosophy point in the direction of an imageless morality. Strip the church and strip your mind as well. Islam forbids some images, Judaism is wary of all images. Of course the danger of idolatry, of taking the shadows for real (and the mythology too literally) is always present. We live by moving beyond our images and can recognise the effort of deliberately moving out into a 'blank' or 'void'. This could be a kind of prayer, or part of an artist's discipline. But we live normally and naturally by metaphors and pictures, some of which are in fairly clear and acceptable ways translatable into less figurative modes, while others seem 'deep' and resist analysis. We may have to use very general and ambiguous terms or other images in answer to the question, 'How do you mean?' 'How do you mean you see the light, what light, what exactly does it show, and what was visible before?' Such are deep ways in which we think about and judge ourselves and explain ourselves to others and try to understand them. Herein too we can understand Plato's picture of the progressive destruction of images. There is a continuous breeding of imagery in the consciousness which is, for better or worse, a function of moral change. This slow constant genesis reflects and affects the quality of our attachments and desires. With St Paul's admonition in mind, I think that what we literally see is important. Perception is both evaluation and inspiration, even at the level of 'just seeing'. Sometimes what we see is 'highly significant', but just looking out of the window is important too. We should also feel socially responsible about what in our society people always or never see. Vision is the dominant sense. Urban poverty can impose relentlessly ugly surroundings. (No trees.) Also of course, and ideally, we should all have the aesthetic training needed to find beauty and interest in apparently charmless and commonplace scenes. Every child should be taught not only how to paint but how to *look* at paintings. The discipline of art, whether in creator or client, stirs and instructs the senses. Here we should also reflect upon the deep effects of television, for instance upon the fact that so many citizens go to bed at night with their heads full of overwhelmingly clear and powerful images of horror and violence. Television can show us beautiful and fascinating things, distant landscapes and works of art, detailed pictures of animals and revealing close-ups of human faces, but it can also commit terrible crimes against the visible world. I am inclined to think that it blunts our general sense of colour and light and reduces rather than enhances our ability to see the detail of our surroundings. It is an instance, and indeed an image or parable, of how the packaged services of increasingly perfected technology reduce our ability to think and imagine for ourselves.

This 'breeding of imagery' is a familiar aspect of our moment-to-moment, minute-to-minute, hour-to-hour 'consciousness', and contributes to giving body to the concept. Our busy minds are (for better or worse) not often empty or idle. Such activity constitutes, in my picture of the matter, a large part of our fundamental moral disposition, it is a function of what we really value, what we love and are magnetised by, and of what we are capable of noticing. I do not want to use the word 'will' (moral will) to describe this deep level, because of its Kantian and existentialist connotations. The distinction between intellect and will is, as I have suggested, misleading. I would (as I said earlier) see 'will', or to be clearer 'effort of will', in a narrower use, as when an act, good or bad, is consciously forced into being against the general tenor of the personality. Obedience to duty may involve force of will. It is also possible for a bad act to be felt as overwhelmingly necessary, even 'as a sort of duty', against the good forces, including the habitual strong desires, of a personality alien to it (as perhaps in the case of Macbeth). When should one speak in terms of a sudden quantity into quality change after a long unseen build-up of a new attitude? Novelists, who 'know' their characters, can confidently describe these deep things, in real life it is more difficult. 'Acts of will', thought of as acts of violence against structures of preformed character, can release fresh good or bad energy. However, moral change for the better happens, if at all, slowly, as new modes of outlook (metaphor) and new desires come into being. Sudden conversions and dramatic new starts can be significant if a new external regime can be established, which then gradually assists the inward change, which cannot happen all at once, upon its way. A new outward landscape assists the imaginative creation of a new inward one. Old associations must be broken in the mind, new ones made. One escapes (often) from really seductive temptation, not by a sudden violent inward 'act of will' which redirects the character, but by an external change such as literally running away, making something impossible, winning time to develop other attachments, to imagine how things might be different. The outward not the inward move may often (as I said earlier) initiate the change; one stops going to a certain place or seeing a certain person. Falling out of love (with a person, possession or activity) is a skill we should all have access to. The background to all such change is our general (moral, spiritual) tendency to descend rather than to rise, which Simone Weil called gravity. Better conduct is often harder and less natural than mediocre or bad conduct. It is not easy to sacrifice strong egoistic attachments or break bad habits. We 'satisfy our conscience' by doing half the task; surely more cannot be required of us. We can always say: well, other people do this. These are among the best-known facts concerning the human condition.

A habit of decent conduct may come by temperament or conditioning or may be consciously achieved. To establish or maintain such habits may be difficult, the requirement to rise above them shocking. One may put it thus, that we cannot see the point of being moral beyond a certain level, we cannot *imagine* it except in terms of pure damaging disadvantage. Kant thought we were all framed by nature to respect what was rational, and that such respect was accompanied by a kind of proud pleasure (in the capacity for free rational thought) as well as by distress at the frustration of desire. He denied that this pleasure could be a moral *motive*, the moral act being essentially a motiveless assent to reason. Desires, carriers of imagination and fantasy, including 'pathological' (as opposed to practical) love, belong to the phenomenal self. If at this point we (I) part company with Kant, it is in the interests of a more realistic and flexible account of moral progress, as a purification and reorientation of desire. That spontaneity of imagination which Kant allows in empirical knowledge (in the 'creation' of an object), and also in artistic genius and sublime experience, has its place in morals too. The good (better) man is *liberated* from selfish fantasy, can see himself as others see him, imagine the needs of other people, love unselfishly, lucidly envisage and desire what is truly valuable. This is the ideal picture. Effective moral motivation, such as may produce 'excellent results' (promotion of justice, good happiness for others, etc.) may be, and admittedly, very mixed, may include magical Gnostic thrills, a wish to please a virtuous mentor, desire to appear good not easily distinguishable from desire to be good. It is at least something if we notice and want to be commended by virtuous people, or have an intuitive sense of what we would be like if we were better! Schopenhauer, who thought moral change was almost impossible, said that virtue usually consisted of pride, timidity, desire for advancement, fear of censure and fear of the gods. Yet, so mixed up are we, pride, fear of disgrace, and intelligent (one might even say well-intentioned) hypocrisy, can lead to genuine change. We flee from one place to another hoping for better 'moral luck'. Hamlet advised his mother to assume a virtue even if she had it not, abstention from sin would then be easier. It is usually, for better or worse, easier to do something a second time. Literature tends to be more interested in dramatic moral change than in good habits, we tend to think more about the former than the latter because it is pleasant to fantasise a rapid easy escape and a miraculous removal of the burden of thickened egoism. Plato pointed out that writers find bad unstable men more interesting than steady good men. The romantic sinner, supposed to be 'really' more saintly than dull well-behaved folk, is a familiar contemporary hero. Pictures of swift (even instant) salvation may also of course be offered in religious contexts to save, or with the effect of saving, sinners from despair and to inspire them to persevere in virtue. Here the idea of forgiveness and reconciliation (with or without God) may properly be detached from the magical prospect of fast moral change. The Prodigal Son is more attractive than his brother, but the latter, who in his dull way never abandoned his decent habits, might also be taken as a model. The retention of innocence is an important and underrated idea in morals. One would also like to know whether, on the whole, Mary or Martha led a better life. Religious mythology which dramatises the spiritual life for purposes of edification can bring sudden insight but may also be looked at with a calm eye. Persisting historical and personal differences in attitude and *style* are involved here: such as, in Christianity, can be seen in the contrast of St Paul with the Gospel writers, and of the first three Gospels with the fourth. Plato's Eros can be seen as a figure of divine grace. Surely there is such a power. Yet is not Eros also a trickster, as Plato suggests in the *Symposium*? Any artist, or thinker, knows of what may be called 'help from the unconscious mind', sometimes called inspiration. One lives for a time with dull intractable material which is suddenly irradiated and transformed by a new vision. Rat-like fantasies or old stale thoughts are metamorphosed or dislodged by the creative force of imagination. Such changes, often so remarkable, explicable some-times, as we may try to see them later, in 'quantity into quality' terms, can appear too as absolute novelty, something which comes 'from beyond', as it might be from God. And if we say this we are speaking too of 'moral inspiration', as in 'conversion', or as in more everyday changes of heart. (Suddenly the resentment ceases, the spring of love returns.) Thus in speculation upon human nature, whether in real life or in moral philosophy or in fiction, we may move from an instructive instance of something exceptional to the thought: But we are all like that.

Of course art and morals have a different status, altogether a different place in human life. Moral and aesthetic imagination are different from each other though often on reflection hard to distinguish. Artists need (as artists) virtues such as courage, patience, etc. On the other hand really good art, rare as it is, is easier and more natural than really good life. Thinking about goodness inclines us to say this; although because all art instinctively aims at visibility, and much virtue at invisibility, it would be hard to prove. Good life is required of us in a sense in which good art is not. Moral seriousness is required of us, we blame frivolity in moral situations. Morality is ubiquitous and we expect a primary recognition of it; whereas we do not have to be, in the ordinary special-ised sense of that word, artists. If we are artists, we are not morally blamed for being bad ones (mediocre, tenth-rate, etc.) unless there are special circumstances. We may (for instance) be blamed for wasting our time; or for producing depraved or pornographic work, or for deliberately and wilfully debasing our talents by producing bad commercially successful work. If an artist who could do better does worse because he needs money to feed his family, we excuse him while criticising his art. If a man takes what is not his own in order to feed his family, if we exonerate him we may also classify his act as blameless. In general, sheer lack of artistic skill is not a fault, there is no harm in cultivating a very modest talent, and we may not feel bound to exhort a mediocre artist to 'try harder', because art (in the ordinary sense) is not compulsory, it does not matter if, here or there, it exists or not. Of course good art benefits a society, but must be allowed to happen spontaneously, and we condemn societies which coerce artists. The contiguous area between art activity and moral activity is, as indicated, complex and variegated, though for ordinary purposes we can usually sort it out fairly easily. I have used an extended sense of the aesthetic in which 'we are all artists': 'use of language is use of imagination', and 'perception is creative evaluation'. These are formulations, designed to evade being tautological or senseless, intended in their context to draw attention to areas of reality which are 'ordinarily' missed or misunderstood. It could for instance be misleading to divide language between dull blunted ordinary language used by ordinary folk, and elegant precise language used by educated or aesthetically sensitive people. Anyone can talk well, anyone (if he can write) can write 'a good letter', many people, whether or not they can write, can dance and sing, more people than we might imagine can draw expressively, everyone can rearrange his possessions (and so on). Anyone can try to imagine someone else's plight. Looked at in this way life can be seen as full of aesthetic imaginative activity which is also, scarcely distinguishably, moral activity. Must we, it might be asked, anxious lest the aesthetic corrupt the moral, always make the distinction?

The apparent area occupied by the concept of imagination is very large and amorphous. Perhaps it would be better just to try to discern the elements of which it seems to be composed. Of course one must attempt this in any case, but the presence of the word, with its strong associations, may too much suggest a unity in diversity. One must ask, at various points, what the concept is doing, and whether it represents an unnecessary emotive mystification. Would it be helpful, for instance, to define imagination as primarily an aesthetic faculty? Kant values genius, but nothing is more fundamental than ordinary morality, and here he enjoins a movement toward cool reason out of the warmer medley of pictures and feelings. (Don't picture Christ, consult your own rational conscience.) Such general advice must always be available; a contrast between an imaginative grasp and a rational grasp of a situation could be illuminating. 'He lacks imagination' is often uttered as a reproach, but 'imaginative activity' is not always what is required. Imagination can 'go too far', 'become too personal', 'be an end in itself'. Here we must avoid the temptation to simplify the problem by a general reference to the distinction between good creative imagination and fantasy imagination. Perhaps in some kinds of moral thinking imagination, in anything like its ordinary senses, is out of place. Imaginative speculation about the consequences of an action may in some cases be irrelevant. (For instance in a straightforward case of keeping a promise.) In some decisions we should not 'think too precisely upon the event'. The doubter is called back from imaginative speculation toward the required form of the act. Imaginative reflection upon a moral choice can become too aesthetic, can tempt us to be stylish rather than to be right. The conception of 'too aesthetic' is recognisable and frequent. On the other hand to distinguish a moral from an aesthetic use of the imagination may be *in general* difficult and indeed undesirable. Consider how difficult it is in a scrutiny of good art. We work roughly in complicated contexts to discern in particular cases whether a writer is too coldly moralistic or a moral agent too self-indulgently imaginative. Metaphors of warm and cool, hot and cold, arise naturally here. Also, we cannot, in considering the 'place' of imagination in morals, avoid considering how and whether we are to separate morality from religion. This is indeed a main question posed by the diverse philosophies of Plato and Kant.

With these questions in mind I return to the problems about 'grace' and moral change which I was discussing just now. The 'redemption' of the (purely) aesthetic, its absorption into the moral and religious, is going on all the time. There are moral illuminations or pictures which remain vividly in the memory, playing a protective or guiding role: moral refuges, perpetual starting points, the sort of thing St Paul was talking about at Philippians 4. 8. A Christian may think here of Christ upon the cross. But at a simpler level the story of his birth, complete with shepherds, kings, angels, the ox and the ass, may be a good thing to have in one's life. Buddhists speak of 'taking refuge'. Such points or places of spiritual power may be indicated by a tradition, suggested by work or subjects of study, emerge from personal crises or relationships, be gradually established or come suddenly: through familiarity with a good person or a sacred text, a sense of renewal in a particular place, a sudden vision in art or nature, joy experienced as pure, witnessing a virtuous action, a patient suffering, an absence of resentment, humble service, persistent heroism, innumerable things in family life and so on and so on. We are turning here to an inexhaustible and familiar field of human resources. Every individual has a collection of such things which might be indicated by various names and images. I have already used some: refuges, lights, visions, deep sources, pure sources, protections, strongholds, footholds, icons, starting points, sacraments, pearls of great price. Our moral consciousness is full of such imagery, kinaesthetic, visual, literary, traditional, verbal and non-verbal, and is full too of images of darkness, of stumbling, falling, sinking, drowning.

Considerations, such as those rehearsed above, about moral change make sense of the notion of our being always 'in the presence of God', being at every moment mobile between good and bad and attracted in both directions. This is a religious picture which belongs where morality and religion spontaneously blend. All my argument assumes that religion is not only a particular dogma or mode of faith and worship, but can exist, and indeed exists, undogmatically as for instance in Buddhism, and potentially everywhere, forming a deep part of morality. Especially now, when we are better able to understand the nature of myth, religious concepts should come home to morals, or let us say be welcomed in the whole area of morality. Liberal political thinking (properly) draws a line between those activities which are the concern of the state and those which are the private concern of the individual. The border of this line is, in democratic societies, much disputed, while its necessity is not. In this context it is sometimes confusingly assumed that morality is public and religion is private. (An alternative view was put by Lord Melbourne who said that religion was all very well provided it did not interfere with one's private life.) Any such distinction between religion and morals, whether offered to protect the one or the other, tends to be somewhat general and unrealistic. It may be said that political thinking has to be in a certain sense 'unrealistic'. Hume said that something could be 'true in politics which was false in fact', and instanced the useful assumption that, politically, every man should be deemed a knave. (Essay 'On the Independence of Parliament'.) Such, and innumerable, rough assumptions and distinctions belong in the necessarily clumsy and often axiomatic mechanics of running a nation-state; in the course of which the 'province' of organised religion is constantly up for debate. In this hurly-burly, religion and morality are equally likely to be 'told off' at intervals for being too public or too private. What may be called the 'soul' of the state, its morale, is (in liberal political terms) a surrounding atmosphere which is essential to the mechanism but not part of it. This is a way of speaking of the status of the individual. I shall shortly discuss these matters in more detail under the heading of 'Politics'. My point here is that familiar distinctions between morality and religion are often artificial or merely (in particular situations) useful.

The idea of reverence is common to what are usually thought of as religious and moral attitudes, connected with art, love, respect for persons and for nature, extending into religious conceptions of the sacred or the holy. The concept is enlivened by our awareness of how it can degenerate, into idolatry, superstition, magic, a preference of what is exciting and charming to what is good. Reverence for life and being, for otherness, is something which can be taught or suggested very early. 'Don't kill the poor spider, put him out in the garden.' Even a use of 'him' or 'her' instead of 'it' may help. Formal religious education in schools tends to disappear, with no positive substitute. Now, if there is any teaching about religion it is likely (except in religiously based schools) to be in a historical or factual mode, and not many teachers are eager to undertake any form of (serious moralistic) 'religious instruction'. The reason for this may be said to be obvious; but children with disparate (or no) religious backgrounds can be taught morality with reference to very general religious images. Formal religion provided ritual and imagery, presenting it as something ordinary and usual. What happens every day is important, images can affect the quality of our thoughts and wishes. The damage done to inner life, to aloneness and quietness, through the imposition of banal or pornographic or violent images by television, is a considerable wound. Teach meditation in schools. Some understanding of, and taste for, exercises in detachment and quietness, the sense of another level, and another place, a larger space, might thus be acquired for life. Simply sitting quietly and calmly can be doing something good; subduing unkind or frenzied thoughts certainly is. Morality, as the ability or attempt to be good, rests upon deep areas of sensibility and creative imagination, upon removal from one state of mind to another, upon shift of attachments, upon love and respect for the contingent details of the world.

The concept of 'imagination' has led towards a discussion of 'pure things' or 'holy images', omnipresent sacraments, rituals, forms of words (as in familiar prayers), and so on. Seeking such refuge or invoking such protection is a human instinct. Religion is always menaced by magic, and yet faith can redeem and transform magic. A Tibetan story:

[ 337 ]

a mother asks her son, a merchant setting off for the city, to bring her back a religious relic. He forgets her request until he is nearly home again. He picks up a dog's tooth by the roadside and tells the old lady it is a relic of a saint. She places it in her chapel where it is venerated. It begins miraculously to glow with light. This story, which may be seen as a version of the Ontological Proof, is itself a religious image or icon: importance of stories in religion. The great religions are full of illuminations and *transferable* images of this kind. We understand by an instinctive grasp how one thing figures another. In this way, and in our most familiar and immediate experiences, we are always deep in art. We understand the imagery of novelists, their descriptions of mental states, because it is sufficiently close to our own 'working images'. Anyone who has studied a subject over a length of time, for instance a foreign language, knows how, when initial difficulties are over and rules have been learnt and internalised, the mind gains a new facility and speeds like lightning to make syntheses and generate forms. *Sprachgefühl*: we grasp general patterns of cognate formulations, instinctively compare and contrast structures in our own language, and so on. Such studies are an image of our understanding of the world, how structures and patterns become spontaneously active in the mind, breaking down more elementary and cruder forms. Imagery of many kinds is at work, there are pictorial and kinaesthetic elements in our mastery of language. Understanding poetry in a foreign tongue exercises these mental muscles. Reflection upon language can help us to understand the edifying power and special status which Plato attributed to mathematics. Mathematical objects as non-empirical individuals may be compared with grammatical forms, the vision of which can joyfully excite the mind. A certain level of structure in any study may be accorded an analogous position, from which indeed we can see how any serious learning is a moral-spiritual activity. Plato, whose words at times must echo those of the real life enquiring Socrates, *shows* his thoughts, his doubts, his hypotheses, his passionately held beliefs and convictions, in a stream of progressive reflection in the context of which the meaning of his myths is clear. 'Scientific explanations' of traditional myths are dealt with at *Phaedrus* 229. The conversation is taking place near the spot where, it is said, Boreas carried off Oreithyia. Phaedrus says, but do you really believe that? Socrates says, well, some clever fellow might explain it away as a gust of wind knocking her off a rock, but then he would have to invent similar explanations for centaurs and chimeras and so on. I prefer not to waste time on such matters, but to accept the usual beliefs and turn my attention to investigating what I am myself. Wittgenstein adopts a somewhat similar attitude when seeing off Frazer's *Golden Bough*.

Our attention to the images of art can provide a point where the distinction of subject and object vanishes in an intuitive understanding. This understanding may be 'lodged' in something particular. The particular, which is saved, held in attention, given being, found to be significant, is not of course meant in any Hegelian sense, where the dialectic casts a light on something taken to be solitary and then destroys it in a higher synthesis. (It eats it.) The particular, which is of course in various ways connected, but also solitary, is thought of here in an empirical-philosophical sense, in an argument appealing in ordinary language to familiar matters. The particular, as art shows us with an exemplary clarity, is not to be left behind, falling out of being, dusty and forgotten, lost in the dark; it must be allowed to glow with light. There is an ordinary mystical discipline which relies upon such insights. Parts of works of art, with and without the intention of the artists, readily acquire, for their clients, a significance which is 'beyond themselves': the man taking off his shirt in Piero della Francesca's baptism, an intensely blue hat in a picture by Bonnard, a line of poetry, or (noted by Proust) Vermeer's yellow wall or Vinteuil's 'little phrase'. Art exhibits, what is less clear elsewhere, the mystery of the synthesis of different levels of cognition, how complexly integrated these levels are, and how therein the 'brute particular' is transcended and retained (known). A case of saving the phenomena. Here we may grasp the ideas of 'transcendence' and 'pure cognition'. This sort of experience and thinking also more clearly exhibits the ubiquitous manner in which one kind of insight or vision, as well as being itself, can image another. The particular can figure the human individual and his rights; and we may say that non-human particulars have rights too. In a sense, everything about us asks for our attention. The aesthetic can image the moral as well as fusing with it. Kant said that beauty was an analogon of good, Plato said it was the nearest clue. The world of nature and of ordinary artefacts is full of potential points of light, of worlds within the world (like Wittgenstein's stove). Schopenhauer explains his Ideas by reference to such experiences. 'The transition . . . from the common knowledge of particular things to the knowledge of the Idea takes place suddenly; for knowledge breaks free from the service of the will, by the subject ceasing to be merely individual, and thus becoming the will-less subject of knowledge which . . . rests in fixed contemplation of the object presented to it, out of its connection with all others, and rises into it.' (*WWI*, Book III, section 34.) He uses the word 'contemplation'; but considering the frequency and ordinariness of such events it is better to speak simply of moments of awareness or heightened cognitive consciousness, wherein too the division between subject and object dissolves. (Compare Heidegger's 'letting be', derived from Eckhart.) In these not unusual situations moral changes may be thought of as taking place, these are ordinary cases of our ability to do what St Paul suggests. We can experience a 'transcendence' at any time in our relations with our surroundings. Particulars are not just potential barriers to thought, as in Plato's picture of the retarded painter and the liberated carpenter. Plato's attachment to mathematics may have contributed to his suspicion of the aesthetic. My examples have suggested good kinds of change. In opposite situations the particular, if it attracts attention, may be degraded, brutalised, not respected, absorbed into private fantasy and fetishistic magic. There are conditions of despair and misery, particularly when hatred and resentment colour these, when particular things become malevolent enemies on whom we want to revenge ourselves. (Smashing plates in a rage, Xerxes thrashing the Hellespont, punishment of things in Plato, *Laws* 873B.) We experience absolute contingency as something horrible or menacingly senseless: as described in Sartre's *La Nausée*, or suggested by Kafka. This sort of literary effect can have the intensity of a kind of fallen or debased sacrament, as for instance in Kafka's story *Die Verwandlung* (*Metamorphosis*) where the father kills his son, who has somehow become a large beetle, by throwing apples at him. Of course we are now safe inside art, but such art is effective because we see through it the real horrors which lurk in life. This can also be seen as a kind of inverted Sublime. Kant's sublime is an experience of moral exaltation, mixed with fear, which we feel (for instance) when gazing at shapeless rocks down which chaotic waters run; and to pursue the idea, we could also experience either a debased or a true Sublime when surveying some humble extremely contingent scene in the kitchen, a burnt saucepan or massive broken crockery accident. Kant suggests a movement of proud withdrawal into a fortress of unconquered rationality as our high reaction to the vast rubble of the world. I would describe this (good) experience on analogy with others I have instanced as a comparatively selfless (unselfing) inspiration drawn from the wild forces of nature or from contingency in other less romantic forms. We may note that art can deal with both the high and the low experience, turning the latter into a kind of exhilarating though fearful surrealism: like the flying apples in Kafka's story. And in life too the absurd contingent, not the waterfall but the broken crockery, may produce a surge of cosmic misery and hatred, or may make us smile and turn the occasion into a sort of rueful aesthetic pleasure: as when we say, unseriously, this is too much, this really is *the end*!

I have been talking about the way in which our moral experience shares in the peculiar density of art, and in its imaginative cognitive activity. The term 'moral experience', comprehensible I trust in this context, is not in general use, whereas the term 'religious experience' is, or was. As used in arguments about religion, 'religious experience' now tends to mean intense personal impressions rather than supernatural visions. Also mentioned in such arguments are interchanges with nature, profound feelings in solitary places, when listening to music, and so on. I say 'such arguments', but perhaps arguments for religion from religious experience are taking place less often. Psychology has suggested to us the ambiguity of this kind of 'evidence', and philosophers and philosophical theologians tend to regard it as obviously peripheral. Perhaps too in a materialistic, scientific, technological, television-dominated atmosphere, people do not have it, or do not *recognise* it. The similarity of religious experience and moral experience, or the ubiquitous moral nature of experience, brings (demythologised) religion closer to us. Perhaps we already have a religious consciousness, not always named as such! Or, we might say that 'religious' concepts have always been part and parcel of morality, but because of some of the specialised claims of the former have not been so recognised by moral philosophers. Such a view would be, in a Buddhist or Hindu context, childishly obvious. To pick up the thread of the argument, all religions make use of our ability to express and experience spiritual and moral aspiration by taking particular contingent things as symbolic of, or signals toward, a reality thought of as more or less veiled from us by our own egoism. This is a characteristic working of imagin-

[ 341 ]

ation, to break through the veil, a natural way of experiencing the interconnectedness of things, their beauty and strangeness, their liveliness in and to our consciousness as 'ours', and yet also as independent witnesses to reality. The bread and wine represent, or are, the body and blood of Christ. Theologians have taken sides on this matter. But ordinary worshippers, even sophisticated ones, have, I should imagine, taken things more in their stride. 'But isn't that condoning superstitions or at least a kind of insincere double-think?' There are superstitions, some harmless, some not. But those who take the bread and wine without caring about the dogma are doing something which we do blamelessly all the time, taking one thing as figuring another and passing swiftly on toward what is important and real; and *mutatis mutandis* in the rituals of other religions. Rituals and ritual objects, sacraments, icons of all kinds, make use of this faculty. Of course there is superstition and obsession, fetishism, paranoia, *nausée* and ordinary familiar states when the world is senseless or filled with images of resentment, fear and magic. There are despairs which can only take refuge in magic and wherein ideas of good and evil are undreamt-of luxuries. But magic is a characteristic nemesis of religion as it is of art; although art also redeems magic, as religion too can transform it. Great art purifies magic. (Prospero's problems, dangerous ground.) In some Protestant worship the absence of images, the plain wooden cross upon the unadorned altar, is a potent image.

In talking about consciousness and imagination and imagery I have come to use the term 'aesthetic' in an extended sense. An analogous and more familiar word which is readily extended by discussion of it in this context is 'love'. 'Love' can be used to mean any desire or tendency. In a more solemn sense we speak of love for people. This love is often distorted by egoism. It is also one of the most important things in any life. Is this a religious, moral, or metaphysical view? Or a psychological generalisation? Religious people speak of love for God, which may be taken ideally to include or subsume love for people. Love can be learnt in family life. We know now of the particular importance of early childhood. Lessons about love may be given to us by religion, or religious atmosphere, but are more likely to come from experiences and examples. Is love a virtue – or a form of energy or a scattered polymorphous concept? Is it 'ultimately' identical with good? God is Love (I John 4. 8) is a sentence that used to be learnt early in life. Plato gives to Good a unique position, above being, real but not contingently existing, *Ens Realissimum*. This is like the *unique* status of the God appealed to in Anselm's Ontological Proof, except that Good is not a god, but an Idea which inspires love. Good is what all men love and wish to possess for ever. (*Symposium* 206A.) What is desired is desired as, genuinely, good; though many desires reach only distorted shadows of goodness. We may love depraved 'goods' (money, power). Good exerts a magnetism which runs through the whole contingent world, and the response to that magnetism is love. The myth in the *Symposium* (203), told by Diotima to Socrates, presents Eros as an ambiguous spirit, the child of Poverty and Ingenuity. Eros is not, as has been suggested earlier in the dialogue, by Agathon, a great god. He is neither a god nor a mortal but a spiritual being residing in between, a daemon, a great spirit (202–3). Love is poor and homeless and without shoes like his mother, but brave and ingenious and aspiring like his father. He lacks goodness and beauty, he is a lover who is forever seeking these, he desires wisdom which is supremely beautiful, he is a creative spirit, he is tension, exertion, zeal (206B). He is, in the strong and eloquent words of Diotima, a terrible magician, an alchemist (*pharmakeus*), a sophist. This creature, appearing amid the funny confused *joie de vivre* of the *Symposium*, is one of the most enlightening images in the mythology of morals. Christ, whom various non-Christians took to be a great daemon, said that he was the way, the truth and the life. Christians are however used to identifying Christ with God as Perfect Love. Love as a deprived and straining seeker, as enchanter and sophist, strikes a different note. The word *pharmakeus* is best translated here as alchemist, spiritual chemist. It means a user of drugs and spells, a sorcerer. A drug, a *pharmakon*, can be either beneficent or malignant. The word 'sophist' is interesting here too. Elsewhere sophists are attacked as charlatans and cheats. Plato separates spiritual energy from spiritual goal. The *goal*, the end, the absolute, is transcendent, impersonal and pure. The *energy* is something more mixed and personal, godlike yet not divine, capable of corruption, aspiring to wisdom, a needy resourceful desire. Eros is a great artist, not a pure being. He seeks goodness and beauty, and works and schemes for the happiness of possessing these. 'Love is the desire for the perpetual possession of the good.' The image exalts perfect good above imperfect love. The theology of the *Symposium* accords here with that of the *Timaeus* and the *Phaedrus*. Beauty is a clue to good. Love is desire for good, virtue is being *in love* with good. As we refine our conception of beauty we discover good. The Artist-Demiurge, moved by his desire for, his vision of, the Forms, creates the World and its Soul. The Demiurge is good but not omnipotent, the Soul is imperfect and confused but desirous of good. Goodness is the perfection of desire. Plato viewed human artists with suspicion, but in these myths portrays the task and impulse of love as a spiritualisation of aesthetic and sexual energy. Here concepts of the aesthetic, and the sexual, are as it were broken by the concept of good. Our desire for beauty leads to and becomes our desire for perfection. The *Ens Realissimum* is impersonal, the desire which seeks it is an impure personal passionate energy, not itself an absolute.

God is Love? The question of love and its metaphysical imagery has come up after a discussion of consciousness, imagination, aesthetic imagery, and relations between the aesthetic and the moral. Beauty can be an image of good, and thus a way to good; or a substitute for it. (Eros as alchemist.) Is not love a better, less ambiguous figure? Such speculations live near to the edge of nonsense, but are valuable, for instance in reflection upon theological pictures. The traditional Judaeo-Christian God is a Person whose main characteristic (though he is also feared) is loving and being loved. In so far as he is a God who is just and who punishes, he does so mercifully and in a loving spirit, always aware of the contrite heart. Christian attitudes and visions which emphasise God's anger usually do so when advocating, and indicating the possibility of, conversion and penitence. Christ represents (or is) the accessibility of God, his closeness and caringness, his love, and the invitation to love in return. The Greeks did not in anything like this sense love their gods. They feared them and placated them and celebrated them. Plato's Good is not a god, it is an impersonal object of love, a transcendent idea, *pictured* as a magnetic centre of vitality (for instance as the sun). It purifies the energy which is directed upon it. We are to love Good for nothing, we may *experience* this lively purification. In the Christian picture we are invited to sense an answering judging rewarding Intelligence and a comforting flow of love. Plato speaks of loving a beautiful person as (potentially) an education which leads on to a love of Beauty as something spiritual, as itself a love of truth and of virtue *and* a capacity (here below) for virtuous and truthful love. (*Symposium* 211–12.) Alcibiades, speaking of his love for Socrates (who was neither beautiful nor, then, young) likens him to a clay figure which is opened to reveal an image of a god. (*Symposium* 215B.)

(The love of Alcibiades for Socrates, the love of Plato for Socrates, the 'light' of the dialogues.) A Christian might speak of loving people in and through God. Love is kind, long-suffering, unenvious, it is not conceited or self-seeking or easily provoked; it thinks no evil and takes no pleasure in ill-doing, it rejoices in truth, it endures and hopes and believes and never fails. (I Corinthians 13. 4–8.) So it is ideally, but not always, found to be. If one reflects: almost all human love fails in some way. Here we use the word 'love' as a normative term, distinguishing it from lust or mere selfish passion. Personal love exists and is tried in impersonal contexts, in a real large world which transcends it and contains other goals, other values, other people. We love in the open air, not in a private room. We know, and this is one of the things we know most clearly of all, which is indeed a knowledge that is 'forced upon us', that the energy of Eros can be obsessive, destructive and selfish, as well as spiritual, unselfish, a source of good life. 'Falling in love' may be our most intense experience, when the world's centre is removed to another place. It is difficult to be unselfishly in love, and the lover who lovingly surrenders the beloved may serve as an image of virtue, of the love that 'lets go', as in Eckhart: emptying the soul to let God enter and even, for God's sake, taking leave of God. Eckhart was loved by Schopenhauer and also influenced Heidegger. Heidegger's concept of *Lichtung* (as portrayed earlier while man was still the Shepherd of Being), a clearing, an opening of space to allow Being to be, expresses Eckhart's denial of self.

Plato envisages erotic love as an education, because of its intensity as a source of energy, and because it wrenches our interest out of ourselves. It may be compared with the startling experience in Zen (perhaps a literal blow) which is to bring about enlightenment. We *may* perhaps thus learn that other worlds and other centres really exist and have rights. But love can be a form of insanity whereby we lose the 'open scene': *lose* our ability to scatter our loving interest throughout the world, to inhabit a large world, to draw good energy from many sources, to have a large and versatile consciousness, to possess many concepts. There is often (as I suggested earlier) a duty to fall out of love, and there are sound techniques for doing so (of which falling in love with someone else is not necessarily the best one). This valuable exercise can occasion a rediscovery of the beauty of the world. Released, we return to our friends, our work, our ordinary pleasures! Successful obsessive love may be accompanied by intense joy, but also by jealousy and fear of loss. There is a better sunnier happiness when together with the beloved we are able to be aware of other things, other people, other joys, illumined by secure mutual love, when we can stand together and look at something else. This is a liberation of which a marriage ceremony is a symbol. In spite of all the warnings mentioned above, love, love of lovers, of family, of friends, is an ultimate consolation and an ultimate saviour. To love and be loved is what we all desire, and what we desire as, as we are able to see it, good. Eros may be wilful, but he is also said to be ingenious, and there are very many ways in which love between persons can exist and endure.

These are matters often written about in works of literature. Human love, the love of persons for other persons, is *sui generis*, and among our natural faculties and impulses the one which is potentially nearest to the highest divine attributes (however these may be understood) though in practice often remote from them. It is unlike our more detached and unthreatened loves for art objects, for work, for nature, for the furniture of the world generally; but art and the world form its natural and proper context and habitat. Aesthetic experience is by definition unpossessive where we speak of contemplation in the ordinary usage of the word. One kind of love can be a figure or analogon for another, and any love can stir up, and reach down into, the deep breeding places of imagery. We see this in the context of religion where the furniture of the world is freely taken as spiritual pointers, and where unpossessive love is pictured as transcending selfish grasping desire. Here Christ is an icon of the irreducible individual endowed with human privacy and inwardness, exhibiting personal yet selfless love and proving that it is possible. Here, as well as, and I think not less than, the familiar story we find enlightening the *atmosphere* of the Gospels. With St Paul we are aware of human pride and passion, in the Gospels all is quieter and simpler. It is true that in Paul's writings, after all they are letters, we see an individual; and we feel the vast energy of a passionate love, the demonic power of a magic force, light blazing in the dark. Whereas the Gospels take place in the open air, lit, in spite of everything they have to tell, by a calm sun. One might say that St Paul is Eros, and the Gospels are the world of the Forms. The human passionate urgency in St Paul makes him (I suspect) for many a more effective teacher. For many temperaments, it is easier to be moved by Paul's warm outcry, by his sinful breast-beating persona with whom one can identify, than with the curious coolness of the

Gospel narratives. The atmosphere of the latter conveys a picture of unpossessive love. Space and light are essential images in the description of morality. What is needful is inner space, in which other things can lodge and move and be considered; we withdraw ourselves and let other things be. Any artist or thinker will appreciate this picture of inner space; not Wittgenstein's 'logical space', but a private and personal space-time. We might think here of spatio-temporal rhythm; a good person might be recognised by his rhythm. An obsessed egoist, almost everyone sometimes, destroys the space and air round about him and is uncomfortable to be with. We have a sense of the 'space' of others. An unselfish person enlarges the space and the world, we are calmed and composed by his presence. Sages in deep meditation are said sometimes to become invisible because of the absence of that cloud of anxious selfish obsession which surrounds most of us. (Let us hope they invisibly edify.)

We must 'give things their rights'. Contingent particulars, objects, in ways which I have mentioned above, can startle us with their reality and arrest obsessive mechanical thought-runs. Particulars which are not art objects or persons, and are thus more unlike us, more resistant to our fantasy, more self-evidently contingent, can play this role. A good consciousness does not ignore or blur these witnesses, or overwhelm their private radiance. Reflection on these rights may also help us to understand the analogous rights of those most important particulars, human individuals. Inner freedom and space, spatio-temporal rhythm, ability to let be, to consider, create, understand, sympathise: these are continually menaced by anxiety, obsessive imagery, base emotions, egoistic illusions. (As well of course as the fear and misery which is the unavoidable lot of so many humans.) This is like, or a case of, the way in which easy bad art drives out difficult good art. Any art form may have an authority which fascinates. Here in talking about love we may return toward the images derived from art which were considered earlier, and to the concept of consciousness. Changes in our desires go along with changes in instinctive imagery, including kinaesthetic images of space and movement, as well as with the more coherent activities of fantasy and imagination. Change occurs it seems automatically, yet also influenced by conscious orientations and decisions. We decide to read this book instead of that, to see this person instead of that, on a particular occasion to indulge or abstain. We decide to stop thinking about something. Can we? Will, as a subsidiary idea, may be connected with such decisions, as in the case I mentioned earlier of literally running away from temptation. The concept of will should be kept under restraint; if it becomes too powerful and abstract and simple it tends to swallow and segregate our ideas of morality, obliterate their omnipresent detail, and facilitate a treatment of 'morality' as a small special subject. The nemesis of an inflated monistic view of moral will is a distinction of fact and value which diminishes the latter. The inner needs the outer and the outer needs the inner. In these pictures I have tried to 'exhibit' the inner; and resist tendencies which give value and effective function only to the outer (thought of as 'moral acts' or as linguistic activity), or regard the 'inner life' as fantasy and dream, lacking identity and definition, even as a fake illusory concept. Such views tend in effect toward a behaviourist moral philosophy, or toward an existentialist or structuralist reduction. Such nullification of the inner may also have a home in utilitarian moral thinking, where it receives understandable lay support from those who hold that 'soul-talk' is a luxury in a world where action to relieve suffering is our main duty. Mill, who cannot find an intelligible place for virtue, shrinks from analysing, though he imagines he can define, 'higher pleasures', a concept which he finds he cannot do without if he is to escape from Bentham. It is difficult to see how higher pleasures can be characterised without reference to states of consciousness. G. E. Moore found it natural to make this move.

The appearance of J. S. Mill in the argument makes a bridge to observations about politics.

> 12 <

# Morals and Politics

Heraclitus, who said almost everything but rather briefly, tells us that: 'Men awake have one common world, but in sleep they turn aside, each into a world of his own.' 'One must follow what is common; but though the word (*Logos*) is held in common, most men live as if they had a private understanding of their own.' (Fr. 2.) Of course, in what we would call a logical sense, my experience is private to me and cannot be experienced by another. This logical or 'grammatical' privacy may be said to have an empirical base, in the sense that there is (it seems) nothing which we could call my having your perceptions. What Heraclitus is speaking of is something more familiar and more puzzling. Language has and must have public rules. Yet we have private insights and cognitions which go beyond what could be described as a private saying of public sentences; and even when we speak aloud may we not to some extent 'make the language our own'? Men dream when they are awake too. The outer and the inner are in a continual volatile dynamic relationship. Such is the creation and growth of the individual, the person who is in innumerable ways special, unique, different from his neighbour. This is the concept for which, in 1989, the people of eastern Europe fought their tyrants. Kierkegaard fought Hegel. And belief in this person is an assertion of contingency, of the irreducible existence and importance of the contingent. Everyday moral decisions normally involve consideration of details; political and social reflections tend to avoid these (*de minimis non curat lex*) but are sometimes felicitously forced to notice them. As we move from generalities toward the accidental and particular we introduce muddle but also variety and space. In obvious, but only generally specifiable, ways we are 'historically conditioned'. Liberal political thinking posits the individual, but accounts of him can vary. Here, as often in moral reflection, one wants to combine 'ought' with 'is' in a way which is not fallacious. When Hume says that 'reason is and ought only to be the slave of the passions' he means that reason is bound, one way or another, whether we like it, or admit it, or not, to be swayed, or coloured, by desires; and moreover this is a good thing of which we should be more fully conscious. We must and can make the best of what happens to be the case. So (*mutatis mutandis*) with the concept of the individual we want to say that every human creature is an individual. We attach some ideas of freedom and reason to the concept 'human' and with these comes an idea of a self-created privacy. The philosophy of Hobbes exhibits such a fusion of ought and is. The individual, pictured as indestructible, is *thereby* pictured as valuable. *Nemo me impune lacessit* is better in politics than in morals. We assume individuality, from our experience of humans, and we add, as properly also present, the potentialities thereof. There are obvious complications in this picture. A man ought to be allowed to be free, and should also possess happiness, and knowledge – and moral sensibility. There are obligations which belong to his environment and others which belong to himself, and these overlap. Moreover, cannot a virtuous ignorant enslaved peasant be a better human being than a sophisticated liberated self-seeker? We move towards developing concepts of 'good', or 'fulfilled', human beings which connect with questions of rights.

Religion and morality, and at certain periods art, have been thought of as having to do with an achieved inwardness, a private personal soul. But parts of human life go on in fashions which, as it might seem unavoidably, neglect the concept of the *moral* individual. For instance in politics we may banish or curtail this concept in the interests of arguing that it is not the duty of the state to make us good. That is *our* business. We distinguish the (moral) ego which retires into privacy from the (political) individual who is irreducible and has inalienable rights. We argue about how far religion and art should play political or 'social' roles. Should the church be enlivening personal spirituality or defending the poor? Should the artist create his own best work of art or advocate a better society? We fight for freedom of religion, and also against ecclesiastical power. As a political property (individual rights, the bourgeois individual, the role of the individual in history) the concept has a fairly new life, though we may also attach the label retrospectively to any human. Are some individuals more individual than others? More, as we say, 'full of themselves'? Different art or social forms may exhibit, in the pages of history and literature, more or less of these distinct beings. Classical Greece (as contrasted with Hellenistic Greece) appears as rich in individuals, its literature develops the idea in a modern sense. We may also associate the ultimate liberated fully individual individual with the 'bourgeois revolution'. Of course whether particular people in the past are remembered or memorable is a matter of chance, and certainly irrespective of merit. Archaeologists, historians and laymen are often more interested in 'the ordinary chaps' and glad to find evidence which identifies one or another of these. Novels were 'novel' because they made much of the histories of obscure individuals.

Varying concepts of the individual have been influential as axiomatic checks and as ideals; discussion of these may throw light on important differences between moral and political thinking, and the role of 'axioms' (e.g. assertions of rights) in the awkward relations between the two. Axioms (in my use of this word) are *sui generis*, unsystematic, may involve acknowledged 'fictions', as when it is argued that in liberal politics the most important picture of man is that offered by Hobbes, the self-contained private being who, within external limitations, does what he pleases, and, because he is fundamental, is valuable. Parolles in *All's Well That Ends Well*: 'Only the thing I am shall make me be.' Hobbes's aggressive selfish individual, and Hume's everyman who for political purposes 'must be deemed a knave', are edifying metaphysical political fictions. We might want to say that political philosophy is about 'advice to princes', or politicians, or citizens, whereas moral philosophy is aimed at each particular thinker or moral agent. This would be over-simple, as great philosophers have usually collected morals and (sometimes by implication) politics, together with epistemology and 'logical foundations', into one metaphysical internally related package. Yet the distinction deserves to be kept in mind. Moreover philosophy is not science, but aims traditionally at a certain (its own) kind of objective detachment. This detachment, or would-be detachment, was what Marx rejected when he said that he did not want to explain the world, but to change it. The term 'commitment' (engagement), which has both political and moral force, for instance in existentialist thinking, expresses this reaction. Hegel's *Phenomenology*, or pilgrim's progress of *Geist*, may be regarded as a dialectic of history or an allegory of the individual soul. Farther on into the age of the novel Kierkegaard and Nietzsche, neither of whom is usually regarded as a philosopher, felt that their work was addressed, 'for edification', to the individual. Linguistic or analytical philosophers who (unlike the great metaphysicians) claim that philosophical accounts of morality can be morally neutral, would classify such thinkers as typical 'preachers', whose task is now to be clearly distinguished from that of philosophy. In fact it is difficult for a moral philosopher to say anything of the slightest interest and be 'neutral'. Thinkers, from preachers through philosophers to scientists, may want to suggest that their ideas both explain and promote some sort of 'good' or 'satisfactory' being; and their arguments are usually addressed to a kind of informed moral *sensus communis* in their readers.

Well, what's wrong, for political purposes, with the Humian man, a relaxed individual, a person of habit and tradition, with a reasonably decent sense of order, but without any lofty moral aspirations? After all, if one appeals to a general notion of human nature, must one not agree that we are on the whole *not* framed to be particularly good? Besides, a utilitarian might add to the argument, ought we not to be primarily employed in removing the misery of others without bothering about our own virtue? The modern 'individual', brought about perhaps by the rise of capitalism, may also claim other inventors, besides Locke, Hume, Kant, (etc.), such as Rousseau, Fielding, Kierkegaard (etc.). He may be described (also with an implication that he is 'finished') as the Romantic man. It may be said that this person is volatile. The man whom Kierkegaard rated highest is an inward conscientious not unpassionate religious man, a calmly unobtrusively good man. Yet is not this ideal also related, perhaps even causally related, to the demonic or Luciferian individual of Nietzsche, or the authentic heroic man of Heidegger and Sartre? Is there not something (for all his apparent 'ordinariness') self-assertive about Kierkegaard's 'best' man, and for a true religious ideal should we not turn to the de-individualised individual of Buddhism or mystical Christianity, the 'empty' soul of Eckhart, the 'decreated' person of Simone Weil? The voice that cries out in the Psalms, and so much affected Saint Augustine, is that of one who, before the divine countenance, 'shrivels like a moth in a flame'. That penitential outcry, with which so innumerably many of us, through the centuries, have identified, is an individual plaint; but is not religious individuality somehow beyond persons? Christ is seen as the guarantor of the irreducible individual, seen in all his particularity by God, and incarnate in a particular man. Yet is Christ himself 'really there', is he not hallowed, in the remarkable accounts of him, out of individuality? Is he not described at last and *seen* (as perhaps other instances are not), as the perfect mystical *non-individual*? This oddness of the figure of Christ is not the least persuasive argument for the truth of traditional Christian claims. He happened to be understood and celebrated by five geniuses. (An accident?) Such images (occurring also in Buddhism and Hinduism) may serve as inspirations, or at any rate remind ordinary folk of the virtue of humility and that, before God, they are nothing.

To return to the importance, in our epoch, of such *imagines*, it could be argued that a dominating figure is that of the demonic individual. Perhaps the individual liberated or created by capitalism had a golden age of integral being and virtuous idealism, reflected in the great art forms of the nineteenth century, but now, it is said, has disintegrated and become unconfident and even corrupt. We see (it may be argued) his demonic descendants in ruthless tyrannical regimes and persons, and, in western democracies, in egoistic materialistic 'go-getters', in pursuit of money, fame, prestige and sex, who are now our most conspicuous citizens. The strong demonic individual whom we associate with Nietzsche, and (*mutatis mutandis*) with Fascism, is of course not a new concept. He was a phenomenon recognised by the Greeks, known as the tyrant and his form of government as tyranny. Greek tyrants, as also later ones, were sometimes politically 'good things', even though they were ruthlessly authoritarian and perhaps, in their private lives, corrupt and vicious. Tyrants' subjects may even admire and value the egoistic anti-moralism of their leaders. That someone very grand exists who can satisfy every caprice may, while causing scandal, produce a warm feeling, and patriotism too can feed on such images. Neither public cruelty nor riotous private living need make a tyrant unpopular in his lifetime or later. Our best-known, best-loved, monarch is Henry the Eighth. Madame Mao Tse-tung was admired as well as envied for the expensive anti-socialist mode of life for which she was later condemned. Of course the satisfaction felt at the overthrow of tyrants is a stronger, and better, emotion! That exceptional (for whatever reason) people are often valued and not hated for living lives of exemplary luxury and selfishness is perhaps a general feature of human societies, such people may be felt to live vicarious lives for the rest of us. In this way film stars, pop stars, television personalities, tycoons, and so on may be expected to live with obvious luxury and even disorder. To take a different though similar example, a majority of people in Britain value the Royal Family, and like to see them dressed up and riding in their coaches. They are not envied. Here the advantages of a hereditary monarchy and head of state are evident. We (now) expect them to observe traditional moral standards but the odd one who is out of line does the institution no harm, rather the contrary. They play a popular symbolic role, and a beneficent political role in so far as by being 'mock tyrants' they are a protection against real tyrants. At the beginning of Plato's *Republic* Thrasymachus suggests that the egoistic all-powerful individual is the highest kind of human being, the happiest and best, whom we all supremely value whether we admit it or not. We would all be like that if we were sufficiently brave and clever. Socrates rapidly dismisses Thrasymachus, but not conclusively enough to satisfy Glaucon and Adeimantus, who then take up the defence of the demonic individual so as to make Socrates explain yet more clearly how it is that the good man is both just and (truly) happy. The persistence of these young persons is an example to us all.

If we reflect upon 'human nature' or wish to use the concept, we may be led to think of 'types' and of the function of various 'ideals'. I have mentioned here the demonic man, the mystical man, the Platonic-Kantian traditional good man, and the Hobbesian-Humian political fiction man. (By 'man' in such contexts throughout, I mean 'human person'.) Of course these roughly posited figures interrelate, overlap and are in tension with each other. The demonic man may have virtues such as (especially) courage. Such courage is romantic, ambitious, egoistic, in contrast with pure heroic selfless courage (Wallenberg, Bukosky, Shcharansky, and numberless other heroes of our time). The demonic man comes before us not only in the extremist arguments of Thrasymachus and Nietzsche, but also as an emanation of existentialism. Some would even connect his modern incarnations with Kierkegaard, and he may certainly be seen in Sartre, where he is even at intervals celebrated. (The character Daniel, called 'archangel', in *Les Chemins de la Liberté*.) We should recall how much popular existentialism meant to the post-1945 generation; and also ask why, as a popular philosophy, it has now waned. Thrasymachus argued that the tyrant was the only completely free man, so the ideal free man, and the person we all really wish to be. Hobbes's imagined sovereign is also the only entirely free being or entity, but his function is precisely to guarantee the necessarily limited freedom of his citizens, whose lives, without his presence, would be 'solitary, poor, nasty, brutish and short'. 'The first and fundamental law of nature . . . commandeth man to seek peace.' 'The liberty of a subject lieth . . . only in those things . . . which the sovereign has praetermitted.' The proper object of every man's will is some good to himself. (*Leviathan*, Part 1, chapters 13 and 15, Part 2, chapters 21 and 25.) Bad government is better than none, and the 'sovereign' can of course be a democratic parliament. Meanwhile, remoter from politics, the theoretical picture of the free solitary self-assertive individual was, and is, a support or consolation to many confused and lonely Parolleses who are far from being Nietzschean. The mystical man, 'decreated' to use Simone Weil's term, who has broken the barriers of the ego, is an ever-present religious ideal, a magnetic moral picture. Eckhart, who suffered for telling Christians that God was in, indeed was, the soul, is a thinker for today. Do not seek for God outside your own soul. Or to put it the other way round,

[ 354 ]

the mystical is an ever-present moral ideal, that of extending ordinary decent morals indefinitely in the direction of perfect goodness. The 'ordinary' good man, aware of the magnetism of good as well as the role of duty, is thus connected to a mystical ideal whether or not he is, in the traditional sense, religious. Kant's Reason, as well as *Imitatio Christi*, recognises perfection as a possibility for every person. Kierkegaard makes a drama of what might be better seen as an intelligible continuum when he contrasts the (decent) Ethical with the (holy) Religious. At least the holy man is (often is) unostentatious ('like a Tax Collector'). One would like to think that it is a matter of experience, rather than of faith or definition, that the mystical man is a good man.

The purpose of this piece of discussion is to situate the concept of what I call 'axioms' in the general argument about morals, connecting it here with a distinction between morals and politics. This distinction can be made fairly clear in many evidently political situations, but can be (properly or improperly) blurred as we find ourselves moving the political model away from its most obvious home in the governing of a state. There are political situations in villages and 'political' situations in families. Nor is the idea of the axiomatic role-playing judgment easily classifiable as moral or political. Axioms can be Hobbesian or Kantian in style, and in the latter case can seem like duties, and we look to their public role to see how axiomatic they are. Utilitarian philosophy is axiomatic. Declarations of rights have (or purport or tend to have) an axiomatic status. Rights must be distinguished from duties. 'A has a right' is not *equivalent* to 'B has a duty'. Rights are simpler, and cruder, than duties. Taking note of the duties of others (which may be complex and private) can take attention away from a basic (axiomatic) fact that someone is being unjustly treated. Assertion of rights is a straightforward way of moral pointing; rights are political flags representing moral ideas in a public political scene. (In family life it may be better to concentrate on one's duties and leave the question of one's rights to be taken up by others! It is certainly often more prudent.) Rights function against a background of axioms. I have preferred the word 'axiom' because of, as I see it, the wider role of this kind of thinking in relation to politics, and to situations deemed political. The ambiguity of 'right', usefully clarified and used in particular situations, needs relationship to a wider background of 'axiomatic' values. The right to be happy is both like and unlike the right to vote. In considering this kind of thinking and argument we are making a place for problems faced by individuals which, as it were, 'hang in space' and are not easily assimilated into inwardness, into the continuous daily moral work of the soul fighting its way between appearance and reality and good and evil. In this context, the general idea of axiom can seem *like* the general idea of duty, but is importantly distinct. There are what we call 'public duties' and there are ordinary duties, related to personal conduct, such as truth-telling and benevolence; and there are very difficult duties where what is public or taken for granted is scrutinised in an unusual personal situation. The idea of duty extends into a personal sphere of potentially minute and not publicly explicable detail. Here, where it loses its automatic or semi-public character, it becomes a part of what seems more like personal moral desire or aspiration, of experience and consciousness and the continuous work of Eros. 'Duty' is like 'axiom' in that it can operate as a battle flag or as a barrier, but in its effective use the concept covers an extremely wide and various area. Whereas I want to relate 'axiom' more narrowly to a kind of political thinking which is, for political ends of convenience and for the moral ends which 'hang around' political decisions, better thought of as separate from personal morals and not assimilable into that sphere. The distinction is important, and of course debatable, for instance in relation to problems about law. When is a bad law a law, is it always a law? The idea of 'natural law' belongs especially in this discussion.

Such theorising is of course a part of our liberal-democratic conception of a decent state, thought of as the best form of government, though not always immediately possible for reasons which are not necessarily bad reasons. The notion of this state as 'best' is always normatively relevant. (This is an axiom.) It is an essential liberal idea that the Utopian concept of a perfect state, even as a distant vision, is radically misleading and damaging. Society, and so the state, *cannot* be perfected, although perfection is a proper ideal or magnet for the individual as moral agent. We set aside the idea of perfection in the one case, not in the other. In society we adjust unavoidable conflicts in view of certain ends of convenience, and not without a continuous concern with (often various and mutually incompatible) moral ends. To set up such a, as it might seem pessimistic, line of thought as in any way authoritative is of course to adopt a political attitude; one which is by no means arbitrary, which can make appeal to experience and to 'human nature', but which cannot claim to be scientifically or otherwise ultimately demonstrable. Here politics rests on values which may be stated in axioms. This attitude was sometimes rhetorically labelled as 'bourgeois' by people who rightly hated the injustices they saw about them, but wrongly imagined that these could not be altered without some total change, and that another more unified style of government (for instance a one-party state) could easily remove them. This example of casual routine Marxist terminology is now increasingly seen to be empty of content. Liberal political thought posits a certain fundamental distinction between the person as citizen and the person as moral-spiritual individual. We are not as real, whole, persons identical with this fictitious citizen, nor are we essentially divided between the two roles. It is often the case that we obey the law, not only as law-abiding citizens, but also as whole-hearted approving moral agents. On the other hand, if the (liberal) state rightly allows itself to account every man (potentially) a knave, does this amount to a licence to be a knave if one thinks one can get away with it? (Is it all right to cheat the Income Tax authorities? If one can cheat them is it not their fault?) In a democracy we may, because we value, and profit from, general obedience to laws made by democratically elected and removable governments, obey laws which we not only dislike but disapprove of. Here the moral agent opposes the citizen, and a certain degree of moral disapproval may occasion conscientious law-breaking. In dealing with this fairly familiar phenomenon a firm distinction (in practice not always easy to observe) is usually made between violent and non-violent abuse of the law. The acceptance of parliamentary democratic government itself involves a deliberate limitation of our moral aspirations, as when we keep our objections to the government within the law. Decisions about illegality and violence in politics live close to an axiomatic background. We distinguish between what is proper in a democratic state, and in a totalitarian state. Violence is not a justifiable political means in a democracy. Terrorism, as defined in liberal political thinking, is not justifiable anywhere.

These heterogeneous and certainly not insoluble problems are usually discussed and solved, against a background of the essential importance of law, by reference to a kind of moral-political common-sense: so far and no further. The liberal state depends upon deep large nebulous good will, something a little, perhaps a good deal, stronger than a minimal understanding of 'government by consent'. National unity, nationalism, patriotism, as exhibited for instance in war-time, is an aspect of this consent, and may or may not be a valuable phenomenon. Politicians constantly argue with each other in moral as well as pragmatic terms, and all kinds of moral idealists criticise and attempt to persuade governments. A high moral as well as intellectual level of political debate is to be hoped for, and lip service at least is paid to its importance. Lip service is not to be despised. The triumph of good causes partly depends on people, at some point, becoming ashamed of saying certain things. (For instance of making anti-Semitic remarks or talking about women in certain ways.) The machinery of the decent state is continually serviced by an atmosphere of moral good will and high ideals which is essential to its survival. This thoroughly mixed-up continually changing atmosphere is kept fresh by innumerable lively moralists, not least artists (especially writers) and their clients.

Equally essential are certain axiomatic notions which distinguish political machinery from moral ideas (e.g. crime from sin), and also allow some moral ideas a special (universal) political status (e.g. the idea of human rights). Of course these axioms live and work on a battlefield. I may hold that a bad law is (anywhere) a law. ('Render unto Caesar' . . . a much disputed remark.) Order is pragmatically (and often morally) better than disorder. In a democracy conscientious law-breaking should be minimal and carefully thought out and explained and controlled, because change can be sought within the law, and too much casualness about law weakens exceedingly important general respect for it. In non-democratic states it may not be easy to distinguish laws from (e.g.) personal decrees of tyrants. In democratic states laws (recognised as such) may (we think) sometimes properly be broken in the name of (axiomatic) rights. Beyond these actions lies an imagined decent, good (not perfect) human society. The aspiration toward democracy is an ideal based on observation of (with all their faults) existing democracies, and is quite unlike Utopian idealism. Problems will also arise about how far into the fabric of society to move the idea of a political situation and a political model. In a Marxist society these situations and this model are (were) omnipresent, and all social machinery related to a single power centre. A liberal democracy contains innumerable groups and power points which are partly or entirely separate from central government. Voluntary groups may depend on a consensus of souls or on strict rules with enforceable penalties, and may sometimes have illegal objectives, but, in relation to them, the borders of state law (law in the strict sense) must always be capable of clarification. The proliferation of other centres of power and social interest is in general good for democracy, indeed essential to it. It is equally important to define the limits of the 'axiomatic' area, and to distinguish (very general) 'natural rights' from 'local rights'. A right not to be tortured is unlike a right to be represented. Democratic arrangements are frail and vulnerable, and the situation which allows these problems to be constantly and intelligibly sorted is volatile and subject to continual pressure and change. Here the idea of law, of positive law and of 'natural law', and of the distinction between the two, is fundamental. Theorists who argue that legal decisions are really political decisions are tending to weaken the fabric of democratic procedure at a very important point; and doing so in favour of what are likely to be, in effect, random ephemeral local political interests. A not dissimilar weakening of the essential fabric of liberal political thinking occurs when, in relation to punishment, the concept of retributive justice is dropped or discredited in favour of (of course very important) utilitarian ideas of rehabilitation, of making the culprit 'better'. It should be remembered that retribution, just equivalence, works both ways, towards leniency as well as towards severity. If we lose sight of it, state punishment may become the tool of political factions, of popular indignation or indoctrination, or of quasi-scientific theorising. Punishment is not only, and not fundamentally, a matter of moral redemption. The idea of just retribution (retribution as justice) also helps us to make sense of much-discussed questions of deterrence. It is unjust to hang a man for stealing a sheep, it is also unjust to shoot a randomly chosen person in order to quell a riot and discourage future ones. Decent law involves continued rational and humane attempts to establish, in very various situations, what a *just* (equivalent) punishment is. Without this bridle, moral improvement may become the 're-education' of the innocent, and deterrence a vindictive retaliation. *Just* (proper) deterrence, rehabilitation and retribution are the three bases of a 'political' theory of punishment, and most fundamental of these is retribution. In the theoretical 'economy' of democratic government there is a pragmatic as well as an axiomatic background to such thinking. Arguments about capital punishment involve a more evident appeal to axiom, when people argue (as I would) that the state should never (legally, in cold blood, etc.) take life. (Hobbes allowed the taking of life as a unique case; the individual had no obligation to obey a sovereign who proposed to kill him.) The argument against capital punishment should, in my view, be stated as an axiomatic matter, and independent of considerations of deterrence.

Not only the influence of Marxism, but other forces, connected for instance with a decline of religious belief, have promoted a 'socialising' of morality, a tendency for a public political morality to seem like the whole of morals. Groups are taken to be more important than individual persons. Persons must seek 'being' by adhering to groups. Of course some kinds of religion, this is very evident in some Christian styles, elevate works above faith. 'Don't study your soul, help your neighbour!' One must no doubt do both and is likely to be tending soul if helping neighbour and vice versa, though this is not always so, and there may be strongly felt choices and tensions. Political idealism and even social earnestness can lead to callousness and cruelty. In the context of politicised morals, a morality of axioms has importance as a presentation of certain independent, *separated*, values. There is nothing new about this configuration. The term 'natural law' names a sort of human and humane standard which accompanies the detail of ordinary (positive) law and provides a critique of the uses of political power. The Greeks thought of the gods (Zeus, the Erinyes) as providers of 'limits'. Roman law recognised a general experiential common-sense. Medieval Christianity saw natural law as the law of God, the Enlightenment as the law of Reason. The American and French declarations of Rights speak of truths which are 'self-evident' and 'simple and indisputable principles'. And we, although our confidence in Reason has been shaken (for instance by Hitler), also appeal to a special kind of intuitive morality connected with an idea of human nature. We are still using the language of Locke and Tom Paine, concerning 'natural rights', 'toleration', the 'rights of man'. Politicians assert 'human rights', law courts listen to pleas for 'natural justice'. The Nuremberg courts (after Hitler's war) used the authority of 'natural law'. The Helsinki Agreement of 1975 spoke of 'human rights'. The definition and role of 'natural law' must always remain in dispute, but its influential presence is of continuing importance and value, even when it receives only lip service. It is a special case of an intuitive axiomatic moral understanding. (I shall discuss similar cases shortly.) Its status (to use Wittgenstein's phrase) 'cuts off the way to an explanation'. It is not deducible from, or *a priori* excluded by, particular political systems or theories. Natural law, natural rights, may be said to have a 'special relation' with utilitarianism, since happiness is the most universally recognisable human value; and through the value of liberty, with liberal theory. But essentially these ideas move around in an atmosphere of their own outside existing legal and political arrangements. D'Entrèves says that natural law 'provides a name for the point of intersection between law and morals' (*Natural Law*, last chapter). It also represents a mode of thinking which can become a morality of its own, and in fact now provides for many people a general ethical viewpoint which is separate both from politicised social theory and from traditional personal morals. I mean the mixed area often 'highly motivated', which includes the promotion of women's rights, black rights, animal rights, the rights of the planet (ecology), one could even add liberation theology where the identification of Christ with the poor inspires a passion for justice which is *sui generis* and not a subsection of either Marxism or dogmatic Christianity. The flag of natural rights or natural law has often been that of revolutionary change. As we have been seeing in the last decade of the twentieth century.

'If we regard man as a being whose existence is a punishment and an expiation we then view him in a right light. The myth of the Fall ... is the only point in the Old Testament to which I can ascribe metaphysical, although only allegorical, truth; indeed it is this alone which reconciles me to the Old Testament. Our existence resembles nothing so much as the consequence of a false step and a guilty desire. New Testament Christianity, the ethical spirit of which is that of Brahmanism and Buddhism, and is therefore very foreign to the otherwise optimistic spirit of the Old Testament, has also very wisely linked itself on precisely to that truth: indeed without this it would have found no point of contact with Judaism at all. If anyone desires to measure the degree of guilt with which our existence is tainted, then let him look at the suffering which is connected with it.'

(*WWI*, Supplement to Book IV, ch. xlvi.)

These words of Schopenhauer may prompt various reactions. The 'Buddhism of the New Testament' is interesting and ambiguous, to be amended perhaps by Christians in the light of Romans 8. 22, 'The whole creation groaneth and travaileth in pain together until now.' The spectacle of the terrible suffering of others may prompt not only sympathy but also a sense of guilt which may be overwhelming. (This was felt by many people in relation to the Holocaust.) So it may be felt that not only 'personal spirituality', but also moral philosophy and traditional theology are out of place in a world tormented by poverty, misery and cruelty: that old-fashioned theoretical generalisations, or calm reflections upon inwardness, are too abstract and dreamy and indeed selfish to be *true* for a post-Hitler post-Stalin over-populated nuclear planet. Such an attitude may make benevolent social fanatics, or could lead to terrorism, where a particular cause, idolised as just, produces a callous indifference to other values. But one does not have to choose between activism and inwardness or feel that one is bound to swallow the other. A morality of axioms needs the intuitive control of a more widely reflective and general morality. In a good society these ways of thinking, while always in tension, know their roles and places, and when they have rights against each other. This procedure belongs with political liberalism. The acceptance of parliamentary democratic government itself involves a deliberate limitation of our morally inspired activity, as when we keep our objections to government policy within the law, or carefully define and delimit occasions of conscientious law-breaking. Decisions about the use of illegality and violence in politics live close to an axiomatic background, but should also depend upon personal moral conscience and common-sense. Law-breaking in a bad unfree state is more excusable than law-breaking in a good free state, where laws and situations can be changed by legal unviolent means. Yet in any state there may be strong grounds for preferring respect for law (even bad law) to alternatives. (See Hobbes.) A habit of law-breaking is a dangerous tendency and conscientious protesting may seem to licence irresponsible, even criminal, activities. (We must be deemed potential knaves.) These are familiar problems. It is not the fundamental duty of the state to make us good. It is the fundamental task of each person to make himself good. Hobbes also suggests that moral philosophers ought to realise that 'virtues' are 'good' because they are 'the means of peaceable, sociable and comfortable living'. (*Leviathan*, Part I, ch. 15.) It is, one might say, the duty of the state to make 'decent arrangements'. Politics concerns large crude decisions affecting large numbers of heterogeneous people. Politics is about other people with individual interests. Think how crude and clumsy all government is and has to be. Of course in modern democracies the liberal (political) individual and the moral individual constantly overlap, as when we argue about pornography, pacifism, abortion, medicine and hundreds of topics which are in the newspapers every day. The discussion and clarification of such topics are often proper tasks of the democratic liberal state, in the context of decisions about what is and what is not 'the state's business' or 'the government's duty'. We recognise and attach importance to sometimes unclear distinctions between public political standards and private personal morals, between sin and crime, between the claims of happiness and goodness, and equality and freedom. We in Britain have many rules to prevent people killing themselves and others in cars, but no rules to prevent them killing themselves and others on mountains; whereas in Russia there are much stricter rules about who is allowed to go up mountains. Reflection upon this could lead us back to the bases of political theory. Modern states, if they are rich enough, may tend toward becoming 'nannies' to their citizens, and we argue about how far this tendency should go. The Welfare State is a good thing, but can it go too far? When does a nanny become a tyrant? We activate the value of freedom against the value of happiness, and for this to be possible the master axioms must be separate. The right to be free is not internally connected with the right to be happy. The explanation that is 'cut off' would be one that attempts to connect where connection is not appropriate, for instance by redefining freedom and happiness in relation to a single social ideal. Faced with political theorising (if told for instance that in obedience to the General Will we are, with Rousseau, 'forced to be free'), we appeal to ideas of freedom or happiness as *sui generis*. This lack of connection, characteristic of liberal political thinking, should be *contrasted* with the way in which private morality discovers the interconnection of the virtues. The lack of internal relations acts as a defence of the citizen as Hobbesian individual. That we, politically, 'are' such individuals is axiomatic.

Citizens of liberal democratic states can argue about whether to be more free and less comfortable or more happy and less rich or more equal and less free and so on and so on, and a great many different kinds of considerations bear on these arguments which are made possible by a certain fundamental *refusal of system*. It is characteristic of totalitarian states to refuse access to such choices and to prohibit such discussion, intimating to the citizenry that (for instance) the system which makes them orderly is also making them happy and good. A denial of human variety and the rights which the *fact* of variety carries, the is-and-ought-to-be aspect of human life, lies behind totalitarian reasoning, which has also relied upon a claim to be scientific and therefore efficient. How false such a claim could be has been demonstrated by the fate of the Soviet Union. The manifest lies involved in the imposition of such a view can produce cynicism and despair, or else simply perpetuate some demoralising simplicity or lack of education in the society. When I was in China I asked a question about 'homosexuality', a word with which our otherwise excellent interpreter was unfamiliar. When I explained its meaning in other terms, I was told that there was no such thing in China. So if homosexuals do not exist they clearly cannot have rights. The famous *Thoughts of Mao Tse-tung* and other pronouncements in this style illustrate a conceptual impoverishment or concept-starvation, a thinking-by-slogans. Orwell's book *1984* exhibits such impoverishment as deliberately fostered by cynical rulers. Of course ordinary idealistic persons can, in various circumstances, readily embrace all kinds of simplified nonsense; and a few crude ideas can inspire unselfish citizens to render genuine service to their society. But in politics a great many people can be led by a few simple notions to bring about a lot of irreversible change. Consider the simplicity of the slogans which prompted or 'justified' the Red Guards who helped to destroy Chinese society in the 'Cultural Revolution'. In any state there are always plenty of motives for destructive activity, but concept-starvation makes it easier for a few leaders to turn their citizens into a centrally directed herd. How true it is that nevertheless the human spirit cannot be quenched is proved by the events of 1989 in eastern Europe which, when I wrote the above, lay in the future.

Mao Tse-tung said that the idea of human nature was a bourgeois concept. Perhaps he had in mind the kind of axiomatic non-systematic non-totalising political theory of which I have been speaking, which tends to disrupt tyranny by a conception of the idiosyncratic individual as valuable *per se*. 'Stop. You can't do that to a person.' Subsequent Marxist explanations of, or apologies for, the Chinese Cultural Revolution, later said to have been a 'mistake', 'incorrect', 'over-enthusiastic', ignored the fact that innumerable people were murdered during this period, and thousands, millions, had their lives permanently ruined. The price paid by individuals for 'socially desirable' change must never be lost sight of. Of course our sort of democracy cannot at present live everywhere (and we cannot know how or whether it will survive into the more than ever unpredictable future) but humane ideas and enlightened axioms and conceptions of human rights can. History is indeed a slaughterhouse and this is in numerous ways an inhospitable planet. Draconian measures may be necessary to prevent people from starving, for example. This too must be remembered. But herein the notion of the fundamental existence and value of the individual should not be, need not be, and ultimately cannot be obliterated. This is where the negativising appeal to an idea of human nature comes in. You must not do this. There are barriers of principle which are not reducible to system; and this irreducibility confronts political systems and theoretical and metaphysical systems of any sort, including religious ones. Human beings are valuable, not because they are created by God or because they are rational beings or good citizens, but because they are human beings.

Slogans, by contrast, are simplified political directives or battle cries addressed to immediate objectives. 'All power to the soviets': a crucial moment in the Russian Revolution aimed at preventing the establishment of bourgeois democracy. 'Struggle, criticism, transformation', the slogan of the Chinese Cultural Revolution. 'In carrying out the proletarian revolution in education it is essential to have working-class leadership . . . The workers' propaganda teams should stay permanently in the schools and take part in fulfilling all the tasks of struggle – criticism–transformation within them.' (*China: the Impact of the Cultural Revolution*, ed. Bill Brugger, p. 97.) Also, and differently, in England in World War II, 'Give us the tools and we will finish the job.' In ordinary (peacetime) situations democracies are not much given to exhortation or direction by slogan. (Except at general elections.) Sloganising has rather become the property of the advertising industry. What I mean by axioms are isolated unsystematic moral insights which arise out of and refer to a general conception of human nature such as civilised societies have gradually generated. Axioms are outside the main moral spectrum, a different and unconnected colour. Utilitarian thinking is in effect axiomatic: attempts to present utilitarianism as a complete moral philosophy fail, for a number of well-known reasons, such as that it does not give a coherent account of virtue. But utilitarian considerations are in general *prima facie* relevant because we all understand the importance of happiness. It is always *a*, not necessarily final, argument against doing something to someone, that it will reduce his happiness. Of course the formulation of such arguments may be difficult because of lack of agreement about the concept. ('But he *enjoys* being miserable' etc. etc.) Did the Greeks have the 'general conception of human nature' referred to above? Yes, only slaves and barbarians did not count. Have we got such a conception? Yes, which may also have, when in use, its tacit exceptions and limitations. General principles of this type may remind us of Kant and of the large maxims which he considers (in the *Grundlegung*) to be so obvious. Do not lie. Be compassionate. Develop your talents. Do not take your life. Kant however regards such commands as fundamental utterances of Reason and thus integrates them into his total system of morality. These orders given 'as if by God' can be internalised as rational moral principles and we may or may not conceive of reason as a single system. (Most modern Kantians probably do not.) We may adopt such principles without holding any particular view of God or reason. One might speak here of 'intuition'; but people who hold unsystematic political or socio-political principles, for instance about capital punishment or abortion or euthanasia, can usually say quite a lot of quite sensible things about them. References to 'reason' as to a single and unified authority are usually rhetorical and otiose and should be victims of Occam's razor. Of course individuals may relate such principles to (for instance) their religious beliefs. But in the context of political argument and activity the absence of metaphysical background is the point. The successful use of persuasion depends on a certain waiving of dogma. A good (decent) state, full of active citizens with a vast variety of views and interests, must *preserve* a central arena of discussion and reflection wherein differences and individuality are taken for granted. (For instance, religious differences.) Here there are no authoritarian final arbiters, certainly not God, Reason or History. Here general good will, *consent*, maintains a kind of justice which is 'intuitively' understood. That this is, in western democracies, something 'obvious' is important too. It is also fragile.

The term 'axiom' points to piecemeal moral insights or principles which are active in political contexts. How far the concept of a political context may reach into peripheral areas, I shall consider later. Talk about 'natural law' and 'natural rights' is axiomatic in this sense, but cannot be accused of being *derived* from an idea of human nature. There is, rather, a mutual relationship between particular insights and general idea. As we 'come to see' that certain things are good and some intolerable these convictions are built into a wider conception of how humans should behave in their societies. It was obvious to Schopenhauer that cruelty to animals was wrong. It was not obvious to previous other and greater philosophers. It is only now becoming obvious in advanced free societies that women have certain rights, including that of being priests. Dr Johnson found the idea of a woman preacher ridiculous. Here again, it would be wrong to attempt to derive these changes from a scientific theory of history. Of course societies change, not as predictably as some might think or wish to think. Who predicted the 1989 liberal revolutions in eastern Europe? History can bring good as well as terrible surprises. Vast complex unplanned changes reveal new vistas and prompt new moral judgments; and of course some of the machinery of this change can be (variously) explained, even controlled. But there is no prior or fundamental metaphysical or scientific system which radically explains it all or provides its general justifications. This is an important commonplace of liberal political thinking. Axioms must be mutually independent (externally not internally related) in order to be able intelligibly to fight each other and to go on existing in defeat. Within a general consensus about what things are right and proper, different views can contend in a reasonable manner. W. D. Ross (*The Right and the Good*), a self-styled intuitionist, used the term '*prima facie* obligation' to picture this aspect of morality, but offered his neo-Kantian theory ('deontological intuitionism') as an explanation of the whole of morals. Some liberal political axioms might appear to indicate *prima facie* obligations (in legislation, always consider happiness), others may be uttered as absolutes (torture is wrong).

Someone may say, so you want to distinguish rough general rules of morality, such as constitute important inspirations and barriers in politics and public life, from a private progressive spirituality, connected with a total change of consciousness? Yes, but the situation is more complicated, since (political) axioms must also be distinguished from imperatives of duty. I certainly want to suggest that the spiritual pilgrimage (transformation–renewal–salvation) is the centre and essence of morality, upon whose success and well-being the health of other kinds of moral reaction and thinking is likely to depend. 'Axioms' appear as part of an assertion that of course political activity is, among other things, or is often, moral activity, but one where values are dealt with in a different way. The idea of a separation is better here than that of a dialectic or a tension within a totality: it both emphasises a very general (liberal) political value, and also helps to make sense of political scenes. Those who organise society so that people do not starve, or so that certain rights are respected, may be acting properly, and we may neither know nor care about their spiritual life or their motives. They too may not care, and may thereby incur criticism from *other* points of view. In politics a dash of cynicism may be an aspect of tolerance, as it is in the thought of Hobbes and Hume. Don't expect too much of the citizens. Everyone is an egoist. Everyone seeks his own private happiness, why not. The privacy and inwardness of the individual are here seen as the justified pursuit of private not social ends. This is the sense in which everyone may reasonably be deemed a knave, and the proper object of every man's will is some good to himself. Government should legislate with human frailty well in view. The citizen whom Hobbes's theory of sovereignty protects is an irreducible atom composed of private ends. The whole cannot be saved. Society must be thought of as a bad job to be made the best of. 'The social domain is unreservedly that of the Prince of this World. We have but one duty in regard to the social element, which is to try to limit the evil contained therein.' Simone Weil, *Notebooks*, p. 296. The individual is contingent, full of private stuff and accidental rubble, and must be accepted as such, not thought of as an embryonic rational agent, or in terms of some social theory. Sovereigns envisaged by Hobbes were of course not endowed with the technical expertise of the modern dictator, they could not *get at* their subjects in the ways now available to technological sovereigns, who may require every citizen to have a television set. So it did not matter too much to Hobbes who the sovereign was, so long as he was strong enough to govern, since he would be unable to destroy the egoistic core of his subject individuals. Looking to the future: the Hobbesian concept of *sovereignty* assumes the existence of the traditional nation state. Will this continue in a more closely integrated world?

So, in political public life, axioms protect values which are irreducible to each other. Axioms can be more or less local, more or less general or particular. No theory could set up a 'king' axiom. 'Be tolerant'? Yet a democratic society is often rightly intolerant. Compare, in morality at large, setting up a single moral guide such as 'Be loving'. Christ reduced the Ten Commandments to two, and moral philosophers have often looked for a single principle. Political liberalism is pluralism, the cost must always be counted and there are different ways of counting. Thinking about politics is in certain special respects different from thinking about private morals. One may be ruthless with oneself but not with others. An acknowledgement of irreducible contingency is an acknowledgement of the rights of individuals. Politics must be concerned with happiness, and is a natural and proper sphere for utilitarian values. Bentham, and James and J. S. Mill, and Marx and Engels were deeply moved by the spectacle of suffering, especially that of the industrial working class. So was Schopenhauer who speaks of work in cotton mills as 'purchasing dearly the satisfaction of drawing breath'. Its utilitarian content made Marxism attractive to people in democratic countries who were not concerned with the whole theory; and many people who were not Marxists became impatient with traditional politics and devoted their idealism to the relief of suffering and the prevention of damage. Help the poor, help the hungry, protect wildlife, ban nuclear waste, save the countryside, save the planet, save whales. These are good political ends, but may replace and exclude wider and deeper thinking about the whole of the political sphere. What will fill the vacuum made by the disappearance of Marxism?

These thoughts about the place of utilitarian thinking in politics may prompt reflection upon later developments in Marxism, in particular the work of the Frankfurt School. It was Marcuse and not Sartre who made Marxism (for a time) a new popular moral philosophy. These thinkers between them divided Marxism into a modified traditional orthodoxy in the style of Lukács and Marcuse, and a neo-Marxist line of more freely philosophical criticism of the thought of Hegel and Marx, which might be said to lead Marxism, deformed by its pragmatic connections with existing regimes, back into the general tradition of European philosophy, where it may cease, or has ceased, to be Marxism. The latter line of thought is represented by Horkheimer, Benjamin and Adorno and I am here mainly concerned with Adorno, who regarded himself as a Marxist, and whose fundamental philosophical idea may be entitled 'the primacy of the object'. Adorno takes his argument back into a critique of Kant's and Hegel's picture of the relation of subject and object. As Adorno sees it, Kant's subject, composed of rigid rules prescribing the form of the object, cannot be regarded as an original spontaneous upsurge of subjectivity, but is really an object itself, framed in the image of the object which it constitutes. The Kantian Thing-in-itself, the inaccessible 'given', is attractive as suggesting the contingent independence of the object, but is not a genuine object for the subject because of its lack of relation with it. Hegel's correction of Kant over-privileges the subject, or *per contra* abolishes the subject by envisaging an ultimate totality in which subject and object merge. The subject is *meanwhile* given complete power over the object, and the dialectical progression is a continual reconstitution of the object by the subject in the interests of a more complete domination. Adorno's 'negative dialectic', which denies the idea of 'the totality', aims to introduce contingency and doubt into this picture, to portray the object as primary, while retaining the necessary connection between subject and object to be thought of as an unsystematic dialectical tension. Adorno here also uses the term 'field of force'. In Kant, contingency is represented by the general, abstract, idea of a timeless unknown, and by the mechanical causality which rules the phenomenal world, including the psychological empirical self. In Hegel contingency progressively vanishes into the ideal totality, as the opposing object is constantly found to be an intelligible part of the subject. In this picture the all-powerful subject might just as well be seen as nothing, a mere moment in the construction of some final perfectly clarified super-object: a thought 'not far from Hegel's mind', as Adorno suggests. Adorno wishes, as metaphysical philosopher and neo-Marxist, to alter these two misleading conceptions and to give a more true, more realistic, account of the relation between subject and object. This he does eloquently and succinctly in his essay 'Subject and Object' (in German in his *Stachworte*, in English in *The Essential Frankfurt School Reader*). The separation of subject and object is both real and illusory. There is the real experienced dichotomy of the human condition; but this separation must not be hypostatised, set up as something invariant and rigid. One might use the world 'reified' here. The relation is 'dialectical' but not in Hegel's sense. Adorno's opponents, it turns out, are not only Kant and Hegel, but also reductionism, positivism, popular (or 'philosophised') science, Freud, and most understandings of Marxism. The object must not be swallowed by the subject; equally it must not be set up as if entirely independent of the subject. This dialectical give-and-take mutually necessary relation between subject and object is not to be understood in a Hegelian manner as taking place within any sovereign determining totality, whether Hegel's Absolute, or a Marxist idea of history as a story with a happy ending. 'The whole is false.' It is in this sense that the dialectic is 'negative': there is no complete self-reflection, no final unity of subject and object, our world is irreducibly contingent. This stand taken by Adorno, which put him at odds with orthodox Marxism, is expressive of the most general philosophical objections to idealism. However, Adorno retains a special place in political thinking for the purely Utopian aspect of Marxism. All thought and knowledge should carry an awareness of its own social conditioning, and of the suffering of individuals, and include the persistent hope of a much better society.

Utilitarian values and ideas informed and supported Marxism from the days of Engels's Manchester and of the philosophy of Bentham. More recently a not unrelated motive was a general hatred of western 'bourgeois' society. Loathing for our society, for its injustice, its vulgarity, its low moral standards, its permissiveness, its hedonism, its materialism, its indifference to the crippled lives which its arrangements bring about, can make people impatient with the weak muddled procedures of democratic government, and angry with the numerous forces, overt or hidden, which tend to keep things as they are. In such arguments, the terms 'bourgeois' and 'late capitalist' are sometimes used to accuse, not only evils which exist also in non-democratic societies, but those which attend upon the human condition itself. It is a paradox of our scene that, inspired by this hatred of the west, intellectuals and artists could (while enjoying the freedom of bourgeois society) embrace the creeds of other societies in which they were well aware that they and their works would be suppressed. Here faithfulness to Marxism whatever the situation and outlook, whatever the record of self-professed Marxist states, appeared as an almost religious last resource of those who could see nothing but evil in the western world. Adorno is (was) a metaphysician and a moralist, one might call him a puritan, he was also an artist, a pianist, a composer, a writer upon the sociology of music. He regarded good art as a redeemer of society. By good art he did not mean art which preached a revolutionary creed (as in the 'committed literature' of Sartre and Brecht), but free individual art which, through its aesthetic honesty and power, could (incidentally) criticise society by exhibiting the deep horrors and sufferings of the human lot (as in Kafka and Beckett). (I like this preference.) For other reasons he was for Schoenberg and against Stravinsky. (Stravinsky was a sentimental romantic.) Adorno objected to Kierkegaard's view which placed 'the aesthetic' at the lowest stage of moral development, below the ethical and the religious, a demotion shared in effect by Hegel.

One may ask, why was all this supposed to be Marxism? Had the

Frankfurt School not shredded up Marxism to such a degree that it could only represent a kind of mood or tendency, if it was not a cover for an authoritarian political programme? The reflections of these *prophetic* neo-Marxists are certainly interesting (more so than those of Sartre in *Critique de la Raison dialectique*), but diverse, in that some (for instance Lukács, Marcuse) adhered to traditional Marxist concepts and programmes (revolution, class consciousness, the liberating role of the proletariat), whereas others (for instance Horkheimer, Benjamin, Adorno) appeared more like independently minded left-wing critics of western society. The 1989 revolutions were effected largely by courageous people uninterested in theory. But there were (for instance in Czechoslovakia) some intellectual leaders. In the long stifling interim the Frankfurt School provided at least a little fresh air. Adorno himself (as I said earlier) was accused by other Marxists of being an ivory tower intellectual, remote from the daily details (*praxis*) of the working-class struggle. Indeed he seems at times to be using Marxist formulations as *imagery* whereby to illuminate the evils of existing societies. He does not claim that any actual society is without them. Marxist thinkers have tried to rewrite the *Phenomenology of Mind*, and reflection on Marx and Hegel certainly led Adorno to his own post-Hegelian metaphysic which has its interest whether or not it can bear a definite political message. For instance, Adorno's views may be seen as a prophetic critique of the Idealist aspects of Derrida's structuralism wherein the subject, as 'language', swallows the contingent object or objects, and becomes an object itself. Adorno speaks eloquently of the 'withering of the subject' under late capitalism, its loss of spontaneity, awareness, truth, its shrunken consciousness, and contrasts this time with the golden age of bourgeois society which produced the great humanistic art of Beethoven and the great literature of the earlier Romantics. This general contrast is a familiar one, not noted only by Marxists. (Why no great novels now, why no great pictures, why no great music?) It is doubtless true that modern industrial society, with all its vast diversity of entertainments and mass of incoherent information (of which television may serve as image and example), has radically changed people's lives and mode of being, bringing some benefits and doing much damage. 'Facts' proliferate, values fade, religion fades, our sense of truth is shaken. A confidence and a certainty, some might say a baseless optimism, carried for us by religion and art, seems no longer present. Benjamin sees the inability of writers to tell stories as a symptom of the fact that 'experience has fallen in value'. (*Illuminations*, essay on Leskov.) Experience, consciousness (where we live) ought to be, it is argued, and increasingly is not, a kind of recollection (*anamnesis*), a calm lively awareness which joins past present and future. These words, consciousness and experience, are constantly used by Adorno in a metaphysical sense to indicate the deep places of human existence. These are the terms which are banished, these are the concepts which are obliterated, by structuralism. Adorno's use of the words is neither Hegelian (as in 'the unhappy consciousness') nor Marxist (as in 'class consciousness') nor of course Freudian or Husserlian. His hostility to the ideas of 'totality', and 'identity' (of subject and object), separate him from Hegel, he rejects the Marxist picture of the proletariat as the redeeming class, he doubts whether alienation can ever be overcome (probably it belongs to human nature), he has no patience with Husserl's essences (his book *Against Epistemology* is largely a refutation of Husserl), or with Freud's conception of the soul which denies religion, instinct and pleasure (*Minima Moralia* 37). He expresses a maverick neo-Hegelian neo-Marxist kind of lucid desperation which is absolutely uncynical. He retains an undogmatic theological religious sense, but has no sympathy with Heidegger's quasi-theological 'ontology'.

Adorno chided everybody, and his positive and passionately held view is not easy to formulate. He expounds what may be called a new philosophy of consciousness. His philosophy lives, dangerously but also fruitfully, in proximity to an ascetic puritanical moral rage, an attachment to some items in the structure and vocabulary of Marxism, and a feeling that human suffering is the only important thing and makes nonsense of everything else. His remark that 'to write poetry after Auschwitz is barbarism' has been much quoted. His main philosophical tenet is 'the primacy of the object', an idea which is explained in relation to consciousness and experience, involving a fundamental doctrine of truth and of the redeeming role of art. Reading Adorno's criticisms of Husserl one may be reminded of Katsuki Sekida, and indeed, in Adorno's work generally, of Buddhist ideas, such as 'pure cognition'. Not only in Kant and Hegel, but (as Adorno holds) in philosophy generally, the role of the subject has been overstated. The subject is degraded by lack of reverence for the object. This is true also of anti-idealist, positivist, theories which, professing objectivity, import a selection of quasi-scientific or philosophical-technical ideas of the world into the subject thus constituted as authoritarian and all-powerful. A similar charge might be levelled at neo-positivist theories of language. Structuralist thinkers, invoking scientific models, 'lose' the subject in the 'objective network' of language, but 'find' it again as omniscient philosopher and scientific literary critic. This is the scene within which consciousness vanishes. The subject annexes to itself a particular concept of objectivity and so of object; herein the object is lost, and the subject is lost too. This sort of loss may indeed be called alienation. The (partial) cure is a change of consciousness in the direction of a patient truthfulness, a selflessness which is at the same time a self-being. There is no metaphysical sovereign power (such as that which haunts Heidegger), no ultimate identity of subject and object, no philosophical beatific vision. All this thinking takes place in an incomplete partly (largely?) unintelligible contingent world. Emphasis upon this aspect of Adorno's view takes him out of Marxism. The quality of his concern with human suffering tends, paradoxically, to do this too: to consider suffering is to consider what is individual, private, unintelligible and contingent. The relation of subject and object is dialectical in a negative sense which is observant of contingency; the relation is one of mutual need, but neither can dominate or 'catch' the other. The subject needs the object more than the object needs the subject; no subject without object, conceivably object without subject, and this 'strength' of the object is an important ingredient in reflection of truth. (This too is a contradiction of Heidegger.) In Idealism truth vanishes together with contingency and the individual mind; structuralist thought tends to be Idealist. The idea of man's domination of nature, and of the exploitation of nature, tolerated in Marxist thinking too, provides another case and image of the hubris of the subject. Adorno turns to art as to a place where we can see the meaning of respect for the object and of a truthful properly constituted subject–object relation. Art respects nature and all its details. Moreover the change of consciousness here in question is also productive of (very important in Adorno's view) *true happiness*, which is *denied* to people by bad societies, by pleasure-loving late capitalism, and by oppressive truth-denying Marxist states. His 'redeeming art' is of course not the cosy kitsch of what he calls the 'culture industry', a phrase used also to make a sweeping judgment against much so-called serious or high-brow art; nor is it dogmatic didactic socialist art with a message, either arcane or popular. Adorno wishes to praise and point out as an

[ 374 ]

example a kind of meticulously artful truthful art which exhibits the disintegration of the world and the pain of crippled alienated beings, as in, often mentioned, Kafka and Beckett. (*Not* Brecht.) Perhaps (it seems) there is not much art which reaches this standard. Adorno also, referring to Benjamin's observation that history is always written from the victor's point of view, and that 'empathy with the victor invariably benefits the present rulers', is prepared to forgive and cherish innocent 'cross-grained, opaque, unassimilated material which . . . has outwitted the historical dynamic'. This is to 'bring the intentionless within the realm of concepts' and 'think at the same time both dialectically and undialectically'. An example he gives here is remarkable, given Adorno's stern aesthetic asceticism. 'In Satie's pert and puerile piano pieces there are flashes of experience undreamed of by the school of Schoenberg, with all its rigour and all the pathos of musical development behind it. The very grandeur of logical deductions may inadvertently take on a provincial quality.' (*Minima Moralia* 98.) This is an interesting concession.

Adorno is a political thinker who wishes to bring about radical change. He is also a philosopher, with a zest for metaphysics, who is at home in the western philosophical tradition. His difficulty is not altogether unlike that of demythologising Christian theologians who are inspired by religious theological thinking, and by warm intuitions of faith, to go onward beyond the bounds of traditional Christianity. After all, Christianity has always been going 'beyond its bounds'. They want to keep the title of Christian, not only out of loyalty and in order to retain authority and influence, but because they believe that their insights are true, or *the* true, understandings of the doctrine. The doctrine and its precious future is in their hands. A difference between the two cases is that, although the church is a visible social institution, religion concerns the individual soul, while Marxism, whatever its Utopian hopes for the development of new individuals, had to retain a pragmatic concern about possible policies. Adorno rejected aspirations of philosophy toward the condition of science, as seen for instance in positivism, structuralism, Husserl. (Even analytical philosophy *à l'anglaise*, as seen for instance in the work of J. L. Austin, has an air of scientific reductionism.) He, together with many others who wanted to present Marxism as a moral philosophy, profited from the rediscovery of Marx's early writings, with their Utopian tone and emphasis upon alienation. Marcuse's *One-Dimensional Man* was the new best-seller of the moral philosophy of Marx. This early moral Marx, more given to philosophical reflection, is to be contrasted with the later more scientific Marx who, less concerned with morals, is struggling to *solve the problem* of how to create a totally viable and efficient economic system. (This problem, it appears, is still with us.) The scientific aspect of Marxism remained essential, indeed primary. A Marxist, however given to philosophising and moralising, was expected to retain some belief in 'scientific socialism', and with this a claim to the generality and objectivity characteristic of science. At this point the demythologising Marxist thinker may feel inclined, or bound, to 'lose hold'. The analogy with a demythologised religion is of course incomplete. A Marxist who becomes a liberal is making a radical change in his political views. A Christian who loses belief in God and resurrection and immortality, while remaining religious, is not necessarily making a radical change in his value world. The difference between morals and politics is different from the difference between (for instance) Christianity and Buddhism. In practice, differences of religious style, though in a sense superficial, stir such deep emotions that those who lose hold of the traditional dogmatic structures of their religion are often unable to carry the concept further and lose religion altogether.

Adorno's deepest criticisms of contemporary society are not specifically Marxist but those of an enlightened and civilised western thinker. He is more evidently a neo-Hegelian than a neo-Marxist. As a neo-Hegelian he is inspired, like many other students of Hegel, by an anti-Hegelian concern for the individual, for the contingent aspects of the world which are lost in the Idealist totality. This concern prompts a corrective analysis of the central Hegelian subject–object relation, in favour of the privileges of the object. This instinct in favour of the contingent, and the 'rights' of what is 'given', what is attended to or referred to or described, the object of cognition, expresses a major objection which can also be brought against the totalising metaphysic of structuralism. 'The given' (contingent, unordered, unconceptualised reality), made inaccessible by Kant except as processed by a rigid subject made in the image of its constituted object, swallowed up by Hegel's evolving all-powerful subject, degraded by Sartre into unassimilable matter inducing disgust and despair, dissolved by structuralists into the 'objective' network of language, and in vulgar dogmatic Marxism ground up by the inevitable historical process with its Utopian culmination, should be restored to the position accorded to it by common-sense and by art, and one might add by western liberal morality and ordinary religious attitudes when these are not deformed by (certain) philosophies. The object, the given, is the magnet of the artist, his inspiration, his joy, also his despair, and that of all of us in our role as artist-thinkers. Such a defence of the object, not only of course by Adorno, but by a variety of thinkers and writers, has as its essential counterpart a defence of the ordinary and traditional conception of *truth*, threatened by Hegel, Heidegger, historicism, and pseudo-science, not only structuralist but post-Freudian. This 'ordinary' truth is also the truth of art, as it emerges when the artist, confronted by the independent other, imagines, that is, *thinks*. Flourishing in this environment are innumerable concerns and respects for innumerable others which civilisation and morality and religion and enlightened politics have gradually and not without difficulty developed: concern for the contingent individual, as social unit, as human person, as idea, as work of art, as plant, as animal, as planet. The details of our world deserve our respectful and loving attention, as artists have always known. There is an attentive patient delay of judgment, a kind of humble agnosticism, which lets the object be. With this goes a perception of the reality and real nature of suffering and a horror of cruelty. Sufferers, victims of injustice and wanton cruelty, are individuals, with unique individual fates. A Marxism which could refer, in a scientific tone of voice, to 'the liquidation of the kulaks' as an incidental necessity in a Utopian programme, is an abominable theory. Sartre's *Nausée* expresses the horror of those who can no longer love or attend to or even really *see* the contingent, and fear it as a threat to their imaginary freedom and self-regarding 'authenticity'. Perception itself must always be held to be an essential part of cognition, not to be swallowed casually into some posited procession of ideas. Modern industrial mass-productive society impairs our power to perceive, not least by continual television. Adorno asks why we are expected to enjoy realistically presented acts of violence as part of our daily entertainment. On the other hand, turning against certain of our 'moral guardians', he attacks a 'false inwardness', as of the 'cantingly emancipated theologian', who 'neutralises the element of danger by internalisation', enjoying a spiritual struggle which, seemingly 'concerned', is only concerned with self. (*Minima Moralia* 87.) Equally self-centred and 'heroic' is the 'authenticity' and 'genuineness' of the existential subject who in seeking personal liberation loses the world of detail and other. Adorno accuses both Kierkegaard and Nietzsche on these two latter counts.

The idea of Utopia is a danger in politics, it hints at a rectification of a primal fault, a perfect unity, it is impatient of contingency. The assertion of contingency, the rights of the object, the rights of the individual, these are connected. The 'perfect state' is an illusory unity. Morality enters politics in an unsystematic way and must carry an awareness of the particular non-totality of political situations. A totalitarian state, intolerant of oddity, loses truth. Many kinds of thought, without claiming the eternal, are indifferent to what is local; one cannot properly generalise about the social duties of all serious thinkers. To argue in this way is to use Adorno's metaphysical ideas against his Marxist ideas. Adorno offers as the centre of his reflection a view of consciousness which is not scientific, either psychologically or sociologically. The Utopianism which leads him to picture a 'good happiness' which is infinitely happier than anything we now call by that name, is a moral aspiration, not a prediction about a perfect society. It is a message to the individual. Even the idea of dialectic, rethought by Adorno, may tie his thinking too closely to a Hegelian model. A view not unlike his might be better stated in a less 'engaged' terminology. Moral existence and moral change connect with, must be explained by use of, the concept of, quality of consciousness. The rescue of the idea of consciousness from its Hegelian and Marxist limitations is an important move. The consciousness in question is that of individuals, not of groups or classes. An emphasis upon consciousness as *perception*, and awareness of detail, presents it as the property of the individual. A good man is truthful, loving, brave, concerned for others, he has overcome the barriers of egoism, he sees clearly, he perceives details (and so on). If we try to describe him we are led also to reflect upon his states of consciousness, his capacity for recollection, for reflection, for *attention*, for the deep intuitive syntheses of moral vision. 'The layer of unpremeditatedness, freedom from intentions, on which alone intentions flourish.' (*Minima Moralia* 150.) Such ideas may be *placed* by philosophy though they cannot be systematised or set up as a clear definition. Philosophy puts things in places and surrounds them with many considerations. The image of a field of force is good here. A passage in Adorno's essay on 'Subject and Object', which presents succinct objections to the views of both Kant and Hegel, also expresses eloquently the quality of a truthful consciousness:

'The subject's key position in cognition is empirical, not formal; what Kant calls formation is essentially deformation. The preponderant exertion of knowledge is destruction of its usual exertion, that of using violence against the object. Approaching knowledge of the object is the act in which the subject rends the veil it is weaving around the object. It can do this only where, fearlessly passive, it entrusts itself to its own experience. In places where subjective reason scents subjective contingency, the primacy of object is shimmering through – whatever in the object is not a subjective admixture. The subject is the object's agent, not its constituent; this fact has consequences for the relation of theory and practice.'

(See *The Essential Frankfurt School Reader*,
ed. Andrew Arato and Eike Gebhardt.)

The 'rending of the veil', the 'fearlessly passive' trust of 'experience', these phrases express a deep, and indeed familiar, moral and moral-religious insight; and the last sentence separates the writer from the prime tenets of Marxist theory and practice.

Political and also legal axiomatic thinking can be important in the various group situations which I mentioned above; but where do such situations end? The church synod, the parish council, the college meeting, the local dramatic society, the family conference, the family row, parents and children? Appeal to separated 'abstract' axioms or rules may have their place in all of these. Then someone will say, surely they have their place everywhere? Is one not now simply referring to the concept of duty? Even if axiomatic rulings are not the deep centre of morality they are its effective crystallisation. Let us look at some cases. Strict Protestants who live with a sense of close literal communication with a personal God may be seen by the outsider as, or may feel themselves to be, living with very definite and general rules. 'Do not lie' means *do not lie*. Such people help us to understand the character of Jeanie Deans in Scott's novel *The Heart of Midlothian*, or of Isabella in *Measure for Measure*. But the place of rules in such lives is unlike

[ 379 ]

the place of axioms in law or politics. If a rule goes deep enough, is surrounded by enough felt or reflective moral or spiritual 'tissue', it is not really a rule, for this service is perfect freedom; and yet, given the frailty of human nature, one is perhaps wise to regard it as, and likely sometimes to feel it as, a rule; whereas axioms are effective through being impersonal and abstract. The internalisation of a rule from the nursery onward is accompanied by the growth of a world. The progressive result for an individual of not lying is that he lives in a particular sort of scene, his patterns of cognition and sensibility are different from those (most of us) who are less careful in this respect. We are perhaps too ready to associate strict morals with rigid and intolerant attitudes, perhaps because we notice the strictness when it is associated with censure. Kant tells us that we ought to tell the truth even to a would-be murderer who asks the whereabouts (which we know) of his intended victim. Kant explains this in an article 'On a supposed duty to lie from altruistic motives' written in reply to Benjamin Constant who had objected to Kant's (already expressed) view that truthfulness is an unconditional duty which holds in all circumstances. Constant says that 'The moral principle "It is a duty to tell the truth" would make society impossible if it were taken singly and unconditionally'. He goes on to say that it is only our duty to tell the truth to those who have a right to the truth, which a violent man would not have. (Schopenhauer agrees.) Kant replies that all men, as rational beings, have this right, one should address the *reason* of the would-be murderer, and any lie harms another person, if not some individual then mankind generally, since it damages our sense of moral law. He adds that if you lie you are morally and also legally responsible for the results, which may be the reverse of your intention: a problem explored in a short story by Sartre called *Le Mur*. In such extreme situations most of us would probably side with Constant, while also regarding 'Do not lie' as a very important *prima facie* rule and one which, among human obligations, stands out with a certain clarity. We may note that both Jeanie Deans and Isabella are saved by their authors from what appeared to be the terrible consequences of their truthful intransigence. Those who (again probably most of us) justify some social lying on utilitarian grounds should certainly reflect that habitual lying of any kind can breed a more general indifference to truth. We might compare this case with that of malicious mockery which is tolerated in polite society, and recall here the stern remarks made about laughter by

Plato in the *Republic* and the *Laws*. Malicious merriment, apparently harmless, can foster more general and sinister spiritual ills: cynicism, cruelty, hatred. The person who regularly refrains from joining in spiteful gossip may be said to 'make it a rule' not to; or we may discern in him an instinctive fastidious dislike of, a shrinking from, such conduct. (It is at the least 'bad form'.) Certainly such a person lives 'in a different world' and sees other people with a difference. The seen world, strengthening the more virtuous desires, reinforces the rule, scarcely now properly called a rule. Of course a vote against malicious laughter is not a vote against laughter, although the border-line involved may sometimes be unclear. Plato's remarks seem less tiresomely puritanical if we also recall the amazingly open happy sunny (Platonic metaphor) atmosphere of the dialogues and how full they are of wit and jokes.

A difference between what I have called, in a political and natural law context, 'axioms', and the ordinary idea of duty (as 'rules'), is that duty merges into, is organically connected with, the hurly-burly of reason-feeling, rule-desire, whereas 'axioms' do not and are not. One could also say that duty recedes into the most private part of personal morality, whereas axioms are instruments of the public scene. Distinctions in philosophy invite attack by regiments of border-line cases. Of course axioms are adopted and employed by individuals who previously and privately, instinctively or reflectively, judged them. The axiom 'in use' lacks the personal particularity of duty, though it may be a man's duty to give public support to an axiomatic formulation. The essential separateness of certain axiomatic values in the area of political thought and political argument and rhetoric is a special and not a general case of a moral pattern. The separateness is to do with the difference between political morality and private morals, and the rough-and-ready unavoidably clumsy and pragmatic nature of the former. Here, moving away from the 'morals and politics' question, though perhaps also throwing light upon it, I want to go on reflecting about the relation of rules to moral cognition. It is said, as a generalisation about moral development, that we learn 'external rules' as a child and then internalise them as values. Or, 'heteronomous subjection' may be followed by 'autonomous rejection', as Tillich suggests has been the fate of the concept of God in the modern world, now felt as an 'external rule' suitable for the nursery. Acceptance and rejection, with appropriate ordering or reordering of the cosmos, may be instinctive or reflective. Moral order is usually not all that orderly, and par-

[ 381 ]

ticular rules, whether learnt in childhood or not, may remain, not fully internalised or integrated with other values, as barriers to certain kinds of conduct. A religious upbringing may leave obstinate traces in a life which, for better or worse, has become remote from such influences. An effect of religion is, often, to make morality attractive, though it can also make it repulsive. Isolated summaries or reminders may appear, pieces of 'abstract morality' out of key with the customary more integrated 'moral world'. Kant's distinction between phenomenal and noumenal lives with Kant's common-sense conviction of the familiarity and obviousness of a sense of duty, and his strong religious sense of the presence of a spiritual reality. Strictly speaking, and evident in the work of neo-Kantians who lack Kant's religious metaphysic and his common-sense, a sharp distinction between fact and value tends to make all morality 'abstract' in relation to an alien world into which no value has been allowed to seep. Socrates's daemon who only told him what not to do may also be seen as an abstract mentor, interfering from elsewhere, although no doubt he was not his only mentor. The voice of duty, announcing the absolute character of certain particular requirements, and their relation to a larger more general world, is often foreign and unwelcome to frail mortals. The concept is both familiar and obvious, and also on reflection vast and ambiguous. In Kant (in the *Grundlegung*) we may see a kind of Protestant (for instance) ethic which envisages the crystallisation out of a mediocre or bad society of a good society guided by very general or rigid rules. Such people would, ideally, live out in the open an unselfish life of moral lucidity and simplicity, and as I said earlier such people exist. There are small 'good societies' of this kind, just as there are others whose rigid morality issues in intolerance and moral conceit. Hawthorne's novel *The Scarlet Letter* depicts the cruelty of such a society, but we may try to observe its merits too. We cannot win all the tricks in the game of morality.

Strictly speaking of course Kant's universal Reason might, while not shedding its universality, offer us rules or maxims of much greater complexity by introducing detailed provisos and specifying particular circumstances. As for instance, 'Always lie to a violent person who, if told the truth, could cause immediate unjustified harm to an innocent person', and so on into more and more detailed cases. Kant would doubtless worry about the inclusion of too much detail because of the danger of self-regarding (heteronomous) specifications creeping in. The end case would consist in the inclusion of one's own character and preferences in the maxim. Of course we readily excuse ourselves as a special case, and unable to resist certain temptations. On the other hand, an aspect of civilised society is the concept of personal character (especially having reference to childhood and environment) as a mitigating circumstance. How far this is carried in particular cases is a moral, and also a legal, problem. (A place where natural law might 'get in'.) Schopenhauer in rejecting Kant's 'duty' as the external heteronomous voice of a postulated God, appears as a theological demythologiser. He refers us away from (what he sees as) this unreflecting undiscriminating narrow-minded voice to the intelligent compassion of the Buddha nature which stirs within each bosom an unselfish concern for other people and a tender and respectful interest in the diversity of the world. Kant's 'universal reason' was a regulative not constitutive idea, its operation was in practice limited by the alien contingent stuff of the phenomenal psyche. It is Hegel's 'reason', with its tempting dream of a potential totality, which retains a philosophical influence. Few non-Hegelian philosophers would now argue in terms of a single faculty of reason. Highly rational people often disagree and it seems better to make use of the ordinary flexible concept of rationality, rather than to define reason as a single system. Even science no longer looks like a single system. But having in mind 'ordinary rationality' is it plausible to suggest that morality consists of rational rules? On the one hand, we are influenced in many situations by very general rules felt as external. On the other hand a 'sense of duty' may exist at any level of generality in the form of a special kind of *certainty* about the absolute importance of morals, and so of *particular* moral acts. Schopenhauer's dismissal fails to regard this distinction. The idea of a network of ordinary duties is an extremely important aspect of morals, it goes with a sense of being always on duty, a conscript not a gentleman volunteer. The actual functioning of this duty-sense is another matter. Also it would be difficult to assert that everyone 'ought' to recognise the concept of duty and the net of duties, on pain of being called (in some sense) morally defective! It is clearly (in my view) inadequate to define morality solely in terms of duty, and without reference to quality of consciousness. It is less clear that one can discuss the phenomenon of morality as a whole without giving an *essential* place to this ubiquitous command. However, a saint has no duties, God has no duties, and good as well as bad people are moral eccentrics. Certainly the idea of moral rules was not invented by Kant, it is one of the most primitive of moral conceptions. A 'sense of duty' may be a sensibility to general rules or an active creation or discovery of detailed ones. Reason seems to dart from the outside into specific situations with an eagle glance which sets all in order. Here the fact–value distinction seems especially out of place. Do we really think there are specifiable sets of neutral facts which in the light of reason give a moral direction? Is it not rather that the prime situation is already to a considerable extent 'read' (or worked upon) when the problem arises? It is certainly often worth saying: Look at the facts! This is a way, *a* way, of directing attention. But what we look at, and attempt to clarify and know, are matters in which value already inheres. In deciding what the initial data are we are working with values. Value goes right down to the bottom of the cognitive situation. Of course we can say, 'Let us establish the facts here', and such an exercise may bring moral enlightenment, but is unlikely to constitute the whole of the situation, even in cases where 'neutral facts' are easily discerned and agreed upon. ('You promised', or 'He's your father!' may or may not end a debate.) These are of course considerations which belong to my general argument. I introduce them here with relevance to the idea of axioms, which I suggested had a special role in politics to be distinguished from the larger ambiguity of moral rules in general. The concept of duty is, as I said just now, of the greatest importance as a formulation of our sense of the absolute nature of moral obligation. It represents a kind of *certainty*, and this concept I shall be discussing shortly. A part of 'duty', but a part only, consists of the ability to act against our natural inclinations, a situation especially interesting to Kant who attaches to it the moral emotion of respect for the law. We are *reminded*. The whole of morality involves the discipline of desire which leads to instinctive good action. This slow discipline, this gradual shift of inclination, is less visible, and indeed less interesting, than the dramatic head-on encounters between duty and interest, or duty and passion, which can be so effectively displayed and explored in literature.

How abstract is 'abstract morality' (rules) even in what might seem like clear cases? A child is not told 'do not lie' in a vacuum. He is living in a moral world, primarily that of his family, where all his antennae are active and he is likely to be learning language, self-control and morality all in one. If we consider *how much* a child learns before the age of six, we may also reflect upon how much of this consists of learning morals. Rules are instantly interpreted in relation to the understood life of the community and its spokesmen, and together with this comes the apprehended difference between appearance and reality. If we think of such cases, in childhood and beyond, we see how appropriate it is to speak of knowledge, of cognitive activity, rather than to use weaker words such as feeling or attitude. As moral agents we have to try to understand the world and thereby to construct 'our world'. Since morality is compulsory (we cannot avoid moral choices) some form of moral *cognition* is compulsory and we have to set up at least the forms of a distinction between what is real and what is not. Bad conduct has its cognate illusions and fantasies. 'Our world' is at best likely to contain large fantasy areas. The idea of truth, not always easily evaded, is active in the training of desire and tends to deepen and strengthen our conception of virtue; whereas would-be neutral descriptions in terms of feelings or moods are themselves morally persuasive and suggestive of a picture. In fact, to speak with the implied seriousness about knowledge or its failure, reality and appearance, accords very much better with our actual experience of morality and the ordinary understanding of it. These are considerations which must be fundamentally important in education, where a good teacher teaches accuracy and truth. The importance of *getting things right*. People who imagine themselves to be relativists, emotivists, existentialists, or determinists have been persuaded by a theory. Cynicism, which may be bred too from a superficial acquaintance with such theories, is often, at first, an affectation, though it can later be a deadly disease. Innumerable metaphors suggest that virtue is knowledge: as when we speak of insight, lucidity, clarity, enlightenment, vision. The child, to return to him, who is led by his observations to conclude that 'Do not lie' is part of an espionage system directed against himself, since the prohibition obviously means nothing to his elders, is being misled concerning the crucial position of truth in human life. We learn language in contexts where our vocabulary is increased and (ideally) refined in the everyday processes of living and learning. We learn moral concepts. Not only 'true' and 'good', but the *vast numbers of secondary* more specialised moral terms, are for us instruments of discrimination and mentors of desire. I mean words like 'generous', 'gentle', 'reckless', 'envious', 'honest', and so on and so on. These are concepts which in turn throw light on other concepts as when we distinguish sympathetic curiosity from impertinent curiosity and a tender smile from a mocking smile. This is the very texture of being and consciousness woven and working

[ 385 ]

from moment to moment in language. 'Do not lie' is clear, general and universal, an understanding and exercise of truthfulness is the required task. Roughly, moral rules are tasks set to individuals, whereas axiomatic statements about rights (etc.) are public banners flown for complex reasons which may be partly, even grossly, pragmatic. Of course politicians and statesmen are ordinary moral agents, and we are moved to claim the rights of others by our own general moral understanding and sensibility; and of course we can construct a series from 'one person, one vote' to the nursery situation of 'Why can't he have an apple too?' But the existence of a series does not legislate for its two ends. Liberal political thinking cannot dispense with the inflexibility of axiomatic morality and the particular kind of exploratory and persuasive language which it generates. The claim to a human right is *designed* to remain in place whatever the situation, and this is not the case with (most understandings of) 'Do not lie'. We do not 'live' the world of politics in the way we 'live' our private lives, and this idea puts a limit (not always easy to determine) upon what the 'world of politics' properly is. We 'cut off the road to an explanation' in order to safeguard the purity of the value, and remove it from vulnerability to certain kinds of argument.

Such assertions constitute liberal-political moral judgments about what politicians ought to value. We also judge the politicians and societies of the past in a certain *light*. Let us consider an example involving the founding fathers of western philosophy. Our distress at the (on available evidence) attitude of the classical Greeks to slavery is a certain kind of distress, unlike our distress about nineteenth-, or twentieth-, century slavery. Both Plato and Aristotle take slavery coolly for granted. By convention of course Greeks did not enslave other Greeks. Barbarians might be regarded as slavish by nature, and so naturally enslavable. A slave was considered to be an irrational being, without *Logos*; people unable to reason were said to be 'like slaves'. (*Laws* 966B). Women might be thought of as like slaves in that respect. *Laws* 720 describes the difference between the sensible free doctor and the stupid slave doctor. At *Laws* 777E Plato says that slaves should be punished justly, but not spoilt by being merely admonished as if they were free persons. On the other hand, Callicles (*Gorgias* 483–4) argues that by nature (as opposed to by moralising convention) it is a worse thing to suffer wrong than to do wrong. Xerxes had no 'right' to attack Greece, he followed nature, a natural right, indeed a natural law. *So a sufficiently spirited slave might rise in revolt and make himself the master, in the 'bright light of natural justice'.* (484A.) Plato lends eloquence to this intelligent dissident voice, but the argument continues without any pause for discussion of 'natural justice'. Callicles condemns philosophy as a rather juvenile pursuit and (like Thrasymachus) applauds the strong man who can enforce his will. Plato uses the word 'slavery' (*douleia*) in picturing other hierarchical situations, in a state, in a soul, even in the cosmos (in the *Timaeus*). Aristotle (*Politics* 1253–60) discusses the institution of slavery, and the use of the slave as a household instrument. At 1253B he says, 'There are some who hold that the exercise of authority over slaves is a form of science. They believe . . . that the management of a household, the control of slaves, the authority of the statesman, and the rule of the monarch, are all the same. There are others, however, who regard the control of slaves by a master as contrary to nature. In their view the distinction of master and slave is due to law or convention; there is no natural difference between them: the relation of master and slave is based on force, and being so based has no warrant in justice.' He does not tell us who those people are who thought that slavery was contrary to nature. At 1260B he says that 'it is clear that the master of a household must produce in the slave the sort of goodness we have been discussing [that is, moral goodness] and he must do so not as a manager giving instructions about particular duties. This is the reason why we may disagree with those [for instance Plato presumably] who are in favour of withholding reasons from slaves, and who argue that only command should be employed. Admonition ought to be applied to slaves even more than it is to children.' And in the *Nicomachean Ethics* VIII xi 7, 'Master and slave have nothing in common: a slave is a living tool . . . Therefore there can be no friendship with a slave as slave, though there can be as human being: for there seems to be some room for justice in the relations of every human being with every other that is capable of participating in law and contract, and hence friendship also is possible with everyone so far as he is a human being.' This may sound a little confusing. However, these extracts show Aristotle as taking slavery for granted, but viewing it in a more humane light than Plato gives evidence of in the *Laws*, his last, and least attractive, work! In general (I think) the Greeks regarded slavery as a *fate*, and one which they too might suffer. To return to Plato, with Callicles's robust views may be read *Republic* 588–92. Socrates tells Glaucon to imagine a creature composed of man, lion, and a beast with many heads, some wild, some tame. The unjust man feeds the lion and the beast, while enfeebling his own nature; the just man is master of the whole, taming the lion and caring for the beast. Law and custom judge between good and bad, deeming good those things which subject our brutish nature to our human nature, or rather perhaps our divine nature. Why is the idea of mechanical or unskilled work a sort of term of reproach? It is so only when the best part of the man is weak and subordinate to the brutish part. Then should not such a one, so that he may gain the self-control which belongs to the best, become the slave of the best man who has the divine governing principle within him? It is better for everyone to be under the control of divine wisdom, which should if possible come from within, but failing that should be imposed from without, so that as far as possible we may all become equals and friends under the same authority. The purpose of the law, which is the ally of everyone in the state, is to use control, as we do with children, fostering the best in them by the best in us, before letting them run free. (I have condensed this passage, so no inverted commas.) This would not please Hobbes or Hume either, though Hume might appreciate the reference to law and custom. The imagery repeats Plato's general theme that the higher part of the soul must discipline the lower part, and that the wisest people, those who partake of the divine nature, are worthy teachers and (ideally) rulers. Taken crudely as 'politics' it certainly offends against the axioms of individualism! On the other hand, if we take it simply, it belongs in many human situations, where one would be glad of the privilege of being the 'slave' of some great scholar or saintly person. We may think here of Plato's relation to Socrates. (And of Alcibiades's passionate homage to Socrates in the *Symposium*.) In any case the end of Book IX, 592B, makes clear (what must always be kept in mind) that the *Republic* is primarily a spiritual guidebook, a myth of the soul, and not (though it instances many practical matters) a political programme. Socrates goes on to describe the good wise man who sets free his higher nature, is indifferent to wealth and honours, and will enjoy only such powers as make him a better man and do not damage the steady tenor of his being. Glaucon says, 'So he won't go into politics!' Socrates says, 'Yes, he certainly will, though not perhaps in the city of his birth, except through some divine event.' Glaucon says, 'You mean the city we have been talking of is an ideal city, not to be found on earth?' Socrates replies, 'Perhaps its pattern is laid up in heaven where he who wishes may see it, and in looking become its citizen.' A final quotation, to cast a kinder light upon the author of the *Laws*: we are 'not precluded from asserting in our doctrine that the female sex must share with the male, to the greatest extent possible, both in education and in all else.' (*Laws* 805C.)

We 'forgive' people in the remoter past because we can (we think) see more clearly the limitations of their situation, whereas we cannot see our own limitations so clearly, and, being still alive and free, do not readily accept the idea of being conditioned. Thinking about the past is moral thinking too, wherein the good historian exhibits a certain delicacy, for instance in describing the (then) tension between morals and politics. That evidence presents the larger issues and the views of the successful, must be kept in mind. Politics is a matter of life and death, but *is* also the language of politics, its modes of justification. A state may be 'placed' by its rhetoric, wherein even hypocrisy can have its value. It can be bad when a politician hesitates to say what he feels; it can also be good. It may be a mark of progress when certain prejudices are not uttered in public. On the other hand, 'this is a free society', surely we can say what we please. The politician who wishes to be re-elected often does not say what he pleases. Here the wavery line runs between private and public; and we may become better, or worse, by 'conforming'. Hypocrisy can be our good friend in a moral situation where we weaken an evil intent by not uttering it. The bad tyrannical state exhibits and imposes itself in an established unchallengeable public value-language in which truth cannot be uttered, and from which many citizens can only 'emigrate' into the more private language of their own souls. Needless to say, there are no good societies, decent societies are partly bad, but there is a crucial difference, here taken for granted, between open societies and others. Observance of human rights is one good test. So, public rhetoric can be decent or false, but in any case occupies a specialised and small area compared with the vast private region of our personal being or soul, wherein we are, to use a religious (variously interpretable) image, alone with God.

The argument led into politics by a consideration of different senses of 'privacy', 'inwardness', and 'individual', and in that context I tried to indicate the concept of 'axioms' as the assertion of isolated intuited general values. The idea of intuition in an 'unexplained' sense seems in place here, where publicity and universality are claimed in contexts which leave private morals deliberately obscure. Utopian political thinking, the *detailed* imagining of an ideal society, set in a political programme, is checked in a liberal scene by tolerance, individualism and (related to these) agnosticism, and by Hobbesian common-sense concerning human nature. Of course people in public political situations may speak from the heart, but must also, if they wish to persuade, consider the actual effect of their words, and the results of being misunderstood. The moralist, in the liberal state, must in this sense play the political game by the political rules. Innumerable moral problems and moral passions touch on and emerge into political situations, and private feeling and reasoning may provide the 'heat' for the forging of political policy. Much political policy *is* the public accommodation of, sometimes socially inconvenient, private wishes. Such struggles and adjustments are always going on. Politics remains the art of the possible, it is engineering; political choices, which concern many and various people, have to be larger and cruder. A better state makes the large choices with a degree of sensibility, as when conscientious law-breakers (or in war time conscientious objectors) are treated with discrimination and understanding. As I said earlier, the point of making a distinction between the political and the private 'moral scene' is itself a political point. The realm of axioms and the realm of densely textured moral cognitive consciousness are (morally) connected through the (limited) operation of abstract rules in private life in the manner I tried to describe earlier, through the work of sympathy and imagination (compassion) which leads us to make certain axioms 'our own'. In practice of course all sorts of reasons of self-interest or idiosyncratic preference lead people to espouse political views and causes. The 'politics' of the individual has a background in his consciousness and his world. The decent state works with a mixture of morality and expediency. It is a *prima facie* duty of any government (sovereign) to defend its citizens' interests. This is in a felicitous sense self-perpetuating in so far as election to political power involves adherence to certain (practical) moral objectives. Citizens wish, for instance, to elect a government which will concentrate on reducing unemployment, or making poor people less poor, or improving education. Politicians who think these goals only minimally feasible have to explain why. Individual voters check their ideals against their self-interest. We may identify with deprived or persecuted people through our imaginative understanding of their plight. Such understanding is an instance of moral knowledge. How much do we know, what do we know, about 'what it is like to be' other people? As moralists, as political moralists, we specialise, we have favourites. We sympathise with, know about, some sufferers not others, we imagine and desire some states of affairs not others. One could reflect on this matter of knowledge and desire in relation to many types of political dissension. There is in ordinary morals a give and take between an axiomatic and abstract level, and the deeper more densely cognitive personal level of my consciousness and my world. The battle between selfishness and unselfishness is enacted in this scenery. Rational argument may persuade us to embrace a cause or adopt a rule which is out of key with what our experience had led us to value and desire. Later on imagination may have 'colonised' the area which at first seemed so alien. Perhaps we trusted some intuitive sense that this might be done. Or, if we do not reject the original argument, the process may work the other way, leaving as dry imperatives, soon to be abandoned, modes of action which once seemed natural.


> 13 <

# The Ontological Proof


'The limits of the ontological arguments are obvious. But nothing is more important for philosophy and theology than the truth it contains, the acknowledgement of the unconditional element in the structure of reason and reality . . . Modern secularism is rooted largely in the fact that the unconditional element in the structure of reason and reality no longer was seen, and that therefore the idea of God was imposed on the mind as a "strange body". This produced first heteronomous subjection and then autonomous rejection. The destruction of the onto-logical argument is not dangerous. What is dangerous is the destruction of an *approach* which elaborates the possibility of the question of God. This approach is the meaning and truth of the ontological argument.'

Paul Tillich (*Systematic Theology*, Part II 'Being and God', section 1.)

The Ontological Argument for, or Ontological Proof of, the existence of God is different in type from other 'proofs', which rely on concep-tions such as cosmic design and a first cause. These latter proofs interest us very little now, and not only because we have other ways of account-ing for the cosmos. The argument from design seems unsound in any case. Even if we leave aside the fact that almost every sentient being seems to be condemned to continual fear and suffering, why should swallows have to fly to Africa every year? And why should we venerate a Supreme Being whose most convincing claim to existence and impor-tance is that of having created an impressive machine? A demon could have created the world. Such reasoning dwindles in the climate of today. The Ontological Proof, though often treated as an absurdity (Schopenhauer called it 'a charming joke' and even Tillich says its limits are obvious), is a deeper and more mysterious matter. Its effective ancestry is Platonic, but its ambiguities give rise to a variety of styles of interpretation. As a formal argument it was put together by a Ben-edictine monk, St Anselm of Canterbury (1033–1109), who in his preface to the Proof speaks, or prays, to God as follows. 'I do not endeavour, O Lord, to penetrate thy sublimity, for in no wise do I compare my understanding therewith; but I long to understand in some degree thy truth, which my heart believes and loves. For I do not seek to understand that I may believe, but I believe in order to understand.' These moving words may seem to indicate a limitation upon the claims of the Proof. Anselm's formulation emerges from a context of deep belief and disciplined spirituality, and may be seen as a clarified or academic summary of what is already known, rather than as an argu-ment to be put to an outsider. It may be seen too as a proof which a man can only give to himself, herein resembling *cogito ergo sum*, to which it is indeed related by Descartes. Yet these reminders do not set the Proof aside as a piece of history or item of private piety, and in spite of having been apparently demolished by Kant it has continued to interest philosophers and theologians. *Credo ut intellegam* (I believe in order to understand) is not just an apologist's paradox, but an idea with which we are familiar in personal relationships, in art, in theoretical studies. I have faith (important place for this concept) in a person or idea in order to understand him or it, I intuitively know and grasp more than I can yet explain. The *Meno* speaks of a kind of 'grace' which brings to us what cannot be said to be either natural or taught. Anselm loves God's truth. Faith (loving belief) and knowledge often have an intimate relation which is not easy to analyse in terms of what is prior to what.

Anselm states the Proof more than once, the second time in reply to objections made by another Benedictine monk. The formulations differ in ways which have interested modern philosophers. For purposes of the Proof God is taken to be the *Ens Realissimum, aliquid quo nihil maius cogitari possit*, the most real Being, than which nothing greater [or more perfect] can be conceived. The first formulation, engaging battle with the Fool in the Fourteenth Psalm who said in his heart that there is no God, distinguishes between what exists (or is conceived of) in the mind (*in intellectu*) and what exists in reality outside the mind (*in re*). To exist *in re* is taken to be a quality (predicate), in the case of something good a perfection, which is *extra* to that of existing only *in intellectu*. It is then clear that if we can understand the idea of God, which we surely can, then we must also understand that God exists, since if he did not then he would lack one important quality or perfection, that of existence, and would fail to be that than which nothing greater can be conceived, *in intellectu* and *in re* being greater than *in intellectu* alone.

'Whatever is understood exists in the understanding. And assuredly that than which nothing greater can be conceived, cannot exist in the understanding alone. For suppose it exists in the understanding alone: then it can be conceived to exist in reality; which is greater.'

In this formulation the idea that God, thought of as supreme perfection, cannot be conceived not to exist, and that if we can conceive of him we know that he exists, appears to depend upon the distinction between *in intellectu* and *in re* and the positing of existence as an extra quality. Critics of the Proof (most famously Kant) argue that existence cannot be so treated. The idea of existence adds nothing to a concept, existence is not a predicate. The conviction that God exists is contained in the believer's initial idea of God which appears in the premises. Anselm's earliest critic, a contemporary monk, Gaunilo, who of course believed in God, anticipates such an objection. He challenges Anselm's assumption that he can frame an idea of God. 'I do not know that reality itself which God is, nor can I frame a conjecture of that reality from some other reality. For you yourself assert that there can be nothing else like it.' If one is going to argue from perfect essence to real existence then could one not argue anything into existence from the imagined idea of a single perfect instance (for example the idea of a perfect island)? 'Whether . . . so long as I am most positively aware of my existence I can conceive of my non-existence I am not sure. But if I can, why can I not conceive of the non-existence of whatever else I know with the same certainty?' In his reply Anselm answers Gaunilo's doubt about whether we can conceive of God. 'Everything that is less good, in so far as it is good, is like the greater good. It is therefore evident to any rational mind that by ascending from the lesser good to the greater we can form a considerable notion of a being than which a greater is inconceivable.' He also enlarges the argument about essence and existence which rests upon the conceptual difference between 'God' and all other cases.

'You often repeat that I assert that what is greater than all other beings is in the understanding, and if it is in the understanding it exists also in reality for otherwise the being which is greater than all would not be greater than all. Nowhere in my writings is such a demonstration found. For the real existence of a being which is said to be greater than all other beings cannot be demonstrated in the same way with the real existence of one that is said to be a being than which a greater cannot be conceived.'

'It is possible to conceive of and understand a being whose non-existence is impossible; but he who conceives of this conceives of a greater being than one whose non-existence is possible . . . What he conceives of must exist; for anything whose non-existence is possible is not that of which he conceives. Of God alone it can be said that it is impossible to conceive of his non-existence.'

Gaunilo's reasonable doubt about whether he can conceive of God is answered by Anselm as follows. We recognise and identify goodness and *degrees* of good, and are thus able to have the idea of a greatest conceivable good. God is taken to be *ab initio* and by definition good, it is moral perfection that we are concerned with, which must be in at the start and cannot be added later. This notion would be supplied by faith or intuition, and supported by metaphysical arguments (yet to be considered) concerning the special status of the concept 'Good'. It must also be assumed that other attributes of God, such as omnipotence and omniscience, should be seen as aspects of, or deducible from, his goodness. Anselm's reply also clarifies his first argument. He is, he says, not speaking of something which is, or *happens to be*, greater than all other beings, but of something than which a greater cannot be conceived, and whose *non-existence is impossible*. This is the respect in which God is unique. To put the matter in the terms in which it has later been handled, God and God alone exists, not contingently or accidentally, but necessarily; what the Proof defines and proves is his necessary existence. In this case alone if you can conceive of this entity you are *ipso facto* certain that what you are thinking of is real. The definition of God has having *necessary* not contingent existence is an important clarification for any interested party. God cannot be a particular, a contingent thing, one thing among others; a contingent god might be a great demonic or angelic spirit, but not the Being in question. Anything that happens to exist, and could perhaps not exist, or about whose existence one might speculate as about empirical discoveries, or about which one could state 'what it would be like' *if* it existed, is not what is thought of here. God's necessary existence is connected with his not being an object. God is not to be worshipped as an idol or identified with any empirical thing; as is indeed enjoined by the Second Commandment.

We are in process of transition here to what may be seen as another and supplementary argument, a metaphysical argument which is also an appeal to experience. Of course good metaphysical arguments are successful appeals to experience, and can be seen too, as this one can, as aspects of other arguments which cluster round in support. Anselm himself makes the transition with natural ease. God is something necessary not contingent, he is not an empirical object in the world. How do we know about him then, and from whence do we derive the unique idea of good which can be extended into a concept of perfection? (Why should not a perfect devil exist non-contingently and necessarily?) God, who is invisible and not an object in the world, can be seen and clearly seen everywhere in the visible things of the world, which are his creatures and shadows. 'So easily then can the Fool who does not accept sacred authority be refuted if he denies that a notion may be formed from other objects of a being than which a greater is inconceivable. But if any Catholic would deny this, let him remember that the invisible things of God, from the creation of the world are clearly seen, being understood by the things that are made, even his eternal power and Godhead.' Anselm is here quoting St Paul, Romans 1. 20. We 'see' God through the morally good things of the world, through our (moral) perception of what is beautiful and holy, through our ability to distinguish good and evil, and through our just God-fearing understanding of what is not good. So we find God both, and inextricably both, in the world and in our own soul. (This is like the argument, or intuition, of Descartes.) We have instinctive faith in God, and also conceive of him by looking at the world; and when we consider what we conceive of we understand that it exists necessarily and not contingently. The idea of *necessity* emerges both from God's evident omnipresent majesty and from his patently non-accidental nature. God exists, he exists necessarily, we conceive of him by noticing *degrees of goodness*, which we see in ourselves and in all the world which is a shadow of God. These are aspects of the Proof wherein the definition of God as non-contingent is given body by our most general perceptions and *experience* of the fundamental and omnipresent (uniquely necessary) nature of moral value, thought of in a Christian context as God. This is essentially an argument from morality not from design. It appeals to our moral understanding, and not to any of the more strictly rational considerations relied upon by Aquinas, who did not accept Anselm's Proof. Some supporters of the Fool might agree that 'God' might name something non-contingent, but in precisely this case something impossible. Others who feel that perhaps the Proof proves something, but not any sort of God, might return to Plato and claim some uniquely necessary status for moral value as something (uniquely) impossible to be thought away from human experience, and as in a special sense, if conceived of, known as real. This claim might be associated with concepts of religion which reject a personal God and other supernatural beliefs. Such a return to Plato leads back into other problems. Anselm's Proof is offered to anybody, even to Fools. Gaunilo, a professional holy man, wondered whether he could conceive of God. God (mythically) seems like a person with a proper name, and this can be, certainly psychologically, important in thinking Anselm's Proof.

Anselm quotes Romans 1. 20 in the course of arguing that of course we can conceive of God, seeing the invisible in the visible, the uncreated in the created, the great Good in the lesser good. The context in Paul, interestingly enough, concerns the inexcusable conduct of those who can or could see God, but turn away. ('Professing themselves to be wise, they became fools': verse 22.) There seems to be no evidence that Paul knew about Plato. Similarities are noted (e.g. by E. R. Dodds, *Pagan and Christian in an Age of Anxiety*, p. 37) between Paul's references to demonic powers and the 'intermediaries' of the *Symposium*, of which Eros is one. But of course the *Symposium* story, and the *Timaeus* story, are myths. Plato was not a Manichaean, and neither was Paul, though both were acutely aware of the power of evil, and lived in societies which believed in ambiguous spirits. Paul was certainly breathing Greek air and his intense mystical religiosity, which has so long and variously fed and disturbed the church, might find a home in Platonism. Romans 1.20: 'For the invisible things of him from the creation of the world are clearly seen, being understood by the things that are made, even his eternal power and Godhead.' Karl Barth comments on this verse, agreeing with Paul about the unrighteousness of those who turn away from what they ought to be able to see clearly.

'This we have forgotten, and must allow it to be brought back once more to our minds. Our lack of humility, our lack of recollection, our lack of fear in the presence of God, are not in our present condition inevitable, however natural they may seem to us. Plato in his wisdom recognised long ago that behind the visible there lies the invisible universe which is the Origin of all concrete things. And moreover the solid good sense of the men of the world had long ago perceived that the fear of the Lord is the beginning of wisdom. The clear honest eyes of the poet in the book of Job, and of the preacher Solomon had long ago rediscovered, mirrored in the world of appearance, the archetypal, unobservable undiscoverable Majesty of God.'

(*Commentary on St Paul's Epistle to the Romans*.)

Barth, although he admits that *our* experience may be darkened, appeals to the 'solid good sense' and 'clear honest eyes' of accessible witnesses. We see in our lower things the shadow of higher things, and thereby our continual (daily, hourly, minutely) sense of the connection between the good and the real can lead us to believe in the supreme reality of what is perfect: the unique place of God, or Good, in human life. The appeal to experience is not just to esoteric strictly contemplative or religiously supernatural experience, since so many situations and activities can suggest this connection. Gaunilo raises doubts about whether we can be said to conceive of God or discover him through knowledge of any other reality, since Anselm says he is unique. Anselm answers that we see him in his creation. If we can see God in the world we can see him everywhere in the world and must be able so to see him. The part played by love in this seeing is implicit, but again need not be thought of as something unusual, specialised or remote. All our best activities involve desires which are disciplined and purified in the process. We often long to understand a truth which we already intuit. Reflection upon our ordinary perceptions of what is valuable, what it is like to seek what is true or just in intellectual or personal situations, or to scrutinise and direct our affections, can thus also lend support to the argument about existence and essence which appeared at first as a kind of logical argument offered to clever sceptically minded Fools.

Anselm's passionate certainty springs from his personal communion with God. His metaphysical argument concerning an *Ens Realissimum* has a background in Plato through Plotinus and Augustine, and the neoplatonic transformations of Plato's Form of the Good into a personified One. Plato's philosophy expounds a fundamental connection between epistemology and ethics; truthful knowledge and virtue are bound together. For purposes of considering the Proof it is important to separate strands in his thought. The Theory of Forms, in so far as it arose out of attempts, such as we see in the early dialogues, perhaps made by the historic Socrates, to define certain moral concepts, is *ab initio* involved with both epistemological and moral problems. The Forms later appear in discussions about 'universals', thought and truth, opinion and knowledge, general ideas and particulars. The connection of the Forms with morality and the spiritual life emerges at the same time naturally, together with their 'ontological' or existential function, out of reflection upon what serious truthful thinking is like. Metaphysics is inspired by a gifted thinker's scrutiny of his own thought. Thought 'aims' at reality, but with varying degrees of success. An object of serious thought must be something real, serious thinking is moral truthful thinking, goodness is connected with reality, the supremely good is the supremely real. Plato pictures objects of thought at different levels of insight as possessing different degrees of reality. The contrast between states of illusion (selfish habits or egoistic fantasy) and honest clarified truthful serious thinking suggests a moral picture of the mind as in a continuous engagement with an independent reality. 'Truth' is not just a collection of facts. *Truthfulness*, the search for truth, for a closer connection between thought and reality, demands and effects an exercise of virtues and a purification of desires. The ability, for instance, to think justly about what is evil, or to love another person unselfishly, involves a discipline of intellect and emotion. Thought, goodness and reality are thus seen to be connected. The intensity of Plato's vision of this connection forces him (if one may put it thus) to *separate* an idea of goodness as the supreme and fundamental requirement, the essential human aim or task, and to separate this idea in a unique manner from the imperfect hurly-burly of the human struggle. The idea of Good cannot be compromised or tainted by its inclusion in actual human proceedings, where its magnetism is nevertheless, and even at the lowest levels, omnipresent. Good is unique, it is 'above being', it fosters our sense of reality as the sun fosters life on earth. The virtues, the other moral Forms, are aspects of this central idea, increasingly understood as interconnected parts of it. The attributes of God may also thus (in Christian theology) be deduced from an original intuitive concept of him. It must be kept in mind that Plato is talking in metaphysical metaphors, myths, images; there is no Platonic 'elsewhere', similar to the Christian 'elsewhere'. What is higher is, as Eckhart observed, inside the soul. The Theory of Forms never really solved 'the problem of universals'. Nevertheless Plato's metaphysic founds a basic connection between knowledge and morals. The unique elevation of the Form of the Good is a metaphysical argument supported, in the *Republic*, by many discussions of various human activities and problems. It is also illustrated by the most memorable of all philosophical metaphors, expressive of the *distance* between good and evil. The argument is also of course a mythical religious vision, which in Plato's mind has nothing to do with a personal God or gods.

In the Cave myth the Theory of Forms is presented as a pilgrimage where different realities or thought-objects exist for individual thinkers at different levels, appearing at lower levels as shadows cast by objects at the next higher level: an endlessly instructive image. The pilgrimage is inspired by intimations of realities which lie just beyond what can be easily seen. The concept of 'an object of thought' has been a source of confusion in philosophy, suggesting intermediary entities necessary to convey thought to reality. In the myth of the *Phaedrus* the disembodied soul sees the moral Forms individually. The Demiurge in the *Timaeus*, creating the world, looks at and (in so far as his alien material will allow) copies the Forms. The virtuous man sees and knows what is more real, the saint what is most real. The idea of the perfect object is one with its reality, which is not the case at other levels, where the light is obstructed and something is always to be intuited beyond. It may be noted that Plato is less democratic, or less optimistic, than Anselm, who thought that anyone could conceive of God. Of course the Christian deity gives to individual pilgrims direct supernatural help, not offered by the Form of the Good. The latter exerts a magnetic force, but is also impersonal and very distant. It would of course be a mistake to interpret Plato's 'objects of thought' in terms of sense data or Husserlian essences or Christian metaphysical being. The best commentary on, or supplementary explanation of, the idea is probably given by Plato himself in the *Meno*, in the myth of *anamnesis*. The slave solving the geometrical problem is orienting himself towards, bringing his attention to bear upon, something dark and alien, on which light then falls, and which he 'makes his own'. He 'sees' an object invisible but grasped as 'there', he is able to concentrate and attend. (To attend is also to wait.) These familiar metaphors are important. It is then as if he always knew it and were remembering it. The process of discovery is to be thought of as accompanied or motivated by a passion or desire which is increased and purified in the process. (As portrayed by Dante in *Paradiso* I, 7–9.) This is something which we can all recognise and which can be illustrated in many different kinds of human activity.

In learning, loving, creatively imagining, we may be inspired or overcome by a sense of certainty at a particular point. (Compare the intuitive leap in Descartes's Proof.) The importance and value of this disturbing experience is not diminished by the fact that 'certainties' or 'recollections' are not solitary revelations, but take place in a general world where they can also be judged by results. As Plato's picture indicates, you can only *see* at your own level and a little above. Perception here is, and properly, the *image* of thought and spiritual insight. Truth and progress (or some truth and some progress) are the reward of some exercise of virtue, courage, humility, patience. The creative artist is like the slave, he attends to the dark something out of which he feels certain he can, if he concentrates and waits, elicit his poem, picture, music: it is as if he remembered it or found it waiting for him, veiled but present. He hopes to be taught, and places himself in a situation where this is possible. In the case of the slave in that moving but in some ways distressing scene, the certainty is assisted by Socrates and his friends. But this too is like life. Paul Valéry, with poetic, and spiritual, inspiration in mind, says that 'the proper, unique and perpetual object of thought is that which does not exist'. 'A difficulty is a light. An inseparable difficulty is a sun.' And, 'At its highest point, love is a determination to create that being which it has taken for its object.' (*Mauvaises Pensées et Autres*, Pléiade edition, vol. II, pp. 785, 795, 818.) This states a kind of Ontological Proof. Valéry's use of the word 'unique' casts a glance, in Platonic style, toward other comparable activities, as if at a certain level of seriousness and love all strivings have not only similar objects but the same object. (End of Dante's *Paradiso*.) Simone Weil, with reference to Valéry, speaks of 'an orientation of the soul towards something which one does not know, but whose reality one does know', and an 'effort of attention empty of all content' which then 'catches' what is certainly its object, as when we try to remember a word. Also: 'Ontological Proof is mysterious because it does not address itself to the intelligence, but to love.' (*Notebooks*, p. 375.) In *Pensées sans ordre concernant l'Amour de Dieu* (p. 136) she puts it more simply: 'For everything which concerns absolute good and our contact with it, the proof by perfection (wrongly called ontological), is not only valid, but the only proof which is valid. It is instantly implied by the notion of good.' Also (more diffidently) Collingwood (*An Essay on Philosophical Method*, p. 124): 'Anselm, putting these two thoughts together, the original Platonic principle that when we really think (but when do we really think, if ever?) we must be thinking of a real object, and the neo-Platonic idea of a perfect being (something which we cannot help conceiving in our minds – but does that guarantee it more than a mere idea?), or rather pondering on the latter thought until he rediscovered the former as latent within it, realised that to think of this perfect being at all was already to think of him, or it, as existing.'

Anselm believed in a personal God, the God of Abraham, Isaac and Jacob, with whom the Psalmist held converse. Anselm prayed to this Person, talked with him and experienced his personal presence. He *knew* that God existed. Plato *knew* that Good was not only real but supremely so, a certainty less apparently simple than belief in God. He knew that morality, an orientation between good and evil, was in a unique sense fundamental and ubiquitous in human life. Anselm was inspired, for the sake of others and to please himself and God, to utter his faith in the form of a metaphysical statement. His argument is striking and memorable because of its condensed form and appearance of being a sort of logical proof which could be offered to sceptics. It contains an appeal to experience which implicitly includes experience of God; as Plato's arguments include appeals to various kinds of moral experiences, in learning, love, politics and so on. Plato knew that mathematics and philosophy were very difficult and that goodness was difficult too. The prisoners in the Cave are pictured as able to get out. But the distance involved is very great. In general Plato was an austere moral thinker. Few could rise high. The 'gravity' of sin compels us. Herein he agrees with Jewish thought, though (as mentioned earlier) it is unlikely that he knew anything about the Jews. How much he was interested in and 'touched' by other forms of oriental wisdom is disputed. The myth of Er recounted at length at the end of the *Republic* is (perhaps) Zoroastrian. (There is a reference to Zoroaster in *Alcibiades* I (122A), but taken by Momigliano (*Alien Wisdom*, ch. 6) to be 'one of the many arguments which make this dialogue almost certainly spurious'.) Plato certainly knew something about oriental religions, and myths about life after death, though his connection with these may have been exaggerated by later Greeks. He may have been (was probably) involved in forms of 'mystical' rites. He recounts myths, and invents his own myths. But he cannot be said to have taken any form of myth literally, and constantly draws attention to its status of an edifying or hermeneutic 'as if'. At *Meno* 86BC (quoted earlier) Socrates, speaking of how *anamnesis* seems like knowledge remembered from a previous life, adds that he cannot be confident that such things could be the case, but if we think about them we shall be braver and better, having faith in our ability to discover the truth. In the *Republic* (592) we are reminded that the 'ideal state' is not to be found on earth but may exist perhaps in heaven. So with the myth of Er, when the long amazing story of the other world and the fate of the soul after death has been completed (621B), Socrates says,

'And the tale is saved, as the saying is, and was not lost. And it will save us if we believe it and we shall safely cross the river of Lethe and keep our souls unspotted from the world. But if we are guided by me we shall believe that the soul is immortal and capable of enduring all extremes of good and evil, and so we shall hold ever to the upward way and pursue righteousness with wisdom always and ever, that we may be dear to the gods, both during our sojourn here and when we receive our reward, as victors in the games go about to gather theirs.'

The idea of the soul's immortality must, if its 'saving power' is to remain pure, be taken in and acted upon *in this life*, whatever may be said, in a story, about another one. This is (in my view) the sense in which the story is *saved*, that is put to its proper use as a spiritual myth or metaphor. And *Phaedo* 114DE: after a long tale of another world, another life where those who have 'purified themselves by philosophy will live henceforth without bodies', Socrates adds:

'But, Simmias, because of all these things which we have recounted we ought to do our best to acquire virtue and wisdom in life ... It would not be fitting for a man of sense to maintain that all this is just as I have described it, but that this or something like it is true concerning our souls and their abodes, since the soul is shown to be immortal, I think he may properly and worthily venture to believe, for the venture is well worth while; and he ought to repeat such things to himself as incantations, which is why I have drawn out the story to such length.'

That is, as it seems to me, these mythical pictures should be kept and used, not as literal factual information, or as magic, but as enlivening spiritual images. As in Buddhism and in mystical or demythologised Christianity. Indeed innumerable Christians probably did and do instinctively use (or save) the Christian stories in this way. Plato, whatever he may in this respect have 'dabbled in', positively excludes theistic magic and belief in gods. The Form of the Good is never identified with God. The author of the *Laws*, with diminished hope for human nature, prescribes picturesque popular religion as suitable for those who cannot rise. It is of course a part of Anselm's faith that an omnipotent God can save any creature, that all, however benighted, may receive grace, distinguish right and wrong, have intimations of light, pray to God and experience his presence. In this respect Anselm is closer to Kant than to Plato. Kant too thinks that anyone can be good; he attacked Anselm's argument but produced his own Proof in the form of the Categorical Imperative. Anselm, like Plato, and indeed

Kant, would see the truth of his picture as everywhere evident to serious reflection on human life.

Stated by itself, as Anselm first states it, the argument may indeed seem frail, only to be given substance by a belief or faith deriving from another source, a specious way of expressing a personal certainty which is already tacitly concealed in its premises. Anselm amends the argument, which he presents twice, the second time in answer to Gaunilo's criticisms. In the first statement he seems to say that the idea of a most perfect being must entail the existence of that being, which would otherwise lack the quality, which in the case of a good being is a perfection, of existence. His fellow monk objected that one could thus argue anything into existence by conceiving of a perfect instance. Anselm replies that the Proof refers to God alone, not just a thing among others which happens to be 'best', but a unique being, existing not contingently but of necessity. The idea of *necessity* here joins the *certainty* of an ardent faith. The difference between the two statements has interested some modern critics who argue that only the first version is vulnerable to Kant's contention that existence is not a predicate. In defending himself at the stage of the second version of the logical argument, Anselm also offers the argument from experience which is omnipresent in Plato. (One may notice a similar progression in modern discussions of the problem, wherein a primary consideration of the essence–existence argument is then joined by a more tentative *ad hoc* appeal to experience.) The argument from the idea of a series, as conveying the idea of the most perfect, is an abstract form of the full Platonic degrees-of-reality argument, the appeal to which provides us with contrasts between illusion and reality as contrasts between good and bad. Anselm resorts to St Paul, and implicitly to Plato, as providing a proof from all the world, proved by the whole of human experience. His definition of God both clarifies his earlier intuitive statement and opens the way for a wider argument.

Anselm, as he now develops his thought, appears to offer two mutually supportive arguments, a 'logical' argument about necessary existence suitably amended, and an ancillary argument from experience to support or enlarge the idea, required by the first argument, that we can conceive of God. The logical argument presents God's existence as being (uniquely) necessary not contingent. The argument from moral experience may be stated in the metaphysical terminology of degrees of reality, or as a more homely *ad hominem* appeal to our sense of

God (Good) as discovered everywhere in the world. Plato uses both methods, presenting large mythical pictures, and explaining them by examples from work, politics, intellectual studies, human relations. The Forms are pure, separate and alone, the Form of the Good is above being. We are saved by Eros and *techné*, by love and toil, by justice, by good desires and by the search for truth, by the magnetism which draws us to innumerable forms of what is good; whether we are philosophers or mathematicians or politicians or lovers, or craftsmen like the carpenter in *Republic* Book X. Thus we are continually shown the reality of what is better and the illusory nature of what is worse. We learn of perfection and imperfection through our ability to understand what we see as an image or shadow of something better which we cannot yet see. The idea of Good, perceived in our confused reality, also transcends it, Good is not a particular, it is not a thing among others. (The mythical Olympic gods are persons, rather like us, but more powerful, and often just as nasty. Good is above gods.) This is what Anselm expresses when he quotes Romans 1. 20, joining Platonic metaphysics, and the neo-Platonic conception of a perfect being, to the Judaeo-Christian experience of the omnipresence of a personal God. The argument from experience emerges as it were under the pressure of the logical argument. If we are able to distinguish necessary and contingent we can see that God cannot be contingent. Experience shows us the uniquely *unavoidable* nature of God (Good, or Categorical Imperative), its omnipresence, its purity and separateness from our fallen world, in which its magnetic force is nevertheless everywhere perceptible. God either exists necessarily or is impossible. All our experience shows that he exists.

Philosophical discussions of the Proof, whether Kantian or modern, have usually tended to take the logical argument, stated by itself, as primary (as if one could talk of God without reference to morality) and in this guise it has attracted some amused observers. It was in this diminished form rejected by Gaunilo and treated by Schopenhauer as a joke. Its more recent (twentieth-century) critics have sometimes felt moved to append an appeal to experience, but as a personal contribution of their own, not quite part of the picture. I would argue that the Proof, as something to be taken seriously, must be understood by looking at Plato. Its deep sense, whose restatement is now of importance in servicing our concept of religion, lies in the degrees-of-reality argument joined to the Platonic, and Pauline, reference to all the world: the argument about necessary existence can only be intelligibly stated in this frame. We gain the concept of this *unique form of necessity* from our unavoidable experience of good and evil. If God (or the 'unconditional element') is a reality anywhere it is a reality everywhere and is in this sense unlike other considerations. Kant makes this point in his distinction between a hypothetical and a categorical imperative: we are not gentlemen volunteers but conscripts in the army of the Moral Law. Much of the tissue of the original Proof is lost in modern views of it. We shy away from Anselm because of Kant's argument, and because Anselm is concerned with a Supreme Being, God as an entity with a proper name, which is unacceptable to modern secularists and also to some modern believers and theologians. A Platonic and Christian idea of love as a, in some sense unitary, positive force is absent from recent 'logical' moral discussions. Kant, whose dualism admits no degrees of reality and no love, more clearly marks the breach with Plato, which is then taken for granted in modern discussions of Kant. Many thinkers believed, and no doubt believe, that Kant finally refuted Anselm by pointing out that existence is not a predicate. (*Critique of Pure Reason*, Transcendental Dialectic, Book II, ch. III, section 4; Kemp Smith translation.) We do not add anything to the idea of something by saying that it exists. 'We do not make the least addition to the thing when we further declare that this thing *is*. Otherwise it would not be exactly the same thing that exists.' Moreover there can be no 'necessary existence', which is to be contrasted with 'contingent existence'. Necessity is *conceptual*. 'Under condition that there be a triangle (that is, that a triangle is given) three angles will necessarily be found in it.' 'To posit a triangle and yet to reject its three angles is self-contradictory; but there is no contradiction in rejecting the triangle together with its three angles. The same holds true of the concept of an absolutely necessary being. If its existence be rejected, we reject the thing itself with all its predicates; and no question of contradiction can then arise.' Kant here expresses something like a modern view of necessity as existing only inside a deductive system, belonging to a sign-system and not to the world. The tautologous, non-empirical, nature of such necessity, which belongs only to definition and cannot be exported to entail anything else, is clear in the case of the triangle. We cannot think something into being simply from the conception of it, as Anselm seems to be arguing. Someone may say when thinking about the Proof, 'What about material objects, aren't they unavoidable, couldn't God be in *that* sense, why should we stay with triangles?' Kant would refer the speaker back to the *Critique of Pure Reason* where the strict limitations of human knowledge are transcendentally deduced. Material objects belong among fundamental conceptual forms of our experience. It is, precisely, the case that God is *not* thus experienced and indeed *cannot* be. We cannot conceive of him in the sense required by Anselm. The borders of empirical knowledge and human reason must be strictly drawn to *make room* for religious faith, which must acknowledge a certain agnosticism. Kant, as I mentioned above, establishes in the space thereby created his own proof of our ineluctable spiritual destiny in the form of the Categorical Imperative, unique, necessary, non-contingent, thereby supplying the 'unconditional element in the structure of reason and reality' to which Tillich wishes us to attend. Kant's command of duty, linked to the concept of freedom, is unavoidable in a sense analogous to that of Plato's Good, and equally to be understood as something which is everywhere in human experience. Thus a (differently stated) philosophical Proof can be said to belong to Kant as well as to Plato. Both reject, and this brings them closer to us today, the concept of supernatural deity as not only irrelevant to the spiritual life, but as harmful to it.

Kant's refutation certainly entertained Schopenhauer who cannot see how the Proof was ever taken seriously. He reproves Descartes for attempting his own version of it. 'We find even the excellent Descartes who gave the first impulse to subjective reflection, and thereby became the father of modern philosophy, still entangled in confusions for which it is difficult to account.' Schopenhauer, who does not share Kant's particular quasi-Christian piety, rejoices in his attack on Anselm and goes on to deride the Proof. 'Oh for the prophetic wisdom of Aristotle! He had never heard of the Ontological Proof, but as though he saw into the night of the coming dark ages, detected in them that scholastic dodge, and wanted to bar the way thereto, he carefully demonstrated in the seventh chapter of the second book of the *Posterior Analytics* that the definition of a thing and the proof of its existence are two different and eternally separate matters.' (*The Fourfold Root of the Principle of Sufficient Reason*, ch. II, section 7; trans. E. F. J. Payne.) Schopenhauer concludes that 'considered by daylight . . . this famous

Ontological Proof is really a charming joke.' It is interesting that Schopenhauer, blinded by Kant, does not seem to have noticed that Anselm is using more than one argument, and that one of his arguments is Platonic, and in this sense close to Schopenhauer's own sympathies. Hegel, in rejecting Kant's sceptical idealism, made the idea of the reality of the rational into an all-inclusive system, which could be described as a huge Ontological Proof. Yet this would (as critics of Hegel could point out) be a misnomer, since Hegel's system excludes the idea, essential to the Proof, and common to Plato and Anselm, and even Kant, of morality as encounter with an (unassimilable) external other. One of the great problems of metaphysics is to explain the idea of goodness in terms which combine its peculiar purity and separateness (its transcendence) with details of its omnipresent effectiveness in human life. This problem (as Kierkegaard contended) 'gets lost' inside Hegel's system, where it is (and *a fortiori* in Marxism) dissolved (some would say solved); it thereby parts company with the aspects of the Proof which I wish to pursue into relationship with contemporary moral and religious problems.

In spite of Kant's authoritative intervention the Ontological Proof has not lost its charm, and has received, with new modes of philosophy, new modes of criticism. Russell and Moore were interested in it. Wittgenstein thought about it. Charles Hartshorne and Norman Malcolm drew attention to the two versions of the argument and suggested that Kant's objections were fatal only to the first version. Both these critics, in attempting to rehabilitate the 'logical' argument, also offer, but as something rather personal and without any major discussion, ancillary arguments from experience. Anselm thought the visibility of God in the world was obvious. Both Kant and Plato appealed to experience in arguing the special status and absolute necessity of their own 'Good'. Malcolm's article, in the *Philosophical Review*, January 1960, initiated a new phase of controversy. Both Malcolm, and Hartshorne who raised the matter earlier, regard the plausible version of the Proof as a sort of hypothesis which might be put (Hartshorne) as 'If "God" stands for something conceivable, it stands for something actual.' In relation to this they agree in finding Kant's argument guilty of a *petitio principii*. Malcolm puts it this way. Kant claims that the subject can simply be rejected, that is, not posited.

'I think that Caterus, Kant, and numerous other philosophers have been mistaken in supposing that the proposition "God is a necessary being" (or "God necessarily exists") is equivalent to the conditional proposition "If God exists then He necessarily exists". For how do they want the antecedent clause "*If* God exists" to be understood? Clearly they want it to imply that it is *possible* that God does not exist. The whole point of Kant's analysis is to try to show that it is possible to "reject the subject". [That is, to refuse to posit it . . .] Let us make this implication explicit in the conditional proposition so that it reads: "If God exists (and it is possible that He does not) then He necessarily exists." '

This, Malcolm says, is a self-contradictory position. Hartshorne, in his book *Man's Vision of God*, phrases the self-contradictory argument thus. 'If the necessary being happens to exist, that is as mere contingent fact it exists, then it exists not as contingent fact but as necessary truth. From this no subject emerges which it is possible to posit or not to posit.' Hartshorne says, 'We should, instead, say "If the phrase 'necessary being' has meaning, then what it means exists necessarily and if it exists necessarily then *a fortiori* it exists".' If we define God as not just existing but as necessarily existing, then we cannot frame a proposition which admits the possibility of his non-existence. This puts God in a different position from the triangle whose possible existence can be denied without contradiction. Malcolm (similarly) says that Kant's assertion that we can 'reject the subject' in the case of God, as in the case of the triangle, neglects an important difference. 'God exists necessarily' must be taken to be an *a priori* truth, it cannot logically be an empirical one. 'A triangle has three angles' is also an *a priori* truth; but one which can be hypothetically stated as: if a triangle exists (and it is possible that none does) it has three angles. Whereas the statement about God cannot be set up in this form without contradiction. Kant's criticism of the Proof is (Malcolm) 'self-contradictory, because it accepts *both* of two incompatible propositions'. The idea of necessary existence, uniquely God's property, cannot be dealt with by pointing out that in other cases (triangles or islands) existence is not a predicate. Kant's argument would only hold against an unclarified or misunderstood version of the Proof, not unlike Anselm's first statement of it, which fails to *insist* upon the difference between contingent and necessary existence. God's relation to the cosmos is *ex hypothesi* unique. A contingent God would be a demon and not God. The God in question, that is God (alone) does not and cannot exist contingently. This may be seen in Hartshorne and in Malcolm, and indeed in Anselm, as an important clarification of the concept of God. But what follows?

This new attention to the Proof, especially Malcolm's article, aroused a certain amount of amused attention among analytical philosophers, many of whom were not interested in God but in the technicalities of the argument. At this point we can hear Schopenhauer saying how right he was to call it a charming joke. A restated hypothetical argument says that if the concept of God is meaningful (not self-contradictory) God must necessarily exist. Hartshorne puts this emphatically by saying that 'where impossibility and mere unactualised possibility are both excluded there remains nothing but actuality if the idea has any meaning at all'. Malcolm summarises the argument as: God (as we understand him) cannot have come into existence, so if he does not exist his existence is impossible, and if he exists his existence is necessary. So if the concept is meaningful, if it is not self-contradictory, God exists. This seems to make the problem, in no trivial way, one of meaning. What is to count as 'any meaning at all'? Is the concept *in intellectu*? Gaunilo, a pious monk, said that he did not know the reality of God, nor could he conjecture it from any other reality. Anselm replied by quoting Paul. And as Barth points out, Paul's argument is Platonic. Malcolm's move brings out the ambiguity of 'meaning' which has, let us say, a strong filled sense, and a weak vague sense. Of course the word 'God' means something, sentences containing it are usually not nonsense, the concept has a history open to believers and unbelievers. (Compare 'Do you really understand what "goodness" means?') Malcolm and Hartshorne have made a point against Kant; but if the argument is to proceed and to establish anything like what was originally promised it is clearly in need of extra help. Such help might come from a strengthening and filling of the meaning of 'God', or to put it in 'demythologised' language, of the idea of an unconditional structure, through a philosophically refined appeal to moral and religious experience. Recent philosophers have resorted to this appeal, as Anselm did when he used Paul's words about how we can apprehend the invisible through the visible.

The ordinary unbeliever or Fool who robustly declares that there is no God does not of course trouble his head about whether or not he is asserting contingent non-existence. The sophisticated unbeliever might counter any attempt to argue necessary existence out of a strong sense of the word, by saying that 'God' is simply the proper name of a pseudo-entity in Judaeo-Christian superstition, effective perhaps as representing an emotive illusion in a localised language of private faith. J. N. Findlay (in *Mind* No. 226, April 1948, pre-Malcolm) used the machinery of the Ontological Proof to establish not the necessity, but the impossibility, of God's existence. His argument contains two complementary strands. If the question of necessity is to be raised then it is clear on both Kantian and modern views of this matter that there can be no such thing as necessary existence:

'Those who believe in necessary truths which are not merely tautological think that such truths merely connect the *possible* instances of various characteristics with each other: they do not expect such truths to tell them whether there *will* be instances of any characteristics. This is the outcome of the whole medieval and Kantian criticism of the Ontological Proof. And on a yet more modern view of the matter, necessity in propositions merely reflects our use of words, the arbitrary conventions of our language. On such a view the Divine Existence could only be a necessary matter if we had made up our minds to speak theistically *whatever the empirical circumstances might turn out to be.*'

'The religious frame of mind . . . desires the Divine Existence *both* to have that inescapable character which can, on Kantian or modern views, only be found where truth reflects a connection of characteristics as an arbitrary convention, *and also* the character of "making a real difference" which is only possible where truth does not have this merely hypothetical or linguistic basis . . . If God is to satisfy religious claims and needs, He must be a being in every way inescapable, one whose existence and possession of certain excellences we cannot possibly think away. And the views in question make it self-evidently absurd (if they do not make it ungrammatical) to speak of such a Being and attribute existence to Him.'

So in fact, Findlay concludes, Anselm's Proof entails, not that God must exist, but that he *cannot* exist. 'It was an ill day for Anselm when he hit upon his famous proof, for on that day he laid bare something that is of the essence of an adequate religious object, but also something that entails its necessary non-existence.' On Findlay's appeal to modern logic, Kant might be said to be intuitively right (as many people no doubt would feel) since 'necessity' could have no sense in the context. And from the nature of the concept itself no appeal to experience could make any 'strong' meaning strong enough. Here the believer may feel that Findlay's general reference to 'empirical circumstances' is too casual. How far may these, for purposes of the argument, be said to exist independently of how the world is seen and understood? Findlay's conclusion that what the concept of God demands is impossible need however, Findlay goes on to explain, cause no grief to the believer since it discredits the idolatry of 'merely existent' things, and brings out clearly, what many religious people actually understand, that any adequate religious object is necessarily non-existent. The concept can then remain, in some new sense, unique. This view of Findlay's of course fits well into arguments for the 'necessity', however understood, of the demythologisation of religion. Imprudently, as sturdy atheists might think, it opens the way toward a special sense of necessity, that of non-existence, in a demythologised religion, or to a renewed belief in *something* which is present 'whatever the empirical circumstances may be'. So Findlay's argument in effect, rather than following Kant and demolishing the Proof, brings out its deep meaning, which may be put thus. Morality is not one empirical phenomenon among others. Morality and demythologised religion are concerned with what is absolute, with unconditioned structure, with what cannot be 'thought away' out of human life, what Plato expressed in the concept of the Form of the Good, and Kant in the Categorical Imperative. What is in question here is something unique, of which the traditional idea of God was an image or metaphor and to which it has certainly been an effective pointer. Ordinary people, whether religious or not, mainly still believe that certain values are 'absolute' and in this sense unique. (See *The Ontological Argument*, ed. A. Plantinga, which usefully indicates various views of the Proof.)

Norman Malcolm replies to Findlay by appealing to a Wittgensteinian line of thought which may be entitled the '*Lebensform* and language-game argument', an argument from forms of life and universes of discourse. Malcolm's formal argument, although bearing in a negative critical sense against Kant, certainly seems in need of some more positive expansion if it is to be interesting to any inquisitive and open-minded Fool. Kant may have been wrong to assimilate God to a triangle, but is not the argument which is thus rescued still an empty one with merely grammatical merits? Kant's intuition may seem right, that idealising something will not make it exist. Malcolm challenges Findlay's assumption that necessity resides only inside sign-systems and uses of words and cannot belong to the real world. As he puts it, 'the view that logical necessity merely reflects the use of words cannot possibly have the implication that every existential proposition must be contingent.' That view requires us to *look* at the use of words and not manufacture *a priori* theses about it. Perhaps if we look we shall see that God is a special case after all. 'In the Ninetieth Psalm it is said, "Before the mountains were brought forth, or ever thou hadst formed the earth and the world, even from everlasting to everlasting thou art God."' 'Here is expressed,' Malcolm says, 'the idea of the necessary existence and eternity of God, an idea that is essential to the Jewish and Christian religions.' 'In those complex systems of thought, those "language-games", God has the status of a necessary being. Who can doubt that? Here we must say with Wittgenstein, "This language-game is played!".' Malcolm is quoting *Philosophical Investigations* 654. Wittgenstein uses the terms '*Lebensform*' and 'language-game' to draw our attention to the localised character of language and the ways in which meaning is determined by communal assent. (I discussed these concepts of Wittgenstein earlier.) In the quest for the meaning of the Ontological Proof the *Lebensformen*, or 'language-game', contextual argument is, in my view, a wrong turning. It ushers in the 'soft' idea, already at large in both theology and ethics, that there is something called 'religious language' which is 'expressive' not 'descriptive'. This path favours structuralism, existentialism, and a renewed life for emotive theories of ethics. Religion is thereby put in a corner, as one possible mode of proceeding. In what one might, in the spirit of Schopenhauer, call the 'game' played here by philosophers, one might wonder whether to start with the 'logical' argument and then invoke the argument from experience, showing *first* that the concept of God is not self-contradictory and *then* that it is full of meaning; or should one start with its meaning, in the hope that it will then be unnecessary to save it from being found to be self-contradictory? Malcolm quotes the Ninetieth Psalm. This escape from the ubiquitous strictness of 'logic', from the postulated unique and absolute nature of God (or Good) into the easier world of language-games and local meanings, is a perilous excursion, not a solution. The truth about 'the unconditional element in the structure of reason and reality', which is contained in the logical argument, should not be abandoned in favour of the notion that if

[ 413 ]

belief in God is 'efficacious' and some people use 'religious language' that is all the 'meaning' that is required.

Malcolm also uses a sort of transcendental argument. God necessarily cannot have come into existence, so if he does not exist his existence is impossible, if he exists it is necessary. God's existence is either impossible or necessary. It can only be impossible if it is self-contradictory or logically absurd. If this is not so he necessarily exists. And 'there is no more of a presumption that it [the concept of God] is self-contradictory than is the concept of seeing a material thing. Both concepts have a place in the thinking and the lives of human beings.' Malcolm's use of the Ninetieth Psalm may suggest that *any* local use of language, by people in church for instance, can offer a kind of 'local necessity'. Is the comparison with the material object more promising? There is an assertion about what we can and what we cannot 'think away' from human life which is in some form essentially contained in the Proof. God may not resemble triangles or islands, but what about objects and causes? Here the strict idea of being self-contradictory *or* necessary blends into some softer notion which involves imagination as well as logic. (Does logical necessity reign on other planets?) The material object example does not help much. We can imagine human life without objects. A minimalising series (without causes? Without coherence?) simply leads on to without humans. (All right, our planet ceases, as no doubt it will – we may or may not imagine God observing its demise.) A more relevant question might be: what about human life without values, without morals, without good and evil? The *goodness* of God is sometimes lost to view in logical discussions of the Proof. It is the argument from *experience* which reminds us that the necessity of God is internally connected with his goodness, that is with morality. At this point the meaning of 'value' (goodness, virtue, good and bad, etc.) is at risk, and the defender of the Proof (whether as proving God or Good) must stiffen the defences against ordinary cheerful cynics and against some linguistic philosophers and metaphysical thinkers who want to remove the concept of moral value from their picture. Another 'soft' deviation at this point could lead toward a vague cosmic sense of God as fate. The proper insistence that God cannot have come into existence and is not a particular could summon up the conception of a sort of cosmic presocratic deity who overwhelms us simply by being everything. Heidegger's 'Being' may be seen as first of all resembling the traditional Judaeo-

Christian God, and becoming later more like a wanton (game-playing) cosmic force. In *Sein und Zeit*, *Dasein* (human being) retires in order to make a space where Being can be. This sounds like Eckhart. But what about *love*? Heidegger does not use that terminology. Perhaps the ability of *Dasein* to encounter (invite) Being is really heroic, at least *aesthetic*, and not an image of some kind of virtue. There is a shadow in *Sein und Zeit* which grows darker later. Heidegger's concept is vulnerable to the fate which ultimately befalls it, when Being is no longer the invited guest of *Dasein* but a (considerably personified) mysterious arbitrary dispenser of fate for whom the human world is a plaything.

Wittgenstein's *Tractatus* expresses in its end section a moral or religious view which owes much to Schopenhauer and resembles a kind of stoicism or *amor fati*. However he also, in various disconnected observations, for instance in *Culture and Value* (*Vermischte Bemerkungen*), talked in a vaguer and more unsystematic way about religion and even God, sketching both logical arguments and appeals to experience.

'A proof of God's existence ought really to be something by means of which one could convince oneself that God exists. But I think that what *believers* who have furnished such proofs have wanted to do is to give their "belief" an intellectual analysis and foundation, although they themselves would never have come to believe as a result of such proofs. Perhaps one could "convince someone that God exists" by means of a certain kind of upbringing, by shaping his life in such and such a way. Life can educate one to a belief in God. And *experiences* too are what bring this about; but I don't mean visions and other forms of sense experience which show us the "existence of this being", but e.g. sufferings of various sorts. These neither show us God in the way a sense impression shows us an object, nor do they give rise to *conjectures* about him. Experiences, thoughts – life can force this concept upon us. So perhaps it is similar to the concept of an "object"'.

(pp. 85–6.)

Similar, that is, in the respect of being overwhelmingly suggested by experience. When Wittgenstein says that life can 'force' the concept of God upon us, he seems to be using a sense of the word less strict, certainly less general, than the sense in which the concepts of material object or cause are forced upon us. He is presumably not just referring

[415]

to the empirical fact that people are instinctively led to console themselves by addressing God. Yet again, who can say, when a man prays, whether this is 'mere superstition' or 'something casual' or 'the real thing'? What Wittgenstein certainly expresses is a very general and intuitive view to the effect that suffering 'deepens' our lives and drives us toward some sense of an absolute.

Norman Malcolm, concerned to establish that the concept of God has meaning, carries his argument further in order to establish a 'strong' sense of 'God' by asking us to reflect on what human life is like, or *really* like. Malcolm's remark that the concept of God, like the concept of an object, has 'a place in the thinking and the lives of human beings', is followed by a more explicit and personal experiential argument about the kind of place which 'God' might occupy. The *Lebensformen* 'rescue' of the concept of God, may be said to involve a very general argument from experience – if 'the game is played' we can observe the circumstances in which it is played – which may profitably be made more explicit. 'Even if one allows that Anselm's phrase may be free of self-contradiction, one wants to know how it can have *meaning* for anyone. Why is it that human beings have even *formed* the concept of an infinite being, a being a greater than which cannot be conceived? . . . I am sure that there cannot be a deep understanding of that concept without an understanding of the phenomena of human life that gave rise to it.' Malcolm's way of putting the matter here may seem to say no more than that 'God' is a concept which we have, at times, motives, such as those mentioned by Wittgenstein, to frame or attend to. In terms of some even tentative sympathy with the argument that if 'God' is meaningful God exists, we might prefer to say that God is a (necessary) being of whom we are implicitly conscious and of whom we learn explicitly through experience. The whole argument is delicately poised at this point. If it is said that we can be ignorant or oblivious of God, some will say that this proves that he does not exist, while others will say that we are 'really' not ignorant and oblivious: the same problem is encountered concerning knowledge of Good (moral sense, conscience). Are we 'really' ever completely unaware of our duty? As an example of one of the phenomena which lead us to frame the perhaps illusory concept, or discover the necessary being, of God, Malcolm instances an overwhelming feeling of guilt, 'a guilt "a greater than which cannot be conceived" ', for which is required an equally measureless power to forgive. 'Out of such a storm in the soul, I am suggesting, there arises the conception of a forgiving mercy that is limitless, beyond all measure. This is one important feature of the Jewish and Christian conception of God.' He goes on to quote Kierkegaard to this effect: 'There is only one proof of the truth of Christianity, and that quite rightly is from the emotions, when the dread of sin and a heavy conscience torture a man into crossing the narrow line between despair bordering on madness, and Christendom.' (*Journals*, trans. A. Dru, 926.) (These are strong words. Only one proof?) Thus Malcolm and Kierkegaard agree with Wittgenstein in mentioning suffering as likely to force the concept of God upon us. Perhaps only one experience (or type of experience) might suffice to suggest a meaning and to enable an individual to administer the whole Proof to himself. I am forced, in a situation which strips me of consolation and compels deep thought, to think in this way and the fact that I am thinking in this way proves that that which I am thinking points to a reality. Descartes wraps up the Ontological Proof in one package with *cogito ergo sum*, but without demanding any special or extreme state of mind. The existentialist line of thought, in the style of Kierkegaard, and *mutatis mutandis* of Sartre, and of some modern theologians, not only suggests that spiritual understanding emerges especially *in extremis*, but also implies that people who lead quiet orderly lives are less spiritual than those who are errant and tormented. And may it not be said that *per contra* great guilt arouses a great desire for forgiveness and with it the *illusion* that it *must* be available. The view of salvation by extremes is consoling, much in evidence in fiction. (Also see Sartre's *Saint Genet*, or Mauriac's *Thérèse*.) Extreme sin *deserves* extreme grace. Malcolm's case may strike us as rather specialised. Wittgenstein too spoke of various sorts of sufferings. But if there is any sort of proof from experience via meaning, should not the relevant phenomena be, not esoteric, but of great generality? What sort of experience can provide a strong enough meaning? If the meaning of 'God' can be learnt from experience might we not expect the lesson to be everywhere visible? In an obvious sense there are religious 'worlds', groups or communities with shared words and feelings; but in another sense all the world must be 'religious'. Malcolm goes on:

'Surely there is a level at which one can view the argument as a piece of logic, following the deductive moves but not being touched religiously? I think so. But even at this level the argument may not be without religious value, for it may help to remove some philosophical scruples that stand in the way of faith. At a deeper level, I suspect that the argument can be thoroughly understood only by one who has a view of that human 'form of life' that gives rise to the idea of an infinitely great being ... It would be unreasonable to require that the recognition of Anselm's demonstration as valid must produce a conversion.'

Whether philosophical scruples are removed by exhibiting the Proof I am not sure. Malcolm connects religion with the idea of an infinite being. The scruples of the modern mind are in general likely to concern the supernatural aspects or 'accidents' of the traditional God, including his claim to be a person; and in removing these by a process of radical demythologisation the idea of experience must play a part. Those who do not want to save the traditional God, but want religion to continue, in a way not unconnected with its past, as an assertion of an absolute (necessary) moral claim upon humanity, will need to see the whole of human experience as indicating this.

This must bring us back to reflect upon the origins of Anselm's Proof in Plato, where we can see the argument as one from the whole of experience, showing how the unique and special and all-important knowledge of good and evil is learnt in every kind of human activity. The question of *truth*, which we are indeed *forced* to attend to in all our doings, appears here as an aspect of the *unavoidable* nature of morality. Here, to speak of 'religious language' as something specialised, supposed to be expressive rather than referential, is to separate religion from the truth-seeking struggle of the whole of life. Religion is not a special subject or one activity among others. Art too is part of the struggle, art is not *either* photographs of facts *or* outbursts of private feeling. In understanding how great art utterly transcends this (version of the fact–value distinction) we exercise our general ability to distinguish what is illusory from what is real. Great art is just and true and deep in ways which are internally connected with its beauty. It inspires unselfish love, and can be seen, as Kant allowed beauty to be, as an analogon of moral good. Praise and worship are not just expressive attitudes, they arise in very various cognitive contexts and are themselves a grasp of reality. In prayer we wait for God (for the spirit and light of goodness) to be made manifest. One image of prayer is the artist who, rejecting easy false mediocre forms and hoping for the right thing, the best thing, *waits*. This too is an image (how constantly in this way the pictures interrelate) of all kinds of stilled attentive situations in work and in human relations where the waiting is intensely collected yet relaxed: 'fearlessly passive', to use Adorno's phrase. Valéry speaks of the sunlight which rewards him who steadily contemplates the insuperable difficulty. What is awaited is an illuminating experience, some kind of certainty, a *presence*: a case of human consciousness at its most highly textured. Of course incoherent desperation can be prayer too.

I think that useless confusion arises from attempts to extend the meaning of our word 'God' to cover *any* conception of a spiritual reality. This move, which 'saves' the concept through a sort of liberal vagueness, clouds over the problem without solving it. 'God' is the name of a supernatural person. It makes a difference whether we believe in such a person, as it makes a difference whether Christ rose from the dead. These differences do not generally, or do not yet, affect whether or not people are virtuous; though wholesale loss of religious belief is likely to remove with it some of the substance of moral thought and action, which was provided for instance by prayer and church-going. Perhaps (I believe) Christianity can continue without a personal God or a risen Christ, without beliefs in supernatural places and happenings, such as heaven and life after death, but retaining the mystical figure of Christ occupying a place analogous to that of Buddha: a Christ who can console and save, but who is to be found as a living force within each human soul and not in some supernatural elsewhere. Such a continuity would preserve and renew the Christian tradition as it has always hitherto, somehow or other, been preserved and renewed. It has always changed itself into something that can be generally believed. Perhaps this cannot be brought about soon enough, that is before Christian belief and practice virtually disappear. To accomplish this leap it might also be necessary for philosophers to become theologians and theologians to become philosophers, and this is not very likely to happen either.

I have been talking as a neo-Christian or Buddhist Christian or Christian fellow traveller. The Jewish religion lacks, or is not burdened by, the attractive figure of Christ who appears in Christianity as a mediator, but might in some strict sense be regarded as an idol or barrier. It could be said that Judaism, the other great religion of the west, is already partly demythologised owing to a more strict observance of the Second Commandment. God is not visible or tangible. Yet what could be more *present* to us than the God of the Psalms? As the hart panteth after water brooks, so panteth my soul after thee, O God. Of course this is not to be lost, it is to be understood. There is a feeling among many religious believers and fellow travellers that it is time to say goodbye to the old literal personal 'elsewhere' God. I want to quote here from a Jewish thinker, Martin Buber, who describes an argument about God with another religious man. This man says to Buber, 'How can you bring yourself to say "God" time after time? How can you expect that your readers will take the word in the sense in which you wish it to be taken? What you mean by the name of God is something above all human grasp and comprehension, but in speaking about it you have lowered it to human conceptualisation. What word of human speech is so misused, so defiled, so desecrated as this! ... All the injustice that it has been used to cover has effaced its features.' Buber replies:

'Yes, it is the most heavy-laden of all human words. None has become so soiled, so mutilated. Just for this reason I may not abandon it. Generations of men have laid the burden of their anxious lives upon this word ... it lies in the dust and bears their whole burden. The races of man with their religious factions have torn the word to pieces; they have killed for it and died for it, and it bears their fingermarks and their blood. Where might I find a word like it to describe the highest! If I took the purest, most sparkling concept from the inner treasure-chamber of the philosophers, I could only capture thereby an unbinding product of thought. I could not capture the presence of Him whom the generations of men have honoured and degraded with their awesome living and dying. I do indeed mean Him whom the hell-tormented and heaven-storming generations of men mean. Certainly, they draw caricatures and write "God" underneath; they murder one another and say "in God's name". But when all madness and delusion fall to dust, when they stand over against Him in the loneliest darkness and no longer say "He, He", but rather sigh "Thou", shout "Thou", all of them the one word, and when they then add "God", is it not the real God whom they all implore, the One Living God, the God of the children of man? Is it not He who *hears* them? And just for this reason is not the word "God", the word of appeal, the word which has become a *name*, consecrated in all human tongues for all time? We must esteem those who interdict it because they rebel against the injustice and wrong which are so readily referred to "God" for authorisation. But we may not give it up. How understandable it is that some suggest that we should remain silent about the "last things" for a time in order that the misused words may be redeemed! But they are not to be redeemed *thus*. We cannot cleanse the word "God" and we cannot make it whole; but, defiled and mutilated as it is, we can raise it from the ground and set it over an hour of great care.'

(*The Eclipse of God*, pp. 17–18.)

This puts with moving eloquence the case for retaining the word 'God', as the name of that *resource*, that *Thou* to whom men turn for help or pardon in their loneliest hours. However, what is envisaged here is, as far as I can see, still an external supernatural person. Even put in Buber's terms it is still the same consoling religious picture. We may hold dialogues or 'dialogues' with other people, with works of art, with animals, with symbolic figures, with parts of our own souls. Here we may well rightly cherish the powerful word 'thou'. Indeed we can erect the concept of dialogue almost everywhere. But Buber wishes to invoke, in the midst of our human tensions, the external and familiar, really existing elsewhere, father figure. Buber's words concerning the cry uttered in the loneliest darkness are very moving. Why can we not simply say 'Yes', as to a mystery? Yet I think it matters how we are to think, and how people now *can* think, about that imagined presence.

In 1931 Wittgenstein wrote some *Remarks on Frazer's Golden Bough*. He also wrote, not appearing as part of the text, the following brief notes. 'I think now that the right thing would be to begin my book with remarks about metaphysics as a kind of magic. But in doing this I must neither speak in defence of magic nor ridicule it. What it is that is deep about magic would be kept – In this context, in fact, keeping magic out has itself the character of magic. For when I began in my earlier book to talk about the "*world*" (and not about this tree or table), was I trying to do anything except conjure up something of a higher order by my words?' This is the A. C. Miles–Rush Rhees translation. The last clause in German is: *was wollte ich anderes als etwas*

*Höheres in meine Worte bannen.* The 'earlier book' must be the *Tractatus*, the book to come presumably the *Investigations*. (The fragment is dated by Rhees 'not earlier than 1936 and probably after 1948'.) *Das Höhere* (*Tractatus* 6. 432) belongs with *das Mystische* (6. 44). ('*How* the world is, is indifferent for what is higher . . . Not how the world is but *that* it is is the mystical.') I think *bannen* here should be taken also in a sense of segregate, meaning that the 'higher' is, not driven away, but *kept* (what is *deep* about magic is to be *kept*), captured, secluded, safe, away from the world, 'indifferent' to the world, indeed 'spell-bound'. (To spell-bind is a possible meaning of *bannen*.) This also defines 'world' as not just a list of trees and tables but a realm, something itself enclosed and complete. So, the *deep* thing which resides in magic is protected by a magical enclosure. What, in general, would Wittgenstein have had to say about metaphysics as magic? A remark in *Culture and Value* (p. 75), speaks quizzically, looking back (to *Notebooks* and *Tractatus*), of metaphysics as something 'seen against the background of the eternal' (with moral and mystical as fundamental). There is very little (genuine) metaphysics, and it is difficult to generalise about it, certainly at the level of Wittgenstein's remarks about magic. It can be motivated by religious passion, by science, by vast brilliant tolerant curiosity, by an obsessional desire to put things in order, or some or all of these (etc.). One might say a metaphysician must have *nerve*, the nerve for instance to rule by decree (by magic). Think of the sheer *nerve* of the *Tractatus* or of Kant's great structure. But there is another way which consists of constructing a huge hall of reflection full of light and space and fresh air, in which ideas and intuitions can be unsystematically nurtured. 'There are, indeed, things which cannot be put into words. They *make themselves manifest*. They are what is mystical.' (*Tractatus* 6. 522; trans. Pears and McGuinness.) The metaphysical magic, the fiat, the confident shameless picture-making of 'the earlier book' magically segregrates what is higher in order to keep it (its own kind of magic) safe, to emphasise its separateness, its inevitably *mystical* character, its silence, its absolute lack of connection with science, that is with the empirical world. 'My propositions serve as elucidations in the following way: anyone who understands me eventually recognises them as nonsensical, when he has used them – as steps – to climb up beyond them. (He must, so to speak, throw away the ladder after he has climbed it.) He must transcend these propositions, and then he will see the world aright. What we cannot speak about we must pass over in silence.' (End of the *Tractatus*.) Philosophy then is to be a *via negativa*, *like* the road to the mystical God which consists of all that He is not, the satisfactions of the material world, and the illusion of its reality. (The Nothing of Nirvana in Buddhism, the Sun in Plato.) Wittgenstein's *via* is of course, in relation to such comparisons, silent. The metaphysics of the *Tractatus*, which confronts other metaphysics, must be seen as nonsense. (Compare Plato's myths which are not to be taken literally.) It is a teaching, a *proper* kind of magic. It is interesting however to see how often the word 'mystical' is allowed to occur. We are also reminded (not of course by Wittgenstein) of Kant's 'magic' which removes God and the noumenal world, keeping them *separate* and *safe* outside the bounds of our knowledge, outside our 'world'. Kant allows, as Wittgenstein does not, a direct line from what is higher in the form of the call of duty. Wittgenstein's distaste for 'duty' is like that of Schopenhauer, who was inclined to allude freely to the mystical in a way in which Wittgenstein was not. The reference to the *Tractatus* serves as a comment upon why Wittgenstein was sufficiently annoyed with Frazer to spend time attacking him – in terms designed to protect what is deep in the magical (and the mystical) from the crude blundering explanations of the scientist. I quote from the *Remarks*:

'Frazer's account of the magical and religious notions of men is unsatisfactory; it makes these notions appear as *mistakes*. Was Augustine mistaken, then, when he called upon God on every page of the *Confessions*? . . . Frazer says it is very difficult to discover the error in magic and this is why it persists for so long – because, for example, a ceremony which is supposed to bring rain is sure to appear effective sooner or later. But then it is queer that people do not notice sooner that it does rain sooner or later anyway. I think one reason why the attempt to find an explanation is wrong is that we have only to put together in the right way what we *know*, without adding anything, and the satisfaction we are trying to get from the explanation comes of itself . . . We can only *describe* and say, human life is like that . . . How could fire or fire's resemblance to the sun have failed to make an impression on the awakening mind of man? But not "because he can't explain it" (the stupid superstition of our time) – for does an "explanation" make it less impressive? . . . Frazer cannot imagine a priest who is not basically an English parson of our times with all his stupidity and feebleness ... An historical explanation, an explanation as an hypothesis of the development, is only *one* kind of summary of the data – of their synopsis. We can equally well see the data in their relations to one another and make a summary of them in a general picture without putting it in the form of a hypothesis regarding the temporal development ... I *can* set out this law in an hypothesis of development [*eine Entwicklungshypothese*], or again, in analogy with the schema of a plant I can give it in the schema of a religious ceremony, but I can also do it just by arranging the factual material so that we can easily pass from one part to another and have a clear view of it – showing it in a *"perspicuous"* way [*in einer "übersichtlichen" Darstellung*]. For us the conception of a perspicuous presentation is fundamental. It indicates the form in which we write of things, the way in which we see things. (A kind of *"Weltanschauung"* that seems to be typical of our times. Spengler.) This perspicuous presentation makes possible that understanding which consists just in the fact that we "see the connections". Hence the importance of finding *intermediate links*. But in our case a hypothetical link is not meant to do anything except draw attention to the similarity, the connection, between the *facts*.'

So, we can only *describe* human life; fire, and fire's likeness to sun, are of course impressive phenomena, one does not have to say why, we are not bound to explain or explain away or treat as an error St Augustine's call upon God. These things are to be looked at, treated with respect. One must just arrange the facts in a clear and intelligible (perspicuous) manner and be satisfied with looking. (*Übersichlichkeit*, translated 'bird's-eye view', in *Philosophical Remarks*, p. 52.) There is much here of what is right in the structuralist revolt against that sort of 'scientific' anthropology. Of course structuralist thinkers, far from being purely negative, have produced a massive counter-theory; whereas Wittgenstein, failing to satisfy the 'other person' of *Tractatus* 6. 53, has simply told us to look at how things are. Not always easy. Possibly he did not intend the remark about the magic of metaphysics for publication. The remarks about the perspicuous representation, the way *we* write and see things, the need to set out the *connections*, and the notion of *Weltanschauung* are repeated at *Investigations* 122.

Wittgenstein says that 'the human body is the best picture of the human soul'. (*Investigations* II iv, p. 178.) I would say that the best picture of most kinds of thinking is perception, and the best picture of serious contemplative thinking is serious contemplative perception; as when we *attend* to a human face, music, a flower, a visual work of art (etc. etc.). Such close mental attention involves the conception of 'presence'. The Ontological Proof is an exercise in serious contemplative thinking of this kind. 'Ontological Proof is mysterious because it doesn't address itself to the intelligence, but to love.' Simone Weil, *Notebooks*, p. 375. (See also pp. 80, 100, 108.) The 'necessity' of the Proof is a certainty which belongs to the battlefield of our existence as humans, and to the creative imagination and love which is part of this. The argument is (may be seen as) transcendental. The definition of God (the necessity and sovereignty of Good) is connected with the definition of a human being. We can 'think away' material objects from human existence, but not the concepts of good, true, and real. Is this an empirical matter? Here the sense of a logical certainty reaches out to join hands with an experiential one. Collingwood described Anselm as pondering upon the unavoidability of the idea of God, and finding 'latent within it' the Platonic idea that 'real thinking' has a real object. (*An Essay on Philosophical Method*, p. 124.) What is at stake here if we wish to abandon 'God' and try 'Good' instead may be taken to interest moral philosophy, or both moral philosophy and theology. Perhaps moral philosophy may in some way be 'forced' to concern itself with the demythologisation of religion; that is with the 'deep' human reality upon which both religion and morality rest, and which may be easier to discern and discuss now that religion is detaching itself from supernatural dogma. This age, which produces pseudo-scientific anti-human 'philosophies', also makes possible new modes of reflection. Certainly theology cannot ignore, indissolubly includes, some form of moral philosophy. With these changes comes a deepened general understanding of great philosophers, such as Plato and Kant, who assumed as obvious the deep connection, indeed identity, between a moral and a religious view. Those who reject 'God' but are attracted by the Proof may do so in order to clarify a central problem in moral philosophy, or may also wish to arrive at some clearer view of a Godless religion. The reasons for rejecting God are themselves clarified by the Proof. No empirical contingent being could be the required God and what is 'necessary' cannot be God either. The concept of an existing personal being is too deeply embedded in the traditional idea of God. One might say that God is impossible, though (in obvious senses of 'meaning') not meaningless. Well, does not the Proof prove *some-*

*thing* to be necessary? It is *about* necessity and certainty and goodness.

Why the quest for certainty, why should *that* be so specially important? Certainty here is the subjective aspect of the necessary existence
of God. It *must* be so. 'I *know* that my Redeemer liveth.' And must
not all morality rest, as Kant felt, upon a similar *certainty*? It is not a
matter of accident or speculation. Yet moral confidence is often mis-
placed. This fact has a fundamental position in political philosophy.
'Be tolerant' is a political axiom. Should not the idea of certainty be
regarded with sceptical caution? 'Certainties' occasion persecutions.
This too must be kept in mind. The good citizen must use his private
wisdom to deal with these public matters. In discussing the Ontological
Proof I have wanted to move from 'God' to 'Good', taking 'religion'
along too. There are various problems about 'religion' and being
'religious', which concern liturgy, rites, styles of meditation and so on.
There is in an ordinary superficial sense a religious outlook, religious
preoccupations, a religious psychology which is detachable from
dogma. The word 'religiosity' might convey an adverse view of such a
field. Religion is a mode of belief in the unique sovereign place of
goodness or virtue in human life. One might put it flatly by saying that
there is something about moral value which goes *jusqu'au bout*. It must
go all the way, to the base, to the top, it must be everywhere, and is in
this respect unlike other things (e.g. sex) of which something apparently
similar might be said. It adheres essentially to the conception of being
human, and cannot be detached; and we may express this by saying
that it is not accidental, does not exist contingently, is above being.
This is a theoretical philosophical way of talking which may or may
not attract religious imagery. Anselm's Proof has interested thinkers
because it seems so concise and 'logical'. But neither its Christian nor
its logical charms must be allowed to conceal its fundamental sense.
The idea of Good (goodness, virtue) crystallises out of our moral activity. The concept of good emphasises a unity of aspiration and belief
concerning the absolute importance of what is done on this heterogeneous scene. What the Proof 'proves' speaks with an especially apt
voice now when traditional supernatural religious beliefs fade, and seem
to be *inevitably* superseded by scientific and technological modes and
conceptions of human existence. The charm and power of technology
and the authority of a 'scientific outlook' conceal the speed with which
the idea of the responsible moral spiritual individual is being diminished.
The fragmentation of morality menaces this individual, as it menaces

the society in which he flourishes. Political utilitarianism may also lead people with high motives into a 'specialised' fragmented morality. In extreme situations of this sort, which may seem to some young people the only 'moral' situations with which they can engage, the idea of the virtuous individual tends to vanish. A cynic (or structuralist) might say of our age that it is the end of the era of 'the virtuous individual'.

The unity and fundamental reality of goodness is an image and support of the unity and fundamental reality of the individual. What is fundamental here is ideal or transcendent, never fully realised or analysed, but continually rediscovered in the course of the daily struggle with the world, and the imagination and passion whereby it is carried on. We may seem to compartmentalise value, but if we look more closely these divisions take place against a base of possible further, better, deeper, understanding and achievement. This is *characteristic* of morality. We *know* of perfection as we look upon what is imperfect. The division of *axiomatic* political morality from private individual morality represents a recognition for general purposes that we cannot achieve a perfect harmonious good society composed of saintly citizens. A liberal view of society wisely imposes a certain modesty upon political idealism. The individual lives against a more extended and ambiguous vision of the impossibility of perfected virtue, and is consciously responsible for any limitation upon his will to be good. The human scene is one of moral failure combined with the remarkable continued return to an idea of goodness as unique and absolute. What can be compared with this? If space visitors tell us that there is no value on their planet, this is not like saying there are no material objects. We would ceaselessly *look* for value in their society, wondering if they were lying, had different values, had misunderstood. At the level of 'no patterns', 'no experience', 'no consciousness' things really break down, but then we cannot set up the example either. There is something here which can be expressed in terms of what is contingent and what is necessary in some non-tautological, not merely linguistic sense. This is where we press language to express the ubiquitous importance of the concept of morality, when it is seriously and strictly considered. This fundamental importance, this kind of (*realissimum*) reality, is what religion in all sorts of ways, with help from art, *reveals* and *celebrates*. What is revealed is 'more important than itself' in the sense of being its 'essence'. Religious mystics have 'taken leave' of their gods to point to something central and mysterious and most real, and difficult to talk about. As for philosophers, they may either ignore the central point, or do the best they can. Religion reveals and celebrates virtue and also exhibits the sense in which its place in human life is mysterious. An ultimate religious 'belief' must be that even if all 'religions' were to blow away like mist, the necessity of virtue and the reality of the good would remain. This is what the Ontological Proof tries to 'prove' in terms of a unique formulation. This is for thinkers to look at. The ordinary fellow 'just knows', for one is speaking of something which is in a sense obvious, the unique nature of morality. The argument for the thinker, after certain clarifications, must largely take the form of a combing-over of experience, with special emphasis upon the connection between the ideas of truth and knowledge and reality, and the place thus made for the concept of love. In the *Symposium*, Eros is not the Good, he is not even a god, he is a spirit which moves toward good. Here, in this combing, the concept of Good may seem to recede while being omnipresent. The idea of perfection haunts all our activity, and we are well aware of how we try to blot it out. Here we see how it matters to talk or think about 'the Good' or 'virtue' as something unitary, rather than just instancing cases of admirable conduct. This 'Good' is not the old God in disguise, but rather what the old God symbolised.

This is Ontological Proof language. In trying to make sense of it we may return to the image of the craftsman and, in spite of Plato, to the artist. Kant, who took the duty of truth-telling to be absolute, also said that 'the beautiful was a symbol of the morally good'. *Critique of Aesthetic Judgment*, Analytic of the Sublime, section 59, 'Beauty as the symbol of Morality'. This work, incidentally, shows Kant at his most engagingly readable, full of examples and jokes and light. The good artist is a sort of image of the good man, the great artist is a sort of image of the saint. He is only a sort of image, since in his whole person he may be a dreadful egoist. Artists have their own specialised temptations to egoism and illusions of omnipotence. Art is power. We are all specialists in morality (after all, we can't be expected to resist *every* sort of temptation!), and it is difficult (impossible) for the whole man to be virtuous. But inside his work, and 'in so far as he is an artist', to use the device employed at the beginning of the *Republic*, he can be humble and truthful and brave and inspired by a love of perfection. Rilke, talking about painting and poetry: 'We must *work*.' There is *always* work to do. We can always work at something, somehow, for someone, for some truth or some good, though this may seem in many contexts a hard saying. Art and craft are formal images of all our busy activities wherein we do well or badly. In general, in the 'combing-through' of experience, good art can figure, not only as an image, but as a kind of evidence, a sort of Ontological Proof, since here we may see more clearly on display how when we connect what is real with what is good we find out what truth means, and how in seeking truth (the right formulation, the better work) we also understand virtue and the 'feel' of reality. Here we may experience the unity of the moral life. In fact the good man, if we can find him, is probably not an artist. Artists have great quasi-spiritual satisfactions, false 'highests', which may arrest progress (Plato's fear). Artists celebrate saints, Plato celebrated Socrates, Paul and the evangelists celebrated Christ. Even this is picturesque. Perhaps some artists can manage it. St John of the Cross was an artist. But what (as I said earlier) do we really know about the detailed lives of famous holy men? What do we even know of Christ, who is and has been for innumerable people the human individual to whom they feel closest? He certainly seems to be a unique case, a *hapax legomenon*, a personal Ontological Proof. (A role, incidentally, in which Kant rejected him: we must look not at Christ, but at our own rational conscience.) But the Christ who saves is the mystical Christ whom we make our own, whose figure is a mixture of essence and accident, partly a creation of art as well as being compact of everything we know about goodness. We look through this Christ into the mystery of good. And so also with the figures and images of other religions including those which, like Judaism and Islam, have made their 'medium' the pointed absence of the image. It may be said that all saints may be used as icons, but are as individuals merely imaginary. There are innumerable unknown saints and martyrs, such as the dissident who is shot down crying out the truth, or perishes incognito in prison. The contingently existing saint who, if we were ever fortunate enough to *meet* him or her, might stand to us in the guise of a demonstration (to show it can be done), might be some quiet unpretentious worker, a schoolteacher or a mother, or better still an aunt. Mothers have many egoistic satisfactions and much power. The aunt may be the selfless unrewarded doer of good. I have known such aunts. In the activity of such workers egoism has disappeared *unobtrusively* into the care and service of others. The egoism of the good artist or craftsman is 'burnt up' in the product. Rilke again, about Cézanne: 'The consuming of love in anonymous work.' And we may also think of Shakespeare. Here we see how Kant's 'practical love' is given warmth by Plato's Eros. The possible saints, aunts, dissidents, social workers and so on, may or may not have any sort of religious vision. How can one know anyway? Some saintly figures are self-evidently 'religious', others may be invisible, buried deep in families or offices or silent religious houses. The vision if any may have been entirely dissolved into the work. 'Christ? Who is he? Oh yes – I forgot.' At the highest level this is practical mysticism, where the certainty and the absolute appear incarnate and immediate in the needs of others.

The proof of the necessity or unique status of good runs through our grasp of an idea of perfection which comes to us in innumerable situations, where we are trying to do something well or are conscious of failure. Kant rightly suggests that there is often a unique 'feel' about such situations. This way of looking at the matter binds together the two arguments in Anselm's Proof. What is perfect must exist, that is, what we think of as goodness and perfection, the 'object' of our best thoughts, must be something real, indeed especially and most real, not as contingent accidental reality but as something fundamental, essential and necessary. What is experienced as most real in our lives is connected with a value which points further on. Our consciousness of failure is a source of knowledge. We are constantly in process of recognising the falseness of our 'goods', and the unimportance of what we deem important. Great art teaches a sense of reality, so does ordinary living and loving. We find out in the most minute details of our lives that the good is the real. Philosophy too can attend to such details, using as examples or 'evidence' experiences which are frequently, and of course emotionally, portrayed in literature. Poets, whose 'evidence' is in their work, may also generalise about it more boldly. 'What the imagination seizes as beauty must be truth, whether it existed before or not.' (Keats.) 'At its highest point, love is a determination to create that which it has taken for its object.' (Valéry.) The appeal to evidence, to reports of experience, and to the direct experience of the reader, is precarious, but is in some regions of philosophy not only the last resort but the proper and best move. A fundamental idea here, and one which in ordinary life is a familiar one, is that of certainty or (its different face) necessity, connected with the sense of a pure untainted source of spiritual power. Herein our most ordinary modes of cognition become connected with strong convictions and vision, of which the conviction and vision of the great artist is both an image and an instance.

# > 14 <

# Descartes and Kant

In continuing the argument I want now to turn away from Plato and look at the same or similar ideas reflected in Descartes and Kant. But before that I shall say something brief by way of introduction. I quote Paul Tillich again:

'The limits of the ontological argument are obvious. But nothing is more important for philosophy and theology than the truth it contains, the acknowledgement of the unconditional element in the structure of reason and reality . . . Modern secularism is rooted largely in the fact that the unconditional element in the structure of reason and reality was no longer seen, and that therefore the idea of God was imposed on the mind as a "strange body". This produced first heteronomous subjection, and then autonomous rejection. The destruction of the ontological *argument* is not dangerous. What is dangerous is the destruction of an approach which elaborates the possibility of the question of God. This approach is the meaning and truth of the ontological argument.'

(*Systematic Theology*, Part II, section 1.)

Heidegger suggested that only now can the concept of divinity be genuinely considered and understood. Perhaps it is true that we are, in this age, really in a general forum considering it openly at last. Tillich glances at the past in speaking of something which was, and is, 'no longer seen'. One may also say that religion involving supernatural beliefs (in a literal after-life etc.) was always partly a kind of illusion, and that we are now being forced by an inevitable sophistication to have a demythologised religion or none at all. In this time of deep change, it seems better to drop the old word 'God' with its intimations

[ 431 ]

of an elsewhere, and of an omniscient spectator and responsive super-thou. Religion can exist without this western concept of a personal God, and does so in Buddhism and Hinduism.

However it may also be said of those who pursue this line of thought that they are changing religion into philosophy before our eyes. Heraclitus said that the one which alone is wise does not want, and wants, to be called Zeus. The *Ens Realissimum* does not want to be called God, but also does. He seems to need and want a persona and a name, and we are but too eager to give it to him, as it brings him closer and comforts us; on the other hand he does not want it because if he be named as an individual he becomes but one more contingent thing among others, even if the grandest one, and subject to the fate of what is contingent. Too great a refinement loses the thing itself. Is not religion to do with going to a shrine and kneeling down and worshipping? Well, worship is something personal and symbolic which each individual must 'make his own'. The outward and visible things show us the inward and invisible things. There are all sorts of ways in which we use the visible for the invisible, life is riddled with metaphor and symbolism, this is not a 'special subject', it is everywhere. Religious ritual (in the strict sense) is both a special case and a delicate plant. Our prejudices about it are very deep and can be very irrational. Catholics and Protestants are amazed and horrified at each other's procedures. I have been arguing in various ways for a moral philosophy which accommodates the 'unconditional element in the structure of reason and reality'. Theology has always had to 'place' (relate to) ethics, whereas ethics has often ignored theology. A changing theology may now more easily relate to a changing ethics. The institutions of religion must of course look after themselves and the argument about morality is independent of historically based speculations about the future of church-going or reactions to the particular activities of religious groups. Moral philosophy must also include political philosophy, must be organised to accommodate the morality of political thinking, a subject which arouses much emotion in popular discussion. Ideally a (western) philosopher should know and consider the whole of philosophy, that is (in the west) from the Greeks to the present day; and also know something about oriental religion (that is, philosophy). Moral philosophy must of course be conscious of the criticisms of traditional metaphysics which have occupied philosophers since Kant, and particularly in this century. If we now call a philosophy 'metaphysics' are we redefining the term? (The Ontological Proof raises the question: What is metaphysics?) A metaphysical argument is characteristically inconclusive and involves an appeal to experience which is partly a use of art. (Metaphysics as a kind of magic: Wittgenstein.) The artist makes us see what is, in a sense manifestly and edifyingly open to discussion, *there* (real), but unseen before, and the metaphysician does this too. Art and philosophy enliven the concept of reality. This is a place where the word 'being' is also used, which I prefer to avoid. The language of ontology may divide the argument from ordinary testable experience just at the point where it is most important to join it. Jargon removes us from our experienced world. The sophisticated language of great art is not jargon. Of course great philosophers generate technical terms, but they also offer them most evidently as explanations and justifications of what is experienced. In my view, the propagation of technical terms should be left to geniuses. (Perhaps the under-labourers of philosophy should aspire to the status of art critics.) And indeed, if we reflect, there are not all that many *essential* technical terms in philosophy.

Even if it should prove to be the case that nothing we would now call religion is destined to survive, philosophical arguments may still properly be offered to the effect that morality must be philosophically defined in terms of an unconditional demand. 'The religious life' often employs ritual, which is not an essential item in 'the moral life'. One may be attracted by various kinds of religious ritual, see and feel them as vehicles of enlightenment, as exercises likely to strengthen good desires; and in wanting religion to survive, want ritual to survive too. This is unlike the idle admiration for great or famous men which, as Kierkegaard says, soothes the soul and induces 'sound sleep'. Holy objects are venerated as pure radiant sources removed from the world yet acting directly upon it. The ritual object speaks directly to the soul, it is meant to be immediately ingested and is itself an image of good and of good persons which is at once an inspiration, and a judgment of oneself. Religion as ritual is a recognition of the oneness of life, and in this sense relates naturally to art and can be a source of joy. So ritual should survive too? Yes. These remarks may seem otiose in a world still full of places and objects of worship. But these precious icons can vanish very quickly, as we see in China, and also in many parts of our western civilisation.

*

Metaphysics shows us the internal relations between concepts of great generality, and in doing so may appeal to experience by using all sorts of particular examples. Metaphysicians speak in quasi-tautologies which can be sources of illumination. What is unconditional demands a sense of certainty. Of course there are false 'certainties'. Certainty may generate hubris. An emphatic sense of the concept of the unconditional as the basis of morals and the highest goal of knowledge is to be found in the philosophy of Descartes and Kant. Descartes was said to have 'perfected' Anselm's Proof, Kant to have destroyed it. Descartes was in a position comparable with that of Anselm in *knowing* that God existed; whereas Kant's thoughts about God belong to, and in a sense begin, the modern age. Anselm quotes St Paul about how the invisible things of God are *clearly seen*, being understood through the things that are made. God is both invisible and clearly seen. Clear seeing: an idea essential to Descartes. His version of the Proof in the *Third Meditation* is a complex structure. Descartes has already argued that *cogito ergo sum*. What follows, intimately connected with the *cogito*, appears as a proof that I give to myself. I am sure that I exist (now) because of the clearness and distinctness with which I apprehend *this*. This unique momentary intuition is one thing I can be absolutely certain is not an illusion. Clear distinct knowledge is also called by Descartes 'the natural light'. (Metaphors of vision.) The truths of mathematics also stand out clearly in this light. Could I be deceived about these? Descartes is reluctant to believe that such clearly and distinctly perceived notions could be false. Mathematics enters as a cautious support to the idea that what is clearly and distinctly perceived is true. Descartes is certain that he possesses the idea of God. He reflects that as the idea of substance has more objective reality than the idea of accidents, so the idea of God has more objective reality than any other idea. I know myself to be imperfect yet I have this idea of perfection, so must it not be derived from elsewhere, and must not the cause be at least as great as the effect? The idea of what is so great must have come from as great an origin.

This may remind us again of the myth of *anamnesis* in the *Meno*. We can only learn what we already know, what we can, as it were, remember. If we have ideas of good or perfection in an imperfect world these must be derived from a higher source. We have to find our certainties for ourselves, in ourselves, and we must believe in our duty and ability to discover and make our own the truths which we first intuit or make out as shadows. We can only be sure of what we have thus personally found out and appropriated. Here we find ourselves close to Kant's Categorical Imperative, the moral confidence which can only be consulted in each individual bosom, not blindly accepted on external authority, and his Ideas of Reason, which constantly inspire us to seek truths which we intuit but have not yet fully discovered. An understanding and practice of goodness clarifies the intuitions of it which arise in the soul. In the *Phaedrus* the disincarnate soul is pictured as seeing the Forms clearly and distinctly. A vision of moral certainty, of a pure light, of the magnetism of truth and access to reality is central and essential in human existence; it is something which each individual can, and can only, discover for and in himself. This is the spiritual force and energy which moves us toward virtue, and it is as if it came from a divine source, and is the form in which, at our different levels of achievement, we can know the divine.

To return to Descartes. Could I exist without God? No. The conservation of a substance requires the same power as is necessary to create it. Some self-subsistent cause must exist. I return to my own mind and find the idea of God innate therein, grasped with the same clarity as that with which I grasp myself and at the same time. It must be grasped at the same time, within the momentary *cogitatio*, since, on the previous argument, *cogito ergo sum* represents a unique self-certifying moment of personal certainty, and anything outside the *cogitatio* may be illusory. God cannot be a deceiver since the natural light tells me that all falsehood springs from some defect. I could not possibly be as I am and yet have the idea of God if God did not exist. I grasp myself and God in one. This argument is an example of the partly circular juggling which the human mind indulges in when determined to *argue* for something which it already *knows*. Such argument is also characteristic of metaphysics. This 'package' combines Platonic conceptions of verification (truth-finding) and degrees of reality with a 'modern' (*new*) conception of the primacy of consciousness, and justifies intuitive faith in God in terms of a basis for morality and empirical knowledge. The idea of God (perfection, most real) must come from elsewhere, mediated to us through some sort of immediate intuitive conception of it, packed up inside the *cogito* and found to be indubitable. It coheres with everything else we know about truth and cognition, and at once goes beyond these and guarantees them. There is an appeal to experience, of knowing and discovering truth, as well as to intuition of the essence of morality (goodness, virtue as God). Descartes *knows* what it is like to perceive something, for instance the truths of mathematics, so clear, so immediately apprehensible, as indubitably true. Plato too chooses a mathematical example in the *Meno* and allots a special status to mathematical objects in the *Republic*. A general acquaintance with tested certainty and truth and clear-seeing, an ability to think seriously and honestly, works to support what is already innately known. Goodness joins with knowledge, moral vision is cognitive. Through learning and striving and truthfulness we are accorded a 'proof' of the divine; and this may be said also to be in the spirit of the *Meno* Socrates. In the *Fifth Meditation* Descartes makes a fresh move. Has he accorded too much value to the clarity of mathematics, could one not doubt even the truths of geometry without being certain that God exists? He is here prodding at the circularity of the argument. He proceeds by adding another kind of circularity. God cannot be a deceiver, we can be confident not only of the specialised and recherché truths of mathematics, but of what is surely even more evident and open to all, the world of material things. He gradually joins his central certainty to his peripheral certainties and allows them to support each other. *Everything* must prove God. Descartes is no longer shut inside his mind but returns to the world where, although he may have illusions and make mistakes, he can confidently trust the 'natural light' of truth-seeking. In this context he looks back to Anselm and 'discovers that existence is a perfection'. Reality must belong to what is most perfect. Just as when I think of a triangle I think of certain essential properties thereof, so when I think of God I must think of him as real:

'Whatever mode of probation I in the end adopt it always returns to this, that it is only the things I clearly and distinctly perceive which have the power of completely persuading me. And although, of the objects I conceive in this manner some indeed are obvious to everyone, while others are only discovered after close and careful investigation, nevertheless after they are once discovered, the latter are not esteemed less certain than the former. Thus, for example, to take the case of a right-angled triangle, although it is not so manifest at first that the square of the base is equal to the squares of the other two sides, as that the base is opposite to the greatest angle, nevertheless, after it is once apprehended, we are as firmly persuaded of the truth of the former as of the latter. And with respect to God, if I were not preoccupied by prejudices and my thoughts beset on all sides by the continual presence of the images of sensible objects, I should know nothing sooner or more easily than the fact of his being.'

Descartes adds, reaffirming his circle of internal relations, that the certitude of all truths depends on the existence of God and that 'without this knowledge it is impossible to know anything perfectly'. The full apprehension of God, like the philosophical argument of the *cogito* with which it is connected, demands a certain reflective concentration. Yet also all clear cognition of what is 'obvious to everyone' (such as material objects) as well as what is only 'discovered after close and careful investigation' (such as properties of triangles) points toward and evidences the existence of God as supremely real. All learning, all cognition, all truth-finding and testing of verification, in perception, in mathematics and (I add) in art, in craft, in love, indicate the connection of the good and the real. Serious reflection is *ipso facto* moral effort and involves a heightened sense of value and a vision of perfection. Certainty and necessity live with intimations of perfection. Descartes' sense of the existence of material things in which the natural light gives him confidence thus reinforces and gives body to his belief in the existence of God. There is here a dialectic or oscillation or ferment within which fundamental ideas enlighten and support each other. This kind of metaphysical argument may displease many critics and never be capable of perfect clarity, but it is the way human beings often tend to think, at less exalted levels also, about serious matters. As when we give a certain weight in a complex situation to our sense of someone as 'truthful', or set aside an instinctive belief for a while when struggling with an alien concept, then welcome the belief back again in a modified form. Descartes, devout Catholic and scientist, worked with passionate ingenuity to fit God and science metaphysically together. At the end of his *Principles* he submits 'all my opinions to the authority of the church', but adds that no one is to believe them unless 'constrained by the force and evidence of reason'.

Kant also argues by juggling together a number of large concepts which give each other mutual support. As he frankly says, in the *Grundlegung*, he assumes freedom and a rational will because of the existence of the moral law, and then proves the reality of the moral law through the concept of freedom. This, he adds, is 'a *petitio principii* which well-disposed minds will readily grant us'. Later he professes to remove this circle by saying that when we conceive of ourselves as free we 'transfer' ourselves to the world of understanding, whereas when we feel we are under obligation we are experiencing our belongingness to the world of sense as well. Kant's division of fact from value is felicitously complicated by the particularity of duty. Reason is a universal faculty, the same for all, but each individual is differently situated and brings spirit into 'his own' world by seeing it in Reason's light. God does not appear in this picture, he is veiled, an object of faith, that faith which Kant's limitation of reason and his rational agnosticism make a space for. We are ourselves moral sources, able to be sure about morality and to be confident judges of our spiritual life. Kant's metaphysic is a model of demythologisation, wherein God, if present, is secluded. The *Grundlegung* hints that, from the existence of the moral law, we can perhaps intuit a supreme lawgiver who will introduce happiness into the *summum bonum*; but strictly speaking this must be regarded as a slip! Kant fears happiness as Plato fears art. A search for happiness here below would be for Kant heteronomous, a surrender to egoistic desires. Happy love can be an ingenious moral cheat. Happiness is not our business, and speculations about what God might do about it are not only empty, but likely to mislead us into giving it a value. Plato's Eros, by contrast, is potentially a happy lover, at many levels, and the joy which breathes in the art of the dialogues is itself a sign or symbol of the possibility of spiritual happiness. Kant's God, who may or may not join happiness to goodness, is a mystery. But the unconditional element in human life is clearly and indubitably visible to all in the categorical imperative of duty. Kant makes an inconclusive attempt to draw human society into the background of the argument by emphasising the generality, as well as the universality, of reason, and connecting certain very general imperatives (such as 'Do not lie') with the bases of human association. Society is not for Kant, in the sense in which it was for Marx, an absolute, a prime reality or goal, a touchstone. Yet the notion of an ideal society or Kingdom of Ends, where the rational purposes of all individuals form a harmony, is an important ancillary member of his system of internally related concepts. The idea of the perfect society has of course a long history in philosophy and theology.

Rousseau, whom Kant admired, and later of course Hegel and Marx, took the idea of perfect social harmony as a conceivably attainable political aim. However, in Kant's metaphysic of morals the shadow of complete social integration appears as an Idea of Reason, a rational inspiration or inspiring image, in the context of individual moral activity. The scattered pieces of such a general harmony are to be found 'crystallising out' wherever peace emerges from conflict as a result of the reasonable unselfish truthful goodwill of any group of persons. And one could imagine that small (for instance monastic or Lutheran) like-minded societies could properly live by principles (such as 'Never lie') which were not only universal but very general. (Remember Jeanie Deans.) But the warnings against heteronomous morality in the *Grundlegung* clearly operate against any social ideal which might override individual conscience.

What is absolute and unconditional is what each man clearly and distinctly knows in his own soul, the difference between right and wrong. It is something intimate, deep in consciousness, inseparable from one's sense of oneself, like the Cartesian sense of one's own existence and as directly grasped. Kant is confident that we all recognise it; and the man in the street, if untainted by theory, would probably assent at once to both ideas, to *cogito ergo sum* and to his ability to discern right from wrong. This is a not unimportant fact. The Categorical Imperative, locked into the concept of freedom, is Kant's Ontological Proof, his established vision of an absolute at the centre of human existence. Intuitive certainty, and a sense of truth which is drawn from experience of testing truth, again work together as in Descartes. Truthfulness is for Kant a *fundamental* virtue; and the rational will, beaming in upon each practical maxim (principle or rule of action) justly discerns and clarifies the particular human situations in which action takes place. Moral good is certainly established as cognitive, the unconditional is seen to belong to the structure of human reality, the evidence is everywhere in our experience. As for God, must we just say that it is *as if* he were there, there is a *space* left for faith? The idea of the empty space might seem attractive but is dangerous, since the conclusion that the space is empty may lead (has led) to some kind of moral relativism. Kant did not (in his main doctrine) think in these terms. There is space for the possibility of religious faith. But the Categorical Imperative is not only evident, it is *enough*. Anselm and Descartes, in different fashions, love God and this love irradiates their speculations. Plato loves Good. Kant reveres Reason, might even be said to fear it, but gives, as far as I can see, no sign of loving God. In later life he observes that God is an Idea of Reason, though one of great practical efficacy. God is not an external substance, but a moral idea in our minds. The idea of God is nothing but the inescapable fate of man. We may recall (perhaps as a warning) the *amor fati* expressed by Wittgenstein in the *Tractatus* and in the 1914–1916 *Notebooks*. The concept of God may be forced upon us. Perhaps some satisfaction is derived from this coercion? Kant allows us a certain thrill when we discipline selfish desire in respecting the moral law, and when, with sublime emotion, we turn from fear of the violence and huge inconceivability of nature to consciousness of our sovereign dignity as rational beings. Scientific law and moral law touched each other in Kant's thought in a way which stirred emotion. Newton and Rousseau. Kant says (late in life) that to think God and to believe in him is one and the same; this sounds like Anselm, but the 'necessity' involved has a different background. For Anselm to think God and to love him were one and the same. Kant, as philosopher, seems to have gone on thinking, perhaps puzzling, about God, but without being moved to report any friendly loving dialogue. God appears as a distant essence without local existence. Kant of course officially consigns the emotions to the world of phenomenal appearances, no question of any Kierkegaardian emotional proof, even at the dangerous border-lines indicated above. His psychology also excludes any sort of purified love-energy, a notion which he would have regarded as a dangerous disguise of heteronomous egoism. One may regret or deplore the way in which Kant's dualism seems to deny to human passion any access to the spiritual. Here a general appeal to experience would scarcely be on his side. The dualism of phenomenal fact and noumenal value when transformed by secularism into a world of technological reality haunted by a small peripheral activity of serious evaluation is a cruel nemesis: Kant without his Ontological Proof. But though one may be uneasy about Kant's picture, especially in the light of these particular results (of course it has many results) one cannot but admire and value the ruthlessness with which, in establishing reason as a pure source, he excludes the least hint of a consoling loving divine father. Nothing here about existential dialogue or the communion of I and thou. The appeal to an experienced certainty is the appeal to the sense of duty. Nothing further is needed.

*

Schopenhauer suggests (*WWI*, Appendix, Criticism of the Kantian Philosophy) that Kant, who was led to his view of the *a priori* nature of the concept of cause by Hume's scepticism, may also have been affected in his criticism of speculative theology by Hume's criticisms of popular theology. (Hume's *Natural History of Religion* and *Dialogues on Natural Religion*.) Hume attacked popular theology, but in the *Natural History* 'points to rational or speculative theology as genuine and worthy of respect'. Kant attacks the latter, but leaves popular theology untouched, even 'establishes it in a nobler form as a faith based upon moral feeling'. This idea was later distorted into religious experience, 'rational apprehensions, consciousness of God', etc., 'while Kant, as he demolished old and revered errors, and knew the danger of doing so, rather wished through moral theology merely to substitute a few weak temporary supports, so that the ruin might not fall on him, but that he might have time to escape'. I do not know if Kant thought in those terms. Such questions were for him a matter of passionate concern. However there may, in a longer run than Schopenhauer (writing here with his usual charm) envisages, be truth in the idea that Kant contributes to establishing popular theology in a nobler form. It is, after all, popular theology which ensures the *de facto* continuation of a faith. Kant's attack on rational theology serves the cause of religion in excluding a 'demonic' (external, material object, literalist, person) God, by showing that the existence of such an entity could not be proved, and by adding that true religion is a matter of free individual belief and practice. The veracity of science is established by Kant in the same movement which limits reason and opens a space of agnosticism which makes way for an untainted faith. We may here compare the (less clearly systematic) way in which Descartes shuffles his counters of 'clear and distinct', 'the natural light', 'veracity' to accommodate God and science in the same picture. Kant here clearly observes the Second Commandment. Any God we could meet or see would be a demon, a mere idol. Even looking at Christ can be dangerous, Kant tells us. Christ can lead back to self. The consoling forgiving figure may weaken the moral fibre and serve as a substitute for moral will. Stories are dangerous. Christianity itself is open to corruption in its role as a story, a drama. Stories can be taken too literally. That way lies weakness and illegitimate consolation. Kant sometimes allowed his teleological dream to occasion hints about how we might proceed from the unconditional moral demand to an *idea* of God as a lawgiver and judge who rewards the good with happiness and (perhaps) blends with natural forces to favour just societies. Kant's examples (in the *Grundlegung*) of what he takes to be fundamental and self-evident maxims which are both universal and very general suggest a confidence (not shared now) in the prompt emergence of social good out of certain inflexible high principles. Modern liberal political thinking employs, for instance in the field of human rights, a small number of very general inflexible universal axioms (about freedom, tolerance, etc.) but without any accompaniment of teleological optimism. Kant's extremely shadowy teleological deity later, of course, became the property of Hegel and Marx. Even the shadow of such a 'God' is, on Kant's part, a lapse. Kant's Ontological Proof lies in his own superb certainty about the fundamental and unconditional nature of the moral demand and the reality of the goodness which this contains. The ordinary man has the capacity of perfection; while at the same time the perfectly fitting transcendental barrier inspires a sense of the silent awe which befits an impenetrable mystery. There is no short cut to salvation through forgiveness offered by a personally friendly God. Kant thus puts us, and deliberately puts us, in the best possible position for denying that God is there at all. We must then do the work ourselves, but under another and higher obedience. The moral will acts necessarily and automatically if barriers to it are removed. No magnetic Other, or desire for God, attracts us toward a glimpsed transcendent object. Kant's absolute is like a Platonic Form in being totally impersonal; and unlike the Christian Trinity, which is a mutually adoring set of thous. Kant and Plato are alike in their intense certainty of the reality of a pure moral source. They are unlike because Kant has no moral role for what Plato calls Eros, the high force which attracts the soul toward Good. Plato's Good is not personal but it is magnetic. Kant had no philosophical concept of Eros, but he has enormous philosophical Eros. As an intellectual, and one may say as a theologian, he is a passionate man. His religious passion together with his critical philosophy bring him near to the deep problems of this age and the turmoil of its theology.


I have been speaking of certainty (a dangerous concept) and its coexistence with ideas of truth and reality. Certainty: clarity. In Anselm's spiritual life these ideas are intimately connected. In Descartes they are a little more loosely joined. Descartes *aims* at connecting them more closely, and does so to his own satisfaction. How could he bear to think that God could falsify his mathematical insights or that he could exist without God, although he can conceive of these things? How could science be without God? In Kant, Anselm's One has virtually ceased to be, and the certainty which *was* faith is on the road toward conviction, even commitment: a very different scene. Kant is a dualist not only because he wishes to picture morality as something pure and real lifted (by metaphysical magic) out of the rat-run of egoism, but because he is a modern scientist, a Newtonian, in spirit, observing how a large part of the cosmos is purely *mechanical*. Many present-day thinkers are impressed and *deeply moved* by scientific discovery in a similar way. In a significant, probably early, fragment Kant joins the names of Newton and Rousseau. 'Newton was the first to see order and regularity combined with simplicity . . . and since then comets move in geometrical paths. Rousseau was the first to discover . . . the deeply hidden nature of man and the concealed law in accordance with which Providence is justified through his observations . . . Since Newton and Rousseau God is justified.' (See H. J. Paton, *The Categorical Imperative*, p. 162.) One might say that such a justification amounts to a discreet removal. For today, if we put Einstein for Newton and Freud for Rousseau the obliteration is even more final. Of course this game begs many questions: Freud is an odd sort of moralist, but then so was Rousseau. Can one suggest a better modern Rousseau? For Kant the severance of science and morality was in itself something thrilling. Wonder at the universe occasions a special (sublime) moral feeling: how can we individual specks be free and moral? We can! This is also the road to Romanticism. Today information technology may tend to make us bored with science, or to take it for granted. Man on the moon was a brief marvel. More deeply perhaps fear inhibits our moral pleasure in the great machine, which now passes human comprehension. In Kant's vision, 'God' who for Anselm was everywhere, is now lodged outside, *present* only, but with supreme certainty, as our sense of duty, intimated perhaps in religious faith, keeping open the empty space made for him in the critical philosophy. Scientific (law of nature) and moral law are mutually alienated, joined only by emotional, almost aesthetic, experiences, and by Kant's unconvincing anthropological teleology. God as a super-scientist could be only a paradoxical symbol. Anselm is innocent of science and his God is omnipresent in a Platonic and Hebrew, not a presocratic, sense. Descartes is a scientific religious thinker, who retains the cognitive moral vision, presocratic and Platonic, which naturally unites all knowledge as God-discovering activity whereby all truth reveals him. Kant's metaphysical machinery deliberately precludes this; certainty about right and wrong, appearance and reality, springs up in the bosom of the conscientious man, who is living as an alien in the factual world of phenomenal causality. The subject of the *cogito* intuited the deity. Kant's dutiful man is a modern individual capable of making free independent judgments on the subject of God.

Kant is one of the greatest systematic 'demythologisers' of Christianity, and in this role, as in others, has a variety of followers. The demythologising theologian has an interesting choice of philosophies. Sartrian existentialism perpetuates Kant's separation of the free will as source of value from the causally determined phenomenal world; except that the will is bereft of the universal rational certainty and spiritual authority with which Kant endowed it, and which Schopenhauer condemned as 'theological', and appears (in Sartre) as individual power, self-assertion, commitment or choice. Virtue lies in the sincerity and courage with which I realise my solitude and make my choices. My free creativity can choose my own 'creation' of God. Cowardly insincerity, lassitude, *mauvaise foi*, is the condition of imagining that I can find values given to me ready-made, by society, or priests, or theological tradition. Here, in some vistas, the enemy appears as the complacent bourgeoisie, also detested by Kierkegaard, who 'institute' an unjust class-divided society and a 'material' God. The determinism which is pertinently contrasted with freedom is not that of a scientifically conceived mechanism, but of the dull lifeless drift of those who will not rethink their fundamental concepts. Here one possible picture is that of a brave sincere 'authentic' individual (as portrayed by Heidegger) as against a spiritless conformer; another that of a decent humble adherent of traditional virtues as against a wilful and conceited adventurer! Modern fiction, as well as modern theology, has explored these themes. The extreme case of the existentialist adventurer would be that of a Dostoevskyan character whose *actes gratuits* may be seen as determined by unconscious forces, *or* as the free activity of God's fool. Dostoevsky too is a modern theologian. A more sober version of existentialism appeared in the work of philosophers who explained morality in terms of a less dramatised and non-universal rational will exercising imperative force. The implicit message of this cool and would-be complete account might be that we can thoroughly under-stand morality, and have no need of God, who can be left aside as an optional private activity. Others who tire of having uncharted freedom as the only fundamental value may turn toward the independent, self-evident (axiomatic) values of utilitarianism; this choice is in effect compatible with religious faith of varying degrees of simplicity, and spiritual energy can be channelled into good works, leaving no time for theological speculation. On the other hand, following the path of John Stuart Mill, the need to distinguish qualities of happiness (*how* does one help people, and to *what?*) leads back to more traditional problems. Thus the drama of fact and value as inaugurated by Kant continues, and enters in various ways into our ethical and theological conflicts. Kant's practical reason mysteriously joined the noumenal world of value and the phenomenal world of fact by framing universal maxims of varying degrees of generality for particular actions. When the light of moral certainty is withdrawn the world of phenomena can appear as an alien scene, outside which the creation of value flashes like intermittent lightning in gratuitous acts, or anguished religious doubts, or possibly in poetic creation. We may see this image too in the metaphysics of the *Tractatus*. The Sartrian world of fact was a wilderness of *mauvaise foi* occasionally lightened by sincere individual free acts. A more alarming wilderness is that of modern technology, so full of brilliant devices and easy entertainments, where numerous self-referential scientific languages shake our belief in old natural lan-guage and old traditional truth.

In the Introduction to the *Critique of Pure Reason* Kant says that 'the proper problem of pure reason is contained in the question: How are *a priori* synthetic judgments possible?' The synthetic *a priori* is a mediating area of thought (reality) which lies upon the border-line of human capacity as a kind of necessary 'reaching further'. Such propo-sitions (judgments), found in mathematics, physics, and metaphysics, are neither analytic (tautologous) nor synthetic (factual), representing a kind of *necessary* unprovable, or unclarifiable, speculation. Every event has a cause. The world had a beginning in time. Such speculations and formulations are 'forced upon us'. Kant's problem concerning the status and truth of metaphysics is indeed difficult and persisting. The metaphysic of morals has its own baffling enigmas. Scientifically, psychologically, we are determined, but spiritually we are free. Moreover, does freedom imply morality, or does morality imply freedom? What is clear is that we all recognise the moral law. But what is its basis? Kant has to speak of what is 'unprovable', and of what 'for us men is impossible to explain' and 'can never be discerned by human reason'. In his later book the *Critique of Practical Reason* Kant puts it as: if our reason had not already distinctly thought the moral law we would not have been justified in assuming freedom, but if freedom did not exist we should never have discovered the moral law. We are also led, through the concept of freedom, to conceive of God and immortality. However, 'we cannot say that we know or understand either the reality or even the possibility of these ideas ... To serve their practical function it suffices that they do not contain any internal impossibility (contradiction).' More firmly, later in the book, Kant says that if we were certain of God's existence and were able to see him, we would have no free will and would be merely puppets. He thus establishes agnosticism as a condition of morality. (*Critique of Practical Reason*, Beck's translation, pp. 119 and 248.) In a yet later book (Kant was nearly seventy when he wrote it), *Religion within the Limits of Reason Alone*, he explains his agnostic position in more passionate and informal and less metaphysical terms, saying in the preface to the second edition that to understand the book 'only common morality is needed'. Here too he repeats that the subjective ground is inscrutable and that if we had certain knowledge of God we would lose our freedom. The words inscrutable, inconceivable, unfathomable, inescapable, occur; also the words God and holy. 'Morality leads ineluctably to religion, through which it extends itself to the idea of a powerful moral Lawgiver outside of mankind.' This 'venturing' *might* even seem to move beyond *respect* for the moral law toward a love for or adoration of the so-naturally postulated God. 'But anything, even the most sublime, dwindles under the hands of men.' We must beware of such instinctive paths which lead us through the comforts of religion toward superstition and illusion. (*Religion within the Limits*, Greene and Hudson trans. pp. 12, 5, 7.) Kant goes on to speak in newly emphatic terms about morality as a struggle between good and evil. The Stoics 'mistook their enemy', who is 'not to be sought in merely undisciplined natural inclinations ... They called out *wisdom* against *folly*' instead of 'against *wickedness*, the wickedness of the human heart'. Kant quotes Ephesians 6. 12, 'For we wrestle not against flesh and blood, but against principalities, against powers, against the rulers of the darkness of this world, against spiritual wickedness in high places.' This adjuration, Kant says, 'is not to extend our knowledge beyond the world of sense, but only to make clear *for practical use* the conception of what for us is unfathomable'. Christianity rightly saw good and evil not as heaven and earth, but as heaven and hell. This prevents us from 'regarding good and evil, the realm of light and the realm of darkness, as bordering on each other and as losing themselves in one another by gradual steps'. (pp. 50, 52, 53.) This warning also has its relevance today. We must *see* evil, and reject any pact (Heraclitus, Jung) between evil and good. Kant looks at Genesis 2. 16–17, and 3. 6. How did sin originate? This remains inscrutable to us. However, humanity is represented as having been *seduced* into evil, and hence as being not basically corrupt but capable of improvement. This, Kant says, is a historical account put to moral use, 'wherefrom we can derive something conducive to our moral betterment'. (p. 39fn.) Religion may thus be thought of as good for us, but only as moral principle. 'Whatever, over and above good life-conduct, man fancies that he can do to become well-pleasing to God is a mere religious illusion and pseudo-service of God.' (p. 158.) The only true church is the *invisible* church, a 'mere *idea* of the union of all the righteous under direct and moral divine world-government, an idea serving as the archetype of what is to be established by men'. Kant adds that 'man must proceed as if everything depended upon him; only on this condition dare he hope that higher wisdom will grant the completion of his well-intentioned endeavours'. (p. 92.) (This 'as if' may remind us of sayings of Plato in the *Meno* and the *Republic*.) Here we are to join with him who cried, 'Lord, I believe, help thou mine unbelief.' (Mark 9. 24.) And also, we might add, with Anselm's 'I believe so that I may understand'. The (awkward) figure of Christ, whom of course Kant cannot take as the founder of religion (that is of the moral law), is hailed by him as 'the founder of the first true *church* . . . Let historical records be what they may . . . in the idea itself is present adequate ground for its acceptance.' Further to convince us Kant quotes at length from the Sermon on the Mount. 'These commands are not mere laws of virtue but precepts of *holiness* which we ought to pursue, and the very pursuit of them is called *virtue*.' (pp. 147–8.)

Of course Kant in his Pietist puritanical childhood grew up with

Christ and God. He continued to live with the Bible. His relation to religion has a kind of immobility, perhaps an expression of the unhistorical statuesque aspect of the Enlightenment. However he speaks passionately from the heart and desires to convince, even to save. Kant is best known, and most influential and important, as the author of the *Critique of Pure Reason*; his thoughts about morality have been of less interest to philosophers, his concept of duty often regarded (as by Schopenhauer and Wittgenstein) as a narrow mandatory account of the moral life. His thoughts about God were more likely to interest theologians. His late book, with its ramblings into detail and its attempted common touch, may be seen as one possible example of a demythologising programme. He establishes firmly the main tenet of an agnostic or demythologising position when he says that if we could *see* God we would be puppets. This perception is also contained in the Ontological Proof. He is stern about (that great resource of all mankind) prayer, which (he says) thought of as an inner formal service to God, is a superstitious illusion, fetishism, mere statement of wishes. However the spirit of prayer as a disposition to act as though in the service of God, should be present with us 'without ceasing'. 'Without ceasing' is good, but 'disposition to act' not so good. Here we see the painful incongruities of Kant's position. Kant reveres the moral law, he surrounds it with emotion (respect, sublime) but the purity of his doctrine must beware of the 'inner life'. The word 'practical' which defends him, may also damn him. Taking a more merciful and modern view, surely prayer (or something like it) is as essential as duty; and is indeed a vital mediating concept, enabling the liberating discovery of the divine in one's own soul. (The church is open for prayer and meditation.) Anyway, who can judge another person's prayer? It may be said of Kant, that for a man who does not (strictly) believe in God, God's name is (especially in later life) embarrassingly often upon his lips. (Many people are in this situation today.) Kant makes use of God. Well, are we to buy an 'as though' or 'as if' religion? Plato's 'as ifs' occur in contexts where it is plain that we are being taught by a story. There is a final reluctance to lose the name of deity. (The One was in a similar dilemma.) Kant is still so close to Christianity that theistic terminology is a natural, perhaps the only clear, mode of explanation. He loves Christ, and speaks of holiness, seen at times as not only an aspect of virtue, but almost as something superior to it (its aura perhaps). His puritanical protestantism favours simplicity and clarity, and shuns the darkness of ritual and 'mysticism' whose magical charms tempt us away from reason and duty and truth. After all, Kant was *fighting* for reason and, like Descartes, got into trouble for doing so. His central concept of truth is continuously at work, quietly supported by his belief in science. Religion is rejected today on the simple charge that 'it isn't true'. Those who reject God but want to keep religion are compelled to discover another conception of truth. Kant stands awkwardly beside the old machinery toward which his deep religious passion constantly returns. His numerous quotations from the Bible express his unquenched faith. Pray without ceasing.

*Postscript.* De Quincey. *The Last Days of Immanuel Kant.* 'The moment that Kant had taken his seat and unfolded his napkin, he opened the business of the hour with a particular formula – "Now then, gentlemen!" The words are nothing, but the tone and air with which he uttered them proclaimed, in a way which nobody could mistake, relaxation from the toils of the morning and determinate abandonment of himself to social enjoyment. The table was hospitably spread; a sufficient choice of dishes there was to meet a variety of tastes; and the decanters of wine were placed, not on a distant sideboard, or under the odious control of a servant . . . but anacreontically on the table, and at the elbow of every guest.'

Kant is chided by those who believe that myth and ritual feed the heart and the understanding, and that religion should be thought of as fundamentally mystical. Von Hügel in *The Mystical Element in Religion* (volume II, p. 260) quotes the following from Kant's *Religion within the Limits of Reason Alone* (pp. 162–3):

' "The delusion that we can effect something, in view of our justification before God, by means of a religious worship, is religious superstition; and the delusion that we can effect something by attempts at a supposed intercourse with God is religious fanaticism . . . Such a feeling of the immediate presence of the Supreme Being and such a discrimination between this feeling and every other, even moral, feeling, would imply a capacity for intuition which is without any corresponding organ in human nature . . . If then a Church doctrine is to abolish or to prevent all religious delusion, it must – over and above its statutory teachings, with which it cannot, for the present, entirely dispense – contain within itself a principle which shall enable it to bring about the religion of a pure life, as the true end of the whole movement, and then to dispense with those temporary doctrines."'

Upon this passage of Kant von Hügel comments: 'It is deeply instructive to note how thoroughly this, at first sight, solid and triumphant view, has not only continued to be refuted by the actual practice and experience of specifically religious souls, but how explicitly it is being discredited by precisely the more delicately perceptive, the more truly detached and comprehensive, students and philosophers of religion of the present day – heirs, let us not forget in justice to Kant, of the intervening profound development of the historical sense, and of the history and psychology of religion.'

Von Hügel proceeds to quote or mention learned thinkers who agree with him and disagree with Kant. Troeltsch for instance says that

'"Kant's theory of knowledge is throughout dependent upon the state of contemporary psychology, so also is his theory of religious knowledge dependent upon the psychology of religion predominant in his day. Locke, Leibniz, Pascal had already recognised the essentially practical character of all religion; and since their psychology was unable to conceive the "practical" otherwise than as the moral, it had looked upon Religion as Morality furnished forth with its metaphysical concomitants. As soon as this psychology had become the very backbone of his concept of Religion, Morality gained an entirely one-sided predominance over Kant's mind – considerably, indeed, beyond his own personal feelings and perceptions."'

For he remains deeply penetrated by 'the conceptions of Regeneration and Redemption; the idea of divine Grace and Wisdom, which accepts the totality of the soul's good disposition in lieu of that soul's ever defective single good works; the belief in a Providence which strengthens the Good throughout the world against Evil; adoring awe in face of the majesty of the Supersensible', and 'all these' conceptions 'are more than simply moral, they are specifically religious thoughts'. Von Hügel (p. 274) tells us that

'we can perceive the difference between the two forces [religion and morality] most clearly in our Lord's life and teaching – say the Sermon on the Mount; in the intolerableness of every exegesis which attempts to reduce the ultimate meaning and worth of this world-renewing religious document to what it has of literal applicability in the field of morality proper. Schopenhauer expressed a profound intuition in the words: "It would be a most unworthy manner of speech to declare the sublime Founder of the Christian Religion, whose life is proposed to us as the model of all virtue, to have been the most reasonable of men and that his maxims contained but the best instruction toward an entirely reasonable life." The fact is that Religion ever insists, even where it but seems to be teaching moral rules and motives as appropriate to this visible world of ours, upon presenting them in the setting of a fuller deeper world than that immediately required as the field of action and as the justification of ordinary morality.'

These attempts to distinguish between morality (as a code of action) and religion (as deep spiritual sensibility) may now sound somewhat old-fashioned. But such reflections remain relevant and their ponderings may at least provide some useful alternative to philosophical attempts to discuss morality in terms of conflicts between (for instance) relativists, consequentialists, absolutists, etc. In such contexts religion is usually ignored, being regarded as something personal, perhaps aesthetic, a more colourful way of looking at morals, or the last repository of a *genuine* belief in absolutes. The place of Christianity among the great religions is unique because of the historical and theological position of Christ. The other two monotheistic religions, Judaism and Islam, are differently placed, partly because of a stricter avoidance of picturesque anthropomorphism and image-making. The figure of Jesus mediates God into humanity and thus into a semblance of empirical being which is difficult to remove from believers' minds without removing the whole substance of belief. It is true that in the Psalms God appears as a Person with whom one can converse. But in general, where the Old Testament is concerned, a distinction between a mythical tribal deity and a nameless spirit can more readily be made. The way is thus more open for a changing view of 'God'. Buddhism and Hinduism, even more 'picturesque' than Christianity, have always provided a variety of *paths* whereby their 'gods' can be seen as images of a higher reality.

A distinction between intellect and will, reason and faith, also expressible as the distinction between fact and value, has appeared in recent theology as an instrument of demythologisation. We must develop a *new mode of speech* to clarify the special nature of what is religious. Ian Ramsey published (in 1957) a book called *Religious Language*, the first chapter of which was entitled 'What kind of situations are religious?' Ramsey wrote under the aegis of plain ordinary-language empiricist philosophy. '"Did the Resurrection occur?" has *not* the same logic as "Did the empty tomb occur?" if for no other reason than that the second can be asserted while the first is denied, and the second might even be, and by some has been, denied while the first has been asserted.' (p. 127.) Ramsey's views were 'bold', as were those of John Robinson (*Honest to God*), but do not amount to a programme for a totally new religious outlook. A more ruthlessly radical position is occupied by Don Cupitt. His book *Taking Leave of God* (published 1980) takes its title from Eckhart (Sermon, *Quis audit me?*): 'Man's last and highest parting occurs when, for God's sake, he takes leave of God.' Cupitt tells us, 'In the Old Testament it was God who appeared to be posturing dramatically, and the believer hid in a cleft of the rock, kept his head down, remained very still and hoped that the divine storm would soon blow itself out. Today God keeps still – and I jump.' (p. 93.) A striking picture with its image of movement, not vision, putting us in mind of Kierkegaard's 'leap', and the 'silence of the Transcendent'. Cupitt, like many others, reminds us that mankind is just emerging from its mythological childhood. Religion must come to terms with autonomy. The traditional self was a given substance, the modern self is more like a self-defining relation, 'generating its own knowledge and its own destiny of becoming a fully-achieved, conscious and autonomous spiritual subject'. Hegel and Feuerbach envisaged the attainment by man of divine attributes. In the traditional Christian story, our first parents, seeking their attributes, were punished by alienation from God; but (*felix culpa*) 'eventually redeemed man attains a higher dignity than fallen man'. Alienation leads on to a higher unity. 'God is the future of man.' The aporia of the new believer is illuminated (in Cupitt's account) by a distinction between 'voluntarism' (will, value) and 'descriptivism' (intellect, fact). Cupitt uses the term 'expressive' to characterise 'religious language'. Modern man cannot accept the old religious story as, literally, descriptive. Nor can he retain the myths as being 'somehow' vehicles of truth. Cupitt says that 'mythical truth is also split in two by the fact–value fork. The descriptive element in mythic truth, when separated out, proves to be false, and the value element we preserve (in so far as it is intrinsically valuable) not because it is in the myth but for its own sake.' Is the Resurrection a fact? It does not matter. Paul did not have our modern conception of fact. Let us ask of the risen Christ not whether he rose, but whether he can save. 'If Christianity were to lose the power of salvation it would not be true any more.' This parting of the ways between descriptivism and voluntarism is also expressed by Cupitt in terms of 'the mythological way' *or* 'the monotheistic way', and the affirmative way, *or* the negative way in spirituality.

'The negative way attempts to do justice to God's transcendence but at the price of making God unknowable. Religious language then perforce becomes expressive, not descriptive, and the relation to God has to be enacted in spirituality because it can in no way be articulated in knowledge. A high and orthodox emphasis on the divine transcendence forces me in the end to a non-cognitive or (as people say) "subjectivist" philosophy of religion. The "higher" God is the more inward God is, and the less we know of him the more he makes us grow spiritually. Alternatively, the affirmative way sees the world as full of images of God and hierarchies pointing to God, but insofar as it moves from the world to God by some sort of extrapolation it can only arrive at an idol and not the true God.'

(p. 51.)

Elsewhere Cupitt says that he wishes to reverse the traditional order,

'putting spirituality first and God second, somewhat as the Buddha put the Dharma above the gods. That is, on our account, the religious imperative that commands us to become free spirit is perceived as an autonomously authoritative principle which has to be freely and autonomously adopted and self-imposed. We choose to be religious because it is better so to be. We must strive with all our might to become spirit, and what God is appears in the striving to answer this call. God is, quite simply, what the religious requirement comes to mean to us as we respond to it. A religion is a cluster of spiritual values.'

(p. 98.)

These are lucid and moving statements, I like and respect the 'high and orthodox emphasis' upon divine transcendence. And that the divine is above the gods (as in Buddhism and Platonism). Yet the point

[ 453 ]

to which the speaker is driven seems unnecessarily extreme. We posit an unknown God; religion (and indeed God), which we have *chosen* as 'better' *is* our personal spiritual striving toward the ultimate goal of free spirit. A subjectivist non-cognitive philosophy of will separates spirituality from knowledge. No myths, no idols. The less we know of God the more spiritual we are made to become. Religion is thus secluded and purified, separated from the world of fact and science, and from the old illusions. This may indeed be a possible form of personal theism. Voluntarism seeks autonomy, human potential, freedom. These are good things; but isolated and in a religious context the programme may remind us more of Feuerbach and Sartre. Agnosticism about God, an unknown God, or a complete denial of God does not (as it seems to me) involve a surrender of the spiritually informed understanding of 'all the world' which traditional theism has implied. The words 'subjectivist', 'expressivist', 'non-cognitive' suggest such a surrender, and a picture of religion as a matter of private (existentialist) choice. The idea of choosing the spiritual or religious as (an item among others) better, seems oddly abstract. Demythologisation is not a single road, nor need it imply or *mean* a disappearance of myths and icons, or some profound 'rectification' of ordinary language. The modern scene includes (I hope) an enlargement of our concept of religion through our greater tolerance and knowledge of other religions. Here the concept of an 'idol' must come under new scrutiny. What can we say about the relation of religious (moral) persons to (in the widest sense) their images? Here we must also think about the difference between the sophisticated and the unsophisticated worshipper. (The Tibetan merchant's problem.) Perhaps the best way to understand idols is to think again about Plato's hierarchy of subjects and their objects. A progressive alteration of 'images' is not in the pejorative sense idolatry, the human imagination engages with the world at many levels. There are many occasions of 'taking leave'. Expressivist voluntarism is, in tune with structuralist formulations, anti-Platonic. Voluntarism, segregating intellectual factual language, forces itself to discover a pure non-factual expressive language appropriate to religion. Jacques Derrida makes a somewhat similar distinction between old ordinary prose and the ecstatic poeticised rhetoric of post-philosophical reflection. Theological crisis no doubt poses linguistic problems. (Does the word 'God' mean something different now, should we go on using it?) But these problems can be dealt with by all the vast resources of our

ordinary reflective procedures and our ordinary metaphorical evaluative language. We are not cut off from St Paul. A division of language
itself between fact and value not only isolates and diminishes value, it
may damage the concept of truth. (As it is damaged by Derrida.) The
picture of religion as a 'cluster of values' suggests a corner, a place
among places, a thing among things. We have not been driven out of
a brightly coloured mythical world which now belongs to a false illu-
sioned past, leaving us with many facts, an imageless striving will and
an expressive language. We still live in the old familiar mysterious
world and explain and clarify and celebrate it in the old endlessly fertile
and inventive modes of speech. We enjoy the freedom of a moral
imagination. The idea of 'the world as full of images of God and
hierarchies pointing to God' is, as I see it, fundamental in religion and
(*mutatis mutandis*) in morality. I think this is what (if we put Good
for God) the world *is* full of! The affirmative way, which can find the
divine everywhere in all the desire-driven burrowings of cognition,
relates spirituality to the whole of our being.

Cupitt has published other works since *Taking Leave of God.* His
brave and ferocious book *Radicals and the Future of the Church* is far
on from the mild tinkerings of Ramsey and Robinson. The book contains many sayings which I like and respect. Religion concerns everything in life, it is not just an occasional or special matter. We have to
learn to think of God in a new way, not as an object, not as a person.
That there is no God is also God. I like too the frequent references to
Buddha and to Void, and in this context to Kierkegaard. Cupitt, in
this respect like Buber, insists upon the retention of the word 'God',
while suggesting various ways in which it can be filled with sense. He
also quotes Bradley that God has no meaning outside the religious
consciousness. I am not so happy with Cupitt's attitude to Plato and
to philosophy generally. 'So far as all the varied movements of the day
have a common theme it is *anti-Platonism.* Plato impressed upon the
entire history of Western thought what now looks like a wholly
unjustified and superstitious supernaturalism of thought, a supernaturalism of our intellectual standards, a supernaturalism of meanings
(essentialism) and of knowledge, and finally *a supernaturalism of
philosophy itself* – all of which has suddenly come to seem utterly
absurd and unendurable. Nietzsche and Heidegger were right after
all . . .' (page 40–1, Cupitt's italics.) To accuse Plato of 'superstitious
supernaturalism' is to misunderstand his philosophy (my view of Plato

need not be repeated here). As for Nietzsche and (late) Heidegger, roughly, I regard those great writers as essentially demonic. Nor do I picture women's liberation in terms of feminine wiles (rhetoric) versus masculine reason (logic)! (p. 50.) 'A number of the most original and creative modern philosophers (including Nietzsche, Wittgenstein and Derrida) have been rediscovering rhetoric and using its wiles against blundering one-eyed theoretical reason.' Here I would rather back analytical philosophy against rhetoric. The conclusion may well be that (p. 22) 'Nietzsche has been vindicated and that we are indeed all aestheticists nowadays' and (p. 13) we 'cannot help but take a thoroughly aesthetic and anarchistic view of meaning and truth'. So, after all, it's a game? However, in spite of these few contentious matters I think Cupitt is a very brave and valuable pioneer and a learned and accessible thinker, who stirs up thought where it is most needed. He speaks *directly*, as few do, about the *necessity of new thinking* about God and religion as something which concerns us all.

It may be said that 'demythologisation' is *ipso facto* hostile to images, to comforting pictures which arrest our progress, and that a certain tough savagery is required in their removal. We may recognise other similar moments in the history of religion; and now, as in some *lutte finale*, the task is given to the Protestant theologians. So a language must be developed for a religion without dogma? But religion has already been 'put into a corner' when we begin to talk of its 'language' or its (special) 'values', which then seem to be wandering aliens in the big world of intellect and fact. The concept of 'freedom' too appears with a difference according to whether or not it is connected to a 'will' which is detached from intellectual knowledge. These concepts are functions of each other. We are all the time exercising and learning freedom and truthfulness as we deal with the whole world. As I have mentioned before the word 'will' should, in my view, in philosophy and strictly speaking, be given a limited use, where something like an 'effort of will' or a 'force' or 'imposition' of will is indicated. This is close to ordinary usage where 'will' often refers to certain kinds of self-consciously effortful movement. Schopenhauer used the word to describe his primal cosmic power which rises through the whole of creation into man where it becomes intellectualised as ideas. This picture, which portrays will as generalised energy, in a sense not unlike that of the presocratics, removes the concept from its ordinary uses, in the interests of (for instance) emphasising our unity with the whole of created being. It also however offers a background in which a sense of, or theory of, determinism can lodge, and indeed Schopenhauer regards the ordinary human state as a determined condition from which rescue, by higher 'Ideas', may be thought of as exceptional. The word 'energy' seems more in place if one is considering some general human 'drive' (such as sex) which is particularised in individuals. Plato's concept of a human energy which joins intellect and (good or bad) desire offers a more satisfactory account of our continuous and unavoidable moral activity. Morality must engage the whole man, being neither an intermittent spring nor a cosmic force. Ordinary language and ordinary cool observation serve best here. A good text-book is St Augustine's *Confessions*. Augustine, here following Plato and Plotinus, and anticipating Freud, was aware of the human soul as a huge area, largely dark. We have to keep moving, working, walking in order not to be enclosed by the darkness. (*Confessions* X 23.) Freedom, as free choice, as right choice, depends upon achieving a certain unity of thought and desire. The pain of *Angst*, the sense of an empty 'freedom', the lack of substance in any path taken, is movingly described by Augustine in *Confessions* VIII 8. He rushes out of the house followed by his friend, they sit at the far end of the garden, Augustine, tormented by indecision, tears his hair, beats his brow. He is conscious of a 'wounded will' which 'staggers and tumbles . . . now on this side, then on that side'. This recognisable state is however not one to which we are condemned, nor is it one which is what it (perhaps) seems. The lonely tortured 'will' of which we are conscious at such moments is not the agent of our freedom and our morality, but rather a symptom of lack of freedom and moral strength. It is indeed not solitary but appearing like a flickering flame before a darker background of habits, principles, ideals, ideas, desires, memories. Out of this substantial region the help must come which unites the choosing self and enables it to be responsible and intelligent and free. We can appeal to a force and a substance which is already within us and always in process of change. Augustine would say we appeal to God. We wait, we reflect, we conjure up good things out of our soul, lights, sacraments, attachments. Seen here, freedom must be thought of as a love of good which enables a unity of thought and desire. A picture which lodges 'the spiritual', and its language, in a detached will may also in effect segregate religion as 'enthusiasm', or a form of drama, to be distinguished from ordinary social 'morals' which inhabit the ordinary 'real' world.

A separation of will from intellect and fact from value may suggest, or go with, a dramatic (or tragic) view of life. The factual world may then appear as a place wherein spiritual heroes live out publicly and edifyingly the contradictions which are less consciously and bravely suffered by the rest of us. This is not far from the spirit of structuralism. We, as spectators in the great arena, see 'the dust cloud of the Olympic battle and the flash of divine spears'. No wonder we are led to conclude that 'the world is the game Zeus plays'. (Nietzsche interpreting Heraclitus, *Philosophy in the Tragic Age of the Greeks*.) A view of art as essentially heroic, challenging, paradoxical, iconoclastic, a sort of *force*, is not by any means always appropriate. It is even less appropriate to use such a terminology about the religious life. The struggle against evil, the love of what is good, the inspired enjoyment of beauty, the discovery and perception of holiness, continues all the time in the privacy of human souls. This process is more like eating or breathing than like a dramatic conflict with clashing swords and contradictions. The word 'tragic' is out of place. Of course there are dramatic moments and situations, but these are, if we look at the long threads of human lives, intermittent. 'Tragic' is another comfort word. We invoke the theatre of the tragic to help us to bear sufferings which it would be too painful to consider in all their detailed structures of accident and muddle. There is no deep analysis of terrible suffering. The horrors of the world recede into darkness.

Anything may become hallowed and be religiously powerful, as in the Tibetan story of the dog's tooth which because it was sincerely venerated glowed with a miraculous light. But can one simply decree this sort of status for the risen Christ and still keep a Christian structure and observance as before, as if it did not matter all that much? The transformation of Christianity into a religion *like* Buddhism, with no God and no literally divine Christ, but with a mystical Christ, may be, if possible at all, a long task, and needs a reflective backing stronger and more complex than that which an existentialist-style voluntarism can provide, as if it were a matter of suddenly choosing a point of view. Or could an individual perhaps decide one day to 'look at it in this way'? Do not people so decide? And suppose a good many of them do? Is one being too rigid and solemn about it all? Do not a large number of those who go to church *already think* in a new non-literal

[ 458 ]

way without bothering about theology and metaphysics? We may relevantly note that in the past literalist thinking was also mythological thinking. Perhaps the term 'demythologisation' is radically misleading; and we only need a shift in our sense of 'myth', rather than radical surgery involving distinctions (for instance between fact and value) and arguments against these distinctions? However that may be, churches are institutions and problems of true and false arise for those in authority, and people ask their priests: is it true? Priests leave their churches because of an unbearable discrepancy between their own beliefs and the beliefs of their flock. Philosophers and theologians have to go on thinking, and laymen are driven to reflect by what they see and hear.

In his poem on the death of W. B. Yeats, W. H. Auden tells us that time worships language and forgives everyone by whom it lives. Those who wish to persuade us that our language is in crisis and already in process of radical change, may try to impress us by reference to the languages of science. Modern biology does not talk about individual creatures, but about things which most people do not understand, such as genes and DNA; and the self-referential systems of modern physics are remote from Newton. These ultimate models of precision affect (and benefit) our lives, but our everyday language (its modes, its truth-conveying structures) is only peripherally touched by them. This language remains as it has been since say (in Europe) Homer and the Psalmist, an instrument which orders and expresses our multiple relations to a reality outside us and to the depths of our own minds. We are mixed into the world around us which we touch and assimilate largely through a vast natural medium of metaphor, and achieve, fundamental to human life, truth, out of which in turn we are able to set up and 'place' the necessary systems of the strictly factual. How we can *do* these things may seem, if we pause and stare at it, a mystery. But out in life we perform all these feats without difficulty. Techniques of political oppression in modern civilisation may tend (as pictured in Orwell's *1984*) to weaken and simplify and starve ordinary speech, depriving it of concepts. However time, mentioned above, will (we hope) continue at intervals to restore the divine power of language (as it has begun to do in eastern Europe since 1989). It may indeed be the case that deep slow changes (only roughly indicated by 'the scientific temper of the age') render it difficult or impossible to think about religion in the old literalistic way. But this need not (must not) imply that we now have to lodge it in a small safe self-protective ball of specialised language. We are still the same people whose dilemmas are described in Greek literature and in the Bible and these descriptions are uttered in our language. Human nature is the abode of spiritual intimations and spiritual imagery and we are not forced by 'science' or 'modernism' to live by the will, by a simple ability to leap right out of a bleak 'factual' world.

The 'demythologisation' of religion is something absolutely necessary in this age. However if it is carried out in too Feuerbachian a spirit it may be in danger of losing too much while asserting too little. The loss of the Book of Common Prayer (Cranmer's great prayer book) and of the Authorised Version of the Bible (which are now regarded as oddities or treats) is symptomatic of this *failure of nerve*. To say that people now cannot understand that 'old language' is not only an insult, but an invitation to more lax and cursory modes of expression. The religious life and the imperfect institutions thereof should continue to represent the all-importance of goodness. At a lower level lies the arcane power-seeking and magic (including spiritualism, scientology, and other forms of gnosticism) toward which human activities naturally tend to fall; and without which thrilling 'fringe', some may argue, institutionalised religion would not continue. 'Spirituality' is always 'breaking away', and is indeed at present 'all over the place'. (Spirit without Absolute: the time of the angels.) This continual defection may in our time favour a self-important autonomy and sense of an available 'instant freedom' presented as a moral ideal: the spirit of Sartrian existentialism joined to the impoverishing reductionism of the structuralists. In this situation religious-minded moralists and new thinkers may be tempted toward a cautious withdrawal, as if this were some meritorious realism, some sensible delimitation of their claims. In general, theology is shaken and there are still new places where thought can go. The 'new theology' of South America, which recognises a live and present Christ who, poor and barefoot Himself, is the champion of the poor, represents something of the openness and vitality of the changing scene. St Paul said we find God everywhere in the world, seeing in material things the spiritual reality which is beyond them. For the spiritual and the holy we are to look toward all the world, not toward our isolated self-will.

# > 15 <
# Martin Buber and God

I want now to look at a different kind of apologist, or 'prophet', a Jewish one, Martin Buber, whom I have mentioned earlier. In common with Heidegger, whom he critically admires, and Jung whom he detests, Buber speaks of the present age as a period of darkness or silence which awaits a new revelation. Like Heidegger, he thinks of Plato as having made a mistake, the substitution of *eidos* for *phusis* as the basis of metaphysics, of visible form for natural growth, of vision for movement or flow. I quote here a passage where Buber tells us that, influenced by Plato, European philosophy has tended to picture spirituality as a looking upward, rather than as a movement or making of contact here below. 'The Greeks established the hegemony of sight over the other senses, thus making the optical world into *the* world, into which the data of the other senses are now to be entered.' They also gave an optical character to philosophy, 'the character of the contemplation of particular objects . . . The object of this visual thought is the universal as existence or as a reality higher than existence. Philosophy is grounded on the presupposition that one sees the absolute in universals.' (*Eclipse of God*, p. 56.) As I have argued in other contexts, the view expressed in the last two sentences represents a misunderstanding of Plato's doctrine. Of course morality is action, not just looking (admiring), but the light of truth and knowledge should be falling upon the path of the agent. For better or worse we look, we see something, before we act. The Forms are magnetic, not just passively stared at, they enliven the energy of Eros in the soul and participate in the world, they are both transcendent and immanent. The activity and imagery of vision is at the centre of human existence, wherein we are conscious

[ 461 ]

of ourselves as both inward and outward, distanced and surrounded. Plato's break with the presocratic tradition: all is patently not one, our human world is not determined by a hidden unity or universal harmony, we are strained and stretched out (like the *Anima Mundi* in the *Timaeus*), we live with intuitions of what we also realise as very distant. *Video meliora proboque, deteriora sequor.* (I see what is better and applaud it, I follow what is worse.) Fundamental moral teaching (which can be given to small children) concerns knowledge and truth. The visual is an image of distance and non-possession. This idea of space and quietness, thinking, seeing, attending, keeping still, not seizing, is important in all education, and not only (where it is of course vital) in the appreciation of art. Reflection, reverence, respect. A picture of an ultimate erotic union as ultimate knowledge, as in union with a god, figures in some religious practice and is a special property of some religious mysticism. It can scarcely be taken as a general picture of moral aspiration, even as mediated through ideas of social participation! Plotinus spoke of union with the One, but Plato spoke only of (perhaps) glimpsing the Form of the Good, not of presuming to touch it. Seeing is essentially separate from touching, and should enlighten and inspire appropriate movement. There are proper times for looking, and, after looking, for touching. (Uzza died because he touched the Ark. Many people touched Christ.) Of course we 'move through life', as upon a 'road', but are required to see our way. Speaking of morality in terms of cognition, the imagery of vision, which is everywhere in our speech, seems natural. Sight is the dominant sense, our world, source of our deep imagery and thought-modes, is a visual world, our idea of the world is of a visual world. St Paul speaks of what is seen as bodying forth what is not seen. Perhaps what is not seen, understood, known, appears as an intimation or orientation, perhaps later it may be understood and visible, while other more distant things begin hazily to appear. These are images of our thinking and our moral life. We speak of the veil of appearance. We know when we are being satisfied with superficial, illusory, lying pictures which distort and conceal reality. Metaphorical preferences are not mere matters of temperament. Dominant metaphors in metaphysics have large implications. By looking at something, by *stopping* to look at it, we do not selfishly appropriate it, we understand it and let it be. We may too, in such looking, take the object as shadow, intuiting what is beyond it. All our most ordinary thinking, in the moral activity of every day involves familiar picturing. Blind desire, of which lust is an image, reaches out to grasp and appropriate. Desire with vision looks first, and in approaching what is near is aware of what is far. Looking can be a kind of intelligent reverence. Moral thinking, serious thinking, is clarification (visual image). The good, just, man is lucid. These persuasive reflections are not exactly philosophical discourse, but are ancillary to a study of metaphysics, arising in connection with Buber's charge that Plato 'opticised thought', a charge to which I shall return.

A powerful religious visual image is the all-seeing eye of God. God sees me. Also the other person (envisaged by Sartre as the enemy) sees me and may turn me to stone. Looking at other people is different from looking at trees or works of art. We may receive deep consolation from knowing that we are 'present', *pictured*, in someone else's loving thoughts or prayers. It matters how we see other people. Such looking is not always dialogue, indeed it is rarely mutual. Others are given to us as a spectacle which we should treat with wise respect. A loving just gaze cherishes and adds substance, a contemptuous gaze withers. A look of hatred designs to kill. I quote from Julian of Norwich, *Revelations of Divine Love*, chapter 76. 'The soul that will be at rest, when other men's sins come to mind should flee from them as from the pains of hell. For the beholding of other men's sins maketh, as it were, a thick mist before the eye of the soul; so that we cannot, for the time, see the fairness of God – unless we behold them with contrition along with the sinner, with compassion on him and with holy desire to God for him.' In our information-ridden society, a prime satisfaction is the spectacle of the misdeeds and misfortunes of others. These reflections, which might proceed further, now lead back to Buber. Buber dislikes visual metaphysics because he wants to use the language of encounter or dialogue, not of contemplation. The deep Judaeo-Christian idea that God is *essentially* invisible is in tension with the natural ubiquity of the visual image. Is vision discredited because of the Second Commandment? 'No images' means no visible or visual images. Do not picture God. Looking at something we may turn it to stone – or be turned to stone ourselves. Buber wishes to present dialogue as encounter, speech. God is that which can only be thou, never it. 'After the imageless era a new procession of images may begin . . . But without the truth of the encounter all images are illusion.' (p. 23.) 'Faith is not a feeling in

[ 463 ]

the soul of man but an entrance into reality, an entrance into the *whole* of reality.' (p. 3.) Buber's pervasive conception of a dialogue involves, certainly suggests, the retention of the word 'God', a personal name, which he explicitly dramatises and defends. God 'is the most heavy-laden of all human words. None has become so soiled, so mutilated. Just for this reason I may not abandon it.' (p. 7.) (Quoted earlier.) It is a word which we must look after during a period of interim or interregnum.

Without encounter images are dead. Buber emphasises minute-to-minute religious experience, consciousness. The 'lived concrete' is the moment, the meeting place of human and divine. 'The religious essence of every religion can be found in its highest certainty, that is the certainty that the meaning of existence is open and accessible in the actual lived concrete, not above the struggle with reality, but in it.' (p. 35.) We experience the mysterious fullness of the concrete situation. When we are most alone we know in our hearts the difference between good and evil. A guiding light (visual image) must be discovered not made. The relation to the moment must be preserved. Here we relate to the divine as to an encountered reality. I do not, as I shall explain, believe in Buber's I–Thou God, or in his fundamental key idea of dialogue. But I like very much what he says about religion being a matter of a continuous consciousness, a preservation of the moment, an entrance into the whole of reality. Also this: 'The ground of human existence in which it' (that is, encountered reality, for Buber God) 'gathers and becomes whole is also the deep abyss out of which images arise. Symbols of God come into being, some of which allow themselves to be fixed in lasting visibility, even in earthly material, and some which tolerate no other sanctuary than that of the soul.' (p. 45.) This abyss is not Jung's or Freud's unconscious mind, though it may be called an unconscious mind or a deep soul. It is, as I see it, more like the dark realm of Plato's *anamnesis*, or St John of the Cross's abyss of faith into which we fall when we have discarded all images of God; or the seething bubbling cauldron in terms of which Eckhart once described God. I quote from Eckhart's *Commentary on the Book of Exodus*.

'The repetition of "am" in the words "I am who I am" indicates the purity of the affirmation, which excludes every kind of negation from God. It indicates too a certain turning-back and reversion of His being into and upon itself and its indwelling or inherence in itself: not only this but a boiling-up, as it were, or a process of giving birth to itself – inwardly seething, melting and boiling in itself and into itself, light in light and into light wholly interpenetrating itself, wholly and from every side turned and reflected upon itself. As the wise man [Hermes Trismegistus] says: monad begets, or begat, monad and reflected its love and ardour upon itself. For this reason it is said in the first chapter of St John's Gospel: "In Him was life." For life denotes a sort of outpouring, whereby a thing, swelling up inwardly, completely floods itself, each part of it interpenetrating the rest, until at last it spills and boils over. This explains the fact that the emanation of the Persons of the Deity is the reason for the creation and precedes it. "In the beginning was the Word" (John 1. 1) comes first and is followed by the words, "All things were made through Him".'

The God celebrated in this mix of sexual and cosmic symbols, and images of light and movement, may seem far from the dark quiet Godhead affirmed by Buber; but there is the same conception of God as a creative fullness of all being, continually engendering Himself. Here we are outside philosophy in poetic theology or mystical poetry. The idea of this image-making abyss is also the concept of a *via negativa*, which is both iconoclastic and fertile of new images.

However that may be (I continue now with Buber), at the present time the God who formerly spoke to us is dumb. We confront 'the silence of the Transcendent'. Images of God appear less spontaneously out of the abyss, which is perhaps after all a dark and ambiguous place containing demons. Buber here (p. 30) quotes Heraclitus's high saying which I quote earlier, that 'the One who alone is wise does not want and does want to be called by the name of Zeus'. (Fr. 32.) Buber takes this as picturing the original relation between religion and philosophy, between meeting and objectifying the divine. I think this saying can, or can also, be taken as referring to a familiar, personal, subjective–objective dialectic in religious experience (of which the contrast between religion and philosophy could then be taken as an image): the sense of being swept to and fro between an absolutely certain sense of a reality, and an instinctive rejection of this reality because it cannot be ultimate, and cannot be that which is sought. To return to Buber, whose point is more specific: the position of the thinker (whether or not philosopher or theologian) is certainly at present a difficult one.

[ 465 ]

Prayer which 'ultimately asks for the manifestation of the divine presence' may lose its spontaneity in this age of 'subjectivised reflection'. (p. 126.) We have lost confidence in certainty and absolute. Buber quotes the words of Hölderlin which are also quoted by Heidegger:

> Aber weh! es wandelt in Nacht, es wohnt wie in Orcus,
> Ohne Göttliches, unser Geschlecht.

Alas, it wanders in night, it dwells as in Orcus, without the divine, our generation. In this interregnum however, Buber sees an important role for philosophy. When images of God obstruct the way to Him, He removes Himself from them.

'Then comes round the hour of the philosopher who rejects both the image and the God whom it symbolises, and opposes to it the pure idea, which he even at times understands as the negation of all metaphysical ideas. This critical "atheism" (*Atheoi* is the name which the Greeks gave to those who denied the traditional gods) is the prayer which is spoken in the third person in the form of speech about an idea. It is the prayer of the philosopher to the again unknown God. It is well suited to arouse religious men and to impel them to set forth right across the God-deprived reality to a new meeting. On their way they destroy the images which manifestly no longer do justice to God. The spirit moves them which moved the philosophers.'

(p. 46.)

Unlike many people who profess to, or attempt to, or seem to, write about religion, Buber really is writing about religion. He is *expressing* religious faith and deploying a context which is to give fresh meaning to the word 'God'. I see and feel what he means about the philosopher who sets up the pure idea. And about God removing himself from the obstructive images. (Actually, this is a Platonic picture.) Religion is always, perhaps essentially, something of a mess. It is the task of some to set up close to it, outside it, intolerably abstract things. However philosophy, as it exists now in the west, apparently lacks the passionate interest in religion which would be needed to generate a new formulation. Can there be, for those who set out across the wasteland, any meetings which are at all like the old ones? We are told that the Absolute is there, but veiled; its time will come again. For the present, to use Buber's own theological language, I–*thou* is in the catacombs,

*I–it* is in charge. The present does certainly appear to be a time of 'angels', of wandering fragmented spirituality. But is there any sense in extending the idea, a traditional one after all, of God's absence and his return, out into this dark fire-illumined void? Of course the idea of such a triumphant return is dramatic and comforting. 'There is no sphere above our moral decisions on the one hand and our relation to the Absolute on the other. Only this is given; and herein religion bestows and the ethical receives.' Buber believes in God and is confident about Absolute and about 'religion'. But can Absolute live without God? We feel, it *must* live, morality must be *fundamental* in human life. But someone may say, we shall have to live now with *spirit* and without *absolute* and be thankful if we still have spirit and if that too is not withdrawn from us. Prophets like drama, after all they want to attract attention. We are dealing with difficult and ambiguous images and may wonder, as we constantly return to them, how much light they shed. Buber believes in a personal God, of whom we may have experience, whom we (indubitably perhaps) *meet*. He wants, as he has said, to preserve and protect the name of God, as naming the purest form of a dialogue which he regards as the essence of religion and morality. (The ethical receives.) He does not want or need a mystical Christ or a mystical Buddha. A mystical Moses would be a contradiction in terms. The idea and name of God brings with it a stricter and more vivid picture of encounter and of prayer. Buber evidently believes that in spite of the Godless darkness of the time, which in his prophetic role he is partly foreseeing, individuals can encounter God. I relate to the divine as to 'Being which is over against me, though not over against me alone'. This Being is personal Being. It is 'permissible for the believer to believe that God became a person for love of him, because in our human mode of existence the only reciprocal relation with us that exists is a personal one'. (p. 97.) Here the person that God becomes for our benefit is of course not Christ or any other human incarnation, but the Person whose presence and loving concern we, with utmost certainty, discover in meditation and prayer. 'The real self appears only when it enters into relation with the Other.' (p. 97.) For Buber, the reciprocal relation is what is absolutely necessary, and in, and as, this necessity he discovers God. The circle of self is broken by what is other. The dialogue of I and Thou 'finds its highest intensity and transfiguration in religious reality in which unlimited Being becomes, as absolute person my partner'. (p. 45.) So, the reality of God is to establish man as *partner*. This might sound, after all, like Feuerbach's triumphant elevation of man; yet Buber's language is that of a traditional piety and his faith, moving in darkness, is in a traditional God. There are here some partings of ways between demythologising thinkers, our prophets, iconoclasts, destroyers and renewers of images. If in the darkness of deep prayer I meet a person may this not be myself in some disguise – and why not? I am indeed, to use Buber's terms, constantly a 'thou' to myself, as well as an 'it'. Morality is loss of egoism. The *tutoiement* between me and myself can be various, and good or bad. I encounter a higher, or a lower, part of my soul. Jung tells us that God and the Unconscious are probably the same thing. This, however one may attempt to raise the status of the Unconscious, seems to remove from God the moral absolutism and separate being accorded to him by Buber. At a simpler more empirical level we may agree that meditation (prayer, attention, with or without God) may enlarge our being by giving power and reality to good impulses. This may serve as a starting point for diverging roads. Should we move on into a theological or religious terminology? If we speak here of an Absolute, is this a 'move' or a tautology? Tradition provides words and pictures and we may wish to benefit from using them. Buddhism provides such language at its least dogmatic when speaking of the Buddha nature within us. (In Platonic terms, the higher part of our soul.) We might speak of the Christ nature within us. Jungian psychology speaks a different language when it speaks of unifying the personality. (At what level?) The absolute as the possible totally harmonised individual (a Hegelian image) cannot be a religious or moral absolute, as these demand a distinction between good and evil. The perfectly *integrated* personality, as presented by Jung as an ideal, must include some notion of a pact with, or somehow reassessment of, what is evil in the soul. Of course we may, and often, feel that we ought to 'harmonise' our personality; but we may also feel that we have to live with disharmony. Amid such variant moral styles and contrasting pictures of the soul, it may be said, Why worry, surely this is a private matter, and are we not out at the edge of language at transcendental barriers? Let each man have his own faith and his own god or absolute, if he can invent one or feel sure he has discovered one. Is there anything for the philosopher to say here about theology, or even about morality, which goes beyond piecemeal conceptual clarifications here and there? What sense can we attach to Buber's 'pure idea' which is to be set up outside, in the desert, or his prayer of the philosopher which is unlike the prayer of the believer? One wants to explain more clearly what it is to have lost the old personal God, and to do this without surrendering the concept of religion. What is meant here by 'absolute' must also show the *essential* mutual connection of religion, as now conceived, and morality. One thing needful is a refreshed conception of transcendence. We may turn here to Plato and Kant, and be edified by the tension between these two mentors.

We are close to problems about 'religious experience'. People who do not hold traditional beliefs may recognise, or be attracted by, or recall from childhood, something like Buber's 'Thou'. How important is this matter of keeping or not keeping a personal God? Is *this*, in whatever disguise, the last piece of supernatural machinery; that which, for a religion likely to survive, must go? Is this an argument about what concepts one can morally, or aesthetically, tolerate, or about when it becomes patently cheating to speak of a personal God? There is a philosophical argument concerning meaning, but this is readily over-whelmed by considerations of experience which are difficult to handle. I mean, the philosopher may well 'give up' and say, religion is a private mystery, what is the point of thinking about it? Of course many philo-sophers take and have taken this view, and have been encouraged to take it, for many reasons, by religious people. Is it just important *now*, when 'demythologisation' proceeds whether we like it or not, to ask the theologian and the philosopher to communicate in a new way? In this context I do not see the eternal Thou as a concept likely to be at home in a demythologised religion. Is there Someone there? Or am I bound, or naturally led, to act as if this is so? Such acting 'as if' would not be like the mythical 'as if' in the *Meno*. The fiction would have to be perilously near to the centre of my faith, hardly discernible from a wishful thought. This is a Judaeo-Christian problem. The well-known contrast made by Buber (originally in his book *I and Thou*) between I –Thou and I–It relations can illuminate morality, the dealings of people with each other, can serve as commentary upon the concept of love. It is instructive too to compare and contrast it with Kant's distinc-tion between treating a person as a means and treating him as an end. Kant's 'practical love' need not involve dialogue. Kant's religious morality does not favour an intimacy with God such as that enjoyed by St Augustine and the Psalmist. Moreover acting rightly toward another person does not necessarily, in fact more often does not, involve face-to-face encounters. There is here a contrast of styles which can be comprehensibly illustrated in everyday terms. One man does good by stealth, attends carefully to the situation of others, sees their needs, helps them without close involvement, even anonymously, admonishes indirectly, by implication and example, shuns close encounter. Only in rare situations would it be a duty, or indeed possible, to achieve complete mutual understanding. Another man prefers to draw people close to him, to have confessions, frank meetings, warmth and friendship, to give support by voice and presence. No doubt the afflicted human race needs both of these philanthropists. There is an essential area of coldness in morality, as there is an essential area of warmth. Seen in a Kantian context, the I–Thou concept can seem (by contrast) thrilling and dramatic, readily compromised by various self-regarding consolations. It holds out a promise of experience and ever-available company.

Buber says that only God can never be an object. 'God can never become an object for me. I can attain no other relation to him than that of the I to its eternal Thou, that of the Thou to its eternal I.' (*Eclipse of God*, p. 68.) This sounds like the language of the Ontological Proof. God exists necessarily not contingently, and his not-ever-being-an-object, a thing among others, is a part of this unique necessary non-contingent being. However, as I have suggested, the Proof need not be tied to the idea of a person, which Buber's I–Thou terminology attempts to make fundamental. Buber's appeal to religious experience is very moving. But suppose we can no longer find this 'necessary' presence? 'But if man is no longer able to attain this relation,' Buber goes on, 'if God is silent towards him and he toward God, then something has taken place not in human subjectivity but in Being itself.' Buber rejects the explanation that we have just subjectively lost the concept, and now find the idea of a personal God incredible, and indicates that the change is, or would be, or could be, something very deep indeed. This must prompt the question, what next? Will God stay silent and 'Being' alter? Must we after all give up the necessary Thou, or consign him (it) to an area of ineffable faith? To refer here to what people generally can or cannot do seems in itself an acceptance of the language of 'it'. Buber is prepared to glance at Heidegger's prophetic notion that, after this dark interlude, the holy will return to us in new and unimaginable forms. Heidegger says that his view is not atheism, but is the making of a place for thought about the divine. Buber's attitude seems ambiguous. He quotes Heidegger (in English see also *The Question concerning Technology*, 'The Word of Nietzsche: "God is dead" ', p. 100):

'The place which metaphysically belongs to God is the place in which the production and preservation as created being of that which exists is effected. This place of God can remain empty. Instead of it another, that is a metaphysically corresponding place can appear, which is neither identical with God's sphere of being nor with that of man, but which, on the other hand, man can, in an eminent relation, attain. The superman does not and never will step into the place of God; the place rather in which the will to the superman arrives is another sphere in another foundation of existing things in another being.'

Buber says of this, 'The words compel one to listen with attention. One must judge whether that which is said or intimated in them does not hold true today and here.' (p. 92.) Buber thus ends one of the essays of which his book consists. He seems here to consider it possible that the deep change in Being, the loss of God, can take place. In such a context the term 'Being' might well be translated into other terms; I would prefer to speak of our ordinary, fairly describable, experiences of 'transcendence', our apprehensions of what is true and good and real. A pessimistic prophecy might suggest that now, or soon, there are or will be fewer of these spiritual experiences and activities available to human beings. A nuclear war or an ecological catastrophe might blot out people and their potentialities. But if we escape such a fate, I see no reason to predict a 'loss of spirit'. The human capacity to seek, and enjoy, the good and the true is versatile and endlessly creative. 'The place which metaphysically belongs to God' is empty in the sense that, in the western world, fewer people believe in the old personal God. The superman cannot fill that place because human frailty forbids the existence of such a being, unless we imagine him as a *de facto* tyrant, or a fake 'religious' superstar. There are of course such 'leaders' or pseudo-supermen. The idea of superman remains with us vaguely however, in the west, set up by Feuerbach, Nietzsche, Sartre, as the free powerful unillusioned fulfilled being. The tyrant of *Republic* Book One. 'The place in which the will to the superman arrives . . . another sphere in another foundation of existing things in another being' might more plausibly, if expressed in less arcane language, be seen as a kind of fatalistic determinism, combined with a superior omniscience, which might emerge through a popularisation of developments in science. One may see this mixture at work in Derrida's nightmarish prophetic theorising. But these matters are parts of human thought and human activity and not, in the sense in which talk of God, his presence or absence, might suggest, the whole basis of it.

Because Buber apprehends what is called 'the silence of the Transcendent', or more mundanely the fact that modern western people have difficulty in believing in traditional supernatural religion, and because he still deeply believes in God, he feels driven to think in terms of an interim or (to use a term employed by Jung) an interregnum. Religious belief then has to become a kind of prophecy. This temptation should be resisted and I think Buber, who comes to the edge of it, does resist it. He rejects of course Jung's style of prophetic psychological historicism, and though fascinated by Heidegger does not follow him. Heidegger's idea, adorned by references to (poor innocent) Hölderlin, of a sort of return of the gods or new undreamt-of renewal of the sacred and the holy is a piece of poetic metaphysical melodrama. The concept of 'Being', used as a substitute for 'God' or 'Absolute', is of dubious value; and in the thinking of late Heidegger becomes a sinister historicised Fate, a posited entity about whose future 'structure' or 'intentions' we may speculate. (A player of games.) Heidegger's search for a universal language, or fundamental basis of language, in the language of poetry is also, whether we regard it as metaphysics, or 'science', or literary criticism, a false path, a search for 'deep foundations' where there are none. (Poetry is written by poets, there are not many of these, poetry is very difficult.) If one does want to believe in what is 'deep' in the form of the old God then let this belief be kept mysterious and separated and pure, and not mixed up with dubious history, or indeed with any history. Buber's writing conveys eloquently what such a belief is like. The renewal of the holy and the sacred is and can only be here and now, and is indeed still happening all the time. To return to I and Thou. It seems to me that if God is a necessary Thou then he must be (in the old sense) a person. One cannot get round this by saying that since we are persons God must be at least a person, or that God becomes a person in order to talk to us. The concept breaks at this point. The eternal Thou that lives in secret, if it is not our own heart or conscience or higher self, or our Buddha nature or Christ nature, speaking back to us, is the old Father God in disguise; and this God (as *a fortiori* the God of the philosophers) is what modern demythologising thought rejects.

Such rejection does not of course involve a choice between 'materialism' and an existentialist theology. There are other paths. Nietzsche's 'God is dead' seems to announce the end of moral as well as religious absolutes. But we continue to recognise moral absolutes just as we continue to use ordinary language. Kant was right to take our recognition of duty as something fundamental. We manage it. Let the philosophers and theologians worry about the background. 'Human subjectivity' may be said to have changed but only in some respects. We can lose God, but not Good. Prophecies about moral-less value-less societies of the future belong to science fiction, or would if science fiction writers could imagine them. We know the difference between a hypothetical and a categorical imperative. Buber's salute to the philosophers is both apt and moving. But he is also of course suspicious of philosophers, who might try to set up an idea of God (as Hegel did). I have quoted his objection to the visual imagery of Plato, which 'opticises thought'. Of course we 'meet with' reality all the time in the sense of 'coming close' to entities, all sorts of entities, and holding opinions and achieving knowledge. We have no difficulty in combining imperfect cognitions with ideas of perfection which haunt them. These are ordinary states of affairs. We grasp these matters all in one, the pure and separated source of light, and the reality which is revealed and imperfectly grasped. Buber says of Plato that he

'gives us a glorious human and poetic account of the mysterious fullness of the concrete situation. He also knows gloriously how to remain silent. When however he explains and answers for his silence, in that unforgettable passage of the seventh epistle, he starts, to be sure, from the concreteness of "life together" where "in an instant a light is kindled as from a springing fire". But in order to explain this he turns immediately to an exposition of the knowing and the known, meaning the *universal*. Standing in the concrete situation and even witnessing to it, man is overspanned by the rainbow of the covenant between the absolute and the concrete. If he wishes in philosophising to fix his glance upon the white light of the absolute as the object of his knowledge, only the archetypes or ideas, the transfigurations of the universal, present themselves to him. The colour-free, beyond-colour bridge

[ 473 ]

fails to appear. Here also, in my opinion, is to be found the reason why Plato changed from the identification of the idea of the good with God, as presented in his *Republic*, to the conception appearing in the *Timaeus* of the Demiurge who contemplates the Ideas.'

(The Eclipse of God, pp. 57–8.)

These are interesting misunderstandings, to which I referred earlier, which appear here given a particular force by the image of the covenant as the rainbow bridge and by the reference to the *Timaeus* Demiurge. Briefly, the term 'universal', often used in explanation of Plato, suggests a logical role, which indeed the Forms also perform. The Theory of Forms (never entirely clarified) is constructed to deal with both 'logical' (or epistemological) and moral problems. 'How does the one relate to the many?', 'how does the universal relate to the particular?' The imagery of the Forms is a *picture* of how we think (use language). How do we *classify* entities as groups under singular concepts and names, and how do we *recognise* these entities as being the *same* in different instances? Wittgenstein worried about this too. The Forms are related to a hierarchy of knowledge *and* morality. Knowledge (language) is essentially related to morality by the idea of truth. Science too depends on truthfulness. There is an orientation toward goodness in the fundamental texture of human nature. We, as individuals, live in different worlds, we *see* (visual metaphor) different things, not just in general but down to last details. The Good is distant and apart, and yet it is a source of energy, it is an active principle of truthful cognition and moral understanding in the soul, the inspiration and love-object of Eros. It is not a logical universal, or a Person, it is *sui generis*. It is a 'reality principle' whereby we find our way about the world. Plato's philosophy offers a *metaphysical picture* of that essential presence, together with (throughout the dialogues) many and various instances and examples of our relations to it. So there is, we may say, a rainbow bridge – but no covenant.

I used the word 'detail' earlier. Our pilgrimage (in the direction of reality, good) is not experienced only in high, broad or general ways (such as in increased understanding of mathematics or justice), it is experienced in all our most minute relations with our surrounding world, wherein our apprehensions (perceptions) of the minutest things (stones, spoons, leaves, scraps of rubbish, tiny gestures, etc. etc.) are also capable of being deeper, more benevolent, more just (etc. etc.). In the *Parmenides* (130) (as I quoted earlier) Parmenides asks Socrates whether there are Forms of little particular things which we think of as absurd and worthless, such as mud, hair, or dirt. Socrates replies, 'No, I think these are just as they appear to us [that is, they have no deeper aspect] and it would be absurd to believe that there is an idea [Form] of them – and yet I am sometimes disturbed by the thought that perhaps what is true of one thing is true of all. Then when I have taken up this position, I run away for fear of falling into some abyss of nonsense and perishing; so when I come to those things which we were just saying do have ideas [such as the good, the just, man, water, fire], I stay and busy myself with them.' Parmenides replies, 'Yes, for you are still young and philosophy has not yet taken hold of you, as I think it will later. Then you will not despise them; but now you still consider people's opinions, on account of your youth.' A whole cloud of philosophy condensed into a drop of dialogue.

To come to the matter of God and the Demiurge. Plato's view of good and virtue is not to be understood in any supernatural sense. He frequently indicates that the pictorial explanations to which he resorts are myths, metaphors. When in the *Meno*, *anamnesis* is explained in terms of how the soul before birth saw the Forms (the exemplars) with perfect clarity, Socrates remarks, 'Well, something like this might be true.' The happy almost playful *ironic light* (invisible to many readers, such as Buber and Heidegger) in which these beautiful world-changing constructions are set out, also and constantly gives us the clue to understand them. Plato's art creates its own atmosphere of understanding, whereby what is deepest and most serious can be grasped with precision. The Form of the Good as creative power is not a Book of Genesis creator *ex nihilo*. The light of Good, as truthfulness and justice and love, gives life to reality for the enlightened knower. The good man perceives the real world, a true and just seeing of people and human institutions, which is also a seeing of the invisible through the visible, the real through the apparent, the spiritual beyond the material. Plato does not set up the Form of the Good as God, this would be absolutely un-Platonic, nor does he anywhere give a sign of missing or needing a real God to assist his explanations. On the contrary. Good is above the level of gods or God.

Buber speculates that Plato wrote the *Timaeus* to exchange the abstract absolute of the *Republic* (the Form of the Good taking the place of God), which excludes the covenant between man and God, for a more personal picture, wherein a personal 'God' appears as man's creator. Plato's motives for writing the *Timaeus* are doubtless complex. If one is to make guesses, one might also imagine that Plato wishes, in this later dialogue, to correct the imagery of the *Republic* by doing justice more overtly to the underlying contingency of the world, to the fact that irreducible non-rational rubble is mixed into the human situation. One might relate this wish to Plato's increasing pessimism about politics and human possibility. The limitations of human powers, of capacities to become rational and knowledgeable and good, are certainly indicated in the *Republic*, but might be thought of there as in principle able to be overcome, rather than as ineluctable and to be taken as given. The *Timaeus* in no way abandons or softens the idea of the separate (implicitly) 'cold' Forms presented earlier. The *love* of the Demiurge for the Forms does not in any way affect, or infect, them, but is a mythical presentation of the energy of Eros as it pervades our world and inspires the creative activities of goodness which make it to be. F. M. Cornford (at the end of *From Religion to Philosophy*) takes a view not totally unlike that of Buber, of Plato's 'abstract absolute' (though of course he does not share Buber's theology), when he speaks of the world of the Forms as a rational 'scheme of classification', a construction of 'the Intellect which can divide and analyse but not create'. Plato then

'is forced to attribute to his deified Intellect an impossible impulse of desire. It is the old religious necessity, realised long before by Phere-kydes, who said that when Zeus set about making the world he changed himself into Eros . . . An immutable passionless Reason may trace the outlines of a scheme of classification . . . but it can do no more. To account for the existence of anything whatever we have to ascribe to it the unworthy and lower faculty of desire, and give this desire an unworthy and lower object – the existence of an imperfect copy of perfection. But that is the language of religion, not of science.'

This curious 'demotion' of Eros represents a misunderstanding not only of the *Timaeus* but of the *Republic* and the *Symposium*. Plato did not encounter or 'fall over' the problem of creative power suddenly at the end of his life, he had already earlier constructed and used his mythology of the imperfect lover and the perfect (impersonal) beloved. Love, as Prometheus, gives arts to men in the *Philebus*. Without the presence and energy of Eros the Forms might indeed seem too awe-

[ 476 ]

somely alone; but that human salvation and the being of the human world depends upon the (unilateral) relation of Eros to the Forms, is an image which is liberally 'cashed' by Plato in his descriptions of human love and of intellectual and moral struggles and aspirations. Eros may be 'lower' (a daemon not a God) but is not necessarily 'unworthy', and is certainly essential. The *Timaeus* differs from the *Republic* in being a semi-scientific, and at the same time mystical, cosmology, wherein scientific speculations mingle with, or inform, mystical religious imagery. But the trinitarian myth which contains this heterogeneous and often obscure material is certainly not a sort of patched-up *pis aller* expressive of Plato's inability to solve his problems. Cornford suggests that Plato, if he could, would have stated it all as *logos* and not *mythos*. The Demiurge, perfectly good but not omnipotent, is clearly presented as a mythical figure, and so far from superseding the Forms is subservient to them. This figure certainly does not represent any yearning in Plato for a conversible personal God or any dissatisfaction of that sort with his own metaphysical imagery. Plato would have found the idea of a supernatural or cosmic Thou, or a covenant with such a being, devoid of sense.

The Demiurge creates the cosmos looking with love towards the Forms. (I invoke my view of the *Timaeus* again here as answering both Buber and Cornford.) The Demiurge, in creating the heavenly bodies and our earth, makes use of necessity, the innate causality of natural law, but since he also designed the good in all existing things, we find ourselves subject to two kinds of cause, a necessary and a divine. We must seek (understand, use) the necessary for the sake of the divine. (68E, 69A.) The wisdom and goodness, which also brings happiness, derives from an understanding of the contingent necessity in our life, guided herein by a love of learning. Philosophy (love of learning and truth and virtue) is the greatest gift the gods have given us. (90B–C, 47B.) Plato's handling of divine and necessary causality is wiser than that of Kant. This creation myth represents in the most elegant way the redemption of all particular things which are, although made of contingent stuff, touched and handled by the divine. The contingent can become spiritually significant, even beautiful, as in art, as in Simone Weil's idea of the beauty of the world as an image of obedience. Plato's myths are the redemption of art. This is an aspect of the return to the Cave, where illusions are not only rejected but understood. The *Anima Mundi* is an image of incarnate mind. It is *as if* the world were created by a being who perceived and loved absolute good, but was only able, because of his given material, to reproduce his model imperfectly. The *Anima Mundi*, being incarnate in the world, partakes of its deficiencies. This is of course not a Manichaean picture; the pre-existing material is just contingent not evil. This extraordinary myth seems to be (in the sense which I have indicated) less optimistic than that of the Cave, where it is conceived of as possible that the prisoner, ascending, might in the end see the Sun itself. In the *Timaeus* (written later than the *Republic* and generally thought to be a very late work) the best we mortals can hope for is the situation of intuiting or glimpsing something beyond through what is here. The mythical Trinity of two persons, Creator and Soul, and impersonal Absolute, is in my view more morally and spiritually eloquent than the mythical Christian Trinity of which it is surely a forerunner. I do not know who baptised the *Timaeus*.

What we see is the Demiurge's model of the eternal reality, made in another material, while he can see the original. This is something which we can imagine, as a picture of our relation to an absolute. The Demiurge sees the Forms, responding to their magnetism, but does not of course converse with them. These magnetic and illuminating objects are separate and unresponsive. They are in and with themselves, simple and eternal (*Symposium* 211B): not the sort of thing with which one holds a dialogue. We do not have dialogues with Goodness. In an important sense Goodness *must* be an Idea. If an incarnate model is proposed we still must judge the model. Only to say 'must' and 'judge' sounds rather too harsh and mechanical. In Platonic terms we recognise what we already know. Goodness is an idea, an ideal, yet it is also evidently and actively incarnate all around us, charged with the love which the Demiurge feels for the eternal Forms as he creates the cosmos. So we are *also* able to evoke mystical Buddhas and mystical Christs who as historical figures were imperfect men, together with innumerable other images and tokens of perfect spiritual ideas. Buber's memorable distinction between the I–Thou relation and the I–it relation seems too simple and exclusive, and may indeed suggest the old fascinating division of fact from value, which makes nothing of the greater part of our ordinary life of knowings and actings. Much, in some cases most, of our spiritual energy and understanding comes from non-reciprocal relationships with what is beyond and other. Our relation with a foreign language which we are learning is not reciprocal. (That we may enjoy what we learn is another matter.) We are helped if we have active principles of diligence and truthfulness standing by. If what we are learning is to love a person unselfishly, we have the privilege of dialogue, and need also the presence of good ideals and desires. In either case the impersonal 'presence' may be felt as external (the voice of duty, the ideal of goodness etc.) or as an instinctive source of relevant power. (Elsewhere in the soul.) Buber wondering (p. 73) how one might give sense to Heidegger's concept of Being, refers to Christian mystics and scholastics who speak of contemplating the Godhead as it is in itself prior to creation. But he adds that Eckhart follows Plato in holding that God is above Being. *Est enim Deus super esse et ens.* Only of course Plato says this of Good, not God. The supreme principle or absolute, the certain unfailing pure source and perfect object of love is not and cannot be an existing thing (or person) and is separate from, though magnetically connected with, contingent 'stuff' however thought of in some contexts as fundamental. God or gods, or a metaphysical conception of History, or a Life Force or Cosmic Rhythm, or protons or genes or DNA, or *archi-écriture*, may be or have been (plausibly or implausibly) said to have some *fundamental* status which is to be contrasted with ordinary existence. But Good would not be a part of this, it would be above it in the position of its judge. Such imagery suggests and defines the unique spiritual element in life, that which religion indicates and to which morality instinctively returns. We have to decide how, whether, why impressive scientific or historical or psychological theories are to affect our way of living. These theories are not gods, and those of us who are not 'specialists' have (for instance in political situations, as citizens) to make judgments, and attempt to make well-informed judgments, about them. The charm of determinism haunts the metaphysical concept of Being. It is a place where attractive quasi-scientific theories of ultimate reality can breed. We are tempted to imagine an alien material which we cannot transcend and where morality and personal responsibility, as it were, stop. Here a general theory reinforces our natural sloth, our weariness and covert despair. Of course, in law courts and in ordinary life, we learn how to forgive people (including ourselves) as victims of forces (psychological or social forces for instance) which are 'beyond control'. But these are properly judgments in individual cases, not instances or evidences of a general human state which must be taken to be beyond challenge. Dramatic pictures of the human situation, as presented by Nietzsche, Freud, Sartre or Heidegger, whose purpose, even when catastrophic or 'austere', is actually consoling, are exercises in hubris, or speculative ultimates which we must judge in the light of something which remains free and untainted beyond them.

*Postscript.* Nietzsche, *The Gay Science*, section 125. '*The Madman.* Have you not heard of that madman who lit a lantern in the bright morning hours, ran to the market place and cried incessantly, "I seek God, I seek God." As many of those who did not believe in God were standing around just then, he provoked much laughter . . . "Whither is God?" he cried. "I shall tell you. *We have killed him*, you and I. All of us are his murderers. But how have we done this? How were we able to drink up the sea? Who gave us this sponge to wipe away the entire horizon? What did we do when we unchained this earth from its sun? Whither is it moving now? . . . What was holiest and most powerful of all that the world has yet owned has bled to death under our knives . . . Is not the greatness of this deed too great for us? Must we not ourselves become gods simply to be worthy of it? There has never been a greater deed; and whoever will be born after us – for the sake of this deed he will be part of a higher history than all history hitherto." Here the madman fell silent and looked again at his listeners; and they too were silent and stared at him in astonishment. At last he threw his lantern to the ground and it broke and went out. "I came too early", he said then: "My time has not yet come. This tremendous event is still on its way, still wandering – it has not yet reached the ears of men." ' The whole of this section is quoted by Heidegger in *The Word of Nietzsche*. Heidegger goes on to say, 'The pronouncement "God is dead" means: The supra-sensory world is without effective power. It bestows no life. Metaphysics, i.e. for Nietzsche Western philosophy, understood as Platonism, is at an end.' This essay (*The Word of Nietzsche*) is based on Heidegger's Nietzsche lectures given between 1936 and 1940.

# > 16 <
# Morality and Religion

In the background of many of these arguments lies a question about
the relation of morality to religion, the difference between them, and
the definition of religion. I have already suggested that my whole argument can be read as moral philosophy. In any case moral philosophy
must include this dimension whether we call it religion or not. Someone
may say that there is only one way to 'acquire' religion and that is
through being taught it as a small child. You have to breathe it in. It
is an ineffable attitude to the world which cannot really be discussed.
People who take up religion as adults are merely playing at it, it remains
at a level of illusion. So someone could speak, being either a believer
or an unbeliever. The unbeliever might add that religion is imbibed in
childhood, when it forms part of the infantile child–parent relationship
now well-known to psychology; only religion, being a soothing drug,
is less easy to give up in later life.

The most evident bridge between morality and religion is the idea
of virtue. Virtue is still treated in some quarters as something precious
to be positively pursued; yet the concept has also faded, even tending
to fall apart between 'idealism' and 'priggishness'. It may be seen as a
self-indulgent luxury. It has, perhaps has always had, many enemies.
Fear of a perverted ideology or of a too fervent 'enthusiasm' may
prevent a positive conception of virtue. Cynicism and materialism and
*dolce vita* can occlude it, also fear, misery, deprivation and loss of
concepts. Even in a religious context 'personal spirituality' may be
something that has to be argued for. A utilitarian morality may treat
a concern with becoming virtuous as a waste of energy which should be
transmitted directly to the alleviation of suffering. Of course numerous

people are virtuous without thinking about it, and sages may say that, if thought about, it may *ipso facto* diminish. A saint may perhaps be good by instinct and nature, though saintly figures are also revered as reformed sinners. Perhaps the word itself begins to seem pretentious and old-fashioned.

An idea (concept) of virtue which need not be formally reflective or clarified bears some resemblance to religion, so that one might say either that it is a shadow of religion, or religion is a shadow of it. The demand that we should be virtuous or try to become good is something that goes beyond explicit calls of duty. One can of course extend the idea of duty into the area of generalised goodness (virtuous living) by making it a duty always to have pure thoughts and good motives. For reasons I have suggested I would rather keep the concept of duty nearer to its ordinary sense as something fairly strict, recognisable, intermittent, so that we can say that there may be time off from the call of duty, but no time off from the demand of good. These are conceptual problems which are important in the building up of a picture; that is, an overall extension of the idea of duty would blur a valuable distinction, and undermine the particular function of the concept. Duty then I take to be formal obligation, relating to occasions where it can be to some extent clarified. ('Why go?' 'I promised.' 'Why go?' 'He's an old friend.' 'Why go?' 'Well, it's somehow that sort of situation.') Duty may be easily performed without strain or reflection, but may also prompt the well-known experience of the frustration of desire together with a sense of necessity to act, wherein there is a proper place for the concept of *will*. Dutifulness could be an account of a morality with no hint of religion. The rational formality of moral maxims made to govern particular situations might make them seem like separated interrupted points of insight rather than like a light which always shines. This could be a picture of human life. Yet Kant also portrays us as *belonging* at every second to the noumenal world of rationality and freedom, the separated pure source. We are orderly because duty is duty, yet also behind the exercise of it we might (surely, after all) glimpse the inspiring light of pure goodness which Kant calls Reason, and sometimes even God. Beyond all this we may picture a struggle in Kant's religious soul over the concept of Reason, so essential, yet so awkward. The rationality (Pure Reason) which enables us to deal with objects and causes *must* be related to that (Practical Reason) which enables us to deal with right and wrong. Well, the concept of truth can relate them. (Compare Plato's relation of epistemological with spiritual.) Perhaps Kant felt no awkwardness – it is we who feel awkward, when we connect morality with love and desire. Certainly it does seem possible to set up a contrast between the dutiful man and the virtuous man which is different from the contrast between the dutiful man and the religious man. Here we may think of Christ saying render unto Caesar what is Caesar's. Duty as order, relating morals to politics. Good decent men lead orderly lives. It might also be said in this context that given the abysmal sinfulness of humans, only a strict list of rules can keep them from mutual destruction! The moral (or spiritual) life is both one and not one. There is the idea of a sovereign good, but there are also compartments, obligations, rules, aims, whose identity may have to be respected. These separate aspects or modes of behaviour occasion some of the most difficult kinds of moral problems, as if we have to move between *styles*, or to change gear. We have to live a single moral existence, and also to retain the separate force of various kinds of moral vision. Jeanie Deans in Scott's novel loves her sister, but cannot lie to save her life. Isabella in *Measure for Measure* will not save her brother by yielding her chastity to Angelo. Duty is one thing, love is another. These are dramatic examples; one can invent many more homely ones of the conflict of moral requirements of entirely different kinds, wherein one seems to have to choose between being two different kinds of person. This may be a choice between two paths in life, or it may be some everyday matter demanding an instant response. We tend to feel that these dissimilar demands and states of mind must somehow connect, there must be a deep connection, it must all somehow make a unified sense; this is a religious craving, God sees it all. What I earlier called axioms are moral entities whose force must not be overcome by, or dissolved into, other moral streams: a requirement in liberal politics. Axioms may not 'win' but must remain in consideration, a Benthamite utilitarian conception of happiness must not, as a frequently relevant feature, be eroded by high-minded considerations about quality of happiness or by theories which make happiness invisible, or of course by political objectives. (The Cultural Revolution, the liquidation of the kulaks.) Equally of course, degraded or evil pleasure cannot count as simple or silly happiness. Such complexities, involving conflicts of moral discernment and moral style, are with us always. So, 'keeping everything in mind' is not an easy matter in morals. This may be an argument for clear rigid rules. Modern clerics who do not feel able to tell newly married couples to be virtuous, tell them to have a sense of humour. This shift is a telling case of a change of style.

Religious belief may be a stronger motive to good conduct than non-religious idealism. Corrupt immoral persons (for instance hardened criminals) who cheerfully break all the 'moral rules', may retain the religious images of their childhood which can, at some juncture, affect their conduct. This idea has been (not unsentimentally) dealt with in various novels and films. Indeed, this retention of images, and sensibility to images, might suggest the importance of a religious childhood. (Is it easier to get out of religion, or to get in?) Parents who have had such a childhood themselves, but have 'given up religion', may often think along these lines. A kind of sensible well-meaning tolerance is involved here. But, a sterner breed may say, what about *truth*? Religion just *isn't true*. A religious man, even a goodish one, is spoilt and flawed by irrational superstitious convictions; and it is held to be ridiculous for lapsed parents to let their innocent children be tainted with beliefs which the parents know to be false. It is no use talking of a 'good atmosphere', what is fundamentally at stake is *truth*. Such arguments come near to familiar problems of today. Is the non-religious good man so like the religious good man that it is merely some point of terminology or superficial style which is at issue? Orthodoxly religious people often tolerantly compliment the unbeliever by saying, 'He is *really* a true Christian'; which may well annoy the unbeliever. More positively attempting a distinction to form part of a definition, it might be suggested that religion is a form of heightened consciousness (Matthew Arnold said it was 'morality touched by emotion'), it is intense and highly toned, it is about what is deep, what is holy, what is absolute, the emotional imaginative image-making faculties are engaged, the whole man is engaged. Every moment matters, there is no time off. High morality without religion is too abstract, high morality craves for religion. Religion symbolises high moral ideas which then travel with us and are more intimately and accessibly effective than the unadorned promptings of reason. Religion suits the image-making human animal. Think what the image of Christ has done for us through centuries. Can such images *lie*? Do we not indeed adjust our attitudes to them, as time passes, so as to 'make them true'? This continuous adjustment is an aspect of the history of religion.

I intended here, thinking about holiness and reverence, not the exclusive property of believers, to quote from Francis Kilvert's Diary (begun in 1870). Kilvert was a parson in country parishes on the Welsh border, a religious good man of simple faith. However, it is difficult to quote from the Diary because of the transparent artless lucidity of Kilvert's account of his days. Any particular quotation can sound naive, or sentimental. 'I went to see my dear little lover Mary Tavener, the deaf and half dumb child. When I opened the door of the poor crazy old cottage in the yard the girl uttered a passionate inarticulate cry of joy and running to me flung her arms about my neck and covered me with kisses.' (12 June 1875.) 'Old William Price sat in his filthy den, unkempt, unshaven, shaggy and grey like a wild beast, and if possible filthier than the den. I read to him Faber's hymn of the Good Shepherd. He was much struck with it. "That's what He has been telling me", said the old man.' (26 January 1872.) 'The road was very still. No one seemed to be passing and the birds sang late and joyfully in the calm mild evening as if they thought it must be spring. A white mist gathered in the valley and hung low along the winding course of the river mingled with the rushing of the brooks, the distant voices of children at play came floating at intervals across the river and near at hand a pheasant screeched now and then and clapped its wings or changed his roost from tree to tree like a man turning in bed before he falls asleep.' (27 January 1872.) Kilvert spent his days walking all over his territory, visiting everyone, noticing everything (people, animals, birds, flowers) and describing it all in simple humble extremely readable detail. 'How delightful on these sweet summer evenings to wander from cottage to cottage and farm to farm.' It may be said that Kilvert was lucky, but also that he deserved his luck. There is a serene light and a natural kindly selfless love of people and of nature in what he writes. He felt secure. He had faith. Wittgenstein was struck by a character in a play who seemed to him to feel safe, nothing that happened could harm him. Wittgenstein's 'Ontological Proof' or 'statement' (*Tractatus* 6. 41) places the sense of the world outside the world, outside *all* of the contingent facts. Thinking of Wittgenstein's picture of the world (all the facts) as a self-contained sphere, a sort of steel ball, outside which ineffable value roams, we might look at something similar but different. 'He showed me a little thing, the size of a hazel nut, which seemed to lie in the palm of my hand; and it was as round as any ball. I looked upon it with my eye of understanding, and thought "What may this be?" I was answered in a general way thus: "It is all that is made." I wondered how long it could last, for it seemed as though it might suddenly fade away to nothing, it was so small. And I was answered in my understanding: "It lasts and ever shall last, for God loveth it. And even so hath everything being, by the love of God." ' (Julian of Norwich, *Revelations of Divine Love*, chapter 5.) Julian's showing, besides exhibiting God's love for the world, also indicates our absolute dependence as created things. We are nothing, we owe our being to something not ourselves. We are enlivened from a higher source.

Kierkegaard would object to a moral–religious continuum. We, existing individuals, therefore sinners, feel guilt, feel in need of salvation, to be reborn into a new being. 'If any man be in Christ he is a new creature: old things are passed away, behold all things are become new.' (2 Corinthians 5. 17.) In Kierkegaard's version of Hegelian dialectic it is not endlessly evolving toward totality, but is a picture of levels in the soul, or of different kinds of people, or of the pilgrimage of a particular person. The aesthetic individual is private, the ethical man, including the tragic hero, is public, the religious individual, the man of faith, is once more private. This dramatic triad also suggests the dangerous link between the two private stages, the aesthetic and the religious, so deeply unlike, so easily confused. The idea of repentance and leading a better cleansed and renewed life is a generally understood moral idea; and the, however presented, granting of absolution, God's forgiveness, keeps many people inside religion, or invites them to enter. Guilt, especially deep apparently incurable guilt, can be one of the worst of human pains. To cure such an ill, because of human sin, God *must* exist. (As Norman Malcolm suggested when discussing the Ontological Proof.) The condition of being changed and made anew is a general religious idea, sometimes appearing as magical instant salvation (as in suddenly 'taking Christ as Saviour') or as the result of some lengthy ascesis. Here salvation as spiritual change often goes with the conception of a *place* of purification and healing. (We light candles, we bring flowers, we go somewhere and kneel down.) This sense of a safe place is characteristic of religious imagery. Here the outer images the inner, and the inner images the outer. There is a literal place, the place of pilgrimage, the place of worship, the shrine, the sacred grove, there is also a psychological or spiritual place, a part of the soul. 'Do not seek for God outside your soul.' Religion provides a well-known well-tried procedure of rescue. Particularly in relation to guilt and remorse or the obsessions which can be bred from these, the *mystery* of religion (respected, intuited) is a source of spiritual energy. An orientation toward the good involves a reorientation of desire. Here a meeting with a good person may bring about a change of direction. If Plato had never met Socrates and experienced his death perhaps western thinking might have been different. The mystical Christ too can be 'met' with. (The idea of redemptive suffering is repugnant to some; but such suffering is everywhere around us, where the innocent suffers through love of the guilty.) Of course it may well be argued that there are sound unmysterious secular equivalents to these devices, there are many resources for the afflicted who may use their enlightened common sense, or go to their friends, doctors, therapists, psychoanalysts, social workers, take refuge in art or nature, or say (as the religious too may say) to hell with it all. Many people hate religion, with its terrible history and its irrationality, and would regard resort to religious rituals as a false substitute for real morals and genuine amendment of life. Judaism and Islam, who have avoided the path of image-making, and have revered the name of [God], avoid many of the problems which now beset Christianity. Buddhists live with the mystical Buddha in the soul. (Like Eckhart's God and Christ in the soul.) The Hindu religion also has its philosophical mysticism above its numerous gods. Religion has been fundamentally mystical, and this becomes, in this age, more evident. So will the theologians invent new modes of speech, and will the churches fill with people who realise they do not need to believe in the supernatural?

Religion (even if 'primitive') is generally assumed to be in some sense moral. Mysticism is also assumed to be, by definition, moral. Thinkers of the Enlightenment however, and many since, have held, often rightly, that organised, institutionalised religion is an enemy of morality, an enemy of freedom and free thought, guilty of cruelty and repression. This has been so and in many quarters is so. Therefore the whole institution may be rationally considered to be discredited or outmoded. Many other influences from the past support such a line of thought. Kierkegaard saw Hegel as the enemy of religion and of, *ipso facto*, the existing individual. The vast force of Hegel's thinking, followed up by Marx, is inimical to both. The Romantic Movement and the liberal political thinking which went with it have tended to look after the individual, and we associate high morality (idealism, selflessness, goodness) with many people in this century and the last who assumed that religion was *finished*. It must be agreed that, in very many ways, western society has improved, become more tolerant, more free, more decently happy, in this period. It may also be agreed that with the decline of religious observance and religious 'consciousness' (the practice of prayer and the fear of God for instance), some aspects of moral conduct may decline also. (Of course this decline can have other causes.) However that may be, Hegel and Marx, Nietzsche and Freud, have had influence. Virtues and values may give way to a more relaxed sense of determinism. There is a more 'reasonable', ordinary, *available* relativism and 'naturalism' about. Hegel's *Geist* is the energy which perpetually urges the ever-unsatisfied intellect (and so the whole of being) onward toward Absolute reality. Everything is relative, incomplete, not yet fully real, not yet fully true, dialectic is a continual reformulation. Such is the history of thought, of civilisation, or of the 'person' who, immersed in the process, is carried on toward some postulated self-consistent totality. Vaguely, such an image as something plausible may linger in the mind. I shall not discuss Hegel here, but look for a moment at a milder form of quasi-Hegelianism in F. H. Bradley's *Appearance and Reality*. According to Bradley both morality and religion demand an unattainable unity. 'Every separate aspect of the universe goes on to demand something higher than itself.' This is the dialectic, the overcoming of the incomplete, of appearance and illusion, the progress toward what is more true, more real, more harmoniously integrated. 'And, like every other appearance, goodness implies that which, when carried out, must absorb it.' Religion is higher than morality, being more unified, more expressive of a perfect wholeness. But both morality and religion face the same insuperable difficulty. Morality-religion believes in the reality of perfect good, and in the demand that good be victorious and evil destroyed. The postulated whole (good) is at once actually to be good, and at the same time to make itself good. Neither its perfect goodness nor its struggle may be degraded to an appearance (something incomplete and imperfect). But to unite these two aspects consistently is impossible. If the desired end were reached, the struggle, the need for devotion, would have ceased to be real. If there is to be morality, there cannot altogether be an end to evil. Discord is essential to goodness. Moral evil exists only in moral experience and that experience is essentially inconsistent. Morality desires unconsciously, with the suppression of evil, to become

[ 488 ]

non-moral. It shrinks from this, yet it unknowingly desires the existence and perpetuity of evil. Morality, which makes evil, desires in evil to remove a condition of its own being; it labours to pass into a super-moral and therefore non-moral sphere. Moral-religious faith is make-believe: be sure that opposition to the good is overcome, but act as if it (the opposition) persists. 'The religious consciousness rests on the felt unity of unreduced opposites.' (Chapters XIV and XXV.)

Bradley, the son of an evangelical Anglican clergyman, was alienated from the church, but interested in religion. His earlier work, *Ethical Studies* (1876), which he refused to have republished in his lifetime, is more liberally and tolerantly empirical (descriptive) about morality. He asks (chapter on 'Ideal Morality'), 'Is evolution or progress the truth from the highest point of view? . . . To whom in England can we go for an answer?' This 'raises problems which nothing but a system of metaphysic can solve'. The question is a good one, and also suggests the kind of situation in which it was felt that metaphysics was needed. *Appearance and Reality* (1893) offers (with various empirically motiv-ated qualms and hesitations) the system. I shall not discuss the details of this large argument. At least, siding with Kierkegaard's anger, one may say that it is very improbable that Ultimate Reality is an apprehen-sible, even describable, total self-enclosed system which forms (ulti-mately) a rational self-harmonious whole excluding nothing. The merits, or charms, of the Hegelian picture lie, one might say initially and genuinely, in having conceived of such an idea in a modern form and having argued it in some detail as psychology, as history, as time, and as science. Parts of these arguments (for instance Hegel's 'unhappy consciousness') are full of substance. The idea of the rational totality, made 'practical' by Marxism, has been widely influential. I am con-cerned here with the account, in Bradley's simplified version, of the self-contradictory nature of morality. Secretly good loves evil, because without evil it would not be good: good appears inconsistently as the absolute good (essential to morals), *and* as the struggle to become good which demands the co-operation of evil. Meditation upon this picture may lead to the conclusion that what ultimately makes sense is not the good but the aesthetic. (We are image-makers, what is finally harmoni-ous is something aesthetic.) A remote ancestry of the Hegelian method is in Heraclitus's creative strife of opposites as the base or matter or origin of being. 'War is the father of all things.' (Fr. 53.) War as creative evolutionary force. (A view held by tyrants.) Hegel returns to

Heraclitus, as do Nietzsche and Heidegger. Plato's dialectic lives in various, not entirely conclusive, debates, in which contingency (becoming) remains unreduced. What we may see in Hegel's *Geist* is more like a (captive, systematised, totalised, utterly demoralised) version of Plato's wild free yet potentially virtuous Eros. Other debased descendants of Eros are the 'Wills' of Schopenhauer and Nietzsche and the libido of Freud. The most obvious objections to Hegel may indeed be to the outrageous implausibility of the whole machine; but more sinister is a lingering shadow of determinism, and the *loss of ordinary everyday truth, that is of truth.* The loss of the particular, the loss of the contingent, the loss of the individual. The same consideration bears against another descendant in this line, the concept of *archi-écriture*. Hegel's system, and Bradley's smaller more confused copy, ignore (destroy, magic away) the essential contingency of human life, its rejection of any idea of rational totality. The life of morality and truth exists within an irreducible incompleteness. The (charming aesthetic) notion of the love affair between good and evil reappears in the work of Jung, presented as a new 'scientific' religious picture. Isn't this (we may be led to feel) worth reflecting upon? Yes, we do live with ideas, ideals, glimpses of some sort of goodness, while we are at the same time aware of ourselves as bad, vain, envious, jealous, struggling with strong selfish impulses. But surely (it is said) we can manage both pictures, both states, the tension between them, often invigorating and exciting, is the stuff of human existence? Did not 'God' perpetuate and hallow this tension? As I suggested earlier, the age of science does tend to introduce us to a certain relativism, we see the 'deep causes of our imperfections', we become more patient with our selfish ego; striving too hard, against our natural impulses, for a virtuous life may be a mistake. Better to be a well-adjusted moderate *happier* person than a would-be-good neurotic. Is there not (it may be argued) some sense in this view, whereby the notions of good and virtue fade in favour of a commonsensical balance between good and evil, wherein even the terms 'good and evil' begin to seem old-fashioned? It may be argued that, if required, 'high morality' can constantly return to us in the form of utilitarianism and political and ecological idealism. A final contention: anyway, really, most human lives are irretrievably sunk in misery and muddle and fear, and to this condition the light of morality is irrelevant. (I shall discuss this too later on.) To return to Bradley, his last chapter (of *Appearance and Reality*), entitled 'Ultimate Doubts', ends with the sentence: 'Outside of spirit there is not, and there cannot be, any reality, and, the more that anything is spiritual, so much the more is it veritably real.' (This is 'the essential message of Hegel'.) This might be read as Platonism or a mystical dictum in the style of Eckhart. But in the context of the busy totalising Hegelian *Geist* it is not to be revered. There is even in it the shadow of a contradiction, the very one which was pointed out in the case of good. The idea of totality (*nothing outside*) is placed in contrast with the idea of search (the discovery of what is more real and more true); and the latter (search) is by definition held to be illusion. What is intolerable here is that the *value* and genuine *existence* of the moral and intellectual struggle is denied in favour of a postulated entity wherein both value and individual being are to disappear. Not all metaphysicians have a sense of humour. Does metaphysics founder on the funny? Not necessarily – a little light and air often improves the scene. Plato continually makes jokes. Heidegger has no sense of humour, and this is one of the reasons why he misunderstands Plato. Funniness mocks totality. (It is forbidden in totalitarian states.) Bradley, for all his brave attempt to gather everything in, admits near the end that there are some things which he has to leave outside in the realm of the contingent. In a footnote (p. 451) he says that he has not included the question of life after death in the argument. What is one to make of that belief, which consoles so many? How can one picture it? 'Friends that have buried their quarrel in a woman's grave, would they at the Resurrection be friends? . . . The revolt of modern Christianity against the austere sentence of the Gospel (Matthew 22. 30) is interesting enough.' (Here Christ says that in the resurrection people 'neither marry nor are given in marriage, but are as the angels of God in heaven'.) 'One feels that a personal immortality would not be very personal if it implied mutilation of our affections. There are those who would not sit down among the angels till they had recovered their dog.'

# > 17 <
# Axioms, Duties, Eros

Philosophers have sought for a single principle upon which morality may be seen to depend. I do not think that the moral life can be in this sense reduced to a unity. On the other hand I do not think that it can be satisfactorily characterised by an enumeration of varying 'goods' and virtues. Of course it is true that, as moral agents, we pick and choose, we find some activities easy, some difficult. A person can be scrupulously honest but unkind, or generous but deceitful and so on. Schopenhauer said that malice was worse than lying. When assessing others and ourselves, we may discriminate between different 'aspects'. But a human being is a whole entity, there is also something essentially one-making about morals, and we may seek to exonerate or accuse on the basis of a seen or felt unity. The idea of good or goodness remains a magnet; the higher part of the soul speaks to the lower part of the soul, the good lightens and reforms the bad, the bad darkens the good. This imagery is readily understood. The image of good here takes the place of God in its connection with a whole being. At our 'deepest' or most serious we may be 'pulled together', not felt as a collection of heterogeneous impulses. When people are morally 'rent in two', the very rending can effect a gathering of the good against the bad. How-ever we may distinguish in philosophy, what in life is more confusedly experienced. I used earlier the image of a field of force, a field of tension, between modes of ethical being, divided under the headings of axioms, duties, and Eros. There is a necessary fourth mode which I name Void, which I have mentioned earlier and will return to. This picture is of course awkward since the entities, besides being of differ-ent types, are internally divided against themselves. I have said a good deal about these modes in preceding pages, and will now add a few brief remarks.

The developed concept of 'axioms' belongs to fairly recent history and is important both in itself and as a clarification of thinking about politics. It is a matter of history when and why something comes to be axiomatic. This is not to say that axioms are merely relative. This is practical morals right up against it. Axioms are designed to be strict and sweeping, ignoring national, racial, etc., barriers. They are connected with justice and with rights, and are essentially of great generality. (Life, liberty and the pursuit of happiness.) They are not to be confused with Kantian statements of duty which may also be very general in form; axioms belong in the Hobbesian rough-and-tumble of the field of 'political morality', which of course has its connections with 'private morality', but is properly to be distinguished. Not exactly under the same heading, yet a close relation, is the much larger and less localised matter of utilitarianism. It might be said that utilitarianism, intimately connected with politics, is an axiomatic philosophy. The actual idea is of great generality and apparent obviousness: every being desires happiness, the absence of pain, happiness is the only good and to promote it the only moral task. Bentham's pure form of the doctrine was modified by Mill who introduced another, different, moral value by speaking of higher and lower happiness. As an axiom the utilitarian idea could be expressed as: 'The question, how will this affect happiness, is *always* relevant to *every* moral decision.' This would be taking a step beyond Mill, and offering a formulation with which many people might agree. As I said earlier, utilitarianism is probably, as an identifiable moral doctrine, the philosophy most widely in practice in the present world. The general command 'Be kind' is also in general use. Utilitarian ideals now support large political ends (ecology, feed the hungry) and might be argued to be (rather than the cultivation of private virtue) what the planet needs. Justice too might, roughly, be considered under this first section, and might indeed have been the title of the section. Justice (indifferent to happiness) should be thought of primarily as retributive, making even: this is not revenge, it works for, as well as against, the accused. Deterrence and reform are, however important, ancillary.

The idea of duty is almost as familiar to us as the idea of happiness. It is perhaps, after the pursuit of happiness, the most evident fact in human life that there are some things we are (morally) required to do irrespective of inclination. Duty (practical reason, the categorical imperative) does not constitute the whole of the moral life. But the concept of duty remains with us as a steady moral force. Duty is formal, and though allowing of many formalisations (from the general to the almost disgracefully particular) can introduce order and calmness. Duty helps the formation of moral habits, partly because certain acts are thereby clearly and publicly defined (and we may be seen to fail), and also of course because we thereby internalise and take for granted certain patterns and values. A good habit of life, reliable decent behaviour, is to be welcomed; on the other hand the 'dutiful man' may be content with too little, with a mere observance of duty, following a rule without imagining that something more is required. (Or in extended Kantian terms, failing to formulate more complex or suitable maxims.) Kant sees the moral life as a struggle (we are aware of a noumenal reality by which we are touched) but he sees the fight in terms of the rational will straining against the massive unregenerate emotional psyche. This is what things are sometimes like, but certainly not always; the concept of duty, taken as the whole picture, identifies the moral agent with the good will. This will, especially when Kant's religious metaphysical background is removed, may be seen as only occasionally active. What is thereby ignored are the ways in which, in so many moments and levels of our experience, we are morally involved.

A large part of what I have been concerned with comes under the heading of Eros. 'All things are full of gods.' (Plato quoting Thales, *Laws* 899B.) Anyone who has been to India will have seen these gods. This is what is deliberately omitted by Kant. 'In every grain of dust there are Buddhas innumerable.' This road may be held to be morally dangerous, strewn with idols and warm emotional consolations and false delusive sacraments. Well, we will ingeniously find such consolations on any moral road, and the performance of duty is not necessarily a cold matter either, as Kant himself handsomely points out. Metaphysics both describes and recommends, and may be embraced or rejected on both counts. When Hume said that reason is and ought to be the slave of the passions he was pointing, in an intelligible way, at a fact and a desideratum. A calm reflective realism about morals suggests a large complex picture which is outlined and underlined in a normative manner and cannot otherwise be adequately presented. This is a case of what (as I have been arguing) is constantly happening

[ 494 ]

outside philosophy and here, as outside philosophy, we know roughly how to treat such pictures so as not to be cheated. Any moral philosopher must (should) appeal to our general knowledge of human nature. Morality is and ought to be connected with the whole of our being. I want here to restate in summary form what I have said earlier in discussing 'consciousness'. The moral life is not intermittent or specialised, it is not a peculiar separate area of our existence. It is into ourselves that we must look: advice which may now be felt, in and out of philosophy, to be out of date. The proof that every little thing matters is to be found there. Life is made up of details. We compartmentalise it for reasons of convenience, dividing the aesthetic from the moral, the public from the private, work from pleasure. We feel we have to simplify, and in our busy lives cannot care about minimals. Yet we are all always deploying and *directing* our energy, refining or blunting it, purifying or corrupting it, and it is always easier to do a thing a second time. 'Sensibility' is a word which may be in place here. Aesthetic insight connects with moral insight, respect for things connects with respect for persons. (Education.) Happenings in the consciousness so vague as to be almost non-existent can have moral 'colour'. All sorts of momentary sensibilities to other people, too shadowy to come under the heading of manners of communication, are still parts of moral activity. ('But are you saying that every single second has a moral tag?' Yes, roughly.) We live in the present, this strange familiar yet mysterious continuum which is so difficult to describe. This is what is nearest and it matters what kind of place it is. This is not to advocate constant self-observation or some mad return to solipsism. We instinctively watch and check ourselves to some extent, but much of our self-awareness is other-awareness, and in this area we exercise ourselves as moral beings in our use of many various skills as we direct our modes of attention. In traditional terms, 'God sees me at every moment' and 'I do not pray just in the morning and the evening, I pray as I breathe.' The word 'spiritual' may be tied to religion, in order to depict other areas as secular or aesthetic and so on, or it may be extended into the moral to connect morality with religion, or it may be taken over by the moral as a way of saying goodbye to religion. This word certainly seems to me to be at home in the moral sphere, suggesting the creative imaginative activity of our mind, spirit, in relation to our surroundings. Religion has no private property here. Thinking about religion throws light upon what morality means and is. And religious thinking too, as well as 'thinking about', should be taken back into moral philosophy, where it used to have a home in the past. Reflection in purely religious contexts, where mystics and artists haunt the borders of theology and enliven and humanise that 'dry' subject, has often revealed the human soul more truly than thoughts in the style of moral philosophy: for fairly discernible reasons concerning intensity of motive and availability of art, the naturalness for instance of working with images. Writers, poets, dramatists, novelists, without formal religious or philosophical aims, have of course done so too. We have many kinds of accessible wisdom. This is not in any way to suggest that philosophy should be softened, or merged or lose its own particular kind of steely rectitude and sense of truth. I think in this respect philosophy can look after itself.

So, in those streets in India, at filthy meaningless street corners, there are images of gods with garlands of fresh flowers about their necks. Of course at every level of sophistication we have to beware, on our way, of idolatry and false deities. This wariness is an essential moral matter, one might almost call it a moral rule. But this too I think we know generally how to handle. On the road between illusion and reality there are many clues and signals and wayside shrines and sacraments and places of meditation and refreshment. The pilgrim just has to look about him with a lively eye. There are many kinds of images in the world, sources of energy, checks and reminders, pure things, inspiring things, innocent things, attracting love and veneration. We all have our own icons, untainted and vital, which we, perhaps secretly, store away in safety. There is nothing esoteric or surprising about this, people know about it, it is familiar. I have taken here the image (concept) of Eros from Plato. 'Eros' is the continuous operation of spiritual *energy*, desire, intellect, love, as it moves among and responds to particular objects of attention, the force of magnetism and attraction which joins us to the world, making it a better or worse world: good and bad desires with good and bad objects. It gives sense to the idea of loving good, something absolute and unique, a magnetic focus, made evident in our experience through innumerable movements of cognition. Good represents the reality of which God is the dream. It purifies the desire which seeks it. This is not just a picturesque metaphysical notion. People speak of loving all sorts of things, their work, a book, a potted plant, a formation of clouds. Desire for what is corrupt and worthless, the degradation of love, its metamorphosis into ambition, vanity, cruelty, greed, jealousy, hatred, or the parched demoralising deserts of its absence, are phenomena often experienced and readily recognised. If we summon up a great energy, it may prove to be a great demon. People know about the difference between good and evil, it takes quite a lot of theorising to persuade them to say or imagine that they do not. The activity of Eros is orientation of desire. Reflecting in these ways we see 'salvation' or 'good' as connected with, or incarnate in, all sorts of particulars, and not just as 'an abstract idea'. 'Saving the phenomena' is happening all the time. We do not lose the particular, it teaches us love, we understand it, we *see* it, as Plato's carpenter sees the table, or Cézanne sees Mont Ste Victoire or the girl in the bed-sitter sees her potted plant or her cat.

So, the carpenter is dealing with wood, tools, measurement, Cézanne is looking at the mountain he knows so well and creating a work of art and saying to himself that he cannot paint what he sees, the girl is comforted by her plant, which is so beautiful and glossy and which she cares for and protects, and also by her cat, whom she also tends, who is a free being, a friend, a privilege to live with, they look into each other's eyes. And the physicist too, whose thoughts we would not understand, loves the beauty of his formulation. Human beings love each other, in sex, in friendship, and love and cherish other beings, humans, animals, plants, stones. Imagination and art are in all of this, and the quest for happiness and the promotion of happiness. The myth in the *Phaedrus* (250) tells us that every human soul has seen, in their pure being, the Forms (Ideas) as justice, temperance, beauty and all the great moral qualities which we 'hold in honour', when dwelling with the gods in a previous existence; and when on earth we are moved toward what is good it is by a faint memory of those pure things, simple and calm and blessed, which we saw then in a pure clear light, being pure ourselves. This seems to me an excellent image of our apprehension of morality and goodness. It also conveys, in brief, a proper understanding of the Theory of Forms in its moral application. (Of course Plato did not think that morality consisted in staring at an abstract idea.) The dialectic descends, returning to the particular. (As in Buddhist views and *Parmenides* 130.) What I have called Eros pictures probably a greater part of what we think of as 'the moral life'; that is, most of our moral problems involve an orientation of our energy and our appetites.

# > 18 <

# Void

This section, which could also be called 'despair' or 'affliction' or 'dark night', concerns a region, or category, which might seem to have been left out of too optimistic a picture. It appears to be different in kind from the other regions or categories, since the latter may, in the context of the argument, be treated as types of moral thinking, whereas this looks more like a tract of experience. As such it might be thought of as an opposing companion piece to happiness. It might also, in a different way, be placed in opposition to 'transcendence', a word that I have used to mean a good 'going beyond' one's egoistic self, as in the Platonic pilgrimage or innumerable ordinary experiences. What I refer to here is something extreme: the pain, and the evil, which occasion conditions of desolation such as many or most human beings have met with.

Someone may say, if you are always noticing images of God or Good or seeing spiritual ladders, or being some sort of artist, you are very lucky. Your view of spiritual refreshment as everywhere available is ridiculously optimistic, even sentimental. It seems to neglect how miserable we are, and also how wicked we are. The average inhabitant of the planet is probably without hope and starving. It is terrible to be human. It is *deinos*. This argument may go on to suggest that any cult of personal spirituality or 'goodness', presented as fundamental reality, is merely selfish pleasure in disguise, and all we can do which is in any way decent is to alleviate suffering whenever we come across it. From here various lines of thought proceed, most obviously utilitarian ones. Why waste time on private morality? There are dreadful human fates, even in 'sheltered' lives there is black misery, bereavement, remorse, frustrated talent, loneliness, humiliation, depression, secret woe. The misery of the world can be seen every day on television. There are places in lives, and geographical places too, where there is nothing but darkness, the devil has his territory, Christ stopped at Eboli. This could be a modern Manichaean morality. And when so many suffer is it not an impertinence to try to think of individual shattered lives? One must think statistically, consider how much money can be spared for relief by one's country and oneself. Can one go on talking about a spiritual source and an absolute good if a majority of human kind is debarred from it?

It is not easy to discuss such a matter or to take it as a single subject. Those who have experienced such black misery and recovered may prefer to forget. Art, which consoles and to which we also return for wisdom, tends to, or may seem to, romanticise despair. Innumerable poems, stories, pictures, portray it in ways we are easily able to tolerate and enjoy. Christ on the cross is an image so familiar and beautified that we have difficulty in connecting it with real awful human suffering. Grünewald's Christ may make us shudder but we admire it as a *tour de force*. Some great novels shake us, Tolstoy, Dickens, Dostoevsky. Attempts by painters, even when producing great pictures, are 'endangered' by either charm or aesthetic frightfulness. (I think the Titian *Pietà* in the Accademia avoids these.) Great tragic poetry and great tragedy seem to succeed best. The Iliad. Lear's pain is not romanticised nor is that of Oedipus. The classical Greeks seem to have been incapable of romanticism and *a fortiori* of sentimentality; they also, a related point, seem devoid of masochism. However and of course Achilles, Hector, Oedipus, Lear are inside works of art. Thucydides' account of the Athenian defeat at Syracuse is great cold tragic writing, and one might even argue that a great historian is best equipped to 'tell us'. Philosophers, even while consigning whole areas of human existence to blindness and suffering, do not feel moved to exhibit distress. Philosophy is supposed to be, in some sense, detached. There is perhaps a certain irony in good philosophical work which avoids appeal to the heart. The existential tradition ('the existing individual') made a point of coming nearer to the heart. But then such a move is in danger from art. Kierkegaard speaks eloquently and with emotion about dread and sickness unto death, but is also a romantic writer. Sartre's *néant*, with its ancestry in Kant's *Achtung* and Kierkegaard's *Angst*, is more like an exciting springboard than a void. At the level of 'human life begins on the other side of despair' we are hearing the voice of the cheerful spectator. (I do not mean that Sartre did not suffer, but that the reality of suffering is not expressed.) A fine writer on the subject, outside art, and *sui generis* philosophical, is Simone Weil. It is just, for reasons which have their own obviousness, very difficult to 'touch' this dark condition. Perhaps art does it best after all, and one need not refer oneself only to the sublimely great. One of the most terrible of human woes, and also the most common, is remorse. Joseph Conrad's novel *Lord Jim* conveys in ruthless detail the horrors of extreme remorse, its coldness, its eeriness, its destruction of the person. Loss of honour, loss of any hope of pardon. Kierkegaard (*Sickness unto Death*, 'Despair over sin') quotes Macbeth's words after the murder:

> For, from this instant,
> There's nothing serious in mortality:
> All is but toys – renown and grace is dead.

Another approach is to say that suffering is good for the soul, the experience of desolation can be a kind of teaching. This may be so, though perhaps (how can one know) more often not so. Any reflection shows that one is dealing, at a roughly recognisable level, with a lot of different states. Jim and Macbeth felt intense guilty remorse without hope of either forgiveness or healing repentance. Norman Malcolm spoke of a guilt so great that it forced us toward belief in God. Kierkegaard thought that sin and guilt could prompt the leap from ethics to religion. Despair induced by sin may be relieved, with or without religious aid, by repentance and restitution. On the other hand, the condition (for instance as humiliation) may, almost automatically, be 'alleviated' by hatred, vindictive fantasies, plans of revenge, reprisal, a new use of energy. There is, which can be no less agonising, a guiltless remorse when some innocent action has produced an unforeseeable catastrophe. A common cause of void is bereavement, which may be accompanied by guilt feelings, or may be productive of a 'clean' pain. In such cases there is a sense of emptiness, a loss of personality, a loss of energy and motivation, a sense of being stripped, the world is utterly charmless and without attraction. Guiltless bereavement can occasion most intense pain, but is often followed by recovery, when, it is said, 'nature' reasserts itself. Duties perceived in this emptiness may be a source of healing. There is no one there, but the pain is there and the tasks. In time the annihilated personality reappears, the victim returns from the strange absolute country of death which he has visited, and resumes his ordinary interests, which in his grief he found senseless. He is made by merciful nature to forget what it was like. Disappointed love or the effortful ending of a relationship may have a similar history. Even extreme guilt may be clouded over as ubiquitous nature prompts the conclusion 'Why bother'. The more terrible pictures are of solitary prisoners with no term of release. Religious belief or a secular equivalent may bring some light. Or a religious faith, strong at first, gradually fades away. In such despairing the idea of death and non-being is made real.

But, it may be said, surely in many cases something good can be retained or learnt from the experience of emptiness and non-being? Should it not be taken as a spiritual icon or subject for meditation? There is nothing that cannot be broken or taken from us. Ultimately we are nothing. A reminder of our mortality, a recognition of contingency, must at least make us humble. Are we not then closer to the deep mystery of being human? When we find our ordinary pursuits trivial and senseless are we not right to do so? The experience of emptiness may be a shock soon forgotten, or a lifelong reminder, a moral inspiration, even a liberation, a kind of joy. Of course one's persona or self-protective personality or 'life illusion' is part of one's working gear as a human being; yet, as we are occasionally given to perceive, it is extremely fragile. Anyone can be destroyed. There is no one there. Loss of personality is loss of ego. Buddhism teaches the unreality of the world of appearance, including the apparent person. (*Phaedo* 67E. Practise dying.) Kafka: '*Es gibt ein Ziel, aber keinen Weg, was wir Weg nennen ist Zögern.*' 'There is an end, but no way, what we call the way is vacillation.' (Hesitation, messing about.) People locked in closed religious houses think longingly of the fruitful happy lives they might have had, and which they have given up *for nothing*. This is, it must be, a familiar phenomenon. It is also, potentially, the dark night spoken of by St John of the Cross, wherein, beyond all images of God, lies the abyss of faith into which one *falls*. (Perhaps as into Eckhart's seething cauldron.) So, we may be told, the experience, whatever its cause, may be an education, may be made use of for good. The victim may be receiving an enforced enlightenment. And even the exempt spectator ought to think: I too could be there; and if so, what am I? (Perhaps the Greeks thought in this way about slavery: a *memento mori*.) Yes, it is possible, but very often just too difficult, to 'learn' from deep despair. One may remind oneself that human beings are remarkably good at surviving and people make jokes in dark situations which would appal the outsider. All the same one's thoughts return (hopelessly) to the imprisoned and the starving and to experiences of loss, ignominy, or extreme guilt.

Simone Weil on this subject. For the extreme state she uses the term *malheur*, meaning not just unhappiness or sorrow. One might translate it as 'affliction'. It is marked ('the mark of slavery') by physical symptoms, 'difficulty of breathing, a vice closing about the heart'. (*Pensées sans ordre concernant l'amour de Dieu*, 'L'Amour de Dieu et le malheur'.) From the *Notebooks*:

'To lose somebody: we suffer at the thought that the dead one, the absent one, should have become something imaginary, something false. But the longing we have for him is not imaginary. We must go down into ourselves where the desire which is not imaginary resides . . . The loss of contact with reality – there lies evil, there lies grief . . . The remedy is to use the loss itself as an intermediary for attaining reality. The presence of the dead one is imaginary, but his absence is real, it is henceforth his manner of appearing.'

(p. 28.)

'To forgive. (Valéry.) One is unable to. When someone has done us harm, reactions are set up. The desire for vengeance is the desire for balance. To accept the lack of balance. To see therein the essential lack of balance.'

(p. 136.)

'Valéry – adherence of painful thoughts (comparison with a burn). So much the better. It makes them real. Let the love of good adhere in this way. See to it that the love of good passes through such a process.'

(p. 51.)

This is joyless imagery. The image of burning is good. Remorse is said to bite, but better said to burn: an adherence of burning stuff. We must experience the reality of pain, and not fill the void with fantasy. The image of balance: the void as the anguished experience of lack of balance. We have been unjustly treated, insulted, humiliated: we want to get our own back, to get even, if need be to hurt innocent people as we have been hurt. We console ourselves with fantasies of 'bouncing back'. We yield to the natural gravity (*pesanteur*) which automatically degrades our thoughts and feelings. (Imagery of the mechanical, in Simone Weil, in Wittgenstein, in Freud, in Canetti's *Crowds and Power*.) Instead of this surrender to natural necessity we must hold on to what has really happened and not cover it with imagining how we are to unhappen it. Void makes loss a reality. Do not think about righting the balance, but live close to the painful reality and try to relate it to what is good. What is needed here, and is so difficult to achieve, is a new orientation of our desires, a re-education of our instinctive feelings. We may think here of Plato's image of the soul as a charioteer with a good horse and a bad horse, struggling with the bad horse and pulling him up violently, 'covering his jaws with blood'. *Phaedrus* 254E.

This partly metaphorical description of *malheur* may be readily recognised as what, in some sense, we have experienced. More difficult to imagine is the reorientation and the relation to good. It may be said that there are many ways out of affliction, the support of friends, the ability to make restitution, or to start a new life elsewhere, or just to rely on forgetting. But a deep, or a real, or a proper, recovery demands, it may be replied, some sort of moral activity, a making a spiritual use of one's desolation. Simone Weil speaks of good and of love. Loving is an orientation, a direction of energy, not just a state of mind. Emptiness: absence of God, absence of Good. This may be felt as the senselessness of everything, the loss of any discrimination or sense of value, a giddy feeling of total relativism, even a cynical hatred of virtue and the virtuous: a total absence of love. Here anything may help, any person, any pure or innocent thing which could attract love and revive hope. The inhibition of unworthy fantasies is perhaps the most accessible discipline. In extreme cases the negative effort of this inhibition may come as a kind of shock, when one is 'brought up short' (like the bad horse). There may be a place here for the idea of an effort of will. This sort of asceticism can of course be an everyday matter, practised at various levels, as when one guards one's tongue or expels bad thoughts. We have (gravity, necessity) a natural impulse to derealise our world and surround ourselves with fantasy. Simply stopping this, refraining from filling voids with lies and falsity, is progress. Equally in the more obscure labyrinths of personal relations it may be necessary to make the move which makes the void appear.

# Metaphysics: a Summary

Metaphysical images, in their travels from obscure books through religious and aesthetic imagery into the daily consciousness of all sorts of people, undergo, in this 'do-it-yourself' process, many changes and reveal many ambiguities. Ambiguity, or call it flexibility, belongs to these curious processes. The idea of void or emptiness, thought of in a moral and religious context, can be seen in various ways and can do various kinds of work. The emptiness can be a 'moment' in a dialectic, as in Kierkegaard's image of creative despair, or in a Platonic iconoclastic pilgrimage. If void continues there can be real ordinary familiar despair. Or this can be made into the kind of asceticism envisaged by Simone Weil, wherein the sufferer, refusing the consolations of fantasy, takes a firm hold upon the painful reality: as in the case of bereavement, for example, or in the terrible situation of waiting for the inevitable death of a loved person. Extreme suffering, from one cause or another, is likely to be the lot of everyone at some time in life; and innumerable lives are hideously darkened throughout by hunger, poverty and persecution, or by remorse or guilt or abandoned loneliness and lack of love. Here every individual is ultimately alone, and in relation to actual cases it seems impertinent to consider what use is made of religious consolation. Theological truth is abstract. Out on the battle-front of human suffering people will use such devices as they have for survival. Experiences of void can also, sometimes perhaps 'in the long run' when they have been lived with, be put to more positive and creative use, or as one may put it, assume a different meaning. The 'dead' void may become 'live', or 'magnetic'. Here I want to look back to, or return toward, the Ontological Proof of which Simone Weil said that it 'is mysterious because it does not address itself to the intelligence, but to love'. (*Notebooks*, p. 375.) I spoke earlier of situations where what is wholly transcendent and invisible becomes partially, perhaps surprisingly, visible at points where the 'frame' does not quite 'meet'. This image describes certain kinds of experience where it is as if, to use another image, the curtain blows in the wind (of spirit maybe), and we see more than we are supposed to. Plato's myths indicate such visions. Here again the activity of the artist or thinker may be taken as an image (or analogy) of, or a case of, the moral life. So deep is imagery in life that one may not always realise or know whether one is regarding something as itself, or as an image. We are all artists and thinkers. We are all poets. Well, surely one will empty the concept by such treatment! If we are all poets, what about real poets? Oddly enough we can manage to think without confusion in these ways, it is a very usual way of thinking. I quoted Simone Weil earlier on the subject of patient attention which waits for the insight which has not yet been given. The artist or thinker concentrates on the problem, grasps it as a problem with some degree of clarity, and waits. Something is apprehended as *there* which is not yet *known*. Then something comes; as we sometimes say from the unconscious. It comes to us out of the dark of non-being, as a reward for loving attention. An insuperable difficulty is a sun. Simone Weil, speaking of *anamnesis*, calls it 'an orientation of the soul toward something which one does not know, but whose *reality* one does know'. The empty space, to pursue one (not the only) picture of the matter, may be found to be full of forms, boiling and seething like Eckhart's God, or like the innumerable divine forms of India, whose proliferation shocks the more puritanical religious of the north. (Perhaps the 'so many' of *Philebus* 16d, as noted by Simone Weil, *Notebooks*, p. 20.) The energy of the attentive scholar or artist is spiritual energy. The energy of the bereaved person trying to survive in the best way, or of the mother thinking about her delinquent son (and so on and so on) is spiritual. One uses this word with a certain purpose, to set up certain pictures, to draw attention to similarities and to explain and clarify the obscure by the familiar. Plato calls such energy Eros, love. Zeus became Eros to create the world. Parmenides said that Genesis (the Creator) invented Love first of all gods. (*Symposium* 178B.) The *Timaeus* Demiurge is inspired to create by love of the Good. Concentrated attention ('loving care') is easily distinguished from the hazy muddled unclarified states of mind wherein one is content with a second best. The second best should be exchanged for void. (Try again. *Wait.*) We intuitively know about perfection. Art and high thought and difficult moral discernment appear as creation *ex nihilo*, as *grace*. The *Meno* concludes that virtue does not come by nature, nor is it teachable, but comes by divine dispensation. Keats says that 'what the imagination seizes as beauty must be truth, whether it existed before or not.' It *must* be *truth*. Simone Weil quotes Valéry: 'The proper, unique and perpetual object of thought is that which does not exist.' Here we may make sense of the idea of loving good. 'At its highest point, love is a determination to create the being which it has taken for its object.' Here indeed we come back to the Ontological Proof in its simpler version, a proof by perfection, by a certainty derived from love. The good artist, the true lover, the dedicated thinker, the unselfish moral agent solving his problem: they can create the object of love. The dog's tooth, when sincerely venerated, glows with light. Compare, God *cannot* be thought of except as real.


The Platonic relation between the different levels of the soul, whereby the higher controls the lower, is not to be understood in a Jungian, Manichaean or Heraclitean way. There is a kind of 'concession' involved in the, in so many ways obviously 'realistic', image of the divided soul. We are divided creatures who must perhaps hope at best to control, not remove, our evil impulses. On the other hand the vision of perfection which condemns them as evil is never absent and there can be no pact between good and evil, they are irreconcilable enemies, and condemned to everlasting war, but not in Heraclitus' sense. There is no harmonious balance whereby we suddenly find that evil is just a 'dark side' which is not only harmless to good, but actually enhances it. Evil may have to be lived with, but remains evil, and we live too with the real possibility of improvement. This Platonic inspiration is like the absolutism of Kant who will not allow that any man lacks the means to be perfectly rational. Common-sense may protest against such a requirement. If we insist on keeping the picture we might be said to have asserted a religious view of the world. This would be one point at which, in the continuity which (as I see it) exists between morality and religion, we might feel that we had crossed the border. The absolute demand remains. As Simone Weil puts it, exposure to God condemns the evil in ourselves not to suffering but to death: a saying worth reflecting upon in relation to a psychology which explores the pleasures of suffering. A characteristically religious saying. The Christian God has been found to be a lovable figure, by believers who are not simply afraid of him. Christ of course is lovable. (So is the Platonic Socrates.) The mystic Christ who is an image of Good is lovable. That we can and do love Good and are drawn towards it is something that we have to learn from our experience, as we move all the time in the continuum between good and bad. This is our everyday existence where spiritual energy, Eros, is all the time active at a variety of levels. Our emotions and desires are as good as their objects and are constantly being modified in relation to their objects. What is good purifies the desire that seeks it, the good beloved ennobles the lover. There is no unattached will as a prime source of value. There is only the working of the human spirit in the morass of existence in which it always at every moment finds itself immersed. We live in an 'intermediate' world. Good as absolute, above courage and generosity and all the plural virtues, is to be seen as unshadowed and separate, a pure source, the principle which creatively relates the virtues to each other in our moral lives. In the iconoclastic pilgrimage, through the progressive destruction of false images, we experience the *distance* which separates us from perfection and are led to place our idea of it in a figurative sense outside the turmoil of existent being. The concept is thus 'forced upon us'. The transcendental proof of it is from all the world, all of our *extremely various* experience. The Form of the Good, herein like Kant's call of duty, may be seen as enlightening particular scenes and setting the specialised moral virtues and insights into their required particular patterns. This is how the phenomena are saved and the particulars redeemed, in this *light*. Plato's Good resembles Kant's Reason, but is a better image, since, by contrast, reason too, if we are to keep any force in the concept, is a specialised instrument. The sovereign Good is not an empty receptacle into which the arbitrary will places objects of its choice. It is something which we all experience as a creative force. This is metaphysics, which sets up a picture which it then offers as an appeal to us all to see if we cannot find just this in our deepest experience. The word 'deep', or some such metaphor, will come in here as part of the essence of the appeal. In this respect metaphysical and religious pictures resemble each other.

\*

We may look back from here to Anselm's Proofs and to the distinction between them which has interested modern philosophers. *Credo ut intellegam*, I believe so that I may understand, represents a faith born out of experience of the relations between truth and good; or, if one wants to extend the picture, out of experience of the internal relations between truth and good and cognition and freedom, and (we may add) beauty. The great artist makes beauty out of necessity (contingency) as the divine cause persuades the necessary cause in the *Timaeus*. The beauty of the world as an image of obedience. The extension of the equation goes beyond Anselm, but in his spirit. As soon as we remove the concept of God the two Proofs co-operate with each other. The second Proof, in terms of necessary existence, proves the (necessary) non-existence of God, thereby, and with its co-operation, leaving the way open for the first Proof, in terms of the idea of perfection, to 'prove' or indicate the real, in a unique mode, existence of good. No existing thing could be what we have meant by God. Any existing God would be less than God. An existent God would be an idol or a demon. (This is near to Kant's thinking.) God does not and cannot exist. But what led us to conceive of him does exist and is *constantly* experienced and pictured. That is, it is real as an Idea, and is *also* incarnate in knowledge and work and love. This is the true idea of incarnation, and is not something obscure. We *experience* both the reality of perfection and its distance away, and this leads us to place our idea of it outside the world of existent being as something of a different unique and special sort. Such experience of the reality of good is not like an arbitrary and assertive resort to our own will; it is a discovery of something independent of us, where that independence is essential. If we read these images aright they are not only enlightening and profound but amount to a statement of a belief which most people unreflectively hold. Non-philosophical people do not think that they invent good. They may invent their own activities, but good is somewhere else as an independent judge of these. Good is also something clearly seen and indubitably discovered in our ordinary unmysterious experience of transcendence, the progressive illuminating and inspiring discovery of *other*, the positive *experience* of truth, which comes to us all the time in a weak form and comes to most of us sometimes in a strong form (in art or love or work or looking at nature) and which remains with us as a standard or vision, an *orientation*, a *proof* of what is possible and a vista of what might be. I see here no need for a dramatic voluntarist 'way' to be pressed upon us by theologians. The ordinary way is the way. It is not in that sense theology, and the 'mysticism' involved is an accessible experience. The 'proof' may be said to resemble the Cartesian *cogito* in that it is an intuitive movement which we may prompt ourselves to make, a proof by morality and by love, not by logic. As an explicitly reflective insight this is something which we might summon to our aid in times of moral difficulty, as when believers might pray especially ardently to God. But our general awareness of good, or goodness, is with us unreflectively all the time, as a sense of God's presence, or at least existence, used to be to all sorts of believers. The proof concerns the unique nature of moral perfection, as contrasted with the relative means-to-an-end (hypothetical) 'perfection' of existing things. We easily distinguish moral from functional uses of 'good', in Kantian terms we recognise *categorical* imperatives. Kant is right to draw attention to our *experience* of the recognition of duty, though he also places reason beyond experience. A picture of humanity must portray its fallen nature. We must keep constantly in view the *distance* between good and evil, and the potential *extremity* of evil. We are ineluctably imperfect, goodness is not a continuously active organic part of our purposes and wishes. However good a life is, it includes moral failure. Is this an empirical hypothesis or a tautology or a synthetic *a priori* proposition? Never mind, let it be in this context a metaphysical conjecture. It is certainly ubiquitously suggested by experience and true enough to exhibit as fundamental our sense of the purely good as essentially *beyond* us. Great saints and avatars may, in this age too and onward, live with us as mysteries, as mythical mystical exemplars and saviours. The *truth*, the *light*, which they bestow 'floats free' from contingent detail and is not at the mercy of history. When, in ordinary life, we are rescued or changed by a meeting with a very good person, we do not assume that he is sinless. With or without avatars, we are perpetually reminded of our natural selfishness and led to see our thoughts and acts as under a judgment which is not a natural part of ourselves. Can we think away the idea of 'the moral', the idea of the authority of good, from human life?

St Paul, Romans 4. 17: 'God, who quickeneth the dead and calleth the things that are not as though they were'. Karl Barth comments: 'Faith beholds life and existence where the man of the world sees nothing but death and non-existence; and contrariwise it sees death and non-existence where he beholds full-blooded life . . . The living

[ 509 ]

must die in order that the dead may be made alive. The things which are must be seen as though they were not in order that the things which are not may be called as though they were ... A similar faith appears on the borderland of the philosophy of Plato, of the art of Grünewald and Dostoevsky, and of the religion of Luther.' Here we find the name of Plato in interesting company. And Schopenhauer's man who has practised dying gives up the existence we know and gets nothing in exchange, because our existence is, by contrast with his gain, nothing. In reflecting upon these sayings we may see too how close to religion certain parts of philosophy can come; Plato and the presocratics would not have made any sharp distinction between philosophy and religious reflection. Nor do thinkers in India make such a distinction now. Plato's work is full of images and myths at which we must work to see what they mean in terms of everyday morals. Plato is not a remote abstract or purely 'intellectualist' thinker. He is very close to our own religious and moral tradition, being indeed one of its founders. The mythology of religion does not necessarily vanish but finds a new and different place as religion is newly understood. As A. N. Wilson says, at the end of his splendidly critical book, 'Jesus has survived'. (*Jesus*, p. 253.)

In thinking about the work of great metaphysicians one has to seek a balance between 'faithfulness to the text' and a tendency to invent one's own metaphysician. If one is too 'faithful' one may merely reproduce unassimilated ideas which remain remote and dead; if one is too 'inventive' one may lose the original and present one's own thoughts instead of the great thoughts to which one should have attended more carefully. This is of course a dilemma which belongs to any sort of interpretation. Structuralism, which tends to emphasise inventiveness at the expense of faithfulness, is also interested in this matter. Theorising about such difficulties can become an end in itself. Such theorising may be another way of losing the original. Methods of interpretation in various fields are all the time under scrutiny by individual thinkers, and sometimes, as in biblical criticism, it is worth while making a large general issue of the matter. Theological discussions of this kind form a background of contemporary problems concerning the 'demythologisation' of religion. In my own case I am aware of the danger of inventing my own Plato and extracting a particular pattern from his many-patterned text to reassure myself that, as I see it, good is really good and real is really real. I have been wanting to use Plato's images as a sort of Ontological Proof of the necessity of Good, or rather, since Plato himself has already done this, to put his argument into a modern context as a background to moral philosophy, as a bridge between morals and religion, and as relevant to our new disturbed understanding of religious truth.

Plato departed from the monistic presocratic view of a self-relating moral-natural cosmos, the cosmos in short as 'God': that is, roughly, *Logos* (intelligibility) is Zeus, and Zeus (not an Olympian god) is the One. I have not in these pages attempted any general account of the great presocratics who 'began it all' and differed considerably among themselves. Modern physics, and philosophical views which derive from it or refer to it, may seem 'close' to these cosmic conceptions. Plato by contrast places, and explicitly places, the Absolute outside the existing cosmos, but *not* in the supernatural sense familiar in traditional Christianity. Christianity now, faced with the withdrawal of belief from the supernatural, may be tempted by various forms of the 'cosmic answer' of which Jung's view is one. Religion as a sort of science. I attach, as I have been arguing, great importance to the concept of a transcendent good as an idea (properly interpreted) essential to both morality and religion. How do you mean essential? Do you mean it is empirically found to be so or are you recommending it? This is the 'beginning' to which such enquiries are frequently returned, except that it is not the beginning. The beginning is hard to find. Perhaps here the beginning is the circular nature of metaphysical argument itself, whereby the arguer combines an appeal to ordinary observation with an appeal to moral attitude. The process involves connecting together different considerations and pictures so that they give each other mutual support. Thus, for instance, there appears to be an internal relation between truth and goodness and knowledge. I have argued in this sense from cases of art and skill and ordinary work and ordinary moral discernment, where we establish truth and reality by an insight which is an exercise of virtue. Perhaps *that* is the beginning, which is also our deepest closest ordinary experience.

Paul Tillich describes theology as a response to 'the totality of man's creative self-interpretation in a particular period'. We need a theology which can continue without God. Why not call such a reflection a form of moral philosophy? All right, so long as it treats of those matters of 'ultimate concern', our experience of the unconditioned and our continued sense of what is holy. Tillich refers us to Psalm 139. 'Whither shall I go from thy spirit, whither shall I flee from thy presence? If I ascend into heaven thou art there, if I make my bed in hell, behold thou art there. If I take the wings of the morning and dwell in the uttermost parts of the sea, even there shall thy hand lead me, and thy right hand shall hold me.'

ACKNOWLEDGEMENTS

I would like to thank the following very kind persons who helped and encouraged the production of this book: Carmen Callil and Ed Victor who patiently nursed it into print, Jane Turner who scanned every page and made valuable suggestions, Anthony Turner as scholarly copy-editor, and Cecily Hatchitt who gallantly typed and retyped the seemingly endless text.

The author and publisher would like to thank the following for permission to reproduce copyright material as follows:

Victor Gollancz Ltd for extracts from *Language, Truth and Logic*, 1936, by A. J. Ayer; HarperCollins Publishers, New York, U.S.A., for extracts from *The Eclipse of God*, 1953, by Martin Buber; SCM Press for extracts from *Radicals and the Future of the Church*, 1989, and *Taking Leave of God*, 1980, by Don Cupitt; Faber & Faber Ltd. for an extract from *Selected Essays*, 1932, by T. S. Eliot; the Hogarth Press, London, and W. W. Norton Inc., New York, for extracts from *The Complete Psychological Works of Sigmund Freud*, 1953–74, translated and edited by James Strachey; Insel Verlag, Frankfurt-on-Main, and Macmillan London Ltd for extracts from *Selected Letters*, 1946, by Rainer Maria Rilke, translated by R. F. C. Hull; Weatherhill Publishers, New York, for extracts from *Zen Training: Methods and Philosophy*, 1976, by Katsuki Sekida, edited by A. V. Grimstone; the University of Chicago Press, Chicago, for extracts from *Systematic Theology*, 1968, by Paul Tillich; Routledge for extracts from *Notebooks*, 1956, by Simone Weil, translated by Arthur Wills; Basil Blackwell Ltd., Oxford, for extracts from works by Ludwig Wittgenstein: *Culture and Value*, amended edition 1980, edited by G. H. von Wright in collaboration with Heikki Nyman; *Lectures*

[ 513 ]

*and Conversations on Aesthetics, Psychology and Religious Beliefs*, 1978, edited by Cyril Barrett; *Notebooks 1914–1916*, 1961, edited by G. E. M. Anscombe and G. H. von Wright; *Philosophical Investigations*, 2nd edition 1958, translated by G. E. M. Anscombe; *Philosophical Remarks*, 1975, edited by Rush Rhees; and also for the following works: *Letters from Ludwig Wittgenstein with a Memoir by Paul Engelmann*, 1967, edited by B. F. McGuinness; *Wittgenstein on Rules and Private Language*, 1982, by Saul Kripke; *Ludwig Wittgenstein and the Vienna Circle*, 1979, recorded by Friedrich Waismann and edited by B. F. McGuinness; the Brynmill Press, Gringley-on-the-Hill, Doncaster, for extracts from *Remarks on Frazer's 'Golden Bough'*, 1979, by Ludwig Wittgenstein, translated by A. C. Miles, revised by Rush Rhees; Routledge for extracts from *Tractatus Logico-Philosophicus* by Ludwig Wittgenstein, in two editions: C. K. Ogden's translation of 1922 and D. F. Pears' and B. F. McGuinness's translation of 1961.

# Index